Formatting SmartIcons

Icon	Name
	OpenFile
	SaveFile
	Print
	PrintPreview
	Undo
	CutToClipboard
	CopyToClipboard
	PasteToClipboard
	Delete
	DeleteStyles
	PasteCellContents
	PasteCellStyles
	Paste1-2-3/DDE/OLE
	PasteFormulaAsValue
	CompleteSequence
	CopyRight
	CopyDown
	TransposeRange
	InsertRow
	InsertColumn
	DeleteSelectedRows
	DeleteSelectedColumns
	DeleteSelectedWorksheets
	NextSet

Editing SmartIcons

Icon	Name
	OpenFile
	SaveFile
	Print
	PrintPreview
	Undo
	CutToClipboard
	CopyToClipboard
	PasteToClipboard
	DeleteStyles
	Bold
	Italics
	Underline
	LeftAlign
	CenterAlign
	RightAlign
	Justify
	RotateData
	AddRangeBorder
	SelectStyleTemplate
	Font&Attributes
	Lines&Color
	FitToWidest
	CopyStylesTo
	NextSet

Understanding 1-2-3 Release 4 for Windows

Understanding 1-2-3® Release 4 for Windows

SECOND EDITION

Douglas Hergert with
Sheldon M. Dunn

SYBEX®

SAN FRANCISCO • PARIS • DÜSSELDORF • SOEST

Acquisitions Editor: Dianne King
Developmental Editor: Sharon Crawford
Project Editor: Brenda Kienan
Editor: Peter Weverka
Technical Editors: Maryann Brown, Erik Ingenito
Assistant Editors: Michelle Nance, Valerie Potter
Production/Chapter Artist: Lisa Jaffe
Screen Graphics Artist: Cuong Le
Page Layout/Typesetters: Stephanie Hollier, Deborah Maizels and Alissa Feinberg
Proofreader/Production Assistant: Janet MacEachern
Indexer:Ted Laux
Cover Designer: Archer Design
Cover Photograph Art Director: Ingalls + Associates
Cover Photographer: Mark Johann

Library of Congress Card Number: 93-85187
ISBN: 0-7821-1181-5

Manufactured in the United States of America
10 9 8 7 6 5 4

ACKNOWLEDGMENTS

AT the outset, we wish to thank Dianne King and David Clark, who were instrumental in getting us started on the book. Sharon Crawford, our developmental editor, helped devise the overall plan for the contents and was always ready with good advice. We are also indebted to Peter Weverka, our copy editor, for his superb and thorough work on the manuscript. Thanks go to project editor Brenda Kienan for seeing this book through the editorial and production processes. Thanks also to technical editors Maryann Brown and Erik Ingenito, who read the manuscript line by line to make sure it was technically accurate—and did a great job of it!

Every computer book is a team effort. We are grateful to all the people at SYBEX who worked so hard to bring this book to completion: proofreader Janet MacEachern; typesetters Stephanie Hollier, Deborah Maizels, and Alissa Feinberg; production artist Lisa Jaffe; screen graphics artist Cuong Le; and assistant editors Michelle Nance and Valerie Potter. Thanks also to indexer Ted Laux.

We also wish to thank all those who worked on an earlier version of this book—Christian Crumlish, Savitha Varadan, and Sheila Dienes. Our thanks to all.

As always, thanks to Claudette Moore of Moore Literary Agency for her counsel, encouragement, and guidance.

CONTENTS
AT A GLANCE

TABLE OF CONTENTS

2   Lotus 1-2-3 and the Windows Interface

PART TWO   **ESSENTIAL 1-2-3 FOR WINDOWS**

3   Worksheet Essentials

4 Worksheet Formatting and Printing

5 Worksheet Formulas and Functions

8   Database Calculations and Operations

9　An Introduction to Macros

PART THREE　**ADVANCED 1-2-3 FOR WINDOWS**

10　Advanced 1-2-3 Worksheet Tools

INTRODUCTION

LOTUS 1-2-3 for Windows Release 4 is the latest release of the world's most popular spreadsheet program for IBM PCs and compatible personal computers. This release, unlike the previous Release 1.0, takes full advantage of the Windows environment and places SmartIcons, tools, and buttons in easy-to-use places on the screen.

This book will guide you through the stages of mastering this powerful new program. In twelve tutorial-style chapters, you'll learn all the essential details of the 1-2-3 software. This book will teach you, among other things, how to:

- Produce clear, accurate, and flexible worksheet documents.

- Generate presentation-quality charts from worksheet data.

- Build accessible databases and perform varieties of query operations on your data.

- Create custom macro SmartIcons.

Who This Book Is For

This book is written for everyone who needs to learn 1-2-3 and is tired of wading through manuals in search of information. You'll find concise, plain-language explanations of Lotus procedures and functions in this book. It is organized so you can find the information you need easily.

If you are a beginner, pay special attention to Part One, which includes many hands-on exercises for learning Lotus basics and the Windows interface. Lotus veterans can learn much from the advanced chapters, which deal with macros, database design, and complex worksheets. This book also includes detailed information about worksheets, functions, formulas, and charts.

For experienced users upgrading to Release 4, this book covers the features of the new release. Look for the "hot stuff" icon. Where you see this icon, you'll find information pertaining especially to Release 4.

Features of This Book

This book serves as both a tutorial and a reference. It is designed so you can find the information you need quickly. To help you learn Lotus 1-2-3 and get the most out of the program, you'll find the following special features in this book.

Hands-On Instructions Step-by-step exercises take you through the procedures for completing important tasks. By doing the exercises, you'll get the experience you need to gain a solid understanding of how 1-2-3 works and the many options available to you.

Notes, Tips, Warnings Where applicable, this book provides special notes, tips, and warnings.

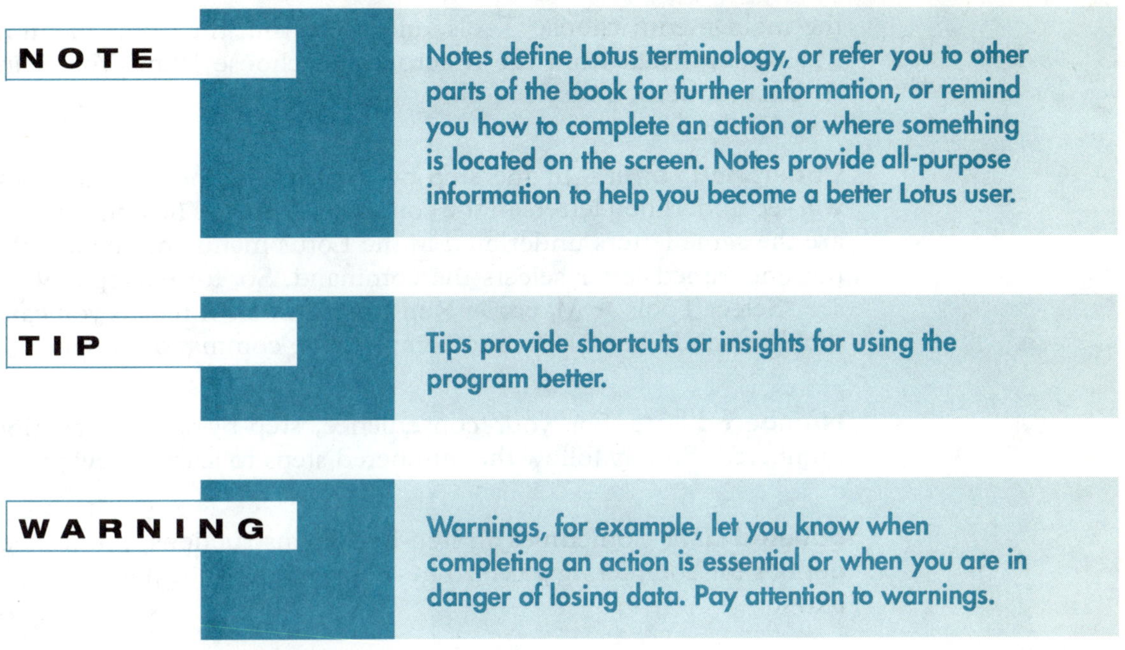

Fast Tracks At the start of every chapter you will find fast tracks. A fast track is a quick, concise explanation of how to do something in Lotus. Next to each fast track is a page number showing where to go in the chapter to find a complete explanation of the task.

Endpapers Inside the front and back cover of this book are charts showing what all the SmartIcons do. Refer to these charts as often as you need to when using the SmartIcons.

"Hot Stuff" The "hot stuff" icon shows you where features new to Release 4 are explained in the book. Look for this icon if you are upgrading to Release 4 and you need information about the new release.

Pull-Down Menus Lotus, like most programs, has a pull-down menu structure. In other words, to complete a task with the menus, you start at the main menu, select an option, and from the next menu that appears you select another option. As a shorthand method of showing you how to use the pull-down menus, this book uses the ➤ symbol to show menu selections. For example, "choose Tools ➤ Macro ➤ Run" means "From the main menu, choose <u>T</u>ools, and then from the Tools menu choose <u>M</u>acro, and then from the Macro menu choose <u>R</u>un." You'll find this shorthand method easy to follow.

Underlined Letters In the step-by-step instructions in this book, you will see underlined letters in the command names. The underlined letters are the same letters underlined in the Lotus menu commands. Pressing the underlined letter selects the command. So, for example, when you see "Select <u>T</u>ools ➤ <u>M</u>acro ➤ <u>R</u>un" in this book, it means you can select the three underlined letters to complete the command sequence.

Numbered Lists For your convenience, step-by-step instructions are numbered. Simply follow the numbered steps to learn a new procedure.

Bulleted Lists Sometimes, in step-by-step instructions, you will be given options for completing a task. These options are shown in a bulleted list, like so:

1. Choose the kind of chart you want to create:

   - a pie chart
   - a bar chart
   - a line chart

Boldface When you see boldface text in a step-by-step instruction list, it means to enter the text in your worksheet or dialog box. For example, an instruction such as "Enter **Computer Conferences, Inc.** in cell A1" means to enter those very words in the worksheet cell.

How This Book Is Organized

This book is divided into three parts and twelve chapters. In Part One, "Lotus 1-2-3 in the Windows Environment," you'll find the following information:

CHAPTER	WHAT YOU'LL LEARN
1	"Getting Acquainted with Lotus 1-2-3 for Windows." Here you'll work on a sample application that previews the many tasks you can accomplish with 1-2-3. You'll get hands-on experience with spreadsheets, charts, and databases.
2	"Lotus 1-2-3 and the Windows Interface." This chapter shows you how to work comfortably and efficiently with Windows. You'll learn about menus, dialog boxes, and the SmartIcons.

In Part Two, "Essential 1-2-3 for Windows," you'll learn the following:

CHAPTER	WHAT YOU'LL LEARN
3	"Worksheet Essentials." This chapter takes you through the initial steps of building a worksheet for a business application. You'll learn how to enter and organize labels and numeric data, how to calculate totals, and how to perform important range operations.
4	"Worksheet Formatting and Printing." Here you continue your basic introduction to spreadsheet formatting. You'll learn to apply type and font styles, and work with date and time values, as well as how to print documents to your specifications.

CHAPTER	WHAT YOU'LL LEARN
5	"Worksheet Formulas and Functions." This chapter guides you through the large library of calculation tools in 1-2-3. You'll learns about all types of formulas. Detailed instructions are given for using the many 1-2-3 functions.
6	"Creating and Refining Charts." You'll learn how to create all varieties of charts in 1-2-3—and how to make them present data just the right way.
7	"Database Essentials." This chapter introduces essential database concepts. You'll learn how to define fields, enter records, and create calculated fields. You'll also master the database tools on the 1-2-3 menu.
8	"Database Calculations and Operations." This chapter delves deeper into 1-2-3's database capabilities.
9	"An Introduction to Macros." This chapter shows you how to create your own macro library to automate the work you do in 1-2-3. This chapter also explains how to attach macros to SmartIcons.

Part Three, "Advanced 1-2-3 for Windows," introduces some of the most powerful tools in the 1-2-3 software package.

CHAPTER	WHAT YOU'LL LEARN
10	"Advanced 1-2-3 Worksheet Tools." Here you'll learn advanced techniques for using 1-2-3's high-level mathematical features. Included are discussions of data regression analysis, using matrices, and performing data distribution analyses.

CHAPTER	WHAT YOU'LL LEARN
11	"Links between Files." This chapter explains how to work with multifile applications in the Windows environment. You'll learn how to work with more than one worksheet at a time, and how to work with and import data from other applications.
12	"Macro Programming." This is an introduction to 1-2-3's complete macro language. You'll learn to use a variety of macros for programming operations such as loops, decisions, subroutines, and branches of control.

This book also includes three appendices:

APPENDIX	WHAT YOU'LL LEARN
A	"Installing Lotus 1-2-3 Release 4 for Windows." This appendix offers complete instructions for installing Release 4.
B	"The @ Functions." Here you'll find explanations and advice for using all @ functions in 1-2-3.
C	"New Features and Tools in Release 4." This appendix describes all the features that are new to Release 4. Read this appendix if you are upgrading from Release 1 and need to know what the new features of the program are.

LOTUS 1-2-3 IN THE WINDOWS ENVIRONMENT

Getting Acquainted with Lotus 1-2-3 for Windows

LOTUS 1-2-3 Release 4 for Windows comprises three interrelated software components, known by the familiar terms *spreadsheet*, *graphics*, and *database*:

- The spreadsheet provides a variety of efficient tools for organizing and working with tables of numbers.

- The graphics component lets you create and print visual representations of numeric data. For example, you can create bar graphs and pie charts.

- The database gives you simple but effective techniques for storing and managing information records.

These remarkable software tools were available in earlier DOS and Windows versions of Lotus 1-2-3. What is new and important about Release 4 for Windows is the seamless way it combines Microsoft Windows' *graphical user interface*, an enhanced @Function language, the Version Manager, and other new tools. Running within the Windows environment, 1-2-3 has many significant advantages. Here are a few of the most important ones:

- Release 4's new and improved interface gives Lotus 1-2-3 the "look" of other Windows applications. All Windows programs have common visual and functional elements, including pull-down menus, dialog boxes, special-purpose keyboard functions, mouse control, and elaborate Help systems. Lotus 1-2-3 for Windows has these features too, which makes the program easier to learn if you are already using Windows programs.

- You can run Lotus 1-2-3 at the same time that you run other Windows programs—a word processor, a desktop publishing program, and even a programming language compiler. Switching back and forth from one program to another is easy.

You can exchange data between Lotus 1-2-3 Release 4 and other applications in a variety of new ways. For example, you can use the Clipboard to copy data or graphs from Lotus 1-2-3 to other Windows programs.

This chapter introduces the three major components of 1-2-3 for Windows—spreadsheet, graphics, and database. We'll examine these three components and learn how they interact with one another. Of course, you will study each component in much greater detail throughout this book. The purpose of this first chapter is to give you an opportunity to gain a general understanding of the product's usefulness and to gather ideas for applying 1-2-3 to your own work.

We'll also explore how Lotus 1-2-3 operates in the Windows environment. This chapter includes many hands-on exercises to help you learn to use the keyboard and mouse and begin exploring the dimensions, features, and appearance of Lotus 1-2-3 for Windows.

Lotus 1-2-3: The Basics

The Lotus spreadsheet provides a system of on-screen menu bars tailored to the tasks you are doing. The spreadsheet is made up of *worksheets*. A worksheet is a large grid of individual data cells for organizing and analyzing tables of information. The terms worksheet and spreadsheet are sometimes used synonymously, but in this book *spreadsheet* refers to one of the three major software components of Lotus 1-2-3 (the other components being graphics and database), and *worksheet* refers to the on-screen grid on which you enter and work with tables of data.

NOTE

Appendix A gives instructions for installing and starting Lotus 1-2-3. If you haven't yet installed the program, do so now.

Figure 1.1 shows the 1-2-3 system *menu bar* and a worksheet. Your screen should look like Figure 1.1 when you start Lotus 1-2-3 for Windows, although there may be some differences between your screen and the figure, depending on the characteristics of your display hardware and how you installed the program.

FIGURE 1.1

A Lotus 1-2-3 worksheet

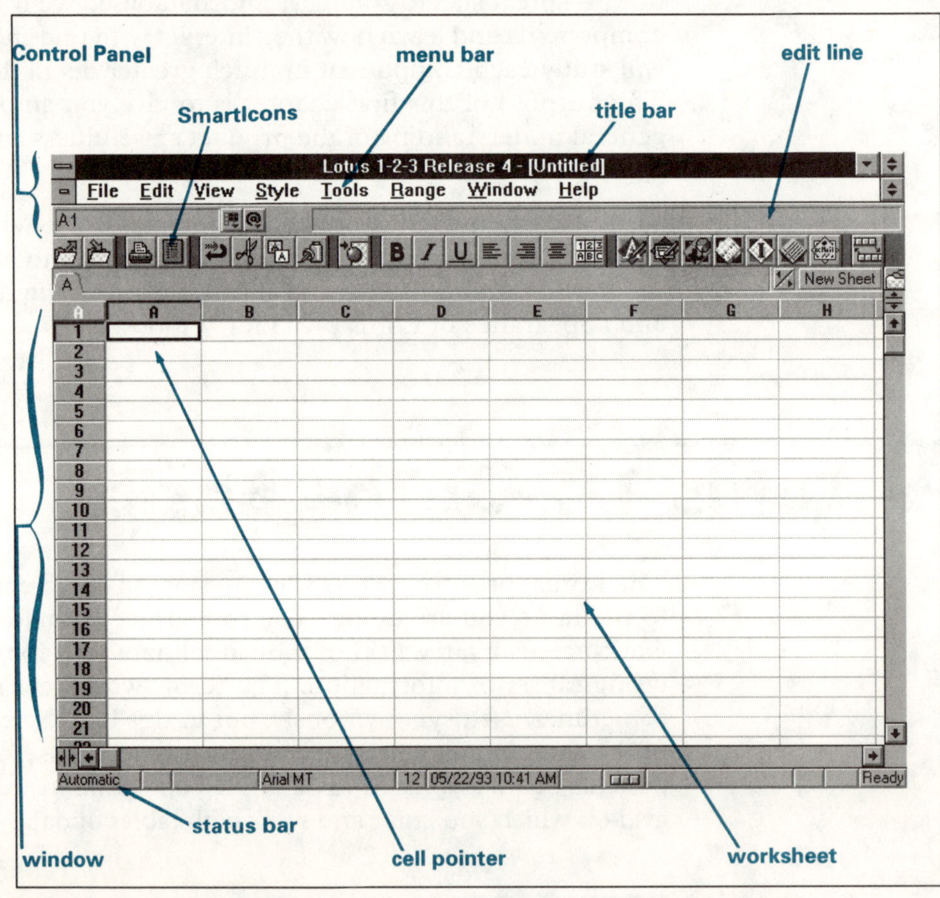

On the top three rows of the screen is the *Control Panel*, which consists of the 1-2-3 *title bar*, the menu bar, and the *edit line*. Immediately below the Control Panel is the set of *SmartIcons*, a row of predefined and customized buttons that provide fast access to 1-2-3 commands, functions, and macros. Worksheets are displayed below the Icon palette in *windows*. At the bottom of the screen is the *status bar*.

Chapter 2 looks at the Windows environment in greater detail.

The worksheet window itself has all the familiar characteristics and features of the Windows environment, including a Control menu, Maximize and Minimize buttons, scroll bars, and a title bar. In Release 4, you can get a graphical representation of worksheets—they appear as folders—and select the one you want to work with from a folder stack by clicking on the folder tab.

The Worksheet

Worksheets are divided into rows and columns. Each row is identified by a number, and each column by a letter. Where a row and a column intersect is called a *cell*. You enter single data values in cells on the worksheet. Each cell has an *address* made up of its column letter and row number. For example, the cell at the intersection of column D and row 9 has the address D9.

The *current cell*—the cell ready to receive a data entry—is highlighted. This highlighted cell is called the *cell pointer*. The cell pointer is the rectangular shading or color that fills the current cell. As you can see in Figure 1.1, cell A1 is the current cell when you begin working in Lotus 1-2-3 or when you open a new worksheet window.

Notice the word *Untitled* in the title bar at the top of the window in Figure 1.1. *Untitled* is the default name of the first worksheet window that Lotus 1-2-3 displays on-screen at the beginning of a new session with a spreadsheet. After you begin developing a data table in a worksheet window, you will want to save the worksheet as a file on-disk. Until you do so, however, the default *Untitled* appears on the title bar.

When the worksheet is *maximized*—that is, when the worksheet is enlarged to full-screen size as it is when you first open it—its title appears in the following form in the title bar:

Lotus 1-2-3 Release 4 - [*Title*]

Moving Around the Worksheet

In maximized worksheets, the *Control-menu box,* located on the left side of the worksheet window menu bar, and the *Minimize* and *Maximize buttons,* located on the right side, are displayed. The *Restore button,* a two-headed arrow icon located at the right side of the menu bar, appears in place of the Maximize button when the worksheet is maximized. Clicking the Restore button returns the worksheet window to its original size. On the right side of the worksheet window is a *vertical scroll bar* for moving the worksheet up and down, and on the left side is a *horizontal scroll bar* for moving it up and down.

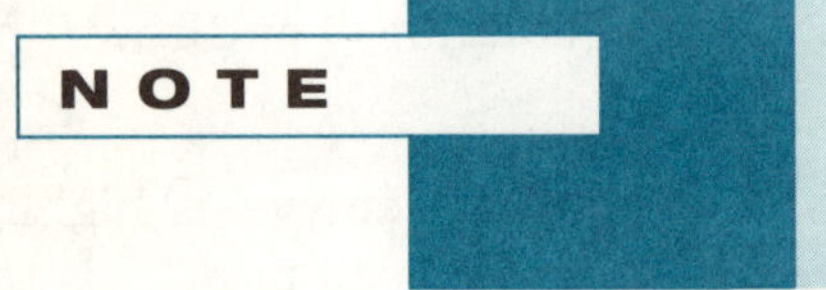

NOTE

Clicking the mouse means to move the mouse pointer to a particular target on-screen and click the left mouse button once.

In the following exercise, you'll use the Maximize, Minimize and Restore buttons, the Control menu, and the scroll bars to explore the dimensions of the worksheet:

1. If the worksheet is not currently maximized, click the Maximize button, the ↑ located in the upper-right corner of the worksheet window. Alternatively, if you don't have a mouse, press Alt-hyphen (-) on the keyboard to pull down the Control menu, as in Figure 1.2, and choose Ma̲ximize. Once the worksheet window is maximized, it fills up all the available space within the 1-2-3 window.

2. Press → once on your keyboard. The cell pointer moves one cell to the right, to address B1. Repeat this action six times to move the cell pointer to H1. Column H is at the right side of the current worksheet window.

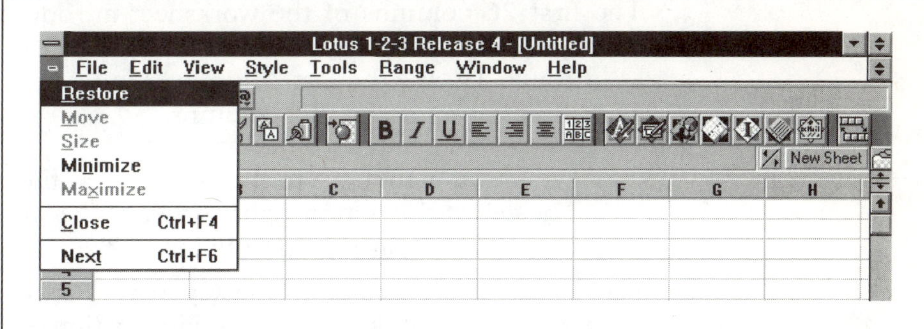

3. Now move the cell pointer one more column to the right and watch what happens to the worksheet. Column A disappears from the left side of the window to make room for column I on the right side. As this action clearly demonstrates, the worksheet contains many more columns and rows than can be displayed in the window at one time.

4. Press ↓ key on the keyboard. Notice how the cell pointer moves down one position, to cell I2. Press ↓ until the cell pointer reaches I20, and then move the pointer down one more cell. Row 1 disappears from the worksheet window to make room for row 21.

Notice the *scroll boxes*, the small, square buttons on the vertical and horizontal scroll bars that show your current position in the *active* part of the worksheet. When the scroll box is located halfway across the scroll bar, it means you are at the approximate center of the worksheet.

NOTE

To *drag* means to move the mouse pointer to a tool or object and hold down the left mouse button as you move the pointer.

5. Drag the horizontal scroll box part of the way across the horizontal scroll bar, the scroll bar at the bottom of the window. The scroll box moves along with the mouse pointer.

6. Press End-→. On this empty worksheet, the cell pointer moves to column IV, the last column in the worksheet.

The first 26 columns of the worksheet are identified by the letters A through Z, the next 26 by AA though AZ, the next 26 by BA through BZ. IA through IV are the last columns. Under this lettering scheme, the worksheet has a total of 256 columns.

7. Press End-↓ to move to the final row on the worksheet, row 8192. The cell at the bottomright corner of the worksheet has the address IV8192, as shown in Figure 1.3.

8. Press the Home key on the keyboard. Pressing Home moves the cell pointer back to its beginning position, cell A1.

A Lotus 1-2-3 worksheet is a huge grid comprising rows, columns, and over 2 million cell addresses (256 columns × 8192 rows). The worksheet window can show only a small part of the worksheet, but you can scroll the worksheet to view any group of cells that you want to work with.

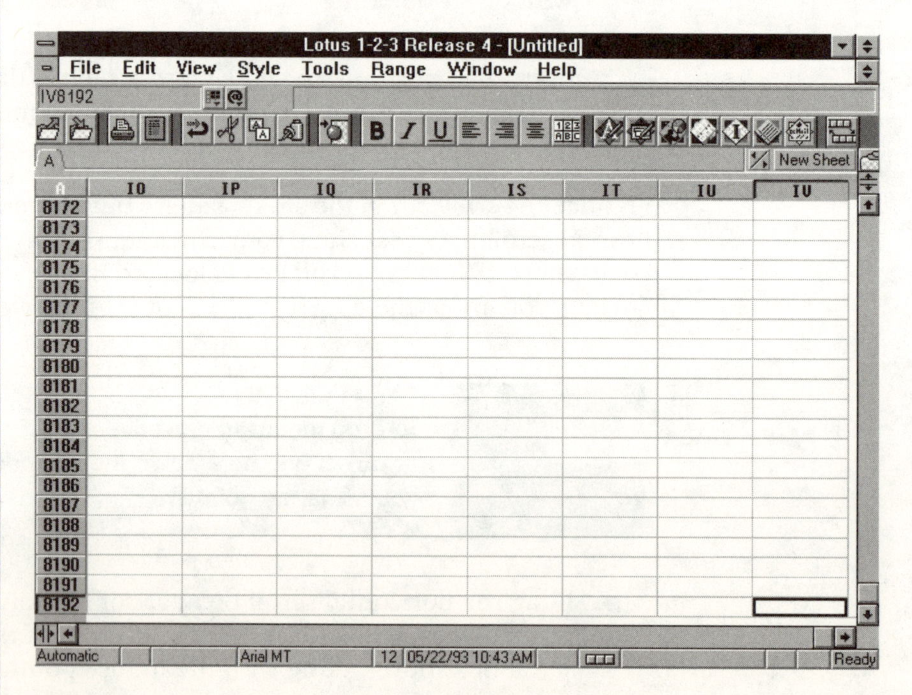

One of the advanced features of Lotus 1-2-3 for Windows is its capacity to show *multiple worksheets* in a single worksheet window. A worksheet window—and when you save the worksheet, an on-disk worksheet file—can contain two or more worksheets. Furthermore, by writing formulas that refer to data values in more than one worksheet, you can establish relationships among multiple worksheets. This useful arrangement is sometimes known as a *three-dimensional worksheet*. In the following exercises, you'll explore three-dimensional worksheets and along the way have your first opportunity to work with commands in the Lotus 1-2-3 menu system.

The Menu Bar

As is the case in most Windows applications, the menu bar is the horizontal row of commands at the top of the screen, just below the title bar:

File Edit View Style Tools Range Window Help

Selecting each of these commands makes a *pull-down menu* appear with a list of options. For example, Figure 1.4 shows the File menu, which appears when you select File. Mastering this system of menus and the dozens of commands they offer is a large part of learning Lotus 1-2-3 for Windows.

Selecting File on the menu bar brings up the File menu.

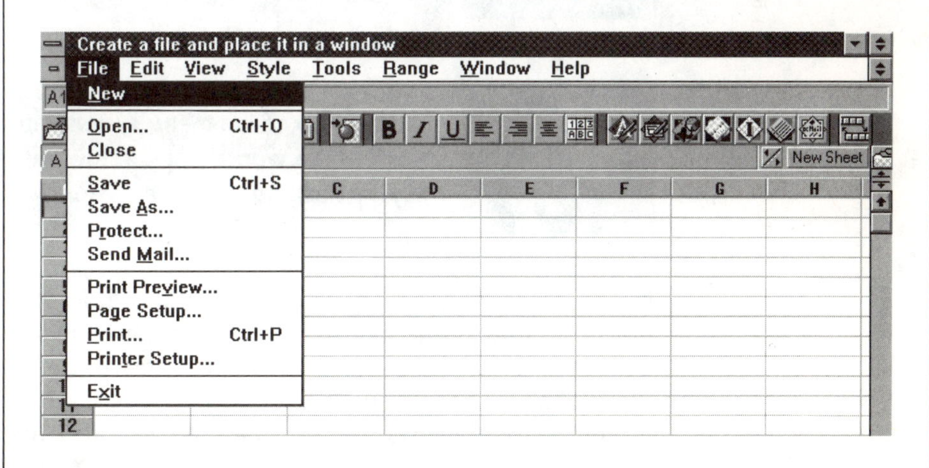

Choosing Menu Commands

Several mouse and keyboard techniques are available for choosing commands from the 1-2-3 menu system:

- Press the Alt key or the F10 key to activate the menu bar. With the menu bar active, you can press → or ← to highlight one of the Main menu commands and ↵ to pull down the menu.

- A keyboard shortcut for selecting a menu command is simply to press the Alt key followed by the underscored letter in the menu command's name. For example, pressing Alt-F pulls down the File menu.

- With the mouse, pull down a menu by simply clicking the corresponding command in the menu bar. For example, to pull down the File menu, position the mouse pointer over File in the menu bar and click the left mouse button.

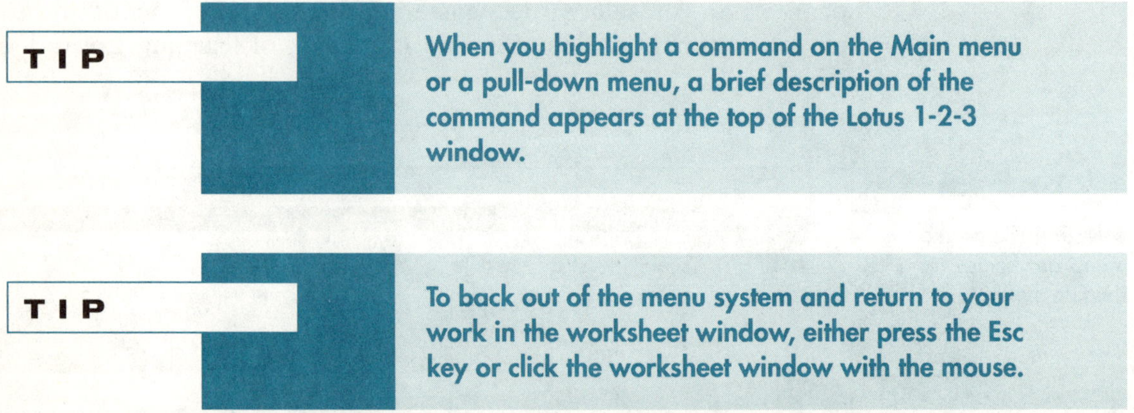

Mode indicator As you switch between menus and worksheets, you'll notice changes in the *mode indicator*, the box in the lower-right corner of the status bar. When the worksheet is active, the mode indicator displays the word *Ready* (see Figure 1.3), but when a menu is active, the mode indicator displays the word *Menu*. Ready and Menu are two of several different *modes* that 1-2-3 operates in. You'll see other changes in the mode indicator later in this chapter.

Using Menu Commands to View Multiple Worksheets

In the following exercise, you'll use menu commands to explore 1-2-3's multiple worksheet feature.

1. Choose <u>V</u>iew by pressing Alt-V or clicking on the View option.

2. On the View menu, choose <u>S</u>plit. This brings up the Split dialog box with options for changing the appearance of the worksheet window.

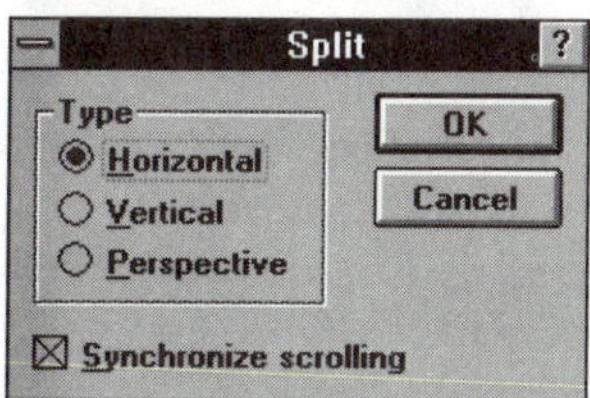

3. Select <u>P</u>erspective. This option allows you to view multiple worksheets inside the current window. When you make the selection, the round button—called a *radio button*—at the left of the option is filled in. To confirm the new option and close the dialog box, press ↵ or click the OK button with the mouse.

Inserting New Worksheets in a Window

When you close the dialog box, the worksheet window appears. Now it is divided into sections for three worksheets, as in Figure 1.5. Notice that

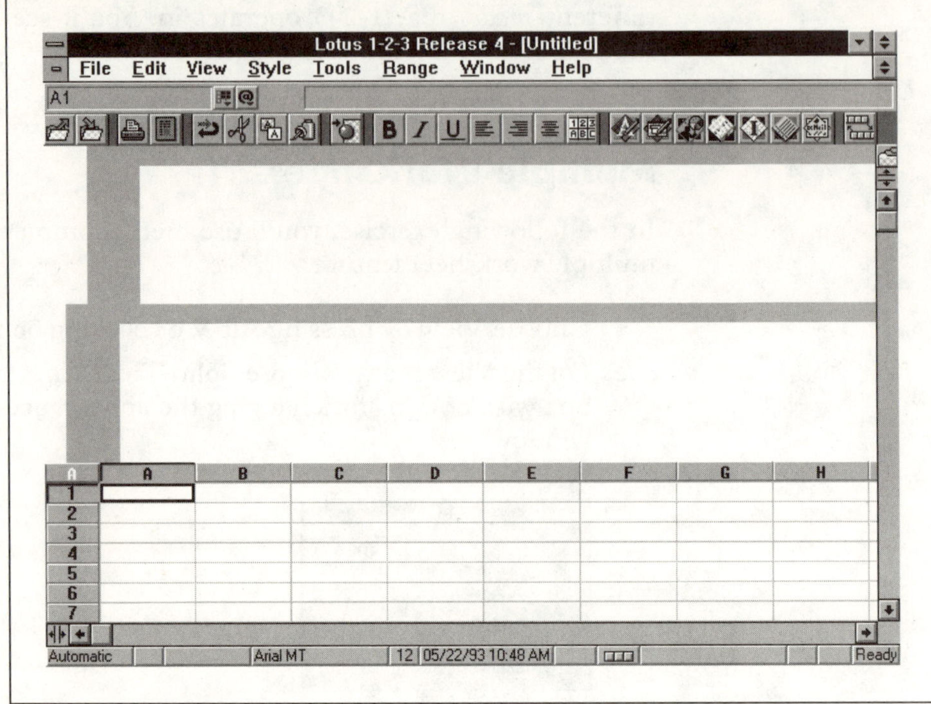

the two worksheet sections on top are empty. To fill them with grids, your next step is to insert two new worksheets in the window.

4. Choose Edit ➤ Insert to open the Insert dialog box.

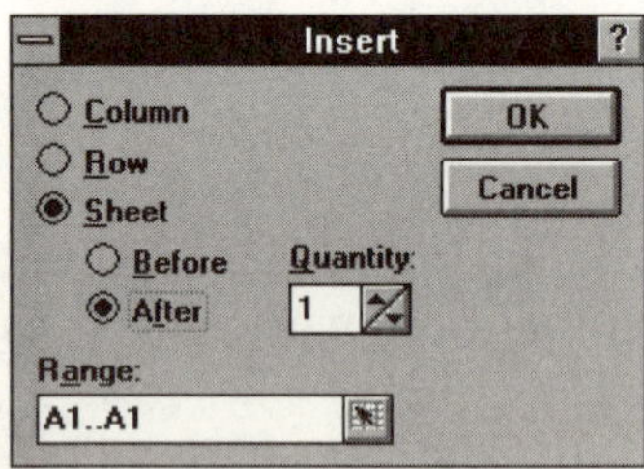

5. Choose Sheet by pressing Alt-S or by clicking Sheet with the mouse. (The Worksheet Insert command also has options for inserting columns or rows at a particular location in a worksheet, but in this case you want to insert entire new worksheets instead.)

If you were not in Perspective mode, you could click on the New Sheet button on the right side of the Edit Line to insert a sheet. Clicking the New Sheet button is an example of using a Smart-Icon for faster access to 1-2-3 command options.

6. Choose <u>Q</u>uantity to open the text box and enter the number of worksheets that you want to insert. As you can see, 1 is the default value displayed inside the box.

7. Enter **2** in the Quantity text box. This tells 1-2-3 to insert two new worksheets into the window. Press ↵ or click the OK button to confirm your entry.

Instead of entering 2 in the seventh step, you could click on the ↑ or ↓ arrows to the right of the Quantity text box to dial up the 2, the value you want to enter.

Now the two additional sections in the window are filled with new worksheet grids, as in Figure 1.6.

8. Press Ctrl-PgUp to activate the top worksheet, and then press Ctrl-PgDn twice to activate the other two worksheets in turn.

Three worksheets in the window, the top two having been inserted

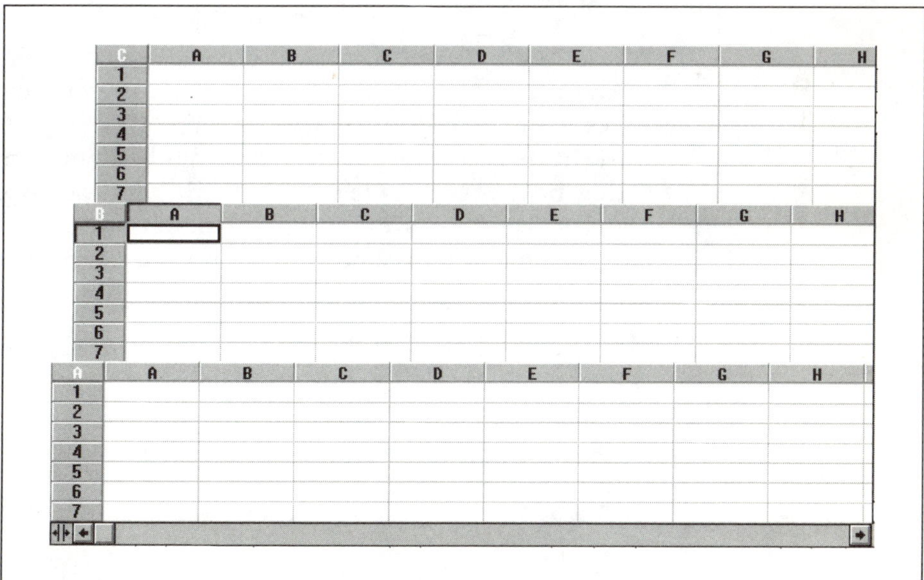

The edit line is found directly below the menu bar.

One worksheet in a window is active at a time. Notice that the worksheets are identified by the letters A, B, and C in the upper-left corner. As you activate each window, you'll see the *current cell address* displayed as A:A1, B:A1, or C:A1 in the *selection indicator*, the box located on the left side of the edit line. After you have experimented with the three worksheets, activate worksheet A, as follows:

9. Choose <u>V</u>iew ➤ C<u>l</u>ear Split to restore the original single-work-sheet display in the window. The two worksheets that you inserted are still there. You can confirm this by pressing CtrlPgUp from the keyboard, or by looking at the folder tabs directly above the work-sheet window.

Reviewing What You've Learned So Far

Take a moment to review what you've learned in these initial hands-on exercises.

Worksheets A worksheet window has the capacity for storing multiple worksheets—actually as many as 256. Every new worksheet window starts out with only one worksheet. You choose <u>E</u>dit ➤ <u>I</u>nsert to add new worksheets to a window. By activating the Perspective option in the Split dialog box, you can view three worksheets at once. Regardless of how many worksheets are actually displayed, you can press Ctrl-PgUp or Ctrl-PgDn to activate and view the previous or next worksheet in a window.

Like the columns in a worksheet, multiple worksheets in a window are identified by letters of the alphabet, from A, B, and C for the first three worksheets, up to IV for worksheet 256.

Cells A *complete cell address* consists of three elements:

- The worksheet letter, followed by a colon
- The column letter
- The row number

For example, the following address refers to the cell at the intersection of column E and row 29, on the third worksheet in a window:

C:E29

Up to now, you have used menu commands—and their dialog boxes—to make changes to the appearance and content of a worksheet window. To make your work easier and more efficient, Lotus 1-2-3 for Windows offers alternative tools for accomplishing particular tasks. Depending on your preferences and work patterns, these alternatives can be quicker and simpler than the standard menu commands. We'll examine some of these tools in the upcoming sections of this chapter.

SmartIcons for Making Your Work Go Faster

<table>
<tr><td>**N O T E**</td><td>You cannot access SmartIcons with the keyboard.</td></tr>
</table>

One of the most engaging new features in 1-2-3 is the SmartIcons—the row of icons above the worksheet area in the top portion of the 1-2-3 window. These tools are onestep shortcuts for accomplishing commonly used menu commands, including file storage, printing, copying, graphing, and formatting. You'll learn what each icon does as you study them in later chapters. To perform the action that an icon represents, you simply click a SmartIcon with the mouse.

In most cases, the pictures that appear on the SmartIcons give you a good idea about their purpose. For example, the second icon from the left in the SmartIcon bar shows an arrow pointing inside a folder. As you may have guessed, this icon saves the current worksheet to disk. In other words, this icon is a shortcut for File ➤ Save. Try clicking this icon with the mouse. You will hear 1-2-3 save the file to disk.

Quickly Learning What an Icon Does

Conveniently, 1-2-3 for Windows offers you a simple technique for finding out the meaning and use of each SmartIcon. To find out what a particular icon does:

1. Position the mouse pointer over the icon you want to learn about.

2. Press and hold down the *right* mouse button. As long as you hold down the button, 1-2-3 displays a brief description of its use on the title bar at the top of the 1-2-3 window.

If you try holding down the right mouse button on the Save icon, you'll see the words "Save the current file" in the 1-2-3 title bar, as shown in Figure 1.7.

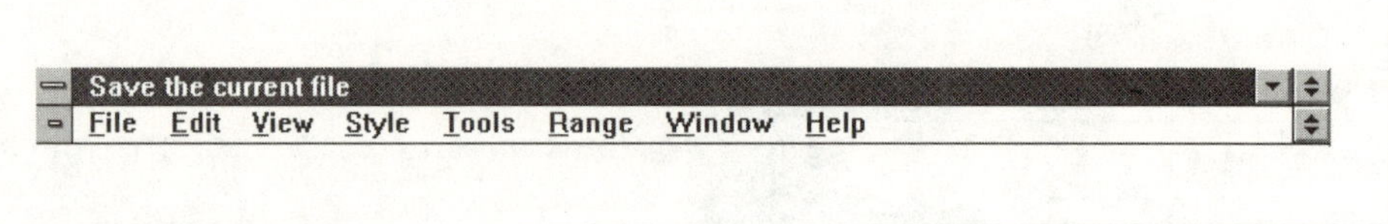

SmartIcons overview Take a few moments now to learn what the other SmartIcons do. Press the right mouse button over each one in turn, and note the description that 1-2-3 displays at the top of the window. Table 1.1 lists the 1-2-3 descriptions of the 24 SmartIcons initially displayed.

TABLE 1.1: The 24 SmartIcons Initially Displayed by 1-2-3

SMARTICON	1-2-3 DESCRIPTION
	Open an existing file
	Save the current file
	Print the selection
	Preview the print selection
	Undo the last command or action

TABLE 1.1: The 24 SmartIcons Initially Displayed by 1-2-3 (continued)

SMARTICON	1-2-3 DESCRIPTION
	Cut to the Clipboard
	Copy to the Clipboard
	Paste the Clipboard contents
	Create and embed data in the worksheet
	Bold data
	Italicize data
	Underline data
	Align data to the left
	Align data to the right
	Center data
	Complete a sequence in a selected range
	Start Ami Pro
	Start Lotus Dialog Editor
	Start Freelance Graphics
	Start Lotus Organizer
	Start Improv
	Start Lotus Notes
	Start cc:Mail
	Select the next set of SmartIcons

NOTE

To learn how to customize SmartIcons, see Chapter 2.

Lotus 1-2-3 for Windows allows you to *customize* the SmartIcon set. Choose Tools SmartIcons to view a large library of predefined *standard icons*. From this library, you can select a group of icons useful for your own work. You can also remove icons that you don't expect to use.

Another special feature included in Lotus 1-2-3 for Windows is the 1-2-3 Classic window, the subject of the next section of this chapter.

The 1-2-3 Classic Window

The 1-2-3 Classic window is a special alternate menu system for users who are upgrading from 1-2-3 Release 3.1 or from an earlier DOS release of the program. This menu appears on the screen when you press the slash key—the key that was pressed to access menus in all previous versions of Lotus 1-2-3. (Alternatively, you can press Shift-<.) Press the slash key now, and you will see the 1-2-3 Classic window at the top of the screen, as in Figure 1.8. If you have worked with a previous version of 1-2-3, the commands in the Classic window will be comfortingly familiar. This alternate menu system is accessible only from the keyboard, not with the mouse.

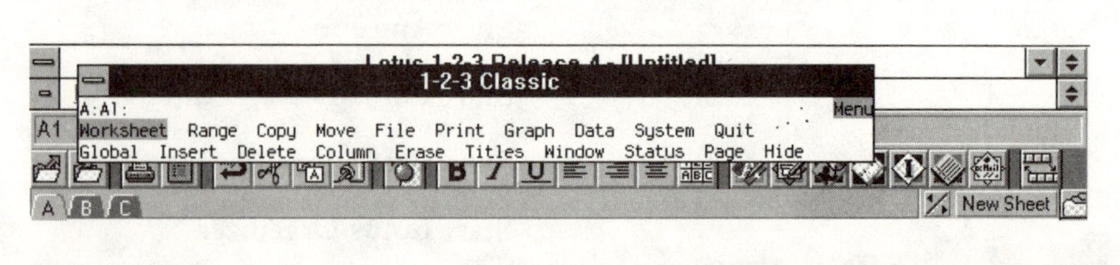

TIP

Use the 1-2-3 Classic window while you are first adjusting to the new 1-2-3 for Windows interface, but try to wean yourself from it as quickly as possible. Learn to use the standard menu bar and the SmartIcons to accomplish tasks in this new environment. In the long run, you'll become a much more efficient Windows user if you adjust yourself to the standard ways of accomplishing tasks in Windows.

As an exercise with the Classic menu system, try switching between the Perspective mode and the single-worksheet view in the current window:

1. Press **/** if you haven't done so already to bring up the 1-2-3 Classic menu. With the menu displayed on the screen, choose the **W**orksheet command.

2. Choose **W**indow.

3. Select **P**erspective. The result is the same as selecting <u>V</u>iew ➤ <u>S</u>plit ➤ <u>P</u>erspective: the current window displays three worksheets. Notice that the 1-2-3 Classic menu disappears after you select the commands.

4. Press the following four keys in sequence: **/WWC**. (This was the traditional notation for representing command selections in 1-2-3. In this case, the notation represents the **/Worksheet Window Clear** command from the 1-2-3 Classic menu.) The current window once again displays a single worksheet.

By the way, if you press Shift-colon (:), another part of the 1-2-3 Classic menu appears on the screen. This second Classic menu offers commands for formatting and preparing a worksheet for printing and publication. By contrast, the standard 1-2-3 for Windows menu offers all of the program's commands in a single convenient system of pull-down menus—another strong argument in favor of using the Windowsstyle menu rather than the Classic menus.

As a final introductory exercise, you'll enter data values into some of the cells of the worksheet you've been examining.

Data Entry and the Mode Indicator

Lotus 1-2-3 recognizes two general types of data for entry into the cells of a worksheet: *labels* and *values*.

- A label is a non-numeric entry beginning with a letter of the alphabet or with one of several special symbols that 1-2-3 recognizes as the first character in a label.

- A value is a number or the numeric result of a formula. (Actually, Lotus also recognizes date and time entries, and translates them into numeric values.)

Entering Data in Cells

Several interesting changes take place in the 1-2-3 program window when you begin entering a data into cells. You'll explore these changes in the following brief exercise, as you enter the word *Profit* as a label in cell A1 and the value 9876 in cell A2.

1. Press the Home key, if necessary, to select cell A1.

2. From the keyboard, hold down the Shift key and type the letter **P**.

Notice the mode indicator in the status bar; it shows the word *Label*, which means that 1-2-3 is accepting your entry as a non-numeric data item.

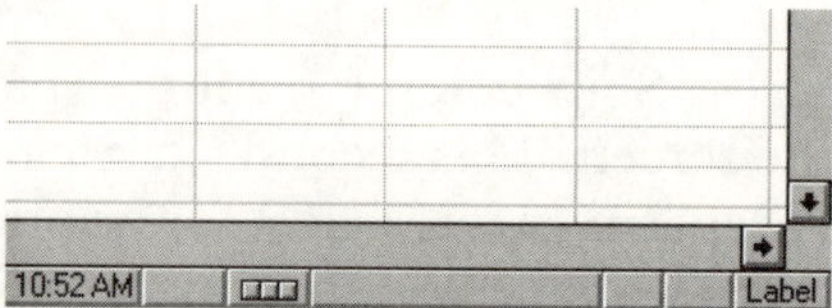

NOTE   As you'll learn in Chapter 2, the contents box is also where you can edit a data item or formula that is already stored in a cell.

The uppercase *P* that you typed appears on the edit line, just below the menu bar, in an area called the *contents box*. The contents box displays data or formulas that you are entering from the keyboard. Just to the left of the contents box appear four boxes. They are, respectively, the Navigator, the Function selector, the Cancel button (the one with an *X*) and the Confirm button (the one with a check mark). You'll learn about these boxes later.

3. Complete the label by typing the remaining letters of the word *Profit*. If you make a mistake, you can press the Backspace key to erase the last character you typed.

4. Confirm the entry either by clicking the Confirm button with the mouse or by pressing ↵.

Once again, notice the changes that occur on your worksheet and in the 1-2-3 window. The Cancel button and the Confirm button disappear, and the data item you entered into the contents box is copied into the current cell, A1. The label is left-justified inside the cell, following the default *alignment* for labels in 1-2-3. The mode indicator now displays the word *Ready*.

5. Press ↓ to select cell A2.

6. Type the four digits **9876** from the keyboard. This time the mode indicator displays the word *Value*, which means that 1-2-3 is accepting your data entry as a numeric value. As before, the entry appears inside the contents box, and the Cancel and Confirm buttons are displayed just to the left of this box.

7. Press ↓ once. This action accomplishes two steps at once: it completes the data entry and moves the cell pointer down to cell A3. Notice that the value 9876 is displayed right-justified inside cell A2. Numeric values are always right-justified in Lotus 1-2-3.

8. In cell A3, begin the following label entry: **ABC**. (Do not press ↵.) Now cancel the entry by clicking the Cancel button with the mouse, or by pressing Esc.

T I P

You can always check the mode indicator during data entry to make sure that 1-2-3 is accepting your data the way you are expecting it to—that is, as a label or a value.

You can complete an entry by pressing ↵, by pressing a direction key (such as ↑, ↓, ←, or →), or by clicking the Confirm button with the mouse. Cancel an entry by clicking the Cancel button or by pressing the Escape key.

Exiting 1-2-3

This is the end of the hands-on portion of this chapter. If you wish to exit 1-2-3 before you continue reading, here are the steps:

1. Choose File ➤ Exit from the menu bar (or press Alt-F4).
2. In the Exit dialog box, choose No to indicate that you wish to exit without saving your current worksheet.

After these steps, you remain in Windows, but the 1-2-3 application window is no longer open.

In the remainder of this chapter, we'll examine a set of example applications. In the context of these examples, you'll begin exploring the three major 1-2-3 components—spreadsheet, graphics, and database.

Planning, Developing, and Creating a Worksheet

As you know, you can enter labels, numbers, and chronological values (dates and times) as the data values on a worksheet. You can also enter *formulas* that instruct Lotus to perform arithmetic operations on your data. Given a table of raw data, a worksheet simplifies all kinds of calculations, from finding bottom-line numeric totals to performing complex statistical and financial formulas.

Perhaps the single most important feature of the Lotus spreadsheet is this: Worksheets automatically recalculate totals and other formulas whenever you make changes to raw data.

This essential characteristic is what distinguishes an "electronic spreadsheet" from making calculations with paper, a pencil, and an eraser. You can make changes to data values whenever you want without having to face the prospect of redoing the rest of your work. If you plan and write your formulas appropriately, Lotus recalculates all numeric values that depend upon the raw data you have changed.

Spreadsheet users sometimes refer to this essential characteristic as 1-2-3's "what-if" capability. You can find out what happens to a specific set of calculations when you make changes to the data that affect the calculations. "What-if" questions come up in an infinite variety of common business applications. Consider the following examples:

- What is the new break-even point in the projected sales of a product if costs increase by a specific amount per unit?

- What happens to a company's projected tax rate this year if it purchases a major depreciable asset, such as a new computer?

- What is the new monthly payment on a business loan if the term of the loan is doubled and the interest rate decreased by 1 percent?

In calculations that are done by hand, finding the answers to questions like these would take a lot of time and effort—especially if many intermediate calculations had to be made leading up to a final value. But in Lotus 1-2-3 you simply change the appropriate data parameters in your worksheet, and the rest of the work is done for you. As you gain experience with worksheets, you'll quickly learn to organize your work to take full advantage of the "what-if" feature, especially when making business calculations.

The upcoming sections of this chapter present example exercises in planning and developing a Lotus 1-2-3 worksheet. The calculations for our sample "what-if" problem are not typical ones like those listed above—but nonetheless they will illustrate the power of 1-2-3. In our example scenario, a company has invited a nutritionist named Barbara Johnson to conduct lunchtime seminars for its employees on the subject of good nutrition for health-conscious working people. The employees are interested in a somewhat confusing diet-related subject that has been in the news lately: the fat content of fast-food lunches and its effect on health. Much has been said about the so-called 30-percent fat diet and many of the employees would like more information.

For the seminars, Johnson is using Lotus 1-2-3 for Windows to prepare a series of handouts on which to base her discussion. These handouts will take the form of worksheets, graphs, and databases. She begins her preparations by designing some worksheets that analyze the caloric and fat content of what she thinks are typical lunches eaten by the employees in her audience.

To acquire a general understanding of the elements of Lotus 1-2-3, keep your own goals in mind and imagine how you would use the program to solve problems as you examine the nutritionist's work. For the moment, focus on 1-2-3's capabilities and features and not on the specific techniques used in these examples.

Developing the Worksheet

Most of the worksheets you create will likely become tools for presenting information to other people. Whether you are sharing data with the person in the next cubicle or communicating ideas to a conference of managers, your data should not only be accurate, it should be organized clearly, presented attractively, and be easy to understand. Lotus 1-2-3 for Windows includes a great many tools designed to help you meet these requirements.

The Stages of Development

Accordingly, creating a successful worksheet typically involves several stages:

1. Place a descriptive title near the top of the worksheet.

2. Enter column headings and row labels that describe the categories of numeric data that you will include in the worksheet table.

3. Enter the numeric data values themselves.

4. Write formulas that perform specific calculations on the numeric data values. When appropriate, copy these formulas to other cells on the worksheet to perform the same calculations on other columns or rows of data.

5. Improve the appearance of the data—both the labels and numbers—by changing display formats and styles in particular cells. For example, you could display certain numbers in a currency or

percentage format. Titles, labels, and numbers can also be displayed in special type styles for clarity and emphasis. For example, you could display data in boldface, italic, and underlined styles.

This progression of tasks is illustrated in Barbara Johnson's worksheet examples. Her initial goal is to explain what the 30-percent fat diet is and, in the context of this diet, to analyze typical lunches that employees eat in fast-food restaurants or bring to work themselves.

Entering the Labels and Data

As the starting point for her research, Johnson visits the fast-food restaurant across the street from the company. She knows that lots of the employees come here for quick, inexpensive lunches. She asks for nutritional information about several items on the menu and is given a nutritional report, one that is always available but only provided on request. A quick glance at the report tells Johnson that the report has the data she will need for her presentation. It lists the calories and fat content of each item on the menu.

Back at her office, she determines what the typical lunch served by this restaurant is: a hamburger, an order of french fries, some cookies, and a diet soda. She starts up Lotus 1-2-3 for Windows and begins designing a worksheet on which to present nutritional information about this particular meal.

The title She begins by entering a title for the worksheet in cells A3 and B3:

LUNCH #1   FAST FOOD RESTAURANT

She entered Lunch #1 because she is planning to create more worksheets for other menus, and this is the first worksheet. Figure 1.9 shows what the first stage of the Lunch #1 worksheet will look like when its done. Notice cells A3 and B3.

Her purpose in this worksheet is to analyze the fat content of a meal and compare it with the recommended fat intake for a healthy adult. Secondarily, she wants to translate nutritional information into meaningful data that employees will find useful when they choose what to eat for lunch.

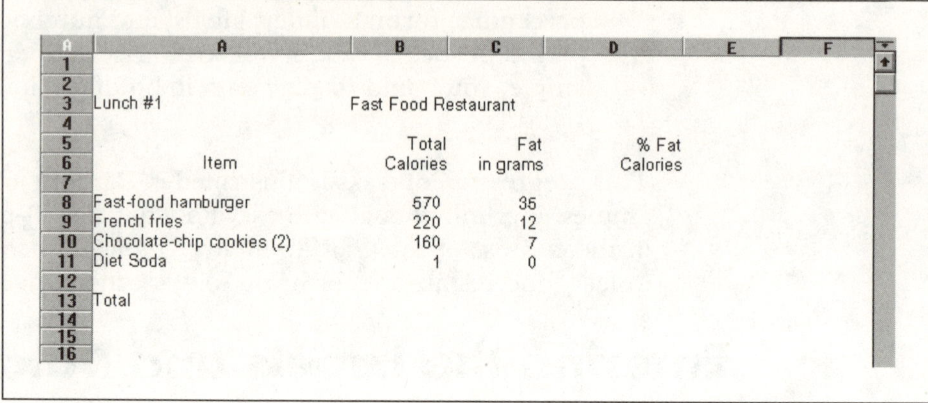

The two major nutritional facts she will present in her seminar are the following:

- Nutritionists recommend that the daily fat intake of healthy adults be 30 percent or less of their total daily caloric consumption (hence the term "30-percent fat diet").

- One gram of fat—regardless of its source—is equivalent to nine calories.

The nutritional panels on food packages usually list the fat content per serving in grams, not as a percentage of total calories. For this reason, the health-conscious consumer needs to do some arithmetic to figure out whether a food item is a reasonable part of a 30-percent fat diet. Johnson will eventually express this arithmetic in formulas and enter them on her worksheet.

The column labels She continues her work by entering labels for four columns in rows 5 and 6 (see Figure 1.9):

	TOTAL	**FAT**	**% FAT**
Item	**Calories**	**in grams**	**Calories**

The first column, "Item," is for the name of the food item. The second and third columns, "Total Calories" and "Fat in grams," will list data acquired from the nutritional report she picked up at the restaurant. The final column, "% Fat Calories," is for values that will be calculated from the available nutritional data: the percent of total calories represented by the fat content in the food item.

Next, Johnson enters four labels for the four food items. She enters the calorie and fat-in-gram numbers. She also places a "Total" line at the bottom of the table for the total figures of each column. At this point, however, she leaves the numeric columns blank.

Figure 1.9 shows Johnson's work up to this point. Notice two interesting features of this worksheet: she has widened column A to accommodate the names of the food items and removed the grid lines, the vertical and horizontal lines that separate columns and rows in a worksheet. Here you see two ways in which Lotus 1-2-3 gives the user control over the appearance of a worksheet.

Now the nutritionist has completed the first few steps of designing her worksheet. She has created a title, entered descriptive column headings and row labels to identify the numeric data in the table, and copied the basic numeric data into the table. Her next step is to write formulas to perform calculations. She'll enter formulas at two different locations on the worksheet, the Total line at the bottom of the table and the % Fat Calories column on the right side.

Writing Formulas

The purpose of a *formula* in a worksheet is to calculate a value. Usually, formulas are calculated by using the existing numbers on the worksheet as the parts of the operation. Lotus 1-2-3 displays the *result* of the formula in the cell where the formula is located. To view the formula itself, select the cell where the result is displayed and look at the contents box in the edit line—it displays the formula itself.

Lotus 1-2-3 recognizes specific formats for formulas and enforces precise rules about the correctness of those formats. Here are some of the most common elements you'll use in writing formulas:

FORMULA FORMAT	DESCRIPTION
Literal numeric values	Examples of literal numeric values are 9 and 365.
Cell addresses	In a formula, a cell address *represents* the value that is stored in the cell whose address is listed. For example, if a formula contains the cell address D5, and the value in D5 is 6, the value 6 will be used in the formula.
Arithmetic operators	Examples of arithmetic operators are + (addition), − (subtraction), * (multiplication), ^ exponentation, and / (division).
Functions	Lotus 1-2-3 lets you use functions from its large function library. A *function* is a built-in tool designed to perform a specific calculation. All of the 1-2-3 functions have names that begin with the at sign (@). For example, the @SUM function—one of the simplest and most commonly used of all the 1-2-3 functions— totals a group of numbers.

You'll find examples of all but the exponentation element in the formulas Barbara Johnson enters into her Lunch #1 worksheet.

Entering Formulas and Values in Cells

Johnson's first task is to find the total calories and the total grams of fat in the meal. To accomplish this, she begins by entering the following formula into cell B13:

```
@SUM(B8..B11)
```

To enter a formula in a cell, move the pointer to the cell and begin typing. As you might have guessed, B8..B11 inside parentheses tells the @SUM function to find the total of all values stored in cells B8, B9, B10, and B11. An expression like B8..B11 represents a *range* of cells. The two periods tell 1-2-3 to include all cells between the two listed cells in the calculation. You'll find many contexts in which ranges are important during your work with 1-2-3.

The result of the @SUM function, displayed in cell B13, is 951. Similarly, Johnson enters an @SUM expression in cell C13 to find the total grams of fat in the meal. (Actually, she has the option of entering a new version of the formula directly from the keyboard, as she did before, or *copying* the formula from cell B13 to cell C13. You'll learn the significance of copying formulas in Chapter 3.) The resulting value in cell C13 is 54.

Next, Johnson has to devise a formula to calculate the fat calories in each food item as a percentage of the total calories. Given that there are nine calories in each gram of fat, here is the formula for finding the ratio of fat calories to total calories:

$$(\text{Fat Grams} \times 9) \div \text{Total Calories}$$

Johnson's task is to translate this into a formula that 1-2-3 can accept and perform. She moves to cell D8 and enters the following:

+C8*9/B8

- Cell C8 contains the number of grams of fat in a hamburger.

- Multiplying this value by 9 gives the total calories of fat.

- Dividing the product by the total calories (stored in cell B8) gives the ratio.

When Johnson first enters this formula into cell D8, this calculated value appears in the cell: 0.55263158.

Changing number formats   This number is the decimal format of the ratio, but Johnson wants to display the ratio as a percentage. With the cell pointer still in D8, she chooses Style ➤ Number Format from the menu bar. She then selects Percent from the Format list and clicks on OK to close the Number Format dialog box. This changes the display format of the value in D8 to a percentage, and 0.55263158 has changed to 55.26%.

Rounding off numbers   Although Johnson appreciates the convenience of this predefined format, she decides that it is not exactly what she wants; she would prefer to display the percent as a rounded integer—that is, with no digits after the decimal point. She chooses Style ➤ Number Format again and enters 0 for Decimal values in the Number Format dialog box. Now, with the percentage of fat calories expressed as a rounded integer, the percentage is displayed simply as 55%.

Johnson has written a successful formula. The fat calories account for 55 percent of total calories in the hamburger. Now she copies this formula down column D—first to find the percent of fat calories for the other food items on the menu, and then to find the total percent of fat calories for the entire meal. Figure 1.10 shows the results of her work. Notice that fat calories for the meal amount to 51 percent of total calories—far above the recommended 30 percent. As Johnson notes with satisfaction, this worksheet will easily prove a point about the nutritional value of fast-food lunches!

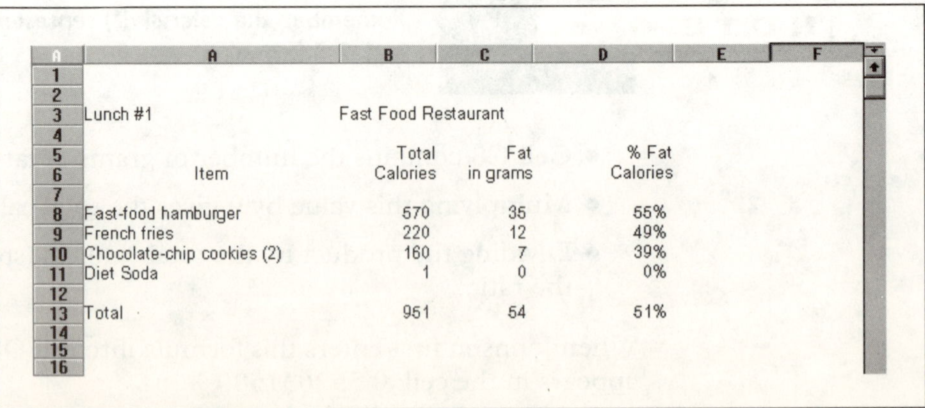

	A	B	C	D	E	F
1						
2						
3	Lunch #1	Fast Food Restaurant				
4						
5		Total	Fat	% Fat		
6	Item	Calories	in grams	Calories		
7						
8	Fast-food hamburger	570	35	55%		
9	French fries	220	12	49%		
10	Chocolate-chip cookies (2)	160	7	39%		
11	Diet Soda	1	0	0%		
12						
13	Total	951	54	51%		
14						
15						
16						

Preparing the Worksheet for Presentation

N O T E *Left-justified* means that the text is aligned along the left margin or left side of the column. *Right-justified* means that it is aligned along the right margin or right side of the column.

Up to now, Barbara Johnson has concentrated on entering data and writing formulas, without worrying much about the appearance of her worksheet. With two exceptions, she left data items in their default formats, alignments, and display styles. She applied the Percent format to the fourth column in her data table, and she also changed the alignment of the four column headings. Can you see in Figure 1.10 that the four column heading labels are not displayed in their default, left-justified positions? Lotus 1-2-3 initially left-justifies label entries in cells, but Johnson's label entries in rows 6 and 7 are right-justified.

Now the nutritionist is ready to give some thought to the appearance of her worksheet. Lotus 1-2-3 for Windows offers a rich variety of options for changing appearances. For example, she can change formats for numeric values, displaying them in the currency, decimal, or percentage format. Values and labels can be displayed in different *styles*—in bold, italics, or underlined characters—to provide emphasis in a worksheet. Furthermore, 1-2-3 offers a selection of type fonts and font sizes for displaying and printing the information in a worksheet.

Changing Fonts and Type Size

Johnson decides to use combinations of bold, italic, and underlined styles—along with larger type sizes for selected data items—to prepare her worksheet for presentation. You can see the result of her work in Figure 1.11.

Some of the options for changing fonts and type size are available with the click of a mouse, thanks to SmartIcons. For example, here are the steps

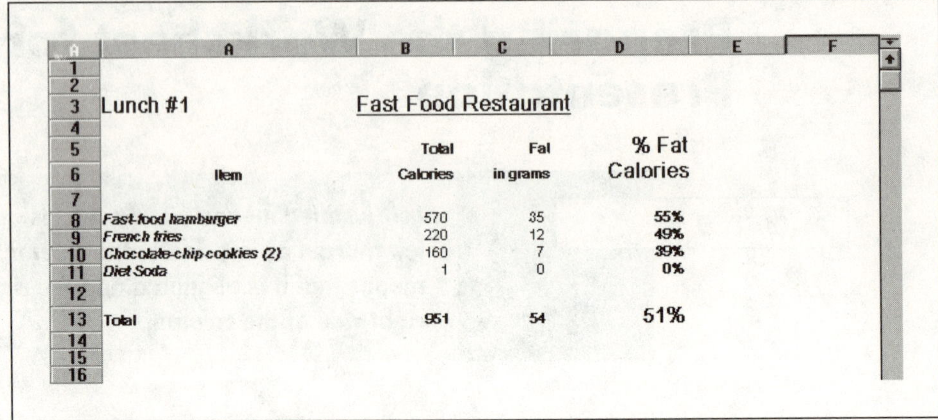

Johnson took to change the column of food items (A8 to A11) to bold italic type style:

1. Select the target range of cells—in this case, A8 down to A11—by positioning the mouse pointer at A8 and dragging the mouse down to A11. Lotus 1-2-3 highlights the entire range.

2. Choose the Bold SmartIcon. The Bold style is applied to all the labels in the range.

3. Click the Italics SmartIcon. The Italic style is applied to the labels.

Notice how these actions were performed. First you select a range of cells on which to perform the action, and then you choose an option to apply to the range. This is the typical way of accomplishing many kinds of tasks in a worksheet. Conveniently, Lotus 1-2-3 for Windows often lets you choose between the following two approaches:

- Select a range first, and then choose a command that applies to the range.

- Choose a command, and then use the command's dialog box to specify the range over which the command will act.

Which method you choose is a matter of personal preference and convenience. The end result is always the same.

Besides changing the food item to italic, Johnson also enlarges the type in column 3 and underlines the Fast Food Restaurant label. She changes the type in the column headings and boldfaces the percentage figures in the third column. Look closely at Figure 1.11 to see these changes.

The nutritionist has now completed her first version of the lunch worksheet. She saves her work to disk by pulling down the File menu and selecting the Save As command. She supplies the name Lunches for her worksheet, and 1-2-3 accordingly saves the file under the name LUNCHES.WK4.

She is now ready to begin formulating other lunch menus to include in her presentation on fat intake in a healthy diet. Clearly, the first menu she studied is not a healthy lunch. She decides to prepare two more menus, the first a combination of items purchased from the fastfood restaurant and food prepared at home, and the second a "brown bag" lunch brought from home.

This is where 1-2-3's "what if" facility becomes central to her work. As you'll see, the nutritionist can create the two new lunch worksheets simply by changing a few data items in the original worksheet. Whenever she enters new numeric data values to describe a particular food item, 1-2-3 automatically recalculates the applicable formulas.

Making Changes in the Data

For Lunch #2, Johnson decides to make two changes in the menu. She substitutes a turkey sandwich for the fast-food hamburger and a carton of milk for the diet soda. She begins by entering the names of the two new food items in cells A8 and A11, as follows:

A8	*Turkey sandwich (with mayo)*
A11	*Lowfat milk (1I2 pint)*

To change the contents of a cell in a worksheet, you can simply select the cell and enter a new label or value. When you confirm the entry pressing ↵, the previous data item disappears, and the new item takes its place. However, if you applied a display style to the cell, it is retained. In this case the two new food items are still displayed in bold italic type.

Next, Johnson determines the approximate caloric and fat contents of these two new menu items. She enters the calories into column B (cell B8 for the turkey sandwich and B11 for the milk). She enters the fat content, in grams, into column C (cell C8 for the sandwich and C11 for the milk).

Playing with "What-If" Factors

Each time Johnson enters a new numeric data value, three changes take place instantly:

- A new column total appears in the Total line at the bottom of the worksheet (row 13).

- A new fat percentage appears in the final column of the worksheet (column D).

- The new total fat percentage for the meal appears in cell D13.

In effect, these are the "what-if" factors for her worksheet. They tell Johnson what happens to the total calories, the total fat content, and the fat percentages if she changes an item in the menu. Because 1-2-3 can recalculate formulas instantly, "what-if" answers appear instantly when the nutritionist makes changes in the worksheet data. Figure 1.12 shows the

	A	B	C	D	E	F
1						
2						
3	Lunch #2	Brown Bag Plus Fast Food				
4						
5		Total	Fat	% Fat		
6	Item	Calories	in grams	Calories		
7						
8	Turkey sandwich (with mayo)	420	18	39%		
9	French fries	220	12	49%		
10	Chocolate-chip cookies (2)	160	7	39%		
11	Low-fat milk (1/2 pint)	181	5	25%		
12						
13	Total	981	42	39%		
14						
15						
16						

second lunch menu, with the revised nutritional information. (Notice that the title of the worksheet has also been changed.) In terms of fat calories, this meal is an improvement over the first one, but it still does not meet the goal of the 30-percent fat diet.

For her third menu, the nutritionist wants to illustrate the importance of making simple but careful dietary decisions. After revising the title again, she makes two more changes to the menu. She removes the mayonnaise from the turkey sandwich and substitutes an apple for the french fries. She enters the new calorie and fat data into columns B and C. Once again, 1-2-3 recalculates her formulas as she changes nutritional data. The final result, shown in Figure 1.13, is a dramatically reduced fat percentage, well below the 30-percent goal.

	A	B	C	D	E	F
1						
2						
3	Lunch #3	Brown Bag				
4						
5		Total	Fat	% Fat		
6	Item	Calories	in grams	Calories		
7						
8	Turkey sandwich (no mayo)	380	7	17%		
9	Apple	81	0	0%		
10	Chocolate-chip cookies (2)	160	7	39%		
11	Low-fat milk (1/2 pint)	181	5	25%		
12						
13	Total	802	19	21%		
14						
15						
16						

For convenience, Barbara Johnson decides to save all three of the lunch worksheets in a single file. She chooses Edit ➤ Insert ➤ Sheet to add two worksheets to the current window, and copies the current version of the lunch menu to each of the two new worksheets. She reformulates the first two menus in worksheets A and B, and retains the final menu in worksheet C. When she saves her work to disk, LUNCHES.WK4 contains three worksheets, one for each lunch menu she will present in her seminar. Figure 1.14 shows how these worksheets appear in the Perspective mode.

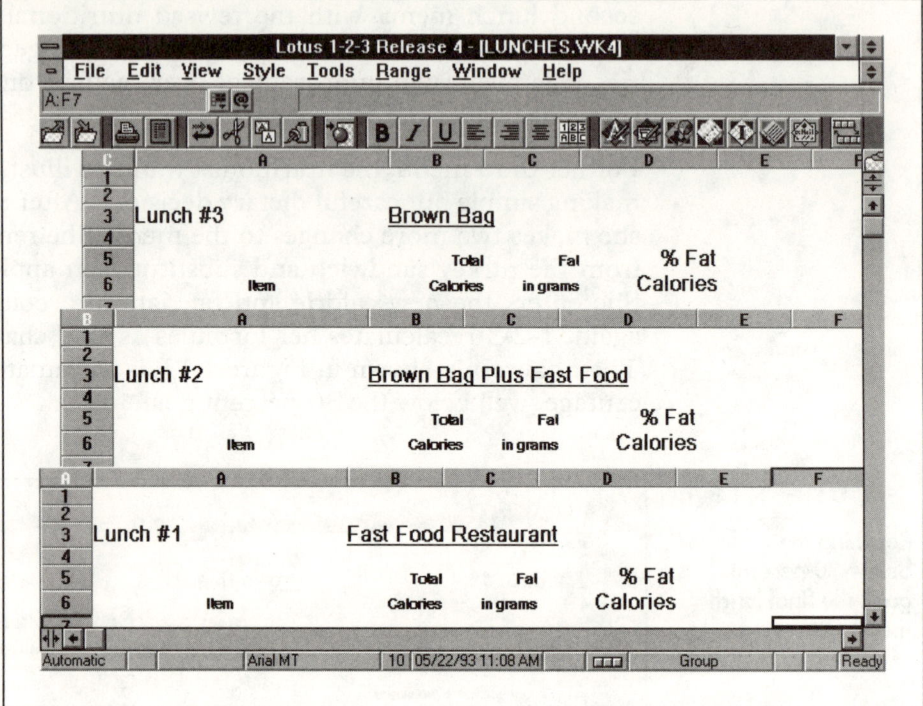

Creating Graphs from a Worksheet

The graphics component of 1-2-3 gives you efficient tools for creating graphs and charts from your worksheet data. Lotus 1-2-3 for Windows supports an impressive variety of two- and three-dimensional graph types, including line graphs, bar graphs, and pie charts. The initial steps for creating a graph are simple:

1. Select a worksheet range with the numbers and labels you want represented in your graph.

2. Issue a command to create a graph from the range you selected.

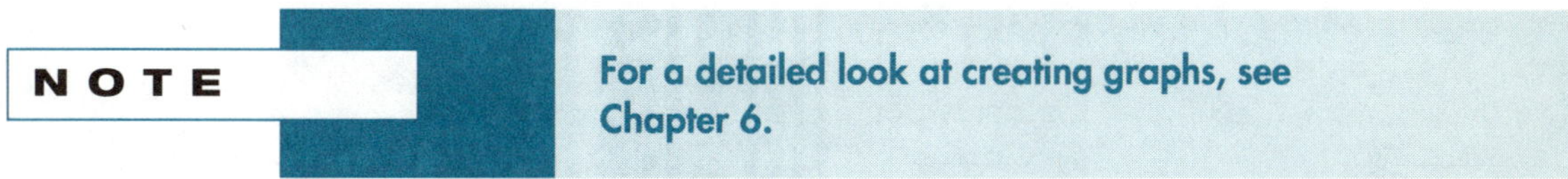

Again, notice the familiar pattern in these steps: first select a worksheet range, and then give a command. Once you've given the command, the graph will appear in a new window on the screen and 1-2-3 will offer both a new set of graphrelated commands on the menu bar and a new set of SmartIcons.

After you have created the initial graph from a table of data, you can change the graph type and customize the graph by adding titles, labels, a legend, and other graph objects, including arrows and frames. The graph menu and SmartIcons offer options for all these features.

Like the formulas in a worksheet, graphs are dependent upon the original raw data. When you make changes to the raw data that the graphs represent, 1-2-3 automatically re-creates the graphs. This is perhaps the ultimate in "what-if" experiments: You can change a data value on your worksheet and immediately see the effect in a graph.

A graph is always associated with the worksheet from which it was originally created. When you save a worksheet file to disk, the graphs you created are saved along with the worksheet. Furthermore, 1-2-3 allows you to copy a graph directly onto a worksheet so that you can view—and print—the worksheet table along with its graph.

Designing a Graph

Barbara Johnson now turns her attention to a new topic that she wants to cover in her seminar. She realizes that many people have trouble interpreting the nutritional information that appears on food labels. In regards to fat content, the problem is simple: labels normally disclose the number of grams of fat per serving, whereas the important factor to consider is the percent of fat calories in the serving. For example, Johnson has found the following information on a package of bologna:

SERVING SIZE: **1 SLICE (30 GRAMS)**

Calories per
serving: 90

Fat per serving: 8 grams

In this example, the fat content (8 grams) is less than a third of the total weight of a serving (30 grams). However, the significant factor is not the weight of the fat, but rather the fat calories in proportion to the total calories. The 8 grams of fat are equivalent to 72 calories, or more than three-quarters of the total caloric content of a serving.

To underscore the importance of this distinction, Johnson decides to create some simple graphics and hand them out at the seminar. The graphs should illustrate clearly the discrepancy between the weight content and the caloric content of fat in a particular food item.

For this second topic, the nutritionist will take advantage of the second major component of Lotus 1-2-3, graphics. She begins by creating a small worksheet table with the information about a slice of bologna. As shown in Figure 1.15, the worksheet has two rows of numeric data, one to record the weight and one to record caloric content of the food serving. There are three columns of numbers. The first two columns display the fat content and the total serving data. The final column is a calculation of the percentage of fat. While the fat is only 27 percent of the weight of a serving, it is a full 80 percent of the caloric content.

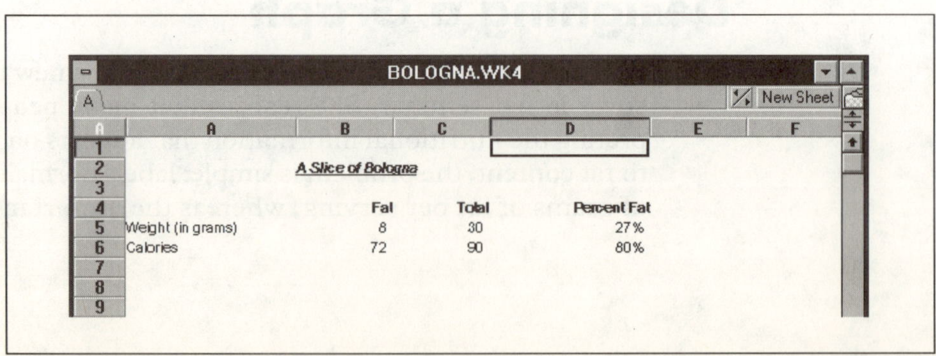

Creating a Graph

After completing this worksheet, the nutritionist follows a quick and easy sequence of steps to create her graphs. She decides to create one bar graph to represent the relationship between the total weight of a serving and the fat weight in the serving. She will create a second graph to represent the relationship between total calories and fat calories.

Chapter 6, which introduces the graphics component of 1-2-3, explains in detail how to create graphs.

For each graph in turn, she selects the range of worksheet data that she wants to include: A5..C5 for the weight and A6..C6 for the calories. These ranges include labels (in column A) that will identify the elements of the graph, along with two columns of numeric data (columns B and C). Next, she clicks the CreateGraph SmartIcon. Lotus 1-2-3 opens a new graph window and displays an initial line graph depicting the data she has selected on the worksheet.

When a chart is the object currently selected on-screen, the Chart menu option appears in the menu bar in place of the Range menu option.

But Johnson decides that three-dimensional charts are the best way to illustrate this particular set of data. She chooses <u>T</u>ools ➤ <u>C</u>hart. In the dialog box, she selects the three-dimensional bar graph type, and she drags open a box on-screen to show where she wants to place the chart.

Next, she uses other commands from the Chart menu to add titles and *legends* to the graphs. A legend identifies the meaning of elements in the graph. In this case, the legend lists the bar colors that represent fat weight and calories, and total weight and calories.

The entire job of creating the graphs takes only a few minutes. The result of Johnson's work appears in Figure 1.16. Each graph contains a cluster of two bars. The first graph shows the relationship between the fat weight and the total weight of a serving, and the second graph shows the relationship between fat calories and total calories. The contrast between these two relationships is dramatic, and the nutritionist is satisfied that this handout will adequately illustrate her point to the seminar participants.

For the final topic in her seminar on lunchtime nutrition for business people, Barbara Johnson wants to apply the 30-percent fat diet to a group of people with different nutritional needs. For this purpose, she has created a database of imaginary, but representative, clients whose daily caloric and fat requirements vary. She wants to compare these individual requirements with the nutritional content of one of the lunch menus she devised earlier. Her goal is to demonstrate the suitability—or inadequacy—of this menu for meeting specific nutritional needs.

The Bologna graphs, showing the weight of the fat and—more importantly—the fat calories in proportion to the total calories

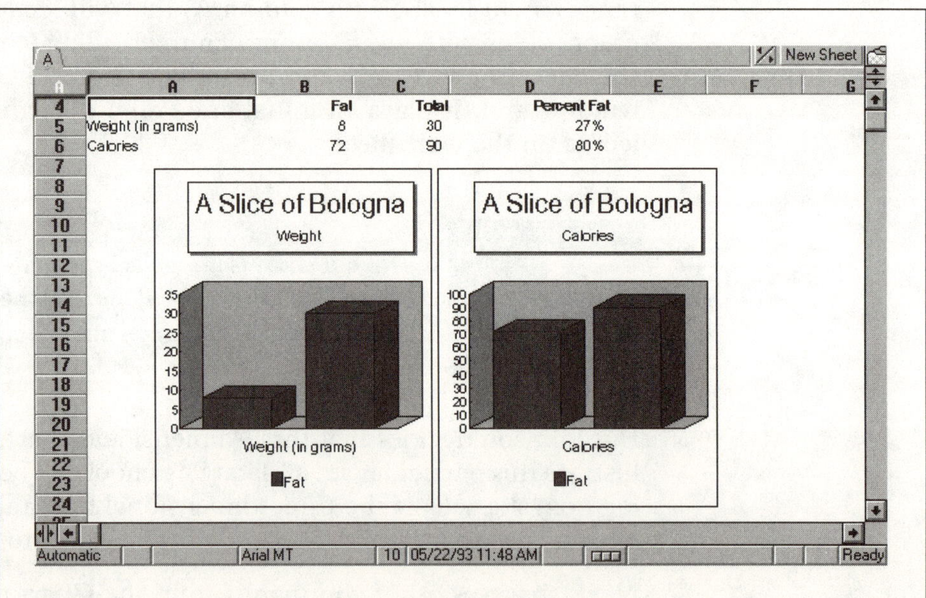

Performing Database Operations

| **N O T E** | Databases are discussed in detail in Chapters 7 and 8. |

A *database* in 1-2-3 is a collection of *records* stored in the rows and columns of a worksheet. For example, a client address directory and a list of inventory items are each a database. Each row in the database contains one record of information. The worksheet columns contain the *fields* of the database—that is, the categories of information within each record. The *field names* are column headings that describe each category of information, or field. For example, an inventory database might include the following fields:

ITEM   **QUANTITY**   **REORDERDATE**   **REORDERAMOUNT**   **PRICE**

Usually a record in the database includes a data entry for each field. Some field items are labels or numbers that you enter directly from the keyboard. Others field items may be *calculated fields*—that is, numeric or chronological items that are calculated from the data in other fields.

The length of a database is equal to the number of records currently stored in the table. For example, an inventory database might have a length of a few dozen, or a few thousand, records. Over time, the length of a database might change, as you insert or append new records, or as you perform operations that delete records.

After you've developed a database in a worksheet, you can perform a variety of operations on the records in the database. A *query* is a database operation that isolates records that match specific *selection criteria*. Commands in the 1-2-3 Database menu are designed to simplify the query process, regardless of the length of your database. After writing expressions that represent your selection criteria, you can choose commands that perform the following queries:

QUERY COMMAND	RESULT
Find Records	Highlights records that match your selection criteria.
Delete Records	Removes selected records from the database.
Extract	Copies matching records from the database to another table location that you specify.
Modify	Also extracts matching records, but keeps track of the locations of the extracted records. You can make changes in the extracted data table and then instruct 1-2-3 to return the modified records to their original places in the database.

Lotus 1-2-3 offers other important database operations. For example, you can rearrange, or *sort*, the database records in alphabetical, numerical, or chronological order. You can also apply statistical functions to selected records. Lotus 1-2-3 offers a complete set of built-in functions that apply specifically to databases.

For the purposes of this introduction, you'll examine a short (and imaginary) database that nutritionist Barbara Johnson might develop to describe the nutritional requirements of a specific group of her clients.

Defining a Database

The first step in designing a database is to determine the number and types of data fields for the table and to choose a name for each field. Field names play several important roles in query operations and criteria formulas. For this reason, you must carefully follow the rules that 1-2-3 establishes for field names. Essentially, a field name is a one-word label (no spaces) consisting of letters and digits.

The nutritionist wants to include seven fields in her database of imaginary clients. On the first row of her database table, she enters seven field names. The first four names— Name, Age, Sex, and Weight—will have personal information about each client. The final three fields—TotalCalories, FatCalories, and FatGrams—will represent nutritional guidelines:

TotalCalories	is the recommended daily caloric intake needed to maintain a person's current weight. The nutritionist will enter this value directly from the keyboard for each client.
FatCalories	is the recommended maximum daily fat consumption for a person. To calculate the value of this field for each client, Johnson will write a formula based on the principles of the 30-percent fat diet.
FatGrams	is the recommended maximum daily fat consumption in grams. This will also be a calculated field and will be found by dividing FatCalories by 9. (You'll recall that a gram of fat is equal to nine calories.)

Entering the Records

After creating the field names, Johnson begins entering the individual records of the database. Each client record occupies one row of the table. She begins by entering data in the fields that are not calculated—Name, Age, Sex, Weight, and TotalCalories. When these fields are entered for each record, she writes and copies formulas for the two calculated fields, FatCalories and FatGrams.

Her completed database appears in Figure 1.17. Notice that the records are entered in alphabetical order by client name. To work more effectively with the information, she may want to view the database in a different order. Lotus 1-2-3 has an efficient Sort command that she can use to rearrange the records quickly. She will also want to perform other database operations to create a meaningful handout for the seminar participants. The 1-2-3 Data menu has a variety of commands that she will use to accomplish specific tasks with her database.

Name	Age	Sex	Weight	TotalCalories	FatCalories	FatGrams
Allen, N.	41	M	135	1650	495	55
Barnes, J.	32	F	120	1350	405	45
Byron, A.	23	M	185	2250	675	75
Everette, Y.	39	F	140	1550	465	52
Giles, C.	25	M	225	2700	810	90
Hall, N.	52	M	160	1950	585	65
Johnson, C.	35	F	155	1700	510	57
Lange, G.	27	F	115	1250	375	42
Paulson, G.	45	M	145	1750	525	58
Ralston, T.	59	F	130	1450	435	48

Daily Calories and Maximum Fat Consumption

Performing Sort and Search Operations in the Database

Sorting a database only requires a few simple steps:

1. Select the range of database records you want to sort, but *not* the database field names.

2. Choose Range ➤ Sort.

3. In the Sort dialog box, specify a *key* field for the sort. A key field is the field by which the records will be reordered. Enter the field value in the Sort by text box.

4. Specify whether you want to sort the database in Ascending or Descending order.

5. Click on the Add <u>K</u>ey button to add the Sort criteria to the All Keys list. When you have created all of the keys you wish, click on OK to close the dialog box and execute the Sort command.

The nutritionist begins her work by performing these four steps to arrange the clients from youngest to oldest—in other words, to sort the database in ascending order by the Age field. Figure 1.18 shows the result of the sort operation.

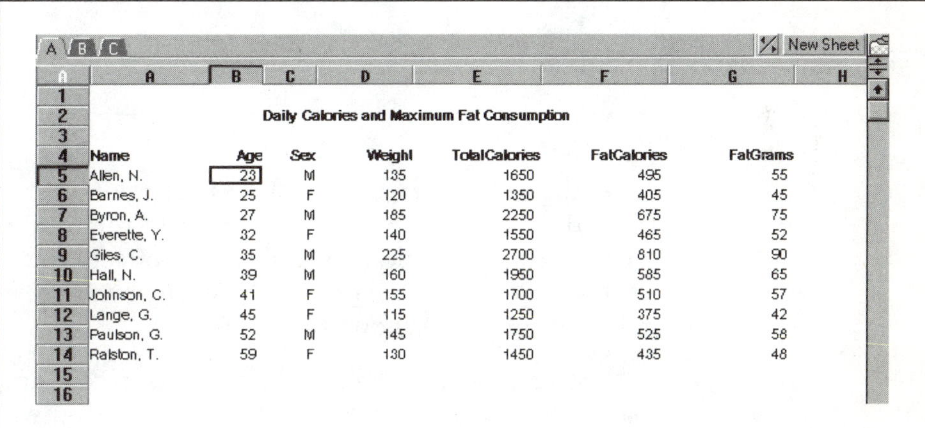

Name	Age	Sex	Weight	TotalCalories	FatCalories	FatGrams
Allen, N.	23	M	135	1650	495	55
Barnes, J.	25	F	120	1350	405	45
Byron, A.	27	M	185	2250	675	75
Everette, Y.	32	F	140	1550	465	52
Giles, C.	35	M	225	2700	810	90
Hall, N.	39	M	160	1950	585	65
Johnson, C.	41	F	155	1700	510	57
Lange, G.	45	F	115	1250	375	42
Paulson, G.	52	M	145	1750	525	58
Ralston, T.	59	F	130	1450	435	48

Johnson realizes that there might be other useful ways to order the records. For example, she could sort the records by the Weight field, but divide the database into male and female patients. In effect, this sort requires *two* key fields: the Sex field is the *primary* key and the Weight field is the *secondary key*. Figure 1.19 shows the database after this two-key sort has been completed.

Formulating Selection Criteria

Finally, the nutritionist would like to produce a second database table, a subset of the first. For this second table, she wants to extract client records that meet a particular selection criterion. To formulate this criterion, she will borrow data from her Lunches worksheet to answer the following question: Which clients can use the menu from Lunch #3 as a satisfactory way of staying within their maximum fat guidelines?

FIGURE 1.19

Sorting the database by two key fields—in this case by sex and weight

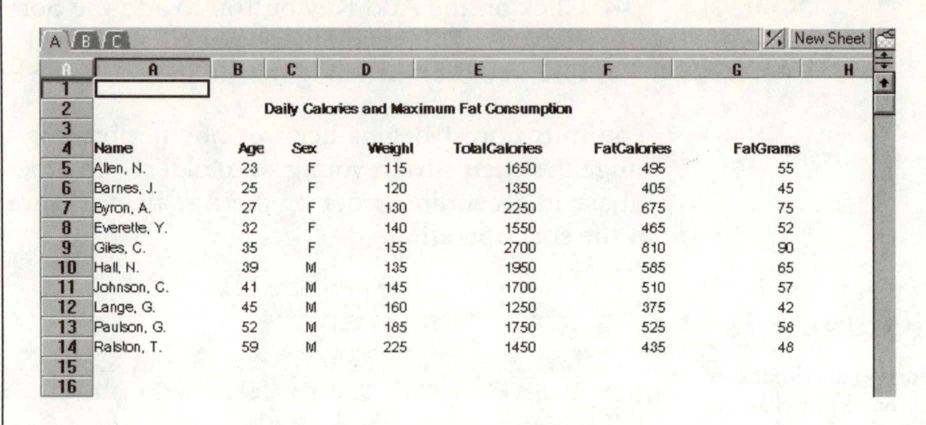

The nutritionist starts with the assumption that fat consumed at lunch should total no more than one-third of the total daily fat consumption. She writes a criterion formula that reflects this assumption, and then chooses Tools ➤ Database ➤ New Query to create the second database table. Figure 1.20 shows the results.

As you can see, only half of the patients in the sample database meet this particular selection criterion. Barbara Johnson will use this database extract table to illustrate a final point to her seminar participants: Each client must look at his or her total caloric and fat intake in relation to nutritional requirements and personal weight goals.

Summary

The three components of Lotus 1-2-3 for Windows—spreadsheet, graphics, and database—have distinct features and yet are designed to work smoothly together in a carefully integrated environment. In many business applications, you will use all components to create interrelated tables and documents.

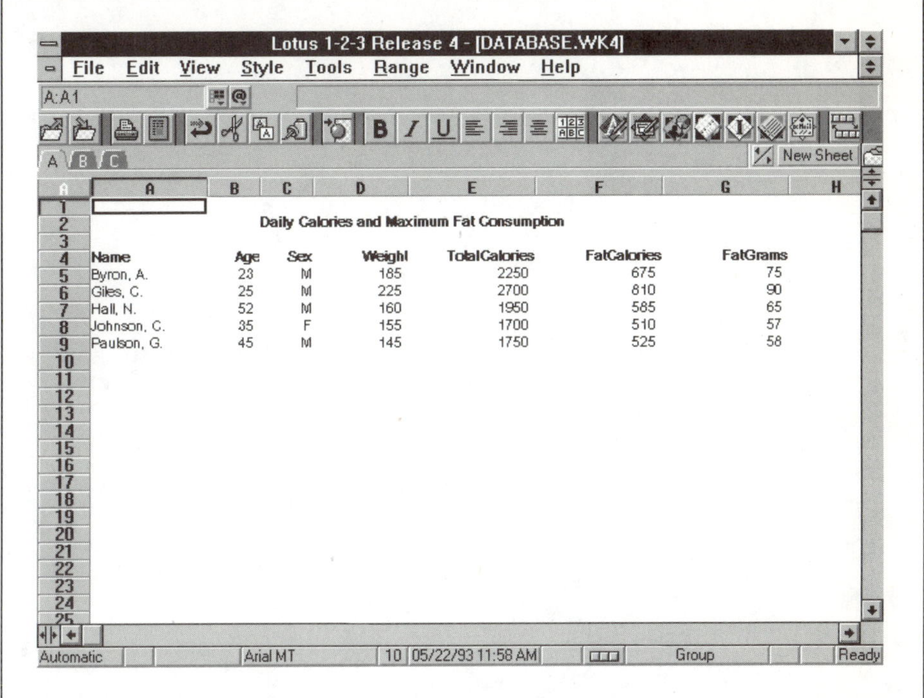

Perhaps the single most important characteristic of a 1-2-3 worksheet is its ability to recalculate formulas based on changes to raw data. This "what-if" capability is a feature you will be seeing in many different forms and contexts throughout this book. In all of your work with 1-2-3 worksheets, graphs, and even databases, you will find ways to take full advantage of formula recalculation.

In Part 2 of this book, you'll begin examining the three components in detail. But first, Chapter 2 will help you orient yourself to how 1-2-3 operates in the Windows graphical interface environment.

2

Lotus 1-2-3 and the Windows Interface

To split a worksheet into two panes,   97

drag the vertical splitter across the horizontal scroll bar, or the horizontal splitter down the vertical scroll bar. Stop dragging where you want the window to be divided. (Alternatively, choose View ➤ Split ➤ Horizontal or Vertical.)

To switch between panes in a split worksheet,   99

press F6 or click a cell in either pane.

To open a new worksheet window,   101

choose File ➤ New.

To view worksheet windows in a tiled arrangement,   101

choose Window ➤ Tile.

To view worksheet windows in a cascading arrangement,   101

choose Window ➤ Cascade.

To get contextsensitive help about almost any command or activity   103

press the F1 function key.

To search for a particular help topic by name,   105

click the Search button in the Help window, and use the Search dialog box to find the topic.

WINDOWS applications are consistent with one another in the way they operate and the way they look. This is not to say that programs developed for Windows lack variety, only that you can usually perform equivalent tasks in similar ways from application to application. As a user, the uniformity of Windows applications gives you a distinct advantage: you can apply much of what you know about one Windows application to other Windows applications. Each new Windows application should be easier to master than the previous one.

In this chapter, we'll review some features that Windows applications share, and you'll see how these features are implemented in Lotus 1-2-3. In particular, you'll examine these features:

- The 1-2-3 application window

- Menus, dialog boxes, and SmartIcons

- Worksheet windows—and mouse and keyboard techniques for performing operations on windows

- The Windows-style Help system

Veteran Windows users can skim this chapter and focus only on unfamiliar areas. But if Lotus 1-2-3 is your first Windows application, read this chapter from beginning to end and carefully work through each exercise.

Exploring the 1-2-3 Application Window

You already know that two windows appear on-screen when you start Lotus 1-2-3 Release 4 for Windows:

- The 1-2-3 application window
- A worksheet window, initially named "Untitled," inside the application window

In Chapter 1 you worked a little with both the 1-2-3 window and the worksheet window. Now we'll examine these two windows in greater detail.

Figure 2.1 shows the various parts of the 1-2-3 application window. Notice the four lines *above* the worksheet window:

- The 1-2-3 window title bar
- The Main menu bar
- The edit line
- The SmartIcons

The first three lines, known collectively as the Control Panel, remain fixed in place at the top of the window at all times. However, you can move the fourth line, the one with the SmartIcons, to different places in the 1-2-3 window. The other line in the application window, the one *below* the worksheet area, is called the status bar.

Throughout this chapter we'll examine the five lines and the many features they offer. As you read this chapter, concentrate on learning what the various 1-2-3 tools are. In later chapters, you'll focus on what these tools can do as you create worksheets, graphs, and databases.

LOTUS 1-2-3 AND THE WINDOWS INTERFACE

FIGURE 2.1

The 1-2-3 application window

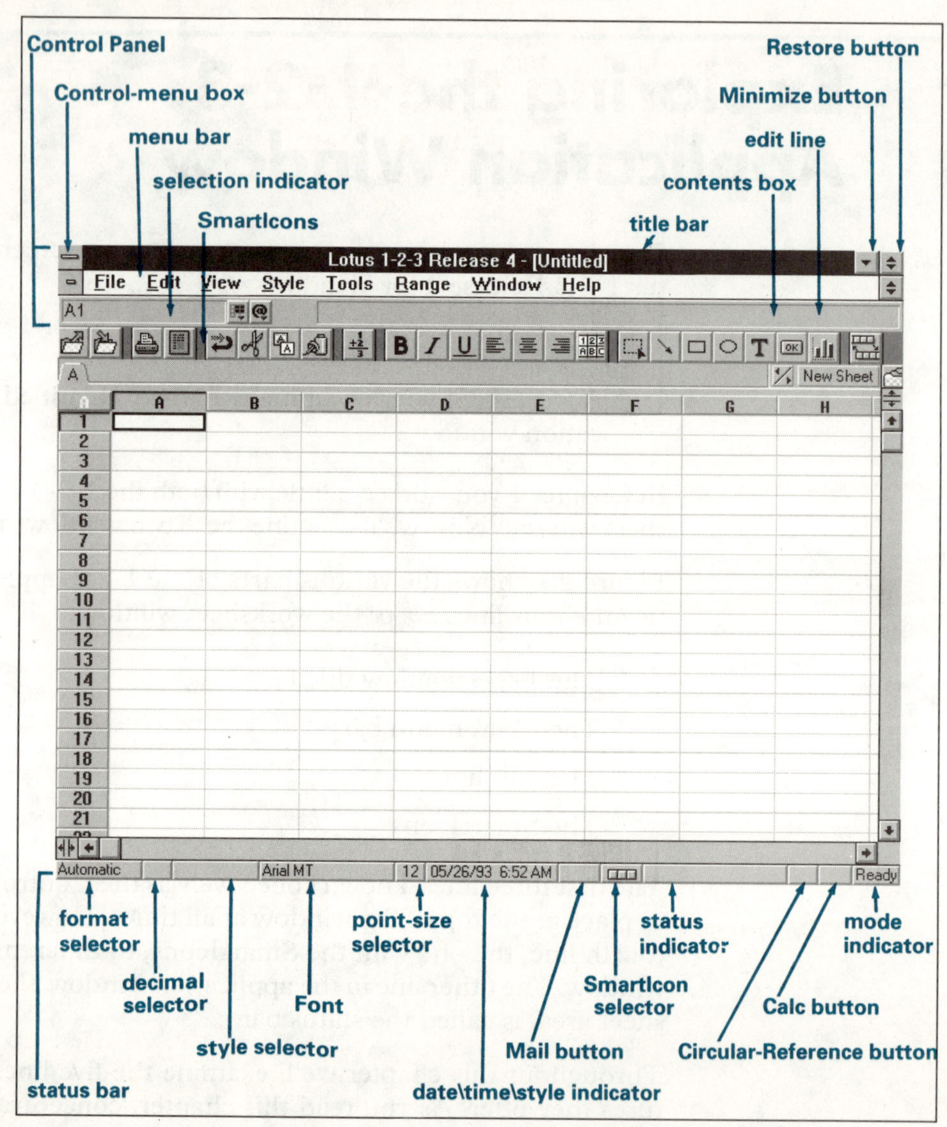

The 1-2-3 Window Title Bar

The title bar identifies the application window and which application is running. At first, the title bar lists the application name:

Lotus 1-2-3 Release 4 - [Untitled]

But when you save a worksheet to disk and maximize the worksheet window, the title bar also lists the name of the worksheet file, like so:

Lotus 1-2-3 Release 4 - [LUNCHES.WK4]

Depending on what you are doing, the title bar lists other kinds of information besides the application and worksheet name. For example, when you choose a menu or command, the title bar describes it. To review this feature, try the following brief exercise:

1. Press the Alt key to activate the menu bar, and press → several times. Each time you highlight a new command in the menu bar, the description in the title bar changes accordingly. For example, when you highlight the Style menu, the title bar provides a general-purpose description of the tools in this menu:

   Control the appearance of data on screen and in print

2. Now highlight the Tools menu and press ↵ to pull down the menu. Press ↓ several times and notice the descriptions in the title bar. For example, the description of the SmartIcons command is

   Reposition, hide, or customize SmartIcons on the icon palette

3. Press the Esc key twice to close the menu and deactivate the menu bar. Now the application name appears in the title bar.

You'll recall from Chapter 1 that when you click a SmartIcon with the right mouse button the title bar provides a description of the icon.

Minimize, Maximize, and Restore Buttons—Sizing and Moving the Window

On the right side of the title bar are two buttons:

- The Minimize button, an arrowhead icon pointing down, reduces the application to icon size so you can work with other Windows applications.

- The Restore button, a double arrowhead, is for changing the size of the 1-2-3 application window.

NOTE

When you click on the Restore button to shrink a window, the Maximize button (an arrowhead pointing up) appears where the Restore button (a double arrowhead) used to be. Click the Maximize button to *maximize* a window to full size. When you do this, the Restore button reappears so you can shrink the window again if you want to.

Experiment with these buttons in the following exercise:

1. Click the Restore button. The 1-2-3 window shrinks to a smaller size and the Restore button itself is replaced by a Maximize button—an arrowhead pointing up.

2. Place the mouse pointer over the right border of the 1-2-3 window. The mouse pointer becomes a double arrowhead, its arrows pointing left and right.

3. Drag the border to the left, toward the center of the screen, and release the mouse button.

You have reduced the 1-2-3 window to about half its horizontal width. Notice how 1-2-3 rearranges the menu bar so that you can still see all of the commands.

4. Position the mouse pointer over the bottom border of the window.

5. Drag the border up to the center of the screen.

You have reduced the vertical length of the window by half. Now you'll use the window's title bar to move the window to a new location on the Windows screen.

6. Position the mouse pointer over the 1-2-3 window's title bar, and click-and-drag the window toward the center of the screen. When you complete this operation, your screen should look like Figure 2.2.

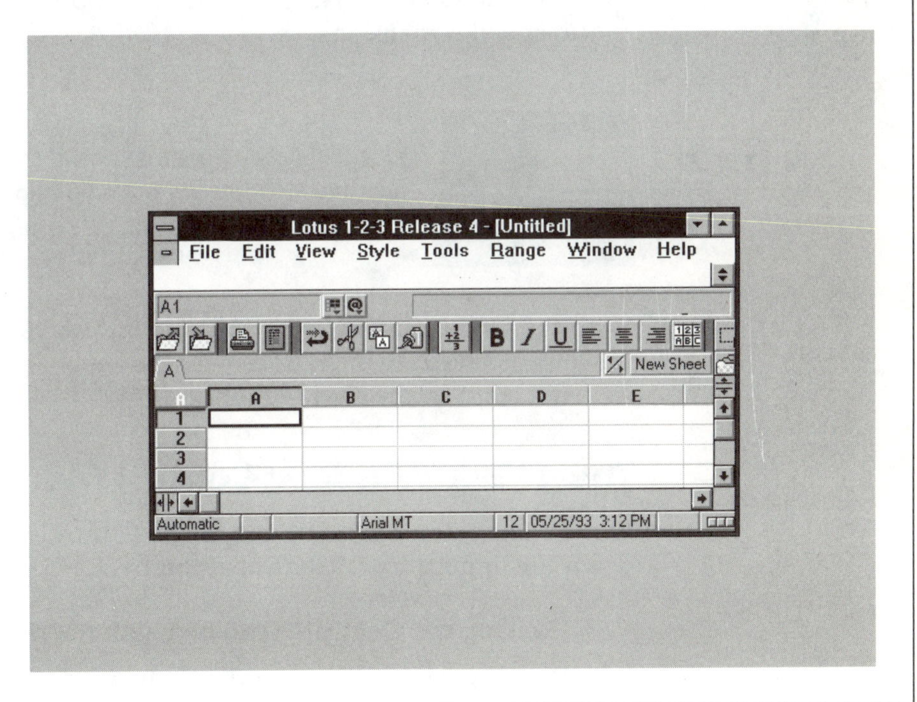

Reducing the size of the application window gives you the opportunity to view more than one application at a time in the Windows environment.

7. Click the Maximize button, the button on the right side of the title bar with an arrowhead pointing up. The 1-2-3 window returns to its full-screen dimensions.

8. Click the Minimize button. The 1-2-3 window disappears altogether and is represented by the 1-2-3 icon near the bottom of the Windows screen.

9. Double-click the 1-2-3 icon. The 1-2-3 window reappears in its original dimensions.

To *double-click* means to position the mouse pointer over the icon, object, or command and click the left mouse button twice in quick succession.

With the Control menu in the 1-2-3 window, you can perform the same moving and resizing operations with the keyboard rather than the mouse, as you'll learn in the next section.

The 1-2-3 Window Control Menu

On the left side of the title bar is the Control-menu box. You can pull down the application's Control menu by

- Clicking the Control-menu box with the mouse, or

- Pressing Alt-spacebar on the keyboard.

Control-menu commands On the Control menu, the Restore, Minimize, and Maximize commands are equivalent to the buttons on the right side of the title bar. The Move and Size commands are for moving and changing the size of the application window with the cursor-movement keys or mouse. Close is for closing 1-2-3 and Switch To is for activating another Windows application. The Control menu offers the following commands:

COMMAND	DESCRIPTION
Restore	Changes the window to its size and location as of the last time it was minimized.
Move	Lets you move the window up, down, or sideways. When you choose this command, a four-headed arrow appears over the window. Press ↑, ↓, ←, or → to move the window up, down, to the left, or to the right. When the window is where you want it to be, press ↵.
Size	Lets you change the size of the window. When you select this command, the pointer becomes a two-headed arrow. Drag the window border to the size you want and press ↵.
Minimize	Reduces the window to icon size. Lotus 1-2-3 is still active, however.
Maximize	Enlarges the window to full-screen size.
Close	Closes the 1-2-3 window and effectively closes the 1-2-3 application as well. The shortcut for choosing Close is to press Alt-F4.

COMMAND

DESCRIPTION

Switch To...

Activates another application in the Windows environment. When you select this command, the Task List dialog box appears with a list of the programs currently running in your Windows environment:

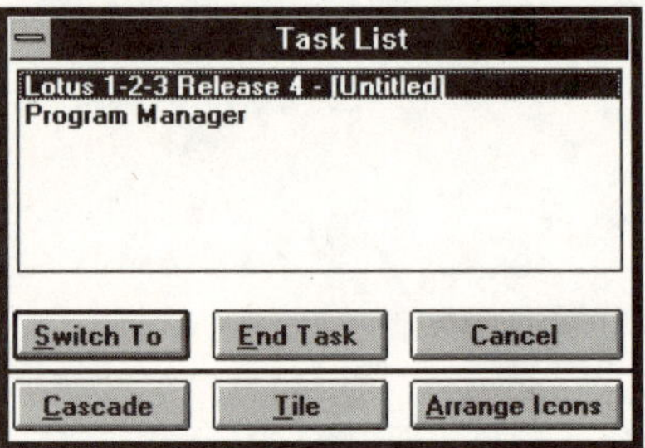

To switch to another application, highlight the program's name in the list and click Switch To (or press Alt-Esc to step through the open application windows). The shortcut for selecting Switch To is to press Ctrl-Esc.

TIP

When you see a dimmed, light gray Control-menu command, it means the command is not available. Dimmed commands in pull-down menus are not available for the type of work you are doing at present.

Try working with the Control-menu commands in the following exercise:

1. Press Alt-spacebar to pull down the 1-2-3 Control menu.

2. Choose _R_estore. The 1-2-3 window returns to the location and size you gave it in the previous exercise (see Figure 2.2).

3. Pull down the Control menu and choose _M_ove. A four-headed pointer appears over the window.

4. Press ↑ on your keyboard. A shadow border appears above the 1-2-3 window. Keep pressing ↑ until the top of the shadow border reaches the top of the screen.

5. Press ← until the left side of the shadow border reaches the left side of the screen.

6. Press ↵ to complete the move operation.

Now try working with the Size command:

7. Pull down the 1-2-3 Control menu and choose _S_ize.

8. Press → and ↓ repeatedly to expand the right and bottom borders of the 1-2-3 window and make them extend almost to the full dimensions of the screen. As you perform the size operation, a shadow border extends beyond the window itself and the pointer becomes a two-headed arrow.

9. Press ↵ to complete the Size operation.

Try this experiment with the Maximize command:

10. Pull down the 1-2-3 Control menu and choose Ma_x_imize. The window returns to its original, full-screen dimensions.

Exiting 1-2-3   The Close command in the Control menu closes the 1-2-3 window and effectively closes the application. Selecting Close is the same as selecting File ➤ Exit. In fact, you can use the following mouse or keyboard techniques to exit from 1-2-3 for Windows:

- Choose _F_ile ➤ E_x_it.

- Pull down the 1-2-3 Control menu and choose _C_lose.

- Press Alt-F4 (the keyboard shortcut for the Close command).

- Double-click on the 1-2-3 Control-menu box.

These actions have the same effect—they end your current session with 1-2-3.

Before closing the file, however, 1-2-3 checks the worksheets to see if you made changes and didn't save them to disk. If you made changes to the file, the Exit dialog box appears on-screen and asks whether you want to save or abandon the changes. You can also click the Cancel button to cancel the Exit and return to your document.

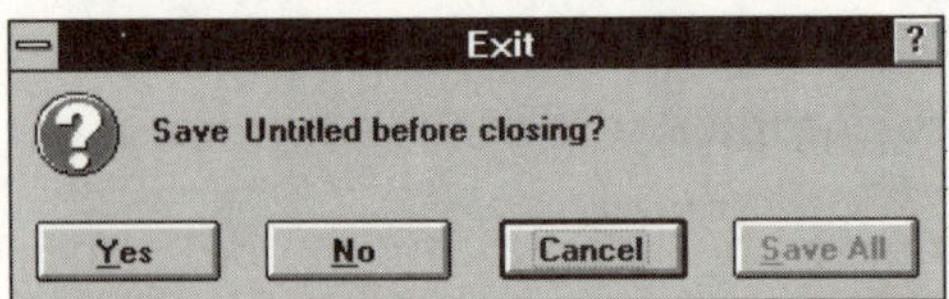

As you saw in Chapter 1, worksheet windows have their own Control menus whose commands are similar to the commands in the 1-2-3 Control menu. You'll learn more about worksheet windows later in this chapter.

The Menu Bar

The menu bar is located just below the 1-2-3 title bar. To activate the menu bar:

- Press Alt,

- Press F10, or

- Click a command in the menu bar to view the commands on its pull-down menu.

The worksheet menu bar offers eight entries. Each one, when you select it, displays a pull-down menu. Table 2.1 gives an overview of the menu commands on the menu bar. Take a few minutes to browse through the Main menu system. Read the brief descriptions that 1-2-3 displays in the title bar for each command in the pulldown menus.

TABLE 2.1: Menu Bar Commands

COMMAND	DESCRIPTION
File	Offers commands for saving worksheets to disk and for retrieving previously saved worksheets. This menu also has commands for printing worksheets and graphs and for previewing pages before printing them. The Send Mail command is for sending and receiving e-mail on a network.
Edit	Offers the extremely useful Undo command for reversing actions in 1-2-3. It also provides commands for cut-andpaste and copy-and-paste operations (via the Windows Clipboard), commands for creating dynamic links between 1-2-3 worksheets and documents from other applications, commands for inserting and deleting worksheets, for performing search-and-replace operations, and for copying formulas across ranges of worksheet cells.
View	Provides ways of controlling how a worksheet appears on-screen. With this menu, you can split the screen into multiple worksheet windows and set your preferences for the appearance of the windows.
Style	Furnishes options for changing the appearance of data on the screen and on the printed page, including font, alignment, color, border style, and shading options.
Tools	Offers the miscellaneous 1-2-3 tools, including the Chart, Draw, Database, Spell Check, Audit, SmartIcons, Macro, and other Add-ins, as well as the User Setup dialog box.
Range	Provides commands for applying formats to specific ranges of data in a worksheet. This command also lets you open the Version Manager and name worksheet ranges.
Windows	Offers commands for controlling how multiple worksheet and graph windows are displayed.
Help	Provides a variety of entry points into the 1-2-3 Help system, as well as two different tutorials, one for beginners and the one for experienced 1-2-3 users who are upgrading to Release 4.

The Release 4 menu bar differs from earlier versions of 1-2-3 in that the Worksheet, Graph, and Data menus are no longer on the menu bar. Commands previously on these menus are now on other menus.

Chart and Transcript menu commands Interestingly enough, the menu commands listed in Table 2.1 are not the only commands you will see in the menu bar. Under certain situations, 1-2-3 alters the menu bar to provide new menus for working with the Transcript window and with graphs.

- You can examine the menu for working with graphs by clicking the Graph SmartIcon. A Chart option will appear on the menu bar—even if your worksheet has no data to graph—so you can define a graph window. Notice the Chart menu in Figure 2.3. Also notice the new set of SmartIcons that appears when a graph window is active. When you are finished examining the Chart menu and SmartIcons, click anywhere on the worksheet (don't click on the Graph workspace). The worksheet will become active again.

- The Transcript window records keystrokes and mouse actions so you can play them back in macros. A macro is a program you create to record a sequence of 1-2-3 commands.

You'll learn about macros and the Transcript window in Chapter 9.

FIGURE 2.3

Lotus 1-2-3 provides a Chart menu option and a new set of SmartIcons for working with graphs.

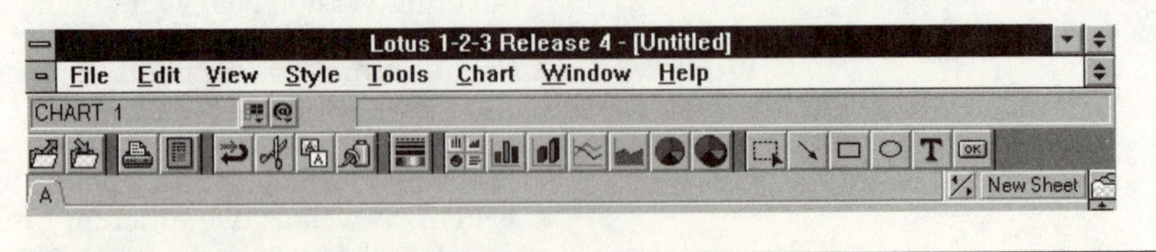

How the 1-2-3 Menu System Works

In Lotus 1-2-3, you'll find a variety of Windows-style tools for choosing menu options and for navigating the menu system. In this part of the chapter, we'll explore how the menu system works.

Cascade Menus

You already know that the Main menu bar offers a horizontal list of menu commands and that, when you choose a menu command, a vertical pull-down menu appears. Pull-down menus sometimes offer additional commands of their own, and these commands appear in the form of *cascade menus*. Commands that bring up a cascade menu have a right-pointing arrowhead (➤) next to them.

Follow these steps to see how cascade menus work:

1. Open the Tools menu. Notice the small right-pointing arrowhead icon next to the Database command. The arrowhead means that a cascade menu with more options will appear when you select Database.

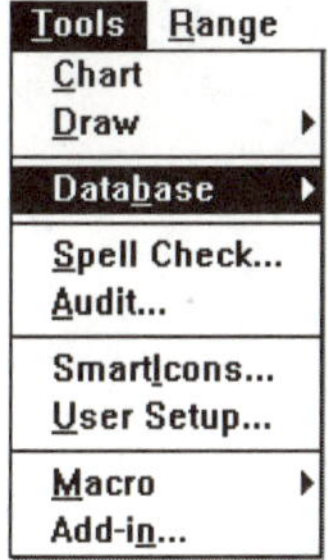

2. Select the Database command. A cascade menu appears with many more commands.

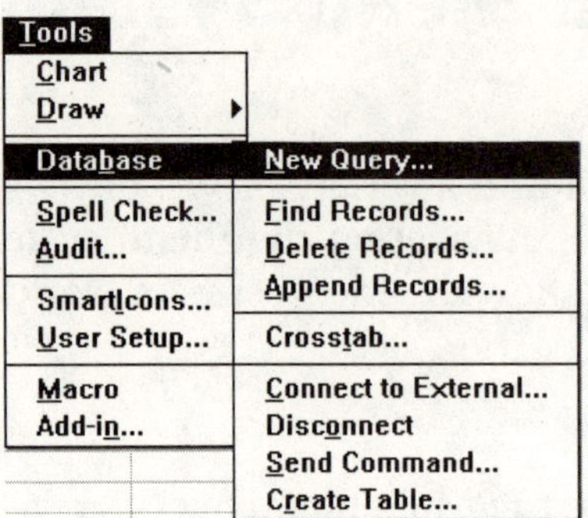

Select a command from a cascade menu in the same way you choose commands from pull-down menus: click a command with the mouse, press the underlined letter on the keyboard, or highlight a command and press ↵.

Dialog Boxes

Dialog boxes prompt you for detailed information so you can carry out operations in 1-2-3. When you see a command followed by an ellipsis (…), it means that a dialog box will appear when you select that command. For example, all twelve commands on the Style menu are followed by ellipses, and all twelve bring up dialog boxes.

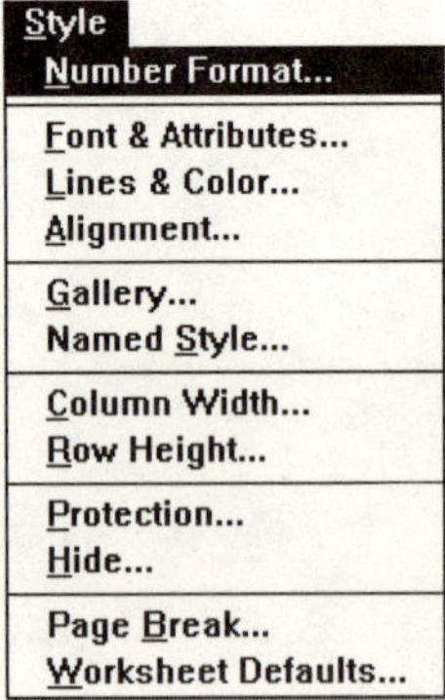

Figure 2.4 shows the dialog box that appears when you select <u>S</u>tyle ➤ <u>N</u>umber Format. To display the Number Format dialog box on your screen:

- Choose <u>S</u>tyle ➤ <u>N</u>umber Format.

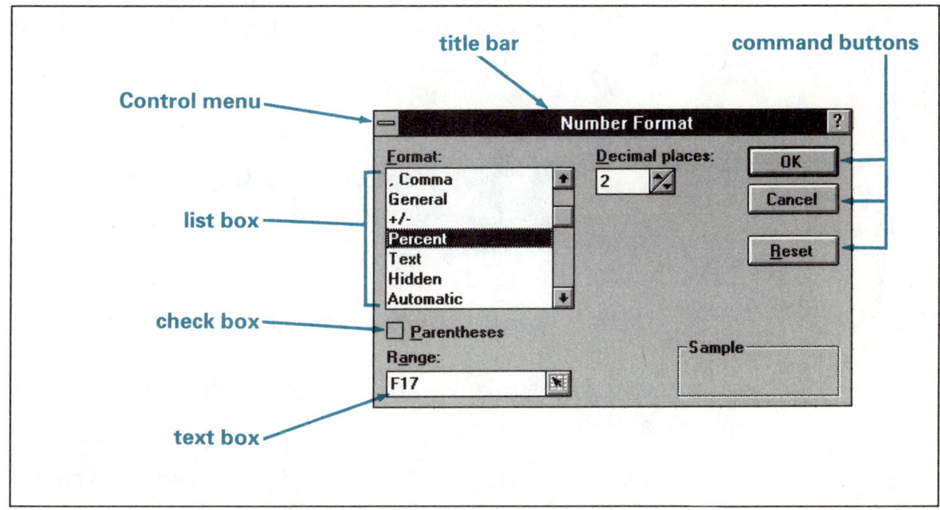

Notice that a dialog box is a window and has its own title bar. Dialog boxes get their names from the sequence of menu commands that you choose to display them. Accordingly, the Number Format dialog box appears when you pull down the Style menu and select Number Format.

Dialog boxes have certain features in common:

- Dialog boxes appear in the center of the screen, but if they keep you from viewing your work you can always move them. To move a dialog box, drag it by the title bar.

- Dialog boxes have their own Control menus. The Control menu is represented by the Control-menu box in the upper-left corner of the window. The Control menu in a dialog box has only two commands, Move and Close.

- Inside all dialog boxes are standard Windows elements that operate in much the same way. These elements include labels, command buttons, text boxes, check boxes, list boxes, frames, option buttons, combo boxes, file list boxes, directory list boxes, and drive list boxes, all of which are explained shortly. A given dialog box may have all or a combination of these elements, depending on the task at hand. As Figure 2.4 shows, the Number Format dialog box includes command buttons, text boxes, a list box, and a check box.

WARNING You cannot resize, minimize, or maximize a dialog box.

Determining which element is active In the sections ahead, we'll look briefly at the Windows elements in 1-2-3 dialog boxes. First, however, you need to learn how to tell which element is *active* and how to activate a dialog box element.

Only one element in a dialog box can be active—and can therefore be changed—at a time. Dialog boxes display a combination of *highlights* and *dotted boxes* to tell you which element is active. For example, when a text box is active, its contents may be highlighted. When a command button is active, its name is enclosed by a dotted box and its border is darkened. You will soon be able to recognize which elements are active.

Activating a dialog box element There are a number of ways to activate a dialog box element:

- Press the Tab key to move forward through the dialog box from one element to the next. Pressing the Tab key is a neutral way of activating an element without completing a particular action.

- Press Shift-Tab to move backward through the elements of the dialog box.

- In some cases you can activate an element by clicking it with the mouse. However, a mouse click can mean different things to different elements in a dialog box, as you'll learn in the sections ahead.

- Press Alt and the underlined letter in a label or caption in the dialog box (in some cases you can also select the option that the element represents by doing this). For example, in the Number Format dialog box (see Figure 2.4), you can press Alt-P to activate the <u>P</u>arentheses check box. Pressing Alt-R here is the equivalent of clicking the <u>R</u>eset command button. Pressing an Alt-key combination in this way is called pressing the *hot key* or *access key*.

As you read the following description of 1-2-3 dialog box elements, don't worry about the specifics of the particular dialog boxes that appear in examples. You'll study 1-2-3 menu commands and dialog boxes in upcoming chapters. For now, focus on how each dialog box element works.

Command buttons A *command button* is one of the simplest and most common elements you'll find in dialog boxes. Command buttons present actions you can carry out with a mouse click. For example, the Number Format dialog box (see Figure 2.4) has three command buttons: OK, Cancel, and <u>R</u>eset. Click one of these buttons and 1-2-3 immediately carries out the action that the button represents.

OK and Cancel buttons are found on most dialog boxes. Choosing OK confirms the specifications you made in the dialog box and closes it. Choosing Cancel closes the dialog box without changing the specifications.

There are several techniques for choosing a command button with the keyboard:

- Press Alt and the corresponding hot key. For example, pressing Alt-R is the same as clicking the <u>R</u>eset button in the Number Format dialog box.

- Press Tab (or Shift-Tab) until the target button is active, and then press ↵.

- In dialog boxes with OK and Cancel buttons, you can press ↵ to select the OK button (except when another command button is active), or press Esc to select the Cancel button.

As an exercise in using command buttons, follow these steps:

1. Choose File ➤ Print. The Print dialog box appears, as in Figure 2.5.

2. Click on the Page Setup button with the mouse, or press Alt-S to choose Page Setup with the keyboard. (As you do so, notice the graphic pushbutton effect that takes place on-screen.) A new dialog box named Page Setup appears on-screen over the Print dialog box.

3. Click the Cancel button or press Esc. The Page Setup dialog box disappears and you once again see the Print dialog box.

4. Click Cancel or press Esc to make this dialog box disappear too.

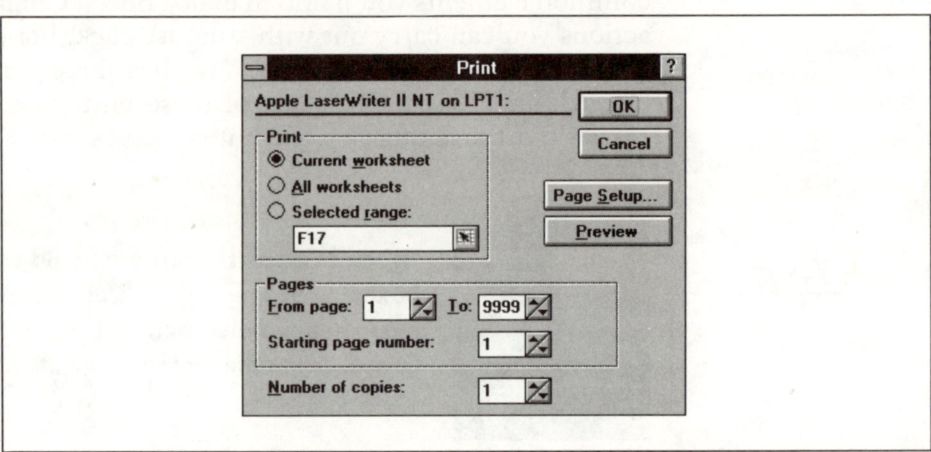

Text boxes A *text box* is a rectangle in which you enter information with the keyboard. You might enter a number, text, or a range, depending on the requirements of the particular dialog box. For example, the Number Format dialog box (see Figure 2.4) has two text boxes, Decimal places and Range. The first is for entering the number of decimal points for a numeric display format, and the second is for entering a range of cells to apply the new format to.

When a dialog box first appears, its text boxes display a *default value*. This value will apply to you if you make no changes in the text box.

To enter a value into a text box:

1. Activate the box by clicking it with the mouse or by pressing Tab until the box is activated.
2. Enter the information with the keyboard.
3. Press ↵ or click OK.

In Release 4 you can enter numeric data in a text box by clicking either the ↑ or ↓ arrow on the right side of the box. Clicking ↑ increases the value with each click, and clicking ↓ decreases it.

Information boxes In some dialog boxes you'll find *an information box*, a box that provides information about options you have chosen. Usually information boxes have labels that tell you what kind of information you can expect to find in the box. You cannot activate an information box or enter data in it.

Range boxes A *range box* is a special kind of text box. If you select a range of cells in the current worksheet *before* selecting a menu command that applies to a range, the range box displays your selected range as its default value. Alternatively, if you want to enter a new range into a text box when a dialog box is already displayed on the screen, 1-2-3 provides special pointing techniques for doing so.

As an introduction to range boxes, follow these steps:

1. Press the Home key, if necessary, to select cell A1 in the worksheet.
2. Choose File ➤ Print.

The cell name, A:A1, is displayed inside the Selected Range box. In the Print dialog box, you specify which parts of your worksheet you want to print in the Selected range box.

3. Type **.** (a period) to anchor the range.

Anchoring simply means to designate the current cell—in this case A1—as the upper-left corner of the range. When you enter the period, you may be surprised to see the Print dialog box disappear temporarily. The range notation A:A1..A:A1 appears in the contents box on the edit line.

4. Press → five times, and then press ↓ five times.

Now the range of cells from A1 to F6 is highlighted on the active worksheet, and the range notation A:A1..A:F6 appears in the contents box, as shown in Figure 2.6. Moreover, a new mode name appears in the mode indicator: *Point*. Point mode means that you are currently selecting a range.

FIGURE 2.6

Selecting a range of cells to print

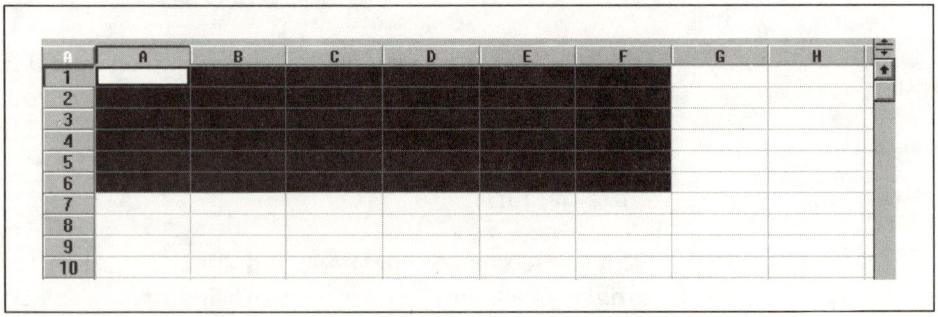

5. Press ↵ to return to the Print dialog box.

In the Print dialog box, the Selected range text box shows a cell notation for the range you selected in the worksheet. Moreover, the Selected range option button, located above the text box, is filled in, which means it has been selected. If you were actually printing your worksheet, 1-2-3 would send the range A1 to F6 to the printer.

6. For now, click the Cancel button or press Esc key to cancel the operation.

You can use the mouse to point to a range. And you can type a range notation with the keyboard directly in a range box. Chapter 3 has detailed information about ranges and how to select them.

List boxes A *list box* is a rectangle with a vertical list from which you may select one item. When a list is too long to be displayed in its entirety, a vertical scroll bar appears on the right side of the list box. Use the scroll bar to bring up the item you want to select.

In the Number Format dialog box (see Figure 2.4), the Format list box offers a set of predefined number formats. You can select a format from this list to change how a range of numbers on a worksheet are formatted.

The general steps for using a list box are:

1. Activate the list box by clicking the box with the mouse, pressing a hot key combination, or pressing Tab until the list box is activated.

2. If necessary, scroll up or down the list until the item you want is visible. To scroll through the box, click the up- or down-arrow on the scroll bar, or drag the scroll box up or down the length of the bar.

3. Click the list item you want with the mouse. Lotus 1-2-3 high-lights it in the list. With the keyboard, press ↑ or ↓ repeatedly to scroll through the list and select the item you want, and press ↵.

Check boxes *Check boxes* present options that you can turn on or off. A check box can be *on*, *off*, or *undetermined*.

- When the option is on, the check box contains an *X*.

- When the option is off, the box is empty.

- When 1-2-3 cannot determine whether the box is on or off, it has undetermined status and 1-2-3 fills it with a dark gray background.

The Number Format dialog box (see Figure 2.4) has one check box, labeled Parentheses. When you check this box, 1-2-3 puts parentheses around numeric values in your worksheet.

When a check box is active, its caption is enclosed in a dotted box. At this point you can change its status—from on, to off, to undetermined—by pressing the spacebar, clicking the check box with the mouse, or pressing the hot key.

In some dialog boxes you'll find lists of check boxes that are grouped together. For example, the Font & Attributes dialog box, shown in Figure 2.7, offers Attribute check boxes labeled Normal, Bold, Italics, and Underline. The check boxes in this group operate independently of one another. You can choose any combination of on, off, and undetermined for these check boxes. Changing the status of one check box has no effect on the others.

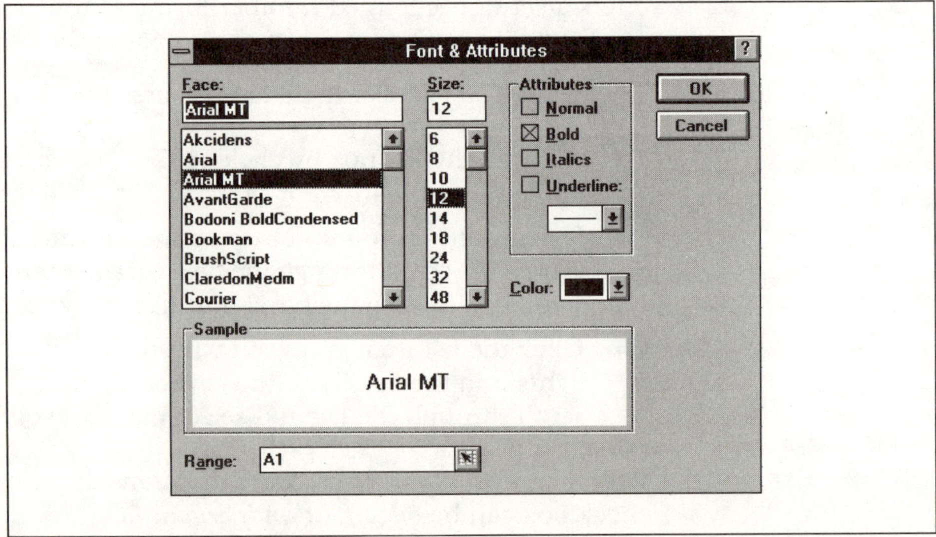

Try this exercise with the check boxes in the Font & Attributes dialog box:

1. Choose Style ➤ Font & Attributes.

2. Press the Tab key five times (or press Alt-B) to move the focus to the Bold check box. Notice that a dotted box encloses the Bold caption.

3. Press the spacebar several times and watch the Bold check box change to on (with an *X*) and off (without an *X*).

4. Press the Tab key again (or press Alt-I) to move the focus to the Italics check box.

5. Press the spacebar several times, this time changing the setting of the Italics check box. Notice that changing the status of Italics has no effect on the current setting of the other check boxes.

6. Click the Cancel button or press Esc to close the dialog box.

Option buttons You can only select one *option button* in a group. In contrast to check boxes, option buttons are mutually exclusive, and when you select an option button, the one that was selected before is "unselected." (Option buttons are sometimes called *radio buttons*.) An option button is a circle with a caption on its right. When the option is *on*, the circle is filled with a bold black dot, but when it is *off*, the circle is empty. On and off are the only possible settings for option buttons.

To select a new option when the group of option buttons is active:

- Press ↑ or ↓,

- Click an option button with the mouse, or

- Press Alt and the underlined hot key.

T I P

The Spell Check dialog box, shown in Figure 2.8, has a set of option buttons for controlling which part of the worksheet to spell-check. The default option is <u>E</u>ntire file, meaning that the entire document will be spell-checked unless you choose another option button.

Try the following exercise with this dialog box:

1. Choose <u>T</u>ools ➤ <u>S</u>pell Check. The Spell Check dialog box appears on-screen with Check option buttons activated.

2. Press ↓ to simultaneously turn the <u>C</u>urrent worksheet option button on and turn off the <u>E</u>ntire file button.

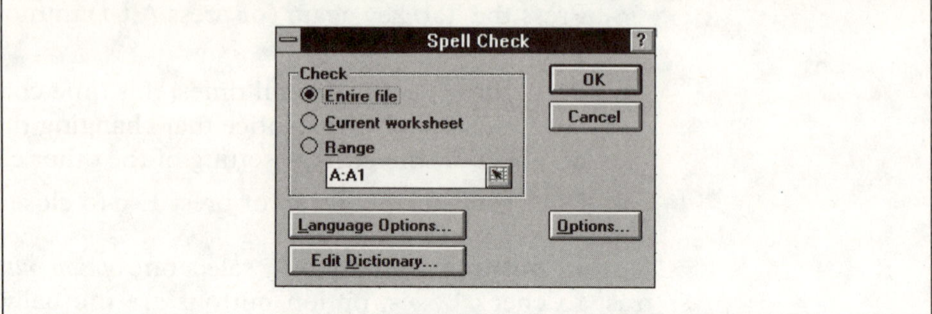

3. Press Alt-E. The <u>E</u>ntire file button is turned on once again.

4. Click the Cancel button or press Esc to close the dialog box.

Frames When a dialog box offers more than one group of option buttons, the groups are usually enclosed in frames. A *frame* is a rectangle with a caption on top. For example, the Alignment dialog box presents two groups of option buttons, Horizontal and Vertical, each inside a frame. In this case, the option groups are independent of each other, and you can select and activate one option in the Horizontal and one in the Vertical group.

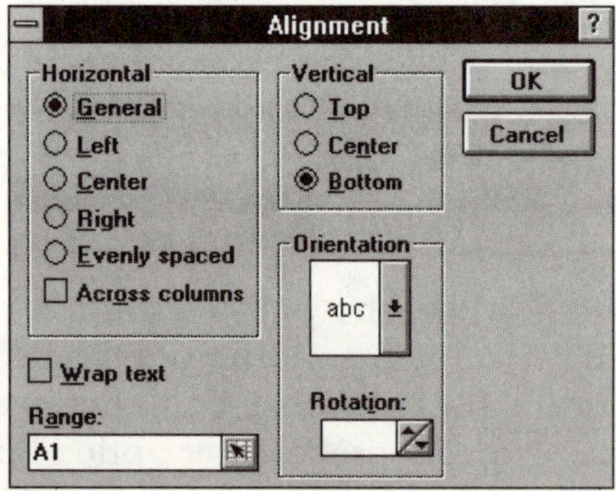

Drop-down boxes A text box with a pull-down list attached is called a *drop-down box* or sometimes a *combo box*. When you see a ↓ scroll button on the right side of a text box, it means the text box is a drop-down box and you can either enter text directly or pull down the list, find the option you want, and choose it.

There are two ways to enter a text value in a drop-down box:

- Enter the text directly with the keyboard (entries are restricted to relevant values).

- Pull down the list and select an entry. To pull down the list, either click the ↓ button with the mouse or press Alt-↓. Your selection is automatically copied to the text box.

A drop-down box appears in the Open File dialog box, shown in Figure 2.9. The Drives drop-down box is for entering the name of the drive (A, B, C, and so on) with the file you want to open.

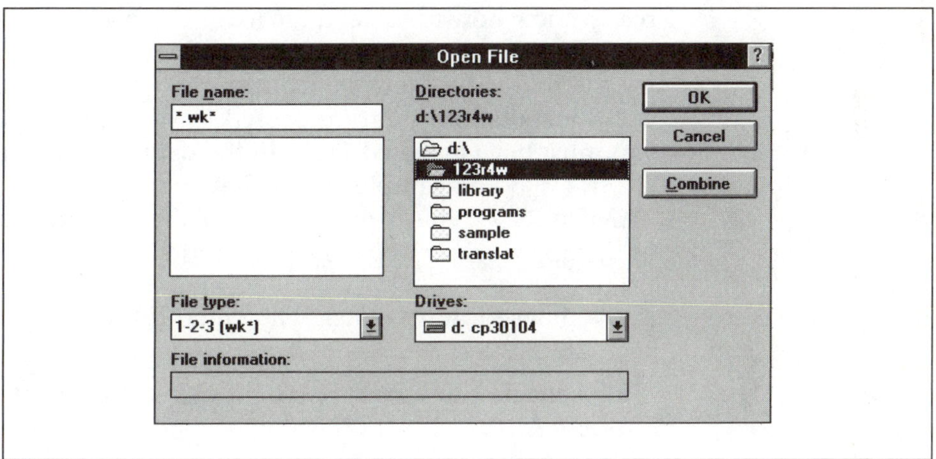

File name, Directories, Drives, and File type list boxes Several 1-2-3 commands require you to identify a file name in order to perform a disk operation. For example, when you select the File ➤ Open command, 1-2-3 asks you for the name of the worksheet file you want to open. One way to specify a file is to enter its complete path and file name in the File name text box. However, if the file you want to open is not located in the current directory and disk, you might have to enter a long and probably difficult-to-remember path and file name, such as

D:\BUDGETS\WORK94\BUDG94.WK4

To make identifying and selecting a target file on disk easier, Windows supplies four dialog box elements: the *File name*, *Directories*, *Drives*, and

File type list boxes. Examples of the four list boxes appear in the Open File dialog box (see Figure 2.9). The four list boxes always appear together and operate in a coordinated manner. When you select a new drive in the Drives list box, the Directories list box automatically lists directories in the new drive. Likewise, when you select a new directory in the Directories list box, the File name list box automatically lists the worksheet files in the new directory. Selecting a different File type makes the File name list change.

Opening and Saving a File

Opening and saving files are basic operations in almost all Windows applications. If you have worked with Windows applications before, you already know how to select a file in an Open File dialog box. But if 1-2-3 is your first Windows application—or if you want to review the procedure—try the following exercise. In this one, you'll open a sample file that the 1-2-3 installation program copied to your hard disk. To do the exercise, you must have installed 1-2-3 in the default installation directory, named \123R4W. (The sample 1-2-3 files are stored in a subdirectory named SAMPLES.) If this is not the case, substitute the correct directory name in the appropriate steps in the exercise.

1. Choose File ➤ Open. The Open File dialog box appears (see Figure 2.9).

2. Activate the Drives box by clicking it with the mouse or by pressing Alt-V.

3. Click the ↓ button on the right side of the Drives box or press Alt-↓ on the keyboard to view a list of the drives available on your system.

4. Select the C drive or the name of the hard drive on which you installed Lotus 1-2-3. The File name box displays the current path on the selected drive.

5. Activate the Directories box by clicking inside it or by pressing Alt-D. At the top of the box is a file folder icon labeled with your drive letter, as shown in Figure 2.10. This entry represents the root directory of the current directory list.

6. As an experiment, doubleclick this icon or highlight the entry and press ↵ to move *up* the directory path—to the root directory in this case. In the new directory list, you will find the 123R4W entry.

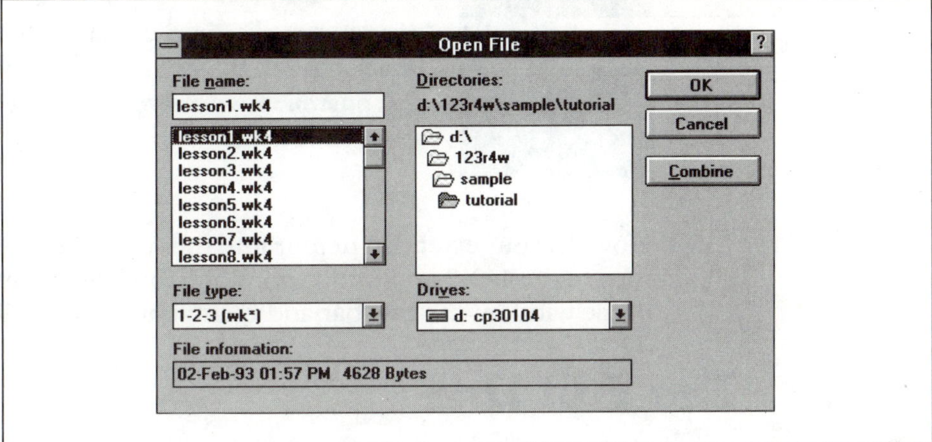

7. To reopen the directory with the 1-2-3 program, double-click the 1-2-3R4W entry or highlight the entry and press ↵.

8. Now find the SAMPLE and then the TUTORIAL subdirectory in the Directories list box. Double-click each entry in turn or highlight the entry and press ↵. The File name box displays a list of all 1-2-3 worksheet files stored in the \123R4W\SAMPLE\TUTORIAL\ path. These are the sample worksheet files that come with 1-2-3 Release 4.

9. Activate the File name by pressing Alt-N.

10. Press Tab and then the spacebar to highlight the file named LESSON1.WK4.

Notice two important changes that take place in the Open File dialog box when you make this selection. First, the File name text box now lists the name of the selected file, LESSON1.WK4, which means that the File ➤ Open command is now prepared to open this file. Second, the File information text box displays specific information about the file you selected—the date and time of its last revision and its size in bytes.

11. Click the OK button or press ↵ to close the Open File dialog box. Lotus 1-2-3 opens the LESSON1 worksheet and displays it as the active window.

12. Examine the worksheet if you wish, and then double-click its Control-menu box to close the worksheet window again.

NOTE Windows applications usually display File name list, Directories list, Drives list, and File type list boxes in disk operations whenever you are expected to select a file name.

Now that our extended detour into menus and dialog boxes is over, let's return to the 1-2-3 application window. You have examined the first two lines of the window, the title bar and menu bar. Next we'll look at the edit line.

The Edit Line

The edit line—the third line in the Control Panel—is divided into two parts, the selection indicator and the contents box.

- **The selection indicator** on the left side gives the complete address of the current cell in the active worksheet. As you know, a complete address includes the letter name of the active worksheet followed by a colon and the column letter and row number, as in A:A1.

- **The contents box** on the right side of the edit line lists the value, label, or formula that is stored in the current cell. The contents box shows you what is actually stored in the cell, not what the cell itself displays. For example, in Figure 2.11 the contents box lists

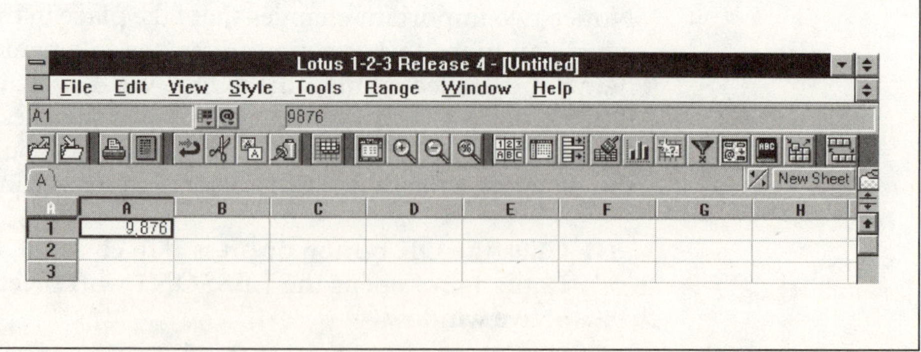

FIGURE 2.11

The contents box, on the right side of the edit line, is where you edit cell entries.

the number 9876, not what is in cell A1, the value 9,876, which has been formatted with a comma.

The contents box also displays new entries as you type them in a cell.

Cancel and Confirm buttons As you know from Chapter 1, when you begin a new cell entry 1-2-3 displays two special buttons, the Cancel button and the Confirm button, just to the left of the contents box.

- Clicking on the Cancel button, the one with a boldface *X*, cancels the current data entry without changing the contents of the cell. (You can also press Esc to cancel a data entry.)

- Clicking the Confirm button, the one with a check mark, completes the current entry and copies the result to the cell. (You can also press ↵ to confirm a data entry.)

Later you'll learn about the two buttons called the @function selector and the navigator located to the left of the Cancel and Confirm buttons. The @function selector displays the @Function menu. The navigator displays a list of named ranges in the current file.

Editing the Contents of a Cell

You can edit the contents of the current cell in the contents box. Rather than reentering a value or label in a cell, you can switch to Edit mode and change the cell contents in the contents box. To edit the current contents of a cell:

1. Select the cell.

2. Press F2 to change to Edit mode. When you press F2,

   - The mode indicator in the lower-right corner of the window displays the word *Edit*.

   - The entry stored in the current cell is copied to the contents box.

   - The Cancel and Confirm buttons appear just to the left of the contents box on the edit line.

   - A flashing vertical bar cursor appears in the cell. This means that 1-2-3 is ready for you to edit the value, label, or formula stored in the cell.

3. Edit the contents of the cell.

4. Select the Confirm button or press ↵ to confirm your edits.

Here is a brief exercise that demonstrates how to switch to and work in Edit mode:

1. Press the Home key to select cell A1.

2. Enter the value **9876** in this cell if you have not already done so in a previous exercise.

3. Press F2. The value of the cell appears in the cell and the word *Edit* is displayed in the mode indicator.

4. Type **0** with the keyboard. This entry becomes the fifth digit at the end of the number in the contents box. Now the number is 98760.

5. Complete the edit by clicking the Confirm button with the mouse, or by pressing ↵ from the keyboard. 1-2-3 returns to Ready mode.

When you complete these steps, the new entry 98760 appears in cell A1.

NOTE   Editing the contents of a cell does not change the formats you applied to the cell. Only the cell's contents are changed.

You can use the contents box whenever you are entering or editing a value, label, or formula in a cell. As you edit, you can use the standard Windows editing keys to move around the cell and make changes. The editing keys are listed in Table 2.2.

TABLE 2.2: The Standard Windows Editing Keys

KEY	USE
←	Moves the flashing cursor to the left one character position at a time.
→	Moves the flashing cursor to the right one character position at a time.

TABLE 2.2: The Standard Windows Editing Keys (continued)

KEY	USE
Home	Moves the cursor to the beginning of the entry in the contents line.
End	Moves the cursor to the end of the entry in the contents line.
Backspace	Deletes the character to the left of the cursor.
Del	Deletes the character at the cursor position.

The SmartIcons

The fourth line in the 1-2-3 Release 4 application window contains a row of useful SmartIcons. Each SmartIcon is a one-click shortcut for selecting a menu command or performing a common keyboard action.

You can customize SmartIcons in three different ways:

- Move the SmartIcons to a different position on the screen. You can even place them in a free-floating window that can be moved to any location.

- Select a new set of SmartIcons—a set composed of the commands you perform the most often.

- Create new SmartIcons. You can write your own macros, attach them to SmartIcons, and carry out actions by clicking your SmartIcons.

Customizing the SmartIcons

This section explains how to move the SmartIcons to new positions on-screen and how to select a new set of SmartIcons. Creating new SmartIcons, an advanced subject, is covered in Chapter 9.

How to create new SmartIcons—and program them with macros—is covered in Chapter 9.

To customize SmartIcons, begin by selecting <u>T</u>ools ➤ SmartIcons. The SmartIcons dialog box, shown in Figure 2.12, appears. This dialog box offers options for changing the location of the SmartIcon set and for removing, editing, and changing the size of SmartIcons.

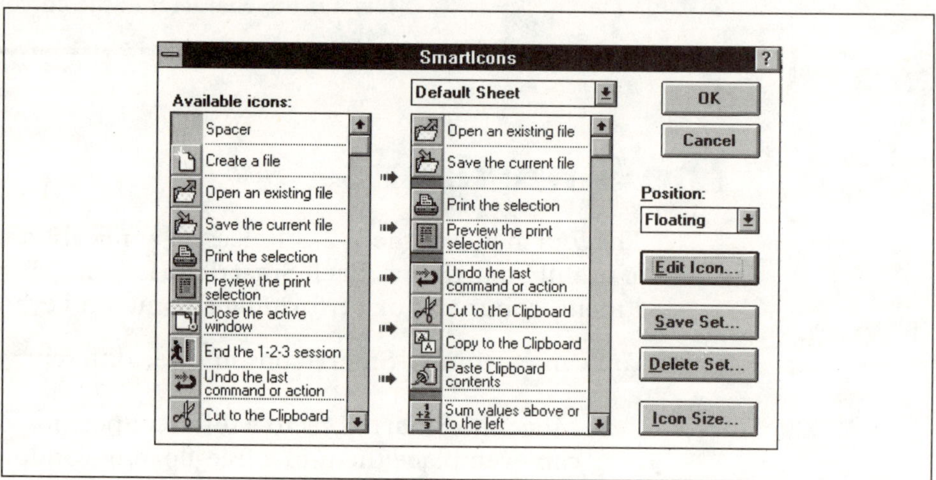

Changing the position of SmartIcons You can change the location of the SmartIcon set in the 1-2-3 window by selecting a new option in the <u>P</u>osition list box. As you can see, Top is the default position.

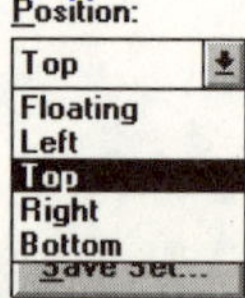

Here are instructions for moving the SmartIcons to the bottom of the screen:

1. Choose Tools ➤ SmartIcons.

2. In the SmartIcons dialog box, click the ↓ button in the Position list box.

3. Select Bottom and either click the OK button or press ↵.

Figure 2.13 shows what happens when you move the SmartIcons to the bottom of the 1-2-3 window. The horizontal set of SmartIcons is arranged across the bottom of the window, just above the status line.

If you want even more control over the position and shape of the SmartIcons, choose the Floating option in the Position list box. The SmartIcons will appear in a free-floating window that you can resize and move anywhere

FIGURE 2.13

Moving the SmartIcons to the bottom of the 1-2-3 window

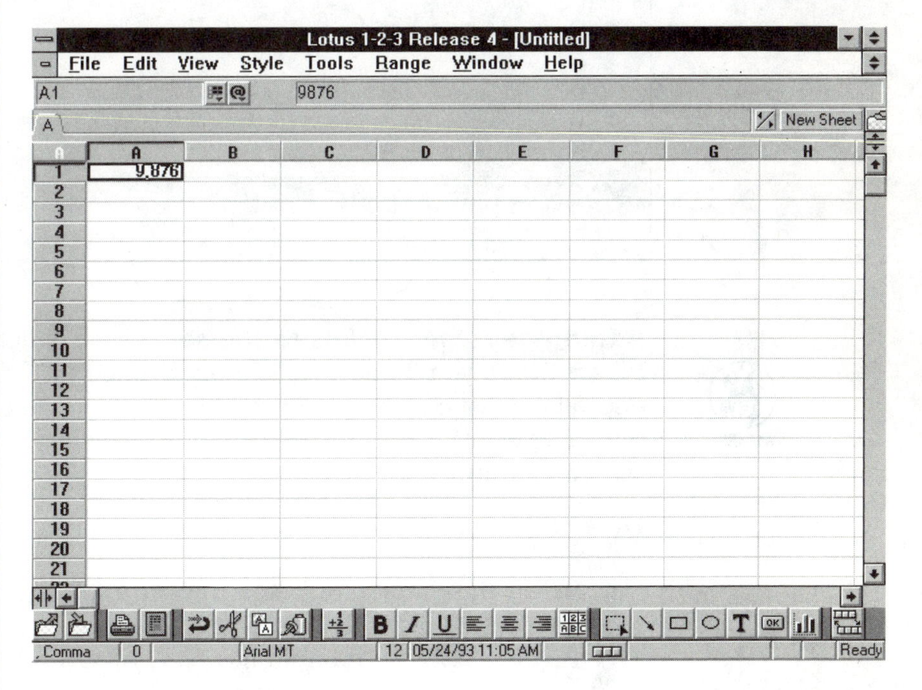

in the 1-2-3 window. Figure 2.14 shows one possible position for a free-floating SmartIcons window.

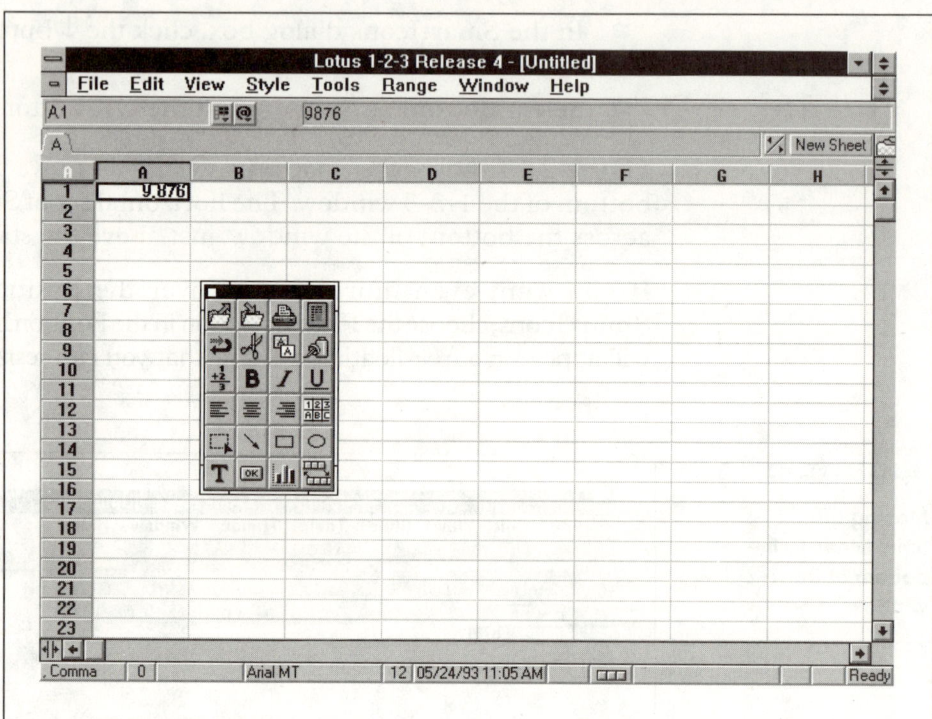

Adding new SmartIcons to the set In the SmartIcons dialog box (see Figure 2.12), you'll find two list boxes. The first, called Available icons, is a scrollable list of dozens of predefined icons you can place in SmartIcon sets. The current set of SmartIcons is displayed in another list box in the center column.

Here are the steps for adding new SmartIcons:

1. Select the SmartIcon set you want to change from the list box above the second column. (This list box is called Default Sheet in Figure 2.12, but it could have any of several other names.)

2. Scroll through the Available icons list box until you find the SmartIcon you want to add.

3. Select the SmartIcon by clicking it with the mouse.

4. Click-and-drag the SmartIcon to the SmartIcon set displayed in the second column. Where you drop the SmartIcon in the set determines where it will be displayed.

Removing a SmartIcon from a set   The current icon palette box displays the selection of icons that are currently in your SmartIcon set. To remove a SmartIcon, follow these steps:

1. Scroll through the list box in the second column until you find the SmartIcon that you want to remove.

2. Click the SmartIcon with the mouse.

3. Click-and-drag the icon from the current SmartIcon set displayed in the second column. Drag it off the list and it disappears.

You can always put a SmartIcon back in a set if you change your mind after removing it. The complete collection of SmartIcons is always available in the Available icons list box.

With the SmartIcons dialog box on-screen, you can add and remove as many SmartIcons as you wish. To confirm your work, click the OK button.

Changing a SmartIcon's color and image   With Release 4, you can edit SmartIcons. You can change their color, shape, and form. To begin doing this, select the Edit Icon button in the SmartIcons dialog box (see Figure 2.12). The Edit Icon dialog box appears, as shown in Figure 2.15. This dialog box provides tools and resources for remaking SmartIcons.

You'll find the SmartIcon you want to edit in the Available icons list box. Here are the steps for customizing a SmartIcon:

1. Scroll through the Available Icons list box until you find the SmartIcon you want to edit.

2. Select the SmartIcon by clicking on it. When you do so, a brief description of the SmartIcon appears in the Description text box at the bottom of the dialog box.

3. Select the colors you want to use to change the icon image from the color palette below the large box that shows the icon. You can

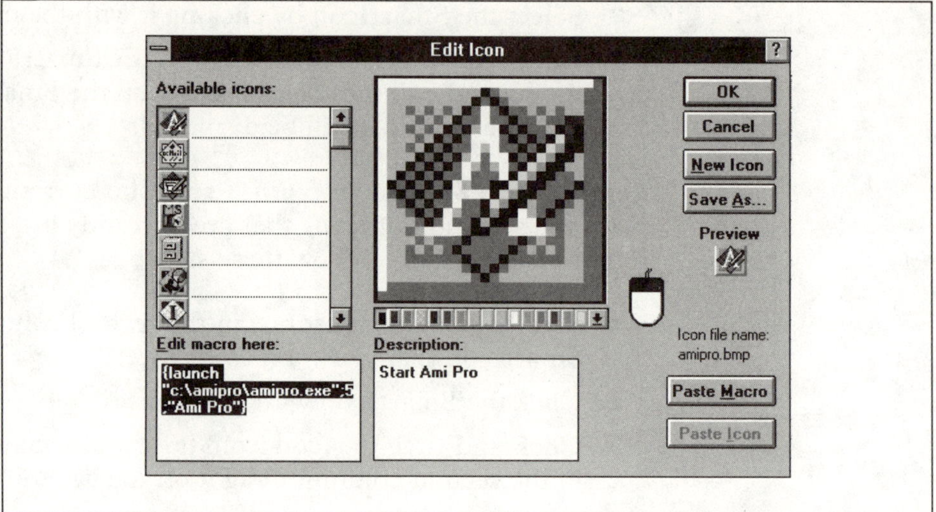

use two colors at a time. Click on a different color with each button of the mouse, and then change individual pixels in the icon by clicking on them with the appropriate mouse button.

4. If a macro command is attached to the SmartIcon and you want to change the macro, choose the <u>E</u>dit macro here text box and change the text of the macro. You can also click on the Paste <u>M</u>acro button to paste text from an existing macro in the <u>E</u>dit macro here text box.

5. If you are editing an existing SmartIcon, you can choose the Save <u>A</u>s button to save the modified icon under a new name.

6. Click OK to close the Edit Icon dialog box and return to the SmartIcons dialog box.

While the Edit Icon box is on-screen, you can customize as many SmartIcons as you wish. To confirm your work, click the OK button, and then click OK on the SmartIcons dialog box.

The Status Bar

The status bar in Release 4 lets you assign formats, decimal places, styles, typefaces, and point sizes to the current cell or range of cells. The status bar also displays SmartIcon sets and information about 1-2-3 operations.

You will be learning about the status bar throughout this book. For now, you need to know that the status bar provides information about any or all of the following properties:

- The number or text format (such as percentage or dollar-and-cent formats)

- The font name and point size

- The named styles

- The date and time

- The SmartIcon sets

- The current time and date from the system calendar and clock settings

- The current mode that you are working in

The Mode Indicator

As you learned in Chapter 1, the mode indicator tells you with a single word what 1-2-3 is currently doing, or gives you information about an activity you are performing. About a dozen different modes exist in 1-2-3 for Windows. You'll learn about other modes in later chapters. You have already seen some of the most common ones:

MODE	MEANING
Label	1-2-3 is accepting your current text entry.
Menu	You are now choosing a menu command or selecting options from a 1-2-3 dialog box.
Point	You are currently selecting a range of cells.
Ready	1-2-3 is ready for your next action—for example, a data entry or a menu selection.
Value	1-2-3 is accepting your current number entry.

As you gain experience in 1-2-3, you'll begin recognizing the most common modes. Check the mode indicator when you get confused about what is happening in your work. Sometimes you'll find that 1-2-3 is in a different mode than you thought. In many cases, pressing Esc or Ctrl-Break takes you back to Ready mode.

A Review of Application Window Elements

You have now examined the fives lines—title bar, menu bar, edit line, SmartIcon set, and status bar—in the 1-2-3 Release 4 window. Take a moment to review what you've learned:

Title bar	Displays the application name, the curent worksheet anme, or a brief description of a menu command or icon, depending on the current activity.
Menu bar	Provides access to the vast system of pull-down menus and Windows-style dialog boxes that represent the 1-2-3 command set.
Edit line	Contains an address box that gives the current cell address, and a contents box that displays the value, label, or formula entry in the current cell.
SmartIcon set	Is a useful and versatile set of tools for streamlining work with databases, graphs, and worksheets.

| Status bar | Displays the date, the current status of keyboard toggles, and other conditions that may be relevant to your work in 1-2-3. |

Aside from these five lines, the worksheet window occupies most of the 1-2-3 Release 4 window. In the next part of this chapter, you'll focus on the worksheet window.

Performing Operations on Worksheet Windows

The mouse and keyboard actions for changing the size and position of a worksheet window and a 1-2-3 window are almost the same. As you know from Chapter 1, a worksheet window has its own title bar, its own Minimize, Maximize and Restore buttons, and its own Control menu—all of which operate in familiar ways.

To pull down the Control menu Pull down a worksheet window's Control menu by pressing Alt-hyphen (-) or by clicking the Control-menu box. (Recall that pressing Alt-spacebar pulls down the 1-2-3 window's Control menu.) You'll see the familiar Control menu commands—Restore, Move, Minimize, etc.

To maximize the worksheet window Maximize the worksheet window by selecting Maximize in the Control menu or by clicking the Maximize button. A worksheet window loses its title bar when you maximize it. Instead of appearing on either side of the title bar, the Control-menu box and Restore button appear on either side of the menu bar, and the name of the window appears in brackets on the 1-2-3 window title bar. Move and Size operations are not available for a maximized worksheet window. To perform these operations, you must first click the Restore button to return the window to its original size.

To move or change the size of a worksheet window Drag a worksheet window by its title bar to move it. To increase or decrease its height or width, position the mouse pointer on a vertical or horizontal border and drag the border. (The mouse pointer turns into a double arrowhead icon pointing vertically or horizontally.) To change both the height and width at the same time, place the mouse pointer on a corner of the window and drag the corner. (The mouse pointer turns into a double arrowhead icon, this time pointing diagonally.)

You can also move or change the size of a worksheet window by choosing Move or Size from the Control menu, Next, press the ↑, ↓, →, or ← key to move or change the size of the worksheet.

TIP The mouse is the best tool for moving a window and changing its size.

To minimize a worksheet window Minimize a worksheet window (or a graph window) by clicking the Minimize button or by choosing Minimize in the Control menu. When you do so, the window turns into a spreadsheet icon and is placed in the worksheet window.

To restore a minimized window to full-screen size, double-click its icon.

To close a worksheet window There are several ways to close a worksheet window:

- Pull down the Control menu and choose <u>C</u>lose.
- Press Ctrl-F4.
- Double-click the Control-menu box.
- Activate the window and choose <u>F</u>ile ➤ <u>C</u>lose.

If you have made changes in the window and not saved them, a dialog box appears, asking you to save the changes before closing the window, abandon the changes, or cancel the Close operation. When you close the last open worksheet window, 1-2-3 automatically opens a new window named "Untitled."

In the following sections, you'll learn two more operations for manipulating worksheet windows: splitting windows into panes, and opening several worksheet windows simultaneously.

Dividing a Worksheet Window into Panes

Suppose you want to examine two distant sections of a worksheet at once. For example, imagine a worksheet with a group of labels in column A and a corresponding group of calculated totals in another column far to the right of A. Many columns of data values separate the two columns, but you want to view the labels and the totals side by side.

A simple way to accomplish this is to divide the worksheet vertically into two panes. A *pane* is an individual view of a single worksheet. By splitting a worksheet into panes, you can look at two different worksheet ranges at the same time. For example, consider the Lunches worksheet that you examined in Chapter 1. As shown in Figure 2.16, the Lunches worksheet

	A	B	C	D	E	F
3	Lunch #1		Fast Food Restaurant			
5		Total	Fat	% Fat		
6	Item	Calories	in grams	Calories		
8	Fast-food hamburger	570	35	55%		
9	French fries	220	12	49%		
10	Chocolate-chip cookies (2)	160	7	39%		
11	Diet Soda	1	0	0%		
13	Total	951	54	51%		

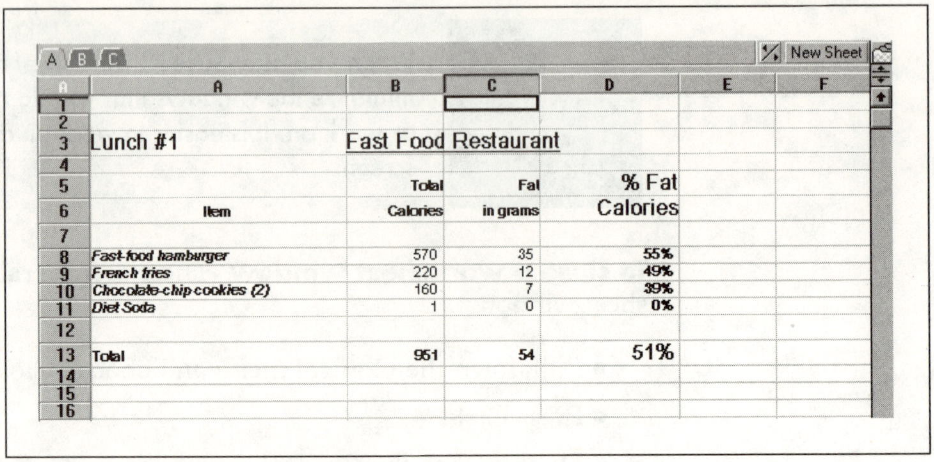

has four columns: the labels in column A, numeric data entries in columns B and C, and calculated fat percentages in column D. Suppose you want to view columns A and D side by side. To do so, you split the worksheet into panes, and you display column A in the first pane and column D in the second pane. The result might look like Figure 2.17.

	A	B	C		A	D	E
3	Lunch #1		Fast Food Restaura	3	nt		
5		Total	Fat	5		% Fat	
6	Item	Calories	in grams	6		Calories	
8	Fast-food hamburger	570	35	8		55%	
9	French fries	220	12	9		49%	
10	Chocolate-chip cookies (2)	160	7	10		39%	
11	Diet Soda	1	0	11		0%	
13	Total	951	54	13		51%	

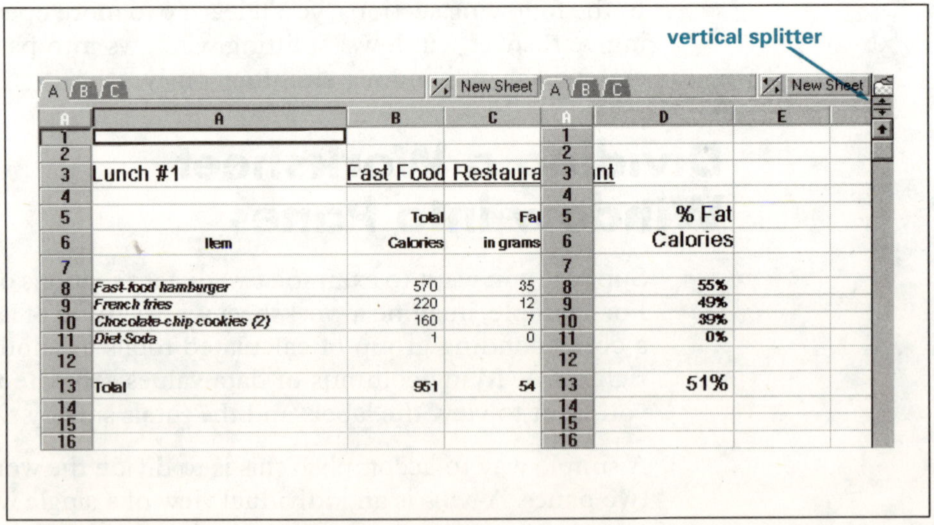

There are two ways to split a worksheet into panes, one with the mouse and one with a menu command. The mouse technique is simpler and more direct. To split a worksheet with the mouse:

1. Place the cursor over a column or row separator to make the splitters appear.

   - The *vertical splitter*, located to the immediate left of the horizontal scroll bar, is a pair of left- and right-pointing arrowheads attached to two short vertical lines (see Figure 2.17).
   - The *horizontal splitter*, located just above the vertical scroll bar, is a pair of up- and down-pointing arrowheads attached to horizontal lines (see Figure 2.17).

2. Point to the vertical splitter to create a vertical split like the one in Figure 2.17, or to the horizontal splitter to create a horizontal split. The mouse pointer becomes a solid black version of the splitter icon.

3. To produce a vertical split, drag the vertical splitter across the horizontal scroll bar until you reach the point where you want to split the panes. To create a horizontal split, drag the horizontal splitter down the vertical scroll line.

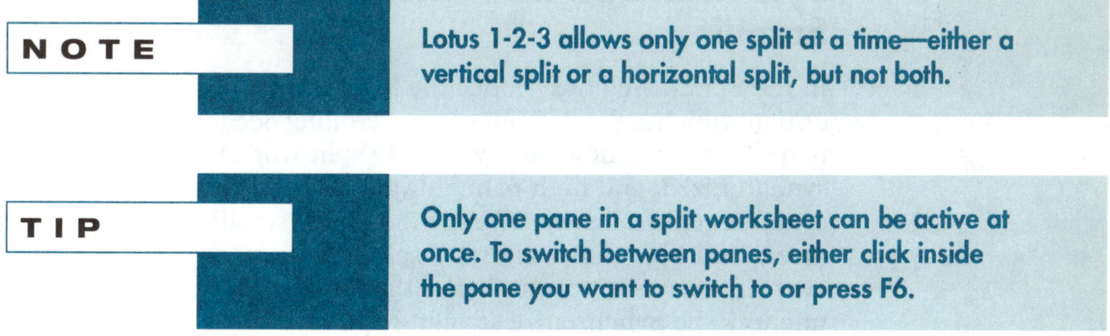

The keyboard method for dividing a worksheet window into panes is to choose <u>V</u>iew ➤ <u>S</u>plit. Here are the steps for creating a split with the keyboard:

1. On the active worksheet, select a cell in the column or row where you want the split to be. (If you are making a vertical split, the column that the cell you selected is in will become the first column in the right-hand pane. If you are making a horizontal split, the row that the cell you selected is in will become the first row in the lower pane.)

2. Choose <u>V</u>iew ➤ <u>S</u>plit.

3. In the Split dialog box, choose either <u>H</u>orizontal or <u>V</u>ertical, and then click the OK button or press ↵ to confirm your selection.

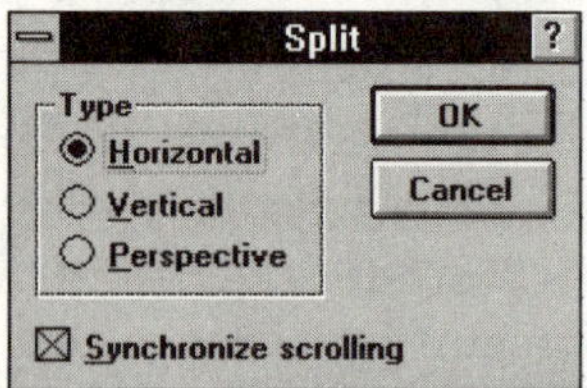

Synchronized and Unsynchronized Scrolling

In the Split dialog box, notice the <u>S</u>ynchronize scrolling check box. This option, which is the default, makes scrolling occur simultaneously in both panes of the window. In a vertically split worksheet, vertical scrolling is synchronized, and both panes always display the same range of rows. In a horizontally split worksheet, horizontal scrolling is likewise synchronized, and both panes always display the same range of columns. However, if you want to scroll in either pane independently of the other, uncheck the <u>S</u>ynchronize scrolling option.

Opening More than One Worksheet Window

In Lotus 1-2-3 for Windows, you can open and work with several worksheet windows at once. This feature is quite different from working with multiple worksheets inside the same window, which you learned about in Chapter 1. Following is a summary of these two capabilities:

- **A window with multiple worksheets.** A single worksheet window can have as many as 256 worksheets. To insert new worksheets in a window, you choose Edit ➤ Insert ➤ Sheet. When you save a window with multiple worksheets to disk, all the worksheets in the window are saved in a single file under one name. In the Perspective view, you can view three worksheets at a time inside the same worksheet window.

- **Windows with multiple worksheets.** Two or more worksheet files can be open concurrently in the 1-2-3 environment, with each open file occupying its own window. To view and manage multiple open windows, you can minimize windows and make them icons, or view multiple windows in *tiled* or *cascading* arrangements.

To experiment with multiple worksheet files, try the following exercise:

1. Choose File ➤ New. A new worksheet window with the default name FILE0001.WK4 opens over the existing worksheet, which is named Untitled.

2. Choose File ➤ New two more times to create two more new files. Their default names are FILE0002.WK4 and FILE0003.WK4.

3. Choose Window to see a list of currently open files.

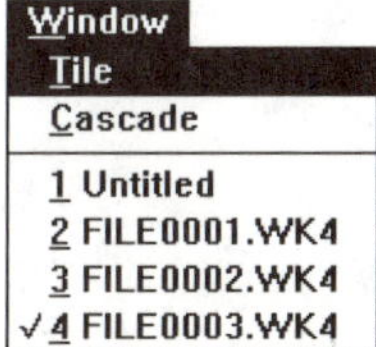

This list tells you which windows are currently open. At this point you could select one of these file names to activate a worksheet window.

TIP

You can press Ctrl-PgUp or Ctrl-PgDn on the keyboard in Ready mode to activate the previous or the next worksheet window in sequence.

4. Select <u>T</u>ile. The open worksheet files are arranged in windows of equal size, as in Figure 2.18.

FIGURE 2.18

A tiled view of four worksheet windows

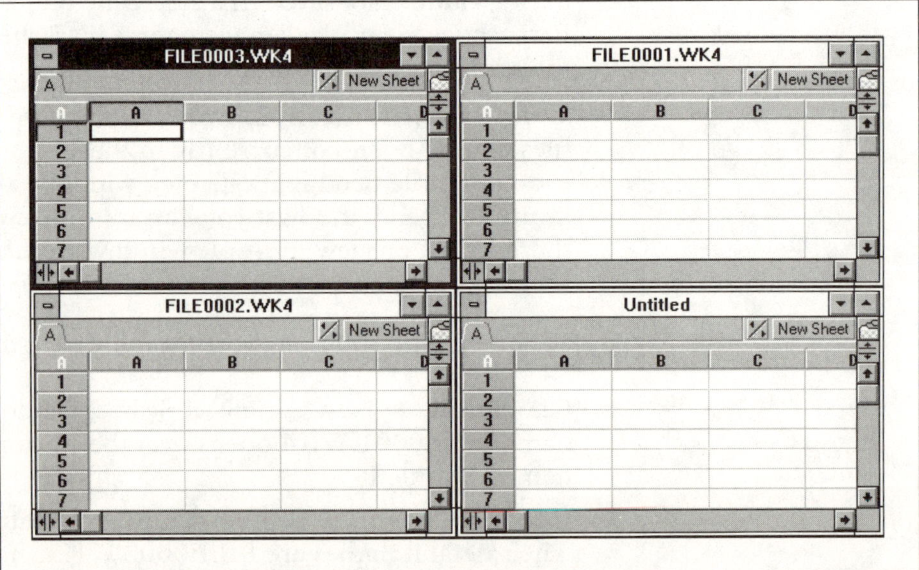

5. Open the Window menu again and choose <u>C</u>ascade. Now the open worksheet files are arranged in windows that overlap, as in Figure 2.19.

One reason for opening multiple files concurrently is to view worksheets that are *linked* by formulas. You'll study this technique in Part 3.

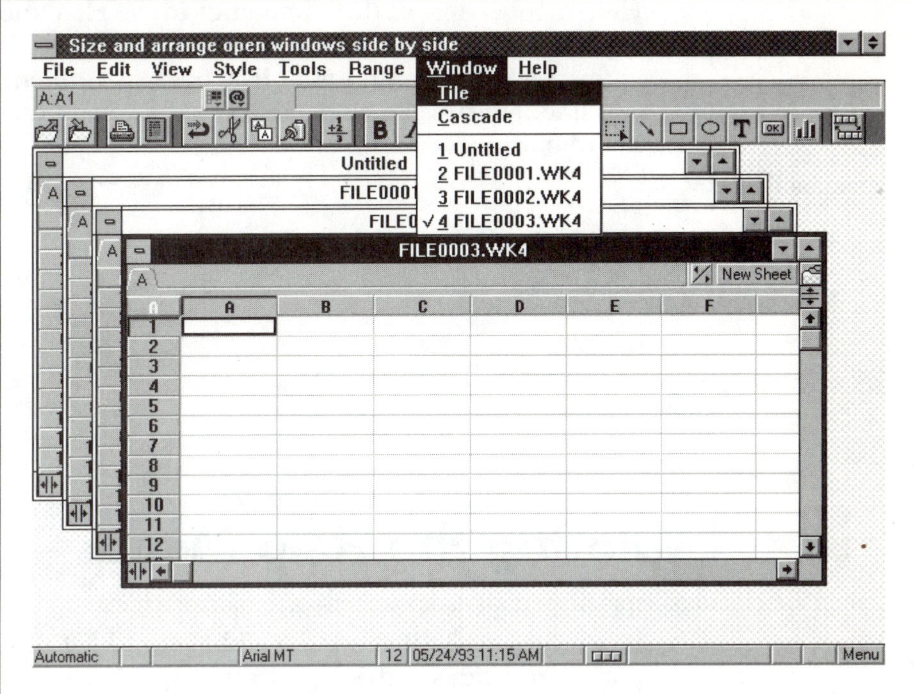

Getting Help in Lotus 1-2-3 for Windows

A complete and systematic help system is vital to Windows applications. You should be able to get clear and relevant on-screen help information with the click of a mouse button or the stroke of a key. Lotus 1-2-3 for Windows meets the highest standards for providing help information. While you are working in 1-2-3, you can bring up detailed information about virtually any topic, command, function, procedure, tool, or technique.

If 1-2-3 is the first Windows application you've used, take the time to explore the help system now. One way to begin is simply to examine the

Help menu. Most of the commands in the Help menu open a special window called 1-2-3 for Windows Help. From this window you can get help with specific topics and view lists of cross-referenced help categories. As you'll see shortly, the help window has its own unique menu bar and command buttons.

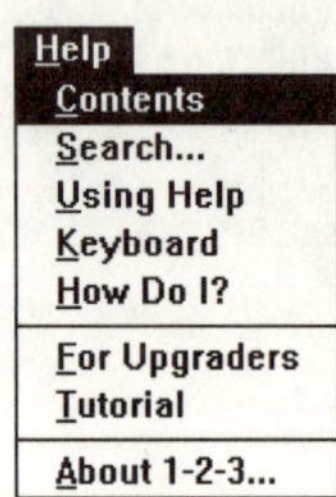

Exploring the Help Menu

Table 2.3 gives a brief summary of the eight commands on the Help menu. Figure 2.20 shows an alphabetized list of all the major help categories. You can see this list by selecting Contents on the Help menu.

TABLE 2.3: Help Menu Commands

HELP COMMAND	DESCRIPTION
Contents	Provides an alphabetized list of all major help categories (see Figure 2.20). Click any underlined category in the list to jump directly to a help topic.
Search	Opens the Search dialog box, where you can either enter the topic you are searching for in the text box or select a topic from the list box in the dialog box.
Using Help	Gives you a general-purpose introduction to the help system (this topic is worth studying carefully). Using Help also provides cross-references to specific help features.

TABLE 2.3: Help Menu Commands (continued)

HELP COMMAND	DESCRIPTION
Keyboard	Displays special purpose lists and indexes of help categories. The Keyboard index provides an introduction to using the keyboard in 1-2-3.
How Do I?	Provides useful lists of general-purpose procedures, organized alphabetically. Under each procedure is a cross-referenced list of relevant help topics. The How Do I? command is a good place to start whenever you need to review a particular task involving worksheets, graphs, or databases.
For Upgraders	Offers an introduction to Release 4 for users of previous 1-2-3 releases. In particular, this help topic explains the 1-2-3 Classic menus, and provides cross-references to commands in these menus.
Tutorial	Opens the on-line 1-2-3 tutorial, where you can choose from eight different lessons in using 1-2-3 Release 4.
About 1-2-3	Is the only command in the Help menu that does *not* open the Help window. Instead, it displays a small dialog box with information about the current release of 1-2-3 for Windows.

Finding Context-Sensitive Help

Context-sensitive help is probably the single most useful feature of a Windows-style help system. You can get help relevant to your current activity by pressing the F1 function key at almost any time during your work in 1-2-3.

For example, imagine that you are selecting options in a dialog box, but you can't recall exactly how to use some aspect of the command in question. To get help you press F1. A Help window appears with specific information about the dialog box you are viewing on-screen.

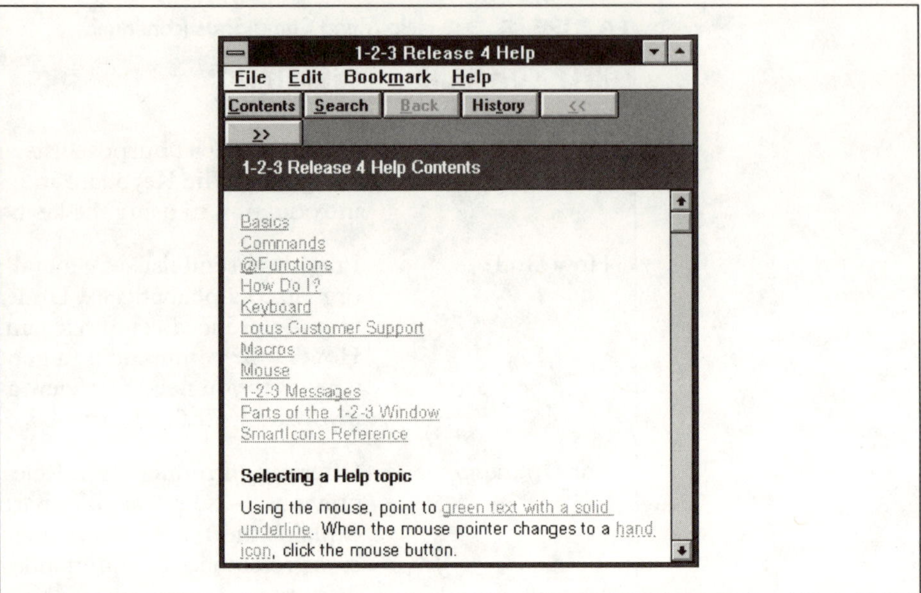

Here is a brief exercise to demonstrate the context-sensitive help feature:

1. Choose Tools ➤ SmartIcons. The SmartIcons dialog box appears.

2. Press F1. The help topic for the SmartIcons command immediately appears, as shown in Figure 2.21. If you wanted to, you could scroll through the topic and read all you needed to know about SmartIcons.

3. Click the Minimize button on the title bar of the Help window. The window disappears. At this point you could make selections in the SmartIcons dialog box.

4. Press Esc to cancel the command and to end this exercise.

TIP

Press F1 to get context-sensitive help whenever you are not sure what to do next in a 1-2-3 procedure.

Getting context-
sensitive help

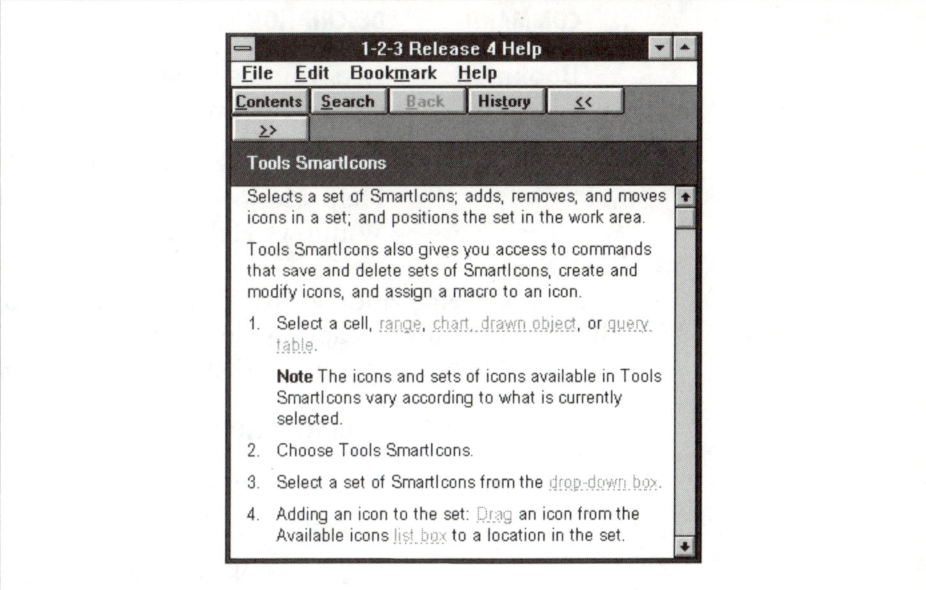

The Help Window

As you saw in the previous exercise, the Help window has its own title bar, Control-menu box, and Minimize and Maximize buttons. These features perform the same way and have the same functions as they do in other windows. For example, if you need to enlarge a Help window so you can read more information at once, just click the Maximize button.

The menu bar in the Help window offers four commands with pull-down menus:

COMMAND	DESCRIPTION
File	Offers commands for printing the current help topic, for opening the help system files for other Windows applications, and for exiting the help system.
Edit	Allows you to copy the current help topic to the Clipboard and to add your own annotations to a help topic.

COMMAND	DESCRIPTION
Book<u>m</u>ark	Lets you mark passages in the help system so you can find them quickly.
<u>H</u>elp	Provides access to the Using Windows Help window, a general description of the Windows Help facility.

Finally, the Help window provides six special command buttons, each with its own icon and caption (see Figure 2.21). The buttons are located right below the Help menu bar. Following is a description of the six buttons.

HELP BUTTON	DESCRIPTION
<u>C</u>ontents	Takes you to the general Help Index.
<u>S</u>earch	Lets you locate information in the help system. When you click this button, the Search dialog box appears on-screen so you can quickly search by name for any topic that you want to read about.
<u>B</u>ack	Returns you to the Help topic that you viewed just before the current topic.
His<u>t</u>ory	Takes you step by step back through the topics you have been examining.
<<	Lets you browse backward through all the topics in a general help category.
>>	Lets you browse forward through all the topics in a general help category.

As an exercise in using the Search button, imagine that you want to review the features of the Control Panel. Here are the steps for using the Search dialog box:

1. Press F1.

2. Select the <u>S</u>earch button. The Search dialog box appears, as in Figure 2.22.

3. In the Type a <u>w</u>ord text box, enter the words **Control panel**. As you do so, the index list beneath the text box automatically scrolls to the Control panel topic.

4. Double-click on this topic. Subjects relating to the one you clicked on appear at the bottom of the dialog box.

5. Select one of the topics and click the <u>G</u>o To button. The Search dialog box closes and the topic you selected appears in the Help window. To see related topics, you can click either of the Browse buttons.

6. When you have finished reading the help topic, click the Mini-mize button on the Help window's title bar to return to your work in 1-2-3.

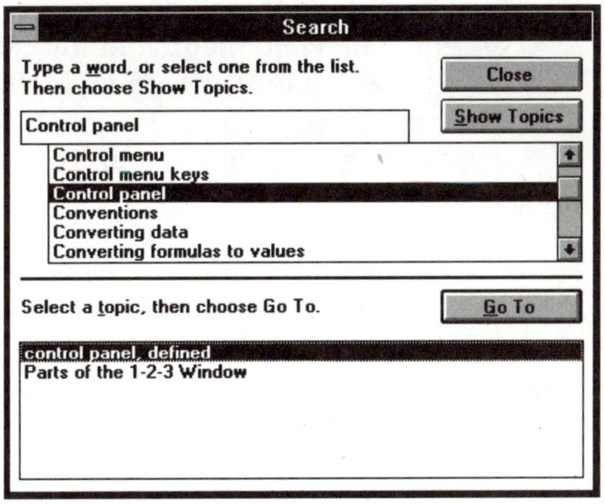

FIGURE 2.22

The Search dialog box for the help system

Summary

The Lotus 1-2-3 Release 4 application window has many tools and properties in common with other Windows applications. If you have worked with almost any other Windows program, these elements will seem comfortably familiar.

The application window itself has six essential lines offering tools and information—the title bar, menu bar, edit line, SmartIcons, and the status bar. Moreover, most windows you encounter in 1-2-3, including the application window, worksheet windows, and even dialog boxes, have Control menus and other common tools designed for managing the windows themselves.

Lotus 1-2-3 gives you two versatile ways to work with multiple worksheets. On the one hand, a single window—representing one worksheet file on disk—can itself hold as many as 256 worksheets. On the other hand, you can open and work with multiple worksheet windows concurrently in the 1-2-3 environment. You can divide a given worksheet window into panes in order to view two distant portions of a worksheet at the same time.

One of the most important resources in 1-2-3 is its comprehensive help system. The Help menu and the Help window itself each give you many ways to search for the help topic that you need information on. Learn to take advantage of the 1-2-3 for Windows Help window as a guide to understanding worksheets, graphs, and databases.

PART

2

ESSENTIAL 1-2-3
FOR WINDOWS

3

Worksheet Essentials

To update an existing file after you have made changes in the active worksheet,   145

click the SaveFile icon or choose <u>F</u>ile ➤ <u>S</u>ave.

To move a range of data from one place to another in a worksheet,   146

preselect the source range, click the Copy SmartIcon, and then click the upper-left corner of the destination range, and click the Paste icon.

To insert a blank row or column at a specific position on the worksheet,   149

select a cell at the target position and choose <u>E</u>dit ➤ <u>I</u>nsert. Select either <u>C</u>olumn or <u>R</u>ow and click OK.

To change the reference type of an address in a formula entry,   159

press F4 in Point, Edit, or Value mode. Each time you press F4, the address changes to the next reference type—from relative to absolute to mixed.

ONE OF the most remarkable qualities of the Lotus 1-2-3 spreadsheet is its flexibility. Instead of arranging your work for you, 1-2-3 offers a multitude of tools and options so you can present data and make calculations the way you want to. From the moment you begin entering information into the empty grid, it reflects your work requirements, your formatting preferences, and your organizational style.

In this chapter, you'll learn basic procedures for entering and calculating data in a worksheet window. You'll learn how to:

- Enter labels and values

- Select ranges on a worksheet

- Calculate totals

- Assign names to ranges

- Copy data ranges

- Save a worksheet to disk

- Insert, delete, and move blocks of data

- Develop formulas and copy them to new ranges

- Select the appropriate reference type—absolute or relative—for addresses in formulas

- Use parentheses to establish the order of operations in formulas

- Explore "what-if" scenarios

In this chapter and in Chapter 4, where you'll learn about formatting and printing, you'll create a sample worksheet for an imaginary company named Computing Conferences, Inc. This imaginary company organizes and conducts one-day training conferences that focus on the computing needs of different businesses. Your sample worksheet will compute the projected revenues, expenses, and profits of a one-day conference.

Figure 3.1 shows what the worksheet will look like when you're get done creating it in Chapter 4. Notice how the worksheet is divided into sections.

- The top section gives general information about a one-day conference: the name, location, date, price of admission, and two attendance estimates, one a minimum and the other a maximum estimate.

- The next two sections show projected revenues and expenses, one projection for minimum attendance and one for maximum attendance.

- The two columns on the right side of the worksheet show financial figures based on the minimum and maximum attendance estimates, respectively.

The final conference worksheet. By the end of Chapter 4, you will have created this worksheet yourself.

Computing Conferences, Inc.
Profit Projection for a One-Day Conference

Conference: *Computing for Video Stores*
Place: *St. Louis*
Date: 16-Oct-93

Expected attendance:

		Minimum	*Maximum*
Price:	$195.00	80	150

	Per Person	Min. Total	Max. Total
Projected Revenues			
Attendance		$15,600.00	$29,250.00
Video Sales	$35.00	$1,400.00	$2,625.00
Total Revenues		$17,000.00	$31,875.00
Projected Expenses - Fixed			
Conference room		$1,500.00	$2,000.00
Video production		$1,000.00	$1,000.00
Promotion		$3,500.00	$3,500.00
Travel		$800.00	$800.00
Total Fixed Expenses		$6,800.00	$7,300.00
Projected Expenses - Variable by Attendance			
Conference materials	$8.25	$660.00	$1,237.00
Coffee and pastries	$3.25	$260.00	$487.00
Box lunch	$4.75	$380.00	$712.50
Total Variable Expenses		$1,300.00	$2,437.50
Projected Profit		$8,900.00	$22,137.50

- The bottom line gives the anticipated profit, again with projections based on minimum and maximum attendance estimates.

The worksheet lists projected revenues, expenses, and profit for a one-day conference in St. Louis for owners and managers of video rental stores. However, the worksheet is carefully designed so it can be used as a general-purpose *template* for all one-day events sponsored by Computing Conferences, Inc. In other words, the company can use this worksheet again to project the expenses, revenues, and profits of other conferences.

In Figure 3.1, the parts of the worksheet with a light gray shading represent input ranges for data about a given conference. The unshaded numeric values are calculated from the input data. A Computing Conferences, Inc. employee simply enters information about a new conference in the shaded ranges, and 1-2-3, based on the data entries, recalculates the formulas in the worksheet to obtain new data in the unshaded ranges.

To prepare for the hands-on exercises that you'll do in this chapter, start 1-2-3 Release 4 if you have not already done so, and click the Maximize button on the default worksheet named "Untitled." In the sections ahead, you'll enter labels, values, and formulas onto the worksheet.

TIP

Think of each new worksheet you develop as a template for other worksheets you will need in the future. Of course, not all worksheets lend themselves to this kind of planning. However, each time you start a new worksheet, ask yourself whether you will need a similar one on a daily, weekly, monthly, quarterly, or even yearly basis. If you will, organize your worksheet so you can reuse it.

Developing a Worksheet

In 1-2-3, it is easy to move blocks of data from one point to another and to insert rows or columns, so you can create the sections of a worksheet in whatever order is most convenient. You don't have to work from the top straight to the bottom.

Accordingly, let's begin the conference worksheet by entering the fixed expenses for the conference. Later, when we are ready to develop other parts of the worksheet, including the projected revenues and projected variable expenses, we can make room for them by moving the fixed expenses section down to its correct position.

Entering Labels

You'll recall that a label is a non-numeric data entry in a cell. Labels are used as titles, column headings, and row descriptions. When you enter a label, 1-2-3 switches into Label mode. By default, 1-2-3 left-justifies labels, but you can change label alignments in a number of different ways.

How 1-2-3 handles long labels Lotus 1-2-3 has an interesting way of handling *long* labels. When a label entry has more characters than will fit in a cell, the label extends across adjacent cells to the right if those cells are empty. But if data appears in the cells to the right of the label, the long label is cut off at the end of its own cell.

To see how long labels work, enter the two title lines at the top of the conference worksheet:

1. Select cell A1, if it is not already selected, by pressing Home.

2. Move to B1 by pressing → or by clicking B1 with the mouse.

3. Type **Computing Conferences, Inc.**, the company name, in cell B1. As you type, your entry appears in the contents box and the mode indicator displays the word *Label*.

4. Press ↵ to complete your entry.

Lotus 1-2-3 copies the entry into cell B1. But because the entry is too long to be displayed completely, the display extends across row 1, into cells C1 and D1, as shown in Figure 3.2.

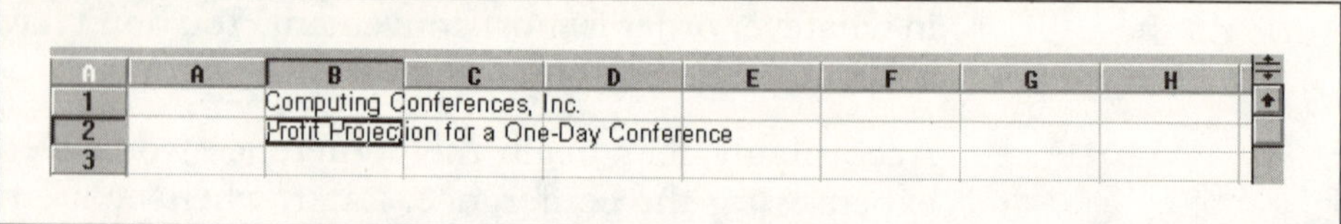

5. Press ↓ to select cell B2, and enter the worksheet title in this cell:
   Profit Projection for a One-Day Conference.

6. Press ↵ to complete the entry.

Again, the long label crosses empty cells C2, D2, and E2. However, as Figure 3.2 shows, the contents box lists the entry in cell B2 in the following way:

'Profit Projection for a One-Day Conference

Although the long label *crosses* cells B2 through E2, its actual storage location is cell B2 alone.

NOTE

In the contents box, a quotation mark (') at the beginning of a label means that the label is left-aligned. Other alignment symbols are explained in Chapter 4.

What happens to a long label when you enter data in the cell to its immediate right? To answer this question, try the following exercise:

1. Press → to select cell C2. Notice that the contents box shows no entry for this cell, because C2 is in fact empty. The long label in cell B2 merely crosses cell C2.

2. Type **abc** as a temporary label in cell C2.

3. Press ↵ to complete the entry. Notice what happens to the long label display in cell B2. It has been cut off in its own cell, so to speak, so that cell C2 can display its label.

4. Press ← to select cell B2 again. The contents box lists the long label that you entered originally in cell B2. However, on the

worksheet, the cell itself displays only the first several letters of the label, as shown in Figure 3.3.

In summary, long labels cross the cells to their right when those cells are empty. But the long label display is cut off, or *truncated*, when the cell to the right contains an entry of its own.

As a result of our experiment, an unwanted label entry appears in cell C2. Deleting entries is quite simple.

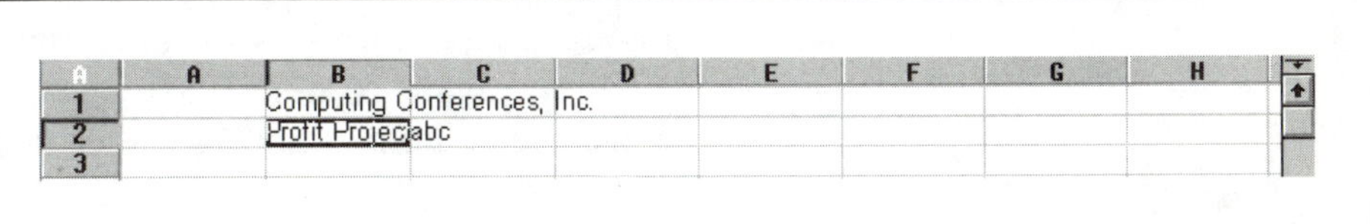

Deleting a Label or Value

To delete a label or value in a cell, either

- Select the cell where the label or value is and press the Delete key on your keyboard.

- Choose <u>E</u>dit ➤ Cl<u>e</u>ar, and in the Clear dialog box, choose <u>C</u>ell contents only.

TIP To delete styles and formats along with the label or value in the cell, select <u>E</u>dit ➤ Cl<u>e</u>ar ➤ <u>B</u>oth.

Follow these steps to delete the "abc" label in cell C2:

1. Press → to select C2.
2. Press the Delete key.

When you delete the label in cell C2, the long label in cell B2 is displayed once again across cell C2, D2, and E2. Now there is no entry in cell C2 to cut off the display.

Other choices for deleting labels and values Open the <u>E</u>dit menu again to see other commands for handling a cell or range of cells. The Edit menu is shown in Figure 3.4. It offers these commands for handling cell entries:

Cu<u>t</u>   Removes an entry and copies it to the Windows Clipboard. Cutting a label or value is the first step in a cut-and-paste procedure.

<u>C</u>opy   Keeps the cell entry intact and copies it to the Clipboard.

Cl<u>e</u>ar   Produces a dialog box for specifying exactly what you want to delete from a cell or range of cells: the cell contents, styles, or a graph. The Clear command deletes entries without copying them to the Clipboard.

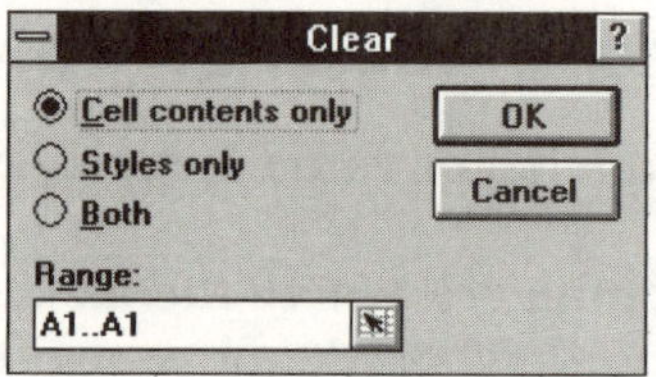

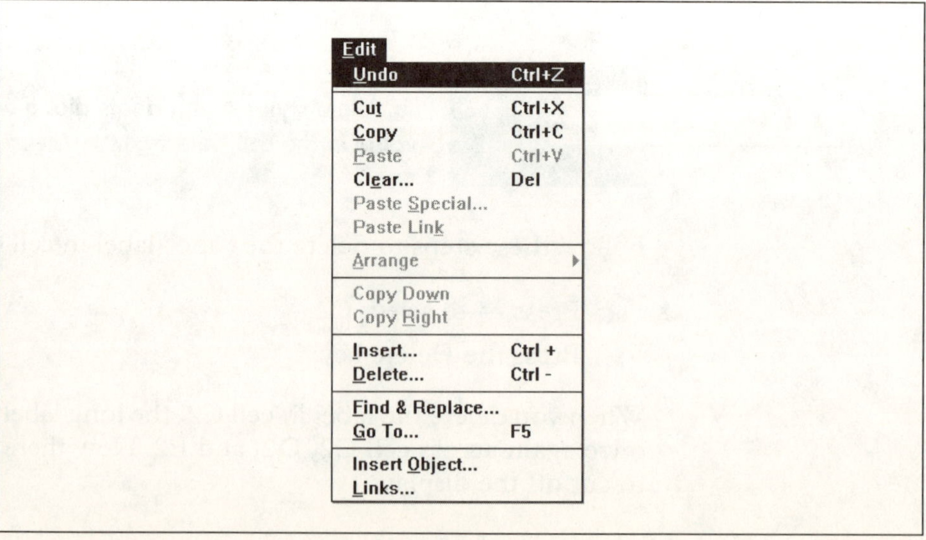

FIGURE 3.4

The Edit menu gives you many options for deleting cell entries.

Putting the Undo command on the Edit menu When you delete a label or value accidentally, or if you make other mistakes in 1-2-3, you can use the Undo command to restore the worksheet to what it was before you made the deletion. Undo should be on the Edit menu. However, if it is not on the Edit menu and you would like to put it there, choose <u>T</u>ools ➤ <u>U</u>ser Setup ➤ <u>U</u>ndo.

Restoring a Deleted Cell Entry

Lotus 1-2-3 gives you four ways to undo the effect of your last action:

- Choose <u>E</u>dit ➤ <u>U</u>ndo
- Press Ctrl-Z
- Press Alt-Backspace
- Click the Undo SmartIcon

The Undo SmartIcon Clicking the Undo SmartIcon is the easiest way to undo an action. On this icon are two arrows, the darker one pointing around to the other to show an action being "undone."

Try this exercise with the Undo command:

1. Press ← to select cell B2, the cell with the label "Profit Projection for a One-Day Conference."
2. Press the Delete key. The entry in the cell disappears. You've made a mistake, and you need a quick way to correct your error.
3. Choose <u>E</u>dit ➤ <u>U</u>ndo, or click the Undo SmartIcon. The label entry in cell B2 reappears.

To use the Undo command successfully, you must correct the mistake before you perform another action. Undo operates only on the action you performed just previous to choosing Edit ➤ Undo.

Entering the Rest of the Labels for the Conference Worksheet

The following instructions tell you how to enter labels in the conference worksheet to make it look like the worksheet in Figure 3.5. As you enter these labels, remember that you can press an arrow key (→, ←, ↑, or ↓) instead of ↵ to confirm an entry.

Pressing an arrow key to confirm an entry helps make your work go faster because it performs two actions at once: it confirms the entry *and* selects a cell for the next entry.

FIGURE 3.5

Labels for the conference worksheet.

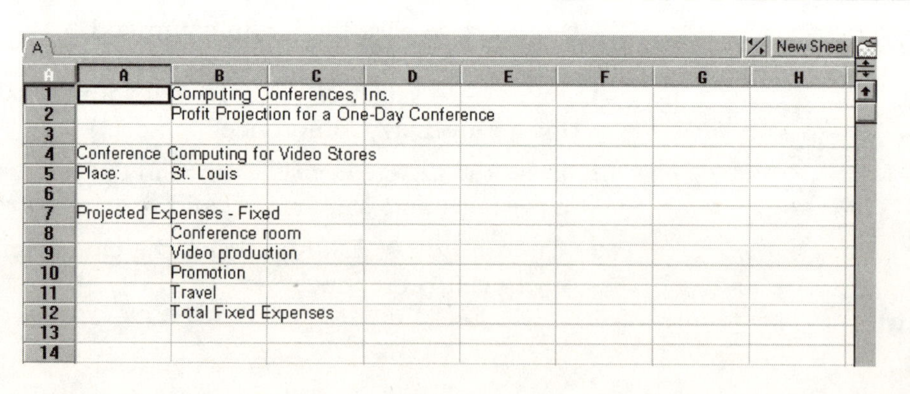

	A	B	C	D	E	F	G	H
1		Computing Conferences, Inc.						
2		Profit Projection for a One-Day Conference						
3								
4	Conference Computing for Video Stores							
5	Place:	St. Louis						
6								
7	Projected Expenses - Fixed							
8		Conference room						
9		Video production						
10		Promotion						
11		Travel						
12		Total Fixed Expenses						
13								
14								

Follow these steps to enter the labels:

1. Enter the label **Conference:** in cell A4 and **Place:** in A5.

2. To the right of these entries, enter the name and location of the conference. In cell B4, type **Computing for Video Stores**. Enter **St. Louis** in cell B5.

3. Enter the subtitle, **Projected Expenses – Fixed**, in cell A7.

4. Finally, enter the fixed-expense labels in cells B8 through B12:

CELL	ENTER
B8	Conference room
B9	Video production
B10	Promotion
B11	Travel
B12	Total Fixed Expenses

Fixed-expense labels represent expenses that do not change no matter how many people attend the conference. These expenses include the fee for the conference room, the cost of producing a video of the conference, the promotion costs, and the amount spent on travel to the conference site. Later, you will enter the variable expenses. How much the variable expenses come to depends on how many people attend the conference.

The next step is to begin entering numeric values for the fixed expenses.

Entering Numbers

Entering numbers in a worksheet is not just a matter of finding the right cell and entering the numbers. You must consider how to enter numbers in labels, how Value and Label mode affect number entries, and how number formats work.

Entering numbers in labels   As you know, a value is a cell entry that 1-2-3 accepts as a number. A value can be used in an arithmetic formula in a worksheet.

WORKSHEET ESSENTIALS

Normally, entries that begin with a number switch 1-2-3 into Value mode. But numbers sometimes represent characters, not numeric values. For example, consider this address:

456 Flower Street

This address is a label, not a value, but it begins with a number. When a label begins with a number, you have to notify 1-2-3 that the entry is a label, not a value. One way to do this is to preface the label with a single quote character, like so:

'456 Flower Street

As soon as you enter the single quote, 1-2-3 switches into Label mode, and you can successfully complete the label entry.

Entering characters in Value mode In previous versions, 1-2-3 would return an error when you entered an alphabetic character after numbers. However, Release 4 assumes that you are intentionally entering a text string and automatically puts in a single quote at the beginning of the entire string.

You'll have an opportunity to experience firsthand what happens when you enter a character in Value mode in the following exercise, as you enter the column of fixed-expense figures in the conference worksheet:

1. Select cell D8, the topmost cell in the column range where you will enter the expense figures.

2. Type **1500** in cell D8. Notice the word *Value* appearing in the mode indicator when you type the first digit of this number. To complete the entry and select the next cell down, press ↓.

3. Type **1000a** in cell D9.

4. Press ↵ to try to complete the entry.

5. Press ↓ to select cell D10.

6. Enter **$3500** into D10 and press ↓ to try to complete the entry.

Lotus 1-2-3 Release 4 ignores the dollar sign, but still recognizes the string as a numeric value. The value displayed in the cell is $3,500, but the entry in the contents box is 3500.

7. Enter the final expense value, **800**, in cell D11.

Now that you have entered an entire column of numbers, you need to compute a total for the column and display it in cell D12. Calculating the total of a column or row of numbers is a common spreadsheet operation—so common that 1-2-3 offers a SmartIcon for calculating row and column totals. But before using this SmartIcon you must select the range of values that you want to total. In the next section, you'll learn more about worksheet ranges.

Selecting Ranges

As you know by now, a range is a rectangular area comprising worksheet cells. You can select and perform an operation on it. Many 1-2-3 menu commands and functions work with ranges. A range can be:

- A single cell

- A group of contiguous cells in a row or column

- A two-dimensional rectangle of cells in multiple rows and columns in a worksheet

- A three-dimensional group of cells, consisting of identically addressed ranges from adjacent worksheets, in a worksheet window

The range notation with which you are familiar is the address of the first cell, followed by two dots, and the address of the second cell, as in B2..F6. If the range is on a single worksheet, this notation can be identified with or without the worksheet name. For example, a range on worksheet A can be identified with the notation A:B2..A:F6 or B2..F6, provided that no one will confuse B2..F6 with the same range on another worksheet, for example B:B2..B:F6.

One-, Two-, and Three-Dimensional Ranges

Figures 3.6 through 3.10 show examples of different kinds of ranges, as follows:

RANGE	FIGURE	DESCRIPTION
B4..B4	3.6	A single cell on a worksheet, at address B4.

RANGE	FIGURE	DESCRIPTION
C5..C10	3.7	A *column range*—a range of cells all in the same column, C in this case. C5 is the top of the range and C10 is the bottom.
A6..E6	3.8	A *row range*—a range of cells all in the same row, row 6 in this case. A6 is the first cell on the left side of the range and E6 is the last cell on the right.
B2..F6	3.9	A *two-dimensional range*. B2 is the upper-left corner of the range, and F6 is the lowerright corner.
A:B2..C:F6	3.10	A *three-dimensional range* consisting of cells from three adjacent worksheets in a window—that is, the range B2..F6 in worksheets A, B, and C.

FIGURE 3.6

A range consisting of a single cell, B4..B4

FIGURE 3.7

A column range, C5..C10

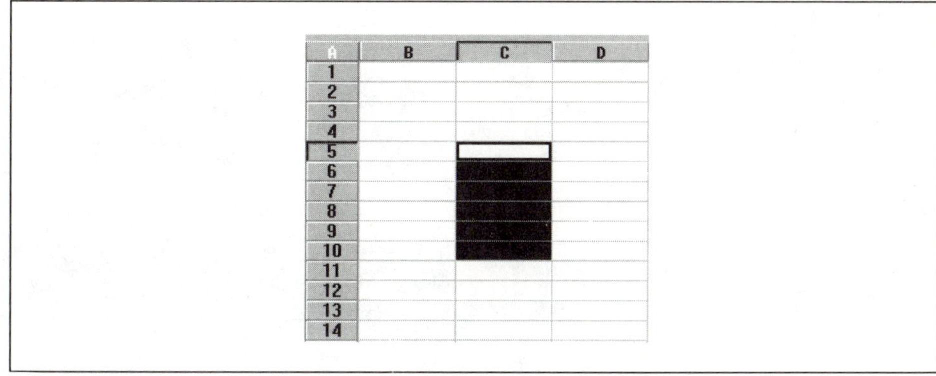

FIGURE 3.8

A row range, A6..E6

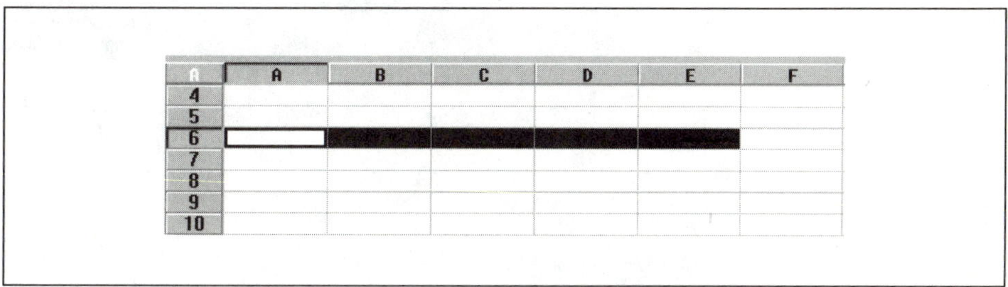

FIGURE 3.9

A two-dimensional range, B2..F6

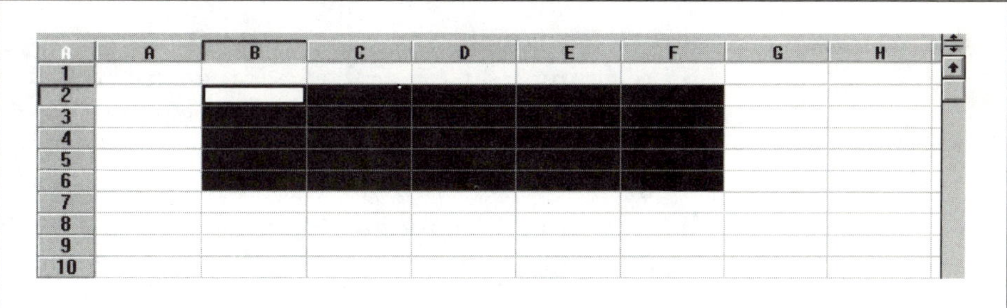

A three-dimensional range, A:B2..C:F6

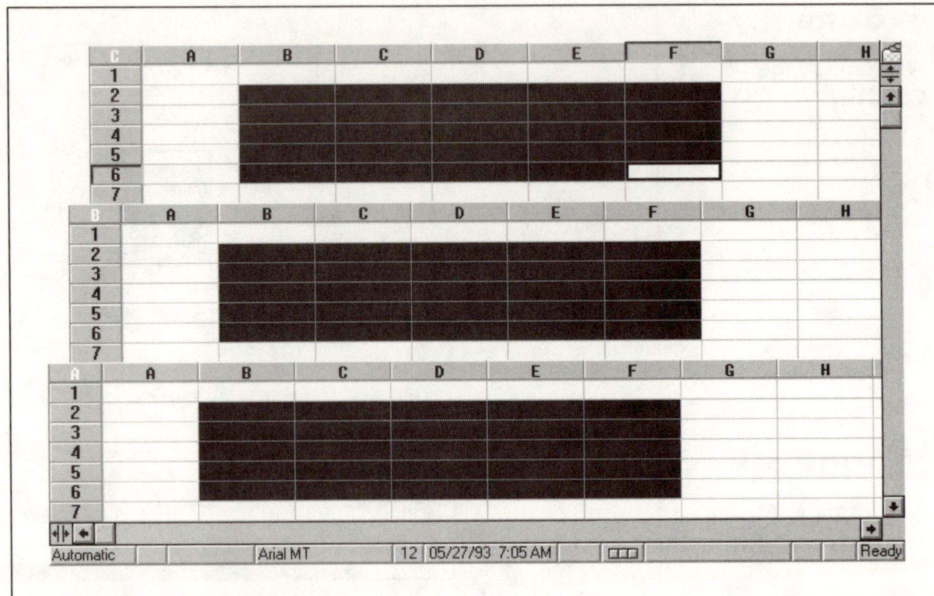

Preselecting a Range

When you choose a menu command that operates over a range, you will usually find a check box for targeting the range in the command's dialog box. For example, the Clear dialog box, which you can bring on-screen by selecting Edit Clear, has a Range check box for telling the program which cells to delete. However, you can choose the range before or after you choose a command that affects a range. When you select the command before selecting the range, 1-2-3 provides special mouse and keyboard pointing techniques for entering the range. Selecting a range before you choose a menu command is sometimes called *preselecting* a range.

TIP

Preselecting a range is usually more convenient than choosing a command first. Sometimes 1-2-3 requires you to select the range first. Moreover, some SmartIcons will not work unless you preselect a range.

When you point to a range of cells to preselect them, 1-2-3 switches from Ready to Point mode. As you point to the cells, your selection is highlighted with a double-line border and the range notation appears in the contents box. There are three ways to preselect a range, one with the mouse and two with the keyboard.

Preselecting a range with the mouse To preselect a worksheet range with the mouse:

1. Position the mouse pointer over the first cell in the range.

2. Hold down the left mouse button and drag the pointer down and/or across until you reach the last cell in the range.

3. To select a three-dimensional range over adjacent worksheets in a window, hold down the Shift key and click the tab of the last adjacent sheet.

4. Release the mouse button when the target range is highlighted.

Preselecting a range with the keyboard With the keyboard, pressing F4 switches 1-2-3 from Ready to Point mode. Here are the steps for preselecting a range with the keyboard:

1. Select the cell you want to be the first in the range.

2. Press F4 to anchor the current cell and make it the starting point of the range. Pressing F4 also switches 1-2-3 to Point mode.

3. Press arrow keys to highlight the target range. For example, press ↓ for a column range or → for a row range.

4. To select a three-dimensional range over adjacent worksheets in a window, press Ctrl-PgUp or Ctrl-PgDn while you are in Point mode.

5. Press ↵ to complete the range selection. This final step switches you back to Ready mode but leaves the range in its highlighted state.

Here is a second keyboard technique for preselecting a range:

1. Select the first cell of the range.

2. Hold down the Shift key as you press →, ←, ↑, or ↓ to define a range on the active worksheet.

3. Press Shift-Ctrl-PgUp or Shift-Ctrl-PgDn to move through multiple worksheets in the active window.

4. Press ↵ to select the three-dimensional range.

You'll have opportunities to practice these techniques as you continue developing the conference worksheet.

Calculating Totals

To use the Summation SmartIcon to calculate totals, you must have preselected a range. The Summation SmartIcon is located near the middle of the SmartIcon set and is labeled with a very simple addition problem, $1 + 2 = 3$.

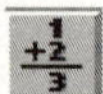

When you preselect the target range of values for a calculation, you must include a final cell in the range so 1-2-3 can store the summation formula. This final cell in the range must be blank. To add a *column* of numbers, select the range of values in the column and a blank cell at the bottom of the column. To add a *row* of numbers, select the row plus a blank cell to the right of the numbers.

Calculating totals with the Summation SmartIcon To calculate totals with the Summation SmartIcon, follow these two simple steps:

1. Preselect the target range. Be sure to include the extra cell at the end.

2. Click the Summation SmartIcon. 1-2-3 sums the values in the range and enters the total value in the blank cell at the end.

In the conference worksheet, cell D12 is reserved for the total of the fixed expenses. Follow these steps to find the total:

1. Preselect range D8..D12.

2. Click the Summation SmartIcon. The value 6800 appears in cell D12. This number represents the total fixed expenses.

3. To view the formula that 1-2-3 has created, select cell D12. (Click the cell with the mouse or press ↓ four times.) The following formula appears in the contents box:

@SUM(D8..D11)

@SUM is one of the tools in 1-2-3's large library of *built-in functions*. In this case, 1-2-3 has entered a formula that finds the sum of the numeric values stored in the range D8..D11.

@SUM and other functions are explained in Chapter 5.

Calculating totals with the keyboard Of course, you can enter the @SUM function directly from the keyboard if you prefer. To try this exercise, select D12 and press Delete to erase the @SUM function already there. Then follow these steps:

1. Enter **@SUM(** with the keyboard. When you do so, 1-2-3 switches to Value mode.

2. You could now type the target range, D8..D11, directly with the keyboard, but the pointing technique is easier: Press ↑ four times to select cell D8. The program switches into Point mode and automatically enters the cell address D8 in the summation formula in the contents box.

3. Enter a period (.) to anchor the range. In this case, D8 is the starting point for the range.

4. Press ↓ three times.

As you press ↓, 1-2-3 highlights the range D8..D11, and the range notation appears in the summation formula in the contents box. At this point, the screen looks like Figure 3.11.

5. Type), the close parenthesis character, to complete the summation formula.

6. Press ↵ to complete the entry.

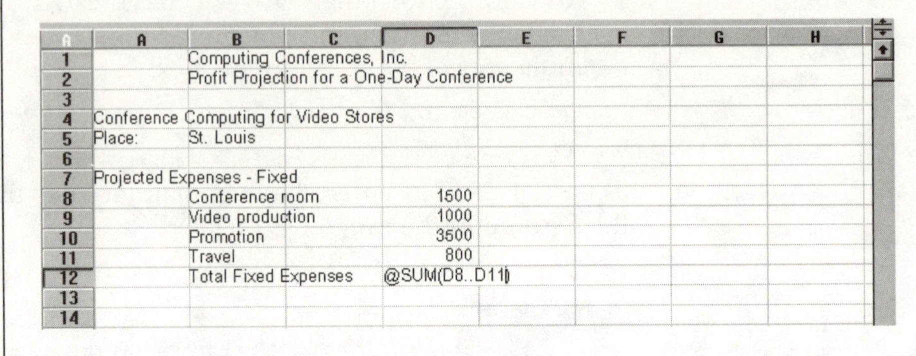

The end result, 6800, is identical to result you got when you used the Summation SmartIcon. After trying both techniques, you can see how much time you save by employing a SmartIcon.

When you enter formulas and functions such as @SUM in a worksheet, you can simplify your work by assigning names to ranges of data. We'll look briefly at this technique in the next section.

Naming a Range

Formulas with the addresses of cells and ranges are sometimes difficult to read and understand. For example, consider the summation formula you just entered in the conference worksheet. Suppose you returned to this worksheet weeks or months from now. Would you understand immediately what the significance of the formula @SUM(D8..D11) is? However, suppose the range notation D8..D11 was replaced with a meaningful name, such as EXPENSES. You would have an easier time recognizing the purpose of a formula that read @SUM(EXPENSES) than you would one that read @SUM(D8..D11).

For this reason, 1-2-3 gives you the option of assigning names to individual cells or to cell ranges in a worksheet. The command for assigning names to ranges is Range ➤ Name ➤ Create. To name a range, follow these steps:

1. Select cells D8..D11.

2. Choose Range ➤ Name. The Name dialog box shown in Figure 3.12 appears.

3. Enter a meaningful name, **EXPENSES**, in the Name text box.

4. Click on the Add button. The new name appears in the Existing named ranges list box below the Name text box.

5. Click on the OK button or press ↵ to confirm your entry.

You use the Name dialog box to assign a name to a particular range. Range names can be as many as 15 characters long. Lotus 1-2-3 automatically converts range names to uppercase letters.

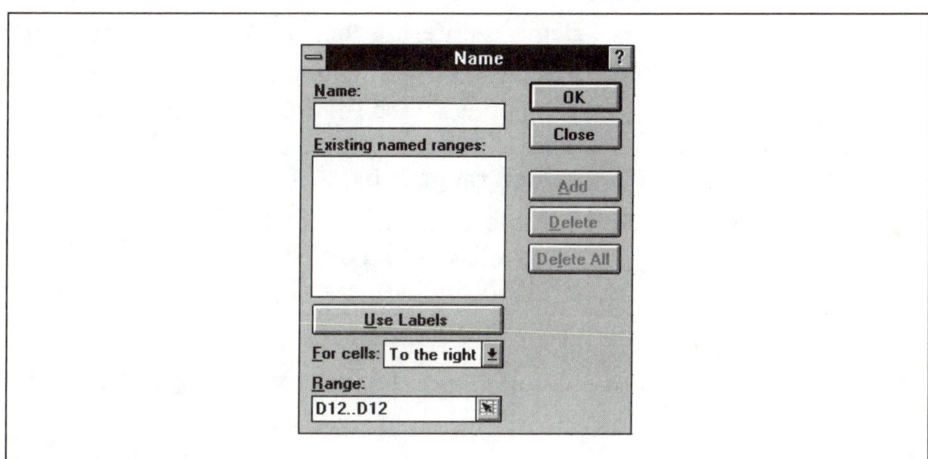

TIP

When you name a range, choose a name that you will be sure to recognize later on. Complicated worksheets can have many range names—you should be able to tell in a glance what a range name signifies.

Copying an existing range name to a formula Giving a range a name does not change the appearance of your worksheet in any way. But the next time you need to write a formula involving the fixed-expenses in column D, you can use the EXPENSES range name. In fact, to help you enter formulas, you can choose a range from a convenient list of existing range names in the current worksheet.

In the following exercise, you'll reenter the summation formula in cell D12, this time using the new range name you just defined:

1. Select cell D12 and press the Delete key to erase the @SUM formula currently in the cell.

2. Begin reentering the summation formula: **@SUM(**.

3. After you type the open parenthesis, press F3. The Name dialog box appears (see Figure 3.12). The name you defined for the column of expense figures, EXPENSES, appears in the Existing named ranges box.

4. Double-click the name EXPENSES in the Existing named ranges list box. The Name dialog box disappears and the name EXPENSES appears in the formula

   @SUM(EXPENSES

5. Complete the formula by typing), the close parenthesis, and pressing ↵.

You'll work with other range names later in this chapter.

Next, you'll copy the fixed-expense figures from column D to column E in the conference worksheet. Looking back at Figure 3.1, you can see that the fixed expenses are almost the same in the two columns. Instead of reentering the figures in the second column, you can copy and revise them in column E as necessary.

Copying a Range of Values

There are three ways to copy a range of data from one place to another in a worksheet:

- Using the CopyRangeRight or CopyRangeDown SmartIcons
- Selecting Copy Down or Copy Right
- Using the Copy and Paste commands

The simplest technique is to use the CopyRangeRight or CopyRange-Down SmartIcons. The CopyRangeRight icon shows a grid with the top row highlighted, and the CopyRangeDown icon shows a grid with the first column highlighted.

Move the mouse pointer to the CopyRangeRight SmartIcon and press the right mouse button. The following description appears in the 1-2-3 title bar:

Copy the leftmost column to a range

In the following exercises, you'll try all three techniques for copying data ranges. All three produce the same results on the worksheet. In each copy procedure, you begin your work by preselecting the range of cells that you want to copy. Preselect the range with the mouse or the F4 function key.

Copying with the CopyRangeRight Icon

Here is how you use the CopyRangeRight icon:

1. Select the range D8..E12, as shown in Figure 3.13, to include both the origin and the destination of the copy.

2. Click the CopyRangeRight icon.

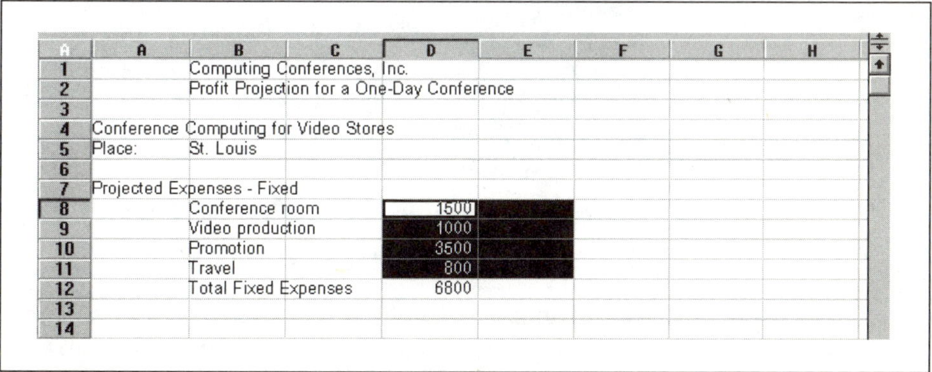

Selecting both the data range and the adjacent cells tells 1-2-3 in which direction the copy will be made. Because the source of the copy is a column of cells, 1-2-3 assumes you want to copy the same column to the right, starting at E8.

How 1-2-3 Copies Formulas

When 1-2-3 makes a copy, it copies formulas as well as cells, and updates the cell range. Move the cell pointer to E12 and look at the contents box. Lotus 1-2-3 has copied the @SUM formula to the cell and has replaced the range D8..D11 with the range E8..E11. This formula was copied from the formula in cell D12, but in the copy 1-2-3 adjusted the @SUM function range to E8..E11. Thanks to this adjustment, the formula in cell E12 now sums the expense figures in column E. Furthermore, the sum in E12 will be recalculated if you make changes to the figures in column E. To see that this is true:

1. Move the cell pointer to E8 and enter the new value **2000**.

2. Look at cell E12. Lotus 1-2-3 has recalculated the formula in this cell, and the new result is 7300.

Later in this chapter, you'll learn much more about the adjustments that 1-2-3 makes in formulas when you copy them from one location to another.

To prepare for the next copy exercise, delete the copy you just made. Select the range E8..E12 and press the Delete key.

TIP

Pressing the Delete key has the same effect on a range of cells as it does on a single cell. Select a range and press Delete to clear all the data away.

Copying with the Copy Right and Copy Down SmartIcons

With Release 4, Lotus added the Copy Down and Copy Right commands to the Edit menu. With these commands, you can copy a single cell and in so doing copy the cells to which a formula refers. Try it in the following exercise:

1. Select the range D12..E12.
2. Choose Edit ➤ Copy Right.

By looking at cell E12, you can see that the @SUM function now applies to the data in column E (to cells E8 to E11), as well as the data in column D. With Copy Right and Copy Down, you simply copy a single cell and in so doing drag across all the adjacent cells as well. To copy cells in a row instead of a column, choose Edit ➤ Copy Down, not Edit ➤ Copy Right.

Copying with Copy-and-Paste

If you are an experienced Windows user, you are probably familiar with the Copy and Paste commands. Copy-and-Paste appear in the Edit menu of most Windows applications and operate in much the same way from one application to the next.

- Copy copies selected data to the Windows Clipboard without deleting or changing it. Choose Copy from the Edit menu or by pressing Ctrl-Ins or Ctrl-C.

- Paste copies what is in the Clipboard to the current document. Choose Paste from the Edit menu or by pressing Shift-Ins or Ctrl-V.

Lotus 1-2-3 also provides SmartIcons for the Copy and Paste commands:

The CopyToClipboard SmartIcon shows as a pair of overlapping squares, each with the letter *A*.

The PasteFromClipboard SmartIcon shows a jar of paste.

The Copy and Paste commands use the Clipboard for storing data in the intermediate stage before it is copied or pasted. Here are the steps for performing a copy-and-paste operation:

1. Select the range, in this case D8..D12.

2. Choose <u>E</u>dit ➤ <u>C</u>opy, press Ctrl-C, or click on the CopyToClipboard SmartIcon.

3. Select cell E8, the beginning cell to which you want to copy the data.

4. Choose <u>E</u>dit ➤ <u>P</u>aste, press Ctrl-V, or click on the PasteFromClipboard SmartIcon.

Once again, examine the formula stored in cell E12 after the copy operation is complete. As before, the @SUM function applies to the data in column E.

In Release 4, you can click the selected range of cells with the *right* mouse button and open a quick menu made up of commands pertaining to range operations. Simply choose a command from this menu instead of having to navigate through the menu system.

To close out the first stage of worksheet development:

- Enter **2000** as the conference room expense in cell E8.

At this point, your worksheet should look like the one in Figure 3.14. In the sections ahead, you'll change the worksheet in several ways to make room for additional data. But first, it is time to save the worksheet as a file on disk.

FIGURE 3.14

After the first stage of development, the conference worksheet should look like this.

A	A	B	C	D	E	F	G	H
1		Computing Conferences, Inc.						
2		Profit Projection for a One-Day Conference						
3								
4	Conference Computing for Video Stores							
5	Place:	St. Louis						
6								
7	Projected Expenses - Fixed							
8		Conference room		1500	2000			
9		Video production		1000	1000			
10		Promotion		3500	3500			
11		Travel		800	800			
12		Total Fixed Expenses		6800	7300			
13								
14								

Saving the Worksheet

You should save your work on a regular basis. How often you save it depends on how much data you are willing to risk losing. Fortunately, you can save a worksheet with the click of a SmartIcon, so it is easy to save worksheets at regular intervals.

Save your work frequently. If you have a hardware or software problem, you can lose the data you entered since the last time you saved your work. So save it frequently!

Saving a Worksheet for the First Time

The first time you save a worksheet to disk, choose File ➤ Save As from the Main menu. Lotus 1-2-3 will ask you to provide a name for the file. File names can be as long as eight characters and consist of letters, digits, underscore characters, or hyphens. (Other characters may be accepted by 1-2-3, but are not advisable.) When you save a worksheet, 1-2-3 supplies the default extension .WK4 to the file and also saves a *format* file with the extension .FM4. Format files contain information about the formatting options that you assign to worksheets. The Save As command also has a password option so you can protect the file with a password.

When you choose File ➤ Save As, the Save As dialog box appears. It is shown in Figure 3.15. Use the Drives and Directories list boxes to find the path location where you want to save your worksheet file. Enter a new file name in the File name text box and click the OK button to complete the save operation.

Follow these steps to save the conference worksheet for the first time:

1. Choose File ➤ Save As. You can save your worksheet file in the default directory or select another location.

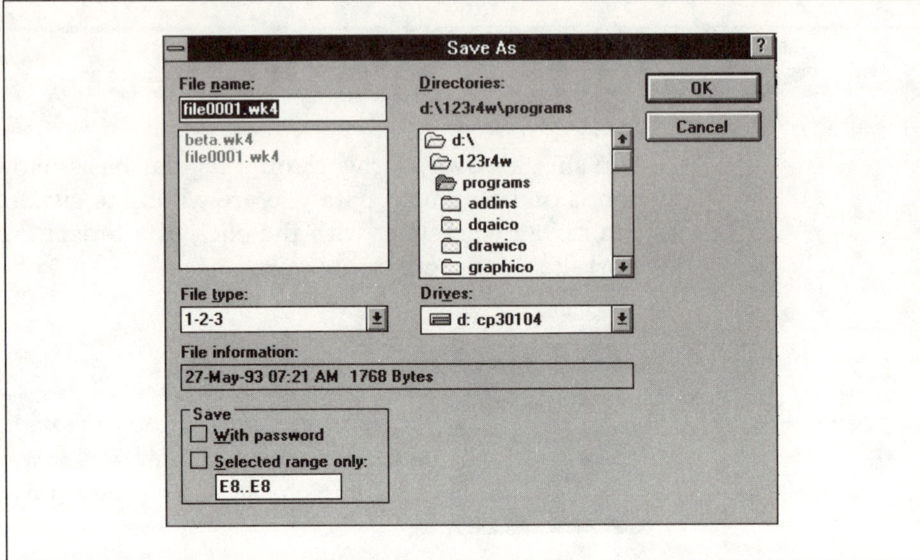

2. Enter the file name **CONF** in the File name text box.

3. Click OK or press ↵ to save the file.

Congratulations! Your worksheet is saved as CONF.WK4. In addition, 1-2-3 creates a format file named CONF.FM4.

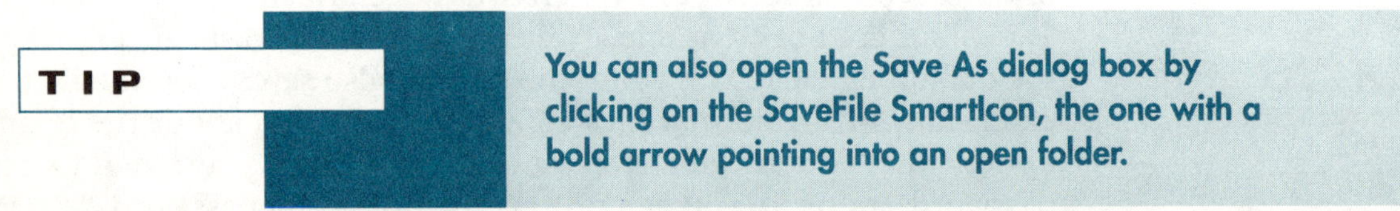

You can enter an existing file name as the name of the file you want to save. When you do so, a second dialog box, the File Save Options dialog box, appears on-screen prompting you for instructions about what to do with the file.

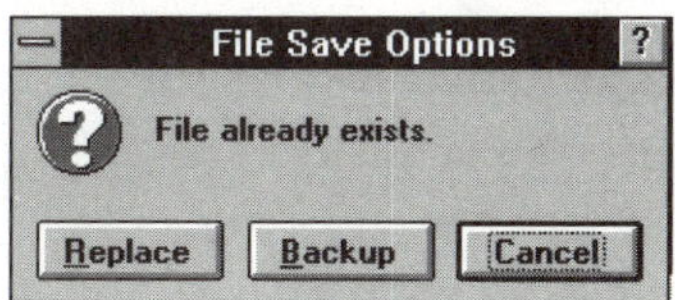

A message, "File already exists," appears in the center of this small dialog box. It gives you three choices:

Replace	Replaces the existing file with the new file you are now saving.
Backup	Retains the existing file on disk as a backup for the worksheet you want to save. The worksheet you are saving gets the extension .WK4 and the worksheet already on disk gets the .BAK extension. (The extension of the existing format file becomes .FMB.)
Cancel	Cancels the save operation under the name you selected.

Assigning a Password to a File

You can assign a password to a file to keep busybodies from looking at it or changing it. When you use the Open command to open a file that has a password, 1-2-3 asks for the password. If you don't know the password, you can't open the file.

WARNING

Protecting files with passwords has one significant drawback: if you forget the password, you can't open the file. Either use passwords you aren't likely to forget or write down your passwords in a secret place.

Here are the general steps for saving a file with a password:

1. Choose File ➤ Save As. The Save As dialog box appears, as in Figure 3.15.
2. Provide a file name.
3. Choose With password. An *X* appears in the option box.
4. Click the OK button.

The Set Password dialog box appears and prompts you for a password to assign to the file.

5. Enter the password in the Password box. A password can be up to 15 characters long. Whether you enter the password in upper- or lowercase letters, or a combination of the two, *is* significant, because you will have to match the password exactly to open your file. Asterisks appear as you enter the password.
6. Enter the same password a second time in the Verify box. Asterisks appear again.
7. Click the OK button to confirm the password, or click Cancel if you change your mind.

Changing a password You can change a password, but to do so you must know the original password.

1. Open the file, supplying the current password when 1-2-3 asks for it.
2. Choose File ➤ Save As, and in the Save As dialog box (see Figure 3.15) make sure that With password is checked.
3. Click OK.
4. Enter the new password twice in the Set Password dialog box.

Saving a Current Copy of a File

After you save a file for the first time, you can *update* it by choosing File ➤ Save. Updating means to store the current version of the worksheet under its existing file name. As you make significant changes to data, formats, or organization, you should update your file regularly.

Here are the steps for updating a file:

1. Activate the window with the worksheet you want to save.
2. Choose File ➤ Save, press Ctrl-S, or click the SaveFile SmartIcon, the one with an arrow pointing inside a folder.

The next step in the development of the conference worksheet is to enter the projected revenues. You will have to move the range of expense data down several rows to make room for the revenues data. In the next part of this chapter, you'll learn how to move a range of data and to insert blank columns and rows in a worksheet.

Changing the Worksheet Organization

You've already learned about several important Edit menu commands for rearranging a worksheet, including Cut, Copy, the Paste commands, and the Clear command. In this part of the chapter, we'll look at how to move ranges of data and insert rows and columns.

Moving Data Ranges in a Worksheet

First we want to open some rows in the worksheet by moving data that is already there. In the following exercise, you'll move the Expenses data down the worksheet to make room for Revenues data.

1. Preselect A7..E12 on the conference worksheet.

2. Choose Edit ➤ Cut.

3. Move the mouse pointer to A15..E20.

4. Choose Edit ➤ Paste. Lotus 1-2-3 moves the range of Expenses data down by eight rows, as shown in Figure 3.16.

	A	B	C	D	E	F	G	H
1		Computing Conferences, Inc.						
2		Profit Projection for a One-Day Conference						
3								
4	Conference Computing for Video Stores							
5	Place:	St. Louis						
6								
7								
8								
9								
10								
11								
12								
13								
14								
15	Projected Expenses - Fixed							
16		Conference room		1500	2000			
17		Video production		1000	1000			
18		Promotion		3500	3500			
19		Travel		800	800			
20		Total Fixed Expenses		6800	7300			
21								

How formulas are affected by range moves You might wonder what happened to the two summation formulas in the range you just moved. To find out, select cell D20 and cell E20 in turn and look in the contents box. Lotus 1-2-3 has adjusted the ranges listed in the cells to accommodate the move. The formula in cell E20 reads @SUM(E16..E19) instead of @SUM (E8..E11). In the case of cell D20, the range represented by the name EXPENSES has been adjusted. Accordingly, the values in D20 and E20 still correctly show the total fixed expenses for a conference with a low and a high attendance rate.

In the area that you opened up by moving the Expenses data, you'll now enter the new labels and values shown in Figure 3.17.

	A	B	C	D	E	F	G	H
1	Computing Conferences, Inc.							
2	Profit Projection for a One-Day Conference							
3								
4	Conference Computing for Video Stores							
5	Place:	St. Louis						
6	Date:			Expected Attendance				
7				Minimum	Maximum			
8	Price:	195		80	150			
9								
10	Projected Revenues							
11		Attendance						
12		Video Sales						
13		Total Revenues						
14								
15	Projected Expenses - Fixed							
16		Conference room		1500	2000			
17		Video production		1000	1000			
18		Promotion		3500	3500			
19		Travel		800	800			
20		Total Fixed Expenses		6800	7300			
21								

1. Make the following entries:

CELL	ENTER
A6	**Date:**
A8	**Price:**
A10	**Projected Revenues**
B11	**Attendance**
B12	**Video Sales**
B13	**Total Revenues**

2. Enter **195** in cell B8. This is the per-person price for attending this conference.

3. Enter the label **Expected Attendance:** in cell D6. Notice that the label display crosses two worksheet columns.

You can right-align a label instantly by entering double quotation marks (") before the label or value itself.

The labels in cells D7 and E7 should each be right-aligned because the numeric values that will appear beneath them will be right-aligned (numbers are right-aligned by default). The simplest way to right-align a label or value is to preface it with a double quotation mark (").

4. Make the following entries to right-align the Minimum and Maximum labels:

CELL	ENTER
D7	**"Minimum**
D8	**"Maximum**

5. Enter **80**, the low estimate of the number of people who will attend the conference, in cell D8.

6. Enter **150**, the high estimate, in cell E8.

Chapter 4 describes other ways to control label alignment in 1-2-3.

If you compare Figure 3.17 with Figure 3.1, you'll realize you need to make space on the worksheet for information that you have not entered yet. You need a blank row for the Per Person, Min. Total, and Max. Total column headings above the Projected Revenues label and a blank column for Per Person revenue and expense figures to the right of column C. So you have to insert a blank row and a blank column on the worksheet. You'll do this in the next section.

Inserting Rows and Columns

You used the Edit ➤ Insert command in Chapter 1 to add new worksheets to a worksheet window. The Edit ➤ Insert command also offers options for inserting columns and rows.

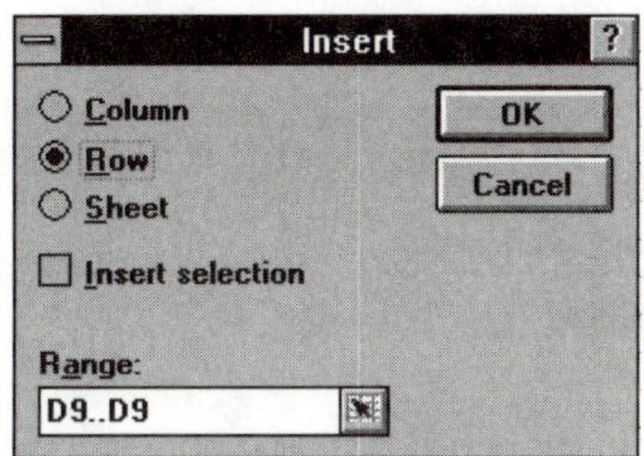

Inserting one column or row To add one new row or column to an active worksheet:

1. Select a cell in the row or column where you want to make the insert.
2. Choose Edit ➤ Insert.
3. Select either Column or Row.
4. Click the OK button or press ↵ to complete the insert operation.

Inserting more than one column or row To insert more than one row or column at a time:

1. Select a range of consecutive cells, one cell for each row or column you want to insert. For example, to insert three rows, select a range of three adjacent columns on the worksheet. To insert three columns, select a range of adjacent cells in a row.
2. Choose Edit ➤ Insert.
3. Click the Column or Row option.

In the conference worksheet, you can select cell D9 as the insert position both for the new row and the new column. Follow these steps to make the insertions:

1. Select cell D9 on the worksheet.

2. Choose <u>E</u>dit ➤ Insert. The default option selection is <u>R</u>ow.

3. Click OK or press ↵ to insert a new row at the current position.

4. Choose <u>E</u>dit ➤ Insert again.

5. Click the <u>C</u>olumn option.

6. Click the OK button or press ↵ to insert a new column.

As before, examine the summation formulas, now located in cells E21 and F21. Again, 1-2-3 has adjusted the ranges in these formulas to accommodate the changes you made to the worksheet.

Now you are ready to enter column headings in row 10 and the perunit price of the conference video in column D.

1. Make the following entries, again starting each label with a doublequote character to achieve right-alignment:

CELL	ENTER
D10	″Per Person
E10	″Min. Total
F10	″Max. Total

2. Enter **35**, the retail price of the conference video, in cell D13.

3. Select cell B8 and choose <u>R</u>ange ➤ <u>N</u>ame. The Name dialog box appears.

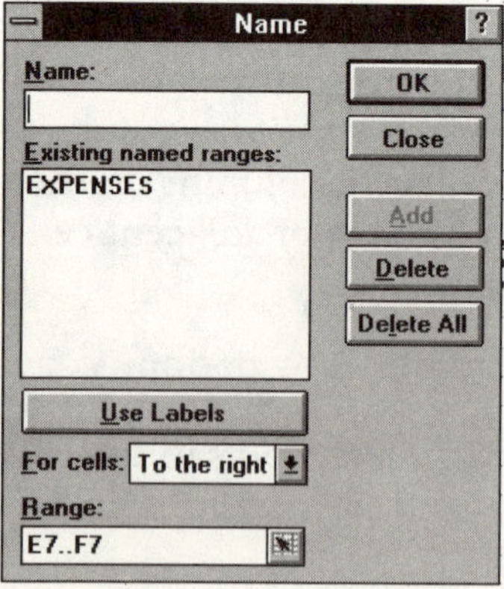

4. Enter **PRICE** in the <u>N</u>ame text box and choose <u>A</u>dd to assign this name to cell B8. Click OK or press ↵ to confirm.

5. Select cell D13 and choose <u>R</u>ange ➤ <u>N</u>ame ➤ <u>N</u>ame.

6. Enter **VIDEO** and click on the <u>A</u>dd button to assign the name VIDEO to cell D13.

7. Preselect range E7..F7, the range with the Minimum and Maximum labels.

8. Choose <u>R</u>ange ➤ <u>N</u>ame, and click on the <u>U</u>se Labels button.

9. Choose <u>F</u>ile ➤ <u>S</u>ave or click the SaveFile icon to save your latest version of the conference worksheet to disk, again under the name CONF.WK4.

Click the Use Labels button in the Name dialog box to use existing labels as range names.

With the Use Labels button, you can use existing column headings or row labels as range names. For example, in step 7 you assigned the name MINIMUM to cell E8 and the name MAXIMUM to cell F8. Now you can use these names as attendance estimates in formulas you will write for the worksheet.

Another way to name a range is to select the range and click inside it with the right mouse button. A quick menu appears from which you can choose Name and open the Name dialog box.

With this second stage of data entry completed, your worksheet should look like Figure 3.18.

The next step is to enter formulas for calculating the minimum and maximum revenue projections, based on expected attendance. When you enter these formulas, you'll use the range names you created.

	A	B	C	D	E	F	G	H
1		Computing Conferences, Inc.						
2		Profit Projection for a One-Day Conference						
3								
4	Conference Computing for Video Stores							
5	Place:	St. Louis						
6	Date:				Expected Attendance			
7					Minimum	Maximum		
8	Price:	195			80	150		
9								
10				Per Person	Min. Total	Max. Total		
11	Projected Revenues							
12		Attendance						
13		Video Sales		35				
14		Total Revenues						
15								
16	Projected Expenses - Fixed							
17		Conference room			1500	2000		
18		Video production			1000	1000		
19		Promotion			3500	3500		
20		Travel			800	800		
21		Total Fixed Expenses			6800	7300		

Working with Formulas in a Worksheet

A worksheet with formulas is not a static collection of data, but a dynamic calculation tool. As you learned in Chapter 1, formulas are made up of various elements, including

- Arithmetic operations, such as +, -, *, and /

- Literal numeric values, such as 2 or 5280

- Cell addresses—or alternatively, range names—that represent the values stored in cells

- Worksheet functions, such as @SUM

When you enter a formula in a cell, 1-2-3 immediately calculates the formula and displays its numeric result. Furthermore, 1-2-3 recalculates formulas whenever the value of a cell that is part of a formula changes. Because 1-2-3 recalculates formulas automatically, you can play around with figures and do "what-if" experiments.

To see how 1-2-3 recalculates formulas, follow these steps:

1. Choose File ➤ New to open a new worksheet window.

2. Enter **92** in cell A1.

3. Select cell B1 and enter the formula **2★A1** with the keyboard. This multiplies the value stored in A1 by 2. The result, 184, is displayed in B1.

4. Select A1 again and enter **32**, a new value, to replace 92. Lotus 1-2-3 recalculates the value in B1, and the result is 2★32, or 64.

5. Enter the following values in cell A1, one at a time, to produce the following results in cell B1. Each time you enter a new value in A1, 1-2-3 instantly recalculates the value in B1.

A1 ENTRY	B1 RESULT
5	10
3212	6424
19	38
543	1086
27	54

6. When you are finished experimenting, pull down the worksheet window's Control-menu box and choose Close. Choose No when 1-2-3 asks if you want to save the worksheet.

The idea is the same whether you are performing simple calculations or doing complex budgeting for a business: when a formula has a cell reference and you change the value in the cell, 1-2-3 recalculates the formula.

Let's return to the conference worksheet for a more practical look at how recalculation works. In an upcoming exercise, you'll enter formulas in cells E12 and F12 to project attendance revenue from the conference.

Entering Formulas

To calculate attendance revenue, you have to multiply the price per person of attending the conference by the number of people who will attend. The price per person, $195, is stored in cell B8 and the first of the two attendance estimates, the minimum attendance estimate, is stored in cell E8. You know that multiplication is represented by the asterisk (*) in 1-2-3, so to calculate the minimum attendance revenue you might expect to enter the following formula into cell E12:

    B8*E8

But there is a problem here. When you type B, the first character of this formula, in the cell, 1-2-3 switches to Label mode, but the correct mode for entering a formula is Value mode. You need to start the formula with a character that triggers Value mode.

Entering Cell Addresses in Formulas

The plus sign (+) is the general-purpose character for starting a formula entry in 1-2-3. Formulas that begin with a number or with the @ symbol do not require a plus sign, but when a cell address is the first entry in a formula, enter a plus sign in front of the cell address to put 1-2-3 in Value mode. Here, then, is the correct format for the projected revenue formula in cell E12:

    +B8*E8

Entering Cell Addresses by Pointing

You can enter a formula directly from the keyboard, but there is an easier way. When you enter the formula, you can press arrow keys on the keyboard or use the mouse to *point* to the cells that you want to include. To see how pointing works, enter the first revenue formula in cell E12:

1. Select cell E12 in the conference worksheet.

2. Type + (the plus sign). A plus sign appears in the contents box and 1-2-3 switches to Value mode.

3. Point to the first cell address in the formula, B8. To do this, press ↑ four times and ← three times to select cell B8. The mode switches to Point while you are pointing to the cell. The contents box now displays the formula +A:B8.

4. Type * (the asterisk) for multiplication. The cell pointer returns to E12.

5. Point to the second cell address in the formula, E8. To do so, press ↑ four times. When the cell is selected, +A:B8*A:E8 is displayed in the Contents box.

6. Press ↵ to complete the formula entry.

Lotus 1-2-3 immediately calculates the formula and displays it in cell E12. The result of multiplying the minimum number of people who will attend the conference by the price of admission is 15600.

Because this formula involves only worksheet A, the contents box displays the formula in its simpler form:

    +B8*E8

Entering Formulas by Using Range Names

Now you need to enter a similar formula in cell F12 to project how much revenue will be returned if the maximum number of people attend the conference. This time, try expressing the formula with range names. Recall that cell B8 is named PRICE and cell F8 is named MAXIMUM. You can therefore write the formula this way:

    +PRICE*MAXIMUM

The formula must still begin with a plus sign to put 1-2-3 in Value mode. You can type it directly into cell F12 or you can press F3 to see a list of range names for the worksheet.

Here is how to enter a formula by choosing a range name from the list:

1. Select cell F12.

2. Type **+** to start the formula.

3. Press F3. The Name dialog box appears with a list of the range names you defined for the worksheet.

4. Double-click the name PRICE in the Existing named ranges list box. This name appears in the contents box as the first reference in your formula: +PRICE.

5. Type * for multiplication.

6. Press F3 to view the Name dialog box and all Existing named ranges.

7. Double-click the name MAXIMUM in the list. This name appears as the second reference in the contents box: +PRICE*MAXIMUM.

8. Press ↵ to confirm the formula entry.

When you complete these steps, 1-2-3 enters the result of the formula in cell F12. Projected revenue if the maximum number of people attend the conference is $195 × 150, or $29,250.

You have to enter two more formulas in the revenue section of the worksheet. In cells E13 and F13, you must project the revenue from sales of the conference video. The planners at Computing Conferences, Inc. know from experience that approximately half of conference participants buy the video tape. Given this expectation, revenue from video sales equals the retail video price times one-half the number of conference participants.

Recall that you assigned the range name VIDEO to cell D13, where the unit retail price of the video is stored. The formula you can enter in cell E13 to project the revenue for video sales if the minimum number of people attend the conference is

    +VIDEO*MINIMUM/2

Likewise, the formula to enter in cell F13 to project sales if the maximum number of people attend is

    +VIDEO*MAXIMUM/2

Enter these two formulas in their respective cells. The result is 1400 for the minimum revenue projection (cell E13) and 2625 for the maximum revenue projection (cell F13).

Entering Two Formulas at Once

Finally, you need to enter summation formulas in row 14 to calculate the minimum and maximum total revenue projections. You may be surprised to learn you can enter both formulas at once. Here are the steps:

1. Preselect range E12..F14.

2. Click the Summation icon in the Edit Line.

When you click the icon, 1-2-3 enters a summation formula in cells E14 and F14. The result is 17000 and 31875, respectively. Figure 3.19 shows what the worksheet looks like at this stage. Click the SaveFile icon now to save your work to disk.

You still have two sections of information left to enter in the conference worksheet. You have to enter the variable expenses and the bottom-line profit. As we do this, we'll explore another important worksheet topic—how to copy formulas from one range to another.

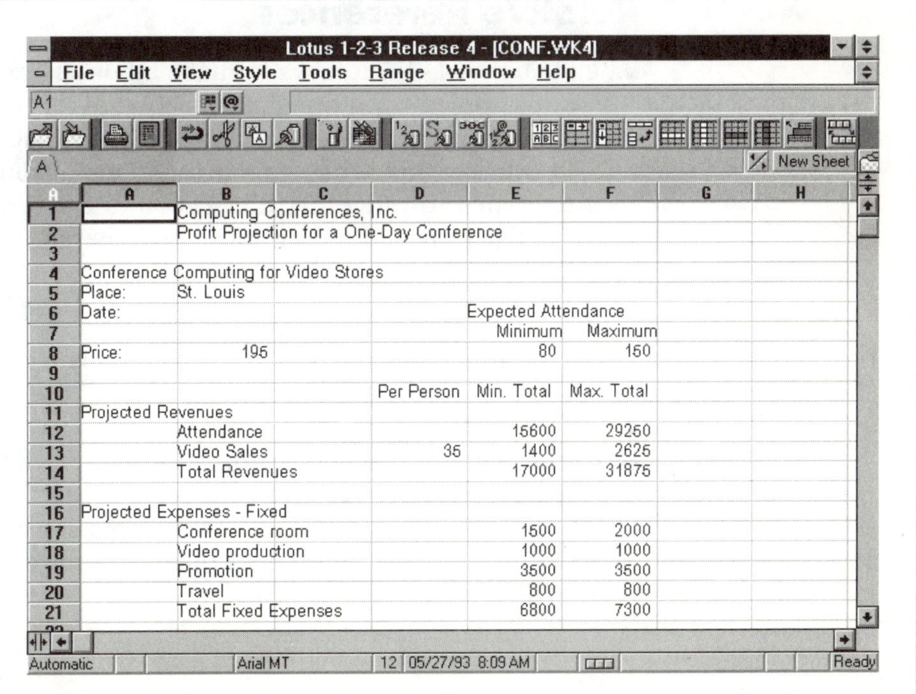

FIGURE 3.19

Completing the revenue formulas

	A	B	C	D	E	F	G	H
1		Computing Conferences, Inc.						
2		Profit Projection for a One-Day Conference						
3								
4	Conference Computing for Video Stores							
5	Place:	St. Louis						
6	Date:				Expected Attendance			
7					Minimum	Maximum		
8	Price:	195			80	150		
9								
10				Per Person	Min. Total	Max. Total		
11	Projected Revenues							
12		Attendance			15600	29250		
13		Video Sales		35	1400	2625		
14		Total Revenues			17000	31875		
15								
16	Projected Expenses - Fixed							
17		Conference room			1500	2000		
18		Video production			1000	1000		
19		Promotion			3500	3500		
20		Travel			800	800		
21		Total Fixed Expenses			6800	7300		

Copying Formulas

In many worksheets, you'll find a formula in one cell that is identical in structure to formulas you need to enter in other cells. Rather than enter similar formulas one at a time, you can copy one formula to other locations. When you copy a formula, Lotus 1-2-3 adjusts references to cell and range addresses as necessary.

You've already seen how cell addresses are affected when a formula is copied. Earlier in this chapter, you copied the summation formula for fixed expenses from one column to an adjacent column. At the time of the copy operation, the expense figures were located in column D and the summation formula in cell D12 was

    @SUM(D8..D11)

When you copied the formula to cell E12, 1-2-3 automatically adjusted the range reference, as follows:

    @SUM(E8..E11)

Relative References

The logic that 1-2-3 follows to make adjustments like these is simple: In a formula copied from one column to another, a reference to a range in the first column becomes a reference to the adjacent range in the second one. In other words, when copying a formula from column D to column E, a reference to range D1..D3 becomes a reference to adjacent range E1..E3. The range address in this copy operation is called a *relative reference*. When you copy a formula containing a relative reference, 1-2-3 adjusts the cell or range address *relative to the location of the copy*.

A similar adjustment occurs when you copy a formula from one row to another. For example, suppose you entered the formula +A3+B3 in cell C3. This formula adds the contents of the two cells located to the left of C3 in row 3. If you copied this formula to cell C4, 1-2-3 would adjust the formula to read +A4+B4. The logic is the same: a formula copied to row 4 should contain references to the data stored in row 4. Accordingly, 1-2-3 adjusts address references relative to the row to which the formula is copied.

Unless you specify otherwise, 1-2-3 treats cell and range addresses as relative references when you copy them. Relative references are the default in copy operations.

Absolute References

Suppose you want to copy a formula that references a *fixed* cell address—that is, a cell address that should remain unchanged when you copy the formula to a new location. In this case, you must express the address as an *absolute reference*. You'll learn how to do this in upcoming exercises.

Absolute vs. Relative Cell References

The difference between relative and absolute references is perhaps the most important concept for you to understand in Lotus 1-2-3. When you have to decide whether to make a reference absolute or relative, consider two important properties of the formulas you create:

- The arithmetic structure. Consider the specific operations and operands in the formula that produce its result.

- The types of address references. Consider the specifications that determine what the formula will contain when you copy it to other locations in the worksheet.

Of course, the second property is relevant only in formulas that you intend to copy. If you write a formula that applies to only one location on a worksheet—a formula that will not be copied elsewhere—then you do not have to worry about relative and absolute references. However, you may be surprised to discover how often you have to copy formulas in 1-2-3.

The $ sign for making relative references absolute Lotus 1-2-3 provides a simple notation for distinguishing between relative and absolute references. So far, you have been using the relative reference format, the default address format. For example, the following address is a relative reference:

B8

To change an address from a relative to an absolute reference, enter a dollar sign ($) before each element. For example, the relative reference B8 looks like this when it is made absolute:

$B$8

You can also create an absolute reference with a range name by placing a dollar sign in front of the name, like so:

$PRICE

F4 for making relative references absolute When you enter a formula, you can create absolute references by typing $ characters at the appropriate locations. But an easier way to make relative references absolute is to place the reference you want to change in the contents box and press F4 in Point, Edit, or Value mode.

NOTE When you are in Ready mode, pressing F4 switches 1-2-3 into Point mode so you can preselect a range. In Point, Edit, and Value mode, pressing F4 changes the cell references in the contents box into absolute references.

In the following exercise, you'll learn the significance of absolute references and practice the mechanical details of changing an address from relative to absolute. For the purposes of this exercise, you're going to backtrack a little in the conference worksheet and redo some work that you completed earlier. You'll reenter the formula for projected attendance revenues in cell E12 and copy this formula to cell F12. You'll recall that the formulas in these cells are designed to multiply the attendance price per person by the anticipated number of people attending the conference. You'll make no change in the *structure* of these formulas. The results will remain the same. What you will change is the reference type that allows you to copy the formula successfully from E12 to F12.

To prepare for this exercise, begin by deleting the contents of cells E12 and F12:

- Select range E12..F12 and press the Delete key.

Now you have an empty range in which to perform the following steps:

1. Select cell E12 and type + to begin the formula entry. 1-2-3 switches into Value mode.
2. Use the keyboard to point to cell B8, which contains the price of attendance. The mode changes to Point and the contents box displays the reference +A:B8.
3. Press F4 to change the address from a relative to an absolute reference.

As you can see in the contents box, +$A:$B$8 is now the contents of cell B8. Notice that 1-2-3 places a $ character in front of all three parts of the address: the worksheet name, the column letter, and the row number.

4. Type * to represent multiplication. The cell pointer returns to E12 and the mode switches back to Value.
5. Use the keyboard to point to cell E8, the minimum estimate of the number of people who will attend the conference. The contents box now displays +$A:$B$8*A:E8. Do not change the reference type of this second address. It must remain a relative reference for the purposes of copying the formula.
6. Press ↵.

The value 15600 appears in cell E12. This is the same as the value produced by the previous version of the formula. But now the formula in the cell reads +$B$8*E8, with the first address being an absolute and the second address a relative reference.

7. Copy the formula to cell F12 by positioning the cell pointer on E12 and choosing Edit ➤ Copy (or clicking on the Copy SmartIcon).
8. Click on cell F12 and choose Edit ➤ Paste (or press Ctrl+V) to copy the contents of the Clipboard into the cell.

To see exactly what you did in this exercise, examine the new formulas in cells E12 and F12. In E12, you see the formula you entered, with an absolute reference to B8 (the address of the attendance price) and a relative reference to E8 (the address of the minimum attendance estimate):

    +$B$8*E8

In F12 is the formula you copied:

    +$B$8*F8

In copying the formula, 1-2-3 made no change in the absolute reference. However, the program adjusted the relative reference appropriately. This is exactly what you wanted to happen: Whereas the original formula in cell E12 calculates the *minimum* expected attendance revenue, the formula copied to cell F12 gives the *maximum* revenue.

In summary, absolute and relative references tell 1-2-3 exactly how to copy a formula:

- An absolute reference is copied without change.
- A relative reference is adjusted according to the row or column to which it is copied.

But this does not give the complete picture. In some worksheets you will want to copy a formula in *two* directions—both down a column and across a row. To perform a double copy operation, you'll use the third type of address format, the mixed reference. You'll learn about mixed references when you complete the final sections of the conference worksheet.

To prepare for the remaining exercises in this chapter, perform the following data entry tasks:

1. Enter the subtitle, **Projected Expenses – Variable by Attendance**, in cell A23.

2. In cells B24 to B27, enter the variable expense categories, the materials and meals provided for each conference participant:

CELL	ENTER
B24	**Conference materials**
B25	**Coffee and pastries**
B26	**Box lunch**
B27	**Total Variable Expenses**

3. Enter the corresponding per-person costs for these items:

CELL	ENTER
D24	**8.25**
D25	**3.25**
D26	**4.75**

4. Finally, enter the profit subtitle, **Projected Profit**, in cell A29.

When you complete these entries, your worksheet should look like Figure 3.20.

	A	B	C	D	E	F	G	H
11	Projected Revenues							
12		Attendance			15600	29250		
13		Video Sales		35	1400	2625		
14		Total Revenues			17000	31875		
15								
16	Projected Expenses - Fixed							
17		Conference room			1500	2000		
18		Video production			1000	1000		
19		Promotion			3500	3500		
20		Travel			800	800		
21		Total Fixed Expenses			6800	7300		
22								
23	Projected Expenses - Variable by Attendance							
24		Conference materials		8.25				
25		Coffee and Pastries		3.25				
26		Box lunch		4.75				
27		Total Variable Expenses						
28								
29	Projected Profit							
30								
31								

Mixed References

A *mixed reference* tells 1-2-3 to adjust one part of an address but leave another part unchanged when the address is copied. In a mixed reference notation, the dollar sign appears to the left of one address element but not the other. In the following reference, the column is absolute but the row is relative:

$D24

If you copied a formula with this address, 1-2-3 would retain a fixed reference to column D but adjust the row reference to match the row of the copy. Conversely, the following example contains a relative column reference and an absolute row reference:

E$8

In making copies of this address, 1-2-3 would adjust the column reference to match the column location of the copy, but would retain a fixed reference to row 8.

Pressing F4 to create mixed references You can use the F4 key to create mixed references as well as absolute references. In Point, Value, and Edit modes, pressing F4 *multiple times* cycles through the different reference types. As you know, pressing F4 the first time creates an absolute reference. But when you press F4 for the second and third times, the address changes into different mixed address forms. You'll see how this works shortly.

The Variable by Attendance part of the conference worksheet is a perfect place to experiment with mixed references. In range E24..F26, you need to enter what is essentially the same formula six times. This formula will calculate the total expenses for each variable expense category—that is, the per-person expense for materials, coffee and pastries, and box lunches times the minimum or maximum number of participants. Using mixed references, you can enter the formula once in cell E24 and copy the formula in two directions: down column E and across rows 24, 25, and 26. Here are the steps:

1. Select cell E24 and type a **+** character to start the formula.
2. Point to cell D24.
3. Press F4 three times. Each time you do so, the address in the contents box changes its format. First it becomes an absolute reference, then a mixed reference with a fixed row and variable column, and then a mixed reference with a fixed column and variable row:

   $A:$D$24

   $A:D$24

   $A:$D24

This final format is the reference you want. When you copy the formula to other rows, column D will remain fixed but the row number will change.

4. Type *.

5. Point to cell E8 (the minimum attendance estimate). You can do this by pressing PgUp once and ↓ four times.

6. Press F4 twice. The address in the contents box becomes an absolute reference and then a mixed reference, like so:

   $A:$E$8

   $A:E$8

   The second format is the one we want. When you copy the formula, the column letter will change, but row 8 will remain fixed.

7. Press ↵ to confirm the formula entry.

The value 660 appears in cell E24. Look in the contents box to see the formula in cell E24. It is +$A:$D24*$A:E$8.

The formula you just created contains only reference formats that allow you to copy the formula successfully in two directions. Here are the steps for copying the formula:

1. With the cell pointer in cell E24, click the Copy icon.

2. Drag the mouse pointer over the destination column range, E25..E26, and click on the Paste icon.

The values 260 and 380 appear in cells E25 and E26. These values represent projected variable expenses for the minimum attendance.

3. Preselect range E24..E26 and click the right mouse button.

4. Choose Copy from the menu that appears.

5. Position the mouse pointer over cell F24 and click the right mouse button.

6. Choose Paste from the menu.

The values 1-2-37.5, 487.5, and 712.5 appear in cells F24, F25, and F26. These are the projected variable expenses for the maximum attendance.

7. As a final step, produce the total variable expense projections: Pre-select range E24..F27 and click the Summation icon. The result of your work appears in Figure 3.21.

The best way to see the effect of mixed references on copy operations is to examine the formulas. In our worksheet, the formulas in range E24..F26 are:

+$A:$D24*$A:E$8	+$A:$D24*$A:F$8
+$A:$D25*$A:E$8	+$A:$D25*$A:F$8
+$A:$D26*$A:E$8	+$A:$D26*$A:F$8

For each row, 1-2-3 has adjusted the row portion of the first reference ($D24, $D25, $D26). Conversely, for each column, the column portion of the second address reference has been adjusted (E$8, F$8).

Now you are ready to enter a formula for projecting the profit. As you do so, you'll learn how to control the order in which operations are performed.

FIGURE 3.21

Copying a formula in two directions

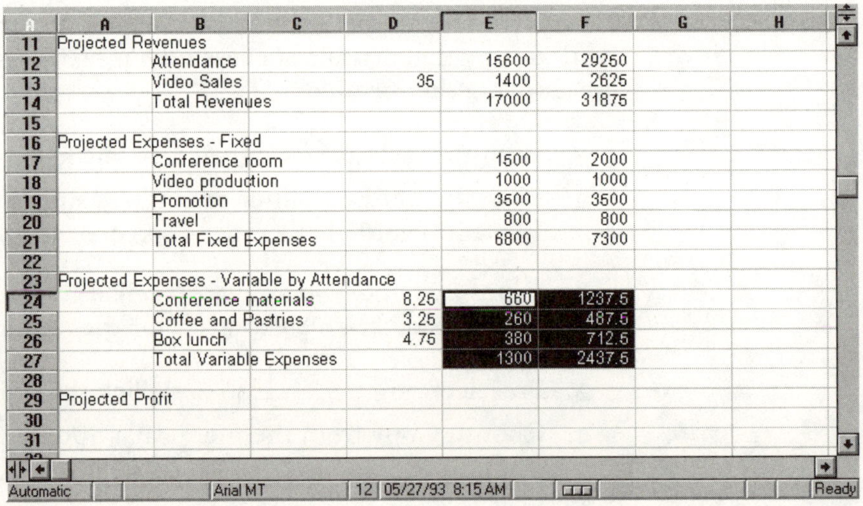

	A	B	C	D	E	F	G	H
11	Projected Revenues							
12		Attendance			15600	29250		
13		Video Sales		35	1400	2625		
14		Total Revenues			17000	31875		
15								
16	Projected Expenses - Fixed							
17		Conference room			1500	2000		
18		Video production			1000	1000		
19		Promotion			3500	3500		
20		Travel			800	800		
21		Total Fixed Expenses			6800	7300		
22								
23	Projected Expenses - Variable by Attendance							
24		Conference materials		8.25	660	1237.5		
25		Coffee and Pastries		3.25	260	487.5		
26		Box lunch		4.75	380	712.5		
27		Total Variable Expenses			1300	2437.5		
28								
29	Projected Profit							
30								
31								

Automatic | Arial MT | 12 | 05/27/93 8:15 AM | | Ready

Controlling the Order of Operations

By default, 1-2-3 follows standard mathematical rules for the *order of precedence*. The order of precedence determines which operation in a formula with more than one operation is calculated first. For example, these two rules govern the most common arithmetic operations:

- Multiplication and division are performed before addition and subtraction.

- Given two operations of equal precedence, the operation on the left is performed first.

Overriding the precedence rules To override the precedence rules, insert pairs of parentheses in a formula. Operations inside parentheses are performed before others. Furthermore, one pair of parentheses can be *nested* inside another pair. When 1-2-3 encounters nested parentheses, it performs the operation inside the innermost parentheses first.

The formula for calculating the bottom-line profit in the convention worksheet requires parentheses. Profit is calculated by subtracting expenses from revenues. However, our worksheet has two groups of expenses, one fixed and the other variable. To add the two expense categories before subtracting total expenses from revenues, we must enclose the expense references in parentheses. For example, here is the formula you'll enter in cell E29 for the first profit projection:

    +E14–(E21+E27)

Cells E21 and E27 contain the two expense subtotals, and cell E14 contains the total revenues. If you were to omit the parentheses from this formula, 1-2-3 would perform the operations from left to right and produce an incorrect calculation.

In this exercise, you'll enter the formula in cell E29 and copy the formula to F29:

1. Select cell E29 and type the **+** to begin the formula.

2. Point to the total revenues figure in cell E14.

3. Type –, the minus sign, and (, the open parenthesis. At this point, the formula looks like this in the contents box:

   +A:E14–(

4. Point to the total fixed expense figure in cell E21.

5. Type +.

6. Point to the total variable expense figure in cell E27.

7. Type), the close parenthesis character. In the contents box, the formula is now

   +A:E14–(A:E21+A:E27)

   Notice that all the address references are relative. The upcoming copy operation does not require absolute or mixed references.

8. Press ↵ to confirm the formula entry.

9. Use the Copy icon or click on the range with the right mouse button to copy the formula from cell E29 to cell F29.

10. Click the SaveFile icon or choose File ➤ Save to save this version of the worksheet to disk.

Your worksheet should look like Figure 3.22.

FIGURE 3.22

Calculating the projected profit

A	A	B	C	D	E	F	G	H
10				Per Person	Min. Total	Max. Total		
11	Projected Revenues							
12		Attendance			15600	29250		
13		Video Sales		35	1400	2625		
14		Total Revenues			17000	31875		
15								
16	Projected Expenses - Fixed							
17		Conference room			1500	2000		
18		Video production			1000	1000		
19		Promotion			3500	3500		
20		Travel			800	800		
21		Total Fixed Expenses			6800	7300		
22								
23	Projected Expenses - Variable by Attendance							
24		Conference materials		8.25	660	1237.5		
25		Coffee and Pastries		3.25	260	487.5		
26		Box lunch		4.75	380	712.5		
27		Total Variable Expenses			1300	2437.5		
28								
29	Projected Profit				8900	22137.5		
30								

Playing the "What-If" Game

The conference worksheet presents many opportunities for "what-if" experiments. For example, suppose you increased the price of attending the conference from $195 to $225. Doing so would boost profits, but it would also cause, let's say, a 15 percent decrease in attendance. Let's see what happens to the projected profit when the admission price is raised to $225 and attendance drops by 15 percent.

To view the results of this scenario, you need only revise three values in the worksheet:

1. Enter a value of **225**, the new admission price, in cell B8.

2. Enter a value of **68**, the new minimum attendance, in cell E8.

3. Enter a value of **128**, the new maximum attendance, in cell F8.

Each time you enter a new value, 1-2-3 instantly recalculates all formulas that reference the revised cell. The split worksheet in Figure 3.23 shows the three revised values and the new profit projections. By comparing this

	A	B	C	D	E	F	G	H
1		Computing Conferences, Inc.						
2		Profit Projection for a One-Day Conference						
3								
4	Conference Computing for Video Stores							
5	Place:	St. Louis						
6	Date:				Expected Attendance			
7					Minimum	Maximum		
8	Price:	225			68	128		
9								
10				Per Person	Min. Total	Max. Total		
11	Projected Revenues							
12		Attendance			15300	28800		
13		Video Sales		35	1190	2240		
14		Total Revenues			16490	31040		

	A	B	C	D	E	F	G	H
27		Total Variable Expenses			1105	2080		
28								
29	Projected Profit				8585	21660		
30								
31								

Automatic　Arial MT　12　05/27/93 8:21 AM　Ready

worksheet to the one in Figure 3.22, you can see that profits in this scenario are down from the original projection. Therefore, Computing Conferences, Inc. decides against raising the price of attending the conference.

You could make other changes in the worksheet to see what happens to profits. For example, consider what you would do in these situations:

- The company is notified of a 10-percent price increase for using the conference room.

- Due to last-minute revisions in the curriculum, some conference materials have to be redone, which increases the cost of materials by five dollars per person.

- The company decides to produce a radio commercial promoting the conference. The commercial adds $2500 to promotion costs, but the company anticipates a possible 25-percent increase in attendance.

These and other experiments demonstrate the flexibility of the worksheet as a tool for exploring the results of "what-if" problems.

When you finish these exercises, exit 1-2-3 *without* saving the latest revisions to disk. You'll continue working with the conference worksheet in Chapter 4, using the original data that you've already saved in the CONF.WK4 file. In the next chapter, you'll begin exploring the variety of formatting and style options available in 1-2-3.

Summary

The first step in creating a new worksheet is to enter the data and consider how to organize the worksheet. To help you with these tasks, 1-2-3 offers many tools for moving and copying data from one location to another and for deleting entries from a cell or range. You perform these procedures by choosing menu commands or—more conveniently—by clicking icons.

With commands that operate over a range of data, you usually have the choice of preselecting the range before choosing the command or of pointing to the range after the command's dialog box has appeared on the screen. Preselecting often seems the more natural approach, and in fact some icons, such as the RangeMove and RangeCopy SmartIcon, require you to preselect a range.

The Save As command in the File menu lets you name your file and add password protection if you wish. For subsequent updates of your worksheet file, you can simply click the SaveFile icon.

Once you've entered numeric data in your worksheet, you can begin adding formulas and producing calculated values. For producing totals at the bottom of a column or at the end of a row, 1-2-3 provides the very convenient Summation SmartIcon.

Using range names in the formulas you write yourself can make your work simpler and clearer. When you write a formula that will be copied to other locations in a worksheet, choose carefully among relative, absolute, and mixed address references. References determine how your formula is copied to other cells.

A well-organized worksheet is the ideal tool for investigating "what-if" questions. Simply by making changes in key data items, you can find out what happens to totals and other calculated values under new assumptions.

4

Worksheet Formatting and Printing

fast TRACK

● **To move the cell pointer quickly to a named cell
or range,** 179

press F5 and select a range name from the list in the Go To
dialog box.

● **To change the width of a column on the worksheet,** 181

select a cell in the column and choose Style ➤ ColumnWidth,
or use the mouse to drag the column's right border.

● **To left-align, center, or right-align the labels
in a range of cells,** 187

preselect a cell that extends over its left or right border and
click the CenterAlign SmartIcon.

● **To center a label over a horizontal range of cells,** 189

preselect the horizontal range, where the first cell in the range
contains the label that you want to center, and then choose
Style ➤ Alignment ➤ Center ➤ Across columns.

● **To remove the display of grid lines from the
worksheet window,** 194

choose View ➤ Set View Preferences and uncheck the Grid
lines check box.

● **To apply a format to a selected range
on the worksheet,** 198

preselect the range, then choose Style ➤ Number Format and
select an entry in the Format list.

To enter a date value in a cell,   206

enter the date in a format that begins with a digit (such as 10/15/94 or 15-Oct-94); 1-2-3 translates your entry into a date number. Next, choose _Style_ ➤ _Number Format and se-lect one of the five available date formats.

To enter a time value in a cell,   213

enter the time in a format that begins with a digit (such as 7:00 PM or 19:00); 1-2-3 translates your entry into a decimal time value. Next, choose _Style_ ➤ _Number Format and select one of the four available time formats.

To establish a protection scheme for a worksheet,   221

choose _Style_ ➤ _Protection, select the range of cells you _don't_ want to protect, check the _Keep data unprotected after file is sealed box, and press ⏎. Then choose _Style_ ➤ _Protect and click the _Seal file check box, enter a password twice, and click OK.

To see a preview of the printed worksheet,   236

click the PrintPreview SmartIcon after you select a print range.

To define a print range,   239

choose _File_ ➤ _Print and enter one or more ranges in the Range(s) box. Back on the worksheet, 1-2-3 encloses your se-lected print range or ranges in a light dashed border. To print the worksheet, click the Print icon.

AFTER you have created a working table with data and formulas, your next task is to refine the worksheet's appearance. Information in a worksheet should be presented as clearly and attractively as possible, both for your benefit when you work with the data on-screen and for the benefit of people who will see the worksheet when it is printed. Lotus 1-2-3 for Windows offers many options for controlling how values and labels look on a worksheet.

In this chapter, we'll concentrate on commands that affect the way a worksheet looks. You'll learn to:

- Change column widths in the entire worksheet and in individual columns

- Align labels in a worksheet

- Hide columns and ranges of data

- Establish numeric formats for the entire worksheet and for ranges in the worksheet

- Enter date and time values in the right formats and perform arithmetic operations on date and time values

- Protect a worksheet from being revised by other users

- Establish styles, fonts, shadings, colors, and borders in data presentations

- Print a worksheet

To learn these procedures, you'll keep working on the conference worksheet you began developing in Chapter 3. As it stands now, the worksheet projects the revenues, expenses, and profit of a business event. What you'll do in this chapter is refine the worksheet so it presents financial data clearly and with the right emphasis on certain categories of information. The first step is to reopen the CONF.WK4 file from disk.

Techniques for Speeding Up Your Work

In Chapter 2, you opened an existing worksheet file from disk by choosing File ➤ Open. An easier way to perform this operation is to click the Open-File SmartIcon, the first icon in the set. It shows an arrow coming out of a folder.

Here are the steps for reopening the CONF.WK4 worksheet that you saved at the end of Chapter 3:

1. Click the OpenFile icon or choose File ➤ Open.

2. If necessary, move to the directory where you saved the file. When you find the correct directory, CONF.WK4 appears in the File name list box, as in Figure 4.1.

3. Double-click the file name to open the file.

The conference worksheet reappears on-screen with all the work that you completed in the last chapter. Press the Maximize button in the worksheet window to make the worksheet fill the screen.

Establishing a New Default Directory

When you select the File ➤ Open command or File ➤ Save As command, dialog boxes appear showing the *default directory*. Which directory this is has to do with how you installed 1-2-3 (see Appendix A). However, you can change the default directory by choosing Tools ➤ User Setup. Make the directory in which you save most of your files the default directory.

If you intend to save most of your worksheets in a single directory, make that directory the default. It will save you a lot of time as you open files and save them to disk.

Here are the steps for establishing a new default directory:

1. Choose Tools ➤ User Setup. The User Setup dialog box appears, as in Figure 4.2.

2. In the Worksheet directory text box, enter the full name of the directory path that you want to make the default. Lotus 1-2-3 saves your new default specification in a file named 1-2-3W.INI in the Windows directory.

3. Click the OK button or press ↵ to complete the operation.

The next time you choose the File ➤ Open or File ➤ Save As command, the new default directory will be the initial selection.

The User Setup command offers many options for controlling 1-2-3's defaults. You'll examine some of them later in this chapter.

In the upcoming exercises, you'll move quickly back and forth to different ranges and cells in the worksheet and change their formatting and styles. Therefore, you need to know about the Go To command on the Edit menu.

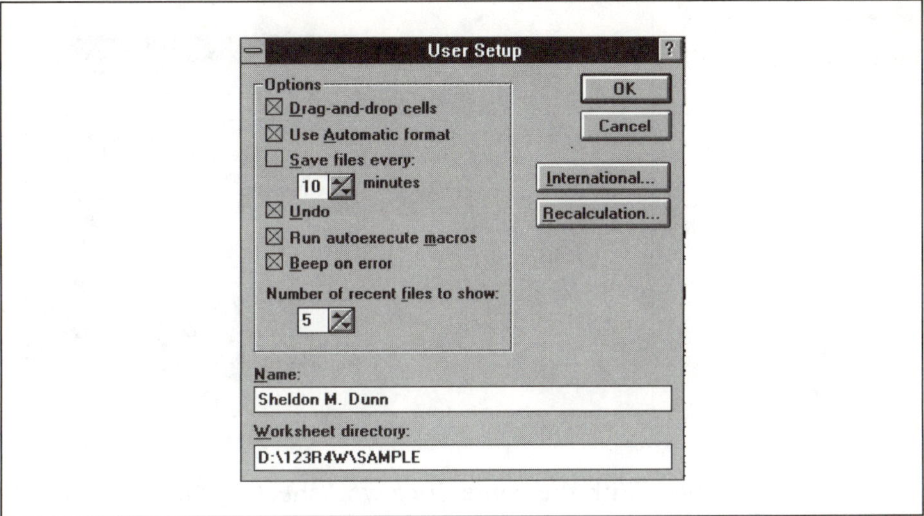

The Go To Command for Moving Quickly Around a Spreadsheet

The Go To command makes the cell pointer jump to a cell or range that you specify. To use the Go To command, either

- Choose Edit ➤ Go To, or
- Press F5.

The Go To dialog box appears on-screen, as shown in Figure 4.3. Here, you can enter the address of a cell to which you want to move or move to a range by selecting its name from the list box.

In Figure 4.3, you can see a list of range names you defined on the conference worksheet. To jump to one of the ranges on the list, highlight its name and either press ↵ or double-click it. Lotus 1-2-3 moves the cell pointer to the upper-left corner of the range.

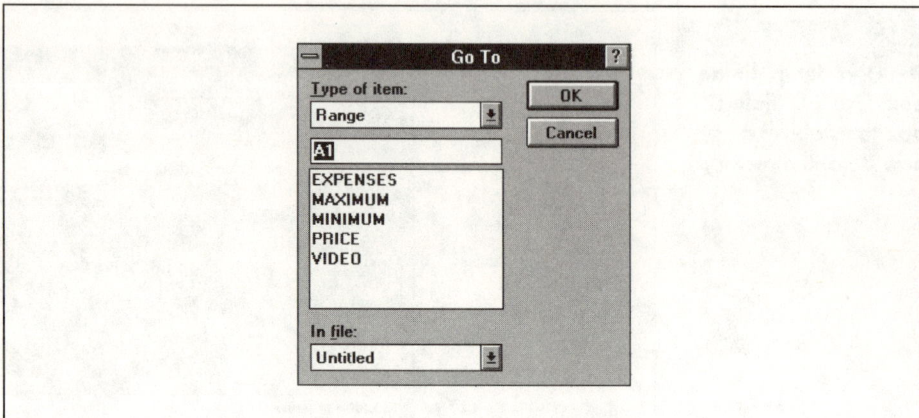

With the conference worksheet open, try using the Go To command:

1. Press F5.

2. Highlight EXPENSES in the range name list.

3. Click the OK button or press ↵.

The pointer jumps to cell E21, the topmost cell in the EXPENSES range, and highlights the range as well.

As you do the exercises in this chapter, you'll discover that the Go To command is the quickest, most convenient way to move to a new location in a worksheet window. Moreover, you can press F5 and activate the Go To command whenever you need to review the list of range names you have defined for a worksheet.

Changing the Layout of a Worksheet

As you refine the appearance of your worksheet, you'll find that some worksheet properties can be changed in two ways:

- Globally, for the entire worksheet
- Selectively, for one or more ranges on the worksheet

The Style menu offers both global and selective commands.

Changing Column Widths

Column width, the next topic in this chapter, is an example of a visual property that you can change globally for the whole worksheet or individually for specific columns.

Globally Changing the Width of All Columns

Increase or decrease the width of all columns with the Worksheet Defaults command on the Style menu. When you select Style ➤ Worksheet Defaults, the dialog box shown in Figure 4.4 appears. Notice that the Column width text box has a default setting of 9. With this default, each column in the worksheet is wide enough to display a nine-digit number in the default font, Arial MT 12-point. (You'll learn about using fonts later in this chapter.) You can enter any value from 1 to 240 in the Column width box to change the worksheet's global column width.

Take the following steps now to increase the global column width of the conference worksheet to 11:

1. Choose Style ➤ Worksheet Defaults.
2. Select the Column width text box and enter a value of **11**.
3. Click OK or press ↵.

The Worksheet Defaults dialog box. This dialog box is for making global changes to a worksheet.

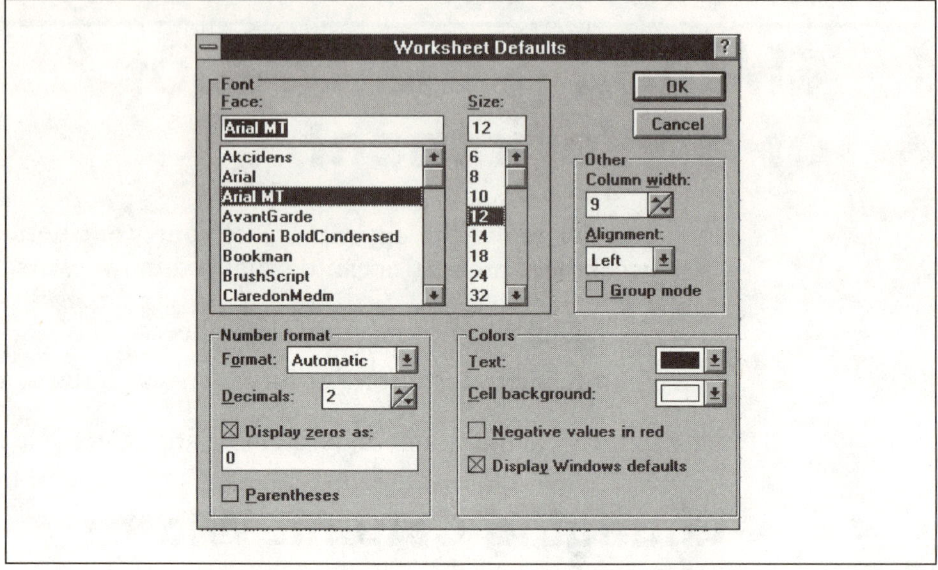

Besides entering a value in the Column width text box, you can change column width by clicking on the ↑ or ↓ arrow to the right of the Column width text box.

Changing the Width of Single Columns

Besides Worksheet Defaults, the Style menu offers another way to change column widths. Choose Style ➤ Column Width to change the width of a single column or a range of columns. The Column Width dialog box appears.

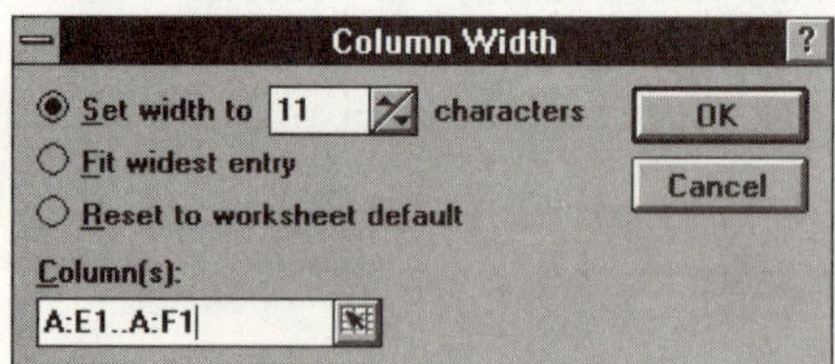

Choosing Style ➤ Column Width is useful when you know precisely what numeric width you want to assign to a particular column or when you want to restore the width of a column to the global default setting.

To experiment with the Column Width dialog box, follow these steps to widen columns E and F to a setting of 14:

1. Preselect range A:E1..F1.

2. Choose <u>S</u>tyle ➤ <u>C</u>olumn Width. In the dialog box, the range you just preselected appears in the <u>C</u>olumn(s) text box.

3. You want to enter a value of 14 in the <u>S</u>et width to text box. To change the column width to 14 characters, either enter **14** with the keyboard or click the ↑ arrow to the right of the Set width to text box.

4. Click OK or press ↵ to complete the operation.

Using the mouse to change column width　Lotus 1-2-3 offers a convenient mouse technique for changing the width of one column at a time: drag the column border to the right to increase the width of the column, or drag it to the left to decrease it.

The advantage of using the mouse to change column width over using the keyboard is that, with the mouse, you can actually see how wide the column will be and you don't have to rely on numeric specifications.

Try increasing the width of column C with the mouse:

1. Place the mouse pointer at the top of the worksheet, over the vertical line that divides the C and D headings. The mouse pointer becomes a double-headed arrow.

2. To widen column C, hold down the left mouse button and drag the border to the right. As you do so, a moving border shows you where the new border will be when you release the mouse button. Move the new border just to the left of the D column heading.

3. Release the mouse button.

4. Press Home to move the cell pointer to A1.

Move the cell pointer to any cell in column C and you'll see that you've increased the width.

You can see the column width in the selection indicator on the right side of the edit line.

Increasing Column Width to View a Number

For the conference worksheet, we changed column widths merely to improve the presentation of data. In other cases, however, you will increase the width of a column for a more basic reason—so your worksheet can display all of its numeric data. When a number is too long to fit in a column, 1-2-3 displays asterisks where you would expect the number to be. When you see a string of asterisks, it means that you must increase the column width in order to see the number itself.

Experiment with this effect in the following exercise:

1. Choose <u>F</u>ile ➤ <u>N</u>ew to open a new worksheet. The cell pointer starts out in cell A1.

2. Click the format selector in the status line at the bottom of the screen and select Currency to assign a dollar-and-cent format to cell A1.

3. Type **1-2-3456789** in the cell. When you press ↵, you'll see the cell fill with a string of asterisks.

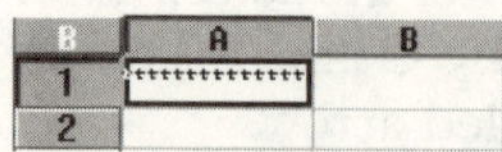

4. Dragging the right border of column A, increase the width of the column by about half. When you release the mouse button, you'll see the number displayed as $1-2-3,456,789.00.

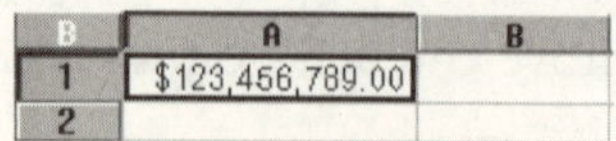

5. After you have examined the number, close the worksheet window
    without saving.

In this experiment, the number in A1 could not be displayed until you increased the column width appropriately.

Another helpful adjustment that you can make in a worksheet is to *hide* a
column completely.

Hiding Columns

You may want to hide columns temporarily so you can concentrate on
other columns of data in your worksheet. Another reason for hiding columns has to do with privacy. If many people will view your worksheet, you
might decide to hide a column of sensitive or private information.

Hiding columns with Style ➤ Hide Whatever your reasons for hiding
columns, you use the Hide command in the Style menu to hide or restore
a column. Suppose, in the conference worksheet, that you've decided to
focus on financial projections concerning the maximum attendance estimate. In order to do this, you have to hide column E, the column containing the minimum estimates. Here is how to hide a column:

1. Preselect cell E1, the topmost cell in the column you want to hide
    on the worksheet.

2. Choose Style ➤ Hide. The Hide dialog box appears.

The Hide dialog box offers options for hiding a column or an entire worksheet. The default selection is Column. The address of the preselected cell
appears in the Range text box.

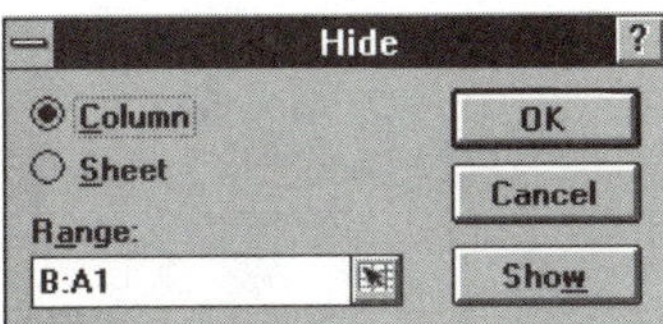

3. Click OK or press ↵ to accept the default Hide option and com-
    plete the Hide operation.

4. Press the Home key to move the cell pointer to A1.

At the end of these steps, column E disappears from the worksheet, as you can see in Figure 4.5. You can now concentrate on the data in column F.

Hiding columns with the mouse You can also use a very fast mouse technique to hide a column.

1. Move the mouse pointer over a border line at the top of the column that divides one column from the next. The pointer changes to a two-headed arrow.

2. Press the left mouse button and drag the column border to the left or right until you reach the next border line.

3. Release the mouse button. The column disappears, just as if you had chosen Style ➤ Hide.

Restoring a hidden column At some point, you'll want to restore the hidden data in column E. To restore a hidden column, follow these steps:

1. Choose Style ➤ Hide. The Hide dialog box appears on-screen.

2. Activate the Range text box and enter **E1** in this box.

3. Click the Show button to confirm the show operation and close the Hide dialog box.

FIGURE 4.5

Hiding column E in order to focus on the data in column F

	A	B	C	D	F	G	H
1		Computing Conferences, Inc.					
2		Profit Projection for a One-Day Conference					
3							
4	Conference:	Computing for Video Stores					
5	Place:	St. Louis					
6	Date:						
7					Maximum		
8	Price:	225			128		
9							
10				Per Person	Max. Total		
11	Projected Revenues						
12		Attendance			28800		
13		Video Sales		35	2240		
14		Total Revenues			31040		
15							
16	Projected Expenses - Fixed						
17		Conference room			2000		
18		Video production			1000		
19		Promotion			3500		
20		Travel			800		
21		Total Fixed Expenses			7300		

The worksheet is restored to its original state, with all its columns in view. Column E has the column width setting you assigned it before the Hide operation.

To "unhide" a column with the mouse, drag the right border of the missing column. For example, to restore hidden column E, place the mouse pointer on the border between the letter headings of columns D and F and drag the border to the right.

Once the column widths are arranged the way you want them, you can start formatting the data on the worksheet. One property you already know about is label alignment. In Chapter 3, you used double quotation mark prefixes to right-align label entries. But sometimes it is easier to apply alignment properties to a range of labels *after* you enter the labels in the worksheet.

Aligning Labels in Cells

Because aligning labels in cells is such an important part of data presentation in a worksheet, Lotus offers many ways of aligning labels. You can change the alignment of individual cells, change the alignment of cells in a range, or change the default alignment of all the cells in a worksheet.

Prefixes for aligning individual cells Three prefixes determine how a label is aligned in a worksheet cell:

PREFIX	PREFIX NAME	DESCRIPTION
'	single quotation mark	Aligns the label on the left side of the cell (this is the default).
^	caret	Centers the label in the cell.
"	double quotation mark	Aligns the label on the right side of the cell.

Aligning cells in a range Moreover, Lotus 1-2-3 offers two ways to change the alignment of labels in a range:

- Choose <u>S</u>tyle ➤ <u>A</u>lignment and select an alignment option.
- Preselect a range and click one of the three alignment SmartIcons:

The LeftAlign icon. Aligns labels on the left.

The RightAlign icon. Aligns labels on the right.

The CenterAlign icon. Centers labels.

Changing the default cell alignment To change the default alignment of all the cells in a worksheet, choose <u>S</u>tyle ➤ <u>W</u>orksheet Defaults and select an option in the <u>A</u>lignment box.

As a quick experiment with label alignments, let's change the alignments of the cells in range A4..A8 on the conference worksheet. The labels in this range all have the default left-alignment, and a single quote appears as the prefix for each label in the contents box. Follow these steps to experiment with other possible alignments:

1. Preselect range A4..A8.

2. Click the CenterAlign icon. The four labels are centered. Notice that the prefix in the contents box changes to a caret.

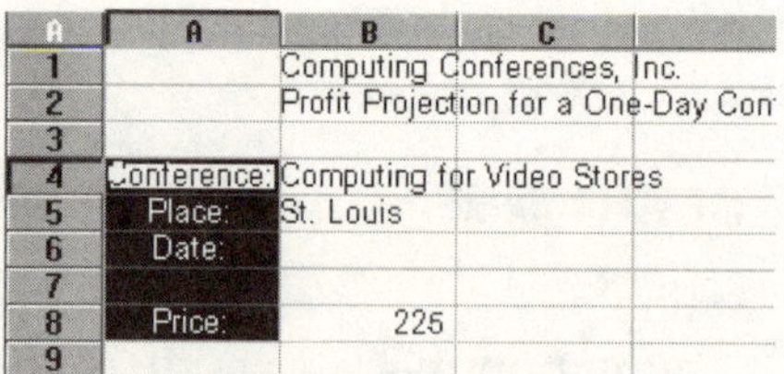

3. Click the RightAlign icon. The labels are right-aligned and the prefix in the contents box changes to a double quotation mark.

	A	B	C	
1		Computing Conferences, Inc.		
2		Profit Projection for a One-Day Con'		
3				
4	Conference:	Computing for Video Stores		
5	Place:	St. Louis		
6	Date:			
7				
8	Price:	225		
9				

Right-alignment is a good choice for these labels, but a small adjustment is necessary. There needs to be a space between the colon and the right cell border to separate the right-aligned labels in column A from the labels in column B.

   4. Use the F2 function key to edit the labels in this range, one label at a time. Insert a blank space after the colon in each label.

Centering labels over a horizontal range of cells In Release 4, cells with long labels can also be aligned. In other words, even a cell that extends beyond its left or right border can be centered, left-aligned, or right-aligned. To see how this works, select cell A11, the cell with the long label "Projected Revenues," and click the CenterAlign and RightAlign icons in turn.

On our worksheet, let's center the two title labels horizontally across columns C through E. As Figure 4.6 shows, centering the two labels over C through E centers them over the entire worksheet. However, the titles themselves are still contained in cells B1 and B2. Selecting each of these cells in turn, you see the following labels in the contents box:

    ^Computing Conferences, Inc.
    ^Profit Projection for a One-Day Conference

Notice that 1-2-3 uses the caret prefix both for labels centered in a single cell and labels centered across a horizontal range.

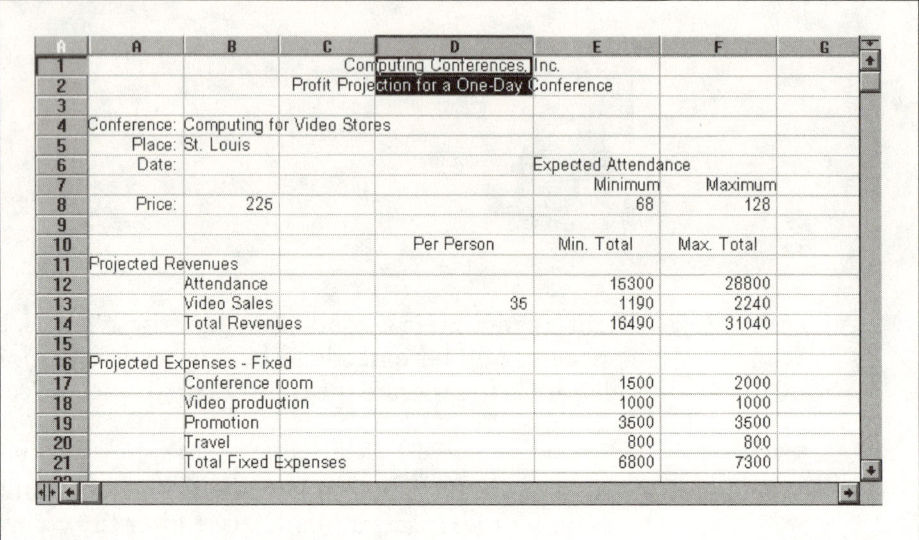

Label Prefixes for Decorating Worksheets and Hiding Rows

Lotus 1-2-3 has two more label prefixes, neither of which is related to alignment:

- **The backslash prefix (\).** This prefix tells 1-2-3 to fill a cell with a single repeating character or a pattern of repeating characters.

- **The vertical bar prefix (|).** When placed before the first cell in a row, this prefix tells 1-2-3 *not* to print the row. You'll learn more about how to use the vertical bar prefix later in this chapter.

You can use the backslash to decorate worksheets with division lines and create other interesting visual effects. For example, in Figure 4.7 the backslash prefix was used to create repeating symbols and patterns. A backslash and the following symbols were placed in cells A1 through A6. Compare the entries below with Figure 4.7.

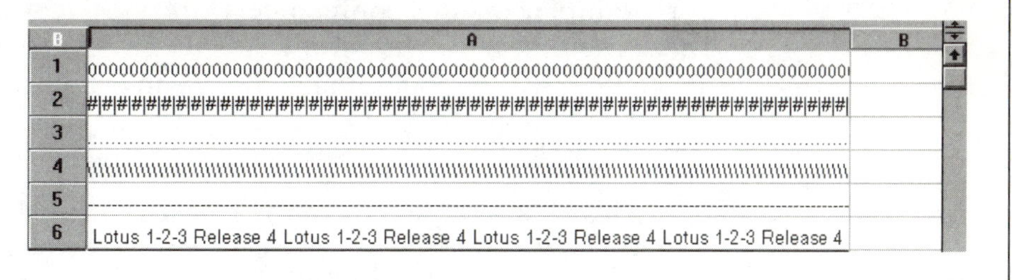

CELL	BACKSLASH AND ENTRY
A1	\( )
A2	\# |
A3	\.
A4	\\
A5	\-
A6	\Lotus 1-2-3 Release 4

Returning to the conference worksheet, you'll now learn about another operation that affects the display of information located at the top of the worksheet.

Keeping Titles and Column Headings in View

As you know, you can scroll down the worksheet by pressing the PgDn key or by using the vertical scroll bar. When you scroll down too far, the rows at the top of the worksheet disappear from view. Likewise, when you scroll to the right by pressing Ctrl-→ or by using the horizontal scroll bar, you can lose sight of the columns on the left side of the worksheet. Suppose you want to keep a range of rows or columns on-screen while you scroll down or across the worksheet. You can do this with the Freeze Titles command on the View menu. Freeze Titles "freezes" beginning rows and/or columns and keeps them in view.

For example, on the conference worksheet it would be convenient to freeze the first ten rows—the worksheet title, general information about the conference, and column headings—in order to view them as you enter data. Here are the steps for freezing rows on a worksheet:

1. Move the cell pointer to the row just *below* the range of rows that you want to freeze. In our case, move the cell pointer to A11.

2. Choose View ➤ Freeze Titles. The Freeze Titles dialog box appears. You can freeze a range of rows at the top of the worksheet, a range of columns on the left side of the worksheet, or both the columns and the rows.

3. You want the Row option, which is selected by default. Click OK or press ↵ to complete the operation.

Now when you press PgDn to scroll down the worksheet, the first ten rows remain in view, and scrolling takes place only in the lower half of the worksheet. In Figure 4.8, the worksheet has been scrolled all the way to the Projected Profit line, giving you a juxtaposed view of the summary information in the first ten rows along with the bottom-line profit.

WARNING

You can't use arrow keys or the mouse to move the cell pointer into a frozen range. The only way to edit cells in the frozen range is to "unfreeze" them.

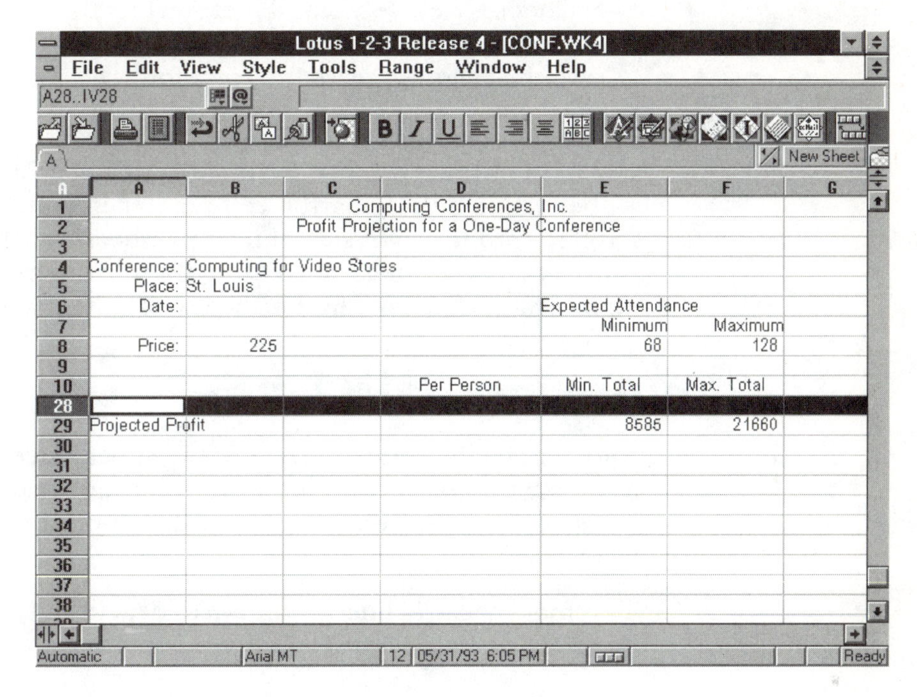

Editing "frozen" cells You can't use arrow keys or the mouse to move the cell pointer into a frozen range. When you press Home, the cell pointer moves to the first cell outside the frozen range, not to cell A1. Furthermore, clicking the mouse inside the frozen range has no effect. If you need to go into the frozen range to edit information there, you have two choices:

- Choose View ➤ Clear Titles to "unfreeze" the titles range. Now you can edit the cells in the previously frozen titles range. When you are finished editing the cells, choose View ➤ Freeze Titles to freeze the title cells again.

- Choose <u>V</u>iew ➤ Clear Titles to clear the frozen views. Now you can press the Home key to select cell A1 or do whatever you want to the cells that were frozen before.

Before you read on, you might want to try freezing columns on the left side of the worksheet. For example, try establishing columns A and B as a titles range by placing the cell pointer in column C. After you do so, scroll toward the right side of the worksheet. What happens as you do so? What is the advantage of freezing these columns? Clear the frozen columns again when you are finished with this exercise.

Removing Grid Lines

Another change you can make to the appearance of a worksheet is to remove the grid lines. Working with or without grid lines is a matter of personal preference. Removing them does not affect operations inside the worksheet.

To remove the grid lines, you have to deactivate an option in the Set View Preferences dialog box. Here are the steps:

1. Choose <u>V</u>iew ➤ Set View <u>P</u>references. The Set View Preferences dialog box appears on-screen, as shown in Figure 4.9.

FIGURE 4.9

The Set View Preferences dialog box

2. Click the <u>G</u>rid lines check box to remove the *X*.

3. Click OK or press ↵.

Lotus 1-2-3 removes the grid lines from the worksheet window, as shown in Figure 4.10. You can restore them by choosing <u>V</u>iew ➤ Set View <u>P</u>references again and checking the Grid lines box.

FIGURE 4.10

The grid lines removed. Removing grid lines makes a worksheet look cleaner, but data entry is harder without them.

Other Worksheet Display Options

Here's a brief look at other options offered in the Set View Preferences dialog box:

<u>W</u>orksheet frame	Checking this box opens a pull-down list with various measurements you can display around the worksheet instead of the column letters and row numbers. You can display Characters, Inches, Metric, or Points/Picas measurements. Uncheck the Worksheet frame check box to remove the border altogether.

Worksheet tabs Check this box to remove the folder tabs you see on the screen from the worksheets. There is also a WorksheetTabs SmartIcon above the splitter in the upper-right corner of the worksheet.

Grid lines Offers a pull-down list with colors for displaying the grid lines on-screen.

Scroll bars Check this box to remove the horizontal and vertical scroll bars at the bottom and right side of the worksheet window. This option is handy when you need to see one or two more rows on-screen.

Page breaks Checked by default, this box controls the display of page breaks. On-screen, a page break appears as a heavy dashed line below the last line of the page.

Charts, drawings, and pictures Check this box to see charts and other graphic elements on the worksheet, if there are any. When this box is checked, you can select the Chart and Draw menu items from the Tools menu. Unless you check this box, these graphics tools are grayed out and can't be selected.

Custom zoom %

This text box lets you change the size of cells as they are displayed on-screen. You can increase their size by as much as 400 percent or decrease the size of the cells to 25 percent of original size. Figures 4.11 and 4.12 show what you can do with this option. Enter a value with the keyboard or click on the $\uparrow$ and $\downarrow$ buttons to dial a value.

Show in 1-2-3

The three options here let you determine which menu bars to see on-screen. You can check SmartIcons, Edit line, and/or Status bar to control their respective display.

FIGURE 4.11

A worksheet with the Custom zoom % option set to 60 percent

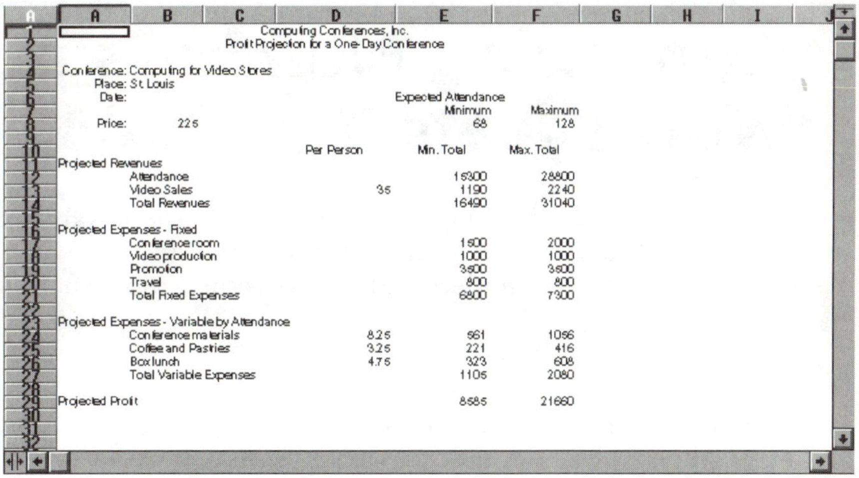

Computing Conferences, Inc.
Profit Projection for a One-Day Conference

Conference: Computing for Video Stores
Place: St. Louis
Date:

	Per Person	Expected Attendance Minimum	Maximum
Price: 225		68	128
	Per Person	Min. Total	Max. Total
Projected Revenues			
Attendance		15300	28800
Video Sales	35	1190	2240
Total Revenues		16490	31040
Projected Expenses - Fixed			
Conference room		1500	2000
Video production		1000	1000
Promotion		3500	3500
Travel		800	800
Total Fixed Expenses		6800	7300
Projected Expenses - Variable by Attendance			
Conference materials	8.25	561	1056
Coffee and Pastries	3.25	221	416
Box lunch	4.75	323	608
Total Variable Expenses		1105	2080
Projected Profit		8585	21660

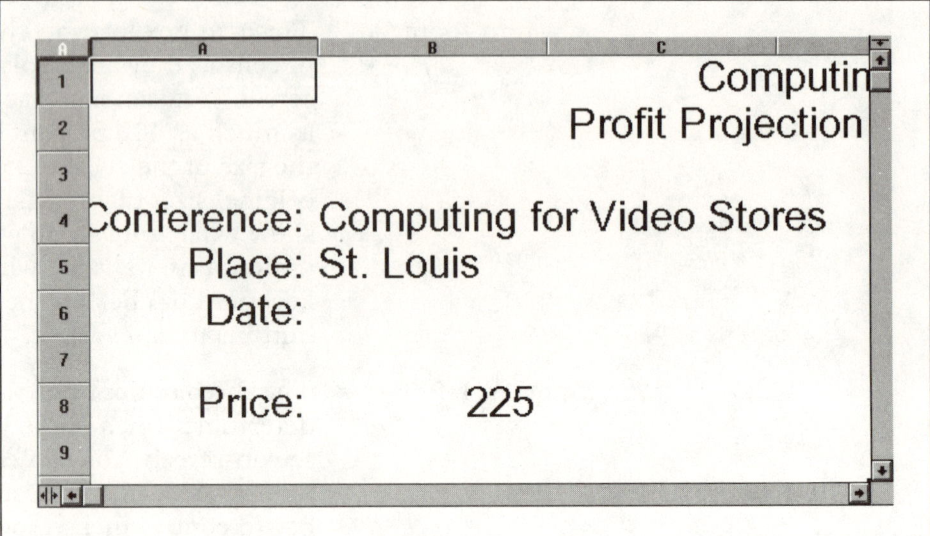

Formatting Numbers in Worksheets

One way to give meaning to a numeric value is to pair the value with a descriptive label. A number and an adjacent label in this way form an easy-to-understand item of information, such as the following:

    Price: 195

But another important technique for establishing the meaning of numbers—and for making a worksheet easier to read—is to apply *formats* to numeric values:

    Price: $195.00

Lotus 1-2-3 for Windows provides standard numeric formats that you can assign to numbers.

Establishing global number formats Like other worksheet properties, formats can be applied globally to the entire worksheet or selectively to cells or ranges. Formats do not change the numeric value entered in the cell, only the way the number is displayed.

You can apply most formats either before or after you actually enter values. To establish global formats for a worksheet, select the Worksheet Defaults command on the Style menu. The Worksheet Defaults dialog box appears on-screen. This dialog box has three main tools:

- The Format box lists global formats that you can apply to the entire worksheet. Click the ↓ button in the Format box to see a list of global formats, as shown in Figure 4.13.

- The Decimals text box controls how many digits are displayed after a decimal point.

- The Parentheses check box gives you the option of displaying numeric values in parentheses.

Establishing number formats for ranges Lotus 1-2-3 presents a dialog box similar to the Format list box when you select Style ➤ Number

Use the Format list box to select a default format for the worksheet.

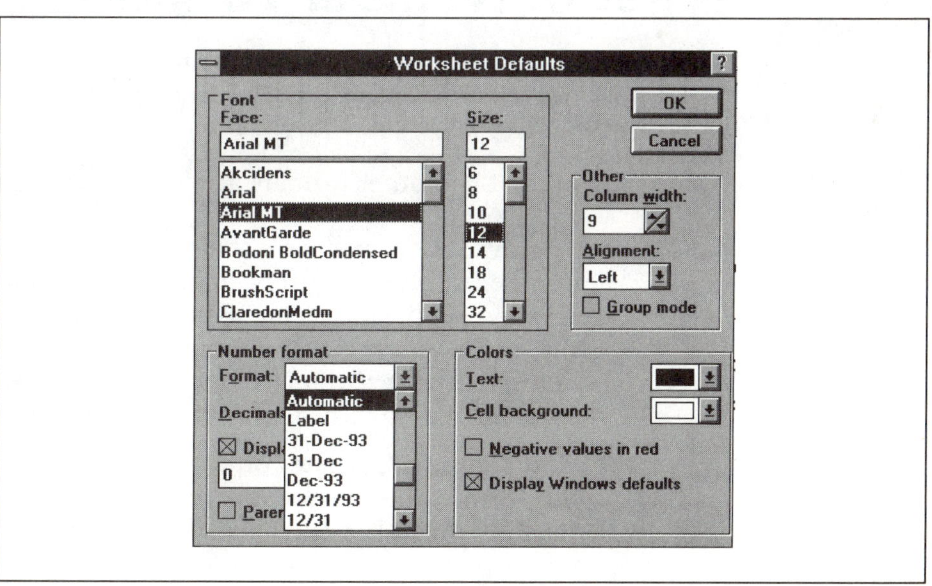

Format. The Number Format dialog box is shown in Figure 4.14. The main difference between this box and the Format list box is that this one is for applying formats to a selected range, not the entire worksheet. The list of format settings, however, is the same as the one in the Format list box. The Number Format dialog box also has a Reset command button. Clicking this button resets the range format to the current global format.

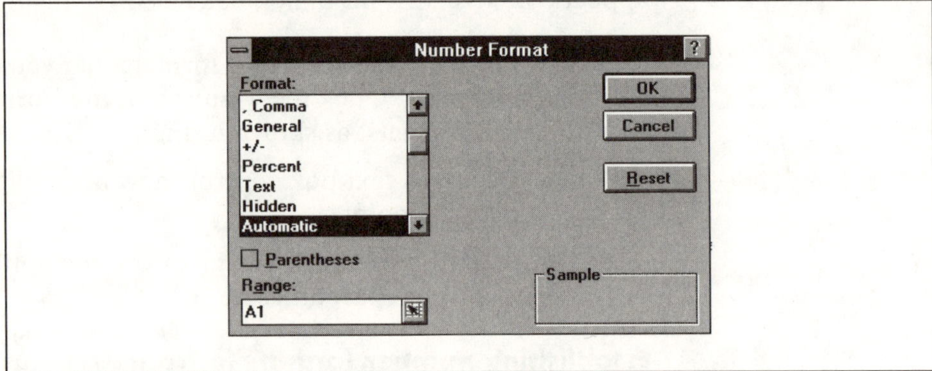

Types of Number Formats

Columns B and D of the worksheet in Figure 4.15 show examples of commonly used number formats. Explanations of these formats can be found in Table 4.1.

Examples of two other formats also appear in Figure 4.15:

- **+/− format.** Transforms the display of a value into an equivalent number of plus or minus characters. This format is useful for creating simple character-based horizontal bar graphs on a worksheet. (In Figure 4.15, column F contains the same positive numbers that are displayed in column G. Likewise, column I contains the same negative values displayed in column J.)

- **Text format.** Operates on a cell that contains a formula. Under this format, the cell displays the text of the formula itself rather than the formula's numeric result, as you can see in Figure 4.15.

FIGURE 4.15

Examples of commonly used numeric formats, +/− format, and text format

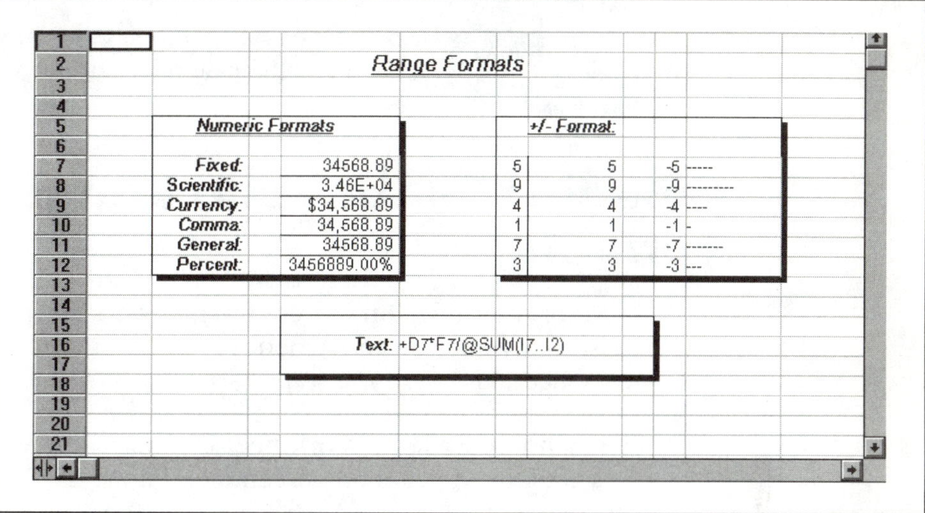

TABLE 4.1:   Numeric Formats Offered by 1-2-3

FORMAT	EXAMPLE	EXPLANATION
Fixed	34568.89	Displays values to a specified number of decimal places, up to fifteen.
Scientific	3.46E+04	Displays numbers in an exponent notation, where the digits after the letter *E* represent the power of 10 by which the base value is multiplied.
Currency	$34,568.89	Displays a dollar sign at the beginning of the number, and a comma before every third digit to the left of the decimal point.
Comma	34,568.89	Displays a comma before every third digit to the left of the decimal point.
General	34568.89	Displays a value without special formatting (the default).
Percent	3456889.00%	Multiplies the displayed value by 100 and appends a percent sign.

Selecting Global and Range Formats

Most of the values on the conference worksheet are dollar-and-cent figures, so it would be convenient to assign a global Currency format to the worksheet. Here are the steps:

1. Choose <u>S</u>tyle ➤ <u>W</u>orksheet Defaults. The Worksheet Defaults dialog box appears on-screen (see Figure 4.13).

2. Click the ↓ next to F<u>o</u>rmat to view the Format list box.

3. Select the Currency format.

4. Click OK to complete the formatting operation.

Now all of the values on the worksheet are displayed as dollar-and-cent values. But the worksheet has two values that are not currency figures but are simple integers: the minimum and maximum attendance estimates in cells E8 and F8. You can use the Comma format to change these two values to an appropriate format:

1. Preselect range E8..F8.

2. Click the format selector on the status bar.

3. Select Comma.

Formatting for International Currencies

If you work with international currencies, you often have to change currency symbols and even reverse the roles of commas and periods to accommodate certain international currency notations. To do so, you can take advantage of a feature that is part of the Tools User Setup command.

1. Choose Tools ➤ User Setup. The User Setup dialog box appears (see Figure 4.2).

2. Click the International button. The International dialog box appears, as shown in Figure 4.16.

3. To change the currency symbol, enter a new character in the Symbol for currency box.

4. To change the comma and period punctuation, make a new selection in the pull-down list attached to the Punctuation box.

Changing the Data-Entry Mode

Two formats, Label and Automatic, represent predefined data-entry modes in 1-2-3:

- **Label format.** This format accepts all new entries to the worksheet as labels, even if they begin with digits or other characters that normally would trigger the Value mode. In label format, 1-2-3 places a single-quote prefix at the beginning of each new entry you make in the worksheet. Label format is useful when you have to enter a series of labels that begin with digits, such as a column of addresses. Without the Label format, you would have to begin each such label by typing a single quotation mark.

- **Automatic format.** This format applies the same format to a cell as the one you initially applied when you entered a value in the cell for the first time. Each time you make a new numeric entry, the value is stored in the cell and the cell is assigned the preexisting format. The Automatic format is useful with worksheets that have a large variety of formatting specifications. With Automatic, you can set each cell's format at the time of data entry and not worry about reformatting when you replace existing numbers with new ones.

In the following exercise, you'll apply Label and Automatic formats to individual cells. You'll also experiment with a format that hides the contents of a range of cells.

1. Choose File ➤ New to create a new worksheet window.
2. With the cell pointer at address A1, choose Style ➤ Number Format.
3. In the Format list box (see Figure 4.14), select the Label format. (While the Format box is active, you can simply type **L** at the keyboard to jump immediately to the target format in the list.)
4. Click OK or press ↵. A1 now operates under the Label format.
5. Type **1–2–3 Maple Drive** into cell A1.

When you begin the entry, 1-2-3 switches to Value mode, but when you press ↵, the entry is stored as a label. Examine the contents box to confirm this: the entry begins with a single quote character.

6. Select cell A2 for an experiment with the Automatic format.

7. Choose <u>S</u>tyle ➤ <u>N</u>umber Format again.

8. Select the Automatic format. (Simply type **A** at the keyboard to jump to Automatic in the Format list.)

9. Click OK or press ↵. Cell A2 is now under the effect of Automatic mode.

10. Type **$1-2-34.56**, without including the comma, in A2.

You did not include a comma in your entry, but entering the dollar sign was enough to tell 1-2-3 to use the Currency format.

11. Press ↵ and note the results.

The cell displays the new entry as $1,234.56. And the status line reports the cell's format as "Currency." Finally, notice that the contents box displays the entry simply as 1-2-34.56.

12. Enter a new numeric value, **6543.21**, in cell A2. The previously assigned format applies to this new entry. In the cell, the new entry is $6,543.21.

13. Preselect range A1..A2.

14. Choose <u>S</u>tyle ➤ <u>N</u>umber Format again and select the Hidden option from the Format list.

15. Click OK or press ↵ to confirm the format selection.

The Hidden format The contents of the two cells disappear. By selecting each cell in turn, you can see in the contents box that the entries have not been deleted, just hidden. The Hidden format is useful when you want to withhold certain sensitive data items from view in a worksheet.

16. When you have finished examining the results of this exercise, close the worksheet window without saving it.

Keep the Label and Automatic formats in mind for special data-entry requirements. In the right situations, they can speed up your work considerably. You'll have another opportunity to experiment with the Automatic mode in the next section of this chapter, as you turn to two other kinds of worksheet data—date and time values.

Entering Date Values in a Worksheet

Lotus 1-2-3 offers many versatile tools for working with calendar dates. For example, you can enter a date on a worksheet as a numeric value and then use the value in *date arithmetic* operations. Here are two date arithmetic operations common to business worksheets:

- Find the number of days between any two dates.

- Find the date that is a certain number of days forward or backward from today's date.

Performing these two operations is quite complicated in some software environments, but in 1-2-3 you can do them with simple arithmetic formulas, as you'll see shortly.

Entering Dates as Labels or Numbers

There are two ways of recording a date in a worksheet.

- **As a label.** If you only need to display a date and have no need to perform arithmetic operations with it, enter it as a label. When you enter a date in a format that starts with the name of a month, 1-2-3 automatically accepts your entry as a label (the same as it accepts any entry that begins with a letter of the alphabet). For example, if you enter July 31, 1994, Lotus will understand that you are entering this date as a label.

- **As a number.** If you anticipate working with the date in arithmetic operations, enter it as a number.

How 1-2-3 handles numeric dates To enter dates as numbers, you have to understand how 1-2-3 handles numeric dates. Lotus 1-2-3 can compute an integer equivalent for every date between January 1, 1900, and December 31, 2099. January 1, 1900, is day 1 in the system, and each day forward from there is numbered consecutively. Here is a sample of date numbers from Lotus's date numbering system:

DATE	DATE NUMBER
January 1, 1900	1
January 2, 1900	2
May 10, 1910	3783
December 1, 1945	16772
March 2, 1976	27821
October 15, 1993	34257
December 31, 2099	73050

When you enter a date and 1-2-3 recognizes it as a date within the 1900 to 2099 range, the entry is stored as a number.

1-2-3 date formats Therefore, after making a date entry, your next task is to reformat the cell in one of 1-2-3's five date formats. Date formats are available in the Number Format dialog box (see Figure 4.14) in the Format list.

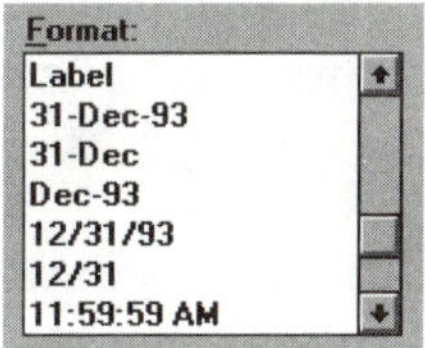

The first three formats use a three-character month abbreviation, along with two digits each for the month and/or the year, like so:

15-Oct-93

15-Oct

Oct-93

The second two formats, called the *Long International Date* and *Short International Date* formats, look like this:

10/15/93

10/15

If you wish, you can select new international date formats in the International dialog box (see Figure 4.16). Bring up this dialog box by selecting Tools ➤ User Setup and clicking the International button.

In summary, to enter a numeric date in a worksheet cell, you enter the date in one of the date formats that 1-2-3 recognizes, such as 15-Oct-93 or 10/15/93. (When you enter a date in the incomplete 15-Oct format, 1-2-3 assumes that the date is in the current year.) The program converts your entry to a date number. Next, you choose the Style ➤ Number Format command and select a date format from the Format list.

Entering Dates in the Conference Worksheet

To practice entering dates, return now to the conference worksheet. Cell B6 is set aside for the date of the conference, but it is still empty. Here are the steps for entering the date:

1. Select cell B6 and type **15-Oct-93**, the date of the conference.

2. Press ↵ and examine the contents box. It shows you the date number, 34257. This same value is displayed in the cell itself, but—somewhat incongruously—it is displayed in the worksheet's global currency format: $34257.00.

3. Choose Style ➤ Number Format.

4. In the Format list box, type **3** to select the 31-Dec-93 date format.

5. Click OK or press ↵ to complete the formatting operation.

Now the date is displayed in the format you selected: 15-Oct-93. The format selector tells you that the format selection is (D1), which stands for date format 1.

When you enter numeric dates, you can save time by setting the format to Automatic. This way, you can enter a date in one of the formats that 1-2-3 recognizes, and the format will be assigned automatically to the cell. Try this technique in the following exercise.

1. Select B6 and press the Delete key to delete the current date entry. (This action also removes the cell's current format setting.)

2. Choose <u>S</u>tyle ➤ <u>N</u>umber Format.

3. In the <u>F</u>ormat list, type **A** to select the Automatic format.

4. Click OK or press ↵.

5. In cell B6, reenter the date in the same format as before: **15-Oct-93**. This time the date display has the same format as your date entry. The date number 34257 again appears in the contents box.

6. Click the SaveFile icon to save the work you have done so far on the worksheet.

Now that you know how to enter and format a date value, you can learn how to perform date arithmetic.

Performing Date Arithmetic

Computing Conferences, Inc, has decided to offer an admission discount to participants who enroll and pay in advance to attend the conference. A 10-percent discount will be offered for payments received 45 days in advance, and a 20-percent discount for payments received 90 days in advance. Naturally, the conference organizers want to develop a small worksheet that formulates and displays the discount schedule.

Entering the Data

In the following exercise, you will begin developing this worksheet by adding a second worksheet to the CONF.WK4 file:

1. Choose Edit ➤ Insert.

2. In the Insert dialog box, select Sheet.

An easier way to add a new worksheet is to click the New Sheet button just below the right side of the title bar.

3. Click OK or press ↵. Worksheet B is added to the window and becomes the current worksheet.

4. Choose View ➤ Split ➤ Perspective to view worksheets A and B in the same window.

5. In cell B:A2, enter the title **Discount Schedule for Advance Enrollment**.

6. In worksheet A, preselect range A:A4..A:B8. (This range contains the basic information about the conference, which you are now going to copy to worksheet B.)

7. Click the CopyToClipboard icon. In worksheet B, select cell B:A4. Click the PasteFromClipboard icon. A copy of the conference information appears in worksheet B. Choose View ➤ Clear Split to toggle back to a view of worksheet B alone. Notice that the range date format in cell B:B6 was copied from worksheet A, but the global currency format was not copied.

8. Select cell B:B8, click the format selector on the status bar, and select Currency.

9. Enter the following three column headings:

CELL	ENTER
B:B10	**If paid by:**
B:C10	**Discount**
B:D10	**Price**

10. Preselect range B:C10..BD10 and click the RightAlign SmartIcon. The alignment of the column headings in these two cells will now

match the alignment of the numeric values that will appear beneath them.

11. Choose <u>S</u>tyle ➤ <u>W</u>orksheet Defaults and enter **11** as the global column width. Click OK or press ↵.

At this point, worksheet B should look like Figure 4.17.

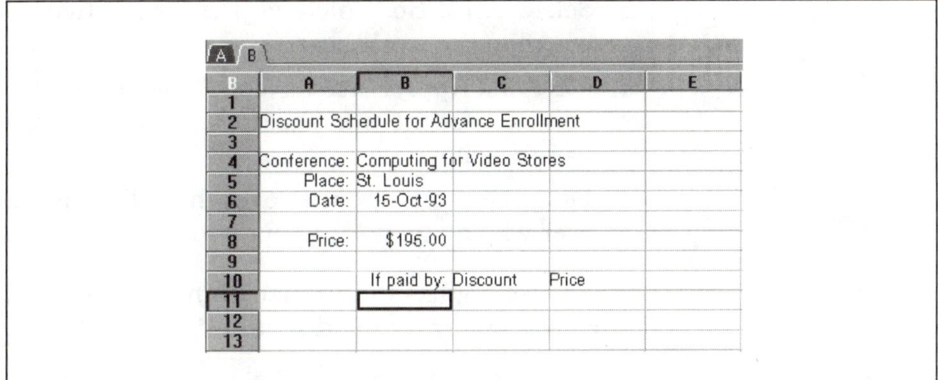

Writing the Formulas

The next step is to write formulas in cells B:B11 and B:B12. You have to display deadline dates for the 10-percent and 20-percent discount rates. Because cell B:B6 contains a numeric date that represents the day of the conference, you can create formulas by subtracting the appropriate number of days from the conference date.

1. Enter the following formula in B:B11:

    +B:B6–90

As you can see, this formula subtracts a value of 90 (representing 90 days) from the date number in cell B6. The result initially displayed in cell B6 is 34167.

2. Enter the following formula in cell B:B12 to subtract 45 days from the conference date:

    +B:B6–45

The initial result is 34212. Now you have to format these two cells so they will look like dates, not numbers. To do so, you can practice using the ApplyFormats icon. This icon, which shows a glue brush over a spreadsheet, copies a *format* from one place in a worksheet to another.

3. Select cell B:B6, which has the format that you want to apply elsewhere in the worksheet.

4. Click the ApplyFormats icon. Now when you move the mouse pointer over the worksheet, the pointer takes on the form of a paintbrush icon.

5. Drag the mouse pointer over the cells B:B11..B:B12, the range over which you want to apply the specified format.

Lotus 1-2-3 applies the format from cell B6 to cells B11 and B12. B11 and B12 now display the discount deadline dates, as follows:

    17-Jul-93
    31-Aug-93

Follow these steps to complete the discount schedule worksheet:

1. Enter a value of .2 in cell B:C11 and a value of .1 in B:C12. These numbers will represent the 20- and 10-percent discount, respectively.

2. Preselect range B:C11..B:C12 and choose Style ➤ Number Format.

3. In the Format list, select the Percent format.

4. Activate the Decimals text box and enter a value of **0**.

5. Click OK or press ↵. The values in C11 and C12 now appear as percentages.

6. Select cell B:D11 and enter the following formula:

    +$B:$B$8*(1–B:C11)

    After typing the plus sign and pointing to the first address in the formula, press F4 to change the address to an absolute reference. The second address can remain a relative reference.

7. Select B:D11..D12 and use the CopyDown icon to copy this formula into cell B:D12. The copied formula—adjusted for its position relative to the original formula—appears as +$B$8*(1−C12).

8. Preselect range B:D11..B:D12, click the format selector on the status bar, and select Currency.

9. Click the SaveFile icon to save your work to disk file CONF.WK4.

Your worksheet should look like Figure 4.18.

	A	B	C	D	E
1					
2	Discount Schedule for Advance Enrollment				
3					
4	Conference:	Computing for Video Stores			
5	Place:	St. Louis			
6	Date:	15-Oct-93			
7					
8	Price:	$195.00			
9					
10		If paid by:	Discount	Price	
11		17-Jul-93	20.00%	$156.00	
12		31-Aug-93	10.00%	$175.50	
13					

Entering Time Values in a Worksheet

Lotus 1-2-3 is just as good at displaying and manipulating chronological, or time, values as it is date values. Like date values, time values are stored as numbers. To display a time number in a recognizable way, you apply one of 1-2-3's time formats. Then you can perform a variety of *time arithmetic* operations. For example, two common time arithmetic operations in business worksheets are:

- Finding the number of minutes between two time values in a 24-hour day

- Finding the point in time a specified number of minutes forward or backward from either the current time or another time

How 1-2-3 handles time values   You have to understand how 1-2-3 translates time values into numbers before you can perform time operations. In 1-2-3, a time number is a fractional value, expressed as a decimal. The fraction expresses the portion of the 24-hour day that has passed at a specific time. For example, the time value for 12:00 noon is .5, because one-half of the day has elapsed at noon. Here is a sampling of other time values and their equivalent time numbers:

TIME	TIME NUMBER	HOW MUCH OF THE DAY HAS ELAPSED
3:00 AM	.125	One-eighth of the day
6:00 AM	.25	One-fourth of the day
9:00 AM	.375	Three-eighths of the day
6:00 PM	.75	Three-fourths of the day
9:00 PM	.875	Seven-eighths of the day

1-2-3 time formats   To enter and display a time value, you use formats that 1-2-3 recognizes for time entries. In the Number Format dialog box in Figure 4.19, you can see the four 1-2-3 time formats in the Format list. The first two are AM/PM formats and the second two are 24-hour international formats:

11:59.59 AM

11:59 AM

23:59:59

23:59

If you wish, you can select new international time formats in the International dialog box (see Figure 4.16). Bring up this dialog box by selecting Tools ➤ User Setup and clicking the International button.

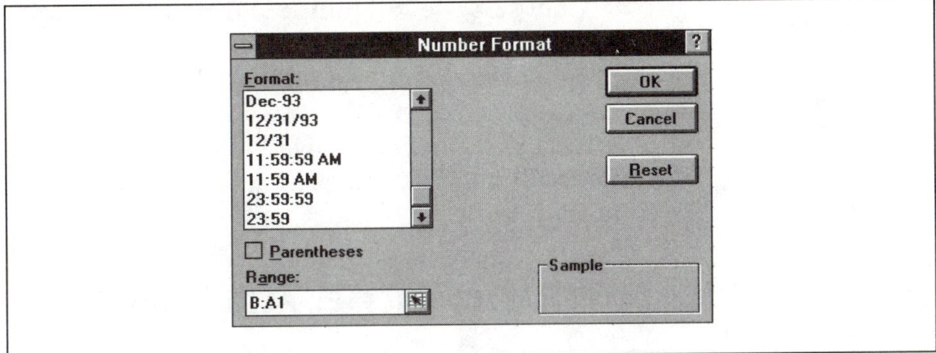

When you enter a value in one of these four formats, 1-2-3 recognizes
your entry as a time and automatically translates it into a decimal time
number. Your next step is to choose Style ➤ Number Format and select
a time format for displaying your entry. Alternatively, you can select the
Automatic format for your worksheet. When you select Automatic, 1-2-3
applies the same time format as the format in which you made your entry.
As you can see, entering time values is much like entering date values.

Entering Time Values in the Conference Worksheet

As your first exercise with time values, you'll insert another worksheet in
the CONF.WK4 file, this time the worksheet named C. You'll begin by
entering one time value in this worksheet, and then you'll use the sheet
to build another document for Computing Conferences, Inc. Here are
the beginning steps:

1. With worksheet B as the active worksheet, choose Edit ➤ Insert.
   Select Sheet and press ↵ to insert the third worksheet into the file.
   When you complete this operation, worksheet C becomes the ac-
   tive worksheet.

2. Select cell C:D8 for this first entry. (You'll see why shortly.) In the
   cell, enter the following time value:

   7:00 AM

1-2-3 displays the time number equivalent of this value, 0.291667, in the
contents box.

3. Choose <u>S</u>tyle ➤ <u>N</u>umber Format. Scroll to the time format you want in the <u>F</u>ormat box and click it.

4. Click OK or press ↵.

The time entry now displayed in cell D8 is 07:00 AM. In the next section, you'll use this time entry as the starting point for an exercise in time arithmetic.

Performing Time Arithmetic

The conference organizers at Computing Conferences, Inc., are ready to begin planning the schedule for the one-day conference in St. Louis. Four presentations will take place during the day, each lasting between one and two hours. Other miscellaneous activities will take place as well, including an introduction, an hour of hands-on demonstrations, coffee breaks, and lunch.

The planners want to develop a worksheet that calculates the day's schedule, given the length of each event. They want to adjust the length of time allotted to the activities to see what effect changing activity times has on the whole schedule.

Entering the Time Data

You'll develop this schedule on worksheet C. Begin with the following formatting and data-entry tasks:

1. Use the ApplyFormats icon to duplicate the format of cell D8 in the cells below it in column D. With the cell pointer located at D8, click the ApplyFormats icon with the mouse. Then drag the paint brush mouse pointer over range C:D9..C:D18. When you release the mouse button, 1-2-3 applies the time format to each cell in this range, although no visible change takes place in the worksheet window.

2. Press the Home key to select cell A1 and enter the title, **Conference Schedule**, in A1.

3. Copy the range containing the conference name, the place, and the date from worksheet B to worksheet C. To do so, press Ctrl-PgDn to activate worksheet B. Preselect range B:A4..B:B6 and

click the CopyToClipboard icon. Press Ctrl-PgUp to activate worksheet C. Select cell C:A3 and click the PasteFromClipboard icon.

4. Choose <u>S</u>tyle ➤ <u>W</u>orksheet Defaults and change the global column width to **11**.

5. Enter the following column headings:

CELL	ENTER
C:A7	**Event**
C:D7	**Start time**
C:E7	**Minutes**

6. Select range C:D7..C:E7 and click the RightAlign icon to align these two column headings with the numeric entries that will appear below them. Then select range C:A7..C:E7 and click the Bold icon.

7. Enter the following list of event descriptions into column A, from C:A8 to C:A18:

CELL	ENTER
C:A8	**Coffee and pastries**
C:A9	**Introduction**
C:A10	**Managing a Video Database**
C:A11	**Coffee Break**
C:A12	**Managing a Customer Database**
C:A13	**Hands-on demonstrations**
C:A14	**Lunch and discussion**
C:A15	**Setting Up a Computer System**
C:A16	**Coffee break**
C:A17	**Software Options**
C:A18	**No-host cocktail hour**

8. In column E, from C:E8 to C:E18, enter values representing the length in minutes of each event:

CELL	ENTER
C:E8	45
C:E9	30
C:E10	90
C:E11	15
C:E12	120
C:E13	60
C:E14	60
C:E15	120
C:E16	30
C:E17	60
C:E18	60

9. Select cell C:D9 to prepare for the upcoming formula entry.

Your worksheet should look like Figure 4.20.

Writing Time Formulas

Now you need to write a formula in D9 that calculates the starting time of the second event. The formula should be simple: Add the length in minutes of the first event (in C:E8) to the starting time of the first event (in C:D8). But there is one complication—the worksheet expresses these two values in incompatible terms. The starting time is stored as a decimal time number, and the length of the event is expressed in minutes. To add the two values you must convert them to common terms.

In this worksheet, the best approach is to convert the minutes to a decimal time value. The following expression calculates the fraction of a 24-hour day represented by the minutes in cell C:E8:

    +C:E8/(60*24)

	A	B	C	D	E	F
1	Conference Schedule					
2						
3	Conference:	Computing for Video Stores				
4	Place:	St. Louis				
5	Date:	15-Oct-93				
6						
7	Event			Start time	Minutes	
8	Coffee and pastries			07:00 AM	45	
9	Introduction				30	
10	Managing a Video Database				90	
11	Coffee Break				15	
12	Managing a Customer Database				120	
13	Hands-on demonstrations				60	
14	Lunch and discussion				60	
15	Setting Up a Computer System				120	
16	Coffee break				30	
17	Software Options				60	
18	No-host cocktail hour				60	
19						
20						
21						

Multiplying 60 by 24 gives the number of minutes in a day. Dividing the value in cell E8 by this number results in the appropriate decimal time value. Given this expression, here is the formula that calculates the starting time of the second event:

```
+C:D8+C:E8/(60*24)
```

In the following steps, you'll use the pointing technique to enter this formula into cell D9. Then, you'll copy the formula down the appropriate range in column D.

1. With the cell pointer positioned at D9, type **+** to start the formula entry.

2. Select cell D8 and type **+** again.

3. Select the value in cell E8 and complete the formula by typing **/(60*24)**. Press ↵ to confirm the formula entry. Cell D9 displays 07:45 AM as the formatted time value.

4. Click the CopyToClipboard icon. Drag the mouse pointer (now in the form of a pointing-hand icon) over range C:D10..C:D18. When you click on the PasteFromClipboard icon, 1-2-3 copies the formula down column D.

Figure 4.21 shows the schedule worksheet at this point. Examine the formulas that 1-2-3 has copied into cells D9 through D18. Do you see why relative references were appropriate for the addresses in this copy operation?

C	A	B	C	D	E	F	G	H
1	Conference Schedule							
2								
3	Conference: Computing for Video Stores							
4	Place: St. Louis							
5	Date: 15-Oct-93							
6								
7	Event			Start time	Minutes			
8	Coffee and pastries			07:00 AM	45			
9	Introduction			07:45 AM	30			
10	Managing a Video Database			08:15 AM	90			
11	Coffee Break			09:45 AM	15			
12	Managing a Customer Database			10:00 AM	120			
13	Hands-on demonstrations			12:00 PM	60			
14	Lunch and discussion			01:00 PM	60			
15	Setting Up a Computer System			02:00 PM	120			
16	Coffee break			04:00 PM	30			
17	Software Options			04:30 PM	60			
18	No-host cocktail hour			05:30 PM	60			
19								
20								

Now the conference planners want to adjust the schedule for the morning events. They want lunch to take place one half-hour earlier than its currently scheduled time of 1:00. To accomplish this, they decide to cut the time for the second presentation—Managing a Customer Database, in row 12—from 120 to 90 minutes.

- Enter a new value of **90** in cell C:E12.

Watch what happens to the schedule. All the starting times from C:D13 down are adjusted for the half-hour change, as shown in Figure 4.22. The schedule worksheet is working according to design.

Click the SaveFile icon now to update the CONF.WK4 file on disk. Then click on the folder tab for sheet A to activate worksheet A. In the next section, you'll learn to protect the conference worksheet from inadvertent revisions or deletions.

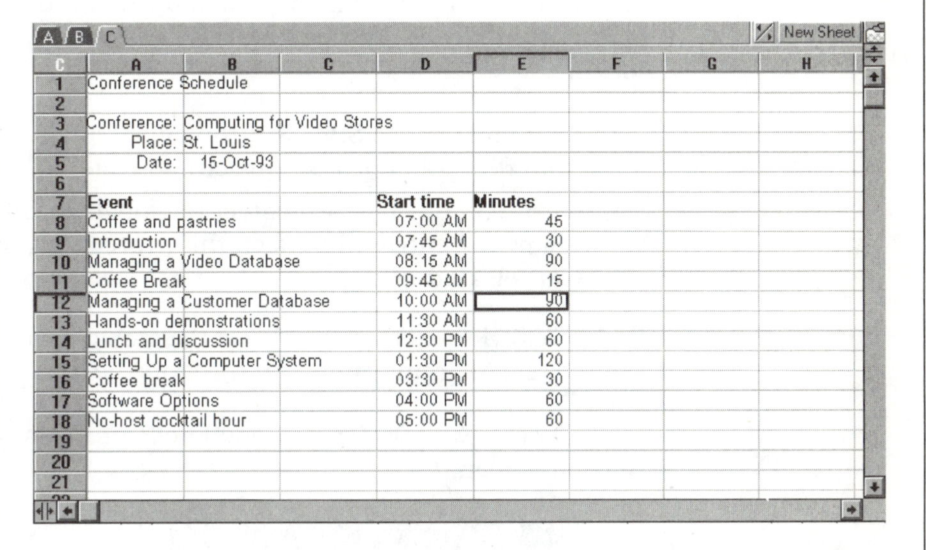

Protecting a Worksheet against Unwanted Revisions

The conference worksheet is designed to be reused. By entering new data values in the "input" ranges, other employees of our fictional company, Computing Conferences, Inc., can quickly project the expenses and profits of future conferences. However, the other employees may not know the difference between worksheet cells that contain simple data entries and cells that contain formulas. They may not understand how carefully designed the worksheet is. By inadvertently making a new entry in a formula cell, they could ruin the structure of the worksheet.

To prevent data entries in certain cells, you can establish a protection scheme for your worksheet. You can prohibit users from making entries in cells that contain formulas, but allow them to enter data in the appropriate "input" cells. Two commands are involved in creating a protection scheme.

1. First you choose <u>S</u>tyle ➤ <u>P</u>rotection to release selected cell ranges from the global protection setting.

2. Next, you use File ➤ Protect to globally protect the worksheet against all entries. In effect, this protects all cells except the ones you released in step 1.

In the following exercise, you'll set the global protection mode. You'll unprotect several input ranges on the worksheet:

1. Choose <u>S</u>tyle ➤ <u>P</u>rotection. The Protection dialog box appears on-screen.

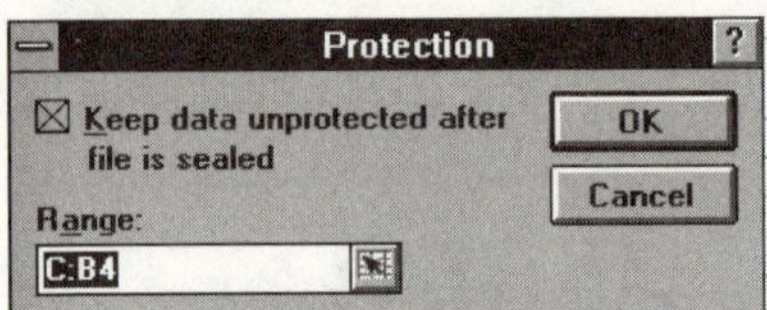

2. We'll use the pointing technique to enter a range into the Range box. Press Tab to make the Protection dialog box temporarily disappear. Use the mouse or keyboard to select range A:B4..A:B8, and press ↵ to confirm the range selection. When the dialog box reappears, A:B4..A:B8 is displayed in the Range box.

3. Click the <u>K</u>eep data unprotected after file is sealed box.

4. Click OK or press ↵ to complete the unprotect operation.

5. Choose <u>F</u>ile ➤ P<u>r</u>otect. The Protect dialog box appears.

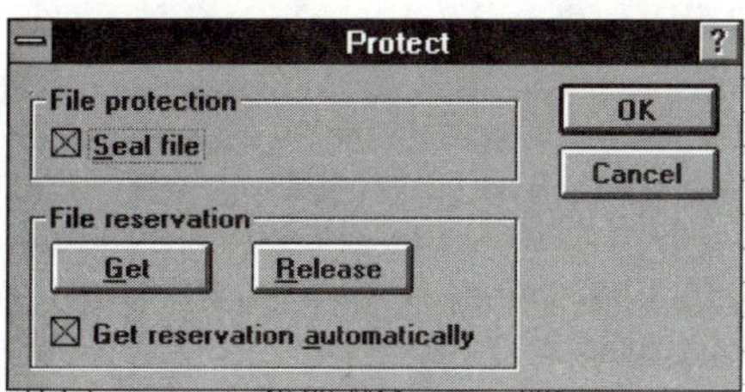

6. Click on the <u>S</u>eal file check box. This protects all cells in the worksheet from being changed *except* for unprotected cells, in our case A:B4..A:B8.

7. Click on OK.

8. Enter a password twice, once in the <u>P</u>assword text box and once in the <u>V</u>erify text box, and click OK to complete the operation.

W A R N I N G

When you set up a protection scheme for a worksheet, don't forget the password. If you forget it, you won't be able to change the scheme—and the cells that are protected now will stay protected no matter what.

Lotus highlights unprotected ranges Now the entire worksheet is protected except for general conference information. Moreover, the unprotected range is now highlighted in blue (or gray if you have a black-and-white display). Highlighting unprotected ranges is 1-2-3's way of letting you know which cells you can enter data in.

To see how unprotected ranges work, try entering a new value into the uprotected range:

- Select cell B8 and enter a new price of **225.00**.

Lotus accepts your new entry and instantly recalculates all the worksheet formulas that depend on it, just as it did before you established protection.

Four more data ranges must be released from protection in the conference worksheet:

RANGE TO UNPROTECT	DESCRIPTION
A:E8..A:F8	The minimum and maximum attendance estimates
A:D13	The retail price of the conference video
A:E17..A:F20	The fixed expenses
A:D24..A:D26	The per-person variable expenses

These ranges all contain data entries that may be changed when the worksheet is used to make projections for another conference.

Releasing a range from protection To release a range from protection, follow these steps with each of the four ranges in the worksheet:

1. Choose Style ➤ Protection for each range in turn.
2. In the Protection dialog box, check the Keep data unprotected after file is sealed box.
3. Click on OK to close the dialog box.

Your worksheet should look like Figure 4.23.

In summary, protecting your worksheet makes it a safer and more valuable tool for distribution to other users. By restricting input to appropriate cells, protection schemes make sure your formulas continue to be reliable.

	A	B	C	D	E	F	G
1			Computing Conferences, Inc.				
2			Profit Projection for a One-Day Conference				
3							
4	Conference:	Computing for Video Stores					
5	Place:	St. Louis					
6	Date:	15-Oct-93			Expected Attendance		
7					Minimum	Maximum	
8	Price:	225			68	128	
9							
10				Per Person	Min. Total	Max. Total	
11	Projected Revenues						
12		Attendance			$15,300.00	$28,800.00	
13		Video Sales		35	$1,190.00	$2,240.00	
14		Total Revenues			$16,490.00	$31,040.00	
15							
16	Projected Expenses - Fixed						
17		Conference room			$1,500.00	$2,000.00	
18		Video production			$1,000.00	$1,000.00	
19		Promotion			$3,500.00	$3,500.00	
20		Travel			$800.00	$800.00	
21		Total Fixed Expenses			$6,800.00	$7,300.00	

"Unprotecting" an Entire Worksheet

For now, deactivate protection mode so you can "unprotect" the worksheet and make more changes to it.

1. Choose File ➤ Protect.
2. Uncheck Seal file and press ↵.
3. Type in your password and press ↵.

Notice that the unprotected ranges are still highlighted in blue (or gray), even though protection is off. If you later decide to restore global protection mode, these unprotected ranges will resume their role as the worksheet's input cells.

The Style Menu: Refining a Worksheet's Appearance

Now it's time to put the finishing touches on the conference worksheet. In this part of the chapter, we'll examine how to use fonts, type styles, borders, lines, and shadings. All of these options are presented in the Style menu, and several are available as SmartIcons as well. In the upcoming exercises, you'll use these SmartIcons and their command equivalents in the Style menu itself:

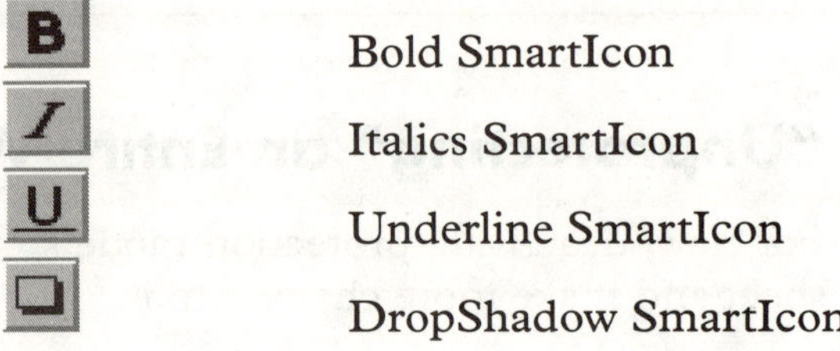

Bold SmartIcon

Italics SmartIcon

Underline SmartIcon

DropShadow SmartIcon

Before we begin making style changes, let's insert blank rows in the worksheet to improve its visual impact.

1. Choose Edit ➤ Insert ➤ Row and insert a blank row in the following four locations (by inserting rows at some of these places you will create two blank rows):

    - Below row 2, which contains the second line of the title
    - Below row 9, which contains the attendance price and the minimum and maximum attendance estimates
    - Below row 16, the Total Revenues line
    - Above row 29, the Projected Profit line

The fastest way to insert a row is to click on the row number and either choose <u>E</u>dit ➤ <u>I</u>nsert or press Ctrl-+.

Fonts, Type Styles, Shadings, and Borders

Begin with the title lines at the top of the worksheet. To place emphasis on these two lines, you'll select a larger font size, display the text in combinations of bold and italics, apply a dark shading to the range, and add a shadowed border called a *drop-shadow*.

1. Preselect range A:B1..A:E2.

2. Choose <u>S</u>tyle ➤ <u>F</u>ont & Attributes. The Font & Attributes dialog box appears, as shown in Figure 4.24.

The Font & Attributes dialog box has three option groups—the Face list, Size list, and Attributes check boxes. The Range box at the bottom tells you the range you preselected.

The Font & Attributes dialog box. Use this dialog box to change typefaces, type size, and font attributes.

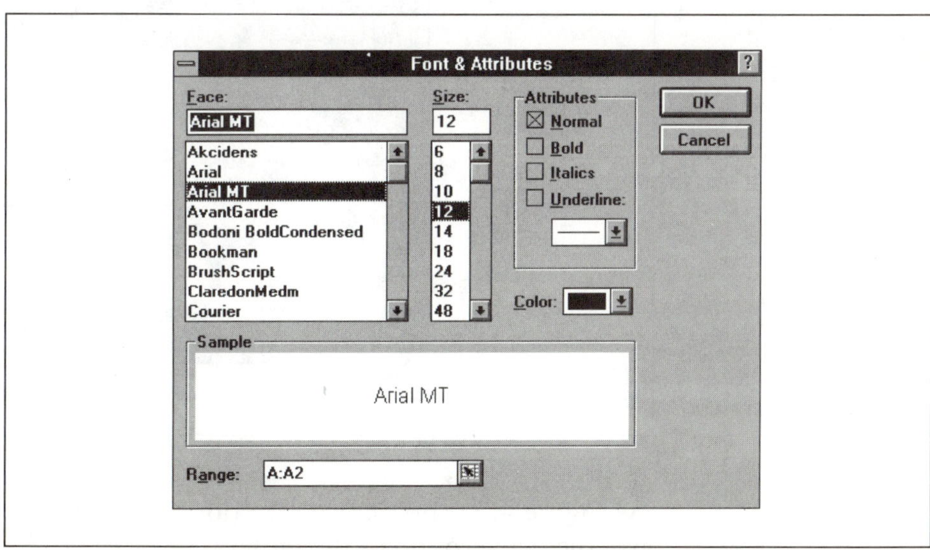

3. In the <u>S</u>ize list, select **14** instead of 10, the default. Now your title will be displayed in Arial MT 14.

4. In the Attributes box, check <u>B</u>old.

5. Click the OK button or press ↵ to confirm your selections.

On the worksheet, the display type of the titles is larger than before. To accommodate this larger point size, 1-2-3 has automatically increased the height of rows 1 and 2.

6. Without changing the range selection, choose <u>S</u>tyle ➤ Lines & Color. The Lines & Color dialog box appears, as in Figure 4.25.

N O T E

1-2-3 automatically increases the height of rows when you increase the type size in a cell.

FIGURE 4.25

The Lines & Color dialog box

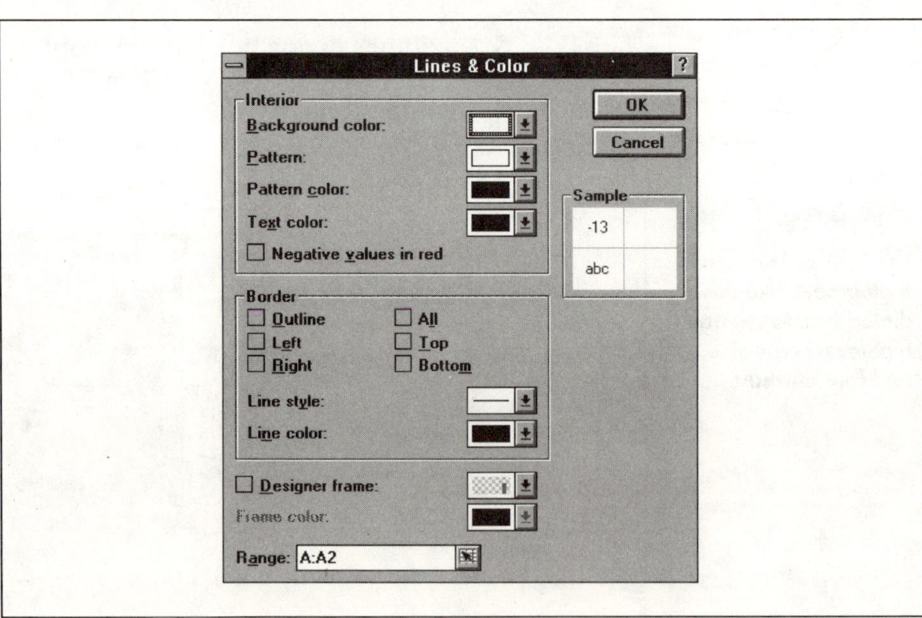

As Figure 4.25 shows, two selections—<u>P</u>attern and Pattern <u>C</u>olor—control the background of the range.

7. Select <u>P</u>attern by clicking the ↓ and pick a background style.

8. Select Pattern <u>C</u>olor and pick a color and shade that you want.

9. Click OK or press ↵ to confirm your pattern and color selection. The Lines & Color dialog box disappears.

10. Click the DropShadow SmartIcon to place a thin border around the selected range and a drop shadow behind the border.

After all these steps, your titles should look like the ones in Figure 4.26.

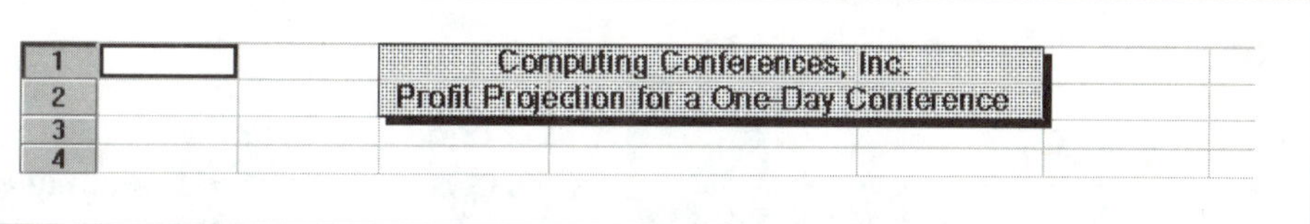

Changing underline styles Besides options for changing typefaces, type size, and attributes, the Fonts & Attributes dialog box (see Figure 4.24) lets you change underlines. Notice the pull-down list below Underline in the Attributes check box. It offers three different underlining styles—a thin line, double line, or bold line.

To activate one of these choices, click the ↓ button to pull down the list and make your selection.

Changing the row height manually As you know, 1-2-3 automatically increases the row height when you select a larger type size than the current one. You can also change the row height manually. To do this, choose <u>S</u>tyle ➤ <u>R</u>ow Height, which produces the Row Height dialog box.

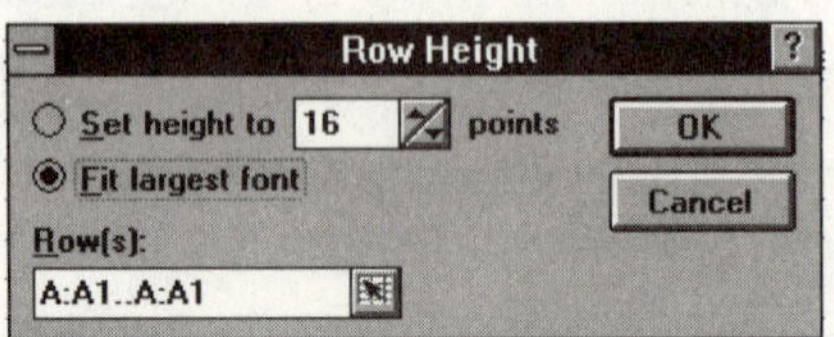

Notice that row height is measured in points, as type size is. Set the height of a row by clicking the up- or down-arrow until you find the row height you want.

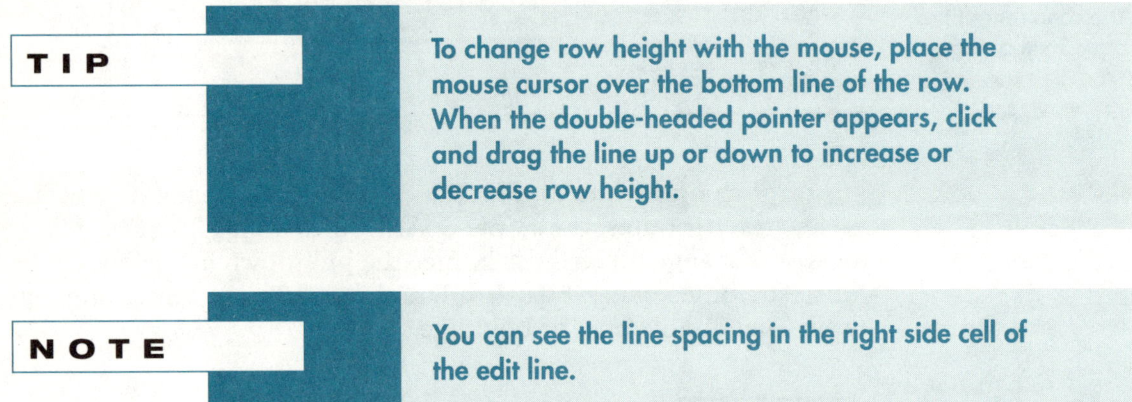

Continue your work by applying the larger font, the bold style, the dark shading, and the drop-shadow border to the Projected Profit line in row 34, just as you did to the titles at the top of the worksheet.

Creating Bold and Italicized Text

Bold and italics are a good way to emphasize or set off text in a worksheet. Practice using the Bold and Italics SmartIcons in the following exercise:

1. Preselect range A:A5..A:A27.

2. Click the Bold icon. Lotus applies the boldface style to all the labels in the range you selected.

3. Select cell B5. Click the Bold icon again, and then click the Italics icon. Now the conference name is displayed in boldface italics.

4. Apply bold and italics to the following cell ranges in the work-sheet: A:B14..A:B15, A:B21..A:B24, A:B28..A:B31, A:E7..A:F7.

Drawing Lines

Next, you'll draw horizontal lines between sections of the worksheet. The Lines & Color dialog box offers a group of border style check boxes (see Figure 4.25). To place a borderline on a worksheet:

1. Choose Style ➤ Lines & Colors.

2. In the Border check box, check Outline, Left, Right, All, Top, or Bottom to tell 1-2-3 where you want the line to appear relative to the current range selection.

3. In the Line Style pull-down list, select the type of line—a thin line, double line, bold line, etc.

4. Click OK to confirm your choices.

Here are the steps for drawing lines on the conference worksheet:

1. Preselect range A:A11..A:F11.

2. Choose Style ➤ Lines & Colors.

3. Select the Top option, and keep the default single-line selection.

4. Click OK or press ↵. Back on the worksheet, a horizontal line now separates the general conference information from the revenues section.

5. Preselect A:A19..A:F19.

6. Once again, choose the Style ➤ Lines & Colors and click on the Top option. After you confirm your selection by clicking OK, a second horizontal line appears on the worksheet. This one sepa-rates the revenues and expense sections.

As a final exercise with the Style menu, you'll learn how to create a name—and a convenient selection method—for frequently used styles or style combinations.

Creating Styles to Simplify Your Work

A *style name* is a single style option or a combination of style effects. You can create a style name—a name for a collection of styles you use often for formatting your spreadsheets—and add it to the Style menu. This way, you can apply formatting changes quickly and be certain that the changes are precisely the ones you want.

To create a style name, you apply styles to a range in a worksheet, choose Style ➤ Named Style, and enter a name for the styles you created in the dialog box. The Named Style dialog box has room for sixteen style names and descriptions.

Here are the general steps for creating a new style name:

1. Using any combination of style SmartIcons or commands from the Style menu, apply one or more styles to a range on the worksheet. Apply styles you use often and would like to apply quickly.

2. With the range still selected, choose Style ➤ Named Style. The Named Style dialog box appears, as in Figure 4.27.

3. Enter a name for the style you are defining. The name can contain up to six characters.

4. Click OK or press ↵.

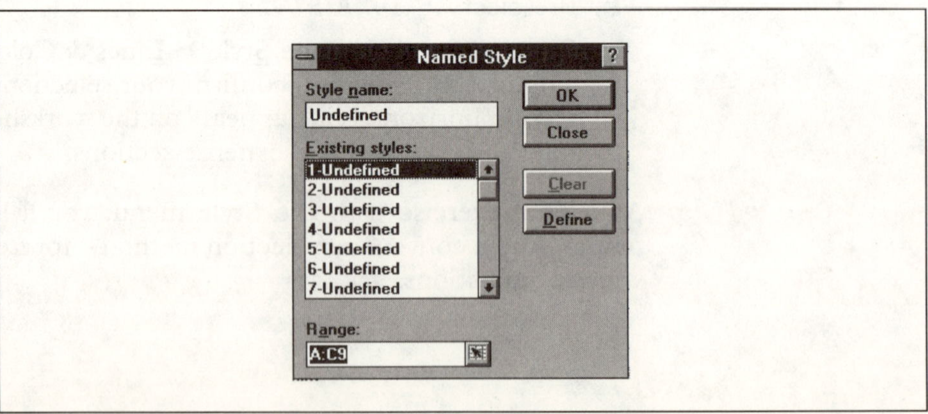

Next time you open the Style menu, the style name you defined will appear in the Named Style dialog box.

To create a standard set of style names for use with all your worksheets, create a master style sheet and save it under a new name each time.

Style names are defined independently for each worksheet file. You can therefore define the style names that are most useful for a given worksheet. As a simple exercise in creating a style name, try defining a name to represent light shading alone:

1. Preselect range A:B5..A:C9.

2. Choose <u>S</u>tyle ➤ <u>L</u>ines & Color.

3. In the Lines & Color dialog box (see Figure 4.25), select a pattern and a light gray pattern color.

4. Click OK or press ↵. Lotus applies a light gray shading to the range you selected.

5. Select cell C9, the bottom-right corner of the shaded range. (In this case, you are going to define a name to represent light shading alone, so you want to make sure that the cell you select does not have any other styles currently applied to it.)

6. Choose <u>S</u>tyle ➤ Named <u>S</u>tyle.

7. In the Name text box, enter the name **LShade**.

8. Click OK or press ↵ to confirm this definition.

9. Preselect A:E9..A:F9, another range to which you want to apply the style shading.

10. Choose <u>S</u>tyle ➤ Named <u>S</u>tyle. Notice that your custom-defined style, LShade, is listed as entry 1.

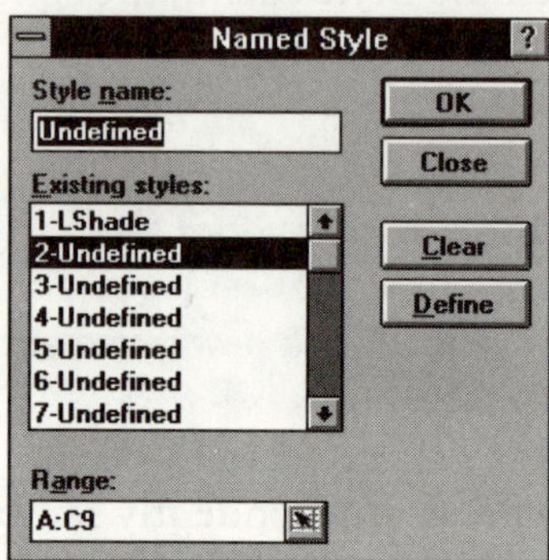

11. Select LShade.

12. Press ↵ to choose LShade. The light shading effect is applied to the preselected range on the worksheet.

13. Apply your new style to create light shading in these areas: cell A:D15, and ranges A:E21..A:F24 and A:D28..A:D30.

So ends your work with the conference worksheet. For more practice with styles, you could apply styles and alignments to the discount and schedule worksheets (B and C) as well. When you complete your work, click the SaveFile icon to update the CONF.WK4 file. In the next section, you'll learn another use for the Lines & Color command.

Applying Colors to a Worksheet

With the Lines & Color command, you can display different parts of a worksheet in different colors. Applying color like this is a good way to mark the differences between sections in a worksheet. In the Lines & Color dialog box (see Figure 4.25), you colorize the labels or values in a range or colorize the background. In addition, by checking the Negative values in red box, you can color negative numbers red and thereby make it easier to distinguish between positive and negative values in a table of numbers.

The best way to gain an appreciation for the Color command is simply to experiment with it in a worksheet.

1. Choose File ➤ New to open a new worksheet window.
2. In cell A1, enter your name.
3. In cell A2, enter your age as a numeric value.
4. In cell A3, enter the negative value **–100**.
5. Preselect range A1..B3.
6. Choose Style ➤ Lines & Color. The Lines & Color dialog box appears.
7. Click the ↓ button next to Text color. A pull-down list of colors appears.

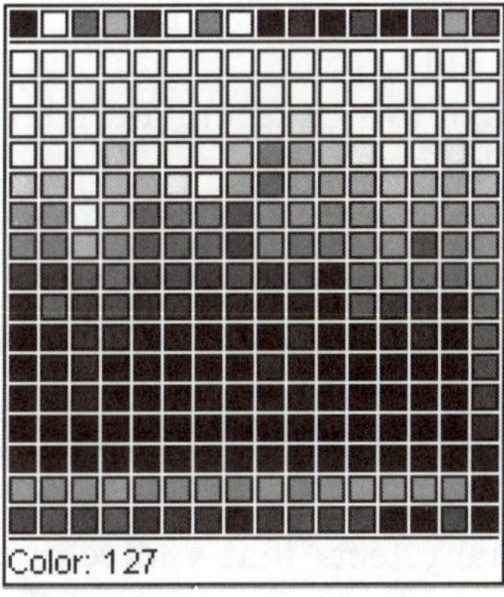

8. Click the dark blue box.
9. Click the ↓ button next to Background color and select the light blue box in the pull-down list. (This color is known as cyan.)
10. Select Negative values in red. An *X* appears in the check box.
11. Click OK or press ↵ to confirm your selections.

On the worksheet, the entire range you selected has a light blue background. Your name and age are displayed in dark blue, but the negative number in cell A3 is displayed in red.

12. Click the Bold SmartIcon and then click the Italics SmartIcon. As you can see, these options have the same effect on color text as they do on black text against a white background.

13. Choose <u>Style</u> ➤ <u>L</u>ines & Color to experiment with other text and background color combinations.

14. When you complete this exercise, close the worksheet window without saving it.

It's easy to overdo colors on a worksheet. But with a little restraint, you can use color to your advantage, clarifying the organization of your work and placing emphasis on particular ranges of labels and values.

In the final sections of this chapter, you'll study the commands that deal with printing a worksheet.

Printing a Worksheet

All the special visual effects that you've created in this chapter can be printed on paper, assuming your printer has the appropriate capabilities. Before sending your worksheet to the printer, however, you'll want to take advantage of several options that affect page layout. Printing the worksheet itself is as simple as clicking the Print SmartIcon. You can see a screen *preview* of the printed page by clicking the Preview SmartIcon. When you take this intermediate step, 1-2-3 displays a preview like the one in Figure 4.28. By examining this screen, you can see the document's layout without actually printing it on paper.

Lotus 1-2-3 offers two SmartIcons for printing, the Print SmartIcon and the PrintPreview SmartIcon. The Print SmartIcon shows a piece of paper

A preview of the printed page. By examining a preview, you can see what a spreadsheet will look like.

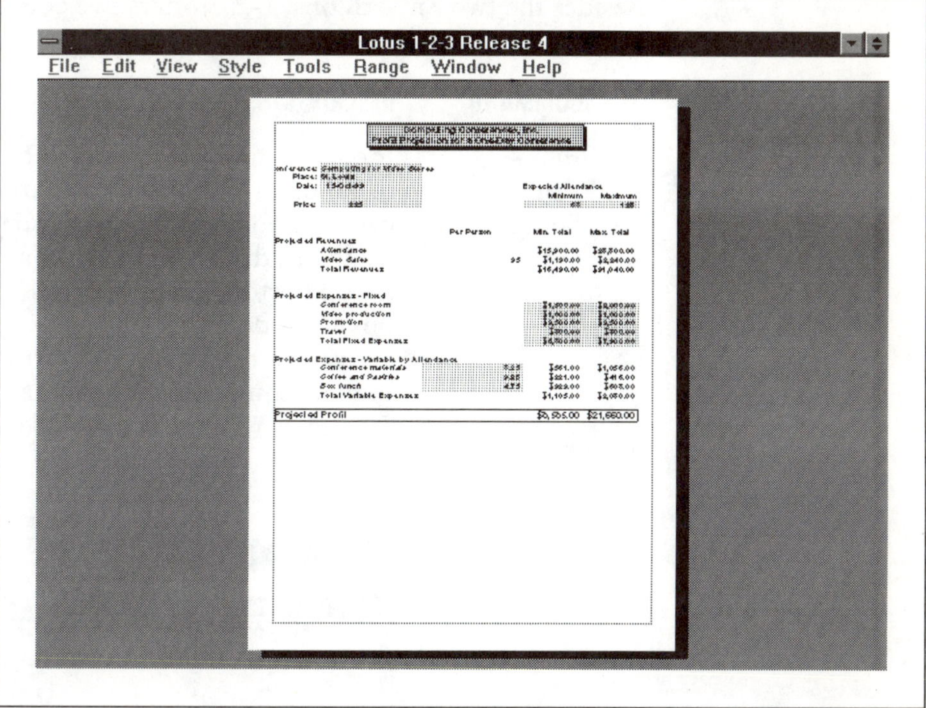

coming out of a printer, and the PrintPreview SmartIcon shows a page similar to the one in Figure 4.28.

Besides the two SmartIcons, 1-2-3 offers five commands for dealing with printing:

COMMAND	DESCRIPTION
File ➤ Printer Setup	Identifies the printer or printers you have installed in Windows. You can select the printer you want to use if two or more are shown in the Printers list box. Clicking the Setup button brings up a Windows dialog box for redefining the characteristics of the active printer. If only one printer is attached to your computer and you have installed it for use in Windows, you will seldom need the File ➤ Printer Setup command.

COMMAND	DESCRIPTION
File ➤ Page Setup	Offers options for controlling how a worksheet is printed.
Style ➤ Page Break	Lets you specify exactly where to place the cut off between pages when printing. In the Page Break dialog box, you can create horizontal (Row) and/or vertical (Column) page breaks, as well as clear previously established page breaks. The Page Break command is useful when printing long single worksheets or printing two or more sheets stored in a single worksheet file.

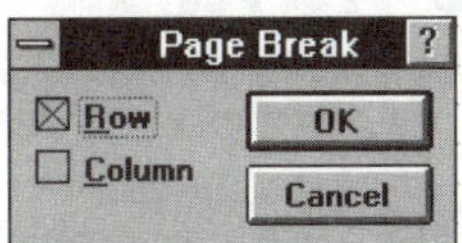

File ➤ Print Preview	Displays an on-screen preview of the page or pages that will be printed. Choosing this command is the same as clicking the PrintPreview icon.
File ➤ Print	Brings up the Print dialog box with many printing options. In the Selected range text box, you can define one or more *print ranges*. A print range is part of a worksheet, either a series of pages or certain columns or rows.

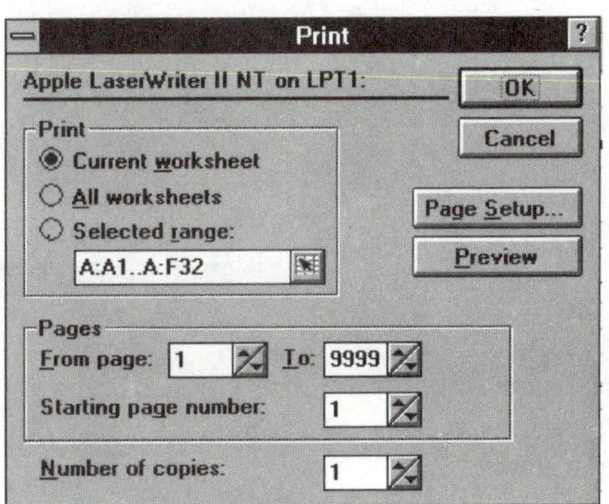

These commands are intuitive and easy to use. However, the Page Setup command options require some explanation.

Establishing the Page Dimensions and Orientations

The Page Setup dialog box, shown in Figure 4.29, includes options for doing the following tasks:

- Creating a header and/or a footer

- Changing the page margins

- Specifying rows or columns of headings that will be printed on every page

- Compressing the print size so the worksheet will fit on a page, or expanding the worksheet so it will fill up a page

- Optionally displaying the worksheet's column letters, row numbers, and grid lines

- Selecting a horizontal (Landscape) or vertical (Portrait) orientation for the worksheet

- Determining whether to print drawings as well as the worksheet

You'll learn about these tasks in turn in the sections ahead.

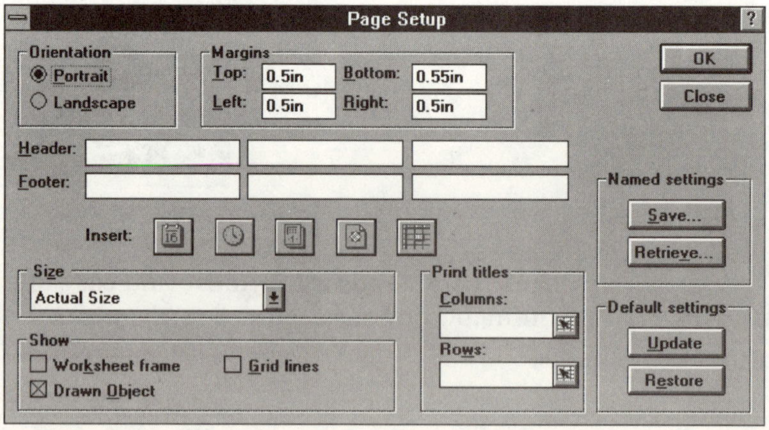

FIGURE 4.29

The Page Setup dialog box. Use this dialog box to define the orientation and dimensions of a page.

Creating Headers and Footers

A *header* is a line of text at the top of each page. A *footer* is a line of text printed at the bottom. Include a header or footer when you print a worksheet to identify the project the worksheet pertains to, the company that developed it, or other information useful to the people who will read the worksheet.

To create a header or a footer, enter the text in the Header and Footer boxes on the Page Setup dialog box.

Using special codes in headers and footers Besides text, you can include five special code characters to represent information in a header or footer:

CHARACTER	ENTERS THIS IN THE HEADER/FOOTER
@	the current date
+	the current time, according to the system clock
#	the current page number
^	the file name of the worksheet
\	the contents of a specified cell

When you enter a backslash (\) in a header or footer to include the contents of a cell, follow the backslash with a cell reference to the cell whose contents you want to print. For example, the following entry in the Header or Footer box tells 1-2-3 to print the contents of cell B2 on each page:

    \A:B2

WARNING The \ code cannot be combined with other text or other codes in a header or footer.

Controlling where headers and footers appear To control the placement of the text or code text in a header or footer, place the text or code in the left, center, or right Header or Footer text box. The text in each box appears on the page in the same relative position. For example, entering @ in the left text box, Conference Planner in the center text box, and Page # in the right text box creates a header or footer that looks something like this:

11-Aug-93   Conference Planner   Page 5

Specifying Margins

In the Margins frame in the Page Setup dialog box (see Figure 4.29) you'll find four text boxes, labeled Top, Bottom, Left, and Right. These boxes are for entering numeric measurements for the four page margins. By default, 1-2-3 assumes that entries are made in inches. For example, if you enter .75 in a box, 1-2-3 converts the entry to 0.75in.

Alternatively, you can use metric measurements instead of inches. To do so, include an mm (millimeter) or cm (centimeter) abbreviation after the number. However, 1-2-3 converts centimeter measurements to millimeters. If you enter .8cm in one margin box, 1-2-3 converts it and all other margin boxes to millimeter measurements.

Printing Headings and Row Labels on Every Page

When you print a long worksheet, you might want to include column headings or row labels from your worksheet on each page of the printout. Imagine a worksheet with 500 rows of data and the column headings displayed in row 1. In the multiple-page printout of this worksheet, you would want the column headings from row 1 at the top of each page. Or imagine a worksheet with dozens of columns and the row labels in column A. You would want the row labels to appear on each page.

To accomplish these effects, you enter references in the Columns and Rows boxes in the Print Titles frame of the Page Setup dialog box (see Figure 4.29). To print one row label or one column head on each page, enter a reference to a single cell in the row or column. For example, a reference to A1 would identify column A in the Columns box or row 1 in the Rows box. Enter a range if you want to print headings from multiple rows or columns. For example, if the column headings in your worksheet are displayed in rows 1 and 2, enter the range A1..A2.

Compressing or Expanding the Printed Worksheet

The Size frame in the Page Setup dialog box (see Figure 4.29) offers a pull-down list box with five options for controlling the page size: Actual size, Fit all to page, Fit columns to page, Fit rows to page, and Manually scale. If your worksheet doesn't quite fit on one page, you can tell 1-2-3 to compress the printout and make it fit a single page. Or, if your worksheet is too small for a page, you can tell 1-2-3 to expand the printout.

Expansion and compression printing options The options for expanding or compressing a worksheet are:

OPTION	DESCRIPTION
Actual size	Does not compress or expand the worksheet in any way (this is the default).
Fit all to page	Compresses the printout so it fits on a single page.
Fit columns to page	Compresses the page in the appropriate dimension to fit all the columns on a page.
Fit rows to page	Compresses the page in the appropriate dimension to fit all the rows on a page.

OPTION	DESCRIPTION
Manually scale	Lets you enter a specific percentage for compressing or expanding. Enter the percentage in the text box. The default value of 100 produces no compression or expansion, a value below 100 compresses the printout, and a value above 100 expands the printout. For example, entering a value of 50 compresses the worksheet size by half (you can enter compression values from 15 to 99). Entering a value of 200 expands the worksheet by a factor of two (you can enter expansion percentages from 101 to 1000).

TIP

Choose File ➤ Preview to view compressed or expanded worksheets before you send them to the printer. Finding just the right percentage usually takes some experimentation.

Printing Grid Lines, the Worksheet Frame, and Drawings

You can print the *worksheet frame* (its column letters and row numbers), grid lines, and drawn objects (drawings, charts, and other graphical elements). To do so, select one or more check boxes displayed in the Show frame of the Page Setup dialog box (see Figure 4.29). Checking Worksheet frame prints the column letters and row numbers, checking Grid lines prints the grid lines, and checking Drawn Objects prints all graphical objects in the worksheet.

Printing in Portrait and Landscape Orientation

By default, 1-2-3 prints a worksheet in *portrait* orientation. Figure 4.28 shows a good example of what portrait orientation looks like. In portrait orientation, the page is longer from top to bottom than it is from side to side. If a table has many columns and fewer rows, you might prefer to print it sideways, with the page longer from side to side than from top to bottom. Printing a page this way is called *landscape* orientation. Figure 4.30 shows a preview of the conference worksheet in landscape orientation.

The Page Setup dialog box (see Figure 29) offers two Orientation buttons, Landscape and Portrait. These options control the orientation of your printout.

FIGURE 4.30

A preview of a page in landscape mode. Print pages in landscape mode if they have many columns and are very wide.

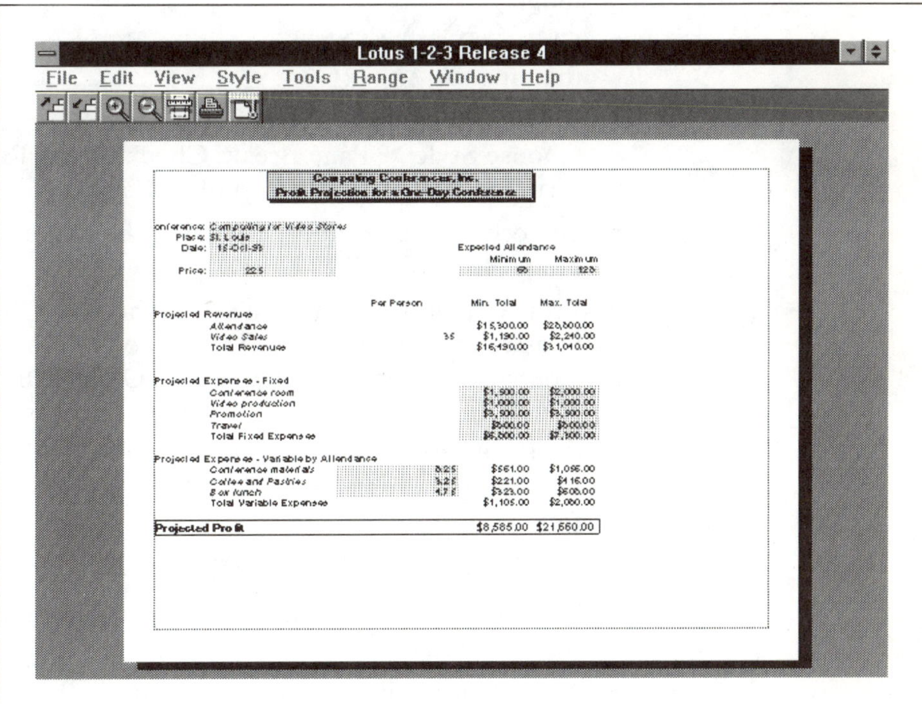

Other Page Setup Options

After you've entered new settings in the Page Setup dialog box, click the Update button to make your settings the defaults, or click the Restore button to keep the old defaults. You can also use the Save and Retrieve buttons to create or read page setup files, containing specific layout settings. Lotus 1-2-3 saves such files with the default extension name .AL4.

Printing the Conference Worksheet

At last, let's print out all the work we've been doing in the last two chapters:

1. On worksheet A, use the mouse to reduce the width of column G to 2. (Because the drop shadow in the profit line intrudes slightly into column G, you'll include this narrowed column in the print range.)

2. Choose Range ➤ Name to assign the name CONFERENCE to the range A:A1..A:G34.

3. Press Ctrl-PgUp to activate worksheet B, and select cell B:A1. Choose Style ➤ Page Break. Checking the Row box, press ↵ to insert a page break at the top of worksheet B.

4. Choose Range ➤ Name to assign the name DISCOUNT to the range B:A1..B:D17.

5. Press Ctrl-PgUp to activate worksheet C. Choose Range ➤ Name to assign the name SCHEDULE to the range C:A1..C:E19. These three new range names—CONFERENCE, DISCOUNT, and SCHEDULE—will simplify the process of specifying a multiple print range, as you'll see in the next step.

6. Choose File ➤ Print. In the Selected range text box, enter the following three names as the multiple print range:

   CONFERENCE;DISCOUNT;SCHEDULE

   Notice the use of the semicolon to separate one range reference from the next.

7. Now click the Page Setup button in the Print dialog box. The Page Setup dialog box appears on the screen.

8. In the Header text box, enter the following coded information:

   @

   in the left text box, and

   Page #

   in the right text box.

9. In the Footer text box, enter the code for printing the contents of a cell in the center text box:

   \A:B1

10. Click the Manually scale option, and enter a value of 110 in the corresponding text box. This setting results in a slightly enlarged printed worksheet.

11. Click OK or press ↵ to complete the Page Setup operation.

12. Back in the Print dialog box, click the Preview button. When the preview screen appears, examine the page layout you are about to print. Press the PgDn key to view page 2 of the upcoming printout.

13. Press Esc to close the preview. Then click the Print icon to print the worksheet.

When you print your worksheet for the first time, you may find that the output is not exactly what you expected it—even if the display from the Preview command seemed correct. You may have to experiment with small adjustments in various settings to achieve the results you want. For example, you might need to make some changes in the Page Setup dialog box, specifically in the margin settings and the Manually scale value. Furthermore, if some values do not print out properly, you might need to increase some column widths on your worksheet. In the end, the best approach to refining the appearance of the printed page is to experiment with the commands and options you've learned about in this chapter.

Summary

In this chapter, you've worked extensively with commands in three different menus—Range, Style, and File.

The Style menu offers commands for applying global property settings to the current worksheet. In particular, the Worksheet Defaults dialog box lets you set the width of all columns on the worksheet, select a global alignment, protect the entire worksheet from inadvertent data entries, and determine whether multiple worksheets in a file will all share the same formatting characteristics.

The Style menu also has commands that apply to selected rows and columns, including the Hide command, which hides one or more columns from view. The Column Width and Row Height commands allow you to adjust the dimensions of columns and rows. The Number Format command contains a list of formats for displaying not only numeric values, but also date and time values.

The View menu offers the Titles commands, Freeze Titles and Clear Titles, for freezing a range of rows or columns on-screen so that they remain in view even when you scroll the worksheet.

The Style menu's Protection command releases selected ranges from the global protection mode. The Edit ➤ Go To command is a useful tool for moving the cell pointer to a cell address or named range on the worksheet.

The Style menu also contains commands that dramatically change the visual properties of a worksheet. In the Font & Attributes dialog box, you can select a display font and choose combinations of bold, italic, and underlined type styles. The Alignment command offers left-alignment, centering, and right-alignment, which can be applied over a single cell or a horizontal range of cells. The Lines & Color command creates lines, borders, and drop-shadow effects on the worksheet, while also allowing you to highlight sections of your worksheet with background and foreground shading.

When you have established all these properties to your own satisfaction, it is time to print the worksheet. The File menu provides four commands for specifying exactly how you want your printed document to look.

Worksheet Formulas and Functions

WRITING formulas is one of the most creative aspects of working with 1-2-3. Without precise and detailed instructions, which are expressed in formulas, a worksheet can do nothing. Formulas establish relationships among data items, supply the steps to complete an operation, produce new values and labels, and define the structure of a worksheet.

Depending upon the task you wish to accomplish, a formula can be succinct and straightforward, or painstakingly complex. To make writing formulas easier, Lotus 1-2-3 includes a library with more than two hundred *functions*. You can include functions in formulas, and in many cases the 1-2-3 functions will serve as substitutes for formulas themselves and do precisely what needs to be done on your spreadsheet. A function is a predefined calculation or operation. Each function is represented by a name that denotes its purpose. All function names in 1-2-3 begin with the at character (@).

Appendix B lists the 1-2-3 functions.

Up to now you've used only one function. To find the total of a column of numbers, you used the @SUM function. Like @SUM, many functions are designed to replace formulas that you would otherwise have to write yourself.

For instance, suppose you had to calculate the monthly payment for a fixed-rate bank loan. You know the principal, the interest rate, and the term in years. You enter loan parameters in a worksheet column and you assign the range names PRINCIPAL, RATE, and TERM to the three cells with the loan data. Next you need to enter a formula for calculating the monthly payment on the loan. Like most people, you cannot produce this formula from memory, so you look it up in a business mathematics book, and carefully enter it in a cell of your worksheet:

```
(PRINCIPAL*RATE/12)/(1–(1+RATE/12)^(–TERM*12))
```

This formula calculates the monthly payment, but at a considerable cost of time and effort on your part.

Fortunately, 1-2-3 offers a much simpler approach for doing this common calculation. The formula for finding a monthly loan payment is @PMT. By using this function, you can calculate the loan payment without having to concern yourself with the details of the formula itself. Here is how you would enter the @PMT function:

```
@PMT(PRINCIPAL,RATE/12,TERM*12)
```

Arguments The three loan parameters are the *arguments* of the @PMT function. In order to make calculations, each function requires at least one argument. In this formula there are three arguments. Moreover, to calculate the *monthly* payment amount, the rate and the term are expressed as monthly values and are divided by 12. As you can see, using the @PMT function is a lot simpler than writing a loan-payment formula yourself.

Functions give you broader options and greater flexibility for designing your worksheet. For example, you can use the @HLOOKUP function to select values from a *look-up table*, a numeric data table organized like an income tax table. With @HLOOKUP, a formula can read data from a two-dimensional data table in a worksheet range.

In short, functions simplify your work and let you do a greater variety of tasks. In this chapter, you'll see examples of @PMT and @HLOOKUP, along with dozens of other functions in several categories.

The Fill command You'll find many exercises to help you understand specific formulas and functions in this chapter. As a quick technique for supplying sample data for these exercises, you'll use a special command on the range menu called Fill. The Fill command enters a sequence of numbers in a range. Following your specifications, each number in a Fill sequence is a fixed amount greater than or less than the one before it. Here is an introductory exercise with the Fill command:

1. On a blank worksheet, preselect range A1..A10.

2. Choose <u>R</u>ange ➤ <u>F</u>ill. The Fill dialog box appears on-screen. Notice the four text boxes.

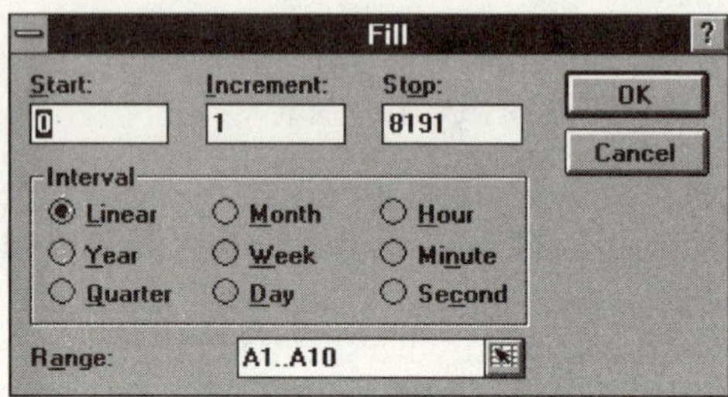

- Start displays the first in the sequence of numbers that Fill will enter in the range. By default, 0 is the start value.

- Increment shows the number by which each subsequent value will either increase or decrease. By default, this value is 1.

- Stop shows the maximum value in the sequence. The Stop value is relevant only if the range you preselected is large enough to display the entire sequence, up to the maximum value. If the range isn't large enough, Fill stops the sequence when the range is full.

- Range displays the notation for the range you preselected.

3. Click OK or press ↵ to accept all the defaults. The Fill command enters a sequence of integers from 0 to 9 in range A1..A10.

4. Preselect the two-dimensional range C2..E6.

5. Choose <u>R</u>ange ➤ <u>F</u>ill again.

6. Type a 5 in the <u>I</u>ncrement text box.

7. Click OK or press ↵.

Fill enters a sequence of values from 0 to 70, incremented by 5, in the three columns in range C2..E6.

8. Preselect the horizontal range A12..F12.

9. Choose <u>R</u>ange ➤ <u>F</u>ill one more time.

10. Enter .75 in the <u>I</u>ncrement text box.

11. Enter a minus sign before the number in the St<u>o</u>p text box.

12. Click OK or press ↵.

Your sheet should look like Figure 5.1. Each value in the new sequence is a fractional amount less than the previous value.

	A	B	C	D	E	F
1	0					
2	1		0	25	50	
3	2		5	30	55	
4	3		10	35	60	
5	4		15	40	65	
6	5		20	45	70	
7	6					
8	7					
9	8					
10	9					
11						
12	0	-0.75	-1.5	-2.25	-3	-3.75
13						

13. When you have examined your work, close the worksheet without saving it.

As the three examples in Figure 5.1 show, the Fill command is a simple but versatile way of entering a series of numbers in a worksheet. You'll use Range ➤ Fill in several exercises in this chapter.

Constructing Formulas

In 1-2-3, you can enter many types of formulas, including numeric formulas, date and time formulas, logical formulas (formulas that return either true or false), and text formulas. You can also check formulas for data errors. All of this is explained in this part of the chapter. But before we learn how to construct formulas, let's look at how to enter the text of the formula itself.

Entering the Text of the Formula

As you know, formulas include a variety of elements:

- Literal data values, such as 3.14 or 1000

- Operators, such as plus (+) and minus (−)

- Functions, such as @SUM and @PMT

- References to cell or range addresses, such as A1, $C$5, and $B$3..$K$7

- References to range names that represent cells or ranges

Lotus 1-2-3 can tell, when you enter certain types of characters, that you are entering a formula. For example, as you learned in Chapters 3 and 4, 1-2-3 knows that a plus sign (+) is often the first character in a formula that starts with a reference to a cell address. Lotus 1-2-3 also recognizes the digits from 1 to 10, a plus sign, a minus sign, a decimal point, an at sign (@), and an open parenthesis as the beginning of a formula.

Formulas that begin with whole numbers Formulas that begin with a number can start with a digit from 0 to 9, an optional plus sign (+), a minus sign (−), or a decimal point (.). You can begin the formula with the first digit of the number, from 0 to 9, if the first element is a positive numeric value. For example, 365*A5 multiplies a positive number, 365, by the value stored in cell A5. If you begin this same formula with the optional plus sign, 1-2-3 will drop the plus sign from the formula after you press ↵. You can enter a minus sign to start formulas that begin with a negative number, as in −19*C2.

Formulas that begin with decimals When the first element in a formula is a decimal value, 1-2-3 makes changes in the format of the entry after you press ↵. For example, if you enter .1-2-3*B1, the number appears this way in the contents box: 0.1-2-3*B1. When the decimal value is very small, 1-2-3 converts it to scientific format. For example, the formula .00001-2-3*B1 becomes 1.23E−05*B1 after you press ↵ to complete the entry.

Formulas that begin with address references You must enter a plus or a minus sign as the first character of a formula that begins with an address reference. For example, +E19*10 tells 1-2-3 to multiply the value in cell E19 by 10, and −E19*10 multiplies the result by −1. After you enter the plus or minus sign, you can type the address reference with the keyboard or use a pointing technique to enter the address.

Formulas that begin with functions Entering an at character (@) tells 1-2-3 that you are entering a formula that begins with a built-in function. A function can stand by itself as a complete entry in a cell or it can be one of several elements in a formula. For example, the following function finds the sum of a range of values:

    @SUM(C5..C10)

 And this formula multiplies the sum of C5..C10 by 25:

    @SUM(C5..C10)*25

In both cases, the result appears where you entered the formula.

Formulas that begin with a parenthesis Any formula can begin with an open parenthesis character, as you learned in Chapter 3. Put parentheses around operations in a formula when you want to override 1-2-3's default order of precedence. For example, the formula (A1+A2)*5 adds two numbers together and multiplies the sum by 5, whereas A1+A2*5 multiplies A2 by 5 and adds A1 to the result.

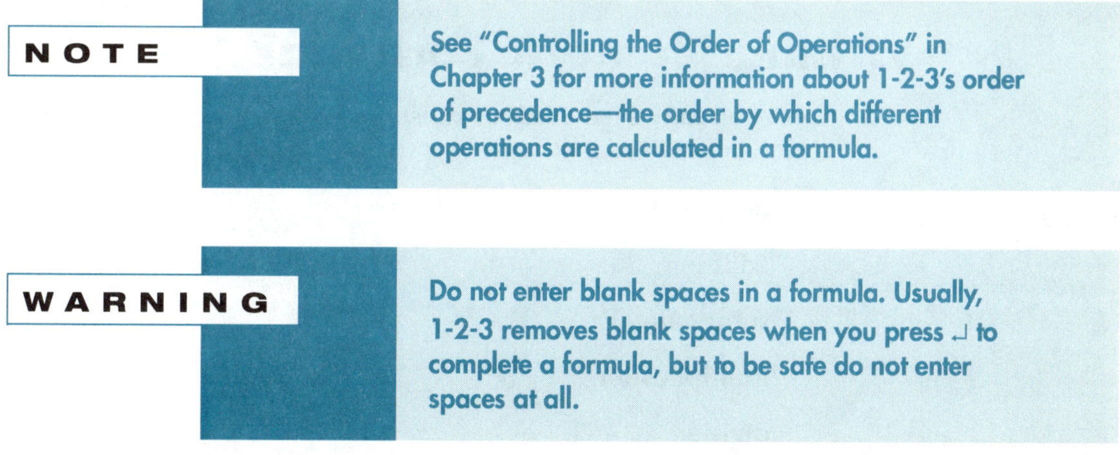

N O T E

See "Controlling the Order of Operations" in Chapter 3 for more information about 1-2-3's order of precedence—the order by which different operations are calculated in a formula.

W A R N I N G

Do not enter blank spaces in a formula. Usually, 1-2-3 removes blank spaces when you press ↵ to complete a formula, but to be safe do not enter spaces at all.

Entering Comments in Formulas

You can include a short note or comment at the end of a formula to help you remember what it does. To place a note at the end of a formula, type a semicolon (;) right after the formula itself and then type your note. For example, consider the following formula and comment:

@PMT(PRINCIPAL,RATE/12,TERM*12); The monthly payment.

Examining this formula later on, you could look in the contents box and see that it is the formula for a monthly mortgage payment. Entering comments is an important feature, especially in a complicated worksheet with many formulas.

Writing notes and comments is a simple way to *document* the structure of a worksheet and be able to see precisely how it is organized. Documenting a worksheet makes revising it easier if you ever want to change the way your formulas operate.

By the way, a formula entry—along with a note or comment—can be as long as 512 characters. You are unlikely ever to reach this maximum, even if you write extensive comments along with your formulas, but you can go to 512 characters if you want to.

Writing Numeric Formulas

You've already seen the four most common numeric *operations* in action and the operators that represent them:

OPERATION	OPERATOR
addition	+
subtraction	−
multiplication	*
division	/

Notice the distinction between *operation* and *operator*. An operation is a calculation that 1-2-3 performs, but an operator is the character or symbol that represents the operation in a formula.

Exponentiation Lotus 1-2-3 has another numeric operation known as *exponentiation*. Given a base value x and an exponent y, this operation finds x to the power of y. In 1-2-3, exponentiation is represented by the caret symbol (^). For example, in the formula 5^3, the result is 125, or 5 to the power of 3. The exponent can also be fractional, in which case exponentiation produces a root value. For example, the formula +A1^(1/4) finds the fourth root of the value in A1. Try this formula on your worksheet:

1. Enter **2401** in cell A1.
2. Enter **+A1^(1/4)** in cell A2.

The result displayed in A2 is 7.

In the order of operations followed by 1-2-3, exponentiation has the highest precedence—that is, exponentiation is performed before all other numeric operations. Table 5.1 shows a complete list of numeric operations in their order of precedence.

TABLE 5.1: Numeric Operations in Their Order of Precedence

ORDER	NUMERIC OPERATION	SYMBOL
1	Exponentiation	^
2	Positive and negative signs	+ and −
3	Multiplication and division	* and /
4	Addition and subtraction	+ and −

As you know, parentheses override this order of precedence. For example, given the formula +A1^(1/4), 1-2-3 performs the division before the exponentiation. Moreover, if there is more than one set of parentheses in a formula, they are worked from left to right, with the innermost equations performed first.

In 1-2-3, date and time arithmetic operations are treated as numeric formulas and the results are displayed in date or time formats. You looked at date and time arithmetic in Chapter 4. In the upcoming section of this chapter, you'll see some further examples.

Writing Date and Time Formulas

In the worksheet that you developed in Chapter 4, you subtracted 90 days and 45 days from a conference date to calculate two different payment due dates. Similarly, on the schedule worksheet you added the length in minutes of each conference activity to the starting time to calculate the starting time for the next activity. Both of these operations involved adjusting *chronological values* (dates or times) by a fixed amount of elapsed time (days or minutes) to produce a new chronological value.

Finding the difference between two dates Another important operation finds the difference between two chronological values. Specifically, you can subtract one date from another in a worksheet. For example, this formula subtracts a range named DATE2 from a range named DATE1 to give the number of days between the two dates:

    +DATE1–DATE2

If DATE1 is later on the calendar than DATE2, the result is a positive value, but if DATE1 is earlier on the calendar, the result is a negative value.

A variety of business calculations require you to find the difference between two dates. For example, suppose you need to calculate the number of days a customer takes to pay an invoice—that is, the difference between the billing date and the payment date. On an employee worksheet, you might want to know the number of days that have elapsed since an employee's last evaluation, or the number of days since the employee was hired.

Finding the difference between two times You can also subtract one time value from another. For example, this formula subtracts a range named TIME2 from a range named TIME1 to give the elapsed time expressed as a decimal fraction:

    +TIME1–TIME2

Again, the result of the subtraction is positive if TIME1 is later than TIME2, or negative if TIME1 is earlier than TIME2. One common use for subtracting time values is to determine the length of time spent on a given task or project.

The following exercise helps you experiment with date and time values:

1. On a blank worksheet, preselect range A1..B5.

2. Choose Style ➤ Number Format, and select the first date format (31-Dec-90) from the Format list. Click OK to confirm.

3. Preselect range A1..A5.

4. Choose Range ➤ Fill and enter **15-Jul-93** in the Start text box, 1 in the Increment text box, **12-Aug-93** in the Stop text box, and Week in the Interval options box. Click OK or press ↵.

A sequence of dates from 15-Jul-93 to 12-Aug-93 appears in range A1..B5 on the worksheet.

5. Enter today's date in cell B1. Use the 31-Dec-93 date format for the entry.

6. Use the CopyToClipboard and PasteFromClipboard SmartIcons to copy the date down column B, to the range B2..B5.

7. Enter the formula **+A1–B1** in cell C1. The result displayed in C1 is the number of days between the dates in A1 and B1.

8. Use the CopyToClipboard and PasteFromClipboard icons again to copy this formula down column C, to range C2..C5.

Your worksheet should look like the upper half of Figure 5.2. Of course, the number of days displayed in column C on your worksheet depends on the date you entered in column B.

9. Preselect range A8..B12 on the same worksheet.

FIGURE 5.2

Experimenting with date and time arithmetic

	A	B	C	D	E	F
1	15-Jul-93	04-Jun-93	41			
2	22-Jul-93	04-Jun-93	48			
3	29-Jul-93	04-Jun-93	55			
4	05-Aug-93	04-Jun-93	62			
5	12-Aug-93	04-Jun-93	69			
6						
7						
8	06:00 AM	07:15 AM	-1.25			
9	09:00 AM	07:15 AM	1.75			
10	12:00 PM	07:15 AM	4.75			
11	03:00 PM	07:15 AM	7.75			
12	06:00 PM	07:15 AM	10.75			
13						

10. Choose Style ➤ Number Format and select the second time format (11:59 AM) from the Format list. Click OK.

11. Preselect range A8..A12.

12. Choose Range ➤ Fill and enter **6:00** in the Start text box, **3** in the Increment text box, **18:00** in the Stop text box, and Hours in the Interval options box. Click OK or press ↵.

A sequence of time values from 6:00 AM to 6:00 PM appears in the range you selected.

13. Enter the current time in cell B8, and then use the CopyToClipboard and PasteFromClipboard icons to copy this time value down column B, to range B8..B12.

14. Enter the formula **(A8–B8)★24** in cell C8.

The result displayed in C8 is the number of hours elapsed between the two time values in A8 and B8. Now you see why the formula multiplies the difference by 24 in order to calculate the elapsed time in hours.

15. Copy this formula down column C, to range C9..C12.

The lower half of the worksheet in Figure 5.2 shows the result. Again, your own worksheet will differ according to the time value you entered in column B. Study Figure 5.2 carefully and make sure you understand the two operations represented in the worksheet. Later in this chapter you'll examine other chronological operations, represented by 1-2-3's built-in date and time functions.

16. Close the worksheet without saving it after you have completed the exercise.

Writing Logical Formulas

The purpose of a *logical formula* is to determine whether a condition is true or false. A *condition* is typically expressed as a relationship between two or more data values on a worksheet. As the result of a logical formula, 1-2-3 generates a numeric value:

- A value of 1 represents *true*
- A value of 0 represents *false*

To build logical formulas, you use 1-2-3's *relational* and *logical operators*.

Relational operators   The six relational operators express relationships of equality or inequality between pairs of numbers. The relational operators are shown in Table 5.2.

TABLE 5.2:   The Relational Operators

OPERATOR	MEANING
=	is equal to
<>	is not equal to
<	is less than
>	is greater than
<=	is less than or equal to
>=	is greater than or equal to

Here is an example of a logical formula that compares the values stored in cells A1 and B1:

```
+A1<B1
```

This formula results in a value of 1 (true) if the number stored in A1 is less than the number stored in B1; or a value of 0 (false) if the number in A1 is greater than or equal to the number in B1.

The logical operators The three logical operators are #NOT#, #AND#, and #OR#. Logical operators are always enclosed by number signs. The #AND# and #OR# operators are *binary*, meaning that they are designed to work with two logical values, whereas the #NOT# operator is *unary*, meaning that its role is to modify the result of a single logical value. In the following descriptions, which help explain logical operators, VAL1 and VAL2 are range names whose cells contain logical values of true or false:

- The expression #NOT#VAL1 results in the opposite value of VAL1. If VAL1 is true, #NOT#VAL1 is false; if VAL1 is false, #NOT#VAL1 is true.

- The expression +VAL1#AND#VAL2 is true if both VAL1 and VAL2 are true. If either VAL1 or VAL2 is false, or if both are false, the #AND# expression is also false.

- +VAL1#OR#VAL2 is true if either VAL1 or VAL2 is true, or if both are true. If both VAL1 and VAL2 are false, the #OR# expression is also false.

NOTE You can begin a logical formula with the # character as long as the formula begins with the #NOT# operator.

Here is an example of a logical formula that uses the #AND# operator:

```
+B1>A1#AND#B2>A2
```

This formula results in a value of 1 (true) if both of the relations are true—that is, if the value in B1 is greater than the value in A1 *and* the value in B2 is greater than the value in A2. If one or both of the two relations are false, the formula itself results in a value of 0 (false). You'll see more examples of #AND# in the upcoming exercise.

Logical formulas are often useful as entries in a worksheet, especially in database applications. Moreover, logical expressions appear as arguments in a 1-2-3 function named @IF. As you'll learn later in this chapter, the @IF function chooses between two values, depending on the result of a logical expression.

Here is an exercise that demonstrates the use of logical formulas:

1. On a blank worksheet, enter the following six integers in range A1..B3:

CELL	ENTRY
A1	73
A2	53
A3	1
B1	0
B2	94
B3	32

2. Enter the following labels in column A, from A6 through A11:

CELL	ENTRY
A6	**A1 less than B1.**
A7	**A2 greater than or equal to B2.**
A8	**Opposite of B1.**
A9	**Opposite of A3.**
A10	**All values in B greater than values in A.**
A11	**Any value in B greater than value in A.**

3. Preselect range A6..D11 and click the Bold SmartIcon to display the six labels in boldface.

4. Choose the <u>S</u>tyle ➤ <u>A</u>lignment command, check the Align over columns option, and click the Right option. Click OK or press ↵.

5. Enter the following logical formulas into column E, from E6 to E11:

CELL	ENTRY
E6	+A1<B1
E7	+A2>=B2
E8	#NOT#B1
E9	#NOT#A3
E10	+B1>A1#AND#B2>A2#AND#B3>A3
E11	+B1>A1#OR#B2>A2#OR#B3>A3

Figure 5.3 shows the results. You can see that each logical formula has produced a value of 1 or 0, representing true or false. By comparison, Figure 5.4 shows the same worksheet with range E6..E11 displayed in the Text format, so you can see the formulas themselves. Study each formula, and make sure you understand why it produces the value it does.

FIGURE 5.3

Using logical and relational operators to create a series of logical formulas

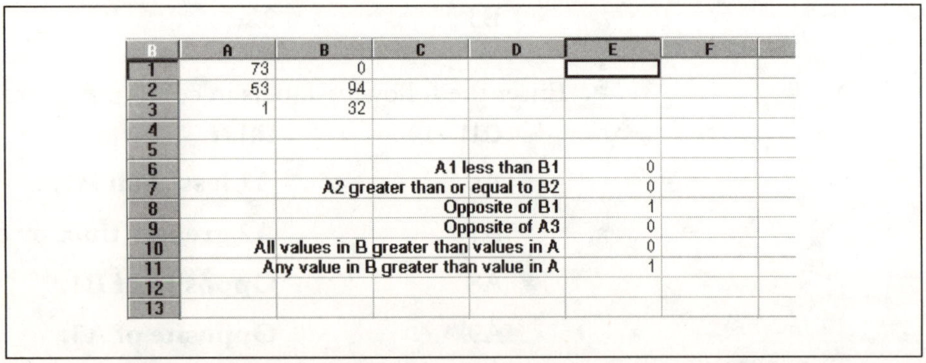

	A	B	C	D	E	F
1	73	0				
2	53	94				
3	1	32				
4						
5						
6			A1 less than B1		0	
7			A2 greater than or equal to B2		0	
8			Opposite of B1		1	
9			Opposite of A3		0	
10			All values in B greater than values in A		0	
11			Any value in B greater than value in A		1	
12						
13						

You'll learn more about logical values when you study 1-2-3's built-in logical functions later in this chapter.

All the formulas you've written up to now have resulted in numeric values. Although date, time, and logical formulas produce results that have special non-numeric meanings, the results are numeric nonetheless. In the next section, you'll learn that 1-2-3 also recognizes formulas that produce labels, or *text* values.

	A	B	C	D	E	F	G
1	73	0					
2	53	94					
3	1	32					
4							
5							
6				A1 less than B1	+A1<B1		
7				A2 greater than or equal to B2	+A2>=B2		
8				Opposite of B1	#NOT#B1		
9				Opposite of A3	#NOT#A3		
10			All values in B greater than values in A		+B1>A1#AND#B2>A2#AND#B3>A3		
11			Any value in B greater than value in A		+B2>A2#OR#B3>A3#OR#B4>A4		
12							

Writing Text Formulas

A text formula combines two or more labels to produce a new text value. Lotus 1-2-3 has one text operation, called the *text operator*. It is represented by the ampersand character (&). The text operator joins two text values. In other software packages, what 1-2-3 calls the text operation is known as *concatenation*.

You may join any of the following in formulas to create a text data item:

- References to cells that contain labels. As always, a cell reference can appear as an address or a range name.

- *Literal strings*—that is, sequences of characters enclosed in double quotation marks

- Built-in 1-2-3 functions that produce text values

Each data item in a text formula is joined to the previous one by the text operator. For example, the following formula joins labels stored in cells A1 and A2 with a literal string value:

    +A1&" and "&A2

Notice that the formula begins with a plus sign, just like a numeric formula, and that the blank spaces are enclosed by the quotation marks. This is the one place where spaces are legal in a 1-2-3 formula.

Here is a brief exercise with a text formula:

1. On a blank worksheet, enter the labels from the first several lines of the conference worksheet, as shown in rows 1 through 5 of Figure 5.5.

FIGURE 5.5

Creating a text formula using the text cells D1, B4, and B5

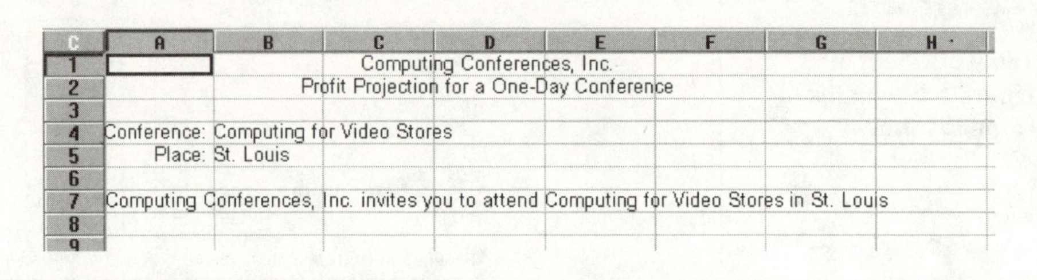

2. In cell A7, enter the following text formula:

   +B1&", invites you to attend "&B4&" in "&B5&"."

   You can use the pointing technique to enter the cell references into the formula. Figure 5.5 shows the result of this formula—a sentence displayed across row 7.

3. Change the label in cell B4 to **Computing for Lawyers**.

4. Change the label in cell B5 to **New York**.

After each one of these changes, 1-2-3 recalculates the value of the text formula in cell A7. The result is shown in Figure 5.6.

FIGURE 5.6

The worksheet after changing the contents of cells B4 and B5

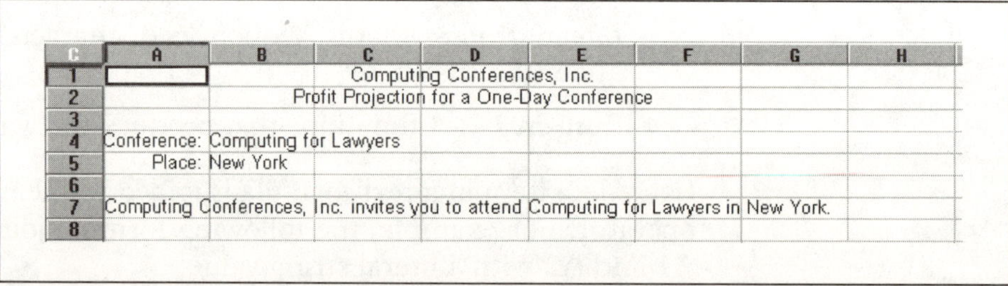

You'll learn much more about text formulas when you examine 1-2-3's built-in string functions later in this chapter.

Correcting Errors in Formulas

Occasionally, 1-2-3 responds to a new formula entry by displaying ERR in the formula's cell. The ERR message means that there is an error in the formula. Because of the error, 1-2-3 cannot calculate the result. Sometimes the error is located in the formula itself, and sometimes the problem is with the data that the formula reads from other cells. In either case, when you see ERR in a cell you must go back and investigate the formula and perhaps other entries in your worksheet.

A number of problems can cause the ERR message. Here are three of the most common:

- A reference to an undefined range name

- An inappropriate mixture of data types in a formula—for instance, a numeric data value in a text formula or a text value in a numeric formula

- An attempt to divide by zero in a numeric formula (division by zero is undefined in 1-2-3)

In the following exercise, you'll simulate these three error conditions by entering formulas devised to produce the ERR value. Then you'll correct the errors by changing values on the worksheet:

1. On a blank worksheet, widen column A to a setting of 16.

2. Enter the following data values:

CELL	ENTRY
A1	**Lotus 1-2-3 Release 4**
A2	**for Windows**
A3	**3**
A4	**0**

D	A	B
1	Lotus 1-2-3 Release 4	
2	for Windows	
3	3	
4	0	
5		

3. Preselect cell A1 and choose <u>R</u>ange ➤ <u>N</u>ame.

4. Enter **TITLE1** as the range name for this cell. Click on <u>A</u>dd and then click on OK or press ↵.

5. Enter the following text formula into cell A6:

+TITLE1&" "&TITLE2

Lotus 1-2-3 responds by displaying ERR in the cell. Can you identify the problem in the formula?

6. Enter the text formula **+A2&A3** into cell A7.

The response is the same—another ERR message. Once again, examine the worksheet's data and try to find the error in the formula.

7. Finally, enter the numeric formula **365/A4** into cell A8. A third ERR message appears in column A.

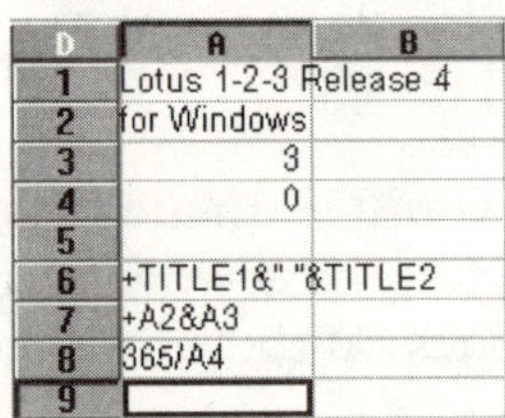

Now begin correcting the conditions that produced the three ERR values. In step 3, we asked 1-2-3 to concatenate two named ranges, but the second range was not named. Let's name the second range.

1. Preselect cell A2 and choose <u>R</u>ange ➤ <u>N</u>ame. Enter **TITLE2** as the range name for the cell.

As soon as you complete this operation, 1-2-3 recalculates the formula in cell A6, which previously contained a reference to an undefined range name. Now the formula's result appears as a text value.

In step 4, we tried to concatenate a text string with a numeric value. Let's fix that.

2. Select cell A3 and enter 3 as a label rather than a value:

    a Press the spacebar to switch 1-2-3 into Label mode.
    b Type **3** and press ↵.

Now 1-2-3 recalculates the text formula in cell A7, which previously contained an unusable reference to a numeric value.

Finally, in step 5 we tried to divide 365 by zero. Many spreadsheet and database programs have problems with *divide-by-zero* operations. To correct this:

3. Select cell A4 and enter a value of 5.

Lotus 1-2-3 recalculates the numeric formula in cell A8. Because the denominator is no longer zero, 1-2-3 successfully calculates the numeric result of the formula.

Here are the results of all three formulas after you complete these corrections:

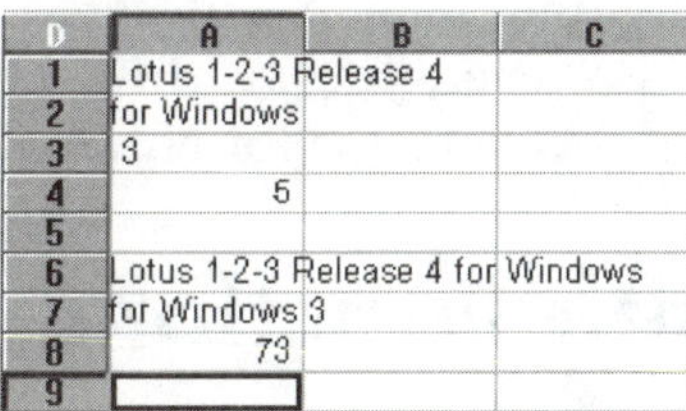

As you know from your experience with the conference worksheet, formulas are often interconnected in a complex system of calculations. When 1-2-3 detects an error in one formula, all dependent formulas are also evaluated as ERR. So a single error condition can produce ERR messages all over your worksheet. Conversely, a single correction can take away all of the ERR messages.

Using Functions

Lotus 1-2-3's function library is one of the program's most important features. The library includes groups of special-purpose functions designed for particular fields of work, such as accounting, engineering, and statistics. Other functions are designed for general use. Functions are among the tools you use most frequently in the 1-2-3 spreadsheet.

A library of over two hundred functions seems hard to master. But over time you'll identify the dozen or so that are most useful to you, and you'll become adept at using them. You can learn about the other functions on occasions when you need to learn them.

The 1-2-3 documentation divides the function library into ten categories: Calendar, Database, Engineering, Financial, Information, Logical, Lookup, Mathematical, Statistical, and Text. In these categories, you can find useful tools in unexpected places. You will also find yourself mixing functions from different categories to solve problems on a worksheet.

This part of the chapter presents a selective survey of the most commonly used worksheet functions. You'll study additional functions in other chapters. Appendix B lists the functions in annotated form. Before studying the function categories, however, you need to see how to get help with functions and what the right format is for entering them.

Getting Help with Functions

Fortunately, 1-2-3 offers you detailed and substantial help when you need to learn how to use a new function. The help comes in two forms:

- **Pressing F3.** After you type the @ character in a cell to enter a function, you can press F3 to view the @Function Names dialog box, shown in Figure 5.7. This dialog box contains a complete list of the 1-2-3 functions. When you select a name from the list, 1-2-3 copies the function directly to the edit line.

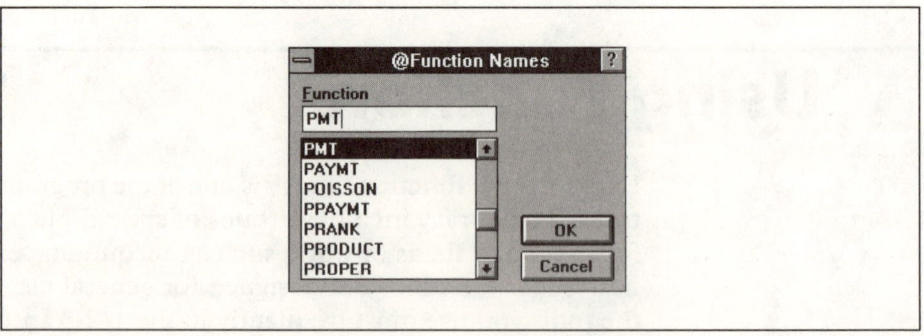

- **Pressing F1.** With a function name displayed in the edit line, you can press F1 to view help information concerning the function.

To see how the @Function Names dialog box works, imagine that you are building a worksheet to calculate the monthly payment on a bank loan. You are ready to enter the formula for the payment, and you know that 1-2-3 has a function that will do the job, but you can't recall its name or how it is used. Here are the steps you take to get help:

1. Type @ to begin a function entry.
2. Press F3. Lotus 1-2-3 displays the @Function Names dialog box.
3. Press the Tab key once to activate the list box.
4. Type **P** to jump to the function names that begin with *P*, and use the arrow keys to highlight the PMT function, as in Figure 5.7.
5. Press ↵ to select this function. Lotus 1-2-3 enters the function into the cell and the Function text box.
6. Move the cursor to the @ sign in either text box and press F1 to view the help topic for this function.

The Help window appears on the screen, as shown in Figure 5.8. This Help topic describes the PMT function in detail, giving you all the information you need to use the function successfully.

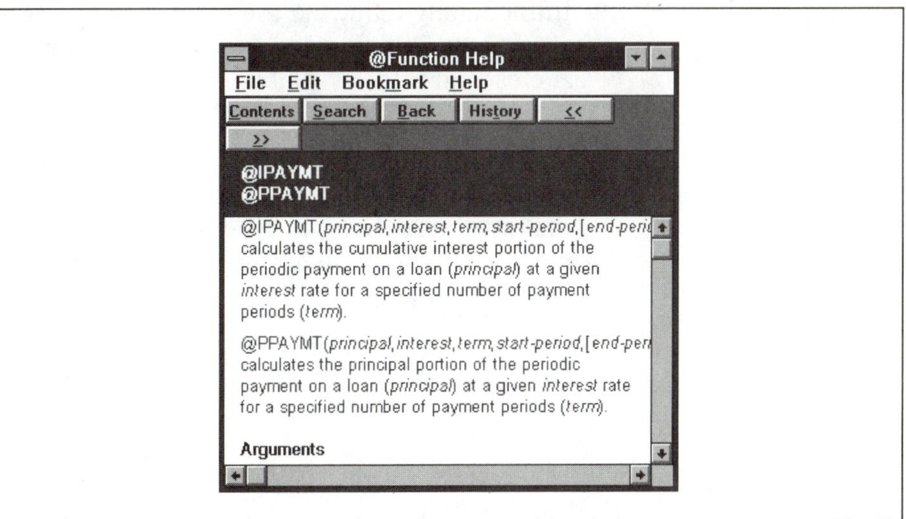

7. After you have read the information, double-click the Minimize button on the Help window. Then continue entering the function in the cell.

Of course, if you already know exactly how a function works, you can enter its name and arguments from the keyboard without using either of these help features. But even experienced users rely on the 1-2-3 Help system for reviewing the details of functions.

The Right Format for Entering Functions

Functions conform to a standard format, with only a few variations. To examine this format, take another look at the function discussed at the beginning of this chapter:

    @PMT(PRINCIPAL;RATE/12;TERM*12)

This @PMT function illustrates the general features of every function:

- A function name consists of the @ character followed by the predefined name of the function itself. If you misspell a function name, 1-2-3 will not recognize your entry. (If you are not sure how a function is spelled, press F3 and select a function from the @Function Names dialog box.)

- Immediately following the function name is an open parenthesis character. This character marks the beginning of the argument list. A close parenthesis character goes at the end of the list.

- Between the parentheses, enter the arguments as required. Each argument is separated from the next by a semicolon, and no spaces are allowed. An argument can be expressed in any form that produces the right type of data—as a cell reference, a range name, an expression, or even as another function name.

- In the 1-2-3 library, you'll find a list of the correct number and type of arguments for each function. A few functions take no argument. Do not enter parentheses after these functions. Moreover, some functions have optional arguments, or varying lists of arguments.

You'll soon grow accustomed to this function format and its variations in upcoming exercises.

Statistical Functions

Statistical functions are used for investigating groups of numbers. For example, you can use the statistical functions to count the number of entries in a list or to find the sum, the average, the largest value, or the smallest value. You can also use statistical functions to calculate the more esoteric statistics known as *variance* and *standard deviation*.

Here are brief descriptions of the ten most commonly used statistical functions:

FUNCTION	DESCRIPTION
@AVG	Calculates the average value in a list of numbers.
@COUNT	Counts the number of cells in a range that contain entries.
@MAX *and* @MIN	Find the largest and smallest numeric values in a list.
@STD *and* @STDS	Give the standard deviation, calculated as the square root of the variance. @STD supplies the standard deviation for a population—that is, the square root of @VAR. @STDS produces the result for a sample, or the square root of @VARS.
@SUM	Finds the total of a list of numbers.
@SUM PRODUCT	Performs, as its name indicates, two operations in one efficient step. First it multiplies corresponding values in a list of ranges, and then it finds the sum of all the multiplication products.

FUNCTION	DESCRIPTION
@VAR *and* @VARS	Represent two different ways of calculating the variance, each a measure of how the numbers in a list diverge from the average. A large variance means a great divergence, and a small variance means little divergence. The @VAR function performs the calculation known as the *population* variance, or the n method, a technique used to analyze a complete list of values from a given application. The @VARS function performs the *sample* variance, or the $n-1$ method, a technique designed for calculating the variance when the list is only a sample of all the values in an application. @VARS produces a larger variance than @VAR.

Statistical function arguments The statistical functions accept lists of numeric arguments that can include ranges, individual cell references, literal numeric values, calculated values, and range names. @SUMPRO-DUCT, however, accepts only ranges as arguments. Statistical functions accept three-dimensional ranges, or ranges across multiple worksheets in a file.

When you use a range reference as an argument in a statistical function, you'll usually want all the cells in the range to contain numeric entries. If a cell contains a label instead of a number, the statistical functions treat the entry as a value of zero. Because this value is then included in the sta-tistical calculation, the result may be inaccurate.

WARNING

Statistical functions treat cells that contain labels as zero. Be careful to use only number values in statistical function calculations. If you include labels, the results will be inaccurate.

The worksheet in Figure 5.9 illustrates the statistical functions. In this worksheet, the conference organizers at Computing Conferences, Inc. have compiled a list of conferences conducted in 1992, along with the number of people who attended each conference. As you can see, column A on the worksheet displays the city in which each conference was held, column B gives the date, and column C the number of participants. Columns D and E supply a variety of statistics about the conferences and attendance, including the number of conferences, the total attendance for all conferences, the average attendance (rounded to an integer), and the largest and smallest attendance records. Moreover, the worksheet shows the variance and the standard deviation calculations, produced with both the *n* and *n–1* methods and rounded to the nearest hundredth. In Figure 5.10, you can see the functions that produce these statistics. Notice that the column of attendance records, C6..C19, has been given the range name ATTENDANCE.

FIGURE 5.9

The statistical breakdown of attendance at 1992 conferences

D	A	B	C	D	E	F	G
1				Computing Conferences, Inc.			
2				Attendance at Conferences Conducted in 1992			
3				*Computing for Video Stores*			
4							
5	Place	Date	Attendance	Statistics			
6	Chicago	09-Jan-92	154				
7	St. Louis	21-Jan-92	119	Number of conferences:	14		
8	Indianapolis	15-Feb-92	174	Total attendance:	1,994		
9	New York	07-Mar-92	201	Average attendance:	142		
10	Boston	25-Mar-92	136	Largest Attendance:	235		
11	Washington, D.C.	03-Apr-92	172	Smallest attendance:	86		
12	Atlanta	11-May-92	112				
13	Miami	28-May-92	97	Variance (n):	1632.53		
14	Dallas	03-Jun-92	86	Standard deviation (n):	40.40		
15	Albuquerque	29-Jun-92	104	Variance (n-1):	1758.11		
16	Las Vegas	05-Sep-92	235	Standard deviation (n-1):	41.93		
17	Los Angeles	11-Oct-92	119				
18	San Francisco	29-Oct-92	137				
19	Seattle	05-Nov-92	148				
20							

Finally, Figure 5.11 demonstrates the use of the @SUMPRODUCT function. Column D shows the attendance price for conferences held in 1992. The following @SUMPRODUCT function appears in cell F11:

```
@SUMPRODUCT(C6..C19,D6..D19)
```

FIGURE 5.10

Compare this worksheet to the one in Figure 5.9. Here, you can see the formulas that produced the numbers in column E.

D	A	B	C	D	E	F	G
1				Computing Conferences, Inc.			
2				Attendance at Conferences Conducted in 1992			
3				*Computing for Video Stores*			
4							
5	Place		Date	Attendance	Statistics		
6	Chicago	09-Jan-92	154				
7	St. Louis	21-Jan-92	119	Number of conferences: @COUNT(ATTENDANCE)			
8	Indianapolis	15-Feb-92	174	Total attendance: @SUM(ATTENDANCE)			
9	New York	07-Mar-92	201	Average attendance: @AVG(ATTENDANCE)			
10	Boston	25-Mar-92	136	Largest Attendance: @MAX(ATTENDANCE)			
11	Washington, D.C.	03-Apr-92	172	Smallest attendance: @MIN(ATTENDANCE)			
12	Atlanta	11-May-92	112				
13	Miami	28-May-92	97	Variance (n): @VAR(ATTENDANCE)			
14	Dallas	03-Jun-92	86	Standard deviation (n): @STD(ATTENDANCE)			
15	Albuquerque	29-Jun-92	104	Variance (n-1): @VARS(ATTENDANCE)			
16	Las Vegas	05-Sep-92	235	Standard deviation (n-1): @STDS(ATTENDANCE)			
17	Los Angeles	11-Oct-92	119				
18	San Francisco	29-Oct-92	137				
19	Seattle	05-Nov-92	148				
20							

The first range argument in this function, C6..C19, represents attendance records, and the second argument, D6..D19, contains the prices. The function multiplies each attendance record by the corresponding price, and finds the sum of all the products. The result is $434,920.00.

FIGURE 5.11

Using the @SUMPRODUCT function to figure the total revenue from all conferences

D	A	B	C	D	E	F	G
1				Computing Conferences, Inc.			
2				Attendance at Conferences Conducted in 1992			
3				*Computing for Video Stores*			
4							
5	Place		Date	Attendance		Price	
6	Chicago	09-Jan-92	154	$195.00			
7	St. Louis	21-Jan-92	119	$195.00			
8	Indianapolis	15-Feb-92	174	$195.00		*Total Attendance*	
9	New York	07-Mar-92	201	$225.00		*Revenues:*	
10	Boston	25-Mar-92	136	$225.00			
11	Washington, D.C.	03-Apr-92	172	$225.00		$434,920.00	
12	Atlanta	11-May-92	112	$225.00			
13	Miami	28-May-92	97	$225.00			
14	Dallas	03-Jun-92	86	$195.00			
15	Albuquerque	29-Jun-92	104	$195.00			
16	Las Vegas	05-Sep-92	235	$245.00			
17	Los Angeles	11-Oct-92	119	$245.00			
18	San Francisco	29-Oct-92	137	$245.00			
19	Seattle	05-Nov-92	148	$195.00			
20							

Financial Functions

Financial functions represent formulas for computing several kinds of calculations, including depreciation, loan payments, present value and future value, and investment analysis.

Functions for Calculating Depreciation

Depreciation is the allocation of the expense of a large purchase over the useful life of the asset. There are many ways to calculate depreciation. Because depreciation is so important in determining how much tax is owed, businesses are always concerned with finding the most advantageous way to calculate depreciation.

Four depreciation functions are available in 1-2-3. The straightlime method, represented by the @SLN function, is the simplist. It depreciates the cost of an asset by the same rate from year to year. The other three methods—@SYD, @DDB, and @BDB—represent various approaches to *accelerated depreciation*. Accelerated depreciation refers to assigning greater partions of the expense to the greater years of useful life, and lesser portions to later years. Table 5.3 explains the 1-2-3 depreciation function

TABLE 5.3: Lotus 1-2-3 Depreciation Functions

FUNCTION	DESCRIPTION
@DDB	The double-declining-balance method. Calculates deviation based on four values—cost, salvage value, life, and period of depreciation.
@SLN	The straight-line depreciation method. Calculates depreciation by assigning equal portions of the asset's cost to each year of its useful life.

TABLE 5.3: Lotus 1-2-3 Depreciation Functions (continued)

FUNCTION	DESCRIPTION
@SYD	The sum-of-the-years'-digits method. Calculates depreciation over a set period of years, given the asset's original cost, its salvage value, and a target period of years for which it will depreciate.
@VDB	The variable-rate declining-balance method. Calculates depreciation over a portion of a year.

Deviation function arguments Functions that calculate deviations have common arguments, which can be represented as *cost*, *salvage*, *life*, and *period*:

- Cost is the original purchase price of the asset.

- Life is the defined useful life of the asset, in years.

- Salvage is the value of the asset at the end of its useful life.

- Period is the target year for which you want to calculate the depreciation.

The @SLN function takes only the first three arguments, because the result of straightline depreciation is the same for each year of useful life:

@SLN(*cost*,*salvage*,*life*)

The @SYD and @DDB functions calculate different amounts for each year of useful life. The target year, therefore, appears as the fourth argument, *period*:

@SYD(*cost*,*salvage*,*life*,*period*)

@DDB(*cost*,*salvage*,*life*,*period*)

The @VDB function is the most complex of all because it takes two *period* arguments, one to represent the start and one to represent the end of the target period. With two *period* arguments, you can calculate the depreciation expense for part of a year. In addition, @VDB takes two optional arguments, *factor* and *switch*:

@VDB(*cost*,*salvage*,*life*,*period1*,*period2*,*factor*,*switch*)

The *factor* argument is the percentage by which the remaining value of the asset is multiplied to calculate the accelerated depreciation for a given period. For example, you might enter a value of 150% or 175% for this argument. If you omit *factor*, the default is 200%, in which case @VDB produces the same result as @DDB. In the *switch* argument, you specify whether you want @VDB to switch to straight-line depreciation at the point when it is advantageous to do so. Supplying a *switch* value of 0 (or omitting the argument altogether) instructs 1-2-3 to make the switch; a value of 1 prevents the switch.

Figure 5.12 shows examples of all four depreciation methods, calculated for an asset with a four-year useful life. Here are the steps for producing this sample worksheet on your own computer:

FIGURE 5.12

You can use four depreciation methods to find out the best way of depreciating an asset.

	A	B	C	D	E	F
1	Asset	Computer system				
2	Cost	$9,600.00			Depreciation	
3	Life	4 years			factor	
4	Salvage	$1,600.00			175%	
5						
6	Year	SLN	SYD	DDB	VDB	
7	1	$2,000.00	$3,200.00	$4,800.00	$4,200.00	
8	2	$2,000.00	$2,400.00	$2,400.00	$2,362.50	
9	3	$2,000.00	$1,600.00	$800.00	$1,328.91	
10	4	$2,000.00	$800.00	$0.00	$108.59	
11						

1. Enter the following labels in cells A1 to A4:

CELL	ENTRY
A1	**Asset**
A2	**Cost**
A3	**Life**
A4	**Salvage**

2. Enter the following data items in cells B1 to B4:

CELL	ENTRY
B1	**Computer system**
B2	**9600**

CELL	ENTRY
B3	4
B4	1600

3. Enter the label **years** in cell C3.

4. Enter the following in cells E2 and E3:

CELL	ENTRY
E2	**Depreciation**
E3	**factor**

5. Enter the @VDB depreciation factor, **1.75**, in cell E4.

6. Enter the following column headings in cells A6 to E6:

CELL	ENTRY
A6	**Year**
B6	**SLN**
C6	**SYD**
D6	**DDB**
E6	**VDB**

7. Enter the year following year numbers in cells A7 to A10:

CELL	ENTRY
A7	1
A8	2
A9	3
A10	4

8. Format all these entries as you see them displayed in Figure 5.12. To do so, preselect range B7..E10, click the <u>N</u>umber Format button, and select Currency. Format them for a decimal point as well.

9. Preselect range A2..A4 and choose Range ➤ Name ➤ Use Labels. Keep the For cells option set on To the Right. Click OK to confirm. Now you've assigned the range names COST, LIFE, and SALVAGE to the appropriate cells in column B.

10. Select cell E3 and choose Range ➤ Name again. This time, set For cells on to Below and click OK to confirm. Now you've assigned the name FACTOR to cell E4.

11. In cells B7 to E7, enter the following formulas:

CELL	ENTRY	TYPE OF DEPRECIATION
B7	**@SLN($COST, $SALVAGE,$LIFE)**	The straight-line depreciation method. Notice the absolute references to range names. This format is necessary for the upcoming copy operation.
C7	**@SYD($COST, $SALVAGE,$LIFE,**	The sum-of-the-years'-digits method.
D7	**@DDB($COST, $SALVAGE, $LIFE,A7)**	The double-declining-balance method.
E7	**@VDB($COST, $SALVAGE,$LIFE, A7–1,A7,$FACTOR)**	The variable-rate declining-balance method.

12. Use the CopyToClipboard and PasteFromClipboard icons to copy the four depreciation formulas down their respective columns. Preselect range B7..E7, click the CopyToClipboard icon, and drag the mouse pointer over range B8..B10. When you click on the PasteFromClipboard icon, the formulas are copied and your work is complete.

Try making changes in the basic data—the cost, the salvage value, and the depreciation factor—and watch 1-2-3 recalculate the depreciation schedules. If you increase the useful life value, you also have to add a new row to the depreciation table for each year's increase.

More Financial Functions

Lotus 1-2-3 offers eight more financial functions:

FUNCTION	USE
@CTERM	Finds the number of compounding periods, or *terms*, required to reach a specific future value from a one-time investment amount.
@FV	Finds the *future value* of a series of equal periodic payments at a fixed periodic interest rate.
@IRR	Finds the *internal rate of return* from a series of positive and negative cash flow amounts.
@NPV	Finds the *net present value* of a series of future periodic cash flow amounts.
@PMT	Finds the *fixed periodic* payment amount required to pay back a loan.
@PV	Finds the *present value* of a series of periodic income amounts.
@RATE	Finds the interest *rate* corresponding to a fixed future return from a current investment amount.
@TERM	Finds the number of equal payments required to reach a specific future value.

Most of these functions take an interest rate in at least one of their arguments. You can enter an interest rate argument as a decimal value, such as .085, or as a percentage, such as 8.5%. Either way, 1-2-3 stores the argument in its decimal format. Of course, you can also provide the interest rate argument by referencing a cell that contains an interest rate. If you enter 8.5% into a cell, 1-2-3 accepts the entry as 0.085. At that point you can format the entry as a percentage or enter the rate as 8.5 in a worksheet cell and then divide the rate argument by 100 in the function itself, like so:

```
RATE/100
```

TIP

If a financial function returns a value you know to be incorrect, double-check the interest rate argument. Make sure you did not accidentally give the function a rate argument that was off by a factor of 100.

@PV function　The @PV function finds the present value of a series of future periodic income amounts, where each amount is the same. The present value calculation takes into account the timevalue of money at a given interest rate. @PV takes three arguments:

```
@PV(payment,rate,term)
```

where

- *payment* is the income amount that will be received at the end of each period in the *term*, and

- *rate* is the periodic rate of return.

The periods of *rate* and *term* must be the same.

@NPV function　The @NPV function finds the net present value of a series of future periodic cash flow amounts, positive or negative. @NPV takes two arguments, representing the rate and a range of cash flow amounts:

```
@NPV(rate,cashflows)
```

The worksheet in Figure 5.13 uses the @PV and @NPV functions to compare the following two five-year investments:

- Investment #1 provides five annual income amounts of $10,000 at the end of each year.

- Investment #2 provides an initial amount of $5,000 at the end of the first year, and then a final amount of $50,000 at the end of the fifth year.

FIGURE 5.13

Use the @PV and @NPV functions to see the value of investments.

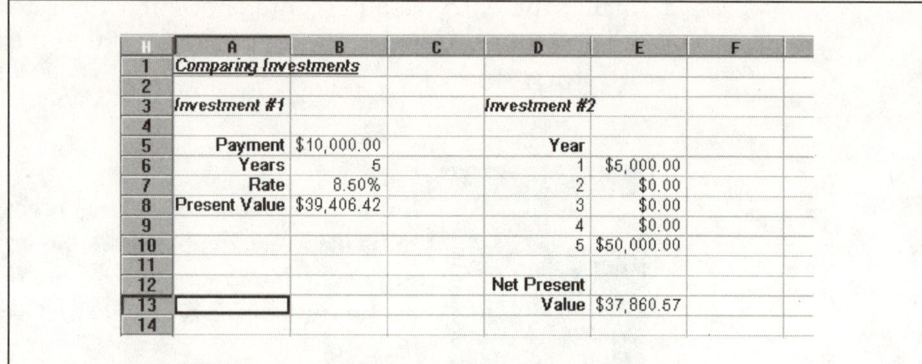

Using a rate of 8.5 percent for the comparison, which is the better investment? The @PV function in cell B8, @PV(B5,B7,B6), gives the present value of the first investment. The @NPV function in cell E13, @NPV(B7,E6..E10), gives the present value of the second investment. As you can see, the first investment has a greater present value, even though the net income of the second investment is $5000 more than the first.

@FV function The @FV function finds the future value of a series of equal periodic payments at a fixed periodic interest rate. @FV takes three arguments:

@FV(*payment,rate,term*)

The future value is equal to the amount of the periodic payments, plus the accumulated interest over the specified term.

Figure 5.14 illustrates the use of @FV in the following situation: the parents of a new baby girl have decided to deposit $1500 in a bank account at the end of each year until their child is ready to go to college. How much will the account be worth at the end of eighteen years if the interest

FIGURE 5.14

Use the @FV function to plan for future financial needs.

	A	B	C	D
1	College Education Fund			
2				
3	Payment	$1,500.00	per year	
4	Rate	8.00%	annually	
5	Term	18	years	
6				
7	Future Value	$56,175.37		
8				

rate is 8 percent, compounded annually? The @FV function in cell B7 is @FV(B3,B4,B5). As Figure 5.14 shows, there will be $56,175.37 in the account at the end of the 18-year term.

@PMT function The @PMT function finds the fixed periodic payment amount required to pay back a loan. @PMT takes three arguments:

> @PMT(*principal,rate,term*)

When you use @PMT to find the monthly payment for a bank loan, you must supply the monthly interest rate and the term in months.

Figure 5.15 shows an example of the @PMT function. The principal of the loan in this example is $35,825. The rate is 11.25 percent (entered into the worksheet as .1125) and the term is 10 years. The formula in cell B6 is @PMT(B3,B4/12,B5*12). Notice that the annual rate is divided by 12 to produce the monthly rate, and the term in years is multiplied by 12 to find the term in months. The rounded monthly payment is $498.57.

FIGURE 5.15

Use the @PMT function to plan payments on a loan.

	A	B	C
1	Monthly Payment		
2			
3	Principal	$35,825.00	
4	Rate	11.25%	
5	Term	10 years	
6	Payment	$498.57	
7			

@CTERM function The @CTERM function finds the number of compounding periods required to reach a specified future value from a one-time investment amount, given a fixed interest rate. This function takes three arguments:

> @CTERM(*rate,futurevalue,presentvalue*)

@TERM function The @TERM function finds the number of equal payments required to reach a specified future value, given a fixed interest rate. Like @CTERM, @TERM takes three arguments, but in a different order:

> @TERM(*payment,rate,futurevalue*)

The worksheet in Figure 5.16 compares @CTERM and @TERM. It analyzes two different scenarios for attaining a future value of $25,000. Under the first scenario, a one-time amount of $15,000 is deposited in a bank account at the beginning of the period. Under the second scenario, $1000 is deposited in an account at the end of each year. In both cases, the accounts yield 8 percent interest annually. How long will it take each investment to reach the goal of $25,000?

	A	B	C	D	E	F
1	Time Needed to Save $25,000					
2						
3	Single Deposit			Annual Deposits		
4						
5	Deposit	$15,000.00		Payment	$1,000.00	annually
6	Rate	8.00%		Rate	8.00%	
7	Goal	$25,000.00		Goal	$25,000.00	
8	Term	7 years		Term	14 years	
9						

The following @CTERM function is stored in cell B8:

    @CTERM(B6,B7,B5)

In this case, the required term is approximately seven years. (The value in B8 has been rounded by formatting.) The following @TERM function is stored in cell E8:

    @TERM(E5,E6,E7)

Given annual deposits of $1000, the account balance would reach $25,000 in approximately fourteen years. (The value in E8 is also rounded.)

@RATE function The @RATE function calculates the interest rate corresponding to a fixed future return from a current investment amount. The function takes three arguments:

    @RATE(*futurevalue,presentvalue,term*)

Figure 5.17 illustrates the @RATE function for the following situation: a friend asks to borrow $15,000 from you now, and promises to pay you $25,000 at the end of four years. What is the annual interest rate that you will earn from the loan?

FIGURE 5.17

Use the @RATE function to figure the interest on an investment.

	A	B	C
1	Calculating the Interest Rate		
2			
3	Present value	$15,000.00	
4	Future value	$25,000.00	
5	Term	4 years	
6	Rate	13.62%	
7			

The @RATE function @RATE(B4,B3,B5) is entered into cell B6. The resulting annual interest rate (displayed in the Percent format, with two decimal places) is 13.62%.

@IRR function The @IRR function gives the internal rate of return from a series of positive and negative cash flow amounts. The *internal rate of return* is defined as the interest rate that gives a net present value of zero. @IRR takes two arguments, a rate and a range of cash flow amounts:

@IRR(*guess,cashflows*)

where

- *guess* is a reasonable guess for the internal rate of return (Lotus 1-2-3 uses the guess as a starting point for the iterative process that calculates the internal rate of return), and

- *cashflows* is a worksheet range that contains the positive and negative cash flow amounts.

Figure 5.18 contains an illustration of the @IRR function that finds the internal rate of return for a six-year investment project. In the first year, an output of $80,000 is required to start the investment. The five subsequent years produce various income amounts: $15,000 at the end of the second year; $20,000 at the end of the third and fourth years; and $25,000 at the end of the fifth and sixth years. What is the calculated internal rate of return for this sequence of cash flow amounts?

	A	B	C
1	Internal Rate of Return		
2			
3	Year	Cash Flow	
4	1	($80,000.00)	
5	2	$15,000.00	
6	3	$20,000.00	
7	4	$20,000.00	
8	5	$25,000.00	
9	6	$25,000.00	
10			
11	IRR	9.00%	
12	NPV	($2.15)	
13			

The @IRR function @IRR(0.1,B4..B9) is stored in cell B11. The guess in the first argument is 10 percent. The range of cash flow amounts is B4..B9. @IRR calculates the internal rate of return as 9 percent. (The value in cell B11 is displayed in the Percent format.) To confirm that this figure matches the IRR definition, the formula @NPV(B11,B4..B9) appears in cell B12. Given the calculated IRR, the @NPV function gives an approximate result of zero.

Mathematical Functions

Lotus 1-2-3 has a standard set of mathematical functions, many of which are used in scientific and engineering applications. These include the trigonometric, logarithmic, and exponential functions. Several mathematical functions, the following included, can be used in everyday business worksheets as well:

- @RAND produces random numbers, which you can use to obtain random data for testing worksheet formulas or to rearrange data in a random order.

- @INT and @ROUND are useful for converting real numbers to integers, or for rounding numbers to a specified decimal place.

- @ABS (absolute value) and @MOD (modulus) have special uses in date arithmetic.

In the sections ahead, you'll get a chance to use some of these functions.

Trigonometric and Inverse Trigonometric Functions

Lotus 1-2-3 has three trigonometric functions, @SIN, @COS, and @TAN; and four inverse trigonometric functions, @ASIN, @ACOS, @ATAN, and @ATAN2. Trigonometric functions take arguments expressed in *radians*. The inverse functions produce radian values. A radian measurement is a multiple of the value π, where the range 0 to $2*\pi$ is equivalent to 0 to 360 degrees. Here are some sample radian equivalents:

RADIAN	EQUIVALENT IN DEGREES
0*PI	0 degrees
PI/4	45 degrees
PI/2	90 degrees
PI	180 degrees
3*PI/2	270 degrees
2*PI	360 degrees

To make it easier to give arguments in radians, 1-2-3 has a built-in @PI function. @PI gives the value of π, accurate to 17 digits:

3.14159265358979324

Trigonometric functions　Figure 5.19 shows @SIN, @COS, and @TAN values for a range of radian arguments from $-\pi/2$ to $+\pi/2$. The sine and cosine values move through their familiar wave patterns in this range: sine goes from -1 to 0 to 1, and cosine goes from 0 to 1 to 0. The result of the tangent function approaches infinity for arguments approaching $+\pi/2$, and negative infinity for arguments approaching $-\pi/2$.

The following exercise tells you how to produce the sine and cosine table on your own worksheet:

1. On a blank worksheet, preselect range A4..A20.

N	A	B	C	D	E	F	G	H
1			Trigonometric Functions					
2								
3		Radians	Sine	Cosine				
4	-0.5000	-1.5708	-1.0000	0.0000			Radians	Tangent
5	-0.4375	-1.3744	-0.9808	0.1951		-0.4375	-1.3744	-5.0273
6	-0.3750	-1.1781	-0.9239	0.3827		-0.3750	-1.1781	-2.4142
7	-0.3125	-0.9817	-0.8315	0.5556		-0.3125	-0.9817	-1.4966
8	-0.2500	-0.7854	-0.7071	0.7071		-0.2500	-0.7854	-1.0000
9	-0.1875	-0.5890	-0.5556	0.8315		-0.1875	-0.5890	-0.6682
10	-0.1250	-0.3927	-0.3827	0.9239		-0.1250	-0.3927	-0.4142
11	-0.0625	-0.1963	-0.1951	0.9808		-0.0625	-0.1963	-0.1989
12	0.0000	0.0000	0.0000	1.0000		0.0000	0.0000	0.0000
13	0.0625	0.1963	0.1951	0.9808		0.0625	0.1963	0.1989
14	0.1250	0.3927	0.3827	0.9239		0.1250	0.3927	0.4142
15	0.1875	0.5890	0.5556	0.8315		0.1875	0.5890	0.6682
16	0.2500	0.7854	0.7071	0.7071		0.2500	0.7854	1.0000
17	0.3125	0.9817	0.8315	0.5556		0.3125	0.9817	1.4966
18	0.3750	1.1781	0.9239	0.3827		0.3750	1.1781	2.4142
19	0.4375	1.3744	0.9808	0.1951		0.4375	1.3744	5.0273
20	0.5000	1.5708	1.0000	0.0000				
21								

2. Choose Range ➤ Fill and enter −.5 as the Start value and **.0625** as the Increment value. Click OK or press ↵. Lotus 1-2-3 fills the preselected range with decimal values from −0.5 to 0.5.

3. Choose Style ➤ Worksheet Defaults and select Fixed in the Format pull-down box. Enter 4 in the Decimals text box and click OK twice.

4. Enter the following in cells B4 to D4:

CELL	ENTRY
B4	@PI*A4
C4	@SIN(B4)
D4	@COS(B4)

5. Use the CopyToClipboard and PasteFromClipboard icons to copy these formulas down their respective columns in range B5..D20. Enter the column headings as shown in Figure 5.19.

Inverse trigonometric functions The inverse trigonometric functions @ASIN, @ACOS, and @ATAN take single numeric arguments.

- @ASIN gives the angle (in radians) corresponding to a sine argument.

- @ACOS gives the angle for a cosine argument.
- @ATAN gives the angle for a tangent argument.

NOTE

@ASIN and @ACOS return ERR for arguments greater than 1 or less than −1.

Figure 5.20 shows the arcsine and arccosine values for a range of decimal arguments between −1 and 1.25. The arcsine value goes from −π/2 to π/2 for this range of arguments, and the arccosine value goes from π down to zero. The function @ASIN(A4) is entered into cell B4, and @ACOS(A4) is entered into C4. To produce the table, these functions were copied down columns B and C.

Figure 5.20 also shows a range of arctangent functions. As you can see, the arctangent approaches -π/2 for large negative arguments, and +π/2 for large positive arguments. The formula stored in cell F4 is @ATAN(E4).

Finally, the @ATAN2 function supplies radian angles in a four-quadrant x-y coordinate system. This function takes two numeric arguments, forming a coordinate pair:

@ATAN2(x,y)

FIGURE 5.20

Use @IRR to figure the interest on cash flow to return a net present value of zero.

	A	B	C	D	E	F	G	H	I	J
1					Trigonometric Functions					
2										
3	Argument	ASIN	ACOS		Argument	ATAN		x	y	ATAN2
4	-1.000	-1.5708	3.1416		-100000	-1.5708		-0.5	-1.0	-2.0344
5	-0.875	-1.0654	2.6362		-10000	-1.5707		-1.0	-1.0	-2.3562
6	-0.750	-0.8481	2.4189		-1000	-1.5698		-1.0	-0.5	-2.6779
7	-0.625	-0.6751	2.2459		-100	-1.5608		-1.0	0.0	3.1416
8	-0.500	-0.5236	2.0944		-10	-1.4711		-1.0	0.5	2.6779
9	-0.375	-0.3844	1.9552		-1	-0.7854		-1.0	1.0	2.3562
10	-0.250	-0.2527	1.8235		-0	-0.0997		-0.5	1.0	2.0344
11	-0.125	-0.1253	1.6961		0	0.0000		0.0	1.0	1.5708
12	0.000	0.0000	1.5708		0	0.0997		0.5	1.0	1.1071
13	0.125	0.1253	1.4455		1	0.7854		1.0	1.0	0.7854
14	0.250	0.2527	1.3181		10	1.4711		1.0	0.5	0.4636
15	0.375	0.3844	1.1864		100	1.5608		1.0	0.0	0.0000
16	0.500	0.5236	1.0472		1000	1.5698		1.0	-0.5	-0.4636
17	0.625	0.6751	0.8957		10000	1.5707		1.0	-1.0	-0.7854
18	0.750	0.8481	0.7227		100000	1.5708		0.5	-1.0	-1.1071
19	0.875	1.0654	0.5054					0.0	-1.0	-1.5708
20	1.000	1.5708	0.0000							
21										

The result of @ATAN2 is the angle formed by two lines in the coordinate system: the x-axis extending horizontally to the right from the origin, and the line from (0,0) to (*x*,*y*). Figure 5.20 shows a range of examples. The formula in cell J4 is as follows:

    @ATAN2(H4,I4)

Exponential and Logarithmic Functions

The exponential and logarithmic functions are @EXP and @LN, both based on the natural constant e; and @LOG, based on 10.

@EXP function The @EXP function calculates exponents of e, where the value of e is represented as

    2.71828182845904524

@EXP takes one numeric argument, *x*, and supplies the value of e to the *x* power.

@LN function The @LN function finds the natural logarithm of its argument. @LN takes one argument, *x*, and supplies the power of e that produces *x*.

@LOG function The @LOG function gives the base-10 logarithm. @LOG takes one numeric argument, *x*, and returns the power of 10 that gives *x*. Figure 5.21 shows a range of examples for all three of these functions.

FIGURE 5.21

The @EXP, @LN, @LOG, and @SQRT functions

P	A	B	C	D	E	F	G	H	I
1		The Exponential, Logarithmic, and Square Root Functions							
2									
3	x	EXP(x)		x	LN(x)	LOG(x)		x	SQRT(x)
4	-1.00	0.3679		0.50	-0.6931	-0.3010		0.25	0.5000
5	-0.75	0.4724		1.00	0.0000	0.0000		0.50	0.7071
6	-0.50	0.6065		1.50	0.4055	0.1761		0.75	0.8660
7	-0.25	0.7788		2.00	0.6931	0.3010		1.00	1.0000
8	0.00	1.0000		2.50	0.9163	0.3979		1.25	1.1180
9	0.25	1.2840		3.00	1.0986	0.4771		1.50	1.2247
10	0.50	1.6487		3.50	1.2528	0.5441		1.75	1.3229
11	0.75	2.1170		4.00	1.3863	0.6021		2.00	1.4142
12	1.00	2.7183		4.50	1.5041	0.6532		2.25	1.5000
13	1.25	3.4903		5.00	1.6094	0.6990		2.50	1.5811
14									

@SQRT The @SQRT function gives the square root of its numeric argument. The argument must be greater than or equal to zero. The last column of the worksheet in Figure 5.21 shows examples of @SQRT.

Producing Random Numbers and Integers with @RAND

The @RAND function produces random numbers. The function takes no argument, and supplies a random decimal value between 0 and 1. If you want to generate random numbers in another range, you can multiply @RAND by the maximum value in the range. For example, the following formula produces random numbers between 0 and 100:

    @RAND*100

@INT function To produce random integers, use 1-2-3's built-in @INT function with @RAND. @INT eliminates the decimal portion of a real number, and supplies the integer portion. For instance, the following formula gives random integers between 0 and 100:

    @INT(@RAND*100)

This is an example of a formula in which one function appears as the argument of another function. You'll see other such examples later in this chapter.

Figure 5.22 shows four columns of random numbers, generated using the @RAND and @INT functions. Column A contains random decimal values between 0 and 1; column B, random numbers from 0 to 100; column C, random integers from 0 to 10; and column D, random integers from 0 to

Q	A	B	C	D	
1			The @RAND Function		
2					
3	@RAND	@RAND*100	@INT(@RAND*10)	@INT(@RAND*1000)	
4	0.983565846	15.156791320	4	20	
5	0.791173466	41.321232003	5	727	
6	0.252441690	85.946271795	9	450	
7	0.787483078	98.990055592	0	417	
8	0.228097470	25.864339120	9	948	
9	0.634172443	1.947584656	6	886	
10	0.536251688	33.055314111	6	279	
11	0.782122907	60.664264979	5	501	
12	0.139700089	84.301504579	1	627	
13	0.939391034	55.387452224	0	642	
14	0.345103324	96.909528504	7	490	
15					

1000. To produce these numbers, the four formulas shown in row 3 were copied down their respective columns. (The Text format was then applied to row 3.)

The @RAND function is used to produce random test data and to arrange records in random order. However, you have to be careful with @RAND because of the way it behaves in 1-2-3's automatic recalculation mode. As you know, 1-2-3 recalculates formulas whenever a change occurs to the data on which the formulas depend. The @RAND function takes no argument and therefore does not depend on data values in a worksheet. However, whenever any formula on the worksheet is recalculated, so are all @RAND entries. This can be a problem if you are trying to perform a test with a fixed set of random numbers.

WARNING

Whenever 1-2-3 recalculates a formula on the worksheet, it also recalculates all @RAND formulas. So random values change whenever the worksheet is recalculated.

Keeping @RAND values from being recalculated There are two ways to keep @RAND values on a worksheet from being recalculated. One way is to switch 1-2-3 out of its automatic recalculation mode and the other is to convert @RAND function entries into simple numeric values.

To switch out of recalculation mode, select Tools ➤ User Setup, and click on the Recalculation button to bring up the Recalculation dialog box.

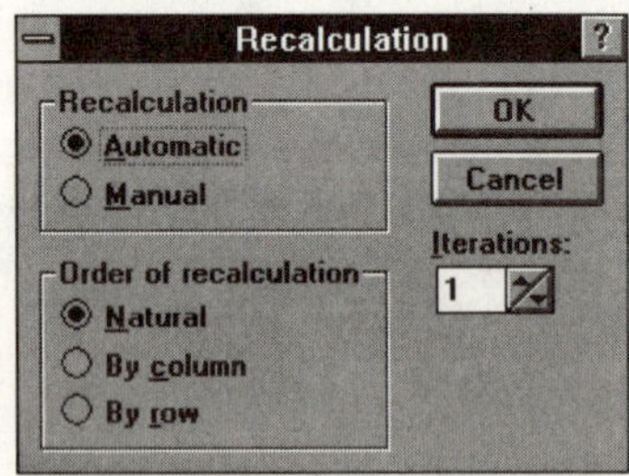

Next, click the <u>M</u>anual option. In manual recalculation mode, 1-2-3 recalculates formulas on the worksheet only when you instruct it to do so. To make 1-2-3 recalculate formulas in manual recalculation mode, press F9. When formulas need to be recalculated—as they usually do after a change in the worksheet's data—1-2-3 displays the word *Calc* on the right corner of the status bar at the bottom of the 1-2-3 window. Ignore the Calc message if you are working with random numbers that you want to keep. Press F9 only when you want to *change* the set of random numbers on your worksheet.

To convert a function or formula to a value as you enter it, simply press F9 before pressing ↵.

Try this exercise with @RAND in manual recalculation mode:

1. On a blank worksheet, enter **@RAND** in cell A1. A random number between 0 and 1 appears in the cell.

2. Select cell A2 and enter a value of **1**.

This new entry has no relationship to the formula in cell A1, yet 1-2-3 recalculates the @RAND function anyway, and a new random number appears in cell A1. Changes like this one would be disconcerting if you were using random numbers as test data on a worksheet. It would be better to be able to examine the results of one random scenario before suddenly jumping to a new one.

3. Choose <u>T</u>ools ➤ <u>U</u>ser Setup, click the Recalculation button, and click on <u>M</u>anual in the Recalculation dialog box to switch to manual recalculation mode. Click OK in both dialog boxes to confirm the change.

4. Enter a value of **2** in cell A2. In manual mode, 1-2-3 does *not* automatically recalculate formulas on the worksheet. The random number in cell A1 does not change.

Notice the word *Calc* at the right side of the status bar. This word tells you that 1-2-3 has not recalculated the worksheet, because of manual recalculation mode.

5. Press F9 to force a recalculation. A new random number appears in cell A1, and the word *Calc* disappears.

6. Continue experimenting with this worksheet in manual mode, if you wish. Then close it without saving.

NOTE By the way, the Recalculation settings apply to all worksheets that are open at the time you select a setting.

Converting @RAND entries to numeric values The second way to prevent 1-2-3 from recalculating random numbers is to convert @RAND function entries to simple numeric value entries. When you make the conversion, worksheet cells with random numbers generated by @RAND continue to displays numbers, but the @RAND function itself is not present in the cell. You can convert a @RAND value to a numeric value either at the time you enter it or after you've completed the @RAND entry. To convert a function or formula to a value as you enter it, simply press F9 before pressing ↵. You'll experiment with these techniques in the following exercise:

1. Select cell A1 on a blank worksheet, and type **@RAND** as a formula entry. Do not press ↵.

2. Press F9. Lotus 1-2-3 converts the @RAND function to a numeric value entry. Specifically, this entry is the first random number that the function would have produced if you had entered the function into the cell.

3. Press ↵. The random number in A1 is now static, because the entry is a value rather than a formula.

4. Select cell A2 and enter the **@RAND** function into the cell. Press ↵ to complete the entry. (Do not press F9 this time.)

5. Use the CopyToClipboard and PasteFromClipboard icons to copy the formula from cell A2 down to range A3..A10. When you complete the copy operation, a different random number appears in each cell in the range.

6. Use the CopyToClipboard and PasteFromClipboard icons to copy the formula from cell A2 down to range A2..A10.
7. Click OK or press ↵ to confirm the new selection.

Back on your worksheet, the entries in the preselected range are now numeric value entries, not functions. Confirm this if you want to by selecting any cell in the range and examining the contents box. You will see a long decimal number in the box, not a @RAND entry.

Using @RAND to rearrange an alphabetical list Now consider a situation in which you might use the @RAND function in a worksheet. Imagine that you have to evaluate a group of employees once a year. You hold evaluation meetings with each employee in September. To avoid meeting employees in alphabetical order each year, you need a way to rearrange the list of employees in random order.

An alphabetical list of employee names appears in columns B and C in the worksheet, as shown in Figure 5.23. Here are the steps you would take to rearrange the list randomly:

1. Enter the formula **@INT(@RAND*50)** in cell A1.
2. Use the CopyToClipboard and PasteFromClipboard icons to copy the formula down column A to each cell in range A2..A15.

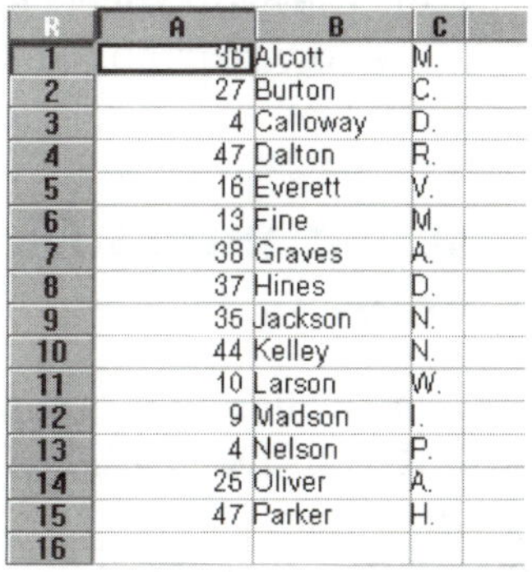

R	A	B	C
1	36	Alcott	M.
2	27	Burton	C.
3	4	Calloway	D.
4	47	Dalton	R.
5	16	Everett	V.
6	13	Fine	M.
7	38	Graves	A.
8	37	Hines	D.
9	35	Jackson	N.
10	44	Kelley	N.
11	10	Larson	W.
12	9	Madson	I.
13	4	Nelson	P.
14	25	Oliver	A.
15	47	Parker	H.
16			

FIGURE 5.23

The inverse trigonometric functions

A random integer between 0 and 50 appears in each cell in column A, as in Figure 5.23. (The random numbers on your worksheet will be different from the ones in the figure.)

3. Preselect range A1..C15 and choose <u>R</u>ange ➤ <u>S</u>ort. The Sort dialog box appears on the screen, as in Figure 5.24.

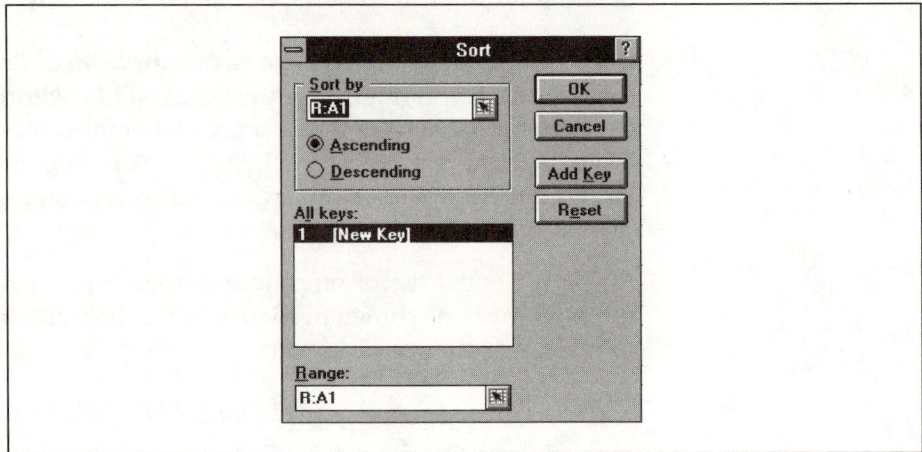

4. Click the <u>A</u>scending option in the <u>S</u>ort by frame and click OK or press ↵ to confirm.

Back on the worksheet, as shown in Figure 5.25, the list of employee names is now rearranged according to the random numbers you entered in column A.

Miscellaneous Mathematical Functions

Three miscellaneous but important mathematical functions remain. They are @ROUND, @MOD, and @ABS.

@ROUND function The @ROUND function rounds out numbers. This function takes two numeric arguments. The first argument, x, is the real number that you want to round, and the second, n, is an integer

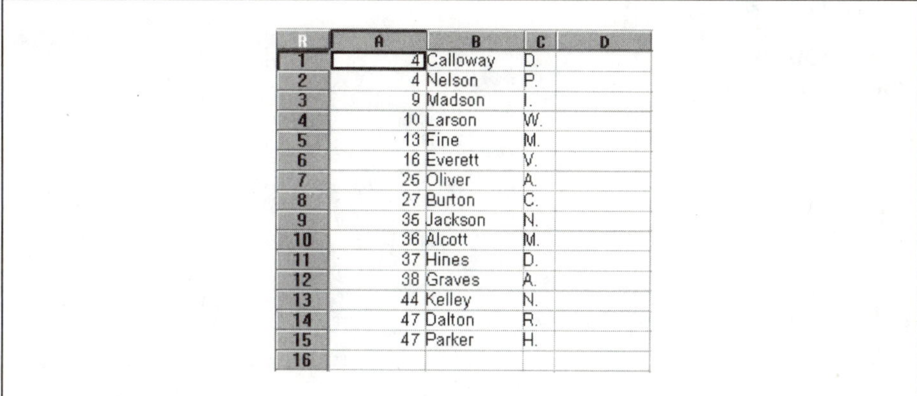

representing the decimal place at which you want the rounding to occur. The arguments are presented like so:

@ROUND(*x,n*)

- If *n* is positive, rounding takes place at the right side of the decimal point. For example, if you enter a value of 2 for *n*, the function rounds the value *x* to the nearest hundredth.

- If *n* is negative, rounding occurs at the left side of the decimal point. For example, if you enter−1 for *n*, the function rounds *x* to the nearest multiple of ten.

- A value of zero for *n* results in rounding to the nearest whole integer.

The worksheet in Figure 5.26 shows examples of the @ROUND function. Column A contains a series of random numbers between 0 and 100. In columns B through E, these numbers are rounded to the nearest thousandth, the nearest hundredth, the nearest integer, and the nearest multiple of ten, respectively. The formulas in cells A4 through E4 are:

CELL	FORMULA
A4	@RAND*100
B4	@ROUND(A4,3)
C4	@ROUND(A4,2)
D4	@ROUND(A4,0)

FIGURE 5.26

The @ROUND
function in action

S	A	B	C	D	E	F
1		The @ROUND Function				
2						
3	RAND	n=3	n=2	n=0	n=-1	
4	85.14688	85.147	85.15	85	90	
5	63.60830	63.608	63.61	64	60	
6	64.71560	64.716	64.72	65	60	
7	75.15490	75.155	75.15	75	80	
8	28.33980	28.340	28.34	28	30	
9	6.94613	6.946	6.95	7	10	
10	43.66886	43.669	43.67	44	40	
11	42.46637	42.466	42.47	42	40	
12	32.23189	32.232	32.23	32	30	
13	21.38864	21.389	21.39	21	20	
14						

CELL	FORMULA
E4	@ROUND(A4,~1)

These formulas were copied down the worksheet to range A5..E13.

@MOD function The @MOD function performs division between two integers. However, unlike the division operator, @MOD supplies the *remainder* from the division, not the quotient. @MOD is known as the *modulus* function. It takes two arguments, the numerator and the denominator of the division operation:

   @MOD(*x,y*)

If *y* divides evenly into *x* with no remainder, @MOD supplies a value of zero. Otherwise, @MOD returns the remainder from the division. For example, if you entered @MOD(25,9) in a cell, the result would be 7, because the division of 9 into 25 gives a quotient of 2 with a remainder of 7.

One of the important applications of the @MOD function is finding the day of the week (Sunday, Monday, Tuesday, and so on) for a date. Given a date number in 1-2-3's date-number format system, here is the formula for determining the day of the week:

   @MOD(*date*,7)

This formula yields an integer from 0 to 6, representing a day of the week from Saturday to Friday (0 is Saturday, 1 is Sunday, 2 is Monday, and so on).

The worksheet in Figure 5.27 shows a series of dates in column C. The following formula in cell B6 finds the day-of-the-week integer for the first of these dates:

    @MOD(C6,7)

This formula is copied down column B to determine the day of the week for each date in the list. You'll work with this list later in this chapter.

	A	B	C	D
1	Place	Day of Wk	Date	
2	Chicago	5	09-Jan-92	
3	St. Louis	3	21-Jan-92	
4	Indianapolis	0	15-Feb-92	
5	New York	0	07-Mar-92	
6	Boston	4	25-Mar-92	
7	Washington, D.C.	6	03-Apr-92	
8	Atlanta	2	11-May-92	
9	Miami	5	28-May-92	
10	Dallas	4	03-Jun-92	
11	Albuquerque	2	29-Jun-92	
12	Las Vegas	0	05-Sep-92	
13	Los Angeles	1	11-Oct-92	
14	San Francisco	5	29-Oct-92	
15	Seattle	5	05-Nov-92	
16				

@ABS function   The @ABS function gives the *absolute value* of a number. @ABS takes one numeric argument, x:

    @ABS(x)

Whether x is positive or negative, @ABS returns the unsigned (positive) equivalent of the argument.

Use this function when the sign of a numeric value is not relevant to your worksheet. For example, when you subtract one number from another, the result may be positive or negative, depending on which number is larger. Applying @ABS to subtraction guarantees a positive result. In the worksheet in Figure 5.28, cell C3 contains a formula for finding the number of days between two dates:

    @ABS(C2–C1)

This formula gives a positive number of days, regardless of which day is later in time. In fact, the formula could be

    @ABS(C1–C2)

and still return the same result.

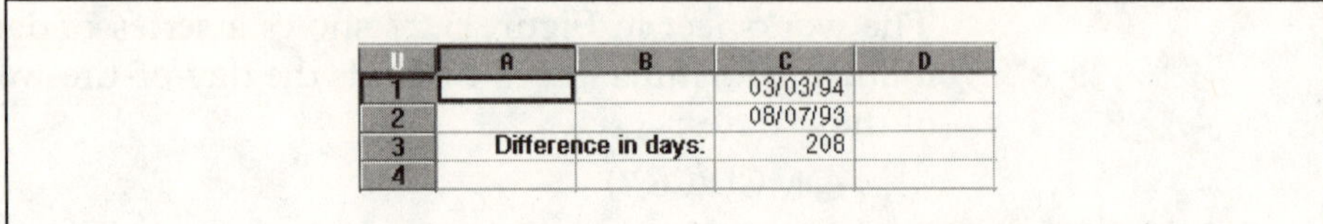

Date and Time Functions

Lotus 1-2-3 has a useful set of calendar functions for working with date and time values. These functions fall into four categories:

- Functions that supply the current date and time

- Functions that give information about existing date and time values

- Functions that convert other types of data into date and time values

- Functions that perform date arithmetic

Functions that give the date and time Two important functions read the system clock and calendar and supply values representing the current date and the current time:

FUNCTION	USE
@TODAY	Returns a number representing the current date. For example, @TODAY gives the integer value 34200 for the date 19Aug93. The @TODAY function takes no argument.
@NOW	Returns a combined date-and-time number representing both the current date and the current time. For example, @NOW supplies the combined value 34200.25, which represents the date 19-Aug-93 at 6:00 AM. @NOW takes no argument.

Functions providing information about date and time values Six
functions supply information about a date value or a time value:

FUNCTION	USE
@DAY	Returns an integer from 1 to 31, representing the day of the month. Takes a date number as its argument: @DAY(*datenumber*).
@HOUR	Returns an integer from 0 to 23, representing the hour. Takes a decimal time number as its argument: @HOUR(*timenumber*).
@MINUTE	Returns an integer from 0 to 59, representing the minutes. Takes a time number argument: @MINUTE(*timenumber*).
@MONTH	Returns an integer from 1 to 12, representing the month. Takes a date number argument: @MONTH(date*number*).
@SECOND	Returns an integer from 0 to 59, representing the seconds. Takes a time number argument: @SECOND(*timenumber*).
@YEAR	Returns an integer representing the year. Takes a date number argument: @YEAR(*datenumber*).

These six functions also accept combined date-and-time arguments, in
the form supplied by the @NOW function.

Functions that convert data into date and time values Four functions convert numeric values or strings into 1-2-3 date numbers or time numbers:

FUNCTION AND ARGUMENTS	USE
@DATE(*year month,day*)	Takes three integer arguments representing the year, the month, and the day to return the corresponding date number. For example, @DATE(93,8,19) gives the date number 34200.
@DATEVALUE (*string*)	Takes a string argument in a format that 1-2-3 can recognize as a date and returns the corresponding date number. For example, @DATEVALUE("19-Aug-93") returns the number 34200.
@TIME(*hour, minutes,seconds*)	Takes three numeric arguments representing the hour, the minutes, and the seconds, and returns the corresponding decimal time number. For example, @TIME(4,30,0) gives the value 0.1875.
@TIMEVALUE (*string*)	Takes a string argument in a format that 1-2-3 can recognize as a time and returns the corresponding time number. For example, @TIMEVALUE("4:30 AM") gives the value 0.1875.

Functions that perform date arithmetic The two functions that perform special date arithmetic operations are:

FUNCTION AND ARGUMENTS	USE
@DAYS360 (*date1*,*date2*)	Takes two date numbers as arguments and calculates the number of days between the two dates, using a standard algorithm based on a 360-day year.
@D360(*date1*, *date2*)	Takes two date numbers as arguments and calculates the number of days between the two dates, based on a year of 12 months with 30 days each.

Practicing with Date and Time Functions

In the upcoming exercises, you'll use some of these functions. To start, here is a simple experiment with the @NOW function and the six functions that supply information about date-and-time values: @DAY, @MONTH, @YEAR, @HOUR, @MINUTE, and @SECOND.

1. On a new blank worksheet, type the **@NOW** function in cell B1. (Recall that @NOW takes no argument.) To convert the function to a value, press the F9 key before you press ↵. A number representing the current date and time appears in B1.

2. Choose <u>R</u>ange ➤ <u>N</u>ame and assign the name DATETIME to this cell.

3. In cells B2 through B7, enter the following six functions:

CELL	ENTRY
B2	**@DAY(DATETIME)**
B3	**@MONTH(DATETIME)**
B4	**@YEAR(DATETIME)**
B5	**@HOUR(DATETIME)**

| | B6 | @MINUTE(DATETIME) |

B6   @MINUTE(DATETIME)

B7   @SECOND(DATETIME)

These six functions give the components of the date-and-time value displayed in cell B1.

The worksheet in Figure 5.29 shows the results of this experiment. (Of course, the date-and-time values in this figure will be different from the value you entered on your worksheet.) Figure 5.29 also includes labels in column A to identify the numbers in column B.

U	A	B	C	D
1	Now	34123.34	03-Jun-93	
2	Day	3		
3	Month	6		
4	Year	93		
5	Hour	8		
6	Minute	9		
7	Second	32		
8				

Calculating time values In the worksheet in Figure 5.30, you can see a practical use of the @MONTH and @DAY functions, along with an example of the @TODAY function in a formula. This worksheet shows a list of employees. The employees' names are in column A, their birth dates are in column B, and column C contains a formula that calculates each employee's age.

The following formula was entered in cell C4—for the first employee— and copied down the column:

    @INT((@TODAY–B4)/365)

Examine this formula carefully. The expression in the inner set of parentheses finds an employee's age in days by subtracting the employee's birth date from today's date (@TODAY–B4). Dividing this number of days by 365 gives the employee's age in years. Finally, @INT eliminates the fractional portion from the result of this division operation.

You can see the result of the formula in column C of Figure 5.30. Notice that this list is arranged by the employees' ages, in descending order—that is, from the oldest employee to the youngest, or from the earliest birth date to the most recent.

	A	B	C	D	E	F
1		Employees' Birthdays				
2						
3	Name	Date of Birth	Age	Mo	Day	
4	Graves, A.	23-Jun-35	57	6	23	
5	Alcott, M.	05-Aug-39	53	8	5	
6	Parker, H.	08-May-45	48	5	8	
7	Dalton, R.	06-Jul-47	45	7	6	
8	Hines, D.	27-Oct-51	41	10	27	
9	Oliver, A.	03-Sep-54	38	9	3	
10	Jackson, N.	19-Jun-59	33	6	19	
11	Everett, V.	02-Dec-59	33	12	2	
12	Larson, W.	07-Aug-65	27	8	7	
13	Nelson, P.	02-Jan-67	26	1	2	
14	Madson, I.	07-Apr-68	25	4	7	
15	Burton, C.	05-Aug-69	23	8	5	
16	Fine, M.	01-Feb-70	23	2	1	
17	Kelley, N.	08-Nov-71	21	11	8	
18	Calloway, D.	03-Mar-72	21	3	3	
19						

Sorting by date Imagine the following situation: the company that these employees work for has a policy of giving each employee an extra vacation day per year on his or her birthday. To monitor birthday vacations, the manager would like to rearrange the employee list in calendar order of birthdays, from the first birthday in January to the last birthday in December. Accomplishing this requires using the @MONTH and @DAY functions:

1. Enter the function **@MONTH(B4)** in cell D4 and the function **@DAY(B4)** in cell E4.

2. Use the CopyToClipboard and PasteFromClipboard icons to copy these two formulas down their respective columns, to the range D5..E18.

Together, these two functions give the month and day of each employee's birthday, as shown in Figure 5.31.

3. Preselect range A4..E18 and choose <u>R</u>ange ➤ <u>S</u>ort. The Sort dialog box appears, as in Figure 5.31.

4. Enter **D4** for the first key, click on <u>A</u>scending, and click the Add Key button to place it in the A<u>l</u>l Keys list.

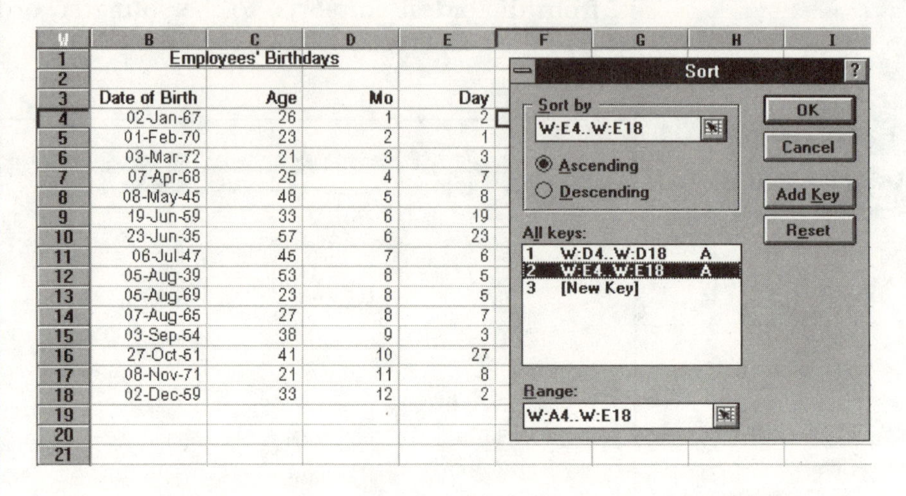

5. Enter **E4** for the second key, click on <u>A</u>scending, and click the Add <u>K</u>ey button to place it in the A<u>l</u>l Keys list. Click <u>A</u>scending for both keys.

6. Click OK or press ↵ to complete the operation.

Lotus 1-2-3 sorts the list of employee birthdays, from January to December. As you can see in Figure 5.31, columns D and E show the month and the day of each birthday through the course of the calendar year. The manager can now use this worksheet to plan for each employee's extra vacation day.

Converting three-column dates into numbers In some worksheet applications, you might prefer to enter the day, month, and year components of dates in three separate columns, as shown in columns A, B, and C of Figure 5.32. Some spreadsheet users find it easier to enter data under this arrangement, especially when dates have to be read from handwritten forms and entered manually in a worksheet. Given a list of dates in this three-column format, you can use 1-2-3's @DATE function to convert the date components into date numbers. With the dates in numbers, you can perform date arithmetic operations on the worksheet. For example, here is the formula entered into cell D2 in Figure 5.32:

    @DATE(C2,B2,A2)

X	A	B	C	D	E
1	Day	Month	Year	Date	
2	31	1	63	31-Jan-63	
3	28	2	61	28-Feb-61	
4	21	3	93	21-Mar-93	
5	5	4	71	05-Apr-71	
6	9	5	88	09-May-88	
7	30	6	55	30-Jun-55	
8	24	7	88	24-Jul-88	
9	17	8	76	17-Aug-76	
10					

After copying this formula down column D, you can choose Style ➤ Number Format and select an appropriate date display format.

Converting date and time labels into numbers You'll need to perform another kind of data conversion on a worksheet that contains date or time values that have been entered as labels. For example, you will find yourself in this situation if you load data into a 1-2-3 worksheet from a different software environment. Column A in Figure 5.33 shows the date and time label formats that 1-2-3 can recognize and convert into numbers. You use the @DATEVALUE function to convert these labels into date numbers. The following formula has been entered into cell B5 and copied down column B:

```
@DATEVALUE(A5)
```

Column D of the same worksheet shows examples of the four time formats that 1-2-3 recognizes. In this case, the @TIMEVALUE function converts these labels into decimal time numbers. The following formula in cell E5 has been copied down column E:

```
@TIMEVALUE(D5)
```


Y	A	B	C	D	E	F
1		String to Number Conversion				
2		for Date and Time values				
3						
4	Date String	Date Number		Time String	Time Number	
5	31-Dec-99	36525		03:30:00 PM	0.6458	
6	31-Dec	36525		03:30 PM	0.6458	
7	Dec-99	36525		15:30:00	0.6458	
8	12/31/99	36525		15:30	0.6458	
9	12/31	36525				
10						

Financial operations with @DAYS360 and @D360   The @DAYS360 and @D360 functions are available for financial operations based on a 360-day year. The worksheet in Figure 5.34 shows examples of these functions. Columns A and B in this worksheet show two lists of dates. Columns C, D, and E demonstrate three techniques for finding the difference in days between pairs of dates in A and B. The three formulas in this worksheet are:

CELL	FORMULA
C4	+B4–A4
D4	@DAYS360(A4,B4)
E4	@D360(A4,B4)

FIGURE 5.34

The 360 date-and-time arithmetic function

	A	B	C	D	E
1		Differences between Two Dates			
2					
3	Date 1	Date 2	ABS	DAYS360	D360
4	01/15/85	05/22/86	492	487	487
5	09/04/86	08/31/83	-1100	-1083	-1084
6	10/31/92	02/28/94	485	478	478
7	07/07/91	11/02/86	-1708	-1685	-1685
8	10/31/93	10/30/93	-1	0	0
9	12/11/85	02/27/82	-1383	-1364	-1364
10	02/18/89	03/06/87	-715	-702	-702
11	02/18/86	08/31/95	3481	3433	3432
12	04/30/95	06/30/93	-669	-660	-660
13	01/21/86	01/05/94	2906	2864	2864
14					

Of course, only the first of these formulas finds the exact number of days between two dates. For the convenience of particular financial applications, the @DAYS360 and @D360 functions only find approximate differences. As you can see, the three formulas produce different results.

Logical Functions

Lotus 1-2-3 has an interesting assortment of logical functions that supply information about a worksheet. Like logical formulas, logical functions give values of 1 or 0, representing true or false. For example, the @IS-NUMBER function takes a cell address as its argument, and returns a value of 1 (true) if the cell contains a numeric value or is blank. @IS-NUMBER returns a value of 0 (false) if the cell contains a label. You are more likely to use functions like this one in macros than in everyday worksheet applications.

@IF function However, one tool in the category of logical functions is very important in worksheets—the @IF function. @IF evaluates a logical expression, and chooses between one of two values, depending on whether the expression is true or false. The @IF function takes three arguments:

@IF(*expression,value1,value2*)

- *Expression* is the logical expression that @IF evaluates. You can use the operators that you studied earlier in this chapter to build a logical expression for the @IF function, both the relational operators (=, <>, <, >, <=, and >=) and the logical operators (#NOT#, #AND#, and #OR#).

- *Value 1* and *value 2* are the data items that the function chooses between. If the logical expression in the first argument is evaluated as true, @IF returns *value1*. If the logical expression is false, @IF gives *value2*. In other words, when you enter the @IF function into a worksheet cell, you can expect the function to display either *value1* or *value2* in the cell.

Using strings as @IF arguments Try the following simple example:

1. Enter a value of **0** in cell A1 of a blank worksheet.
2. Enter the following formula in cell A2:

   @IF(A1=0,"zero","not zero")

   The word *zero* appears in cell A2.
3. Now select cell A1 again and enter a value of **10**. The display in cell A2 changes to *not zero*.

The @IF function evaluates the expression A1=0 to decide which label to display in cell A2.

If you can't get your @IF function to work, check for the word *Calc* on the status bar. You may have to reset the recalculation mode to Automatic.

The *value1* and *value2* arguments in the @IF function can be strings enclosed in quotes, as the previous example showed, or they can be values or calculations.

Using @IF with other functions For a more interesting example of the @IF function, consider the worksheet in Figure 5.35. This worksheet shows part of a billing application. Column A contains a list of dates on which a company has sent bills to its customers. Normally, each invoice is payable in 30 days, as shown in column B. However, if a 30-day due date falls on a Sunday, the formula in column B adds an additional day to produce a Monday due date. Here is the @IF function that performs this calculation in cell B2:

FIGURE 5.35

Using the @IF with the @MOD function

AA	A	B	C
1	Billing Date	Due Date	
2	15-Jan-93	15-Feb-93	
3	17-Jan-93	16-Feb-93	
4	27-Jan-93	26-Feb-93	
5	03-Feb-93	05-Mar-93	
6	10-Feb-93	12-Mar-93	
7	13-Feb-93	15-Mar-93	
8	17-Feb-93	19-Mar-93	
9	26-Feb-93	29-Mar-93	
10	06-Mar-93	05-Apr-93	
11	18-Mar-93	17-Apr-93	
12			

```
@IF(@MOD(A2+30,7)=1,A2+31,A2+30)
```

This formula is copied down column B, to range B3..B11. The first argument in the @IF function is an expression that determines whether the 30-day due date falls on a Sunday:

```
@MOD(A2+30,7)=1
```

The @MOD function adds 30 to the date in column A, and performs the modulus 7 operation on the result. If this @MOD function gives a value of 1, representing Sunday, the @IF function chooses the *value1* argument, a 31-day due date:

    A2+31

But if the @MOD function shows that the 30-day due date is not a Sunday, the *value2* argument is chosen:

    A2+30

Uses of the @IF function can be even more complex than this example. In some applications, you might write additional "nested" @IF functions in the positions of the *value1* and *value2* arguments of an initial @IF function. This can result in multifaceted decision-making processes for a worksheet.

String Functions

Lotus 1-2-3's large library of string functions gives you the power to manipulate labels and strings in your worksheets. Like the logical functions, most string functions are more likely to be used in macros than worksheets. String-related tasks require careful attention to detail, and are more often the concern of programmers than everyday spreadsheet users. But some of the string functions are very useful worksheet tools, as you'll see in upcoming exercises.

Essentially, string functions come in four categories:

STRING FUNCTION CATEGORY	USE
Substring	For working with sequences of characters inside existing strings or labels
Alphabetic case	For changing letters to uppercase or lowercase
Conversion	For producing strings from numeric values, or numbers from strings
Miscellaneous	For working with strings in a variety of ways

Examples of many of these functions appear in the worksheet in Figure 5.36. At the top of the worksheet, in cell A1, is the label "Lotus 1-2-3 for windows." Each function example in the worksheet uses this label to illustrate a particular string operation. (Notice two odd details about the string in cell A1: there are four spaces between *for* and *windows*, and the word *windows* is not capitalized. This was done on purpose to demonstrate how certain functions correct these details.) The results of the function examples appear in column B. Column G shows complete text copies of the functions in column B.

FIGURE 5.36

Different types of string functions at work

	A	B	C	D	E	F	G	H	I
1	Lotus 1-2-3 for	windows							
2									
3	Left	Lotus					@LEFT(A1,5)		
4	Right	windows					@RIGHT(A1,7)		
5	Mid	1-2-3					@MID(A1,6,5)		
6	Find	6					@FIND("1-2-3",A1,0)		
7	Replace	Lotus 1-2-3 for Windows					@REPLACE(A1,16,10,"Windows")		
8									
9	Proper	Lotus 1-2-3 For Windows					@PROPER(A1)		
10	Upper	LOTUS 1-2-3 FOR WINDOWS					@UPPER(A1)		
11	Lower	lotus 1-2-3 for windows					@LOWER(A1)		
12									
13	Length	26					@LENGTH(A1)		
14	Exact	0					@EXACT(A1,G9)		
15	Repeat	Lotus 1-2-3 for windowsLotus 1-2-3 for windows					@REPEAT(A1,2)		
16									
17	Trim	Lotus 1-2-3 for windows					@TRIM(A1)		
18									
19	S	Lotus 1-2-3 for windows					@S(A1..A1)		
20	N	0					@N(A1..A1)		

Substring functions The first five examples in the worksheet show the substring functions:

FUNCTION	USE
@LEFT	Supplies a copy of a substring from the beginning of a string. @LEFT takes two arguments, a string and an integer: @LEFT(*string,n*). The function supplies the first *n* characters of *string*. For example, @LEFT(A1,5) displays the string "Lotus" in cell B3 of the worksheet.
@RIGHT	Supplies a copy of a substring from the end of a string. @RIGHT also takes two arguments: @RIGHT(*string,n*). The function supplies the last *n* characters of *string*. For example, @RIGHT(A1,7) displays the string "windows" in cell B4 of the worksheet.
@MID	Supplies a copy of a substring from a position inside a string. @MID takes three arguments, a string and two integers: @MID(*string,pos,n*). The function copies *n* characters from *string*, starting from the position identified as *pos*. For example, @MID(A1,6,5) displays the string "1-2-3" in cell B5. Note that the first character in a string has a *pos* value of 0; this value is sometimes called the *offset* number. The offset number for a character in a string is one less than the character's actual position in the string. For example, the seventh character in a string has a *pos* value of 6.

FUNCTION	USE
@FIND	Identifies the position of a substring inside a larger string. @FIND takes three arguments: @FIND(*substring,string,pos*). The function searches for a *substring* inside *string*, starting the search at the *pos* character in *string*. If the search is successful, @FIND returns the offset location of the substring. For example, @FIND("1-2-3",A1,0) searches for the string "1-2-3" in the label stored in cell A1. The search begins at the beginning of the label. It results in a value of 6, the offset where the substring is found.
@REPLACE	Writes a sequence of characters over existing characters in a string. @REPLACE takes four arguments: @REPLACE(*string,pos,n,substring*). The function replaces *n* characters of *string*, starting from *pos*. The *substring* argument supplies the replacement characters. For example, @REPLACE(A1,16,10,"Windows") replaces the final characters of the string.

Figure 5.37 demonstrates an interesting application of the @MID function. The following formula has been entered into cell B6 and copied down column B to display the day of the week of each date in column C:

```
@MID("SatSunMonTueWedThuFri",@MOD(C6,7)*3,3)&"."
```

The first argument is a string containing three-character abbreviations for the days of the week. The second argument calculates a starting point in this string, to extract the abbreviation for a particular day. As you saw back in Figure 5.27, the function @MOD(C6,7) supplies an integer from 0 to 6 representing the day of the week, in this case the day of the week in cell C6. Multiplying this value by 3 gives the correct starting point in

AB	A	B	C	D
1	Place		Date	
2	Chicago	Thu.	09-Jan-92	
3	St. Louis	Tue.	21-Jan-92	
4	Indianapolis	Sat.	15-Feb-92	
5	New York	Sat.	07-Mar-92	
6	Boston	Wed.	25-Mar-92	
7	ington, D.C.	Fri.	03-Apr-92	
8	Atlanta	Mon.	11-May-92	
9	Miami	Thu.	28-May-92	
10	Dallas	Wed.	03-Jun-92	
11	lbuquerque	Mon.	29-Jun-92	
12	Las Vegas	Sat.	05-Sep-92	
13	os Angeles	Sun.	11-Oct-92	
14	n Francisco	Thu.	29-Oct-92	
15	Seattle	Thu.	05-Nov-92	
16				

the string. Finally, the third @MID argument is the value 3, the length of each day name. To complete the abbreviation, the formula joins the selected name with a period.

Alphabetic case functions Returning to Figure 5.36, the next three examples show the alphabetic case functions, @PROPER, @UPPER, and @LOWER. These three take a single string argument and return a copy of the same string with specified changes in the alphabetic case:

FUNCTION	USE
@PROPER	Capitalizes the first letter in each word of its string argument. An example appears in cell B9.
@UPPER	Capitalizes all the letters in the string, as shown in cell B10.
@LOWER	Changes all the letters in the string to lowercase, as in cell B11.

Miscellaneous functions In Figure 5.36, the six functions in cells B13 to B20 perform a variety of string operations:

FUNCTION	USE
@LENGTH	Supplies the length, in characters, of a string. @LENGTH takes one string argument. For example, @LENGTH(A1) displays 26 as the length of the string.
@EXACT	Compares two strings and determines whether or not they are the same. @EXACT returns a value of 1 (true) if its two string arguments are identical, or a value of 0 (false) if they are different. For example, @EXACT(A1,B9) returns a value of 0.
@REPEAT	Generates a new string consisting of multiple copies of a string argument. The function takes two arguments: @REPEAT(*string,n*). The first argument is the string to be repeated, and the second argument is an integer that specifies the number of repetitions. For example, @REPEAT(A1,2) produces the display shown in cell B15.
@TRIM	Removes extraneous spaces from a string—that is, spaces at the beginning and the end of the string, and multiple consecutive spaces inside the string. For example, @TRIM(A1) in cell B17 removes the extra three spaces between *for* and *windows*.

FUNCTION	USE
@S	Returns the label located in the first cell of a range. If this cell does not contain a label, @S returns an empty string. For example, the function @S(A1..A1) in B19 copies the label from cell A1.
@N	Returns the numeric value located in the first cell of a range. If this cell does not contain a value, @N returns a value of zero. For example, the function @N(A1..A1) in B20 returns a value of zero.

Conversion functions Four string functions in Figure 5.36 perform conversions from one data type to another, and give you access to the character code used in Lotus 1-2-3 Release 4 for Windows:

FUNCTION	USE
@CHAR	Takes an integer as its argument, and from the integer supplies a character from the *Lotus Multibyte Character Set*. This character code, known by its abbreviation LMBCS, represents all the characters that can be produced and displayed in Lotus 1-2-3. Figure 5.38 shows an excerpt from the LMBCS code.
@CODE	Supplies the LMBCS code number of a given character. @CODE takes one string argument, and gives the code number of the first character in the string.

FUNCTION	USE
@STRING	Produces a string from a numeric value. @STRING takes two arguments: @STRING(*value*,*n*). The *value* argument is the number to be converted to a string, and the *n* argument specifies the number of decimal places that will be displayed in the result. For example, @STRING(1-2-3.456,1) produces the string "1-2-3.5" as its result.
@VALUE	Performs the opposite conversion, producing a number from a string of digits. The single argument in @VALUE must be a string that 1-2-3 can read as a number. For example, @VALUE("9876") produces the number 9876.

Incorporating numeric values in strings The worksheet in Figure 5.39 shows two short experiments with the @STRING and @VALUE functions. The @STRING function is important in situations where you need to incorporate a numeric value into a string. The & operation will not join a string and a number; before you can perform the concatenation, you must convert the number into a string. This is the job of the @STRING function. For example, cell A4 in Figure 5.39 contains the calculated number of days between today's date and December 25. The following string formula combines this number with two strings to form the sentence displayed in cell A5:

    +"There are "&@STRING(A4,0)&" shopping days 'til Christmas."

Changing a string of digits into a number Conversely, you may sometimes need to convert a string of digits into a number so you can perform arithmetic operations on the value. The @VALUE function does this. For example, consider the sentence in cell A9 of Figure 5.39: "We received 107 units @ $1.25 per unit." In order to perform arithmetic operations on the two numbers in this string, you have to extract the strings of digits

FIGURE 5.38

An excerpt from the LMBCS character set, the set of all characters that can be produced and displayed in 1-2-3

	A	B	C	D	E	F	G	H	I	J
1	33	!	52	4	71	G	90	Z	109	m
2	34	"	53	5	72	H	91	[	110	n
3	35	#	54	6	73	I	92	\	111	o
4	36	$	55	7	74	J	93	]	112	p
5	37	%	56	8	75	K	94	^	113	q
6	38	&	57	9	76	L	95	_	114	r
7	39	'	58	:	77	M	96	`	115	s
8	40	(	59	;	78	N	97	a	116	t
9	41	)	60	<	79	O	98	b	117	u
10	42	*	61	=	80	P	99	c	118	v
11	43	+	62	>	81	Q	100	d	119	w
12	44	,	63	?	82	R	101	e	120	x
13	45	-	64	@	83	S	102	f	121	y
14	46	.	65	A	84	T	103	g	122	z
15	47	/	66	B	85	U	104	h	123	{
16	48	0	67	C	86	V	105	i	124		
17	49	1	68	D	87	W	106	j	125	}
18	50	2	69	E	88	X	107	k	126	~
19	51	3	70	F	89	Y	108	l		

FIGURE 5.39

Using the @STRING and @VALUE functions

	A	B	C	D
1	Experiments with @STRING and @VALUE			
2				
3				
4	81			
5	There are 81 shopping days 'til Christmas.			
6				
7				
8				
9	We received 107 units @ $1.25 per unit.			
10				
11	107	units		
12	$1.25	per unit		
13	$133.75	total cost		
14				
15				
16				

and convert them into numeric values. The formulas in cells A11 and A12 illustrate the technique:

CELL	FORMULA
A11	@VALUE(@MID(A9,12,3))
A12	@VALUE(@MID(A9,25,4))

The argument in each of these @VALUE functions is a @MID function that extracts a string of digits from the sentence in cell A9. @VALUE then makes the conversion from string to number. After this conversion, the numbers can be formatted and used in numeric formulas; for example, cell A13 contains the formula +A11*A12.

Special Functions

Like the logical and string functions, the special functions include several tools that are more relevant to macros than to spreadsheets. But there is a group of very important worksheet functions in this category, known as *lookup functions*. They are called @CHOOSE, @INDEX, @HLOOKUP, and @VLOOKUP. Lookup functions allow you to select a data item from a table that you enter into a range of your worksheet—or, in the case of @CHOOSE, from a list that is contained within the arguments of the function itself. Lookup functions require careful planning on your part, because you have to begin by developing the list or table of data. But once you have organized your worksheet appropriately, lookup functions prove to be very powerful tools, as you'll see in the next exercise.

The @CHOOSE Function

@CHOOSE is the easiest function to use in the group. It takes one numeric argument, n, followed by a list of data values or references to cells:

@CHOOSE(*n,datalist*)

The purpose of n is to select one of the values in *datalist*. The elements of the list are separated by commas. The value of n must be within the range from 0 up to the number of entries in the list minus 1. Using n as an offset number, @CHOOSE returns the nth value in the list.

@CHOOSE provides an interesting alternative to the formula used in Figure 5.37 to produce the days of the week. You can generate exactly the same day names by entering the following @CHOOSE formula into cell B6 and then copying the formula down column B:

    @CHOOSE(@MOD(C6,7),"Sat","Sun","Mon","Tue","Wed","Thu","
    Fri")&"."

In this function, @MOD(C6,7) produces the value from 0 to 6 that serves as a selector value for the list of names. For example, if the @MOD function returns a value of 3, the @CHOOSE function returns "Tue" as its string result.

The @INDEX Function

By contrast, the @INDEX function selects a label or value from a table on your worksheet. @INDEX takes three required arguments and one optional argument. Here is its format:

    @INDEX(*range,column,row*)

The *range* argument is the location of the table where @INDEX reads a data item. The *column* and *row* arguments identify column and row offsets within *range*. The *column* argument ranges from 0 up to the number of columns in the table minus 1. Likewise, the *row* argument ranges from 0 up to the number of rows in the table minus 1.

The fourth optional argument is an integer representing the worksheet that contains the lookup table:

    @INDEX(*range,column,row,worksheet*)

This argument allows you to build the lookup table in a different worksheet location from the function itself.

An example of the @INDEX function appears in Figure 5.40. This worksheet illustrates a technique for producing a complete date string from the date numbers that appear in column A. As you can see in the lower part of the worksheet, columns B and C contain lists of day names and month names. The worksheet reads these as one-column @INDEX tables. The column of day names, B7..B13, is assigned the range name DOW; and the column of month names, C7..C18, is named MO.

	A	B	C	D
1	32946	Wednesday, March 14, 1990		
2	34132	Saturday, June 12, 1993		
3	32129	Friday, December 18, 1987		
4	16705	Tuesday, September 25, 1945		
5				
6		DOW	MO	
7		Saturday	January	
8		Sunday	February	
9		Monday	March	
10		Tuesday	April	
11		Wednesday	May	
12		Thursday	June	
13		Friday	July	
14			August	
15			September	
16			October	
17			November	
18			December	

Formulas in cells B1 to B4 use the @INDEX function to read names from the DOW and MO ranges. Here is the formula in cell B1:

```
@INDEX($DOW,0,@MOD(A1,7))&", "&
@INDEX($MO,0,@MONTH(A1)-1)&" "&
@STRING(@DAY(A1),0)&", 19"&
@STRING(@YEAR(A1),0)
```

This is the most detailed formula you've seen yet, but it's easy to understand if you study it one part at a time.

- The first @INDEX function uses the expression @MOD(A1,7) as a row offset in the DOW range to select the day of the week.

- The second uses the expression @MONTH(A1)−1 as a row offset in the MO range to select the name of the month. In both @INDEX functions, the column offset is 0, because both tables have only one column.

- The two @STRING functions are used to convert the results of @DAY and @YEAR to strings.

When all of these substrings are joined together, the result is a full date display:

Wednesday, March 14, 1993

The formula in cell B1 is copied down to the range B2..B4. (Notice the use of absolute references to make this copy procedure possible.)

The @HLOOKUP and @VLOOKUP Functions

The @HLOOKUP and @VLOOKUP functions read values from specially organized lookup tables. The first row or column of a lookup table contains a range of reference values that are central to the search for a target data item in the table.

For example, look at the Conference Room Price Table, shown in the lower part of the worksheet in Figure 5.41. The conference planners at Computing Conferences, Inc. use this table to determine the price of a downtown conference room for a one-day event. As you can see, the price of a conference room varies according to the number of people attending and the date of the event. To find the correct price for attendance size n, you begin by looking across the first row of the table, which contains a range of attendance figures from 1 to 300. Find the *largest* value in this row that is less than or equal to n. This value heads the column in which you will find the price for the conference room. Next, look down the column to the row containing the date of the conference. The correct price is found in the cell at the intersection of the attendance column and date row.

@HLOOKUP function The @HLOOKUP function automates this search. The function takes three arguments—a lookup value, a table range, and a row offset:

@HLOOKUP(*n,table,row*)

The first argument, n, is the value that the function looks for in the first row of the lookup table. The second argument, *table*, is the range of the lookup table itself, and the third argument, *row*, is the target row offset in the table.

In Figure 5.41, the @HLOOKUP function is used in cells E11 and F11 to find the conference room costs corresponding to the minimum and maximum attendance estimates. The table in the range B16..H19 is assigned the

AC	A	B	C	D	E	F	G	H
1			Computing Conferences, Inc.					
2			Profit Projection for a One-Day Conference					
3								
4	Conference:	Computing for Video Stores						
5	Place:	St. Louis						
6	Date:	15-Oct-93			Expected Attendance			
7					Minimum	Maximum		
8	Price:	$195.00			80	150		
9								
10								
11			Conference Room Cost		$1,750.00	$2,300.00		
12								
13								
14								
15	Conference Room Price Table							
16	Attendance	1	35	75	100	150	200	300
17	1992 price	$400.00	$600.00	$1,500.00	$1,750.00	$2,000.00	$3,000.00	$3,500.00
18	1993 price	$450.00	$700.00	$1,750.00	$1,900.00	$2,300.00	$3,400.00	$3,700.00
19	1994 price	$500.00	$750.00	$1,900.00	$2,000.00	$2,500.00	$3,500.00	$3,850.00
20								
21								

name ROOM. The two attendance estimates are in E8 and F8. Here is the function in cell E11:

    @HLOOKUP(E8,$ROOM,2)

In this example, E8 is the attendance estimate that the function looks for in the first row of the ROOM range. A row offset of 2 gives the correct row for a 1993 conference date. In short, the @HLOOKUP function finds the conference room price corresponding to an estimated attendance of 80 people: in the first row of the lookup table, the largest value that is less than or equal to 80 is the attendance figure of 75 in cell D16. Searching down column D to the 1992 row, the function finds the correct price for the conference room, $1,750.00, in cell D18.

@VLOOKUP function The @VLOOKUP function performs an equivalent data search, but in a vertically organized lookup table:

    @VLOOKUP(*n,table,column*)

This function searches for *n* in the first column of *table*. The third argument, *column*, gives the column offset in the lookup table.

You can also enter labels rather than numbers in the first row or column of a lookup table. In this case, the first argument in the @HLOOKUP and @VLOOKUP functions is a string:

@HLOOKUP(*string,table,row*)

@VLOOKUP(*string,table,column*)

The @HLOOKUP function looks for a label that exactly matches *string* in the first row of the lookup table. Likewise, the @VLOOKUP function looks for a match for *string* in the first column of the table.

The @HLOOKUP and @VLOOKUP functions are versatile and powerful, especially in applications that require very large lookup tables. Of course, the classic example is an income tax table, in which the first column contains a range of income levels, and the first row contains taxpayer categories. The @VLOOKUP function is ideally suited to reading tax amounts from such a table.

Summary

Each major category of formulas in 1-2-3—numeric, logical, and text—has its own set of operators:

- Numeric formulas use the familiar *, /, +, and − operators, along with the ^ operator for exponentiation.

- Logical formulas produce values of true or false, represented numerically by 1 and 0. There are two groups of logical operators. They are =, <>, <, >, and <=, which determine equality or inequality, and #NOT#, #AND#, and #OR#, which modify or combine logical expressions.

- Lotus 1-2-3 has one text operator, &, which joins two labels or strings.

The 1-2-3 function library includes over two hundred functions that can be entered into cells by themselves or used in formulas. Here is a brief summary of the function categories you have studied in this chapter:

FUNCTION TYPE	USE
Statistical	Includes tools designed to calculate totals, averages, counts, and maximum and minimum values, along with the more advanced statistical calculations known as variance and standard deviation.
Financial	Includes calculations for depreciation methods; present value and future value; payment, term, and rate values; and the internal rate of return.
Mathematical	Includes built-in formulas for trigonometric, logarithmic, and exponential values, plus an assortment of other important tools: a random number generator, integer and rounding functions, and the absolute value and modulus operations.
Date and time	Includes tools that supply the current date and time; functions that give information about date and time values; conversion functions; and date arithmetic functions.
String	Includes tools that work with substrings; alphabetic case functions; and functions that convert between numeric and string values.
Special	Includes four important lookup tools that read values from tables and lists on the worksheet.

Creating and Refining Charts

**To update a chart after changing the figures
on which it is based,**   350

simply click on the chart. 1-2-3 redraws the chart automatically.

To add a legend to a chart,   351

activate the chart and choose Chart ➤ Legend. In the Legend
dialog box, click [all ranges] in the Series list box, click the
Legend entry range button, and select the data range you
want to represent the legend.

To change fonts in legends, titles, and footnotes,   354

click on the chart object you want to change and click on the
right mouse button. A menu appears with commands associated with the object. Choose Font & Attributes. In the dialog
box, choose a new font and press ↵.

To delete an object from a chart,   360

click on the object to select it and either choose Edit ➤ Cut
or press the Delete key.

To add grid lines to a chart,   361

activate the chart and choose Chart ➤ Grids, click Y-axis and
select an interval option for the grids. Then click OK.

To print a chart,   362

simply click the Print SmartIcon.

IN BUSINESS, technology, and everyday life, charts have a universal appeal. People prefer to look at pictorial representations of numbers rather than the numbers themselves. Grasping what is in a table of numbers requires time, effort, and concentration, but charts have an instant impact. When you look at a chart, you can answer questions about the data almost before you can even ask the questions: Which data item is the smallest and which is the largest? Is there a downward or upward trend? Are there atypical values that don't conform to the trends shown in the other data? How significant is one value in relation to the total? The answers to these and many other questions are plain to see in a chart.

Producing a chart in 1-2-3 is simple, and you can create an extraordinary variety of visual effects. You can choose from eight major chart types. Besides the familiar bar charts, line charts, area charts, and pie charts, which are available in both two- and three-dimensional versions, you can create XY charts, mixed charts, and high-low-open-close (HLOC) charts for special kinds of data. Release 4 offers a new kind of chart called a *radar chart*. Once you have chosen a chart type, you use 1-2-3's powerful collection of graphics tools to refine and clarify its message.

HOT STUFF

In Release 4 for Windows, you can place charts on a worksheet. All you have to do is select a range of data, choose Tools ➤ Chart, and make room on your worksheet for the chart. Whenever a chart is active, a new menu choice—Chart—appears on the menu bar in place of the Range menu. The Chart menu is shown in Figure 6.1. This chapter will teach you how to create and refine charts.

In Release 4, Chart is a menu option on the menu bar when a chart is active.

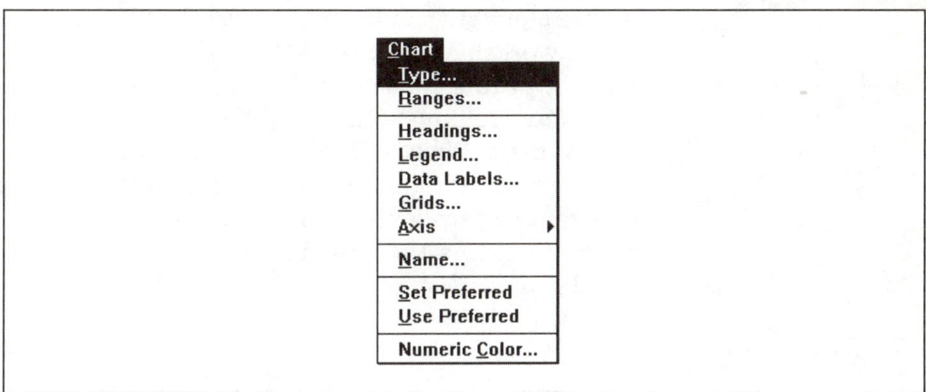

Creating a Chart from Worksheet Data

In 1-2-3 Release 4, charts are embedded directly in worksheets. They are saved to disk as part of the worksheet file. A worksheet can have multiple linked charts.

To create a chart, begin by developing a table whose data the chart will represent. Once the worksheet is ready, you follow these steps to develop the chart:

1. Preselect the data range from which the chart will be created.

2. Choose Tools ➤ Chart.

3. The mouse cursor changes to a miniature graph. Click and drag the mouse to make room on the worksheet for the chart.

4. Use the Chart commands and Chart SmartIcons to refine the chart's appearance. You can include titles and footnotes, arrows and shapes, free-floating text, or a legend on a chart.

5. When the chart is complete, click outside of the chart to deselect it.

6. Print the worksheet with the chart.

In this chapter, you'll create several different kinds of charts from one simple worksheet. The worksheet, shown in Figure 6.2, is a one-year summary of profits earned by Computing Conferences, Inc. Profits earned from four regions—Eastern, Western, Northern, and Southern—are shown in the chart columns. The rows represent the different types of computer-training conferences. In 1992, Computing Conferences, Inc. held conferences for accountants, doctors, lawyers, retail businesses, and video stores. As the title shows, the different kinds of conferences are called "topics."

FIGURE 6.2

The conference profits worksheet. In this chapter, you'll create charts from the data found here.

	A	B	C	D	E	F
1		Computing Conferences, Inc.				
2		Conference Profits by Region and Topic				
3		1992				
4						
5		Eastern	Western	Northern	Southern	Total
6	Accountants	$111,200	$79,300	$59,500	$64,200	$314,200
7	Doctors	$131,900	$116,900	$77,500	$96,700	$423,000
8	Lawyers	$63,500	$81,500	$54,000	$88,400	$287,400
9	Retail Business	$92,800	$88,600	$57,900	$78,400	$317,700
10	Video Stores	$88,300	$63,200	$41,900	$61,900	$255,300
11	Total	$487,700	$429,500	$290,800	$389,600	$1,597,600
12						

To prepare for the exercises ahead, your first job is to enter this data table in your own worksheet. Here are the steps:

1. On a blank worksheet, enter the following titles into cells A1 to A3:

CELL	ENTRY
A1	**Computing Conferences, Inc.**
A2	**Conference Profits by Region and Topic**
A3	**'1992**

Remember, you enter a label that begins with a number, such as 1992, with a single quotation mark so that 1-2-3 will not accept it as a value.

2. Preselect range A1..F3. To center the titles horizontally over this range, choose <u>S</u>tyle ➤ <u>A</u>lignment, select <u>C</u>enter, and select Acr<u>o</u>ss columns. Click OK to confirm. Then click the Bold and Italics SmartIcons to set the display style for the titles.

3. Choose <u>S</u>tyle ➤ <u>W</u>orksheet Defaults and click on the ↓ button next to <u>F</u>ormat. Select Currency from the pull-down list, and enter a value of **0** for <u>D</u>ecimals.

4. Enter the following labels in cells A6 to A11:

CELL	ENTRY
A6	**Accountants**
A7	**Doctors**
A8	**Lawyers**
A9	**Retail Business**
A10	**Video Stores**
A11	**Total**

5. Drag the border of column A to the right to increase the column width to 13.

6. Enter the following column headings in cells B5 to F5:

CELL	ENTRY
B5	**Eastern**
C5	**Western**
D5	**Northern**

E5	**Southern**
F5	**Total**

7. Right-align these five headings in their respective cells.

8. Enter the numeric profit values into range B6..E10, as shown in Figure 6.2.

9. Preselect range B6..F11 and click the Summation SmartIcon once. In response, 1-2-3 enters all the appropriate @SUM functions in cell F11.

10. Select all titles and totals, as shown in Figure 6.2, and apply boldface to them with the Boldface SmartIcon.

11. Your worksheet should look like the one in Figure 6.2. Choose File ➤ Save As and save the worksheet as PROFITS.WK4.

You're now ready to create a chart from this worksheet.

Selecting Data Ranges for Charts

The first step in creating a chart is to preselect the data range from which the chart will be created. By default, 1-2-3 reads your data range selection in *columnwise* mode. In columnwise mode, each column in the range plays a specific role in the chart, either as the *X-axis labels* or as *Y-data ranges*:

- **The X-axis labels.** The x-axis is the horizontal line at the bottom border of a chart. The first column in the data range will provide the X-axis labels, since the first column is where 1-2-3 expects to find the labels that identify the numeric data in the columns to the right. Where appropriate, 1-2-3 displays these labels along the chart's x-axis.

- **The Y-data ranges.** The adjacent columns provide the Y-data ranges. In these columns, 1-2-3 expects to find the numeric data that will be represented in the chart.

X-axis labels and Y-data ranges apply when you are constructing area charts, line charts, and bar charts. Other chart types impose more requirements on the data range, as you'll learn later in this chapter.

On the profits worksheet, the data range for your first chart is A5..E10. The first column in this range, A5..A10, represents the X-axis range labels. As you'll see shortly, these labels will appear along the x-axis of the chart. The four adjacent columns, the one-year profit figures for the four regions in which the company does business, will be the Y-data ranges.

- Select range A5..E10 on your worksheet now.

Notice what this range does *not* contain. You are not including the column of topic totals (column F), or the row of regional totals (row 11). Including either would make no sense in the resulting chart. Furthermore, you have included the row of column headings (row 5) from the data range. These headings will be used to create a legend for your chart. In Release 4, creating a legend is a separate step.

Now that you have selected an appropriate data range, you can create the chart. That is the subject of the next section.

Creating a Bar Chart

When you make a chart the active element on a worksheet (by clicking anywhere inside it), the Range option on the menu bar is replaced by the Chart option. You can also make the Chart option appear on the menu bar by selecting Tools ➤ Chart. Open the Chart menu and you see a list of eleven commands. The commands on the Chart menu are described in Table 6.1.

TABLE 6.1: Chart Menu Commands

COMMAND	DESCRIPTION
Type	Changes the chart to a different style. With this command, you can choose a different *chart orientation* or create a *table of values* from the data range in the chart.
Ranges	Specifies a new data range for the chart. Enter a new range in the Range text box or click the ↓ next to the Range text box to select a new range.
Headings	Lets you enter text for creating or changing titles and footers in the chart.

TABLE 6.1: Chart Menu Commands (continued)

COMMAND	DESCRIPTION
Legend	Lets you create legend labels. These labels, along with different colors and patterns, identify rows or columns of data in the chart.
Data Labels	Lets you create data labels, the text titles that identify the *data points* on the chart.
Grids	Lets you add add or remove grids from the chart. These grids differ from the grid lines on worksheets.
Axis	Controls the creation of axis titles and sets the axis scale for the chart. With this command, you can change the x-axis, y-axis, or the second y-axis.
Name	Lets you name the charts attached to a worksheet. By default, these charts are named Chart 1, Chart 2, and so on.
Set Preferred	Lets you change the default chart settings to the ones you've established for the currently selected chart. Once the settings become the default, you can apply them to charts you create in the future simply by selecting Chart ➤ Use Preferred.
Use Preferred	Lets you change the chart settings to those you've established with the Set Preferred command on the Chart menu.
Numeric Color	Lets you change the color or pattern for a data series in the chart.

Release 4 provides a quick way to select any menu command on the Chart menu. Select an element of a chart on-screen—a legend or a heading, for example—and click the right mouse button. Lotus 1-2-3 will display a menu with Chart options.

Creating a Bar Chart with the Chart Menu

For your first chart, you will create a bar chart with the Chart menu. *Bar charts*, the default chart in Lotus 1-2-3, depict bars of different lengths to show the relative differences between different kinds of data. Our bar chart will depict the relative profit levels generated by the five different conference topics.

1. With range A5..E10 still preselected on your worksheet, choose <u>T</u>ools ➤ <u>C</u>hart.

The Graph cursor　The cursor changes to a miniature graph. Use this cursor to specify the area on the worksheet where the new chart will be.

2. Click on the upper-left corner of the area where you want to place the chart and drag the cursor. A box appears. Drag the box out until it is the size you want the bar chart to be, and release the mouse button.

If the window is too small for the chart, simply drag the chart display beyond the border window. The window will scroll in the direction you push it out.

When you release the mouse button, 1-2-3 immediately creates a new chart from your preselected data range, as shown in Figure 6.3. As long as the chart is active, the Chart option appears in the menu bar and the Chart SmartIcons appear as well. As Figure 6.3 shows, the profit data is represented by sets of bars. Each set represents one of the four regions. In each set, the bars represent a different conference topic.

Naming a chart　Now it is time to give the chart a name:

3. Choose <u>C</u>hart ➤ <u>N</u>ame, and specify a name for the chart in the Name dialog box.

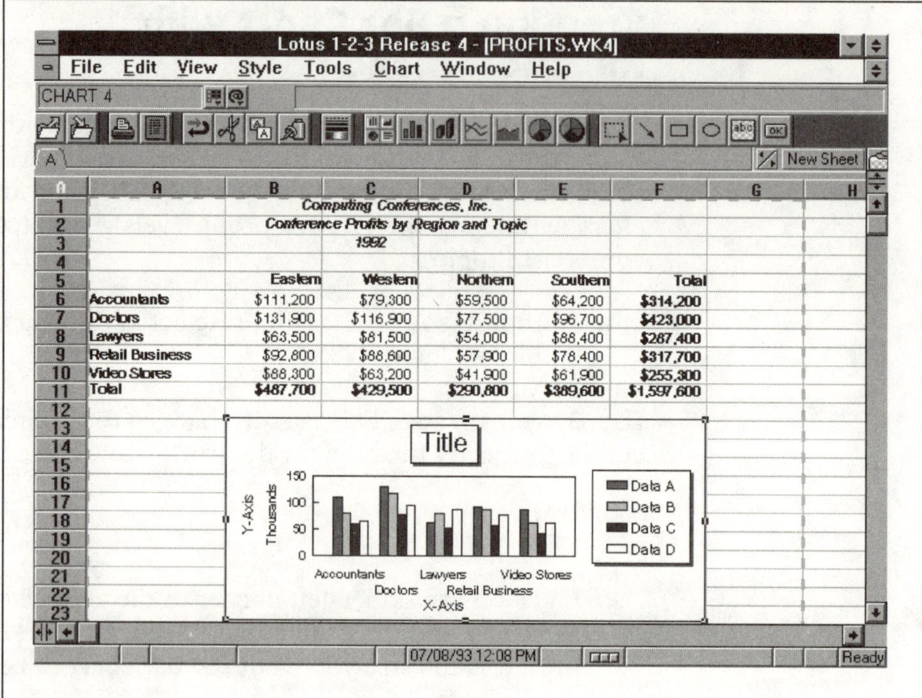

The spreadsheet in the figure shows:

	A	B	C	D	E	F	G	H
1			Computing Conferences, Inc.					
2			Conference Profits by Region and Topic					
3			1992					
4								
5		Eastern	Western	Northern	Southern	Total		
6	Accountants	$111,200	$79,300	$59,500	$64,200	$314,200		
7	Doctors	$131,900	$116,900	$77,500	$96,700	$423,000		
8	Lawyers	$63,500	$81,500	$54,000	$88,400	$287,400		
9	Retail Business	$92,800	$88,600	$57,900	$78,400	$317,700		
10	Video Stores	$88,300	$63,200	$41,900	$61,900	$255,300		
11	Total	$487,700	$429,500	$290,800	$389,600	$1,597,600		

Specify a descriptive chart name. Chart names can be as long as 15 characters. Use letters of the alphabet, not special characters (such as +, –, and &), so that the chart won't be confused with a formula or range address. You can enter the chart name in uppercase or lowercase letters, but 1-2-3 converts your entry to all uppercase letters.

Switching back to the worksheet   Let's return to the worksheet in order to experiment with the other tool available for creating a chart, the CreateChart icon. To reactivate the profits worksheet:

4. Click the worksheet window with the mouse. The familiar worksheet menu bar reappears at the top of the 1-2-3 window, along with the familiar worksheet SmartIcons.

Creating a Bar Chart with the CreateChart Icon

The CreateChart icon is located on the right side of the SmartIcon set. It shows three bars in a bar chart.

In the following exercise, you'll create a new chart with the CreateChart icon, and then you'll delete the chart.

1. Preselect range A5..E10 on the profit worksheet once again.
2. Click the CreateChart icon.
3. Click the mouse and drag the graph cursor to the shape you want the chart to be.
4. Release the mouse button. Lotus 1-2-3 creates a bar chart like the one in Figure 6.3.
5. To delete the chart that you just created, click on the chart and press Del (the delete key on your keyboard).

Clearly, the advantage of the CreateChart icon is its one-step efficiency.

After deleting the chart you created with the CreateChart icon, only one chart is linked to the profits worksheet, the one you created and named with Tools ➤ Chart. Activate this chart now:

- Click on the chart with your mouse.

In the next exercise, you'll select a 3D bar chart type as the new format for the chart.

The Chart SmartIcons

Soon you will familiarize yourself with the Chart SmartIcons. You can click a Chart SmartIcon with the right mouse button to view a brief description of what it does. The description appears temporarily in 1-2-3's title bar.

Furthermore, the Chart SmartIcons are conveniently arranged in easy-to-distinguish groups. For example, the following list identifies the seven icons that produce the most common chart types. Just by clicking one of these icons, you can change the chart type displayed in the graph window. For example, clicking the 3DBarChart icon changes the current chart to a vertical three-dimensional bar chart. These icons represent the same options available when you choose Chart ➤ Type, which you'll do shortly. The first icon in this group, ChartType, actually displays the Type dialog box on-screen.

CHART SMARTICON	ICON NAME
	ChartType
	BarChart
	3DBarChart
	LineChart
	AreaChart
	PieChart
	ExplodedPie

The Chart SmartIcons in the list below are the equivalents of commands found on the Draw menu. They are found on the right side of the Chart SmartIcon set. Each allows you to place a new object on your chart: an arrow, a line, an ellipse, a polygon, a rectangle, a text item, or a freehand drawing. You'll experiment with these icons later in this chapter.

CHART SMARTICON	ICON NAME
	ObjectSelector
	Arrow
	Rectangle
	Oval
	Text

Changing to a New Type of Chart

For now, the current chart selected is a bar chart. Your next step is to transform this chart and make it a 3D bar chart. Lotus 1-2-3 lets you change to a new type of chart quite easily with the Type dialog box.

1. Choose Chart ➤ Type. The Type dialog box appears, as in Figure 6.4.

The Type dialog box. With this dialog box, you can change a chart from one type into another.

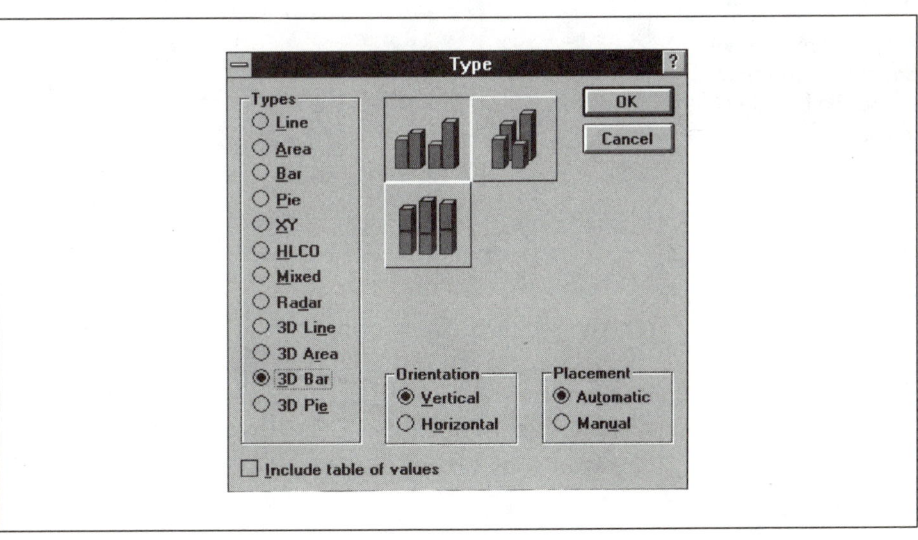

CREATING AND REFINING CHARTS

The Type dialog box offers a complete list of 1-2-3's chart types, represented as a column of option buttons. When you click one of these buttons, the dialog box displays pictures of the formats available for the chart type you selected.

Creating a 3-D Bar Chart

Change the bar chart you created earlier into a 3-D bar chart:

2. Click the option labeled 3D Bar (for "three-dimensional bar chart"). As you can see in Figure 6.4, three formats are available for three-dimensional bar charts:

   - one with the bars in a given category grouped together in adjacent positions (this is the default),
   - one with the bars clustered together and overlapping,
   - one with bars stacked one on top of another.

3. Click OK or press ↵ to accept the default 3D Bar format. Lotus 1-2-3 redraws the bar chart, as shown in Figure 6.5.

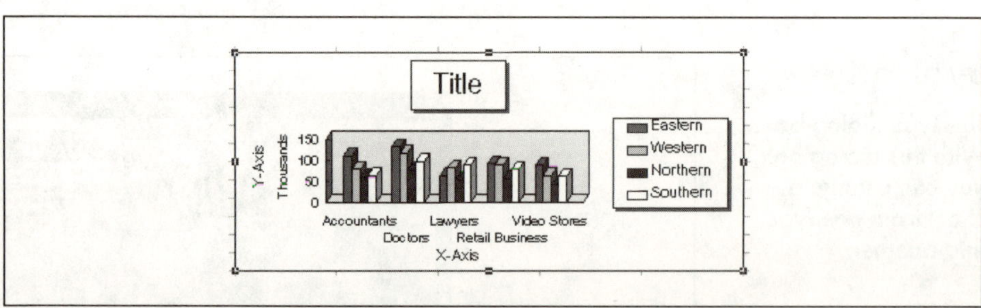

In the three-dimensional format, each set of vertical bars represents the profit figures from one of the five training-conference topics. Within each topic, one bar represents one of the four regions. Now you have a good visual representation of the data. You can see which conference topic brings in the largest profits and which region brings in the most revenue.

Displaying table values beside a chart Interestingly, 1-2-3 lets you view a data table along with a chart by clicking the option labeled _I_nclude table of values at the bottom of the Type dialog box. To see what this option does, try the following exercise:

1. Choose _C_hart ➤ _T_ype.
2. Click the _I_nclude table of values option. An *X* appears inside the check box.
3. Click OK or press ↵.

The chart window shown in Figure 6.6 appears on the screen. Beneath each group of bars, you can now read the exact data values that the bars represent.

4. To get ready for the next exercise, click the SaveFile icon to save your work to disk.

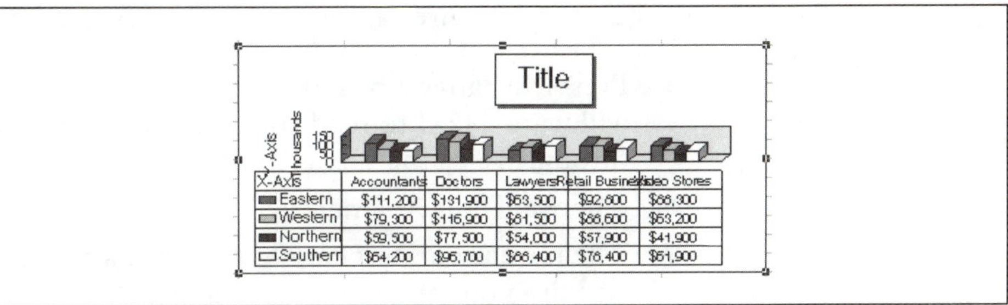

X-Axis	Accountants	Doctors	Lawyers	Retail Business	Video Stores
Eastern	$111,200	$131,900	$63,500	$92,600	$66,300
Western	$79,300	$116,900	$61,500	$66,600	$53,200
Northern	$59,500	$77,500	$54,000	$57,900	$41,900
Southern	$64,200	$96,700	$66,400	$76,400	$51,900

NOTE   When you save a worksheet, 1-2-3 saves all the charts linked to the worksheet as well.

Creating Charts in the Rowwise Format

You learned earlier in this chapter that the columnwise method is 1-2-3's default way of translating a table of data into a chart. In the columnwise chart you've been working with, each group of bars on the chart represents data values found in a column of the worksheet. Consequently, the focus of the chart is on the conference topics and on the profits generated from each topic category. But what if you wanted to create a chart that focused instead on the regions? Because columnwise charts are the default, you might consider reorganizing the worksheet itself, entering the regional data values into rows and the topic profits into columns.

Fortunately, 1-2-3 offers a simpler approach. You can select a series of rows as the data range for a chart, and, once the chart is displayed, choose Chart ➤ Ranges to instruct 1-2-3 to reorganize the chart in a *rowwise* format.

Your task in the next exercise is to create a stacked bar chart in which you can compare the total profits from each of the four regions. Each regional bar will consist of five stacked components representing the five conference topics. The labels along the x-axis—that is, the X-data range—will identify the four regions. The A-, B-, C-, D-, and E-data ranges will be the profit figures from each of the five topics.

Looking at the profits worksheet (see Figure 6.2), it's easy to see that this arrangement requires a rowwise chart. Here are the steps for creating it:

1. Preselect range A5..E10 on the profits worksheet. Ultimately, you will want 1-2-3 to read row 5 as the X-data range, and rows 6 through 10 as the Y-axis data ranges.

2. Choose Tools ➤ Chart.

3. The mouse cursor changes to a miniature graph. Click the mouse and drag out an area for the chart.

4. Choose Chart ➤ Ranges. The Ranges dialog box appears, as in Figure 6.7.

The Ranges dialog box gives you control over the data ranges portrayed in the chart. By examining the Ranges dialog box, you can see in the Assign ranges box that 1-2-3 has created the current chart in the columnwise mode. Column A on the worksheet has been selected as the X-data range, and columns B, C, D, and E have been selected as the remaining data ranges. This is not the arrangement you want for your new chart.

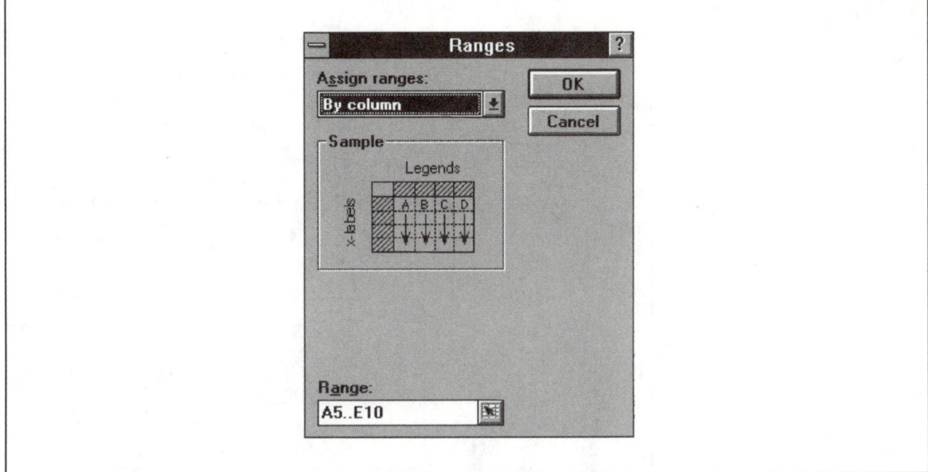

5. To change the ranges, click the ↓ button on the A_ssign ranges box. In the pull-down list are three options, By row, By column, and Individually. The default selection, as you have guessed, is Individually. Select By row.

6. Click OK or press ↵ to confirm.

Now 1-2-3 has correctly reorganized the data ranges, as you can see on your screen and in Figure 6.8. The labels in row 5 are identified as the X-data range, and the five rows of profit figures beneath these labels are identified as data ranges A through E.

Creating stacked bar charts Now create a stacked 3-D bar chart:

7. Choose C_hart ➤ T_ype. The Type dialog box appears.

8. Select the 3D Bar option, and click the picture of the stacked bar chart, the one on the bottom.

9. Click OK or press ↵ to confirm your selections.

10. Select C_hart ➤ N_ame and give your chart the name REGIONBARS.

The stacked bar chart appears in Figure 6.9. You have achieved the effect that you wanted: each stacked bar represents one of the four regions, and each portion of a given bar represents one of the conference topics. This presentation makes it easy to compare the profits of the four regions.

Changing the range orientation from columnwise to rowwise

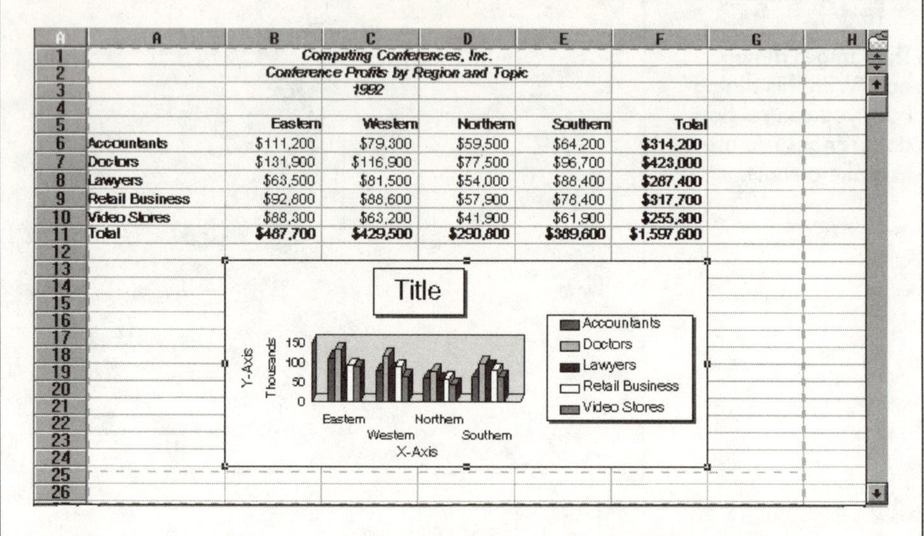

Performing "What-If" Experiments with Charts

What happens now if you make a change to the original data on the worksheet to which the charts are linked? Suppose, after creating these charts, one of the managers at Computing Conferences, Inc. discovered an unfortunate clerical error. The profit of Video Stores training conferences in

This rowwise 3-D bar chart is stacked.

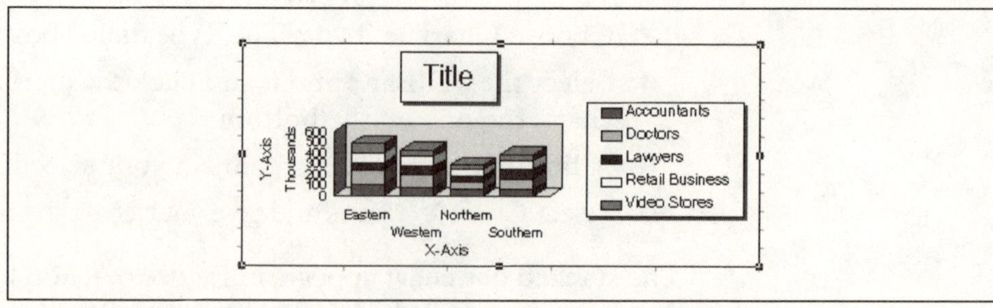

the Southern region had been underreported by $100,000. Instead of the current $61,900, the figure should be $161,900. What will the charts look like when this figure is corrected? To find out, follow these steps:

1. Click anywhere on the data in the PROFITS.WK4 worksheet.

2. Select cell E10 and enter the correct profit value, **$161,900**.

3. Click anywhere on the REGIONBARS chart. Lotus 1-2-3 redraws the chart in response to the correction. Now the Southern region has the highest profits of the four regions.

4. Activate the worksheet again, and click the SaveFile icon to save the profits worksheet to disk, along with its linked charts.

Refining a Chart by Adding New Features

Your next job is to improve the presentation of the chart. You'll add a variety of new elements, starting with titles and a legend. The commands for adding titles and a legend are in the Chart menu.

Adding Titles and a Legend

You choose Chart ➤ Headings and Chart ➤ Legend commands to create new elements at fixed positions on a chart.

- **Chart ➤ Headings.** In the Headings dialog box are text boxes for entering a title and a subtitle. The title and subtitle are displayed at the top of the chart. There are also text boxes for entering one or two "footnotes." Footnotes are displayed in the lower-left corner of the chart.

- **Chart ➤ Legend.** In the Legend dialog box, in the Series list box, are six labels. In place of these labels, you can enter labels of your own for the legend that 1-2-3 displays beneath your chart.

In many cases, you will want to copy titles and labels from your worksheet. For example, the REGIONBARS chart titles are in cells A1, A2, and A3 of the profits worksheet, and the labels for the legend are the conference topics, in cells A6 through A10. Lotus 1-2-3 supplies a special notation for selecting a worksheet cell as the source of a title or legend. In this notation, you simply click on the Cell check box next to the cell reference. For example, clicking A1 tells 1-2-3 to copy the text from cell A1. In the next exercise, you'll supply entries like this one in the Headings dialog box to identify the text for headings and footnotes.

The Legend dialog box has an additional feature for entering a legend. Text entries for the legend usually come from a row or column of a worksheet, so 1-2-3 lets you identify a *group range* as the legend.

Adding the Legend

Here are the steps for adding the legend, titles, and footnotes to the REGIONBARS chart:

1. Click on the REGIONBARS chart to activate it, and choose Chart ➤ Legend. The Legend dialog box appears, as in Figure 6.10.

2. Click [all ranges] in the Series list box.

3. Click the Legend entry range button and select the data range A6..A10.

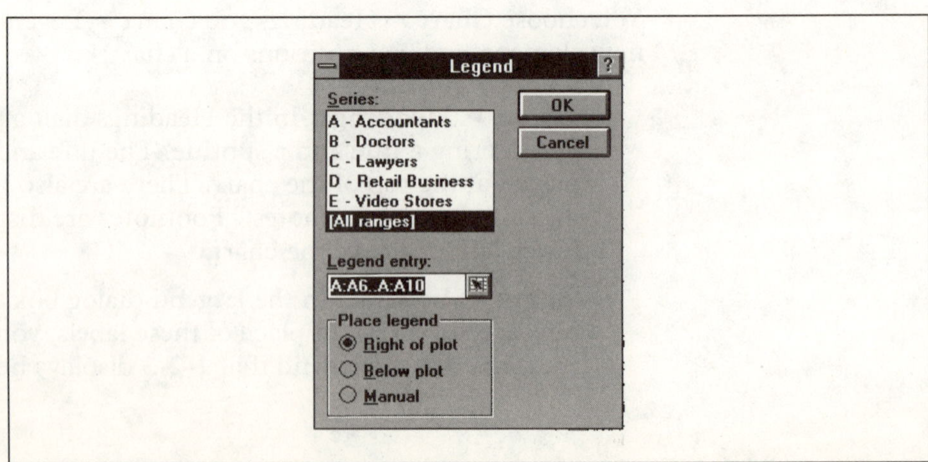

As Figure 6.10 shows, five cell references containing legend labels have been entered in the text boxes labeled A through E.

4. Click OK or press ↵.

The legend appears on the right side of the REGIONBARS chart. For this chart, the legend consists of the five topic labels, each paired with a small rectangle that identifies its color in the stacked bar chart.

Adding Titles and Footnotes

Now let's add titles and a footnote to the chart:

5. Choose Chart ➤ Headings. The Headings dialog box appears, as shown in Figure 6.11.

6. Make the following entries:

- Enter **A2** in the Title Line 1 text box. (Cell A2 is "Conference Profits by Region and Topic.")
- Enter **A3** in the Title Line 2 text box. (Cell A3 is "1992.")
- Enter **A1** into the Note Line 1 text box. (Cell A1 is "Computing Conferences, Inc.")

Your Headings dialog box should look like the one in Figure 6.11. Leave the Note Line 2 text box empty.

7. Click OK or press ↵.

FIGURE 6.11

The Headings dialog box. This is where you enter titles and footnotes for a chart.

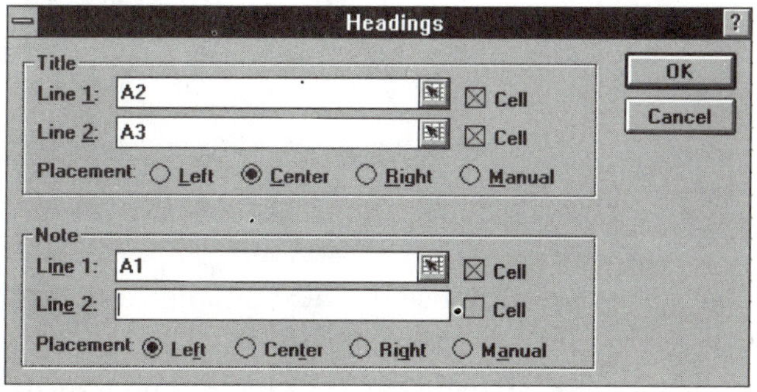

HOT STUFF

Changing fonts and type sizes in titles and footnotes A title and subtitle now appear at the top of the chart, and "Computing Conferences, Inc." appears as a footnote in the lower-left corner. Unfortunately, the title and the legend labels are displayed in a font size that seems too big for the rest of the chart. You'll correct this problem next.

8. Click on the chart object that you want to change, in this case the first line of the title. When you click on the chart object, a box appears around it.

9. Click on the object with the right mouse button. A menu of commands associated with the object you clicked on appears.

10. Choose the Font & Attributes command. The Font & Attributes dialog box appears, as shown in Figure 6.12.

The Font & Attributes dialog box gives you a selection of fonts for the chart object you have selected. (The fonts that appear on your screen may not be the same as those in Figure 6.12.)

FIGURE 6.12

The Font & Attributes dialog box

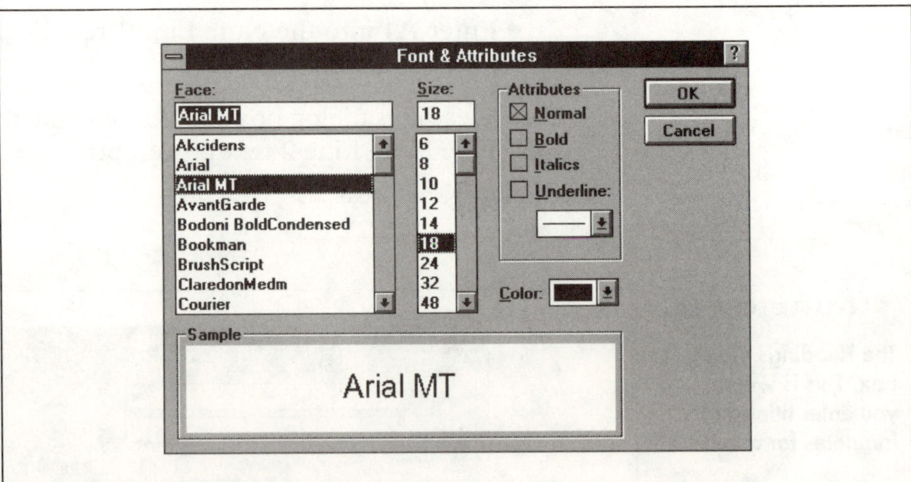

11. Choose the next smaller font size, located above the current font selection in the list.

12. Click OK or press ↵. The REGIONBARS chart now looks like Figure 6.13.

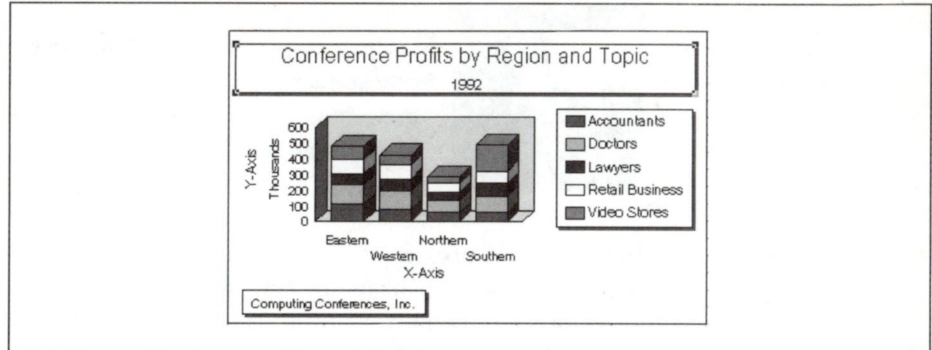

NOTE See Chapter 4 for more information about the Font & Attributes dialog box.

These new entries make your chart much more complete. The legend clarifies the meaning of the five data ranges, and the titles and footnote give general information about the chart. As a formal presentation of the data, this chart is nearly ready to be printed and distributed. However, to spruce up the document even more, you could add more features to it. That is the subject of the next part of this chapter.

Adding Chart Objects, such as Arrows and Text Boxes

For informal documents, such as memos to staff members or notes to colleagues, you may want to add more elements to your chart. For example, to focus attention on part of a chart, you can add a line of text explaining what it is, along with an arrow pointing from the text to the part of the chart to which the text refers. Arrows and text are examples of *chart objects*. Unlike titles and the legend, you can place chart objects anywhere you want on the chart. To add objects, choose Tools ➤ Draw or click the corresponding SmartIcons.

Objects can be displayed in any size and at any position in the chart, so you may have to experiment with objects before your chart looks the way you want it to look.

In the next exercise, you'll draw a rectangle on the chart, place text inside the rectangle, and draw an arrow from the rectangle to the chart. These additions will call attention to the unusually high profits generated by the Video Stores conferences in the Southern region.

Drawing a Rectangle on a Chart

Start by drawing the rectangle:

1. Choose <u>T</u>ools ➤ <u>D</u>raw ➤ <u>T</u>ext. The mouse pointer becomes a small cross.

Take a look at Figure 6.14 to see the position and size of the rectangle you'll be drawing. The rectangle will go between the title and the chart itself.

2. Using Figure 6.14 as your guide, hold down the left mouse button and drag the mouse down and to the right. As you do so, an outline of the rectangle appears over the chart. When the outline is the correct size and shape, release the mouse button.

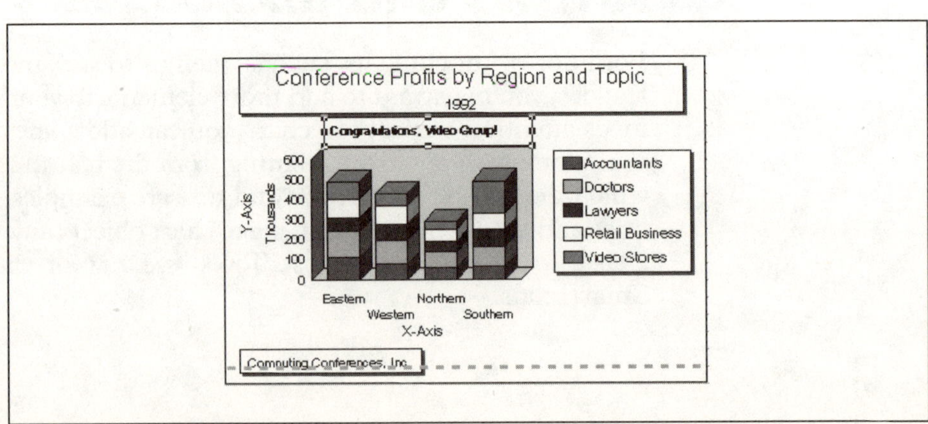

3. In the text box, enter **Congratulations, Video Group!**, as shown in Figure 6.14. When you have finished entering the text, click anywhere outside of the text box.

The text that you entered in the text box appears inside the dotted rectangle. Don't be concerned if it's in the right place. Later you'll adjust this text.

Changing the color of chart objects Now we'll change the color of the text box to help call attention to it:

4. Click on the text box with the right mouse button and choose Lines & Color. The Lines & Color dialog box, shown in Figure 6.15, appears. With the Lines & Color dialog box, you can change the color of the selected object in the chart.

5. Open the Pattern list in the Interior frame. When you do, a color palette appears on the screen. Click the white selection, at the upper-left side of the color palette.

Changing the font of chart objects The default font size of the text may be too large for the chart. To change the font:

6. Choose Style ➤ Font & Attributes. The Font & Attributes dialog box appears (see Figure 6.12) with a list of the available fonts.

FIGURE 6.15

The Lines & Color dialog box. Use this dialog box to change the color of chart objects.

(The list on your screen may not be the same as the one in Figure 6.12.)

7. Select a font that is smaller than the current font and click OK or press ↵ to confirm. You may have to repeat this step one or more times until you find an appropriate font size.

8. Select <u>B</u>old from the Attributes box.

9. Position the mouse pointer over the box, and hold down the left mouse button. The mouse pointer becomes a white hand as soon as you begin moving the mouse. Drag the box that you placed on the chart earlier until it is centered over the chart. Then click the mouse at some other position inside the chart to deselect the text.

Drawing an Arrow

To draw an arrow:

10. Choose <u>T</u>ools ➤ <u>D</u>raw ➤ <u>A</u>rrow or click the Arrow icon, the fifth icon from the right in the palette. The mouse pointer becomes a small cross.

11. Position the pointer along the lower border of the white rectangle, hold down the left mouse button, and drag the mouse down and to the right, into the top stacked bar portion for the Southern region.

12. Double-click the mouse pointer to both deselect the arrow and to finish drawing it.

The new objects that you've created appear approximately as shown in Figure 6.16.

TIP

Place the mouse cursor over a worksheet or chart object and click the *right* mouse button to bring up a menu of commands specific to the object you clicked. This is a quick way to work with objects.

The chart with a box, text, and an arrow added

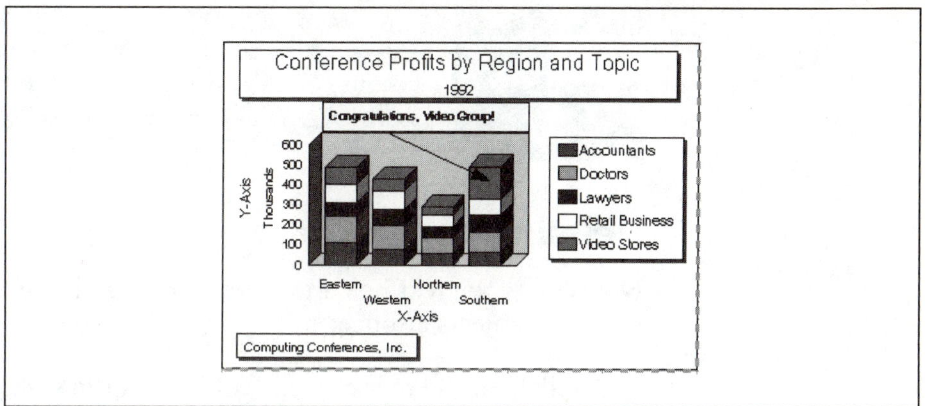

Working with the Draw SmartIcons

Sometimes you'll add an object to a chart, only to discover that you liked your chart better without the object. Lotus 1-2-3 conveniently allows you to change your mind about any detail of your chart's presentation. In an upcoming exercise, you'll delete the arrow, the text, and the rectangle from the REGIONBARS chart. But before you do so, let's experiment briefly with some of the commands in the Draw SmartIcons. These commands change the size and orientation of objects.

1. Click the arrow object with the mouse. A handle appears on the arrow, meaning that this object is the selected object. The Draw SmartIcons operate on the currently selected object only.

2. Choose the FlipHorizontal icon. Now the arrow points to the lower-left corner of the chart.

3. Choose the Rotate icon. The cursor changes to an arrow with a dotted line perpendicular to its axis. Now when you move the mouse it will rotate the arrow around a central point. Click the mouse when the arrow is pointing where you want it to point.

4. Choose Edit ➤ Undo, or press Ctrl-Z. The arrow returns to its original position on the chart.

You can tell when an object has been selected because handles appear around it. You cannot work with an object until you select it.

Deleting an Object

Now delete the text box and arrow you just created. First you have to select both objects at once:

1. Click on the text object. Hold down the shift key and click on the arrow object. Now you have selected both objects, the text and the arrow. Handles appear on both objects.

2. To delete the objects, take any one of these actions:

   - Choose Edit ➤ Cut.
   - Press the Delete key on the keyboard.

   The objects disappear from the chart.

3. As an experiment, choose Edit ➤ Undo. The objects reappear.

4. Delete the objects once again by following steps 1 and 2.

TIP

You can always press Edit ➤ Undo to reverse your latest action in 1-2-3.

Changing Number Formats and Adding Grid Lines

The Chart menu offers other options for controlling the appearance of a chart. For example, you can change the scale and appearance of the axes (with Chart ➤ Axis) or add borders and grid lines (with Chart ➤ Grids). In the following exercise, you'll change the format of the numbers along the Y-axis and add horizontal grid lines to the chart.

Changing number formats To change number formats on a chart:

1. Click on one of the Y-axis labels. You'll change the number format of these numbers. Handles appear around the Y-axis objects.

2. Click one of these objects with the right mouse button and choose Number Format. The Number Format dialog box appears, as in Figure 6.17.

3. Select the Currency option and enter a value of 0 in the Decimal places text box.

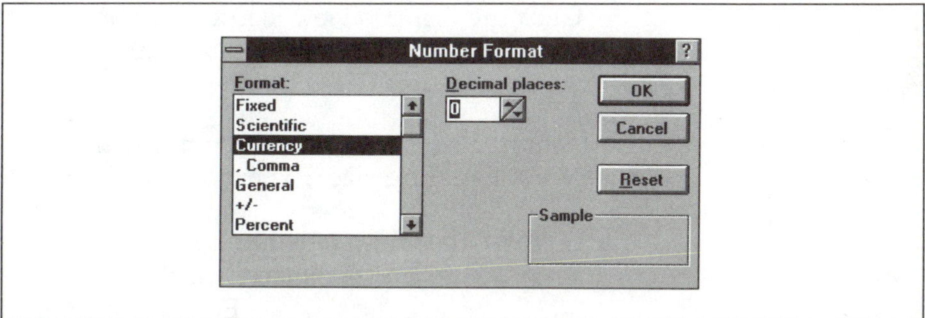

4. Click OK in the dialog box. Back on the chart, the values along the Yaxis are now displayed as dollar amounts.

Adding grid lines Now add the grid lines:

1. Choose Chart ➤ Grids. The grid dialog box appears.

2. Click the Y-axis option.

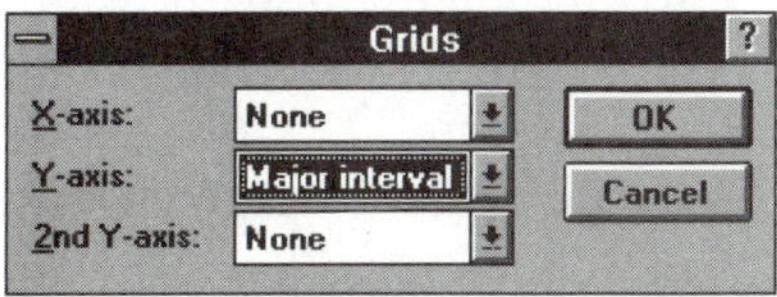

3. Select Major interval to displays horizontal grid lines across the width of the chart at numeric intervals.

4. Click OK or press ↵.

5. Click the SaveFile icon to update your worksheet and chart on disk.

Printing a Chart

In Release 4 of 1-2-3 for Windows, charts are an active part of the worksheet they were created in. To print a chart in 1-2-3, you just print the worksheet.

1. Make sure that you can see the chart somewhere on-screen. If the chart is not visible, choose View ➤ Set View Preferences and make sure that the check box next to Charts, drawings, and pictures is checked. Exit Set View Preferences.

2. Click the PrintPreview icon to see approximately how the printed document will look when it is printed. Press Esc to return to the worksheet.

If the chart does not look quite right, there are several simple ways to change its shape and size. Experiment with the following techniques:

- Increase the width of column F on the worksheet. When you do so, 1-2-3 widens the chart over the new width of the range.

- Choose File ➤ Page Setup. In the Size pull-down list, choose Fill Page and enter a value greater than 100 percent. This will increase the overall dimensions of the spreadsheet and chart on the printed page.

When the chart is ready for printing:

3. Click the Print SmartIcon.

If you are not satisfied with the results, keep making adjustments in the worksheet until you get what you want. Figure 6.18 shows one version of the worksheet, printed after several such adjustments.

4. Click the SaveFile SmartIcon to save your work to disk.

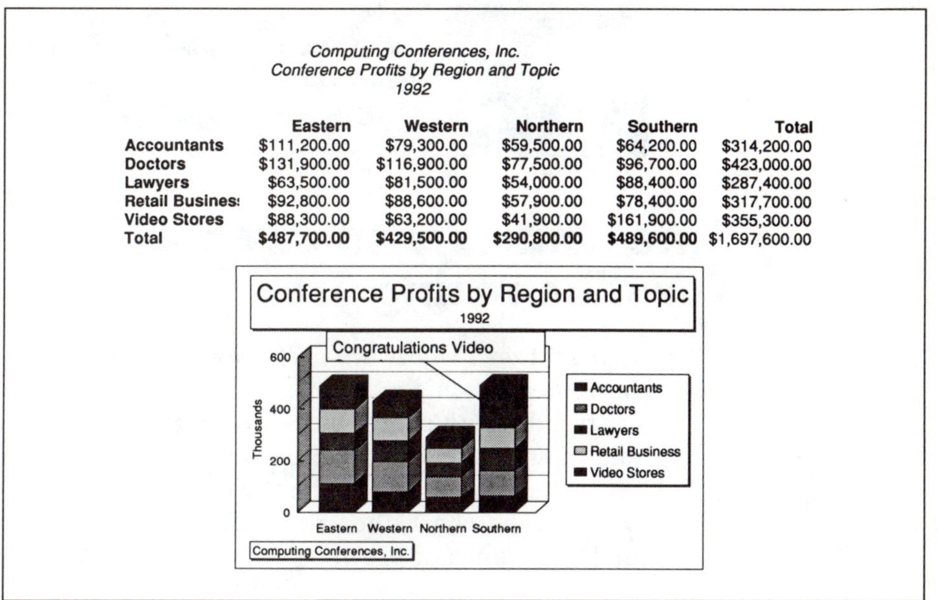

	Eastern	Western	Northern	Southern	Total
Accountants	$111,200.00	$79,300.00	$59,500.00	$64,200.00	$314,200.00
Doctors	$131,900.00	$116,900.00	$77,500.00	$96,700.00	$423,000.00
Lawyers	$63,500.00	$81,500.00	$54,000.00	$88,400.00	$287,400.00
Retail Business	$92,800.00	$88,600.00	$57,900.00	$78,400.00	$317,700.00
Video Stores	$88,300.00	$63,200.00	$41,900.00	$161,900.00	$355,300.00
Total	$487,700.00	$429,500.00	$290,800.00	$489,600.00	$1,697,600.00

Working with Different Kinds of Charts

To complete your introduction to the 1-2-3 chart component, you'll now look at other types of charts. As you learned earlier in this chapter, 1-2-3 uses the X-, A-, B-, C-, D-, E-, and F-data ranges in a variety of ways to make charts. To create a useful chart, you need to plan your worksheet according to the appropriate data range requirements.

Fortunately, the Chart ➤ Range command gives you some leeway. You can begin by creating a chart in one way, and then use Range to make adjustments to the way in which 1-2-3 interprets the data ranges. You saw how useful Chart ➤ Range is when you transformed REGIONBARS from a columnwise to a rowwise chart. You'll see other examples of its usefulness in the upcoming exercises.

Line Charts and Area Charts for Illustrating Trends

Line and *area charts* are useful for illustrating the downward or upward movement of data over time. In other words, they are useful for illustrating trends. Both chart types come in two- and three-dimensional formats, and in unstacked and stacked versions. In an unstacked chart, each point on a line represents an actual value from the corresponding data range. In a stacked chart, the values of each data range are added to the accumulated values of previous data ranges, so that the top line of the chart represents the total value of all the data ranges.

Both line and area charts use the standard data range definitions: the X-data range contains the labels along the X-axis, and the Y-data ranges contain the numeric data. Figure 6.19 shows a table of yearly regional profit figures from a five-year period and a line chart created from this data. There are four lines and each represents profit fluctuations over the five-year period. Notice that some of the lines cross each other more than once. This is typical of an unstacked line chart.

By contrast, Figure 6.20 shows a stacked area chart created from the same data. An area chart is the same as a line chart, except the areas beneath the lines are filled in with shading or color. In this stacked area chart, the area between one line and the next represents the variations in profit for a given region. But the area between the x-axis and the top line of the chart represents the *total* annual profit for all four regions.

Pie Charts for Showing Data Comparisons

A pie chart depicts one range of numeric data. The wedges, or "slices," of the pie show how individual data values compare to one another and

A line chart. Line charts are useful for illustrating trends.

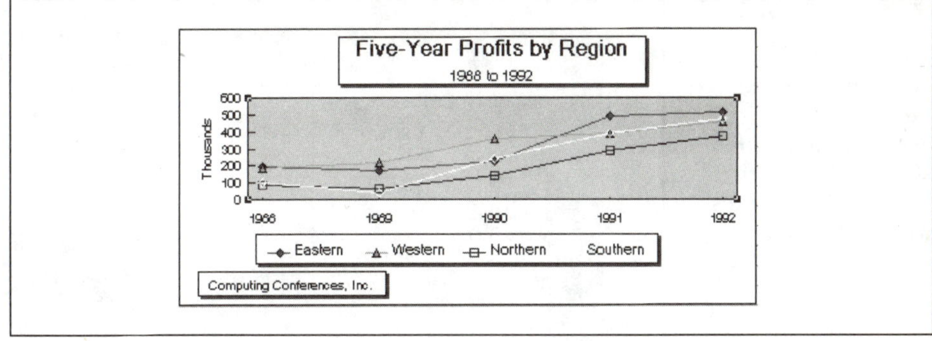

A stacked area chart. Stacked charts are good for showing data totals, as in this case, where the stack shows total profits.

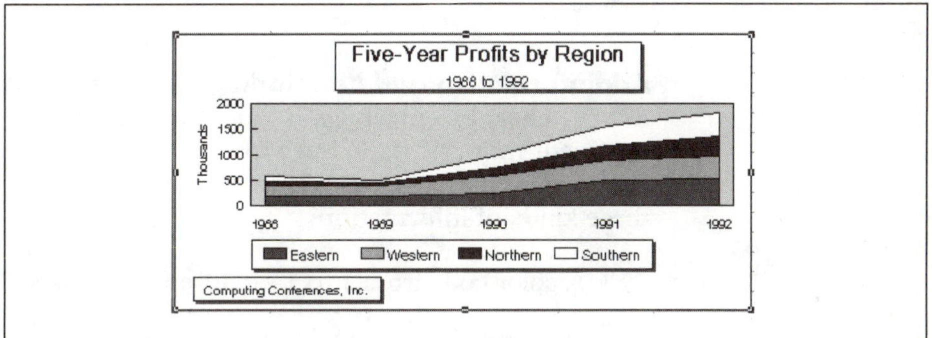

to the total. Pie charts are available in two-dimensional and three-dimensional formats.

In its simplest organizational scheme, a pie chart uses only two columns of data—an X-range and an A-range. The X-range represents the labels displayed beside the wedges of the pie, and the A-range represents the numeric data depicted in the chart. For example, Figure 6.21 shows profit figures for a region over a one-year period and a pie chart created from this data. By default, 1-2-3 displays a label from the A-data range and its percentage of the total pie next to each slice. For example, you can see in Figure 6.21 that Video Stores conferences represent 18.1 percent of annual profit in the Eastern region.

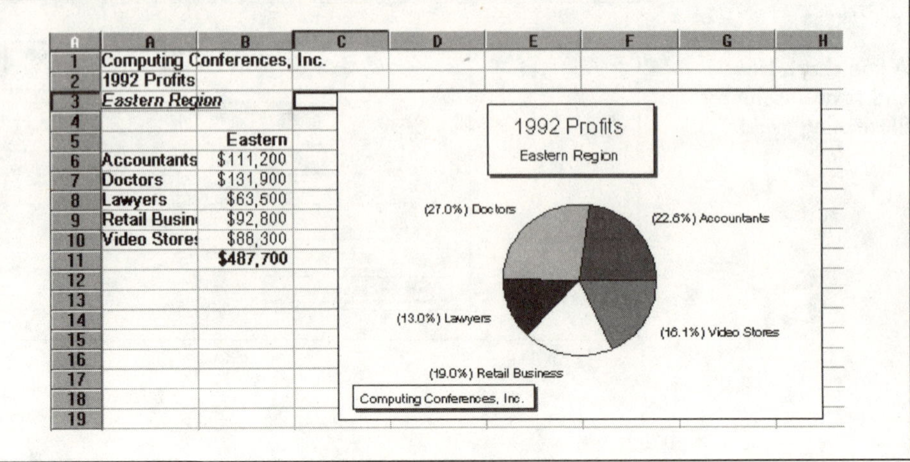

Adding color to and "exploding" the pie chart You can add color to a pie chart by entering a B- and C-range. The B- and C-ranges do not represent numeric data, but rather instruction codes that 1-2-3 reads to create the chart. The B-range, also known as the *color range*, can give three kinds of information:

- A color code from 1 to 14 that represents a color for a given wedge.

- A negative color code that leaves a blank space where a wedge belongs.

- A value of 100, added to the color code, which tells 1-2-3 to "explode" the wedge—that is, to display the wedge slightly outside the circumference of the pie.

Percentage labels in a pie The C-range, also known as the *percent-labels range*, tells 1-2-3 whether or not to include the percentage in the pie slice label. Entering a value of 0 (false) in each cell in the C-range omits the percentage that 1-2-3 normally displays with the label. A value of 1 (true) instructs 1-2-3 to include the percentage.

For example, Figure 6.22 shows an expanded worksheet table that includes appropriate instructions for modifying the pie chart. The column of color codes includes a value of 105 in cell C10—an instruction to explode the Video Stores wedge. The percent-labels range contains values of 0 in each cell, which instructs 1-2-3 to omit the percentage figures.

Figure 6.22 shows a pie chart created from a worksheet. As you can see, the Video Stores wedge is "exploded" and no percentages are displayed.

A pie chart with no percentage labels and one "exploded" wedge

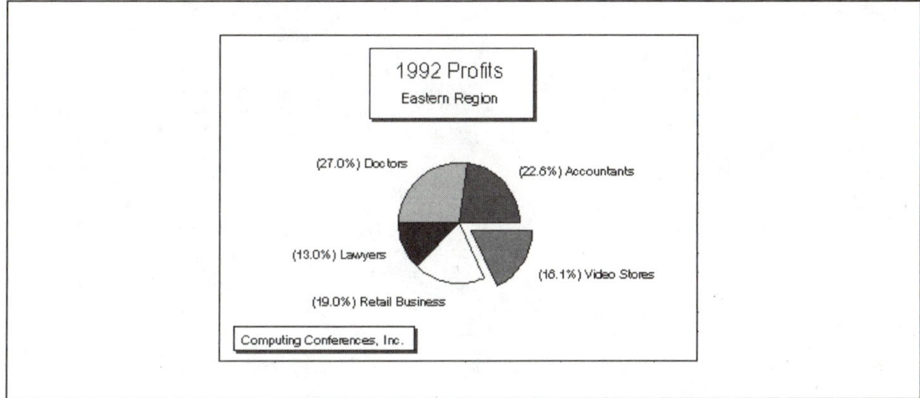

XY Charts for Correlating Data Relationships

The XY and mixed charts are perhaps the most complex kinds of charts. An XY chart plots points in a true X-Y coordinate system. XY charts are the only charts that do not use the X-data range for labels. Instead, the X-data range supplies the x-coordinate of each plotted point in the chart. The A- through F-data ranges supply y-coordinates.

For example, the worksheet in Figure 6.23 is an attempt to discover a correlation between conference attendance and advertising expense. Column C shows the amount that Computing Conferences, Inc. spent for advertising in advance of each conference, and column D shows the number of people who attended each conference. The XY chart in Figure 6.24 was created by using the advertising figures as the X-data range and the attendance figures as the A-data range. Each point on the chart therefore represents the amount spent for advertising and the corresponding attendance figure as an ordered pair (x,y) of values in the coordinate system.

FIGURE 6.23

A worksheet with data on attendance and advertising expenses

	A	B	C	D	E
1	Computing Conferences, Inc.				
2	Attendance at Conferences Conducted in 1992				
3	Computing for Video Stores				
4					
5	Place	Date	Advertising	Attendance	
6	Chicago	09-Jan-92	$5,000.00	154	
7	St. Louis	21-Jan-92	$3,500.00	119	
8	Indianapolis	15-Feb-92	$6,000.00	174	
9	New York	07-Mar-92	$6,000.00	201	
10	Boston	25-Mar-92	$3,500.00	136	
11	Washington,	03-Apr-92	$5,000.00	172	
12	Atlanta	11-May-92	$3,500.00	112	
13	Miami	28-May-92	$1,000.00	97	
14	Dallas	03-Jun-92	$1,000.00	86	
15	Albuquerque	29-Jun-92	$1,000.00	104	
16	Las Vegas	05-Sep-92	$7,500.00	235	
17	Los Angeles	11-Oct-92	$1,500.00	119	
18	San Francis	29-Oct-92	$2,500.00	137	
19	Seattle	05-Nov-92	$3,500.00	148	
20					

FIGURE 6.24

An XY chart correlating conference attendance with advertising dollars

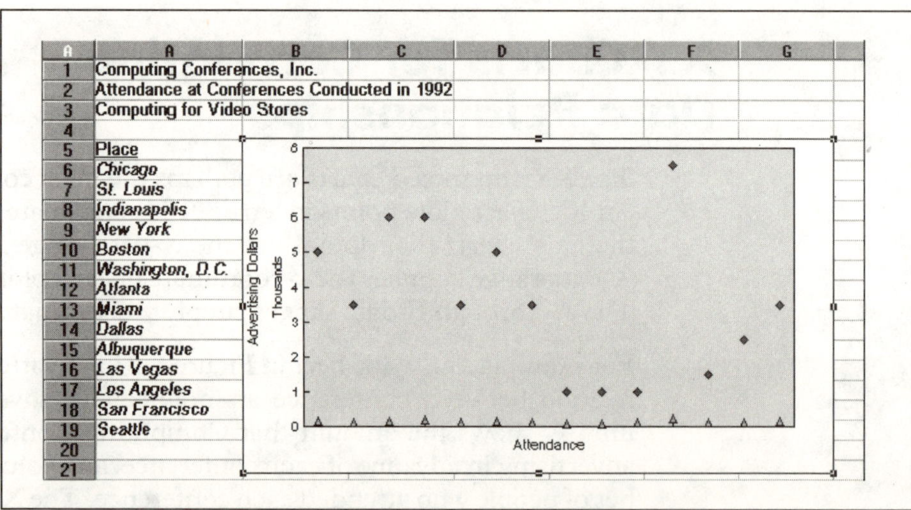

	A	B	C	D	E	F	G
1	Computing Conferences, Inc.						
2	Attendance at Conferences Conducted in 1992						
3	Computing for Video Stores						
4							
5	Place						
6	Chicago						
7	St. Louis						
8	Indianapolis						
9	New York						
10	Boston						
11	Washington, D.C.						
12	Atlanta						
13	Miami						
14	Dallas						
15	Albuquerque						
16	Las Vegas						
17	Los Angeles						
18	San Francisco						
19	Seattle						
20							
21							

Creating Titles on the X- and Y-Axes

By the way, you'll notice that this chart displays titles along the X-axis and the Y-axis. Here are the steps for creating these titles:

1. Choose <u>Chart</u> ➤ <u>Axis</u>.

2. In the cascade menu, choose <u>X</u>-Axis or <u>Y</u>-Axis.

3. In the dialog box, enter a title in the A<u>x</u>is title text box.

4. Click OK to confirm your entry.

Mixed Charts which Combine Line and Bar Charts

Figure 6.25 shows a mixed chart. This chart, like the XY chart, was created from the attendance-advertising worksheet in Figure 6.23. A mixed chart superimposes a line chart, which represents one or more numeric data ranges, over a bar chart, which represents another set of numeric data ranges.

FIGURE 6.25

A mixed chart. Mixed charts combine the features of line charts and bar charts.

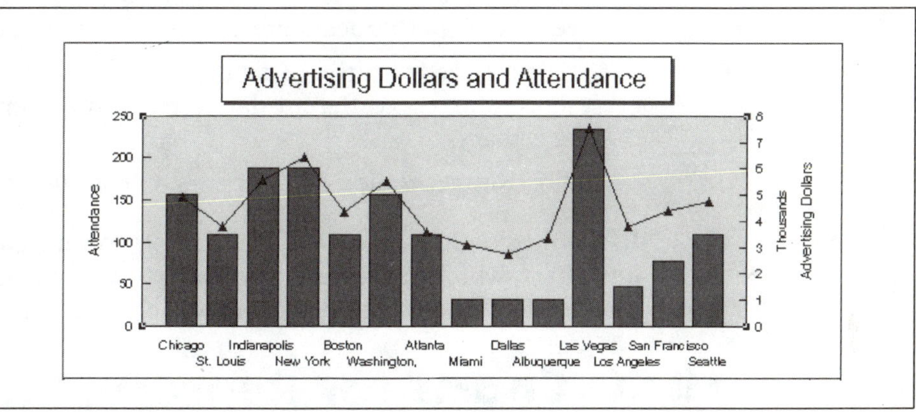

Mixed charts use data ranges in a unique way:

- The X-range supplies labels for the x-axis, as usual.

- Some ranges become bars in the bar chart.

- Some ranges become lines in the superimposed line chart.

Here are the steps for creating the mixed chart in Figure 6.25 from the worksheet data in Figure 6.23:

1. Preselect range A6..D19 on the attendance-advertising worksheet, and click the CreateChart SmartIcon.

2. Drag the cursor on the worksheet to create the chart. The initial chart needs several adjustments in its data range definitions.

3. Choose Chart ➤ Ranges. The Ranges dialog box appears (see Figure 6.7).

4. Select the range A6..A19 as the A-axis labels data range if necessary.

5. Enter C6..C19 for the A-data range and D6..D19 for the B-data range. Delete the entries in all the other data range boxes.

6. Highlight the A-axis labels and click the second Y check box. A second Y-axis appears at the right side of the chart.

7. Select Line from the Mixed type list. Because a mixed chart represents two different data sets, the two vertical axes are often necessary.

8. The Ranges dialog box appears. Click OK or press ↵.

In the mixed chart, the y-axis on the left contains a scale of values for the line chart, which represents attendance. The y-axis on the right contains a scale of values for the bar chart, which represents advertising dollars.

HLCO Charts for Representing Values within Values

A *high-low-close-open chart*, also known as a *stock-market-chart*, has vertical lines representing pairs of high and low values. On each vertical line, special markings represent opening and closing values. The HLCO chart is a special form of the mixed chart. HLCO charts use data ranges as follows:

- The X-data range supplies labels along the x-axis.

- The A- and B-data ranges represent high and low values, respectively.

- The C- and D-data ranges represent closing and opening values, respectively.

- The E-data range becomes an additional bar chart, located beneath the high-low lines.

- The F-data range becomes a horizontally oriented line chart, which runs through the high-low lines.

All of these ranges have typical uses for reporting stock market data:

- The high-low lines represent stock prices, as do the opening and closing values.

- The bar chart beneath the lines represents trading volume.

- The horizontal line chart represents stock averages.

However, you may find other uses for the HLCO chart. For example, consider the HLCO chart in Figure 6.26. It displays daily high and low temperatures, morning and evening readings, daily rainfall, and average temperatures.

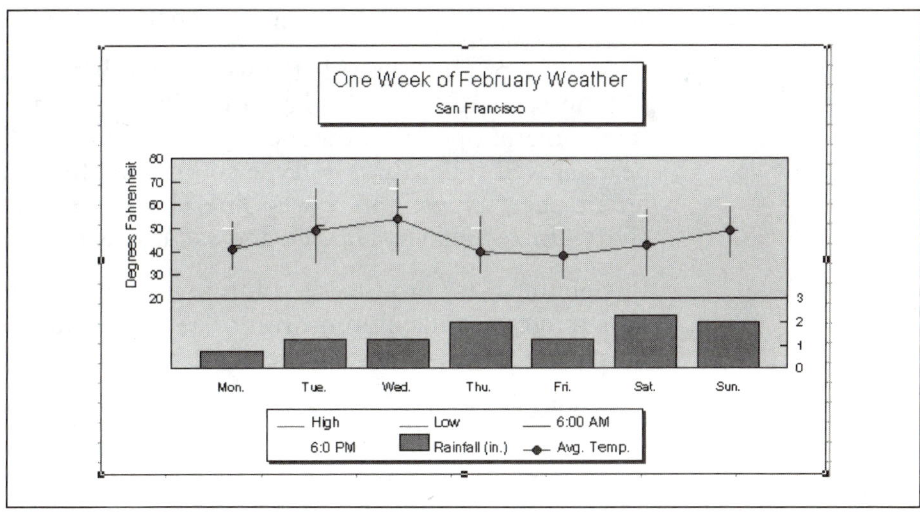

Radar Charts for Comparing Actual and Projected Data

The newest addition to 1-2-3 charts is the radar chart. Radar charts plot data around a central point. The data is plotted from the central point outward, just as a radar scope in the control tower of an airport tracks aircraft. The radar chart is a good tool for showing actual figures against projected figures over a given period of time.

Summary

A chart is linked to a worksheet in 1-2-3, and is saved on disk as part of the worksheet file. Charts are produced from columns of numbers, known as data ranges, plus a column of labels, known as the X-data range. First you preselect the range containing these columns, and then you choose Tools ➤ Chart to create the chart.

Charts are produced inside the worksheet. When a chart is the active object on-screen, 1-2-3 displays the Chart menu option instead of the Range menu option on the menu bar, and a set of Chart SmartIcons appears as well. The Chart ➤ Type command offers variations on seven different chart types: bar charts, line charts, area charts, pie charts, XY charts, mixed charts, HLCO, and radar charts.

By default, 1-2-3 produces a columnwise chart, meaning that the selected data ranges are all columns. But once you create a chart, you can choose Chart ➤ Ranges to redraw the chart in a rowwise fashion.

Typically, the first elements you add to a new chart are titles and the legend. Select Chart ➤ Headings and Chart ➤ Legend to enter them. Use the commands on the Tools ➤ Draw menu (or the Draw SmartIcons) to add geometric shapes to a chart. These shapes are known as objects.

Each of the seven chart types is suited to a particular kind of data. For example, line and area charts typically depict data values that change over time. Pie charts show the importance of individual data items in relation to a total. In an XY chart, sets of paired data values are plotted as points against an x-y coordinate system. Lotus 1-2-3 offers many different charts.

CHAPTER 7

Database Essentials

● **To create a database table,**   **377**

enter a row of field names at the top of the table range, and then enter the records in consecutive rows immediately after the field names.

● **To create a calculated field,**   **384**

enter the formula as the field entry in the first record, then copy the formula down to all the records in the database table.

● **To sort a database,**   **390**

preselect the range containing all the records in the database, *but do not include the field names*. Then choose Range ➤ Sort. In the Sort by box, enter references to cells contained in the fields you have chosen as keys to the sort. Click Ascending or Descending for each key.

● **To prepare for database queries,**   **400**

create a criteria range containing a row of field names from the database table followed by one or more rows of criteria. For convenience, assign range names to the criteria range, the output range, and the database table itself.

● **To find records that match the stated criteria,**   **402**

choose Database ➤ Find Records. Enter the database table range in the Find records in database table range box. Enter the criteria range reference by pressing F3 and double-clicking the range name. Click the Field range button and click the field to enter it as a criteria range. Click OK. Press Ctrl-↵ to move to the next matching record, or Ctrl-Shift-↵ to move to the previous matching record.

A *database* is a collection of information that has been systematically organized so that records can be accessed conveniently. Business databases are created for a variety of subjects, including inventory, product lines, sales transactions, business assets, employees, customers, regional divisions, and salespeople.

The 1-2-3 database component is ideal for building small to medium-sized databases. Choose Tools ➤ Database to examine the many options—and many ways of accessing data—available with 1-2-3. As shown in Figure 7.1, the Database menu offers many different options. The options on this menu will be the focus throughout much of this chapter.

With the commands on the Database menu, you can perform a variety of operations on a database. In this chapter, you will explore the following Database menu commands:

DATABASE MENU OPTION	USE
New Query	Makes a copy of records that match selection criteria

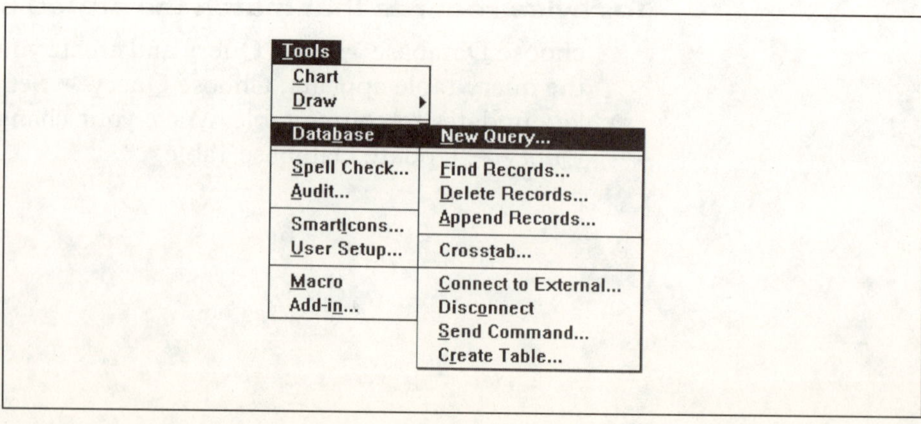

DATABASE MENU OPTION	USE
Find Records	Finds records that match stated conditions.
Delete Records	Deletes records that you no longer need.

You will also look at two Query commands. Query ➤ Sort arranges the records in a table in a different order and Query ➤ Set Options ➤ Allow updates a table with new information.

You can perform queries on one or more data tables. You'll begin your work in this chapter by learning how to organize a 1-2-3 database. Then you'll study essential database operations.

Basic Database Concepts

Before you can begin building a database, you have to know how databases operate. You also have to understand some of the concepts and terminology. Following is a brief overview of databases.

Records and Fields

The basic structural components of a database are known as *records* and *fields*.

- **Records.** A record comprises all the information pertaining to a single item or person in a database. Each row in a database makes one record. For example, in the following small table, the second row is a single record. It comprises all information about a person named Liz Victor:

ID	LAST	FIRST	CITY	REGION
S-127	Victor	Liz	Hemet	W

- **Fields.** A field is one category of information. Fields are the equivalents of columns in a worksheet. Usually there are several fields in each record. For example, here are the five fields that make up Liz Victor's record:

ID   LAST   FIRST   CITY   REGION

In 1-2-3, a database is stored in the rows and columns of a worksheet. Specifically, here is how a database is stored in a worksheet:

- Records are stored in consecutive rows. All information on a given record is displayed across one row.

- Fields appear side by side in adjacent columns. All entries down a given column belong to the same field and the same data type. At the top of each field, just above the first record in the database, is a *field name*. The field name identifies the field.

What Is a Database Table?

A *database table* is a collection of records organized into distinct information fields and stored in a single worksheet. Database tables begin with a row of field names. For successful query operations, entering a consistent data type in each field is essential. You have to design databases so that information of the same kind is entered in the same field.

The best way to clarify these terms and concepts is to consider an example. In this chapter, you'll once again do exercises involving the business files of Computing Conferences, Inc. This time you'll examine a database the company maintains for tracking conference instructors. In this database table is information about all the computer specialists who signed contracts and agreed to present topics at conferences.

In Figure 7.2, you can see the beginning of the database table inside a worksheet window.

- Each record is stored in a row. Each record contains all the information about one instructor. The first record is in row 4.

- There are eleven fields, displayed across the worksheet in columns A through K. The field names are in row 3.

	A	B	C	D	E	F	G	H	I	J	K
1				Instructor Database							
2											
3	ID	Last	First	City	Region	Specialty	Rate	Hrs	Contract	Yrs	Ok
4	D-140	Abrams	P.	Atlanta	S	Database	$125	29	20-Oct-90	1.3	B
5	W-154	Alexamder	E.	Los Angeles	W	WP	$150	10	14-Jun-93	0.6	New
6	S-125	Ashford	W.	Washington D.C.	E	Spreadsheet	$150	145	10-May-87	1.6	A
7	S-126	Ballinger	I.	Boston	E	Spreadsheet	$150	40	12-Feb-87	5.0	C
8	W-145	Banks	S.	St. Louis	S	WP	$150	55	10-Jun-90	1.6	A
9	W-130	Burke	C.	Miami	S	WP	$100	41	22-May-88	3.7	B
10	D-141	Cheung	F.	Las Vegas	W	Database	$125	61	15-May-92	1.7	A
11	D-143	Cody	L.	Los Angeles	W	Database	$75	43	20-Jun-90	1.6	B
12	A-146	Daniels	A.	Atlanta	S	Accounting	$125	24	09-May-91	0.7	New
13	W-119	Davis	G.	San Francisco	W	WP	$150	149	09-Jul-87	4.6	A
14	N-115	Dixon	G.	Las Vegas	W	Networks	$150	59	09-May-87	4.6	B
15	S-120	Edmunds	R.	Indianapolis	N	Spreadsheet	$75	35	27-Sep-87	4.3	C
16	T-128	Eng	R.	Albuquerque	S	Telecomm	$75	75	11-Oct-87	4.3	B
17	S-131	Garcia	A.	Seattle	N	Spreadsheet	$100	17	02-Jul-88	3.6	C
18	W-114	Garrison	V.	Boston	E	WP	$125	207	06-May-86	5.7	A
19	S-127	Gill	P.	Los Angeles	W	Spreadsheet	$100	35	22-Jun-87	4.6	C
20	S-149	Harris	P.	Dallas	S	Spreadsheet	$150	17	12-Feb-91	1.0	New
21	W-124	Meyer	J.	New York	E	WP	$150	85	05-May-87	4.7	B
22	A-103	Perez	D.	Las Vegas	W	Accounting	$100	5	11-Jul-86	5.6	C

As you can see, a complete record consists of one entry for each of the eleven fields.

Here are descriptions of the fields in the instructor database:

FIELD NAME	DESCRIPTION
ID	The identification number assigned to the instructor
Last	The instructor's last name
First	The instructor's first initial
City	The city where the instructor prefers to work
Region	The instructor's home region, represented by a single letter N, S, E, or W for North, South, East, or West
Specialty	The instructor's primary area of expertise: Spreadsheet, Database, WP (for word processing), Accounting, Networks, or Telecomm (for telecommunications)

DATABASE ESSENTIALS

FIELD NAME	DESCRIPTION
Rate	The instructor's hourly pay rate for making presentations at conferences (this amount is established individually for each instructor, in negotiation with the company, and fees range from $75 to $150)
Hrs	The total number of conference hours that the instructor has worked for the company
Contract	The date of the instructor's first contract with the company
Yrs	The number of years since the instructor's first contract was signed
Ok	A rating of A, B, or C for the instructor's level of experience (if he or she has worked for Computing Conferences, Inc. for less than a year, the entry in this field is New)

Rules for Naming Fields

As you'll see later in this chapter, field names play an important role in query operations. For this reason, you must follow the rules when you create field names:

- Write each field name as a one-word label without including any spaces.

- Do not use characters or formats that would make a field name look like a formula or a cell address.

- Most important of all, create a unique name for each field in a database table. You'll be using field names in formulas and operations. For your own convenience, write field names that are clear, reasonably short, and easy to remember.

Figure 7.3 shows the complete database table with information about all the instructors who work for Computing Conferences, Inc. There are over fifty records, and over fifty instructors, in all. In this particular listing, the records are arranged in alphabetical order by instructors' last names.

FIGURE 7.3

The complete instructor database table. These records are in alphabetical order by last name, but you can arrange—or sort—database records based on any field you want.

Instructor Database

ID	Last	First	City	Region	Specialty	Rate	Hrs	Contract	Yrs	Ok
D-140	Abrams	P.	Atlanta	S	Database	$125	29	20-Oct-90	1.3	B
W-154	Alexander	E.	Los Angeles	W	WP	$150	10	14-Jun-91	0.6	New
S-125	Ashford	W.	Washington, D.C	E	Spreadsheet	$150	145	10-May-87	4.7	A
S-126	Ballinger	I.	Boston	E	Spreadsheet	$150	40	12-Feb-87	5.0	C
W-145	Banks	S.	St. Louis	S	WP	$150	55	10-Jun-90	1.6	A
W-130	Burke	C.	Miami	S	WP	$100	41	22-May-88	3.7	B
D-141	Cheung	F.	Las Vegas	W	Database	$125	61	15-May-90	1.7	A
D-143	Cody	L.	Los Angeles	W	Database	$75	43	20-Jun-90	1.6	B
A-146	Daniels	A.	Atlanta	S	Accounting	$125	24	09-May-91	0.7	New
W-119	Davis	G.	San Francisco	W	WP	$150	139	09-Jul-87	4.6	A
N-115	Dixon	G.	Las Vegas	W	Networks	$150	59	09-May-86	5.7	B
S-120	Edmonds	R.	Indianapolis	N	Spreadsheet	$75	35	27-Sep-87	4.3	C
T-128	Eng	R.	Albuquerque	S	Telecomm	$75	75	11-Oct-87	4.3	B
D-105	Fitzpatrick	P.	New York	E	Database	$125	164	07-Nov-86	5.2	A
S-131	Garcia	A.	Seattle	N	Spreadsheet	$100	17	02-Jul-88	3.6	C
W-114	Garrison	V.	Boston	E	WP	$125	207	06-May-86	5.7	A
S-127	Gill	P.	Los Angeles	W	Spreadsheet	$100	25	22-Jun-87	4.6	C
S-156	Hale	S.	San Francisco	W	Spreadsheet	$75	28	09-Jun-91	0.6	New
S-149	Harris	P.	Dallas	S	Spreadsheet	$150	17	12-Feb-91	1.0	New
D-109	Hayes	S.	San Francisco	W	Database	$75	95	07-Feb-86	6.0	B
T-138	Hermann	J.	Los Angeles	W	Telecomm	$125	74	24-May-89	2.7	B
S-132	Jones	L.	Atlanta	S	Spreadsheet	$125	5	10-Feb-88	4.0	C
W-116	Jordan	E.	Dallas	S	WP	$100	17	06-Oct-86	5.3	C
W-117	Kim	E.	Washington, D.C	E	WP	$100	137	11-Oct-86	5.3	B
N-144	King	T.	New York	E	Networks	$75	13	06-Jan-90	2.1	C
D-136	Koenig	O.	Albuquerque	S	Database	$125	20	02-Jun-89	2.7	C
S-111	Kwan	O.	New York	E	Spreadsheet	$100	71	21-Jun-86	5.6	B
D-123	Lambert	S.	Dallas	S	Database	$150	145	26-Jun-87	4.6	A
D-134	Lee	H.	Seattle	N	Database	$150	21	17-Dec-88	3.1	C
W-150	Leung	M.	Chicago	N	WP	$100	16	26-Mar-91	0.9	New
W-112	Manning	P.	Atlanta	S	WP	$75	71	09-Nov-86	5.2	B
W-107	Martinez	G.	Las Vegas	W	WP	$150	178	15-Mar-86	5.9	A
N-129	McKay	J.	Washington, D.C	E	Networks	$150	35	09-May-87	4.7	C
W-124	Meyer	J.	New York	E	WP	$150	85	05-May-87	4.7	B
A-135	Meyer	L.	New York	E	Accounting	$100	57	17-Aug-88	3.5	B
T-148	Miranda	O.	Las Vegas	W	Telecomm	$75	9	04-Jan-91	1.1	C
S-153	Nichols	B.	Albuquerque	S	Spreadsheet	$150	19	28-Feb-91	0.9	New
N-118	O'Neil	P.	Atlanta	S	Networks	$75	5	01-May-87	4.8	C
A-103	Perez	D.	Las Vegas	W	Accounting	$100	5	11-Jul-86	5.6	C
W-113	Porter	D.	Seattle	N	WP	$125	59	02-Aug-86	5.5	B
D-139	Porter	M.	Washington, D.C	E	Database	$150	26	28-Mar-89	2.8	B
T-133	Ramirez	F.	Boston	E	Telecomm	$150	73	08-Feb-88	4.0	B
S-155	Roberts	P.	Chicago	N	Spreadsheet	$100	10	21-Aug-91	0.4	New
D-137	Sanchez	W.	Indianapolis	N	Database	$100	47	16-Apr-89	2.8	B
N-101	Schwartz	B.	Boston	E	Networks	$150	178	02-Mar-86	5.9	A
W-151	Schwartz	P.	Indianapolis	N	WP	$150	23	10-May-91	0.7	New
D-104	Taylor	F.	Boston	E	Database	$100	17	24-Oct-86	5.3	C
D-142	Thomas	T.	St. Louis	S	Database	$150	35	23-Dec-90	1.1	A
S-108	Tong	C.	St. Louis	S	Spreadsheet	$150	35	12-Nov-86	5.2	C
N-152	Tong	P.	San Francisco	W	Networks	$150	23	13-May-91	0.7	New
N-110	Tong	W.	Los Angeles	W	Networks	$150	83	09-May-86	5.7	B
S-122	Vasquez	T.	Las Vegas	W	Spreadsheet	$75	5	27-Apr-87	4.8	C
T-102	Vaughn	A.	Washington, D.C	E	Telecomm	$75	53	11-Sep-86	5.4	B
T-147	Webb	F.	New York	E	Telecomm	$125	32	27-Jan-91	1.0	A
D-106	Weinberg	P.	Miami	S	Database	$75	59	18-Jan-86	6.0	B
D-121	Williams	C.	Chicago	N	Database	$150	30	02-Oct-87	4.3	C

Notice that the entries in a each column belong to the same data type and are formatted consistently. The first six fields—the ID, Last name, First name, City, Region, and Specialty—are labels, but the next four are numeric fields—the rate (formatted as a dollar amount), the hours (formatted as an integer), the contract date (a date number formatted in a date display format), and the years (formatted as a numeric value with one decimal place). The last field, Ok, is a label.

Entering the Database

For the exercises in this chapter, you need a copy of the instructor database table in a worksheet of your own. However, to avoid having to enter all the records in Figure 7.3, you will enter the shortened form of the database shown in Figure 7.4. It contains only 17 records in rows 4 through 20.

To create the shortened database, start with a new blank worksheet and follow these steps:

1. Choose <u>E</u>dit ➤ <u>I</u>nsert and click the <u>S</u>heet option to insert worksheet B into the window. Click OK or press ↵ to complete the Insert operation.

You'll enter the instructor database into worksheet B. We'll save worksheet A for a later exercise.

FIGURE 7.4

The short version of the instructor database table. Here the records are not in any order whatsoever—the way records are usually entered.

	A	B	C	D	E	F	G	H	I	J	K
1				Instructor Database							
2											
3	ID	Last	First	City	Region	Specialty	Rate	Hrs	Contract	Yrs	Ok
4	S-149	Harris	P.	Dallas	S	Spreadsheet	$150	17	12-Feb-91		
5	A-146	Daniels	A.	Atlanta	S	Accounting	$125	24	09-May-91		
6	A-103	Perez	D.	Las Vegas	W	Accounting	$100	5	11-Jul-86		
7	W-113	Porter	D.	Seattle	N	WP	$125	59	02-Aug-86		
8	N-101	Schwartz	B.	Boston	E	Networks	$150	178	02-Mar-86		
9	S-155	Roberts	P.	Chicago	N	Spreadsheet	$100	10	21-Aug-91		
10	S-125	Ashford	W.	Washington, D.C.	E	Spreadsheet	$150	145	10-May-87		
11	D-106	Weinberg	P.	Miami	S	Database	$75	59	18-Jan-86		
12	W-119	Davis	G.	San Francisco	W	WP	$150	139	09-Jul-87		
13	W-124	Meyer	J.	New York	E	WP	$150	85	05-May-87		
14	W-145	Banks	S.	St. Louis	S	WP	$150	55	10-Jun-90		
15	D-137	Sanchez	W.	Indianapolis	N	Database	$100	47	16-Apr-89		
16	D-139	Porter	M.	Washington, D.C.	E	Database	$150	26	28-Mar-89		
17	T-133	Ramirez	F.	Boston	E	Telecomm	$150	73	08-Feb-88		
18	D-143	Cody	L.	Los Angeles	W	Database	$75	43	20-Jun-90		
19	S-127	Gill	P.	Los Angeles	W	Spreadsheet	$100	25	22-Jun-87		
20	T-128	Eng	R.	Albuquerque	S	Telecomm	$75	75	11-Oct-87		

2. Choose <u>S</u>tyle ➤ <u>C</u>olumn Width to adjust columns A through K to the following widths: A, **6**; B, **8**; C, **4**; D, **13**; E, **6**; F, 10; G, **5**; H, **4**; I, **9**; J, 4; K, **4**.

3. Enter the title **Instructor Database** in cell A1. Select columns A through K and choose <u>S</u>tyle ➤ <u>A</u>lignment ➤ <u>C</u>enter ➤ Across columns to center the title horizontally over columns A through K. Click the Bold and Underline SmartIcons to apply these styles to the title.

4. Enter the field names in row 3, cells A3 through K3. You can copy them from Figure 7.4. Then select the range A3..K3 and click the Bold icon. Right-align the Rate, Hrs, and Yrs field names, and center the other field names.

5. Enter the data of the first six fields into columns A, B, C, D, E, and F. Copy each entry exactly as you see it in Figure 7.4. Center the entries of the Region field in column E.

6. Enter the numeric data of the next two fields, Rate and Hrs, into columns G and H. Format the entries of column G as Currency, with no decimal places.

7. Before entering the dates into column I, select the range I4..I20 and choose <u>S</u>tyle ➤ <u>N</u>umber Format. Select the 31-Dec-93 date format and click OK. Now enter the dates into column I just as they appear in Figure 7.4.

8. Choose <u>F</u>ile ➤ Save <u>A</u>s, and save this file to disk as INSTRUCT.WK4.

Remember, 1-2-3 converts date format entries into date numbers, which you can use in date arithmetic operations.

The Yrs and Ok fields, in columns J and K, remain blank in Figure 7.4. Yrs and Ok are *calculated fields* in the instructor database.

Including a Calculated Field in a Database Table

You can write a formula to calculate data and enter it in any field in a database table. To create a calculated field, enter the formula in the first record at the top of the column, in the first field entry, and copy it down the field column. This is the same procedure you follow to enter a formula in a worksheet column. Formulas in calculated fields often contain references to values in other fields. As it does worksheet formulas, 1-2-3 recalculates field formulas whenever you change the data in a cell to which the formula refers.

The Yrs field in the instructor database table lists the number of years that have passed since an instructor signed his or her first contract with Computing Conferences, Inc. To calculate this number, you obtain the difference between today's date and the date in the Contract field. So you would normally enter the following formula in the first record of the Yrs field:

    (@TODAY–I4)/365

This formula finds the difference, in days, between today's date (@TODAY) and the contract date (I4), and divides the result by 365 to calculate the difference in years. The advantage of putting a formula like this in a database is that 1-2-3 recalculates the Yrs field each time the value of @TODAY changes—that is, every day. So the values in the Yrs field are always up to date.

For the exercises in this chapter, however, you'll replace this formula with one that gives a fixed date:

    (@DATE(92,1,31)–I4)/365

By making this small adjustment, you will be able to duplicate the database examples exactly as you see them in this chapter.

1. Enter the following formula into cell J4, to calculate the number of years since the initial contract:

    (@DATE(92,1,31)–I4)/365

The value in the Ok field for a given instructor is based on the instructor's experience level—specifically, the average number of conference hours the instructor has worked, per year, since signing his or her first contract.

- An instructor who has worked an average of 30 hours or more per year receives an Ok rating of A.

- An instructor who has worked fewer than 30 hours but at least 9 hours per year receives a rating of B.

- An instructor who has worked fewer than 9 hours per year receives a rating of C.

- A new instructor receives no rating, and the word *New* appears in his or her Ok field.

Here are the steps for entering the Ok formula in column K:

2. Enter this formula carefully into cell K4:

```
@IF(J4<1,"New",@IF(H4/J4>=30,"A",@IF(H4/J4<9,"C","B")))
```

NOTE

You may want to turn briefly back to Chapter 5 to review the structure and use of 1-2-3's built-in @IF function.

This formula uses a sequence of *nested* @IF functions to select a label of New, A, B, or C for the Ok field:

- The outermost @IF function enters a label of New if the value of the Yrs field is less than 1.

- Otherwise, the middle @IF function enters A if the average yearly work hour amount (H4/J4) is greater than or equal to 30.

- Finally, if neither of these first two conditions is true, the innermost @IF function chooses between labels of C or B, depending upon whether the average work hour figure is less than or greater than 9.

Now you need to copy the two formulas down columns J and K, respectively:

3. Preselect range J4..K4, and click the CopyToClipboard Smart-Icon. Drag the mouse over range J5..J20.

4. Click the PasteFromClipboard SmartIcon.

5. Preselect range J4..J20 and choose Style ➤ Number Format. Select the Fixed format and enter a value of **1** in the Decimal places text box.

6. Click the SaveFile SmartIcon to update the file on disk.

The two calculated fields, Yrs and Ok, appear as shown in Figure 7.5.

FIGURE 7.5

Columns J and K calculated to show the number of years' experience and the Ok rating

	A	B	C	D	E	F	G	H	I	J	K
1						Instructor Database					
2											
3	ID	Last	First	City	Region	Specialty	Rate	Hrs	Contract	Yrs	Ok
4	S-149	Harris	P.	Dallas	S	Spreadsheet	$150	17	12-Feb-91	1.0	New
5	A-146	Daniels	A.	Atlanta	S	Accounting	$125	24	09-May-91	0.7	New
6	A-103	Perez	D.	Las Vegas	W	Accounting	$100	5	11-Jul-86	5.6	C
7	W-113	Porter	D.	Seattle	N	WP	$125	59	02-Aug-86	5.5	B
8	N-101	Schwartz	B.	Boston	E	Networks	$150	178	02-Mar-86	5.9	A
9	S-155	Roberts	P.	Chicago	N	Spreadsheet	$100	10	21-Aug-91	0.4	New
10	S-125	Ashford	W.	Washington, D.C.	E	Spreadsheet	$150	145	10-May-87	4.7	A
11	D-106	Weinberg	P.	Miami	S	Database	$75	59	18-Jan-86	6.0	B
12	W-119	Davis	G.	San Francisco	W	WP	$150	139	09-Jul-87	4.6	A
13	W-124	Meyer	J.	New York	E	WP	$150	85	05-May-87	4.7	B
14	W-145	Banks	S.	St. Louis	S	WP	$150	55	10-Jun-90	1.6	A
15	D-137	Sanchez	W.	Indianapolis	N	Database	$100	47	16-Apr-89	2.8	B
16	D-139	Porter	M.	Washington, D.C.	E	Database	$150	26	28-Mar-89	2.8	B
17	T-133	Ramirez	F.	Boston	E	Telecomm	$150	73	08-Feb-88	4.0	B
18	D-143	Cody	L.	Los Angeles	W	Database	$75	43	20-Jun-90	1.6	B
19	S-127	Gill	P.	Los Angeles	W	Spreadsheet	$100	25	22-Jun-87	4.6	C
20	T-128	Eng	R.	Albuquerque	S	Telecomm	$75	75	11-Oct-87	4.3	B

What Is a Database?

Lotus 1-2-3 makes an important distinction between a *database table* and a *database*. A database table, as you've seen, is a collection of records stored in consecutive rows in a single worksheet. A database is defined as a collection of one or more database tables.

With 1-2-3, you can perform special query operations on multiple database tables. In this sense, 1-2-3 is a *relational* database system. In relational databases, two database tables with a common field can match records and build new tables by comparing and combining data.

In the next exercise, you'll create a new database table in worksheet A, which you've left empty up to now. This new table, shown in Figure 7.6, stores information about the four regional offices of Computing Conferences, Inc. Consequently, it has four records, one for each regional office. There are seven fields in the database:

FIELD NAME	DESCRIPTION
Region	North, South, East, or West—N, S, E, or W
Address	The street address
City	The City
State	The State
Zip	The zip code
Phone	The telephone number
Manager	The name of the regional manager in charge of each office

Notice that the office database table has one field in common with the instructor table—the Region field. Because both tables have the same field, you can correlate records in the two tables. For example, imagine the steps you might take to find the name of the regional manager who is in charge of a particular instructor:

1. You would begin by searching for the instructor's name in the instructor database table.

	A	B	C	D	E	F	G
1	Regional Offices						
2							
3	Region	Address	City	State	Zip	Phone	Manager
4	E	222 Allen Street	New York	NY	10103	(212) 555-4678	Campbell, R.
5	N	Mills Tower, Suite 992	Chicago	IL	60605	(312) 555-8803	Logan, C.
6	S	11 Maple Street	Dallas	TX	75210	(214) 555-6754	Harvey, J.
7	W	432 Market Avenue	Los Angeles	CA	90028	(213) 555-9974	Garcia, M.

DATABASE ESSENTIALS

2. After locating the correct record, you would take note of the instructor's region.

3. Then you would switch to the office database, look up the office record corresponding to the same region, and find the manager's name in the Manager field.

In Chapter 8, you'll learn how 1-2-3 automates this sequence of steps in a special kind of query operation that *joins* data from multiple database tables.

For now, take the following steps to enter the office database table in worksheet A:

1. Click the folder tab for worksheet A.

2. Choose <u>S</u>tyle ➤ <u>C</u>olumn Width command to set the correct widths of columns A through G: A, **6**; B, **17**; C, **11**; D, **4**; E, **7**; F, **12**; G, **12**.

3. Enter the title **Regional Offices** in cell A1. Click the Bold and Underline icons to apply these two styles to the title.

4. Enter the seven field names in row 3, as shown in Figure 7.6. Then preselect range A3..G3 and click the Bold icon. Center the Address and Zip field names.

5. Choose <u>S</u>tyle ➤ <u>W</u>orksheet Defaults and click the <u>F</u>ormat ↓ button. In the pull-down list, type **L** to select the Label format. Click OK to confirm the selection. Note that all seven of the fields in the office database table are label fields.

NOTE

Recall that the Label format gives you a convenient way to enter labels into a worksheet, even when an entry begins with a digit or some other character that 1-2-3 would normally read as the beginning of a value entry.

6. Enter the four regional office records into rows 4 through 7 of the worksheet. Thanks to the default Label format, you don't have to worry about starting addresses, zip codes, and phone numbers with special label prefixes.

7. Center the Region and Zip field values in their respective columns.

Now the INSTRUCT.WK4 database file consists of two database tables—the office table in worksheet A and the instructor table in worksheet B. Adding range names to the file will simplify your work in upcoming exercises with these two tables. In the following steps, you'll assign two range names to each table:

1. On worksheet A, preselect range A:A3..A:G7. This range contains the entire database table, including the field names. Choose Range ➤ Name and assign the name **OFFICEDB** (for "office database") to this range.

2. Preselect range A:A4..A:G7. This range contains the four regional office records, without the field names. Choose Range ➤ Name and enter **OFFICERECS** (for "office records") as the name for this range.

3. Click the B tab to move the cell pointer to worksheet B.

4. Preselect range B:A3..B:K20. This range contains the entire instructor database table, including the field names. Choose Range ➤ Name and assign the name **INSTRUCTDB** (for "instructors database") to this range.

5. Preselect range B:A4..BK20. This range contains the instructor records, without the field names. Choose Range ➤ Name and enter **INSTRUCTRECS** (for "instructor records") as the name for this range. Press Home to deselect the range.

6. Click the SaveFile icon to update the database file to disk.

You'll use the OFFICEDB and INSTRUCTDB range names in query operations that require references to the entire database tables, including field names. In contrast, the OFFICERECS and INSTRUCTRECS names will prove convenient in procedures for sorting the database records.

Rearranging, or Sorting, a Database

Once you create a database, you may want to rearrange its records. For example, records aren't usually entered in alphabetical order, but you might want your database in alphabetical order. Rearranging records this way is called *sorting*. You accomplish it by choosing Range ➤ Sort. As you learned in Chapter 5, Range ➤ Sort is not exclusively for use in databases. You can use this command to sort the data in any range of rows, whether or not they form a database.

You can probably imagine several useful new arrangements for the records in the instructor database. You could sort the database by instructor ID numbers (the ID field). Or you could sort it in numerical order by hourly rates (the Rate field). Or in chronological order by contract dates (the Contract field). In each of these examples, the specified field—ID, Rate, or Contract—is called the *key* to the sort.

Ascending and Descending Sorts

Given a sorting key and a database range to be sorted, the Range ➤ Sort command can arrange the records in *ascending* or *descending* order. The difference between these two sorting directions depends on the type of data stored in the key field:

- **Labels.** If the key field contains labels, an ascending sort arranges the records in alphabetical order, from A to Z. A descending sort produces the reverse alphabetical order, from Z to A. By default, 1-2-3 ignores uppercase and lowercase distinctions during a sort operation.

- **Numeric values.** If the key field contains numeric values, an ascending sort arranges the records from the smallest value to the largest. A descending sort arranges the records from the largest to the smallest.

- **Date numbers.** If the key contains dates that have been entered as 1-2-3 date numbers, an ascending sort arranges the database from the earliest to the latest date. A descending sort arranges the records from the latest to the earliest date.

The Sort dialog box appears in Figure 7.7. For a one-key sort, you need to specify three pieces of information:

BOX/FRAME	INFORMATION
<u>S</u>ort by box	A reference to a cell inside the selected key field.
<u>S</u>ort by frame	<u>A</u>scending or <u>D</u>escending.
<u>R</u>ange box	The range of records that you want to sort.

Do not include field names in the sort! Keep this important rule in mind when you sort a database: do not include the row of field names in the range to be sorted. If you do, the field names will leave their positions at the top of the database during the sort and end up somewhere in the range of records. If you mistakenly sort field names, click the Undo SmartIcon or press Ctrl-Z to correct the error. Lotus 1-2-3 will restore your database to its original order. (For this corrective action to work, however, the Undo option must be enabled in your system, and you must

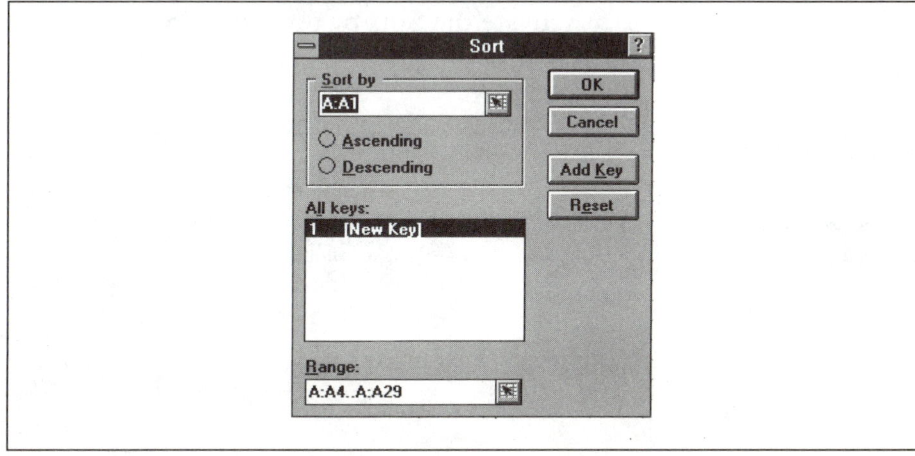

click the icon immediately after the sort—before you choose any other menu command.)

WARNING Do *not* include the row of field names in the sort range. If you do, the names will be sorted along with the other data.

A Chronological Sort

In the following exercise, you'll sort the instructor database in ascending chronological order by contract dates:

1. Select worksheet B if it is not already selected, and choose <u>R</u>ange ➤ <u>S</u>ort. Initially, click in the <u>R</u>ange text box.

2. Press F3. 1-2-3 displays the Range Names dialog box, as in Figure 7.8, with a list of all the range names you have defined up to now in your database.

3. Double-click the name INSTRUCTRECS. This name represents the range of records *without* the row of field names. The Range Names box disappears and 1-2-3 enters the name into the Range box.

4. Use the mouse to drag the dialog box window further down the screen from its original position, so you can see the field names and the first few records in the instructor database.

5. Activate the <u>S</u>ort by text box. The Sort dialog box appears, as in Figure 7.9.

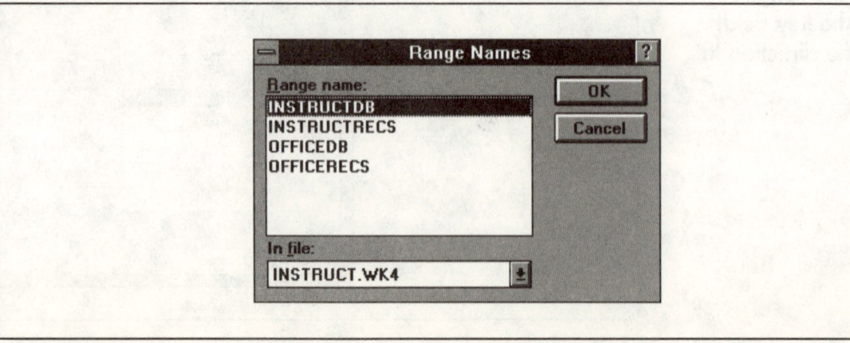

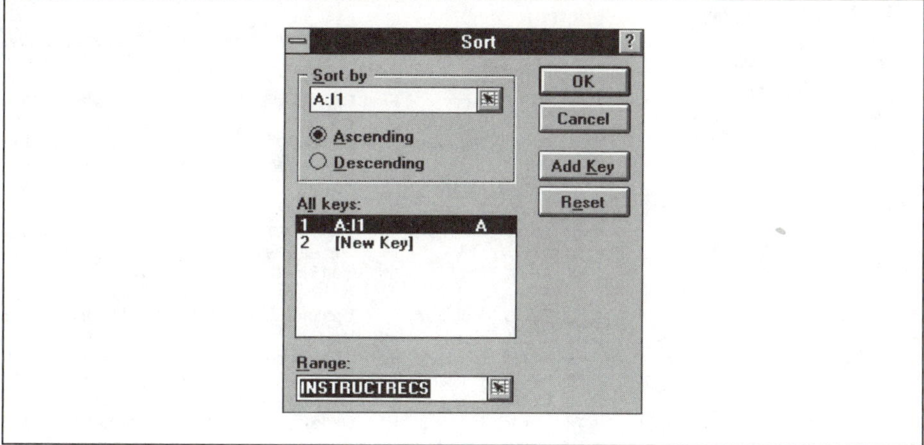

6. Click cell I4 in the instructor database. This cell contains the contract date for the first record in the database. In response to your mouse click, 1-2-3 enters a reference to this cell in the Sort by box. This reference is sufficient to select the Contract field as the key to the sort.

7. Click the Ascending option button, located just beneath the Sort by box.

8. Click OK or press ↵ to complete the sort operation.

Your sorted database should look like Figure 7.10. As you can see, 1-2-3 has rearranged the instructor records in order of contract dates, from the earliest to the most recent.

Sorting on More than One Field

Sometimes a single key is not enough to produce a complete or useful sort. For example, suppose a database table has a number of people whose last name is Smith. In an alphabetical sort by last name, 1-2-3 needs to sort the Smiths by first as well as last name to put them in alphabetical order. When two or more records have the same entry in the primary key field, as is the case with the Smiths, you need to choose a secondary key to decide the order of matching records.

	A	B	C	D	E	F	G	H	I	J	K
1				Instructor Database							
2											
3	ID	Last	First	City	Region	Specialty	Rate	Hrs	Contract	Yrs	Ok
4	D-106	Weinberg	P.	Miami	S	Database	$75	59	18-Jan-86	6.0	B
5	N-101	Schwartz	B.	Boston	E	Networks	$150	178	02-Mar-86	5.9	A
6	A-103	Perez	D.	Las Vegas	W	Accounting	$100	5	11-Jul-86	5.6	C
7	W-113	Porter	D.	Seattle	N	WP	$125	59	02-Aug-86	5.5	B
8	W-124	Meyer	J.	New York	E	WP	$150	85	05-May-87	4.7	B
9	S-125	Ashford	W.	Washington, D.C.	E	Spreadsheet	$150	145	10-May-87	4.7	A
10	S-127	Gill	P.	Los Angeles	W	Spreadsheet	$100	25	22-Jun-87	4.6	C
11	W-119	Davis	G.	San Francisco	W	WP	$150	139	09-Jul-87	4.6	A
12	T-128	Eng	R.	Albuquerque	S	Telecomm	$75	75	11-Oct-87	4.3	B
13	T-133	Ramirez	F.	Boston	E	Telecomm	$150	73	08-Feb-88	4.0	B
14	D-139	Porter	M.	Washington, D.C.	E	Database	$150	26	28-Mar-89	2.8	B
15	D-137	Sanchez	W.	Indianapolis	N	Database	$100	47	16-Apr-89	2.8	B
16	W-145	Banks	S.	St. Louis	S	WP	$150	55	10-Jun-90	1.6	A
17	D-143	Cody	L.	Los Angeles	W	Database	$75	43	20-Jun-90	1.6	B
18	S-149	Harris	P.	Dallas	S	Spreadsheet	$150	17	12-Feb-91	1.0	New
19	A-146	Daniels	A.	Atlanta	S	Accounting	$125	24	09-May-91	0.7	New
20	S-155	Roberts	P.	Chicago	N	Spreadsheet	$100	10	21-Aug-91	0.4	New

In the instructor database, two instructors have the last name Porter. When you sort the records alphabetically by instructor name, you should select the First field as the secondary key to sort Porter, D. before Porter, M.

To specify a secondary sort key for "breaking the tie" when matches occur in a sort:

1. Choose Range ➤ Sort to see the Sort dialog box (see Figure 7.9).

2. Highlight [New Key] in the All keys dialog box

3. Click on the Sort by list box, choose a secondary key to sort on, and click OK or press ↵.

The Range ➤ Sort command allows you to select more than two key fields to sort on. Suppose you sorted the database by making the Region field the primary key and the City field the secondary key. However, in examining the result of this sort (shown in Figure 7.11), you realize that you would like to sort the records in each city in alphabetical order by Specialty. In other words, your goal is to sort the database three ways: first by the Region field, then by the City field, and finally by the Specialty field.

Entering extra sort keys in the dialog box To sort by more than one key, begin in the Sort dialog box (see Figure 7.9) by entering references

Row	A	B	C	D	E	F	G	H	I	J	K
1				Instructor Database							
2											
3	ID	Last	First	City	Region	Specialty	Rate	Hrs	Contract	Yrs	Ok
4	T-133	Ramirez	F.	Boston	E	Telecomm	$150	73	08-Feb-88	4.0	B
5	N-101	Schwartz	B.	Boston	E	Networks	$150	178	02-Mar-86	5.9	A
6	W-124	Meyer	J.	New York	E	WP	$150	85	05-May-87	4.7	B
7	S-125	Ashford	W.	Washington, D.C.	E	Spreadsheet	$150	145	10-May-87	4.7	A
8	D-139	Porter	M.	Washington, D.C.	E	Database	$150	26	28-Mar-89	2.8	B
9	S-155	Roberts	P.	Chicago	N	Spreadsheet	$100	10	21-Aug-91	0.4	New
10	D-137	Sanchez	W.	Indianapolis	N	Database	$100	47	16-Apr-89	2.8	B
11	W-113	Porter	D.	Seattle	N	WP	$125	59	02-Aug-86	5.5	B
12	T-128	Eng	R.	Albuquerque	S	Telecomm	$75	75	11-Oct-87	4.3	B
13	A-146	Daniels	A.	Atlanta	S	Accounting	$125	24	09-May-91	0.7	New
14	S-149	Harris	P.	Dallas	S	Spreadsheet	$150	17	12-Feb-91	1.0	New
15	D-106	Weinberg	P.	Miami	S	Database	$75	59	18-Jan-86	6.0	B
16	W-145	Banks	S.	St. Louis	S	WP	$150	55	10-Jun-90	1.6	A
17	A-103	Perez	D.	Las Vegas	W	Accounting	$100	5	11-Jul-86	5.6	C
18	D-143	Cody	L.	Los Angeles	W	Database	$75	43	20-Jun-90	1.6	B
19	S-127	Gill	P.	Los Angeles	W	Spreadsheet	$100	25	22-Jun-87	4.6	C
20	W-119	Davis	G.	San Francisco	W	WP	$150	139	09-Jul-87	4.6	A

for the primary key in the Sort by text box. Next, click on the Add key button. Then you create each additional key in the Sort by box (remembering to select each new range in the Range text box) and click on Add key for each key. As a result, 1-2-3 displays a list of additional sorting keys in the All keys box.

Try it for yourself:

1. Choose Range ➤ Sort. If necessary, press F3 to enter the INSTRUCTRECS range name to the Range box. Enter a reference to cell E4 into the Sort by box, click the Ascending option, and click on the Add key button.

2. Enter a reference to cell D4 into the Sort by box, click Ascending, and click on the Add Key button again.

3. Use the mouse to drag the Sort dialog box window down the screen, creating a clear view of the field names and the first few records in the database.

4. Enter a reference to cell F4 into the Sort by box, click Ascending, and click on the Add Key button again.

5. Click on OK to accept the sort keys and execute the sort command. Lotus 1-2-3 carries out your instructions for the database sort.

The sorted database appears in Figure 7.12. You can see that the database has indeed been sorted by three keys: first the records are arranged by region; within each region they are arranged by city; and where there are duplicate city entries—specifically, Boston, Washington D.C., and Los Angeles—the records are arranged by specialty.

According to the 1-2-3 documentation, you can have as many as 253 extra sorting keys, but it's hard to imagine a database that requires so many. Suffice it to say, 1-2-3 supports as many keys as your database requires.

	A	B	C	D	E	F	G	H	I	J	K
1				Instructor Database							
2											
3	ID	Last	First	City	Region	Specialty	Rate	Hrs	Contract	Yrs	Ok
4	N-101	Schwartz	B.	Boston	E	Networks	$150	178	02-Mar-86	5.9	A
5	T-133	Ramirez	F.	Boston	E	Telecomm	$150	73	08-Feb-88	4.0	B
6	W-124	Meyer	J.	New York	E	WP	$150	85	05-May-87	4.7	B
7	D-139	Porter	M.	Washington, D.C.	E	Database	$150	26	28-Mar-89	2.8	B
8	S-125	Ashford	W.	Washington, D.C.	E	Spreadsheet	$150	145	10-May-87	4.7	A
9	S-155	Roberts	P.	Chicago	N	Spreadsheet	$100	10	21-Aug-91	0.4	New
10	D-137	Sanchez	W.	Indianapolis	N	Database	$100	47	16-Apr-89	2.8	B
11	W-113	Porter	D.	Seattle	N	WP	$125	59	02-Aug-86	5.5	B
12	T-128	Eng	R.	Albuquerque	S	Telecomm	$75	75	11-Oct-87	4.3	B
13	A-146	Daniels	A.	Atlanta	S	Accounting	$125	24	09-May-91	0.7	New
14	S-149	Harris	P.	Dallas	S	Spreadsheet	$150	17	12-Feb-91	1.0	New
15	D-106	Weinberg	P.	Miami	S	Database	$75	59	18-Jan-86	6.0	B
16	W-145	Banks	S.	St. Louis	S	WP	$150	55	10-Jun-90	1.6	A
17	A-103	Perez	D.	Las Vegas	W	Accounting	$100	5	11-Jul-86	5.6	C
18	D-143	Cody	L.	Los Angeles	W	Database	$75	43	20-Jun-90	1.6	B
19	S-127	Gill	P.	Los Angeles	W	Spreadsheet	$100	25	22-Jun-87	4.6	C
20	W-119	Davis	G.	San Francisco	W	WP	$150	139	09-Jul-87	4.6	A

Clearing All Sort Instructions

Each time you choose the Range ➤ Sort command, the Sort dialog box shows sorting instructions from the previous sort. If you want to start over again with a fresh set of sorting instructions, click the Reset button and clear all instructions from the dialog box.

To see how this works and to sort the database by instructor names in preparation for upcoming exercises, follow these steps:

1. Choose Range ➤ Sort and click the Reset button in the dialog box. This clears the current entries from the Sort dialog box.

2. Enter **INSTRUCTRECS** in the Range box, **B4** in the Sort by box, click Ascending, and click on the Add Key button. Then enter **C4** in the Sort by box, click on Ascending and again click on Add Key. Then click OK or press ↵.

3. Click the SaveFile icon to update the INSTRUCT.WK4 worksheet on disk.

Changing the Default Sort Order to Letters First

The *sort order* refers to 1-2-3's default technique for sorting a database when a key field has some label entries that begin with digits and others that begin with letters. In Figure 7.6, three entries in the Address field begin with numbers and one begins with a letter. If you were to sort this table by the Address field, what would the resulting order be?

By default, 1-2-3 uses the *numbers first* sort order. To demonstrate that this is so, try the following exercise:

1. Click the A tab to move the cell pointer to worksheet A.

2. Choose Range ➤ Sort command and click the Reset button to clear all previous sorting instructions.

3. Enter the range name **OFFICERECS** into the Range box. Then enter a reference to cell A:B4 in the Sort by box. Click the Ascending option, and then click OK.

Figure 7.13 shows the office database, sorted by the Address field. You can see that 1-2-3's default sort order is to place the addresses that begin with digits first and the address that begins with letters next.

Except to complete this experimental exercise, you would not likely sort the office database by the Address field, because the four addresses in the table are all in different cities. But you might sort a field with numbers and letters if you had to sort a database of addresses all in the same city—and in such a case you would want to control the default sort order.

To change the default order:

1. Rerun the 1-2-3 Install program. The Main Menu appears on the screen, as shown in Figure 7.14.

DATABASE ESSENTIALS

2. To change the sort order, click the option labeled Choose country driver and sort order. The Choose Country and Sort Order dialog box appears, as in Figure 7.15.

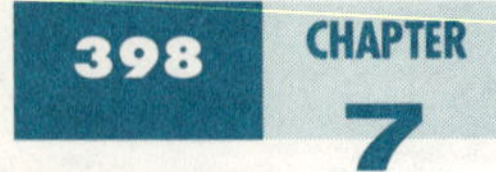

FIGURE 7.13

In fields with numbers and letters, 1-2-3 sorts numbers before letters, although you can change this default specification.

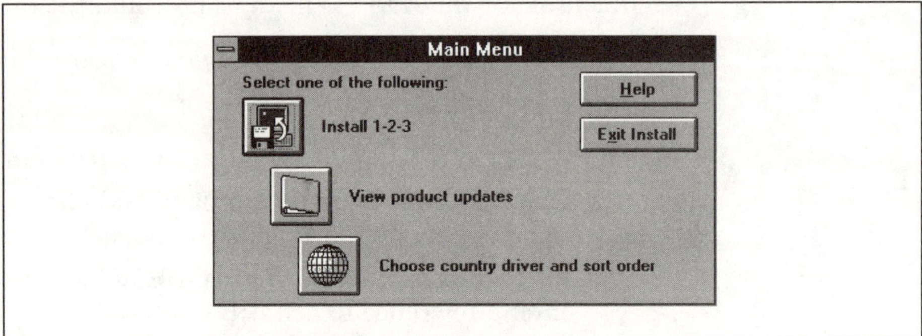

FIGURE 7.14

The Main Menu of the 1-2-3 Install program

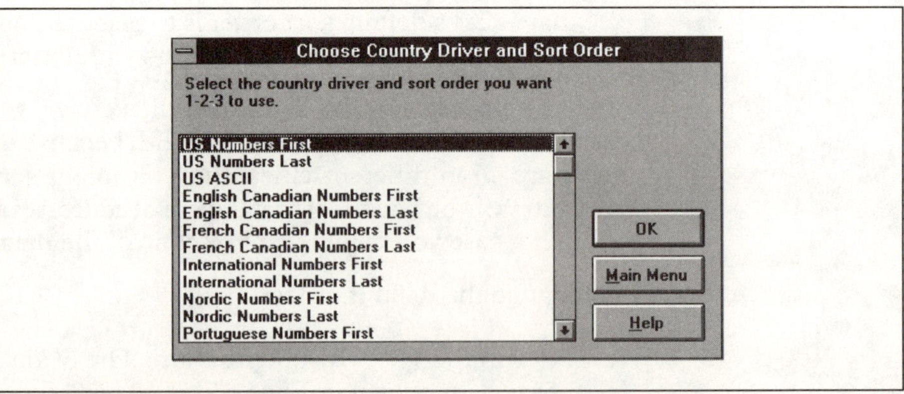

FIGURE 7.15

The Choose Country and Sort Order dialog box

3. From this dialog box you can select from a list of 1-2-3's sort orders, including Numbers First, Numbers Last, and ASCII.

NOTE See Appendix A for information about the Install program.

Querying a Database

As you learned at the beginning of this chapter, you use the Database commands when you want to find, list, delete, or revise records that match certain conditions in your database. The conditions for selecting records in a query operation are known as *criteria*. The expressions for criteria can be simple or complex. For example, in the instructor database, you could perform query operations to find one of the following:

- Instructors in the Southern region

- Instructors who specialize in word processing

- A Los Angeles instructor who specializes in spreadsheets

- Cities that have telecommunications or networking experts

- Western region instructors whose hourly rate is less than or equal to $100

- Spreadsheet experts who have an A rating in the Ok field

- Southern or Eastern database experts who have an A or B rating and work for less than $100 per hour

- Eastern region instructors who signed their first contracts with Computing Conferences, Inc. at least four years ago and have an A or B rating.

The criteria, input, and output ranges To perform queries like these, you write a single criterion or a combination of criteria, and you store them in a specially designated worksheet range called the *criteria range*.

A criteria range consists of a row of field names from your database, plus one or more rows of criteria that 1-2-3 can use to select records from the database.

Actually, the Database commands require you to identify as many as three special worksheet ranges. Besides identifying the criteria range, you must specify

- an *input range* that contains the database table from which you want to select records, and

- an *output range* (in some operations), where 1-2-3 can copy records that match your criteria.

The output range, like the criteria range, contains a row of field names; 1-2-3 uses this row of names to determine which fields to copy from the database. One convenient way to organize queries in a 1-2-3 worksheet window is to create separate worksheets for the input range, the criteria range, and the output range. In the next section, you'll begin developing these ranges for the instructor database.

Preparing the Input, Criteria, and Output Ranges

The INSTRUCT.WK4 file already includes two worksheets, one for the office database table and one for the instructor database table. For the upcoming query exercises, you'll make the instructor database table the input range. It will be the one from which you select records. This table has already been assigned the range name INSTRUCTDB. In the following steps, you'll insert two more worksheets in the file, one for the criteria range and one for the output range:

1. Click the B tab to move to worksheet B.

2. Choose <u>S</u>tyle ➤ <u>W</u>orksheet Defaults. Click the <u>G</u>roup mode option to place an *X* in the check box. Click OK to confirm.

3. Choose <u>E</u>dit ➤ Insert ➤ <u>S</u>heet and enter a value of **2** in the <u>Q</u>uantity box. Click OK or press ↵.

Lotus 1-2-3 inserts worksheets C and D in the file. Worksheet C is active initially. Thanks to the Group mode option, 1-2-3 has duplicated the column widths from worksheet B in the two new worksheets.

4. Click the A tab to view worksheet A. Unfortunately, the column widths from worksheet B have also been imposed on worksheet A.

5. Choose Style ➤ Worksheet Defaults again, and disable the Group mode option. (The *X* disappears from the check box.) Click OK to confirm.

6. Reestablish the correct column widths for the office worksheet: A, **6**; B, **17**; C, **11**; D, **4**; E, **7**; F, **12**; G, **12**. In exchange for this repeated effort on worksheet A, you saved time on new worksheets C and D.

7. Click the B tab to move to worksheet B. Now choose View ➤ Split and select the Perspective option button. If Synchronize scrolling is checked, click the Synchronize scrolling option, removing the *X* from the check box. (Disabling the Synchronize option allows you to scroll each of the worksheets independently.) Click OK or press ↵ to confirm. Now you have a perspective view of worksheets B, C, and D.

8. On worksheet B, select the range of field names, B:A3..B:K3. Click the CopyToClipboard icon or press Ctrl-C.

9. Move to worksheet C and select cell C:A3. Click the PasteFrom Clipboard icon, or press Ctrl-V. The row of field names appears in row 3 of worksheet C. Now move to worksheet D, select cell D:A3, and perform the same paste operation. A copy of the field names appears in worksheet D.

10. Move the cell pointer to worksheet C again. Enter the name **Criteria Range** in cell C:A1. Now preselect the two-row range C:A3..C:K4. Choose Range ➤ Name and enter the name **CRITERIA1** for this range. Click OK to confirm.

11. Move to worksheet D. Enter the name **Output Range** in cell D:A1 of worksheet D. Now preselect the one-row range D:A3..D:K3. Choose Range ➤ Name and enter the name **OUTPUT1** for this range. Click OK to confirm. Click elsewhere on the worksheet to deselect the range.

12. Click the SaveFile icon to update INSTRUCT.WK4 on disk.

When you complete all these steps, your worksheet window appears as shown in Figure 7.16. You are now ready to begin experimenting with the Database Query commands.

Output Range

ID	Last	First	City	Region	Specialty	Rate	Hrs	Contract	Yrs

Criteria Range

ID	Last	First	City	Region	Specialty	Rate	Hrs	Contract	Yrs

	A	B	C	D	E	F	G	H	I	J	K
1				Instructor Database							
2											
3	ID	Last	First	City	Region	Specialty	Rate	Hrs	Contract	Yrs	Ok
4	S-125	Ashford	W.	Washington, D.C.	E	Spreadsheet	$150	145	10-May-87	4.7	A
5	W-145	Banks	S.	St. Louis	S	WP	$150	55	10-Jun-90	1.6	A
6	D-143	Cody	L.	Los Angeles	W	Database	$75	43	20-Jun-90	1.6	B
7	A-146	Daniels	A.	Atlanta	S	Accounting	$125	24	09-May-91	0.7	New

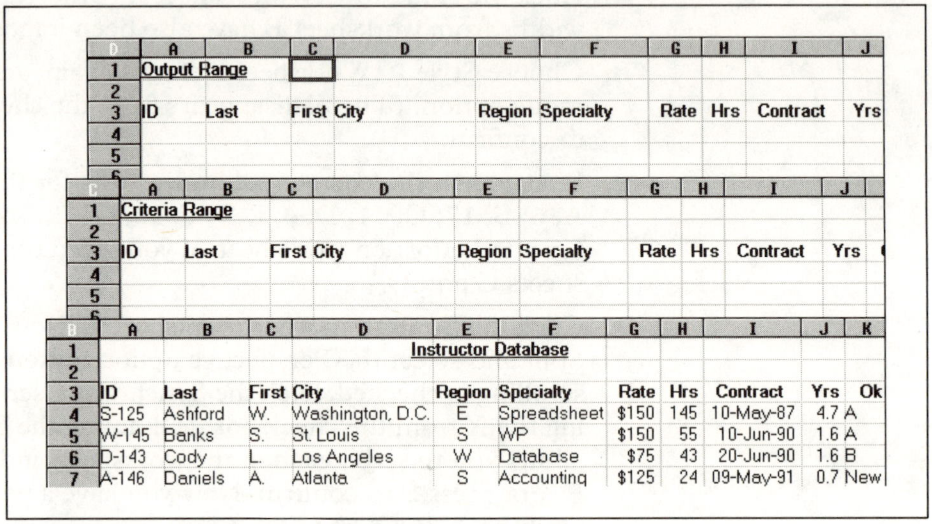

Finding Specific Records

In worksheet C, you have established a criteria range that includes the row of field names copied from the database, plus the row just beneath the names. When you perform your first query operations, and you identify CRITERIA1 as the criteria range, 1-2-3 will look in this range for values or expressions representing criteria. You can use several kinds of criteria to generate queries. The simplest kind is a label or a value that you enter below a field name in the criteria range. This kind of criterion instructs 1-2-3 to find all records with the same label or value in the field. For example, if you enter the label E under the name Region in the criteria range, 1-2-3 will find all records that have a Region entry of E.

As your first database query, try this Find Records operation:

1. Move the cell pointer to worksheet C, and enter the label **E** in cell E4, just beneath the Region field.

2. Choose <u>T</u>ools ➤ <u>D</u>atabase ➤ <u>F</u>ind Records. The Find Records dialog box appears, as in Figure 7.17.

This dialog box has four text boxes: <u>F</u>ield, Op<u>e</u>rator, <u>V</u>alue, and Find records in <u>d</u>atabase table.

3. In the Find records in <u>d</u>atabase table range box, press the F3 function key to view the Database Names box. Double-click the name INSTRUCTDB. 1-2-3 copies this name into the range box.

4. Click the <u>F</u>ield range button. Click the field name Region to enter it as the criteria range. When you do so, Region=E appears in the Criteria list box. At this point in your work, the Find Records dialog box should look like Figure 7.17.

5. Click the OK button.

Lotus 1-2-3 finds records that match the single criterion in the criteria range. 1-2-3 places a frame around the first record in the instructor database that matches the criterion. It also highlights all records that match the criterion, as shown in Figure 7.18.

N O T E

To move from selected record to selected record, press Ctrl-↵ to move forward, or Ctrl-Shift-↵ to move backward.

FIGURE 7.17

The Find Records dialog box. This is where you specify which records to find.

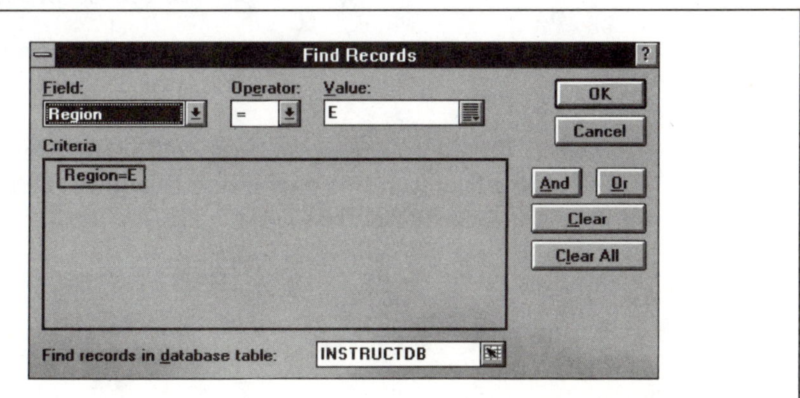

The results of a Find Records operation

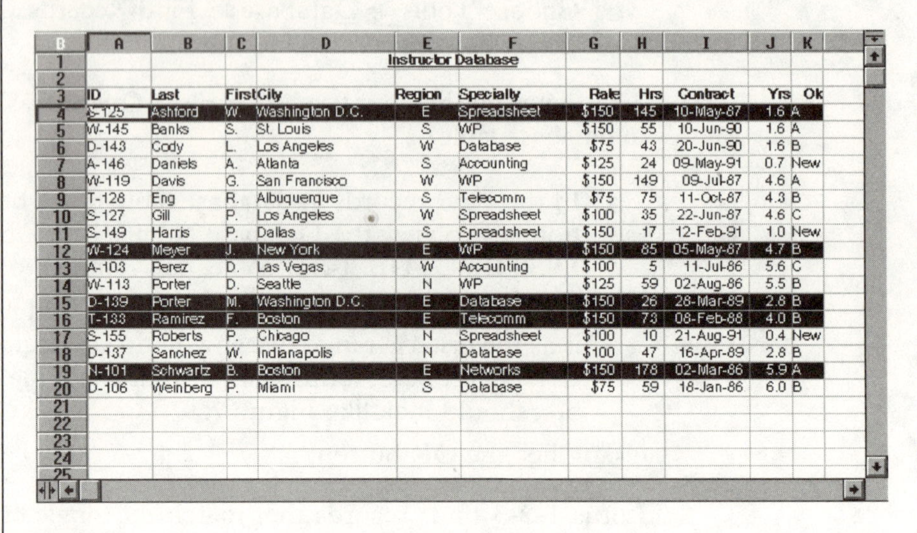

	A	B	C	D	E	F	G	H	I	J	K
1				Instructor Database							
2											
3	ID	Last	First	City	Region	Specialty	Rate	Hrs	Contract	Yrs	Ok
4	S-125	Ashford	W.	Washington D.C.	E	Spreadsheet	$150	145	10-May-87	1.6	A
5	W-145	Banks	S.	St. Louis	S	WP	$150	55	10-Jun-90	1.6	A
6	D-143	Cody	L.	Los Angeles	W	Database	$75	43	20-Jun-90	1.6	B
7	A-146	Daniels	A.	Atlanta	S	Accounting	$125	24	09-May-91	0.7	New
8	W-119	Davis	G.	San Francisco	W	WP	$150	149	09-Jul-87	4.6	A
9	T-128	Eng	R.	Albuquerque	S	Telecomm	$75	75	11-Oct-87	4.3	B
10	S-127	Gill	P.	Los Angeles	W	Spreadsheet	$100	35	22-Jun-87	4.6	C
11	S-149	Harris	P.	Dallas	S	Spreadsheet	$150	17	12-Feb-91	1.0	New
12	W-124	Meyer	J.	New York	E	WP	$150	85	05-May-87	4.7	B
13	A-103	Perez	D.	Las Vegas	W	Accounting	$100	5	11-Jul-86	5.6	C
14	W-113	Porter	D.	Seattle	N	WP	$125	59	02-Aug-86	5.5	B
15	D-139	Porter	M.	Washington D.C.	E	Database	$150	26	28-Mar-89	2.8	B
16	T-133	Ramirez	F.	Boston	E	Telecomm	$150	73	08-Feb-88	4.0	B
17	S-155	Roberts	P.	Chicago	N	Spreadsheet	$100	10	21-Aug-91	0.4	New
18	D-137	Sanchez	W.	Indianapolis	N	Database	$100	47	16-Apr-89	2.8	B
19	N-101	Schwartz	B.	Boston	E	Networks	$150	178	02-Mar-86	5.9	A
20	D-106	Weinberg	P.	Miami	S	Database	$75	59	18-Jan-86	6.0	B
21											
22											
23											
24											
25											

Moving the cursor to selected records To move between records, press these keys:

PRESS	TO MOVE
Ctrl-↵	Forward one record at a time
Ctrl-Shift-↵	Backward one record at a time
↵	Forward to the individual cells (or fields) of each record in sequence
Shift-↵	Backward through the individual cells (or fields) of each record in sequence

When you are at the first cell of the first matching record and you press Shift-↵ to move backward, the active cell becomes the last cell of the last matching record.

Finding Records that Match More than One Criterion

To further define the conditions for selecting records, you can place more than one label or value in a row of the criteria range. If you enter two criteria in a given row, 1-2-3 reads the entries as *And* conditions. In this case, a record must match both criteria to be selected. For example, if you now enter an A beneath the Ok field in the CRITERIA1 range, 1-2-3 combines this new entry with the E that is already beneath the Region field. As a result, the Database ➤ Find Records operation selects all Eastern region instructors who have a rating of A.

You'll try using more than one criterion in the next exercise:

1. Move to worksheet C and select cell C:K4. Enter the label **A** in the cell.

2. Choose <u>T</u>ools ➤ <u>D</u>atabase ➤ <u>F</u>ind Records. In the Find records in <u>d</u>atabase table range box, press F3 to view the Names box. Double-click the name INSTRUCTDB. 1-2-3 copies this name into the range box.

3. Click the <u>F</u>ield range button. Click the field name Region to enter this name as the criteria range. When you click on Region, Region=E appears in the Criteria list box.

4. Click on the <u>A</u>nd button on the right side of the dialog box. The Region=E criterion changes.

5. Click on the <u>F</u>ield range button again and select Ok. At this point in your work, the criteria box looks like Figure 7.19.

6. Click the OK button.

Lotus 1-2-3 finds records that match the double criterion currently expressed in the criteria range. A frame appears around the first record in the instructor database that matches the criterion, and all records that match the criterion are highlighted.

DATABASE ESSENTIALS

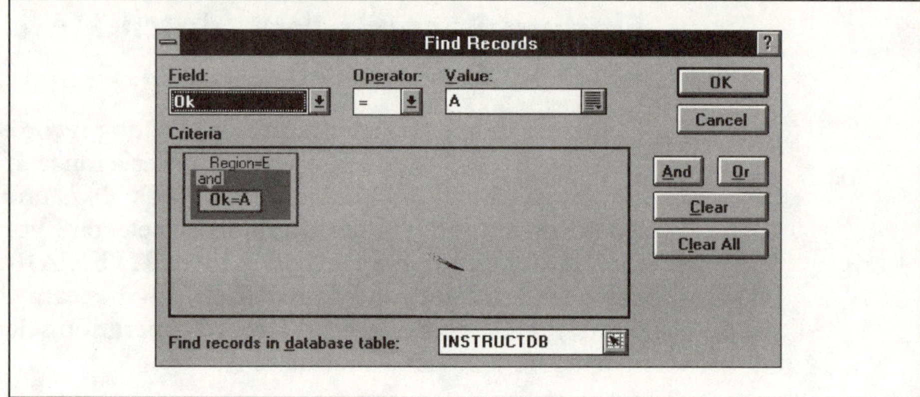

Copying Records that Match Selection Criteria

Unlike the Find Records command, which merely highlights selected records, the New Query command makes a copy of the records that match
the selection criteria. New Query copies the records to the output range.
To perform a New Query operation, you therefore need to go to the New
Query dialog box. From there you enter a range name in the Select location for new query table range box, as well as provide the source range
and criteria.

In the following steps, you'll use the current criteria to create an output
list of all Eastern region instructors with A ratings:

1. Choose <u>T</u>ools ➤ <u>D</u>atabase ➤ <u>N</u>ew Query.

2. In the Select <u>d</u>atabase table to query range box, press F3 and select
   INSTRUCTDB from the pull-down list that appears.

3. Click on the Set <u>C</u>riteria button.

4. Click on the ↓ button next to <u>F</u>ield and click on Region.

5. Click on the <u>A</u>nd button to the right side of the Set Criteria
   dialog box.

6. Return to <u>F</u>ield and select OK. Then click on OK to return to the New Query dialog box.

N O T E

In the Field text box, just press the first letter of the field name to jump to it immediately. If there is more than one field name starting with the same first letter, keep pressing the letter until the right name appears.

7. Click in the Select location for new <u>q</u>uery table text box.

8. Press F3 and double-click the name OUTPUT1 in the Range Names dialog box. In response, 1-2-3 copies this name to the Output range box, as shown in Figure 7.20.

9. Click on the OK button.

FIGURE 7.20

Entering a name for the output range

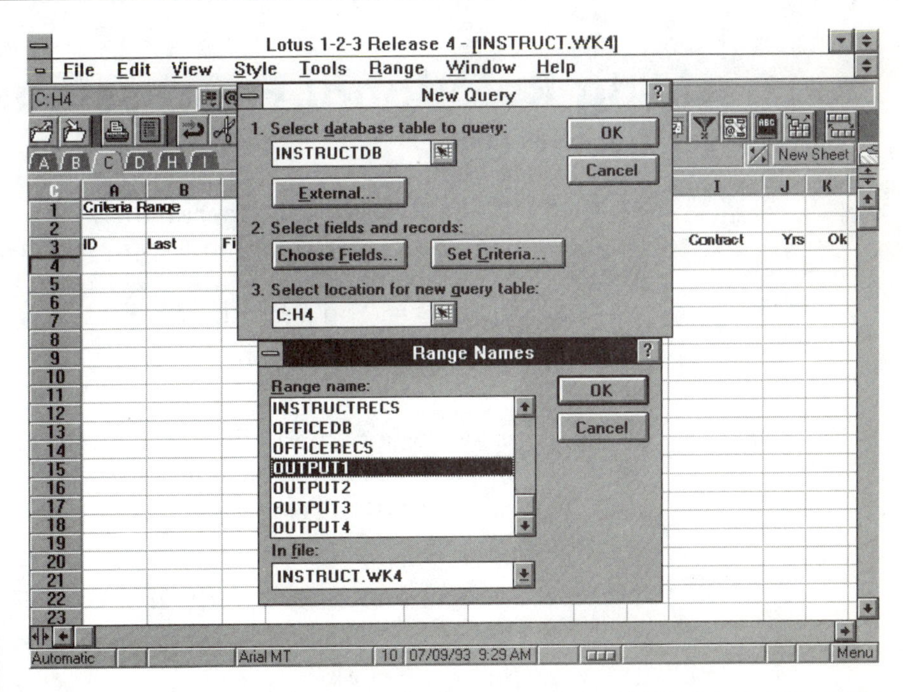

10. You will notice that the cell pointer has automatically moved to worksheet D as a result of the query. Now scroll the worksheet horizontally so that you can see columns B though K.

When you complete these steps, the worksheet file appears as in Figure 7.21. As you can see, the table brought forward has a heavy frame around it. You activate the data in the table for Query operations by clicking on the frame. When the table is highlighted, you will notice that the Range option on the Main menu bar is gone and the Query option is now in its place. We will use the Query menu in a following section. In the output range of worksheet D, 1-2-3 has selected and copied the two matching records.

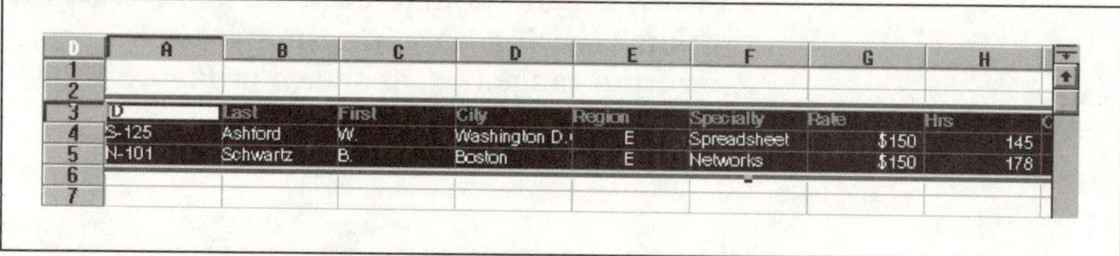

Using Relational Expressions in Queries

In the next exercise, you'll experiment with a new kind of criterion expression. You can enter relational expressions in the criteria range—that is, expressions beginning with one of the relational operators, such as <, >, <=, and >=. You enter these expressions as labels. For example, if you enter the expression

    >100

as the criterion for a numeric field, 1-2-3 selects all records that have a value greater than 100 in that field. This kind of criterion also works with date fields. The criterion expression

    <=15-Jun-86

prompts 1-2-3 to search for records that have date values on or before June 15, 1986.

Less-than (<) as a label expression   There is one problem with entering a label expression that begins with the less-than character (<). Pressing < normally opens the 1-2-3 Classic window, as you learned in Chapter 1. To avoid this response, you must begin the < label with a label prefix such as the single quotation mark.

Follow these steps to try using relational criteria in a sequence of extract operations:

1. In sheet D, clear the entries from the previous Query operation. Go back to sheet C of the worksheet and delete the two criteria currently displayed in the criteria range. Choose <u>D</u>atabase ➤ Delete Records, enter ranges in the Delete records from data<u>b</u>ase table, and click OK.

2. Select cell C:H4 in the Hrs field and enter the criterion **'>100**. This criterion instructs 1-2-3 to find all instructors who have worked for more than 100 hours.

3. Choose <u>T</u>ools ➤ <u>D</u>atabase ➤ <u>N</u>ew Query.

4. In the Select <u>d</u>atabase table to query range box, press F3 and select INSTRUCTDB from the pull-down list that appears.

5. Click on the Set <u>C</u>riteria button. Click on the ↓ button next to Field and click on Hr. Then click on the Op<u>e</u>rator button and select the > symbol. Finally, enter **100** in the <u>V</u>alue text box and click on OK to return to the New Query dialog box.

6. Click on OK to close the New Query dialog box and execute the Query operation.

7. Examining the output range in worksheet D, you can see that 1-2-3 has found three records that match this criterion. Select worksheet D and scroll the worksheet vertically so you can see all three selected records. When you do so, your worksheet will look like Figure 7.22.

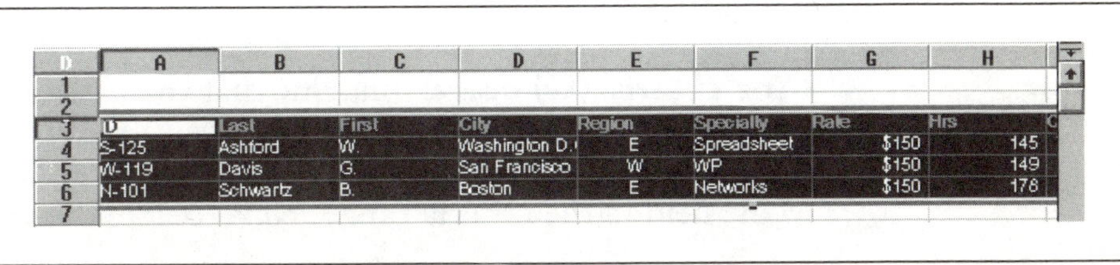

D	A	B	C	D	E	F	G	H	C
1									
2									
3	ID	Last	First	City	Region	Specialty	Rate	Hrs	
4	S-125	Ashford	W.	Washington D.	E	Spreadsheet	$150	145	
5	W-119	Davis	G.	San Francisco	W	WP	$150	149	
6	N-101	Schwartz	B.	Boston	E	Networks	$150	178	
7									

8. Delete the criterion from cell C:H4, and then select cell C:I4 in the Contract field. Enter the expression **'<=15-Jun-86** in this cell.

9. Repeat the Tools ➤ Database ➤ New Query process, setting **Contract** in the Fields box, **<=** in the Operator box, and **15-Jun-86** in the Value box of the Set Criteria dialog box.

Lotus 1-2-3 searches for instructors who signed contracts on or before June 15, 1986. As you can see in Figure 7.23, there are two such records.

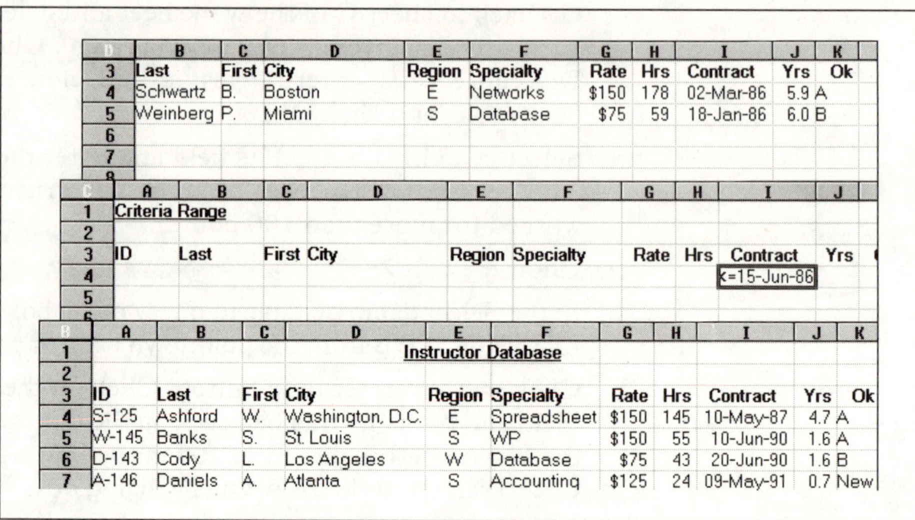

Using Wildcard Characters in Searches

Label criteria can appear in additional forms. For example, you can use wildcard characters to search for labels that contain certain combinations of characters. Lotus 1-2-3 lets you use the wildcard characters shown in Table 7.1

The asterisk wildcard Imagine that you are searching for an instructor whose name begins with *P*, but you can't recall the rest of the name. To find all the names that begin with *P*, enter P★ as a criterion under the Last field in the criteria range. Next, delete the criterion from cell C:I4,

TABLE 7.1: Lotus Wildcard Characters

WILDCARD CHARACTER	USE
?	Represents any single character in a label.
*	Represents an unspecified number of characters.
~	Identifies a value that you want to *exclude* from the selected records.

and then rerun Database ➤ New Query. Figure 7.24 shows the response: 1-2-3 finds the three instructors whose names begin with *P* and copies the records to the output range.

The tilde wildcard (~) An entry of ~E in the Region field of the criteria range instructs 1-2-3 to select all the records *except* those of the Eastern region.

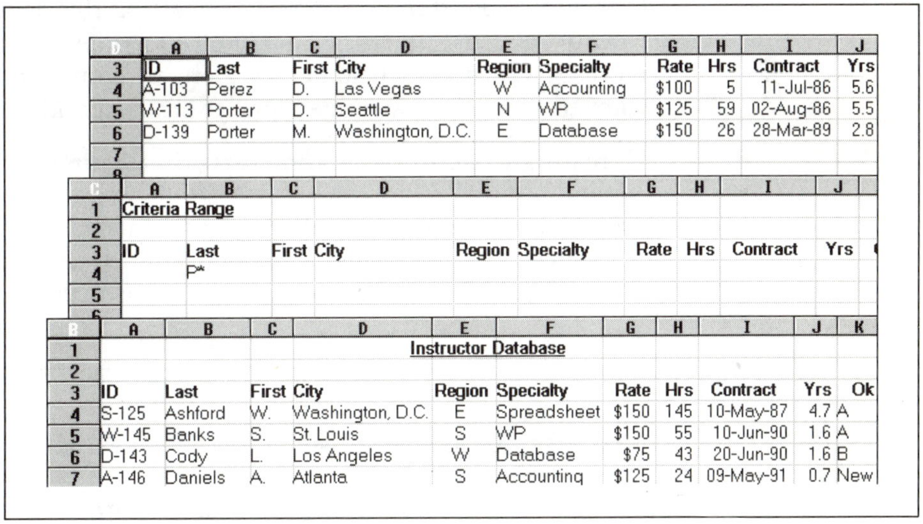

FIGURE 7.24

Using wildcard characters in criteria. Here, the asterisk was used to represent unknown or unspecified characters.

Using Or Conditions in Queries

In the upcoming exercise with the Query command, you'll work with yet another variation in the criteria range. Up to now, you've entered each criterion in a single row, just beneath the field names in the criteria range. You've seen that 1-2-3 treats multiple criteria in a row as And conditions. To be selected, a record must match all the criteria. In contrast, expressions entered on different rows of the criteria range are treated as *Or* conditions. This means that a given record from the database will be selected if it matches any one of the criteria.

For example, imagine that you want to examine the records of all Western region instructors who specialize in either spreadsheets or word processing. Figure 7.25 shows the criteria range that you will prepare for this query. In the Specialty field, one row has an entry of Spreadsheet and the other WP. In addition, an entry of Wappears in both rows beneath the Region field. (If you were to omit the *W* from the second row, 1-2-3 would select Western region spreadsheet specialists along with word processing instructors from *all* regions.)

One additional step is required to establish this as the criteria range. You can no longer use the name CRITERIA1 to identify the range. CRITERIA1 represents the row of field names, along with only one row of criteria. You'll want to create a new range name for the expanded criteria range.

Here are the steps for creating this criteria range on your worksheet:

1. Click the Perspective SmartIcon, if necessary, to view three worksheets at once. Select cells C:K4 and B4. Press the Delete key to delete the criterion from the previous exercise.

C	A	B	C	D	E	F	G	H	I	J	K
1	Criteria Range										
2											
3	ID	Last	First	City	Region	Specialty	Rate	Hrs	Contract	Yrs	Ok
4					W	Spreadsheet					
5					W	WP					
6											

2. Make the following entries:

CELL	ENTRY
C:E4	**W**
C:E5	**W**
C:F4	**Spreadsheet**
C:F5	**WP**

3. Preselect the range C:A3..C:K5. Choose <u>R</u>ange ➤ <u>N</u>ame and enter the name **CRITERIA2** for this new criteria range. Click OK or press ↵ to confirm.

4. Click the SaveFile icon to save your work to disk.

You'll make use of this new criteria range in the next section, as you explore the use of the Query command.

Placing Revised Records Back in the Database

The Query command gives you a convenient way to revise records you've taken from a database and return them to the original database from which they came. With this technique, you can work on selected records in a database—records that match a certain criterion—all at once without having to move back and forth through the database.

As was mentioned earlier, when you create a table with Tools ➤ Database ➤ New Query, it is surrounded by a heavy frame, and when this table is active and highlighted, the Query option replaces the Range option on the Main menu bar. To revise selected records and place them back in the database, you follow this general procedure:

1. Use the New Query command to remove records that match a given set of criteria. The records appear in your output range.

2. Choose Query ➤ Set Options.

3. Select the Allow updates to source table check box.

4. Activate this range and revise the records in any way necessary.

5. Choose Query ➤ Update Database Table and instruct 1-2-3 to copy the revised records back to the database.

DATABASE ESSENTIALS

When you use the Query command, 1-2-3 keeps track of the original locations of the extracted records.

Suppose the Western region has just completed a series of conferences focusing on spreadsheets and word processing. The regional instructors specializing in these fields each worked for ten hours. Your job is to locate the records for these instructors and increase the entries in their Hrs fields.

You have already entered the correct criteria into worksheet C for accomplishing this task, and you have assigned the name CRITERIA2 to the new criteria range. This is what you do next:

1. Choose <u>T</u>ools ➤ <u>D</u>atabase ➤ <u>N</u>ew Query and create the query table of records that you want to modify.

2. Choose Query ➤ Set <u>O</u>ptions. The Set Options dialog box appears.

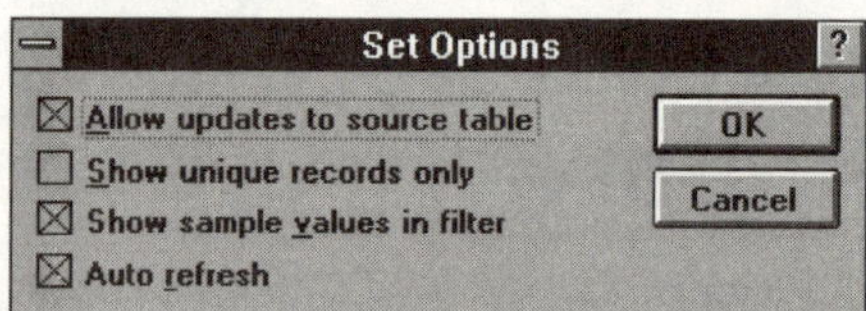

3. Click on <u>A</u>llow updates to source table to place an *X* in the check box. Click on OK to return to the table.

4. Select cell D:H4. Enter a new value of **149**, ten hours more than the previous entry.

5. Select cell D:H5 and enter a new value of **35**.

6. Choose Query ➤ <u>U</u>pdate Database Table. Lotus 1-2-3 copies your revised records from the output range back to the database.

If you look at the original table, you will see the changes to the records that you pulled out for modifications.

7. Preselect range D:A3..D:K3 and choose Range ➤ Name. Enter **OUTPUT1** in the Name box and click OK. (Renaming this range is necessary after the Query command.)

8. Click the SaveFile icon to save your work to disk.

Figure 7.26 shows your database after the Query operation is complete. By scrolling vertically down the database in worksheet B, you can see the two records that have been revised in rows 8 and 10. They contain the correct new entries for the Hrs field.

Output Range

	ID	Last	First	City	Region	Specialty	Rate	Hrs	Contract	Yrs
4	W-119	Davis	G.	San Francisco	W	WP	$150	149	09-Jul-87	4.6
5	S-127	Gill	P.	Los Angeles	W	Spreadsheet	$100	35	22-Jun-87	4.6

Criteria Range

	ID	Last	First	City	Region	Specialty	Rate	Hrs	Contract	Yrs
4					W	Spreadsheet				
5					W	WP				

	A	B	C	D	E	F	G	H	I	J	K
8	W-119	Davis	G.	San Francisco	W	WP	$150	149	09-Jul-87	4.6	A
9	T-128	Eng	R.	Albuquerque	S	Telecomm	$75	75	11-Oct-87	4.3	B
10	S-127	Gill	P.	Los Angeles	W	Spreadsheet	$100	35	22-Jun-87	4.6	C
11	S-149	Harris	P.	Dallas	S	Spreadsheet	$150	17	12-Feb-91	1.0	New
12	W-124	Meyer	J.	New York	E	WP	$150	85	05-May-87	4.7	B
13	A-103	Perez	D.	Las Vegas	W	Accounting	$100	5	11-Jul-86	5.6	C
14	W-113	Porter	D.	Seattle	N	WP	$125	59	02-Aug-86	5.5	B

Writing Formulas as Criteria

In some database applications, you may not be able to express all your selection criteria as simple labels, values, or relations. For more complex queries, 1-2-3 allows you to write logical formulas as criteria. As you'll recall from Chapter 5, a logical formula is an expression that results in a value of true or false. You build logical formulas with the relational operators (=, <>, <, >, <=, and >=) and the logical operators (#NOT#, #AND#, and #OR#).

In a formula criterion, you use field names as the operand. For example, suppose you want to find all the instructors who charge hourly rates that are greater than $75 but less than $150. To do so, you could enter the following formula in the Rate field of the criteria range:

    +RATE>75#AND#RATE<150

DATABASE ESSENTIALS

Figure 7.27 shows how this formula works as a criterion in a query operation. As you can see in worksheet D, 1-2-3 has copied the records of instructors who charge $100 or $125. Notice that the formula in the criteria range (in cell C:G4) is displayed in the Text format. When you enter a formula like this one into the criteria range, 1-2-3 may respond by displaying ERR in the cell. This does not mean that there is anything wrong with the formula as a criterion. To clarify your worksheet—and to avoid displaying ERR—you will probably want to choose Range Format and select Text format for the cell.

Here is another example. Imagine that you want to review all the contracts that were signed during the last half of 1987 and all of 1988. To find the names of instructors who signed contracts in this period, you enter the following formula below the Contract field name in the criteria range:

```
+CONTRACT>@DATE(87,6,30)#AND#CON-
TRACT<=@DATE(88,12,31)
```

Figure 7.28 shows how this formula works in a Query operation. Three records match the criterion expressed in the formula.

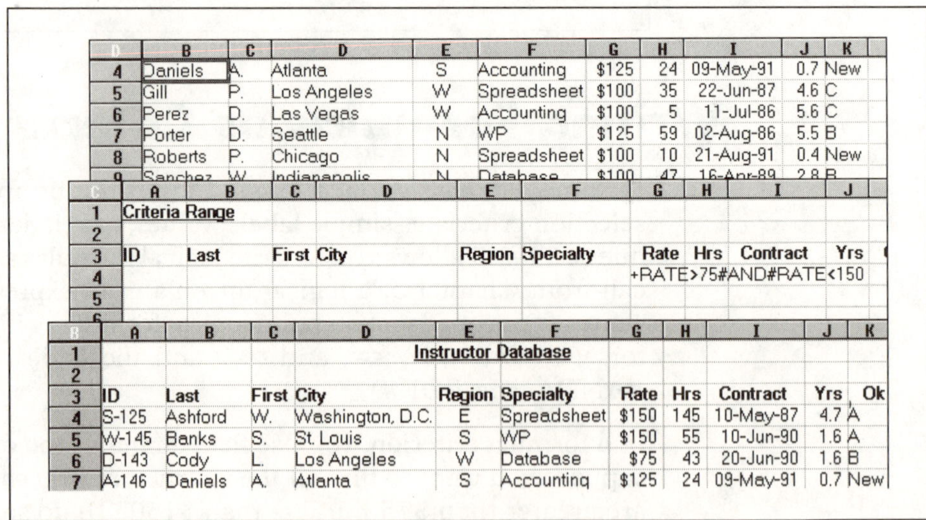

Worksheet D:

	B	C	D	E	F	G	H	I	J	K
4	Daniels	A.	Atlanta	S	Accounting	$125	24	09-May-91	0.7	New
5	Gill	P.	Los Angeles	W	Spreadsheet	$100	35	22-Jun-87	4.6	C
6	Perez	D.	Las Vegas	W	Accounting	$100	5	11-Jul-86	5.6	C
7	Porter	D.	Seattle	N	WP	$125	59	02-Aug-86	5.5	B
8	Roberts	P.	Chicago	N	Spreadsheet	$100	10	21-Aug-91	0.4	New
9	Sanchez	W.	Indianapolis	N	Database	$100	47	16-Apr-89	2.8	B

Worksheet C:

	A	B	C	D	E	F	G	H	I	J
1	Criteria Range									
2										
3	ID	Last	First	City		Region	Specialty	Rate	Hrs	Contract	Yrs
4								+RATE>75#AND#RATE<150		
5										
6										

Worksheet B:

	A	B	C	D	E	F	G	H	I	J	K
1				Instructor Database							
2											
3	ID	Last	First	City		Region	Specialty	Rate	Hrs	Contract	Yrs	Ok
4	S-125	Ashford	W.	Washington, D.C.	E	Spreadsheet	$150	145	10-May-87	4.7	A
5	W-145	Banks	S.	St. Louis	S	WP	$150	55	10-Jun-90	1.6	A
6	D-143	Cody	L.	Los Angeles	W	Database	$75	43	20-Jun-90	1.6	B
7	A-146	Daniels	A.	Atlanta	S	Accounting	$125	24	09-May-91	0.7	New

	Last	First	City	Region	Specialty	Rate	Hrs	Contract	Yrs	Ok
3	Last	First	City	Region	Specialty	Rate	Hrs	Contract	Yrs	Ok
4	Davis	G.	San Francisco	W	WP	$150	149	09-Jul-87	4.6	A
5	Eng	R.	Albuquerque	S	Telecomm	$75	75	11-Oct-87	4.3	B
6	Ramirez	F.	Boston	E	Telecomm	$150	73	08-Feb-88	4.0	B

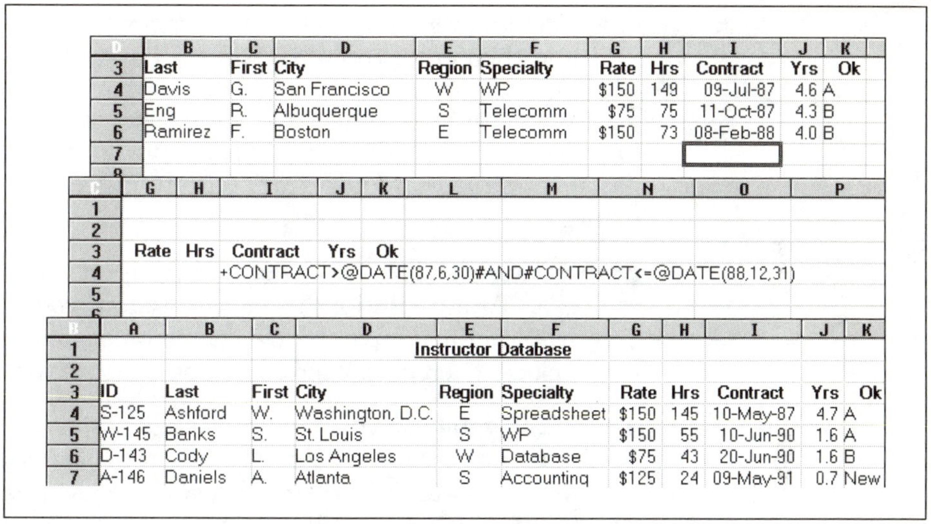

	G	H	I	J	K	L	M	N	O	P
3	Rate	Hrs	Contract	Yrs	Ok					
4			+CONTRACT>@DATE(87,6,30)#AND#CONTRACT<=@DATE(88,12,31)							

	A	B	C	D	E	F	G	H	I	J	K
1				Instructor Database							
3	ID	Last	First	City	Region	Specialty	Rate	Hrs	Contract	Yrs	Ok
4	S-125	Ashford	W.	Washington, D.C.	E	Spreadsheet	$150	145	10-May-87	4.7	A
5	W-145	Banks	S.	St. Louis	S	WP	$150	55	10-Jun-90	1.6	A
6	D-143	Cody	L.	Los Angeles	W	Database	$75	43	20-Jun-90	1.6	B
7	A-146	Daniels	A.	Atlanta	S	Accounting	$125	24	09-May-91	0.7	New

Summary

A 1-2-3 database table is a collection of records that you enter into consecutive rows of a worksheet. Each database table begins with a row of field names. The entries within a field all belong to the same data type.

You use Range ➤ Sort or Query ➤ Sort to rearrange the records of a database table in alphabetical, numeric, or chronological order. The Sort dialog box allows entries for primary and secondary sorting keys, and options for ascending or descending sorts. To define additional key fields, you simply keep creating new keys and clicking on the Add Key button until you have specified all of the keys you need.

The Database and Query commands are the central features of the 1-2-3 database component. You use options in these commands to perform these database operations:

- Highlighting records that match specific criteria.
- Copying matching records to an output range.
- Deleting records from a database.

DATABASE ESSENTIALS

- Copying records to an output range, where you can work on them and then enter them back in the database.

To prepare for these query operations, you create a criteria range containing a row of field names and one or more rows of criteria. In addition, the Query command requires an output range containing a row of field names.

In the criteria range, 1-2-3 reads a group of criteria arranged in a single row as an And condition; to be selected, a record must match all of the criteria. Criteria in separate rows of the range are taken as an Or condition; to be selected, a record need match only one of the criteria.

The 1-2-3 database component recognizes a variety of criteria formats. You can enter simple labels or values in the criteria range to find records that contain matching entries. Or, you can use relational operators (<, >, <=, >=) with labels or values to find records that contain a range of field entries. To express more complex criteria, you can enter complete logical formulas into the criteria range.

A database in 1-2-3 consists of one or more database tables. The database component can perform special query operations on multiple tables in a database. In this sense, 1-2-3 is a relational database system. You'll learn more about this in Chapter 8.

8

Database Calculations and Operations

f a s t TRACK

To establish a connection to an external database,   437

> choose <u>T</u>ools ➤ Data<u>b</u>ase ➤ <u>C</u>onnect to External. In the Select a driver text box, type three items of information separated by spaces: the name of the DataLens driver, the name of the directory where the external database is stored, and the name of the database file. Press ↵. In response to the next prompt, <u>R</u>efer to as, enter a range name to represent the external table, or press ↵ to accept the default range name. Click OK to complete the connection.

To perform a New Query operation on an external database,   443

> choose <u>T</u>ools ➤ Data<u>b</u>ase ➤ <u>C</u>onnect to External to establish the connection and to define a range name for the database. Create an output range where 123 can copy records from the database. Choose <u>T</u>ools ➤ Data<u>b</u>ase ➤ <u>N</u>ew Query. In the Select <u>d</u>atabase table to query range box, enter the range name defined for the external database. Click the Set <u>C</u>riteria button and enter your criteria in the dialog box. Then set the Select location for new <u>q</u>uery table range, and click the OK button.

BESIDES the query operations you learned about in Chapter 7, Lotus 1-2-3 has several more important features to help you extract information from a database. Using a variety of tools, you can:

- Calculate statistical values and other numeric data from groups of records.

- Join data from two database tables.

- Perform queries on an *external database*. An external database is a file created in a database-management program, such as dBASE IV, dBASE III Plus, and Paradox.

These operations make use of the same three kinds of database ranges you've prepared for other queries: the input range, which contains the database itself; the criteria range, which expresses conditions for selecting records; and the output range, which displays the information that 1-2-3 copies from the database.

To explore these operations in this chapter, you'll continue working with the instructor database you developed for Computing Conferences, Inc.

1. Open the INSTRUCT.WK4 file from disk and briefly review what is inside it.

Worksheets A and B contain the office and instructor database tables, respectively. Worksheets C and D contain the current criteria and output ranges. You have defined several range names for query operations already:

- OFFICEDB is the name of the office database table
- INSTRUCTDB is the instructor database table

- OUTPUT1 is the output range

In upcoming exercises, you'll reuse these same ranges, and you'll also add new worksheets to the file for additional criteria and output ranges.

Performing Calculations on Database Records

You perform a variety of numeric and statistical calculations on a database table with one or more numeric fields. Suppose you were trying to find answers to questions like these about one of the four regions in the instructor database:

- What is the average number of hours an instructor has worked in this region?

- How much has each instructor in the region earned from working at conferences?

- What is the average hourly rate for instructors in the region? What are the highest and lowest rates?

You can take two different approaches to answering questions like these. Lotus 1-2-3 has a useful group of statistical functions that operate on database records. You could use these tools along with selected criteria and formulas to perform statistical calculations on selected groups of records. Or you could perform calculations as part of a Database ➤ New Query. You'll study these tools and techniques in the upcoming sections of this chapter.

Calculating Statistical Values with the Database Functions

Lotus 1-2-3 supplies the following *database functions* for calculating statistical values with records in a database:

@FUNCTION	USE
@DAVG	Computes the average of all values in a field.
@DCOUNT	Counts the entries in a field.
@DGET	Reads and returns individual field entries from a database. This function is useful when you need to build a worksheet that lists values from a single record.
@DMAX	Finds the largest value in a field.
@DMIN	Finds the smallest value in a field.
@DQUERY	Is for use only on external databases (you'll study external databases in the second half of this chapter).
@DSTD	Computes the standard deviation using the population method.
@DSUM	Totals the numeric entries in a field in a group of records you select.
@DVAR	Computes the variance using the population method.

NOTE

See Chapter 5 to review the difference between @DST and @DVAR.

Database functions, which begin with a *D*, perform the same statistical formulas as their worksheet equivalents, @SUM, @COUNT, @AVG, and so on. But the difference is that database functions perform calculations on a *selection* of records. To define this selection, you write specific criteria in a criteria range associated with the database.

Database Function Arguments

In their simplest form, each statistical database function takes three arguments:

- *The input range.* The first argument is the input range—that is, the range of the database itself.

- *The target field.* The second argument identifies which field is the target of the calculation. This argument can be either a field name enclosed in quotation marks or an offset number. Offset numbers range from 0 to $n-1$, where n is the number of fields in the database.

- *The criteria range.* The third argument is the criteria range from which the records in the database are selected.

For example, consider the following @DSUM function:

    @DSUM(INSTRUCTDB,"Hrs",CRITERIA1)

This function selects all the records in the instructor database that match a criterion expressed in the CRITERIA1 range. Then, within this selection of records, the function finds the sum of all the entries in the Hrs field.

Figure 8.1 shows the result of this @DSUM function. Shown also are the results of five other database functions—@DCOUNT, @DAVG, @DMIN, @DMAX, and @DSTD. Worksheet E, at the top of the worksheet window, contains the function entries; the calculations focus on the work hours recorded for instructors in the Southern region. As you can see, this worksheet shows

- The number of instructors in the region (5)

- The average number of conference hours these instructors worked (46)

- The total hours they worked (230)

- The smallest number of hours worked by an individual instructor (17)

- The largest number of hours worked (75)

- The standard deviation calculated for this set of data (displayed as 21.98).

The six database functions that produce these calculations all use the CRITERIA1 range to select records. Notice that the CRITERIA1 range contains a single criterion, an *S* in the Region field.

Worksheet E

E	A	B	C	D	E	F	G	H
1	Conference Hours in Region:		S					
2								
3	Number of instructors		5		Lowest instructor hours		17	
4	Average instructor hours		46.00		Higest instructor hours		75	
5	Total instructor hours		230		Standard deviation		21.98	
6								

Worksheet C

C	A	B	C	D	E	F	G	H	I	J
1	Criteria Range									
2										
3	ID	Last	First	City	Region	Specialty	Rate	Hrs	Contract	Yrs
4					S					
5										
6										

Worksheet B

B	A	B	C	D	E	F	G	H	I	J	K
1					Instructor Database						
2											
3	ID	Last	First	City	Region	Specialty	Rate	Hrs	Contract	Yrs	Ok
4	S-125	Ashford	W.	Washington, D.C.	E	Spreadsheet	$150	145	10-May-87	4.7	A
5	W-145	Banks	S.	St. Louis	S	WP	$150	55	10-Jun-90	1.6	A
6	D-143	Cody	L.	Los Angeles	W	Database	$75	43	20-Jun-90	1.6	B
7	A-146	Daniels	A.	Atlanta	S	Accounting	$125	24	09-May-91	0.7	New

Creating a Sample Database

To create this example for yourself in the upcoming exercise, you'll begin by adding the E worksheet to the INSTRUCT.WK4 file. Then, to see worksheets B, C, and E together in perspective view, you'll hide worksheet D. Here are the steps for producing this worksheet:

1. Use the PerspectiveView icon, if necessary, to view worksheets B, C, and D in the worksheet window.

2. In worksheet C, the criteria range, delete any expressions currently displayed in rows 4 and 5. Enter the label **S** in cell C:E4 under the Region field.

3. Move to worksheet D and choose <u>E</u>dit ➤ <u>I</u>nsert ➤ <u>S</u>heet. Click OK or press ↵ to add the new worksheet to the file.

4. Move to worksheet D again and choose <u>S</u>tyle ➤ <u>H</u>ide ➤ <u>S</u>heet. Click OK or press ↵ to hide worksheet D. Now you can see worksheets B, C, and E in the worksheet window.

5. Enter the title **Conference Hours in Region:** in cell E:A1.

6. Enter the formula **+C:E4** in cell E:D1. This formula copies the label representing the selected region from the criteria range. Preselect range E:A1..E:D1 and click the Bold and Underline icons.

7. Enter the following three labels into range E:A3..E:A5:

CELL	ENTRY
E:A3	**Number of instructors**
E:A4	**Average instructor hours**
E:A5	**Total instructor hours**

8. Enter these three labels in range E:E3..E:E5:

CELL	ENTRY
E:E3	**Lowest instructor hours**
E:E4	**Highest instructor hours**
E:E5	**Standard deviation**

9. Enter these six functions into the worksheet:

CELL	ENTRY
E:C3	**@DCOUNT(INSTRUCTDB,"Hrs", CRITERIA1)**
E:C4	**@DAVG(INSTRUCTDB,"Hrs", CRITERIA1)**
E:C5	**@DSUM(INSTRUCTDB,"Hrs", CRITERIA1)**
E:G3	**@DMIN(INSTRUCTDB,"Hrs", CRITERIA1)**

| E:G4 | **@DMAX(INSTRUCTDB,"Hrs",** **CRITERIA1)** |
| E:G5 | **@DSTD(INSTRUCTDB,"Hrs",** **CRITERIA1)** |

10. With the cell pointer at E:G5, choose <u>S</u>tyle ➤ <u>N</u>umber Format and select the Fixed format. Keep the default value of 2 in the <u>D</u>ecimal places box. Click OK or press ↵. Apply the same format to cell E:C4.

11. Move to worksheet B and press the Home key. Click the SaveFile icon to save your work to disk.

Now your worksheet should look like Figure 8.1.

Database Functions Are Recalculated Automatically

In a sense, each database function performs a type of query. Database Functions use the criteria range to select records from the database and read data from a specific field. But there are a couple of important differences between a database function and a query. First, you don't have to choose Database ➤ New Query to make the function work. Second, 1-2-3 automatically recalculates the function when you make changes to the criteria range.

To see how this recalculation works:

- Enter the new label **E** in cell C:E4 and examine the result in worksheet E.

The worksheet now contains statistical data about the instructors in the Eastern region, as shown in Figure 8.2.

Try other selection criteria on this application if you wish.

1. Select records from the remaining two regions, Northern and Western.

2. Enter a second criterion, **Spreadsheet**, in cell C:F4.

Given the combined criteria of W in the Region field and Spreadsheet in the Specialty field, 1-2-3 selects only one record. Notice what happens

FIGURE 8.2

Applying the database functions to a different selection of records

	A	B	C	D	E	F	G	H
1	Conference Hours in Region:			E				
2								
3	Number of instructors		5		Lowest instructor hours		26	
4	Average instructor hours		101.40		Higest instructor hours		178	
5	Total instructor hours		507		Standard deviation		53.91	

	A	B	C	D	E	F	G	H	I	J
1	Criteria Range									
2										
3	ID	Last	First	City		Region	Specialty	Rate	Hrs	Contract	Yrs
4					E					

	A	B	C	D	E	F	G	H	I	J	K
1				Instructor Database							
2											
3	ID	Last	First	City	Region	Specialty	Rate	Hrs	Contract	Yrs	Ok
4	S-125	Ashford	W.	Washington, D.C.	E	Spreadsheet	$150	145	10-May-87	4.7	A
5	W-145	Banks	S.	St. Louis	S	WP	$150	55	10-Jun-90	1.6	A
6	D-143	Cody	L.	Los Angeles	W	Database	$75	43	20-Jun-90	1.6	B
7	A-146	Daniels	A.	Atlanta	S	Accounting	$125	24	09-May-91	0.7	New

to the results of the statistical functions in this case: the @DAVG, @DSUM, @DMIN, and @DMAX functions all produce the same value, and the @DSTD returns a value of 0.00.

The @DGET Function for Retrieving Specific Labels and Values

The @DGET function takes the same three types of arguments as other database functions—an input range, a field name, and a criteria range. However, to use the @DGET function successfully, the expressions in the criteria range must select a single record from the database. @DGET returns a label or a value from a specific field in a record.

NOTE　If two or more records match the criteria, @DGET returns an ERR value.

Worksheet E

	A	B	C	D	E	F	G	H
6								
7			Name:	Cody				
8			City:	Los Angeles				
9			Specialty:	Database				
10			Rate:	$75				
11								

Worksheet C

	A	B	C	D	E	F	G	H	I	J
1	Criteria Range									
2										
3	ID	Last	First	City	Region	Specialty	Rate	Hrs	Contract	Yrs
4		Cody								
5										
6										

Worksheet B

	A	B	C	D	E	F	G	H	I	J	K
1					Instructor Database						
2											
3	ID	Last	First	City	Region	Specialty	Rate	Hrs	Contract	Yrs	Ok
4	S-125	Ashford	W.	Washington, D.C.	E	Spreadsheet	$150	145	10-May-87	4.7	A
5	W-145	Banks	S.	St. Louis	S	WP	$150	55	10-Jun-90	1.6	A
6	D-143	Cody	L.	Los Angeles	W	Database	$75	43	20-Jun-90	1.6	B
7	A-146	Daniels	A.	Atlanta	S	Accounting	$125	24	09-May-91	0.7	New

The worksheet window in Figure 8.3 shows a simple exercise with the @DGET function. The criteria range in worksheet C contains one criterion, a name in the Last field that selects one instructor's record from the database. The @DGET functions entered in worksheet E read labels and values from this one record.

Here are the steps for setting up this example on your own worksheet:

1. In worksheet C, delete criteria from row 4 of the criteria range.

2. Enter the name **Cody** in cell C:B4 under the Last field.

3. Move to worksheet E and scroll down the worksheet by several rows, so that row 6 is displayed at the top of the worksheet window.

4. Enter the following labels:

CELL	ENTRY
E:C7	**Name:**
E:C8	**City:**
E:C9	**Specialty:**
E:C10	**Rate:**

5. Preselect this range of cells and click the Bold icon.

6. Enter the formula **+C:B4** in cell E:D7. This formula copies the selected instructor's name from the criteria range.

7. Enter the following three @DGET functions:

CELL	ENTRY
E:D8	**@DGET(INSTRUCTDB,"City", CRITERIA1)**
E:D9	**@DGET(INSTRUCTDB,"Specialty", CRITERIA1)**
E:D10	**@DGET(INSTRUCTDB,"Rate", CRITERIA1)**

8. Choose <u>S</u>tyle ➤ <u>N</u>umber Format to apply the Currency format and set <u>D</u>ecimal places to zero for cell E:D10.

9. Click the SaveFile icon to save your work to disk.

When you complete these steps, your worksheet appears as shown back in Figure 8.3.

Now try changing the criterion in worksheet C to select a new record from the database.

- Enter the new name **Daniels** in cell C:B4.

As shown in Figure 8.4, 1-2-3 immediately recalculates the @DGET functions in worksheet E to display entries from the record for the instructor named Daniels.

Finally, try one more experiment with this worksheet:

- Enter the name **Porter** as the criterion in C:B4.

As you may recall, the database contains two instructors named Porter. Because this criterion selects more than one record, the three @DGET functions in worksheet E all return values of ERR, as you can see in Figure 8.5. Whenever you use the @DGET function you have to keep in mind this important fact: the function operates successfully only on a single selected record.

FIGURE 8.4

Selecting a new record for the @DGET function

	C	D
7	Name:	Daniels
8	City:	Atlanta
9	Specialty:	Accounting
10	Rate:	$125

Criteria Range

ID	Last	First	City	Region	Specialty	Rate	Hrs	Contract	Yrs
	Daniels								

Instructor Database

ID	Last	First	City	Region	Specialty	Rate	Hrs	Contract	Yrs	Ok
S-125	Ashford	W.	Washington, D.C.	E	Spreadsheet	$150	145	10-May-87	4.7	A
W-145	Banks	S.	St. Louis	S	WP	$150	55	10-Jun-90	1.6	A
D-143	Cody	L.	Los Angeles	W	Database	$75	43	20-Jun-90	1.6	B
A-146	Daniels	A.	Atlanta	S	Accounting	$125	24	09-May-91	0.7	New

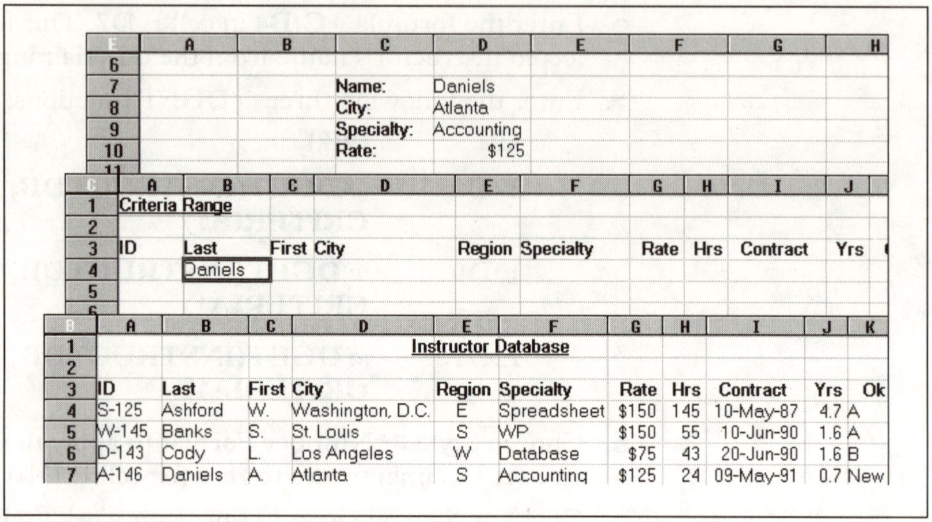

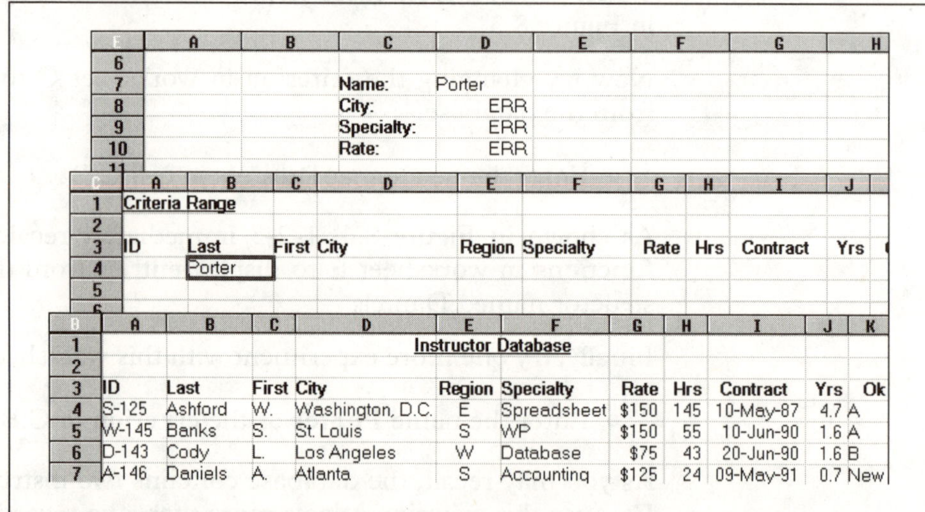

FIGURE 8.5

@DGET returns ERR when multiple records are selected.

	C	D
7	Name:	Porter
8	City:	ERR
9	Specialty:	ERR
10	Rate:	ERR

Criteria Range

ID	Last	First	City	Region	Specialty	Rate	Hrs	Contract	Yrs
	Porter								

Instructor Database

ID	Last	First	City	Region	Specialty	Rate	Hrs	Contract	Yrs	Ok
S-125	Ashford	W.	Washington, D.C.	E	Spreadsheet	$150	145	10-May-87	4.7	A
W-145	Banks	S.	St. Louis	S	WP	$150	55	10-Jun-90	1.6	A
D-143	Cody	L.	Los Angeles	W	Database	$75	43	20-Jun-90	1.6	B
A-146	Daniels	A.	Atlanta	S	Accounting	$125	24	09-May-91	0.7	New

WARNING

@DGET works only on one selected record.

The database functions are not the only tools for producing calculations on a database table. For some applications, you'll prefer to use the Data Query Extract command, which creates output tables that include calculations. In the following two sections, you'll learn about *output computed columns*.

Computing Columns in a Database

Worksheet D, currently hidden from view, contains the output range that you used for the query exercises in Chapter 7. To reexamine this output range now, bring the worksheet back into view:

1. Choose <u>S</u>tyle ➤ <u>H</u>ide ➤ <u>S</u>heet.

2. Enter **D:A1** in the <u>R</u>ange text box and click the Sho<u>w</u> button to confirm.

3. Move the cell pointer to worksheet D and press the Home key.

Row 3 in this worksheet lists the complete group of field names from the instructor database. As you know, this output range contains all the fields from each record selected in the database query operations we just completed. This is not the only way to design an output range, however. If you want to extract information from a smaller group of fields, you can enter the corresponding selection of field names in the Choose fields list box of the New Query dialog box. Lotus will copy a column of data for each field you include.

You can enter formulas by using the Formula button in the Select fields dialog box. A typical formula includes one or more references to fields in the database. As the response of such a formula, 1-2-3 creates a computed column in the output range. The computed column appears under a new field name that you create. In the following exercise, you'll create a new output range, OUTPUT2, and a computed column labeled Total Paid. The new column will show the total amount each instructor earned from conference jobs.

1. Move the cell pointer to worksheet E.

2. Choose <u>E</u>dit ➤ <u>I</u>nsert ➤ <u>S</u>heet. Click OK or press ↵. A new work-sheet named F appears in the worksheet window.

3. Move to worksheet F. Then select F:A2..F:F2 and click the Bold icon. Adjust the widths of columns C through F to the following settings: C, 11; D, 6; E, 5; F, 11.

4. Select range F:F3..F:F6. This is the column in which 1-2-3 will enter computed values corresponding to the formula you will construct. Choose Style ➤ Number Format to apply the Currency format, with no decimal places, to the range.

5. Select F:A2..F:F2. Choose Range ➤ Name and enter OUTPUT2 in the Name text box as the new name for this range. Click OK or press ↵. Then press the Home key to move the cell pointer to F:A1.

6. Choose Tools ➤ Database ➤ New Query. The New Query dialog box appears, as in Figure 8.6.

7. Enter INSTRUCTDB in the Select database table to query range box. Click on the Set Criteria button and select Region, =, and W in the Field, Operator, and Value list boxes.

8. Click on the Choose Fields button. In the Choose Fields dialog box, select Clear all, then click on Add.

9. In the Add fields dialog box, hold down the Ctrl key and click on Last, Specialty, Rate, and Hrs. (ID was already selected.) Press ↵ or click Okay

10. Click on the Formula button. Type **+Rate*hrs** in the Enter Formula text box. Press Tab and type **Total Paid** in the Show field as text box. Click Insert or press ↵. Click on +Rate*hrs in the list of field names and click the ↓ beneath the list box to move the computed field to the end of the list. Press ↵ or click Okay.

11. Enter OUTPUT2 in the Select location for new query table range box. Your New Query dialog box should look like Figure 8.6.

FIGURE 8.6

A query using the new output range

You can also press F3 to select each range name in turn from the Range Names list.

When you complete these steps, your worksheet appears as shown in Figure 8.7. In worksheet F, 1-2-3 has copied records from the Western region, with an entry for each field in the output range. In addition, column F in this output range now displays the calculated total earnings of each instructor in the region.

FIGURE 8.7

A completed column in the output range

F	A	B	C	D	E	F	G	H
1						Total Paid		
2	ID	Last	Specialty	Rate	Hrs	+RATE*HRS		
3	D-143	Cody	Database	$75	43	$3,225		
4	W-119	Davis	WP	$150	149	$22,350		
5	S-127	Gill	Spreadsheet	$100	35	$3,500		
6	A-103	Perez	Accounting	$100	5	$500		

C	A	B	C	D	E	F	G	H	I	J
1	Criteria Range									
2										
3	ID	Last	First	City		Region	Specialty	Rate	Hrs	Contract	Yrs
4						W				
5										

B	A	B	C	D	E	F	G	H	I	J	K
1				Instructor Database							
2											
3	ID	Last	First	City	Region	Specialty	Rate	Hrs	Contract	Yrs	Ok
4	S-125	Ashford	W.	Washington, D.C.	E	Spreadsheet	$150	145	10-May-87	4.7	A
5	W-145	Banks	S.	St. Louis	S	WP	$150	55	10-Jun-90	1.6	A
6	D-143	Cody	L.	Los Angeles	W	Database	$75	43	20-Jun-90	1.6	B
7	A-146	Daniels	A.	Atlanta	S	Accounting	$125	24	09-May-91	0.7	New

You can now perform additional Query operations to view the same computed column for other selections of records. When you change the selection criterion in Set Criteria and select OK or press ↵, 1-2-3 copies new records to the output range and recalculates the formula in the computed column. For example, try entering N as the new criterion in the Set Criteria ▶ Value. Then press ↵ or click OK to repeat the Query operation. In response, 1-2-3 creates the output in Figure 8.8, showing the total earnings of the three instructors in the Northern region.

	A	B	C	D	E	F	G	H
1						Total Paid		
2	ID	Last	Specialty	Rate	Hrs	+RATE*HRS		
3	W-113	Porter	WP	$125	59	$7,375		
4	S-155	Roberts	Spreadsheet	$100	10	$1,000		
5	D-137	Sanchez	Database	$100	47	$4,700		

	A	B	C	D	E	F	G	H	I	J
1	Criteria Range									
2										
3	ID	Last	First City		Region	Specialty	Rate	Hrs	Contract	Yrs
4					√					
5										

	A	B	C	D	E	F	G	H	I	J	K
1				Instructor Database							
2											
3	ID	Last	First	City	Region	Specialty	Rate	Hrs	Contract	Yrs	Ok
4	S-125	Ashford	W.	Washington, D.C.	E	Spreadsheet	$150	145	10-May-87	4.7	A
5	W-145	Banks	S.	St. Louis	S	WP	$150	55	10-Jun-90	1.6	A
6	D-143	Cody	L.	Los Angeles	W	Database	$75	43	20-Jun-90	1.6	B
7	A-146	Daniels	A.	Atlanta	S	Accounting	$125	24	09-May-91	0.7	New

Working with External Databases

Finally, you can use the 1-2-3 database component to gain access to external databases created in programs like dBASE, Paradox, or SQL Server. To work with an external database, you begin by establishing a connection between the database on disk and the current worksheet. At the time that you create this connection, you also define the equivalent of a 1-2-3 range name for the external database. This range name represents the database as long as the connection is active. Using this range name, you can perform a variety of operations on the external database file, as though the database were stored in an open worksheet file. For example, you can use the 1-2-3 database functions to perform statistical calculations on selected records of the external database; and you can perform any variety of Database Query operations to copy records from the external database to an output range.

DataLens driver The software that makes this kind of connection possible is called a *DataLens driver*. Lotus 1-2-3 Release 4 for Windows comes with DataLens drivers for dBASE, Paradox, Informix, IBM Database

FIGURE 8.9

A dBASE database

ID	LAST	FIRST	CITY	REGION	SPECIALTY	RATE	HRS	CONTRACT
D-140	Abrams	P.	Atlanta	S	Database	125	29	10/20/90
W-154	Alexander	E.	Los Angeles	W	WP	150	10	06/14/91
S-125	Ashford	W.	Washington, D.C	E	Spreadsheet	150	145	05/10/87
S-126	Ballinger	I.	Boston	E	Spreadsheet	150	40	02/12/87
W-145	Banks	S.	St. Louis	S	WP	150	55	06/10/90
W-130	Burke	C.	Miami	S	WP	100	41	05/22/88
D-141	Cheung	F.	Las Vegas	W	Database	125	61	05/15/90
D-143	Cody	L.	Los Angeles	W	Database	75	43	06/20/90
A-146	Daniels	A.	Atlanta	S	Accounting	125	24	05/09/91
W-119	Davis	G.	San Francisco	W	WP	150	139	07/09/87
N-115	Dixon	G.	Las Vegas	W	Networks	150	59	05/09/86
S-120	Edmonds	R.	Indianapolis	N	Spreadsheet	75	35	09/27/87
T-128	Eng	R.	Albuquerque	S	Telecomm	75	75	10/11/87
D-105	Fitzpatrick	P.	New York	E	Database	125	164	11/07/86
S-131	Garcia	A.	Seattle	N	Spreadsheet	100	17	07/02/88
W-114	Garrison	V.	Boston	E	WP	125	207	05/06/86
S-127	Gill	P.	Los Angeles	W	Spreadsheet	100	25	06/22/87
S-156	Hale	S.	San Francisco	W	Spreadsheet	75	28	06/09/91
S-149	Harris	P.	Dallas	S	Spreadsheet	150	17	02/12/91
D-109	Hayes	S.	San Francisco	W	Database	75	95	02/07/86
T-138	Hermann	J.	Los Angeles	W	Telecomm	125	74	05/24/89
S-132	Jones	L.	Atlanta	S	Spreadsheet	125	5	02/10/88
W-116	Jordan	E.	Dallas	S	WP	100	17	10/06/86
W-117	Kim	E.	Washington, D.C	E	WP	100	137	10/11/86
N-144	King	T.	New York	E	Networks	75	13	01/06/90
D-136	Koenig	O.	Albuquerque	S	Database	125	20	06/02/89
S-111	Kwan	O.	New York	E	Spreadsheet	100	71	06/21/86
D-123	Lambert	S.	Dallas	S	Database	150	145	06/26/87
D-134	Lee	H.	Seattle	N	Database	150	21	12/17/88
W-150	Leung	M.	Chicago	N	WP	100	16	03/26/91
W-112	Manning	P.	Atlanta	S	WP	75	71	11/09/86
W-107	Martinez	G.	Las Vegas	W	WP	150	178	03/15/86
N-129	McKay	J.	Washington, D.C	E	Networks	150	35	05/09/87
W-124	Meyer	J.	New York	E	WP	150	85	05/05/87
A-135	Meyer	L.	New York	E	Accounting	100	57	08/17/88
T-148	Miranda	O.	Las Vegas	W	Telecomm	75	9	01/04/91
S-153	Nichols	B.	Albuquerque	S	Spreadsheet	150	19	02/28/91
N-118	O'Neil	P.	Atlanta	S	Networks	75	5	05/01/87
A-103	Perez	D.	Las Vegas	W	Accounting	100	5	07/11/86
W-113	Porter	D.	Seattle	N	WP	125	59	08/02/86
D-139	Porter	M.	Washington, D.C	E	Database	150	26	03/28/89
T-133	Ramirez	F.	Boston	E	Telecomm	150	73	02/08/88
S-155	Roberts	P.	Chicago	N	Spreadsheet	100	10	08/21/91
D-137	Sanchez	W.	Indianapolis	N	Database	100	47	04/16/89
N-101	Schwartz	B.	Boston	E	Networks	150	178	03/02/86
W-151	Schwartz	P.	Indianapolis	N	WP	150	23	05/10/91
D-104	Taylor	F.	Boston	E	Database	100	17	10/24/86
D-142	Thomas	T.	St. Louis	S	Database	150	35	12/23/90
S-108	Tong	C.	St. Louis	S	Spreadsheet	150	35	11/12/86
N-152	Tong	P.	San Francisco	W	Networks	150	23	05/13/91
N-110	Tong	W.	Los Angeles	W	Networks	150	83	05/09/86
S-122	Vasquez	T.	Las Vegas	W	Spreadsheet	75	5	04/27/87
T-102	Vaughn	A.	Washington, D.C	E	Telecomm	75	53	09/11/86
T-147	Webb	F.	New York	E	Telecomm	125	32	01/27/91
D-106	Weinberg	P.	Miami	S	Database	75	59	01/18/86
D-121	Williams	C.	Chicago	N	Database	150	30	10/02/87

- The 1-2-3 range name that you will use to represent the external database table.

As an illustration of Connect to External, the following steps show you how to establish a connection with a dBASE file named C:\DBASE\IN-STRUCT.DBF. Use these same steps on an external database file of your

Manager, and SQL Server. You can include one or more DataLens drivers in your system at the time you install 1-2-3. The appropriate driver must be available on your hard disk if you want to use 1-2-3 to access an external database. For complete information about the DataLens drivers, read the *DataLens Drivers for 1-2-3* in your 1-2-3 package.

W A R N I N G — SHARE must be loaded from DOS before you can access an external database with 1-2-3 Release 4 for Windows.

In the final sections of this chapter, you'll learn how to conduct an external database query. For these exercises, imagine that the original instructor database from Computing Conferences, Inc. is a dBASE III Plus database file stored on disk as INSTRUCT.DBF in a directory named C:\DBASE. Figure 8.9 shows the complete database listing, printed from the dBASE program. In upcoming sections, you'll learn how to connect a file like this one to a 1-2-3 worksheet, and how to perform a variety of queries on the database.

Making the Connection with the External Database

The starting point for working with an external database is the Connect to External command in the Database menu. When you choose this command, the Connect to External dialog box appears on-screen, as shown in Figure 8.10. This dialog box lists the DataLens drivers that you have installed in your system.

To establish a connection with an external database, you have to supply four items of information:

- The name of the appropriate DataLens driver.
- The directory location of the database file. In the context of the Data Connect to External command, this directory is known as the "database."
- The database file name. This file is known as the *external table*.

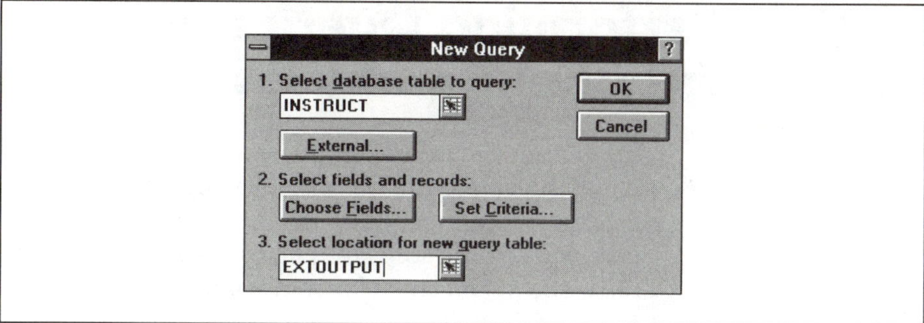

5. Click on the Set Criteria button and set a multiple criteria to match that shown in cells A3..C4. Click the OK button.

Lotus 1-2-3 finds the matching records in the external database and copies the appropriate fields to the output range, as shown in Figure 8.14.

You can repeat the previous query operation on an external database. For example, Figure 8.16 shows a revision in the criteria for the external database. Here, the selection is for *Northern* region word processing instructors who signed contracts before January 1, 1990. After you make a change like this one, press ↵ or click on OK to perform the extract operation again. Lotus will read matching records from the external database and display them in the output range. In this case, only one record matches the criteria, as you can see in Figure 8.16.

	A	B	C	D	
1	Connection to External Database:			INSTRUCT.DBF	
2				(dBASE III Plus)	
3	Region	Specialty	Contract		
4	N	WP	<1-Jan-90		
5					
6	ID	Last	City		
7	W-113	Porter	Seattle		
8					
9					
10					

Performing Queries on External Databases

To extract records from an external database, you use the Database ➤ New Query command. Once again, you begin the procedure by establishing the connection with the external database. Except for this initial task, the general steps for performing a query on an external database are the same as the steps for performing one on a 1-2-3 database:

1. Choose Tools ➤ Database ➤ Connect to External command. Establish the connection with the external database, and define a range name to represent the database.

2. Choose Tools ➤ Database ➤ New Query.

3. In the Select database table to query range box, enter the range name that represents the external database. Enter the criteria and set the output ranges.

4. Click the OK button to execute the query.

Figure 8.14 shows a worksheet in which an output range has been prepared for the external database INSTRUCT.DBF. The output range is defined by the three field names in row 6. The range A6..C6 is named EXTOUTPUT. In Figure 8.15, these range names—INSTRUCT and EXTOUTPUT—appear in the New Query dialog box.

	A	B	C	D	
1	Connection to External Database:			INSTRUCT.DBF	
2				(dBASE III Plus)	
3	Region	Specialty	Contract		
4	S	WP	<1-Jan-90		
5					
6	ID	Last	City		
7	W-130	Burke	Miami		
8	W-116	Jordan	Dallas		
9	W-112	Manning	Atlanta		
10					

Performing Other External Database Operations

Most of the database operations that you've learned to perform on 1-2-3 databases are also available for external databases. For example, you can use Database ➤ Send Command to send a command to remove matching records from an external database.

The Tools ➤ Database command offers more commands that apply to external databases. You'll find these commands at the bottom of the cascade menu. As shown in Figure 8.17, this section of the cascade menu offers four commands—Connect to External, Disconnect, Send Command, and Create Table.

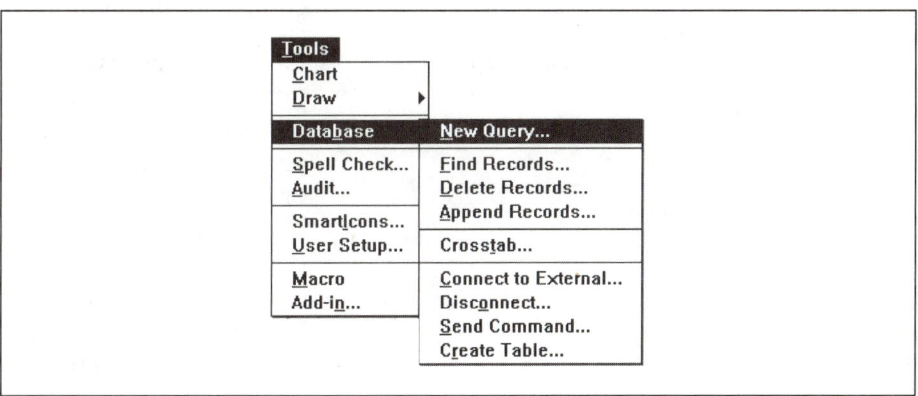

Here are brief summaries of the three commands we have not discussed yet:

COMMAND	USE
Disconnect	Closes the connection between 1-2-3 and an external database. When you select this command, the Disconnect dialog box appears with a list of all current database connections. To disconnect, select a name from this list.

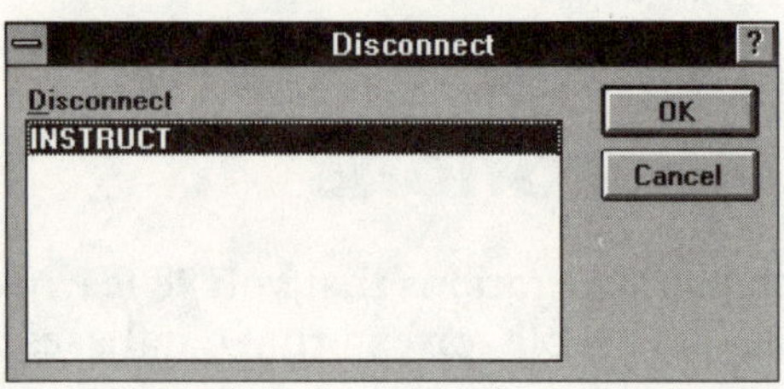

COMMAND	USE
Send Command	Lets you send program-specific commands to the external database. The commands available for this option depend upon the DataLens driver you are using. See the *DataLens Drivers for 1-2-3* documentation for complete information.
Create Table	Creates a new external database table in the file format used by a particular database management program, such as dBASE, Paradox, or SQL Server. You can use this command to create an external database from an existing 1-2-3 database table. After you choose this command, the Create Table dialog box appears. Use the Select a driver box to establish the connection with the database. In the Model Table range box, supply the range name of the 1-2-3 database you want to use as the "model" for the new external database.

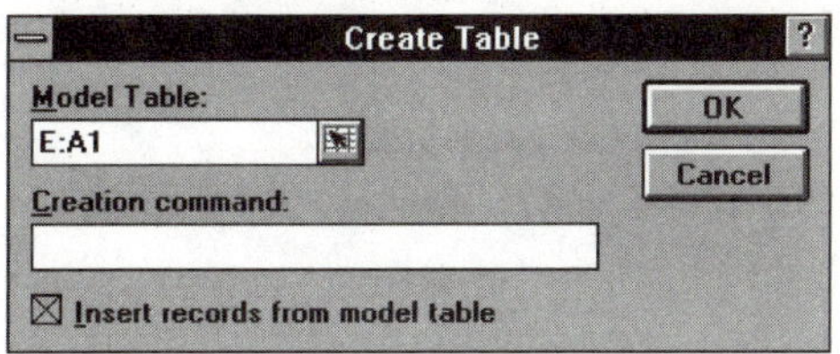

SQL Server DataLens Finally, with the SQL Server DataLens you can use the @DQUERY function to call functions available in SQL Server. @DQUERY takes a string argument representing the name of the external function, followed by any arguments required by the external function itself:

@DQUERY("*FunctionName*",*ArgumentList*)

Summary

To calculate statistics from a database, you can use database functions such as @DSUM, @DAVG, @DCOUNT, @DMIN, and @DMAX. These functions calculate totals, averages, or other statistical values from numeric field entries in selected database records. Each statistical database function takes three arguments: an input range, a field name or offset number, and a criteria range.

Another kind of database calculation, known as computed, results from the New Query operation. To produce a computed column, you enter a formula in the first row of the output range. The formula typically expresses an arithmetic operation on one or more fields in the database.

An external database is a file that originates from a database management program such as dBASE IV, dBASE III Plus, or Paradox. To establish a connection between an external database and a 1-2-3 worksheet, you use Tools ➤ Database ➤ Connect to External. As long as the connection is active, you can apply 1-2-3 database functions to the external database, and you can use Database ➤ New Query to read or modify the database.

An Introduction to Macros

fast **TRACK**

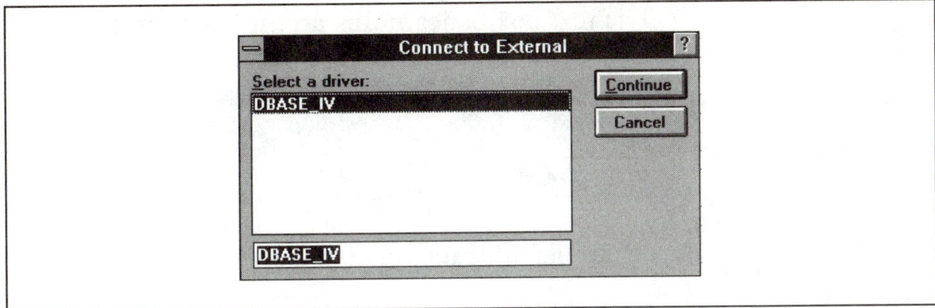

own or the EMPLOYEE.DBF sample database installed with 1-2-3 in
the SAMPLE\DBASE subdirectory. To do so, substitute the appropriate
driver, directory, file, and range name.

1. Open the 1-2-3 worksheet file to which you want to connect the
   database.

NOTE   Even if the worksheet file was formerly connected to
an external database, you must reestablish the
connection every time you reopen the file.

2. Choose Tools ➤ Database ➤ Connect to External.

3. Type the driver, directory, and file names into the Connect to
   driver text box, as follows:

   dBASE_IV C:\DBASE INSTRUCT

NOTE   The driver named dBASE_IV also handles database
files originating from dBASE III Plus.

4. Press ↵.

The dialog box next displays the prompt "Refer to as:."

The text box beneath this prompt lists the external file name INSTRUCT

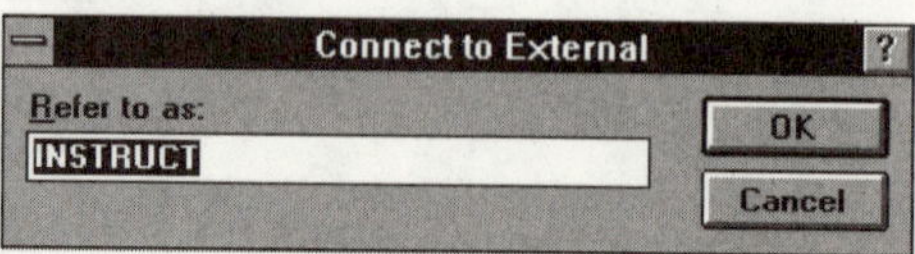

as the default range name.

5. Click OK to complete the connection.

After you complete these steps, the range name INSTRUCT represents the external dBASE file. Now, for example, this name can appear as the first argument in a database function, as you'll learn in the next section of this chapter.

Using Database Functions with External Databases

To use database functions on an external table, you begin by preparing a criteria range to select records from the connected database. In the first row of the criteria range, you enter one or more field names from the external database. For example, in Figure 8.11, you select the field and criteria needed in the Set Criteria dialog box (selected from the New Query dialog box) for selecting data from the INSTRUCT database.

Column C in the same worksheet contains a set of database functions that compute statistics from the external database. Figure 8.12 displays these functions in the text format. As you can see, each function uses the external database name INSTRUCT as the input range, the field name Hrs as the target field, and EXTCRIT1 as the criteria range. For example, the following function computes the total work hours recorded in the external database for the selected region:

@ DSUM(INSTRUCT,"Hrs",EXTCRIT1)

If you revise the criterion for selecting data, 1-2-3 reads a new selection of records from the external file, and recalculates the database functions accordingly. For example, in Figure 8.13 a new criterion, N, appears in

In this chapter, you'll create and run a dozen small macros. Along the way, you'll become familiar with many of 1-2-3's macro tools. You'll learn about macro key names and work with some of the macro commands.

NOTE To learn more about macros, see Chapter 12. It examines concepts and techniques of macro programming.

Creating Keystroke Macros

Macros are created and saved in 1-2-3 worksheet files. Conveniently, you can store a collection of your favorite macros in a worksheet and open it whenever you need access to a macro or to the entire macro collection.

A worksheet that stores a macro collection is sometimes called a *macro library*. In 1-2-3, many worksheet files can be open at once, which means you can keep your macro library worksheet open for when you need to run a macro. Most keystroke macros are designed to be run on an active worksheet.

Entering the Macro Instructions

To create a macro, you enter macro instructions into consecutive cells of a worksheet column. Two basic steps are necessary for creating a macro:

1. Entering macro instructions into a column of cells.
2. Assigning a range name to the first cell of the macro.

The range name is the key to running a macro. For convenience, macro range names consist of only two characters: a backslash (\) followed by a letter from A to Z. For example, \C, \N, and \H can all be macro names. Once you've assigned a backslash-letter range name, you can run the macro simply by pressing the Ctrl key and the letter key. For example, pressing Ctrl-C runs a macro that has been assigned the range name \C.

WARNING

Macro keystrokes supersede predefined keystroke shortcuts. For example, Ctrl-C is the shortcut key for selecting the Edit ➤ Copy command, but if you assign Ctrl-C to a macro and press Ctrl-C, Lotus will run your macro, not select the Edit ➤ Copy command.

In the following brief exercise, you'll create your first macro and assign it a name. This simple macro will enter a company name in a cell you select on a worksheet.

1. Select cell B2 on a new blank worksheet.

2. Enter the following label in the cell: **Computing Conferences, Inc.~**.

The tilde as Enter key The last character you typed is called a *tilde*. In a macro, a tilde represents ↵, the Enter key. Entering a tilde is the same as pressing ↵ to tell 1-2-3 to accept a cell entry.

3. With the cell pointer still at B2, choose <u>R</u>ange ➤ <u>N</u>ame.

4. Enter \C as the two-character range name. Click on OK to place the name in the <u>E</u>xisting named ranges list box and close the dialog box.

NOTE

When you enter a macro range name, enter a double quotation mark first. Otherwise, 1-2-3 reads the backslash character as a label prefix and enters repeating characters.

5. Choose <u>F</u>ile ➤ Save <u>A</u>s and save the worksheet file as COM-PANY.WK4.

6. Pull down the worksheet window's Control menu and choose Mi<u>n</u>imize or simply click the window's Minimize button to reduce the worksheet to an icon. (Macros in a minimized worksheet are still available for use.)

7. Choose <u>F</u>ile ➤ <u>N</u>ew to open a second new worksheet.

8. With the cell pointer positioned at cell A1, hold down the Ctrl key and type C. The macro you just created enters the company name as a label in the current cell.

9. Select cell D8 and press Ctrl-C again. As you can see in Figure 9.1, the macro again enters the company name as a label in the cell.

In this first exercise, you created a simple keystroke macro. Except for the final tilde character, the keystrokes you entered were the very same ones the macro ran when you pressed Ctrl-C. Used in a macro, the tilde character completes the entry and is the equivalent of pressing ↵ when you finish typing a label onto the edit line.

	A	B	C	D	E	
1	Computing Conferences, Inc.					
2						
3						
4						
5						
6						
7						
8				Computing Conferences, Inc.		
9						

Using Macro Key Names in Macros

Used in macros, some keys and commands are represented by names enclosed within curly braces ({ }). Recognizing and remembering the macro key names is usually easy because most are the same as the names that appear on your keyboard. For example, the following macro key names correspond to the keys located on the number pad at the side of your keyboard:

{Home}	{Up}	{PgUp}
{Left}		{Right}
{End}	{Down}	{PgDn}
{Ins}		{Del}

Other readily identifiable macro key names include {Backspace}, {Esc}, and {Tab}.

Some variations are allowed in the way you write the name of a macro key. For instance, you can enter macro key names in any combination of uppercase or lowercase letters: {Down}, {DOWN}, and {down} all represent the ↓ key. With some key names, you can use the full or the abbreviated name:

- {Ins} or {Insert}
- {Del} or {Delete}
- {BS} or {Backspace}
- {UP} or {U}
- {DOWN} or {D}
- {RIGHT} or {R}
- {LEFT} or {L}

Other macro key names also represent key combinations. For example, the Ctrl-→ and Ctrl-← combinations are represented by the names {BigRight} and {BigLeft}, respectively.

Function Keys in Macros

The first nine function keys, F1 to F10, have macro key names corresponding to the tasks they perform in 1-2-3. Macro key names of the F1 to F9 function keys are shown in Table 9.1.

TABLE 9.1: Macro Key Names of the Function Keys

FUNCTION KEY	MACRO KEY NAME	USE IN 1-2-3
F1	{Help}	Open the 123 Help system.
F2	{Edit}	Edit the contents of the current cell.
F3	{Name}	Request a list of range names, function names, graph names, and so on.
F4	{Anchor} or {Abs}	In Ready mode, {Anchor} represents what happens when you press F4 to preselect a range on the worksheet. In Edit, Point, and Value modes {Abs} represents what happens when you press F4 to create an absolute, relative, or mixed reference.
F5	{Goto}	Move the cell pointer to a selected location.
F6	{Window}	Move the cell pointer between panes and worksheets.
F7	{Query}	Repeat the previous Query command.
F8	{Table}	Repeat an operation from the Range ➤ Analyze ➤ Whatif Table command.
F9	{Calc}	Recalculate the worksheet.

With some of the key names, 1-2-3 allows you to include an integer to represent repetitions of the keystroke. For example, the instruction {Down 3} is equivalent to pressing {Down} {Down} {Down}. You'll see how to represent repetitions in a key name in an upcoming exercise.

Building a Macro Library Worksheet

In the next part of this chapter you will build a macro library worksheet. You will format the worksheet so you can access your macros easily and understand precisely what they do. When you are done studying macros in this chapter, you might consider adding your own macros to the macro library you will build here.

The Three-Column Format

Macros can become complex and difficult to read, so you should make room for brief comments and explanations on macro worksheets. A common way of organizing macros is to use the following three-column format:

- Enter each macro name in the first column (you'll enter the macro itself in the second column). As you'll see shortly, putting macro names in the first column lets you use Range ➤ Name to assign names to macros.

- In the second column, enter the macro instructions themselves. Each macro entry is a label and consists of keystrokes, macro key names, and macro commands. To run a macro, 1-2-3 reads down the column from one instruction to the next. When 1-2-3 comes to a blank cell or a cell with a numeric value rather than a label, it stops reading. Blank cells and numeric values are used to mark the end of a macro. For this reason, be careful not to include blank cells or cells with value entries inside a macro range.

WARNING　Do not include blank cells or cells with numeric values in a macro entry. They are used to mark the end of a macro.

- In the third column, enter brief comments that explain the lines and instructions in the macro. Lotus 1-2-3 does not read these comments. The third column is for your benefit or that of another person trying to understand what your macros do. To describe short macros, you can write a single comment, but to describe long and complex macros, write one comment for each row of instructions.

As shown in Figure 9.2, the macros you'll write in this chapter each begin with a *macro title* displayed in boldface. Titles appear above the first line of macro instructions. Each title is inside the macro column, but is not part of the macro.

Figure 9.2 shows the three-column macro format. The first macro, "Company Name," has the following new elements:

- A macro title in cell B1

- A range name in cell A2

- A brief explanation in cell C2

A second macro, titled "Address of Northern Office," is located one line beneath the first one. This second macro performs another simple data-entry task: it enters a two-line address in consecutive cells of a worksheet column.

FIGURE 9.2

Macros in the three-column format

A	A	B	C
1		Company Name	
2	\C	Computing Conferences, Inc.~	Enter the company name.
3			
4		**Address of Northern Office**	Enter the address
5	\N	Mills Tower, Suite 992{Down}	of the northern
6		Chicago, IL 60605~	regional office.
7			

Tips for Entering Macros on a Worksheet

Maximize your own copy of the COMPANY.WK4 worksheet now, so you can complete the first macro and enter the second one. Here are some tips to guide you as you enter macros in the worksheet:

- Begin by adjusting the widths of the three columns appropriately. For example, in Figure 9.2 the width settings are as follows: A, 3; B, 27; and C, 27.

- When you enter the macro range names in column A, begin each entry with a double quotation mark in order to right-justify the label. (Otherwise, 1-2-3 reads the backslash character as a label prefix and enters repeating characters.)

- Make sure you enter the names in their correct cells, just to the left of the first line of instructions in each macro. Do not put the names to the left of the boldfaced macro titles.

- Don't enter any extraneous spaces or other characters in the macro instructions. For example, notice that there is no space between the end of the address and the {Down} instruction in cell B5. When you run a macro, 1-2-3 assumes that every letter, character, and space is significant.

- In column C, initially enter the comment for each macro as a long label in a single cell. Then use Style ➤ Alignment and check the Wrap text check box to break the long label into lines that are easier to read. For example, type the entire comment for the second macro into cell C4 as follows:

Enter the address of the northern regional office.

Then, while C4 is still the current cell, choose Style ➤ Alignment ➤ Wrap text and click OK to close the dialog box. In response, 1-2-3 increases the height of the row and rearranges the descriptive text in cell C4, as shown in Figure 9.2.

Linking the Range Names to the Macros

When you finish entering the macros, your next task is to apply the range names in column A to the adjacent cells in column B. (Actually, you have already named the first macro, but for the purpose of the next exercise you'll proceed as though you hadn't done so yet.) Here are the steps:

1. Preselect range A2..A5.

2. Choose Range ➤ Name. The Range Name dialog box appears.

3. Notice that For cells is set to the right as the default. Click the Use labels button to accept this selection and click on OK to close the dialog box.

4. Click the SaveFile icon to update COMPANY.WK4 on disk.

As a result of the Range ➤ Name command, the name \C is assigned (or reassigned in this case) to the first cell of the Company Name macro, and \N is assigned to the first cell of the Address of Northern Office macro.

Running the Macros

Now you can try running the macros:

1. Activate the other open worksheet, the one on which you have already been experimenting with the first macro.

2. Select cell A3 and press Ctrl-C to make sure the first macro still works properly.

3. Select cell A4 and press Ctrl-N to run the second macro.

4. Press Home and examine the result, which is shown in Figure 9.3.

Notice that the second macro enters two labels into consecutive cells of the column. The {Down} instruction performs two tasks in the first line of this macro: it completes the entry of the street address and it moves the cell pointer down by one row for the city, state, and zip code entry. (You use the ↓ key for this same purpose when you are entering a sequence of data values into a column.)

	A	B	C	D	E	F
1	Computing Conferences, Inc.					
2						
3	Computing Conferences, Inc.					
4	Mills Tower, Suite 992					
5	Chicago, IL 60605					
6						
7						
8				Computing Conferences, Inc.		
9						
10						

Running Macros from the Main Menu

By selecting <u>T</u>ools ➤ <u>M</u>acro ➤ <u>R</u>un, you can view a list of all macros currently available in all open worksheets. You can also run a macro with this command. To run a macro that has a backslash-letter name, using <u>T</u>ools ➤ <u>M</u>acro ➤ <u>R</u>un is normally unnecessary. It's easier to simply press the Ctrl-letter keyboard sequence. But 1-2-3 also allows you to assign an ordinary range name to a macro. If the name is not a backslash with a letter, you must use <u>T</u>ools ➤ <u>M</u>acro ➤ <u>R</u>un to run the macro.

With the worksheet on which you have been testing the macros still current, try the following exercise with <u>T</u>ools ➤ <u>M</u>acro ➤ <u>R</u>un:

1. Choose <u>T</u>ools ➤ <u>M</u>acro ➤ <u>R</u>un. The Macro Run dialog box appears on the screen, as in Figure 9.4.

This dialog box displays the currently selected data range in the <u>M</u>acro name text box, a list of all defined macros in the <u>A</u>ll named ranges list box, and the name of the worksheet file that is currently serving as your macro library—COMPANY.WK4—in the In <u>f</u>ile text box.

2. Click the ↓ button on the right of the In <u>f</u>ile text box. Lotus displays a list of open files.

FIGURE 9.4

The Macro Run dialog box

3. Select a different file, and all the macros stored in that file are displayed in the <u>A</u>ll named ranges list box, as you can see in Figure 9.5.

You can now run any macro in the list by selecting the macro's name.

4. Select the \N macro and click OK. Back on the worksheet, the macro once again enters the two lines of the address.

5. After you have examined the results, close this worksheet without saving it; the macro library worksheet, COMPANY.WK4, remains open.

FIGURE 9.5

Now the Macro Run Dialog box displays the list of macros in the selected macro library.

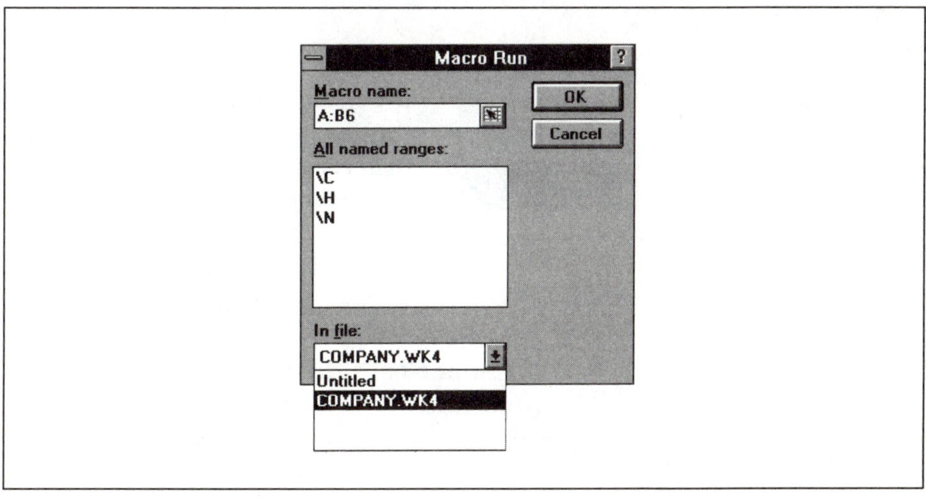

The two ways to run a macro You have seen two ways to run a macro. To run a macro that has a backslash-letter name, press Ctrl and the letter. To run any macro, regardless of its range name, choose Tools ➤ Macro ➤ Run. By the way, the keyboard shortcut for Tools ➤ Macro ➤ Run is Alt-F3.

Interestingly enough, you can also run one macro from within another macro. In programming terms, this is known as a *subroutine*. When one macro uses another to perform tasks, that macro is said to be *calling* the other one.

Subroutines: Using Macros within Macros

When one macro calls another, 1-2-3 performs all the instructions of the called macro and then returns control to the original macro. To write a call instruction, you simply enclose the range name of the macro in braces. For example, the instruction {\C} inside a macro calls the macro named \C.

A call instruction works successfully regardless of the format of the macro name, because alphabetic case is not significant in a call instruction. For instance, suppose you assign the range name SCHEDULE to a macro you have written; the instruction {Schedule} represents a call to this macro.

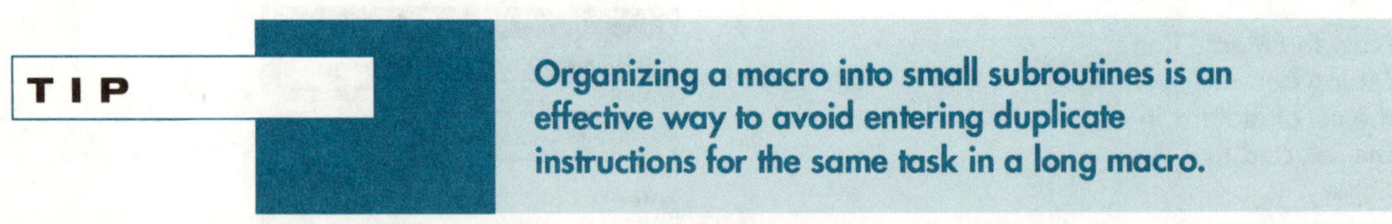

Figure 9.6 displays a third macro in the COMPANY.WK4 worksheet. This new macro contains three lines of instructions.

- The first line calls the macro named \C, and then moves the cell pointer down by one row:

{\C}{Down}

To create a keystroke macro from the steps of an activity you have just completed,   469

> choose Tools ➤ Macro ➤ Record, do a formatting operation using the Style menu, and choose Tools ➤ Macro ➤ Stop Recording. Then choose Tools ➤ Macro ➤ Show Transcript to view the Transcript window. Then perform a copy-and-paste operation to copy some or all of the window's contents to your macro library worksheet.

To attach a macro to a SmartIcon,   472

> start the Windows Paintbrush program and create your own icon; save the new icon file in the directory \1-2-3R4W\PROGRAMS\SHEETICO. Back in 1-2-3, select the worksheet range containing the macro you want to attach to the new icon, and then choose Tools ➤ SmartIcons ➤ Edit Icon. Select your new icon in the Edit Icons box, and click the Paste Macro button. The text of your preselected macro appears in the Macro box; click OK to assign the macro to the icon. Select the final position in the SmartIcons frame and click on OK.

To create an autoexecute macro,   483

> assign the macro the special name \0 (backslash, zero).

MACROS are tools for streamlining activities in 1-2-3 and for customizing the working environment. You can design macros to perform a variety of tasks, from simple keystroke repetitions to sophisticated programming procedures. How you use macros is a matter of individual choice and preference. Some users employ macros in all their daily operations, while others do all their work without macros. The best way to decide how to use macros in your work is to experiment with them and choose the macro techniques that seem useful to you.

At its simplest, a macro is a record of a sequence of commonly used keystrokes. When you *run* a macro, 1-2-3 repeats the keystrokes as though you were typing them from the keyboard. Besides common keystrokes, a macro can consist of data entries or instructions for choosing menu commands. For example, you could write one macro to enter your company's name and address in a worksheet column and another to choose formatting options from the Range or Style menus. Or, you could write a longer macro to do both in one step.

Macro key names To choose commands and perform worksheet operations in a macro, you use 1-2-3's special *macro key names*. In macros, macro key names such as {PgUp} and {PgDn} represent the keys and the key combinations that you press at the keyboard to carry out particular actions.

Macro commands You can also create macros that accomplish more complex jobs. Along with macro key names, 1-2-3 supplies a complete set of *macro commands* that represent specific programming tasks. For example, you can design macro programs that make decisions, perform repetitive actions, read or write worksheet data, and elicit data from the user at the keyboard. In effect, the macro commands provide a complete programming language that operates within the 1-2-3 environment.

FIGURE 8.11

Setting up a criteria for the external database

𝔸	A	B	C	D	E
1	Connection to External Database:			INSTRUCT.DBF	
2				(dBASE III Plus)	
3	Region				
4	S				
5					
6	*Statistical Database Functions:*				
7					
8	Number of instructors		16		
9	Average instructor hours		40.75		
10	Total instructor hours		652		
11	Lowest instructor hours		5		
12	Highest instructor hours		145		
13	Standard deviation		34.06		
14					
15					

FIGURE 8.12

Using database functions with the external database

𝔸	A	B	C	D	E	F
1	Connection to External Database:			INSTRUCT.DBF		
2				(dBASE III Plus)		
3	Region					
4	S					
5						
6	*Statistical Database Functions:*					
7						
8	Number of instructors		@DCOUNT(INSTRUCT,"Hrs",EXTCRIT1)			
9	Average instructor hours		@DAVG(INSTRUCT,"Hrs",EXTCRIT1)			
10	Total instructor hours		@DSUM(INSTRUCT,"Hrs",EXTCRIT1)			
11	Lowest instructor hours		@DMIN(INSTRUCT,"Hrs",EXTCRIT1)			
12	Highest instructor hours		@DMAX(INSTRUCT,"Hrs",EXTCRIT1)			
13	Standard deviation		@DSTD(INSTRUCT,"Hrs",EXTCRIT1)			
14						
15						

cell A4 of the criteria range. The new results in column C are the statistics for the Northern region. As you might expect, 1-2-3 takes a little more time to recalculate these functions for an external table than it would for a database in an open worksheet.

A	A	B	C	D	
1	Connection to External Database:			INSTRUCT.DBF	
2				(dBASE III Plus)	
3	Region				
4	N				
5					
6	*Statistical Database Functions:*				
7					
8	Number of instructors		9		
9	Average instructor hours		28.67		
10	Total instructor hours		258		
11	Lowest instructor hours		10		
12	Highest instructor hours		59		
13	Standard deviation		15.03		
14					
15					

Reestablishing a connection with a database If you close this worksheet, 1-2-3 will disconnect the external database. When you later reopen the worksheet, the database functions return values of ERR, because the range name INSTRUCT is no longer defined. To reestablish the connection with the external database, choose Database ➤ Connect to External again. When you complete the connection, 1-2-3 correctly recalculates the database functions.

A	B	C
1		Company Name	
2	\C	Computing Conferences, Inc.~	Enter the company name.
3			
4		**Address of Northern Office**	Enter the address
5	\N	Mills Tower, Suite 992{Down}	of the northern
6		Chicago, IL 60605~	regional office.
7			
8		**Heading for Northern Office**	Enter a complete
9	\H	{\C}{Down}	heading for the
10		Northern Region{Down}	northern region.
11		{\N}{Down 3}	
12			

- The second line enters a label into the current cell and then moves the cell pointer down again:

  Northern Region{Down}

- The third line calls the macro named \N and moves the cell pointer down by three rows:

  {\N}{Down 3}

Enter this macro into your own copy of the COMPANY.WK4 worksheet. Also enter the macro name, \H, in column A, and the comment in column C. Select cell A9, and choose <u>R</u>ange ➤ <u>N</u>ame ➤ <u>U</u>se Labels to designate \H as the name of the macro. Click the SaveFile icon to update COM-PANY.WK4 on disk. Then choose <u>F</u>ile ➤ <u>N</u>ew to open a new blank worksheet, and press Ctrl-H to run the new macro. Figure 9.7 shows the result, a four-line heading with the company name, the region name, and the regional office address. As you can see, the output from the \H macro includes labels produced by calls to the \C and \N macros.

Take a moment to reexamine this third macro before you move on. The instructions of the macro are divided into three parts, which you entered into three consecutive cells of column B. But this division is actually

	A	B	C
1	Computing Conferences, Inc.		
2	Northern Region		
3	Mills Tower, Suite 992		
4	Chicago, IL 60605		
5			
6			
7			
8			
9			

arbitrary. Lotus 1-2-3 would run the macro in exactly the same way if you divided its instructions into only two parts, like so:

```
{\C}{Down}Northern Region
{Down}{\N}{Down 3}
```

You could even enter the entire macro into a single cell:

```
{\C}{Down}Northern Region{Down}{\N}{Down 3}
```

The purpose of dividing the instructions into smaller sections is to make the macro easy for *people* to read. For 1-2-3, how macro instructions are divided is irrelevant, as long as you follow the few simple rules you have learned for entering a macro:

- Enclose macro key names in braces.

- Don't enter any extraneous spaces or characters in the macro instructions.

- Use a blank cell to mark the end of the macro.

In preparation for the next exercises, close both the COMPANY.WK4 file and the worksheet you have used to test the third macro. In the new Untitled worksheet, you'll develop a second library of macros.

Writing Macros as Menu Shortcuts

You can create a useful variety of menu-shortcut macros—that is, macros that choose commands from 1-2-3 menus. Like a SmartIcon, a menu-shortcut macro does in one step what pulling down a menu, choosing a command, and selecting options from a dialog box takes three or more steps to do. Instead of going through these steps, you can simply press the Ctrl-letter keyboard combination that runs your macro.

A macro that chooses a command from a pull-down menu consists of the following elements:

- A sequence of menu choices and one or more commands

- Dashes to separate each menu choice and/or command from the following one

For example, consider the following macro:

    {Range-Name-Label-Create "Right"}

The default selection in the Range ➤ Name ➤ For cells box command sequence is the To the right option. What this macro does, therefore, is to define a label in the current cell as a range name for the adjacent cell at the right. As you'll see shortly, this macro is an ideal tool to use while developing other macros in the three-column macro library format. To assign a name to a macro, all you have to do is move the cell pointer to the cell in the first column that contains the name, and run this macro.

Here is another example of a menu-shortcut macro, also useful in the development of other macros:

    {Style-Align-Horizontal Left;;;On}

This macro chooses Style ➤ Alignment, sets the horizontal alignment to Left, and checks the Wrap text box in the dialog box. You can use this command to rearrange a long label that you have entered as a comment in an adjacent cell at the right of a macro. Select the cell that contains the comment, and run this macro; in response, 1-2-3 increases the height of the row.

Figure 9.8 shows these two menu-shortcut macros in a worksheet. In the following exercise, you'll enter them into a worksheet of your own, as the first two tools of a new macro library that you'll save on disk as MACRO-LIB.WK4.

To start creating the new macro library:

1. Adjust the width of the first three columns of the Untitled worksheet as follows:

COLUMN	WIDTH
A	3
B	27
C	27

2. Enter the macro names \R and \J in cells A2 and A6, and click the Bold icon for each cell. Then enter the titles and the macro instructions themselves in column B, exactly as you see them in Figure 9.8.

3. Select cell A2 and choose <u>R</u>ange ➤ <u>N</u>ame ➤ <u>U</u>se labels. Click OK to assign the name \R to the macro. The Right Label macro is now ready to use.

4. Select cell A6, and press Ctrl-R to run the Right Label macro. As a result, 1-2-3 assigns the name \J to the Justify in Column macro. To confirm that this has actually happened, press Alt-F3 to choose <u>T</u>ools ➤ <u>M</u>acro ➤ <u>R</u>un and examine the list of defined macro names in the current worksheet. The two macro names have both been defined successfully.

	A	B	C
1		Right Label	
2	\R	{Range-Name-Create-Label "Right"}	
3			
4			
5		Justify in Column	
6	\J	{Style-Align-Horizontal Left;;;On}	
7			

5. Enter the following long label as a comment in cell C1: **Assign a label name to the cell on the right**. Initially, the label is displayed across the width of two columns, as shown in Figure 9.9.

6. With the cell pointer still positioned at C1, press Ctrl-J. The macro increases the height of row 1, as in Figure 9.10.

7. Enter the following long label into cell C5: **Justify a long label within the current column**. With the cell pointer at C5, press Ctrl-J again.

8. Choose File ➤ Save As and save this worksheet on disk as MACROLIB.WK4.

FIGURE 9.9

Entering a long label as a comment

	A	B	C
1		Right Label	Assign a label name to the cell on the right
2		\R{Range-Name-Label-Create "Right"}	
3			
4			
5		Justify in Column	
6		\J{Style-Align-Horizontal Left;;;On}	
7			
8			
9			

FIGURE 9.10

Using the Justify in Column macro to fix the long label

	A	B	C
1		Right Label	Assign a label name to the cell on the right
2		\R{Range-Name-Label-Create "Right"}	
3			
4			
5		Justify in Column	
6		\J{Style-Align-Horizontal Left;;;On}	
7			
8			
9			

Developing Macros with the Transcript Window

You have now created two macro libraries—COMPANY.WK4 and MACROLIB.WK4—by entering instructions directly from the keyboard.

After this much experience, you may be happy to learn that 1-2-3 offers a simpler method for planning and writing macros. The central tool in this method is called the Transcript window.

The Transcript window records the latest keystrokes you type as you record a macro. When you select Macro ➤ Record, the Transcript window begins recording keystrokes. When it reaches its maximum capacity, it releases the oldest characters it has recorded but continues recording new characters. All recordings are made as macro entries with the macro key names you've been working with in this chapter.

You can view the Transcript window at any time by choosing Tools ➤ Macro ➤ Show Transcript. When the Transcript window is active, the Transcript menu option appears on the main menu bar where the Range menu option used to be. Using Transcript commands, you can perform important operations. For example, you can rerun a selection of keystrokes from the current recording and examine the actions they represent.

A macro you create by copying a selection from the Transcript window may not always be identical to an equivalent macro that you write yourself. There are almost always several different ways to structure a macro for a particular task, and the Transcript window has its own way of recording events.

The following exercise serves as a brief introduction to the Transcript window. In the course of this exercise, you'll create an Insert Sheet macro:

1. Close both the MACROLIB.WK4 worksheet and the other worksheet on which you were testing the macros. 1-2-3 opens a new blank Untitled worksheet.

2. Choose Tools ➤ Macro ➤ Record and format a range of cells with any of the options from the Style menu.

3. Choose Tools ➤ Macro ➤ Stop Recording to stop recording to the Transcript window.

4. Choose Tools ➤ Macro ➤ Show Transcript.

The Transcript window appears as a small window located at the lower-left corner of the screen. It contains the recording of your most recent activities. The Untitled worksheet is still the current window, and the spreadsheet menu bar is still displayed at the top of the 1-2-3 window.

5. Activate the Transcript window by pressing Ctrl-F6 or by clicking the window's title bar with the mouse.

Some interesting changes occur in the 1-2-3 window when you do this. The Transcript Menu bar appears, and only six pull-down menus—File, Edit, Tools, Transcript, Window, and Help—have active options. Moreover, a special set of SmartIcons appears in the window.

6. Choose Window ➤ Tile. The Transcript and Untitled windows are resized and take up equal halves of the worksheet area.

7. Choose Edit ➤ Clear All. The current contents of the Transcript window are deleted.

8. Activate the Untitled worksheet window by pressing Ctrl-F6 or by clicking the window's title bar with the mouse. The SmartIcons and the familiar main menu return to view.

9. Using the mouse or the keyboard, choose Edit ➤ Insert and select the Sheet option. Click OK or press ↵ to confirm. When you complete the operation, worksheet B is added to the Untitled window, and a sequence of macro instructions appears in the Transcript window.

10. Activate the Transcript window. Use the mouse or the keyboard to select the entire current recording in the window: drag the mouse pointer over the contents, from beginning to end. Next, choose Transcript ➤ Playback, as shown in Figure 9.11. The command reads the highlighted recording and runs the selection as a macro.

FIGURE 9.11

Running the recording as a macro

11. In response, 1-2-3 activates the Untitled worksheet window, and inserts worksheet C into the window. As this action demonstrates, you can use the menu's Transcript ➤ Playback command to test a selected portion of the current recording.

12. Now activate the Transcript window again; the recording is still highlighted. Choose Edit ➤ Copy, or press Ctrl-Insert from the keyboard. This copies the selected recording to the Clipboard. Notice that no changes take place in the contents of the Transcript window; 1-2-3 does not record your actions while the Transcript window itself is active.

13. Activate the Untitled window. The cell pointer is currently located at cell C:A1. Click the PasteFromClipboard icon; in response, 1-2-3 pastes the selected recording into column A as a macro. (However, 1-2-3 does not record any keystrokes for the paste operation; the Transcript window never records mouse clicks on SmartIcons.)

14. Choose Range ➤ Name and enter \W as the name for this new macro. Click OK or press ↵ to complete the operation. This action is duly recorded in the Transcript window.

15. Press Ctrl-W twice. Worksheets D and E are added to the Untitled window.

Continue experimenting with the Transcript window if you wish: perform other worksheet commands and note how 1-2-3 records them, or create additional macros from selected portions of the recording.

16. When you are finished experimenting, close the Transcript window by choosing Tools ➤ Macro ➤ Hide Transcript, pulling down its Control menu and choosing Close, or pressing Ctrl-F4. Also close the Untitled worksheet window without saving it.

Of course, you are free to edit and modify any recording that you paste from the Transcript window. You can also combine recorded passages from the window with macro instructions that you write yourself. This is a common way to build a large macro project.

Attaching a Macro to an Icon

Perhaps the ultimate step in customizing 1-2-3 is to create a new SmartIcon that represents a macro you've written yourself. Macros that you use often are good candidates for being assigned to SmartIcons, as are macros that are convenient to use or whose names are difficult to remember. In the upcoming exercise, you'll create a new icon to represent a Value Conversion macro. When you complete the exercise, the ValueConversion icon, the "V" icon shown below, will be the right-most SmartIcon in the set. You'll be able to click this new icon to convert formulas to their current calculated values.

Developing an icon for a macro is a detailed process and requires many steps, but is not really very difficult. You start out by temporarily leaving 1-2-3 and starting up the Windows Paintbrush program to create the icon itself, then you save this new icon as a .BMP file in a directory named \1-2-3R4W\PROGRAMS\SHEETICO. When you return to 1-2-3, you open your macro library and select the macro you want to assign to this new icon. Then you choose Tools ➤ SmartIcons and click the Edit Icon button; the icon you've created shows up in the dialog box. You select the icon and assign the macro.

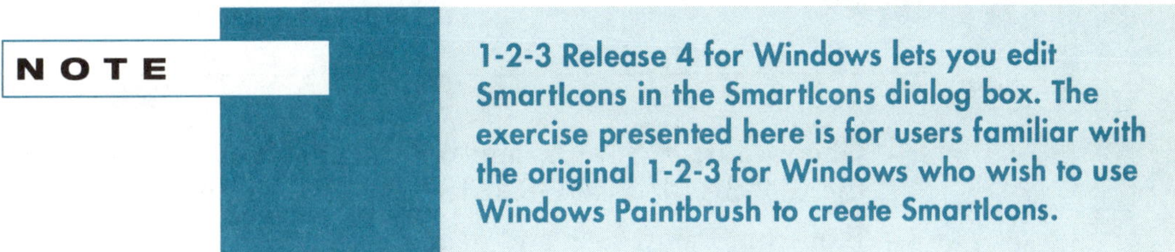

Here are the steps for creating the ValueConversion icon as a new SmartIcon:

1. Minimize the 1-2-3 window and start up the Paintbrush program from the Windows Program Manager. (Paintbrush is a Microsoft program that comes packaged with Windows 3.1. It is part of the Accessories program group by default.)

2. In Paintbrush, choose File ➤ New, and navigate to the \1-2-3R4W \PROGRAMS\SHEETICO directory. This is the directory from which 1-2-3 reads customizable icon files. Create a small blank

icon with a gray background in the upper-left corner of the Paint-brush work area.

3. As a simple way of developing a graphic to represent the Value Conversion macro, you can simply enter a large bold *V* inside the blank icon:

   a Click on the Paintbrush abc tool.

   b Select a suitable font from the Text ➤ Fonts menu.

   c Choose Bold from the Font Style list box.

   d Select a point size from the Size list.

   e Click inside the blank icon button and enter an uppercase V, as shown in Figure 9.12. (The font for the V in the figure is 26point Helvetica Bold.)

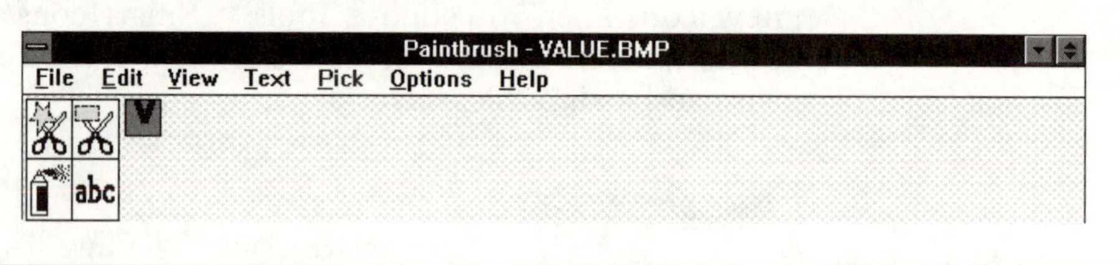

4. Choose File ➤ Save As and save the new icon as VALUE.BMP in the \1-2-3R4W\PROGRAMS\SHEETICO directory.

5. Exit from Paintbrush and maximize the 1-2-3 window to return to the spreadsheet program.

6. Open the MACROLIB.WK4 worksheet and preselect range B19..B20, which contains instructions for the Value Conversion macro.

7. Choose Tools ➤ SmartIcons.

Your new V icon appears in the SmartIcons dialog box, as shown in Figure 9.13.

The new ValueConversion icon appears in the SmartIcons dialog box

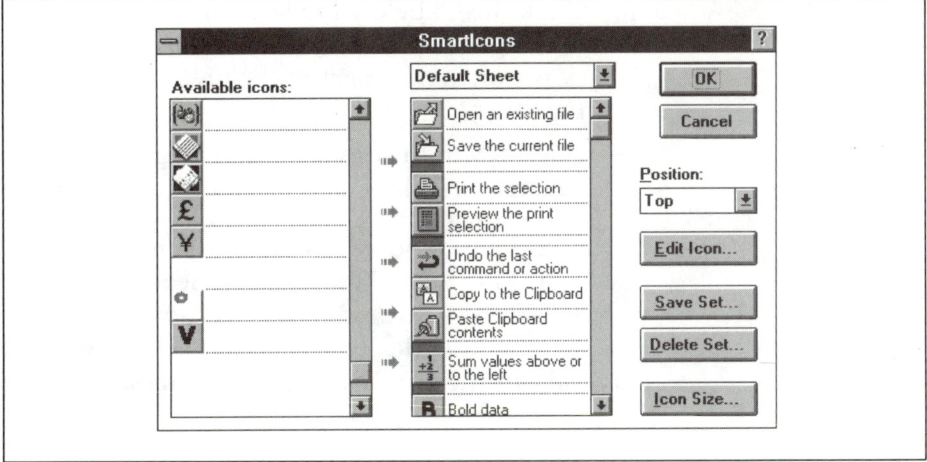

8. Click the Edit Icon command button.

9. Click on the Paste Macro button. 1-2-3 copies your preselected macro from the MACROLIB.WK4 file to the Edit macro here text box, as shown in Figure 9.14.

10. Click OK to assign this sequence of macro instructions to the icon. The SmartIcons dialog box becomes active again.

11. Scroll horizontally to the end of the SmartIcons frame and click the V icon again in the Available icons frame.

Assigning a macro to the new SmartIcon

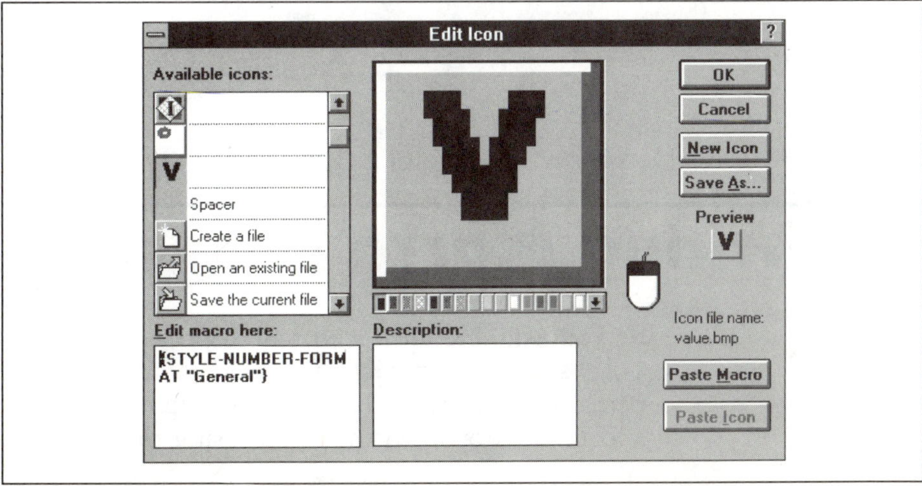

12. Click the → below the last icon in the SmartIcons frame, or drag to the position you want with the mouse. The new ValueConversion icon is now part of the palette collection, as you can see in Figure 9.15.

13. Click OK in the SmartIcons dialog box. When you complete this procedure, the ValueConversion icon appears with the other SmartIcons.

In this exercise, you've assigned a simple menu-shortcut macro to the new icon. This SmartIcon will reappear each time you start a new session with 1-2-3. To restore the original SmartIcon set, return to the SmartIcons dialog box, delete the V icon by dragging it out of the SmartIcon bar, and put the CutToClipboard icon back in the SmartIcon bar.

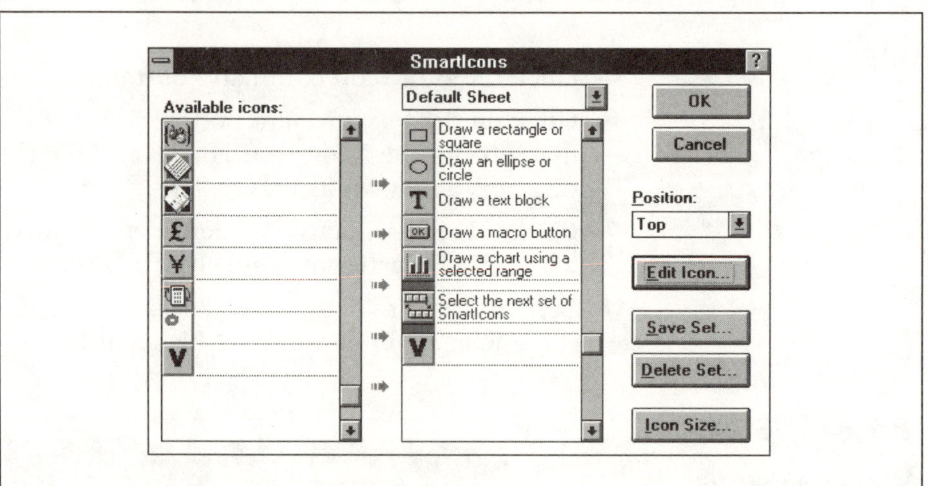

Writing Macro Programs

As you examine advanced macro programs, you'll begin learning about 1-2-3's significant vocabulary of macro commands. Macro commands perform programmed operations, such as decision making, repetition, and interaction with the user during the program run. Like macro key names, macro commands are enclosed in curly braces ({}). But a macro command represents a predefined action rather than a simple keystroke. Most macro commands require arguments, which you supply inside the braces after the command itself. Depending on the requirement of the macro command, arguments can be any of the following:

- values or labels

- arithmetic, string, or logical expressions

- functions

- cell or range references

- range names

Getting User Input with Interactive Macros

One interesting example of a macro command is {Get-Label}. This macro command is a central element in *interactive* macros, which are programs that pause one or more times during the run to get keyboard input from the user. The {Get-Label} macro command displays a custom text-input dialog box in the center of the screen. Instead of offering menu commands, the input dialog box presents a *prompt* asking the user for a particular item of information. After the user types the information and presses ↵, {Get-Label} copies the input as a label to a pre-specified worksheet cell.

As you might expect, {Get-Label} takes four arguments:

{Get-Label [*string*];*reference*;[*default*];[*title*]}

- *string* is the prompt that {Get-Label} displays in the dialog box.

- *reference* is the cell location to which {Get-Label} copies the input.

- *default* (an optional argument) is the text displayed by default.

- *title* (also optional) is the text displayed in the title bar of the dialog box.

The entire command, with its arguments and braces, must appear in a single cell of the macro column. You cannot spread a marco command across multiple cells.

You'll see examples of {Get-Label} in the sample macro presented in the next section of this chapter.

Constructing Interactive Macros

The Memo macro, shown in Figure 9.16, is a useful office tool for writing quick memos to business associates and co-workers. The program asks you to enter three strings of information from the keyboard, one at a time:

- The name of the person who is to receive the memo
- The name of the sender
- The text of the message itself

FIGURE 9.16

The Memo macro. This is an example of an interactive macro.

	A	B	C
1		Memo Maker	
2	\M	{Select A:A1..A:C9;A:A1}	Select the text range on sheet A.
3		{Edit-Clear ;"Contents"}	Delete the previous text on sheet A.
4		{Home}Memorandum~{Down 2}To:~{Right}	Enter the title and "To:" labels.
5		{Get-Label "To:",@CELLPOINTER("address")}	Get the recipient's name.
6		{Left}{Down}From:~{Right}	Enter the "From" label.
7		{Get-Label "From:",@CELLPOINTER("address")}	Get the sender's name.
8		{Left}{Down 2}Date:~	Enter the "Date" label.
9		{Home}{Anchor}{Down 5}~{Style-Font-All "",,On}	Display the labels in boldface.
10		{Right}{Down 5}	Select a cell for the date.
11		{Cell-Enter "@TODAY"}	Enter the date.
12		{Style-Number-Format "DD-MMM-YY"}{Right}	Format the date.
13		{Cell-Enter "@NOW"}	Enter the time.
14		{Style-Number-Format "HH:MM AM/PM"}{Down 3}	Format the time.
15		{Get-Label "Message:",@CELLPOINTER("address")}	Get the text of the memo.
16		{Style-Align-Horizontal Left;;;On}	Justify the text over a range.
17			
18			
19			
20			
21			

Given this information, the macro organizes the memo neatly on a worksheet, along with entries for the current date and time. When the macro run is over, you can simply click the Print icon to print the memo.

The Memo macro is designed to be saved on disk as a self-contained program file. The file contains two worksheets: worksheet A is reserved for the text of the memo created during a program run, and worksheet B contains the Memo macro itself. The contents of worksheet A change each time you run the macro. Follow these steps to create your own copy of this macro:

1. On a blank worksheet, use Range ➤ Name to assign the range name MEMO to cell A:A1.

2. Choose Edit ➤ Insert ➤ Sheet and add worksheet B to the window. Carefully enter the three columns of the Memo macro into worksheet B. (Copy the macro text from Figure 9.16.)

N O T E

If you would like to read descriptions of the macro steps you're entering as you enter them, see later in this chapter under the heading "Step-by-Step Review of the Memo Macro" for a complete explanation.

3. Select cell B:A2, where the macro name \M is displayed. Choose Range ➤ Name and click OK to assign this name to B:B2, the first cell of the macro.

4. Select cell B:B2, and choose Range ➤ Name. Assign the second range name \0 (backslash, zero) to the cell. You'll learn the purpose of this second range name later in this chapter.

5. Save the file as MEMO.WK4.

Now you can try running the macro. Press Ctrl-M to start. The macro moves to worksheet A and displays a custom dialog box in the center of the screen. The window displays a one-word prompt, *To:*, along with the vertical bar cursor. At this point, you enter the name of the person to whom you are sending a memo:

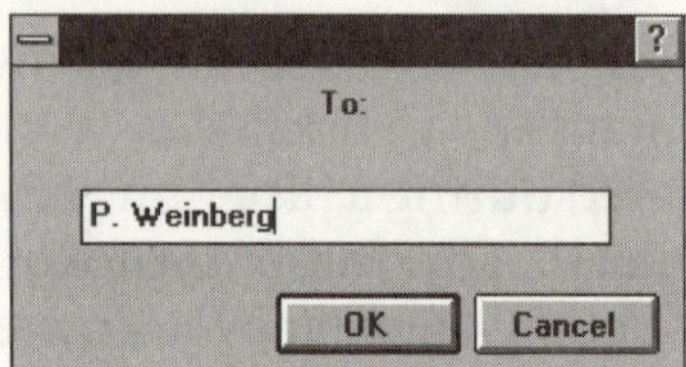

When you press ↵, the macro enters the name onto the memo worksheet. Then a new custom dialog box appears with a new prompt, *From:*. Here, you enter your own name. The macro does some more work on the memo worksheet, and then displays a third prompt in yet a third custom dialog box, *Message:*. To complete your memo, you enter the text of your message in the input window. The message can be as long as 511 characters.

When you press ↵ at the end of the message text, the Memo macro enters and formats the message text in cell C9 below the heading. This is the end of the macro run. Press the Esc key to return to the memo worksheet. Figure 9.17 shows an example of a memo worksheet that the macro creates. As you can see, the heading includes the names of the recipient and the sender, and the date and time when the memo was written. To print the memo, click the Print icon. When printed, it will look something like Figure 9.18.

Step-by-Step Review of the Memo Macro

The Memo macro is longer than the macros you created earlier in this chapter, but it is really not more complicated. Its major new element is the {Get-Label} command. Here is a brief line-by-line explanation of

FIGURE 9.17

A memo created by
the Memo macro

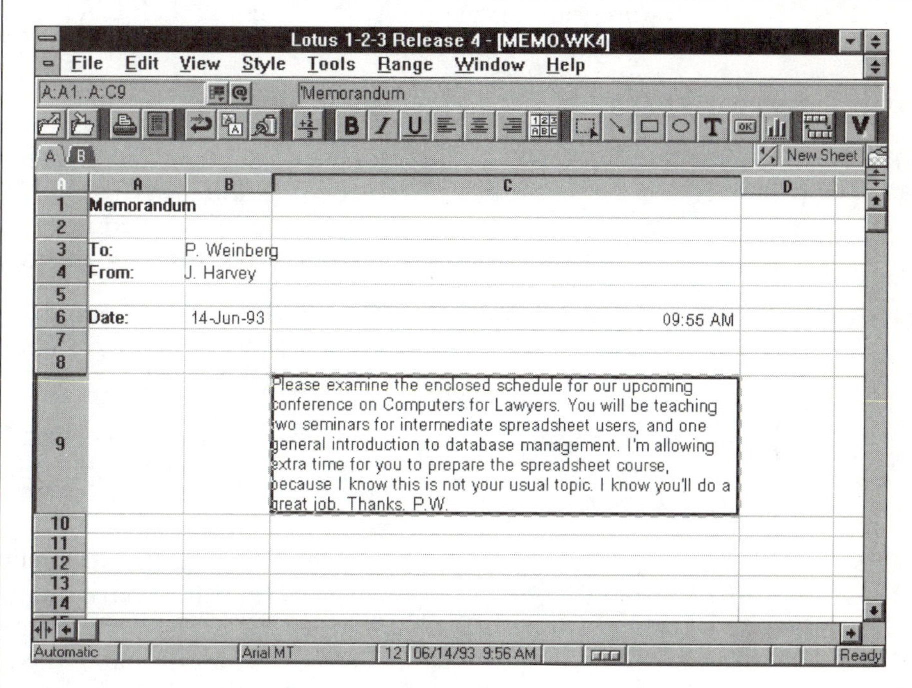

FIGURE 9.18

The printed memo

Memorandum

To: P. Weinberg
From: J. Harvey

Date: 17-Feb-92   04:36 PM

Please examine the enclosed schedule for our upcoming
conference on Computers for Lawyers. You will be teaching two
seminars for intermediate spreadsheet users, and one general
introduction to database management. I'm allowing extra time
for you to prepare the spreadsheet course, because I know this
is not your usual topic. I know you'll do a great job. Thanks.
P.W.

program instructions, identified by their cell locations in worksheet B, as shown in Figure 9.16:

CELL	MACRO COMMAND	STEP DESCRIPTION
B2:	{Select A:A1..C9;A:A1}	First a {Select} instruction moves the cell pointer to the beginning of the MEMO range. This instruction is included in case worksheet B is current at the time the macro run begins.
B3:	{Edit-Clear;"Contents"}	Then the macro command {Edit-Clear;"Contents"} erases the contents of the selected data range.
B4:	{Home}Memorandum~ {Down 2} To:~{Right}	The labels *Memorandum* and *To:* are entered into their respective cells in the memo worksheet.
B5:	{Get-Label "To:", @CELLPOINTER ("address")}	A {Get-Label} instruction elicits the name of the person who is to receive the memo. The first argument, "To: ", is the prompt displayed in a custom text input dialog box. The second argument is a call to the special function @CELLPOINTER. Given an argument of "address", this function supplies a reference to the address of the current cell. Once the input is complete, the {Get-Label} command copies the input to the current location of the cell pointer.
B6:	{Left} {Down}From:~ {Right}	The label *From:* is entered onto the worksheet macro.
B7:	{Get-Label "From:", @CELL-POINTER ("address")}	Another {Get-Label} command elicits the name of the person who is writing the memo.
B8:	{Left} {Down 2}Date:~	The label *Date:* is entered onto the memo worksheet.
B9:	{Home} {Anchor} {Down 5}~ {Style-Font-All "",,On}	The macro applies the boldface style to the range of labels in column A.

CELL	MACRO COMMAND	STEP DESCRIPTION
B10:	{Right} {Down 5}	The cell pointer is moved to the location for today's date.
B11:	{Cell-Enter "@TODAY"}	The value of the @TODAY function is entered into the current cell. This instruction is equivalent to pressing F9 while @TODAY is still displayed on the edit line.
B12:	{Style-Number-Format "DD-MMM-YY"} {Right}	The date is formatted with the {Style} macro and a {Right} instruction then moves the cell pointer one cell to the right, for the time entry.
B13:	{Cell-Enter "@NOW"}	The current value of the @NOW function is entered into the cell.
B14:	{Style-Number-Format "HH:MM AM/PM"} {Down 3}	Then the cell is formatted for time display. Then the cell pointer is repositioned for the message text.
B15:	{Get-Label "Message:", @CELLPOINTER ("address")}	Now, a {Get-Label} is used to open the custom text input dialog box for the memo message.
B16:	{Style-Align-Horizontal Left;;;On}	The Style ▶ Alignment ▶ Wrap text to command sequence is used to increase the height of the row that the message is in.

Autoexecute Macros

You'll recall that you assigned two different range names to the first cell in the Memo macro: \M and \0. You saw why you created the first of these names when you pressed Ctrl-M to run the macro for the first time.

The second name has a different purpose. Assigning \0 to a macro in a worksheet file creates an *autoexecute* macro. When you open a file from disk, 1-2-3 looks to see if the range name \0 exists anywhere in the worksheet. If it does, the macro with this name is automatically run as the first event on the newly opened worksheet.

You can see how this works with the MEMO.WK4 file:

1. Close the file now, without saving the current changes.
2. Choose <u>F</u>ile ➤ <u>O</u>pen and reopen the file. As soon as you do so, 1-2-3 runs the Memo macro.

As you've seen, the macro begins by clearing the previous memo from worksheet A. Then it displays the custom text-input dialog box in the center of the screen to elicit the first input label.

If you don't want to complete the macro run, you can stop it prematurely by pressing Ctrl-Break and clicking OK in the message box that appears.

Opening the file without running the macro   To open a file like MEMO.WK4 without performing the autoexecute macro that it contains:

- Choose <u>T</u>ools ➤ <u>U</u>ser Setup and remove the *X* from the Run autoexecute <u>m</u>acros option.

When you next open the file, the macro will not be performed automatically.

Opening a macro library automatically   Another way to automate macros is to create a library file named AUTO1-2-3.WK4 in the default directory. You'll recall that the default directory is defined in the Worksheet directory box of the User Setup dialog box. If a worksheet file named AUTO123.WK4 exists in this directory, 1-2-3 automatically opens the file at the beginning of each session. Furthermore, if the file contains an autoexecute macro named \0, the macro is run as the first action in the new session.

Summary

A macro is a program that records and performs a particular operation in the 1-2-3 environment. Macros can include literal keystrokes, specific menu commands, or detailed sequences of programmed activities. Lotus 1-2-3 has two categories of special reserved words that you can use in macros: macro key names and macro commands. Macro key names represent nonprinting keyboard operations, such as {Right}, {Alt}, {Home}, and {Select}. Macro commands perform specific programming activities. For example, {GetLabel} elicits input from the user during a macro performance.

You enter the instructions of a macro as labels in consecutive cells of a worksheet column. Assign a range name to the first cell of every macro and include a column of range names at the left side of the macro and a column of explanatory comments to the right. A worksheet that contains a collection of macros is sometimes known as a macro library. When you open such a worksheet, all the macros in the library are available for use.

There are two ways to run a macro, depending upon the macro's range name. For convenience, you can assign a special two-character range name consisting of the backslash character followed by a letter from A to Z; this name allows you to run the macro directly from the keyboard. For example, you press Ctrl-M to run a macro named \M. Alternatively, if a macro has an ordinary range name (not the backslash and a letter), you must use Tools ➤ Macro ➤ Run to run it.

Macros can be automated and integrated into the 1-2-3 environment. A macro with the name \0 (backslash, zero) is an autoexecute macro; 1-2-3 starts a run of this macro as soon as you open the worksheet that contains it. A macro library stored in the default 1-2-3 directory with the file name AUTO123.WK4 is automatically opened at the beginning of each session with 1-2-3.

The Transcript window can help you develop certain kinds of macros. This window displays your recorded activities during a given session with 1-2-3; the recordings appear in macro format.

PART
3
ADVANCED 1-2-3
FOR WINDOWS

Advanced 1-2-3 Worksheet Tools

To copy a range of data from a worksheet file on disk,   521

choose File ➤ Open. Specify the name of the file, and optionally, the source range within the file, and click on Combine. Then click on OK in the Combine 1-2-3 File dialog box.

To create a one-way what-if table,   522

enter a column of input values at the left side of the table range, and enter one or more formulas at the top of each column in the table range. Preselect the table range, and choose Range ➤ Analyze ➤ What-if Table. Enter 1 in the Number of variables box, specify the input cell, and click OK.

To recalculate a defined what-if table,   526

press the F8 function key.

To find the input value that yields a target result from a worksheet formula,   532

choose Range ➤ Analyze ➤ Backsolver. Specify the formula location, the target result and the adjustable cell, and click OK.

To analyze a complex data problem on a worksheet,   534

create a range of logical formulas to represent the constraints. Then choose Range ➤ Analyze ➤ Solver. Specify the adjustable cells, the constraint cells, and the optimum formula cell, and click OK.

N THE Range menu, 1-2-3 furnishes some exceptionally powerful commands to help you analyze values, variables, and calculations on a worksheet. This chapter starts with a discussion of the Range ➤ Analyze commands, but it looks at other advanced worksheet tools as well in the Range, Tools, and File menus. Choose Range ➤ Analyze to view the Analyze menu.

Analyze	What-if Table...
	Solver...
	Backsolver...
	Distribution...
	Regression...
	Invert Matrix...
	Multiply Matrix...

It offers the following seven commands:

COMMAND	DESCRIPTION
What-if Table	Calculates worksheet formulas multiple times while varying the data in one, two, or three input cells.
Solver	Produces worksheet scenarios from a system of variables, formulas, and constraints that you specify. Solver is the most sophisticated of all the Analyze commands.
Backsolver	Finds the numeric input value that produces a desired result in a selected worksheet formula.

COMMAND	DESCRIPTION
Distribution	Counts the number of entries that belong to specific numeric categories.
Regression	Examines the correlations between sets of numeric data, in a series of calculations known as *regression analysis*.
Invert Matrix	Produces the *inverse* of a square matrix. Along with the Multiply Matrix command, this command lets you find solutions for *simultaneous equations*.
Multiply Matrix	Performs *matrix multiplication* between two matrices. You can use this command with Invert Matrix to solve simultaneous equations.

You'll explore these important features through the examples and exercises presented in this chapter. Along the way, you'll also learn about other commands in the Range, Tools, and File menus:

- Range ➤ Transpose changes the orientation of a table, exchanging rows for columns and columns for rows.

- Tools ➤ Draw is for inserting a graphic shape such as an arrow, a rectangle, or an oval into a worksheet range.

- Range ➤ Parse converts the lines of an imported text file into a table with values and label entries.

- File ➤ Open reads the rows of a text file and displays them as entries in a worksheet column.

- File ➤ Open ➤ Combine reads data from a worksheet file and incorporates it into the current worksheet window.

What the Analyze Commands Can Help You Accomplish

A group of numbers arranged in rows and columns is called a *matrix*. In mathematics books, a matrix is represented by a rectangular array of numbers enclosed by a large pair of parentheses. But in a 1-2-3 worksheet a matrix is an ordinary table of numbers to which you can successfully apply the Range ➤ Analyze commands.

Analyze commands let you solve simultaneous equations in business, financial, or technical applications. A set of simultaneous equations has a common group of unknown values called *variables*. In a typical set, each equation has the same number of variables, and the number of equations is equal to the number of variables. For instance, in a set of four simultaneous equations, each equation has the same four variables. To *solve* simultaneous equations, you must find a set of four numeric values that satisfy all four equations.

Consider the example in Figure 10.1. As the figure shows, the central office of Computing Conferences, Inc. has incurred expenses for curriculum development in four topic areas. Namely, it has had to pay for computer training courses for accountants, doctors, lawyers, and video store owners. Curriculum expenses will be shared among the company's four regions in proportion to each region's profits. The table of numbers in the range B5..E8 represents the profits earned from regional conferences in the four topic areas. Column F shows the expenses for curriculum development. The problem of this worksheet is to find the percentage of each region's profits to charge for curriculum costs.

The curriculum expense problem can be expressed as a group of four simultaneous equations with four unknowns. In this case, the unknowns are the percentages to charge the four regions—that is, the amount by which each profit figure in B5..E8 should be multiplied to find the correct

FIGURE 10.1

Setting up the curriculum expense worksheet

	A	B	C	D	E	F	G
1	Distributing the Cost of Curriculum Development						
2						Cost of	
3		Profits by Region				Curriculum	
4	Topic	Eastern	Western	Northern	Southern	Development	
5	Accountants	$111,200	$79,300	$59,500	$64,200	$8,058.76	
6	Doctors	$131,900	$116,900	$77,500	$96,700	$10,852.33	
7	Lawyers	$63,500	$81,500	$54,000	$88,400	$7,376.34	
8	Video Stores	$88,300	$63,200	$41,900	$161,900	$9,619.99	
9							
10							
11							
12							
13							
14							
15							
16	Region	% of Profit					
17	Eastern						
18	Western						
19	Northern						
20	Southern						

share of the curriculum expense. In the following equations, these unknowns are represented as E, W, N, and S:

$$111200*E + 79300*W + 59500*N + 64200*S = 8058.76$$

$$131900*E + 116900*W + 77500*N + 96700*S = 10852.33$$

$$63500*E + 81500*W + 54000*N + 88400*S = 7376.34$$

$$88300*E + 63200*W + 41900*N + 161900*S = 9619.99$$

Accordingly, the goal of the worksheet in Figure 10.1 is to find values for E, W, N, and S that satisfy all four equations.

To prepare for the upcoming exercise, enter the values and labels in the Figure 10.1 worksheet in a new blank worksheet of your own, and format the data as shown in Figure 10.1. Save the worksheet under the name CURREXP.WK4.

Solving Problems with Matrix Arithmetic

Before you start using the Range ➤ Analyze commands, you may find it helpful to review the mathematics of matrices. The worksheet in Figure 10.2 shows a group of matrices generated from the curriculum expense problem. In range A2..D5 is the *coefficient matrix*, in this case the table of regional profits, whose number are multiplied by the four variables in the simultaneous equations. The constant matrix, shown in range F2..F5, is the column of values from the right side of each equation, the expense amounts for curriculum development.

Here is a summary of the two operations you can perform on matrices using the Range ➤ Analyze commands:

- The Range ➤ Analyze ➤ Invert Matrix operation can be performed only on a *square matrix*—that is, a matrix that contains an

FIGURE 10.2

Matrices and matrix arithmetic. Range A2..D5 is the coefficient matrix, and range F2..F5 is the constant matrix.

	A	B	C	D	E	F	
1	Coefficient Matrix					Constant Matrix	
2	111200	79300	59500	64200		8058.76	
3	131900	116900	77500	96700		10852.33	
4	63500	81500	54000	88400		7376.34	
5	88300	63200	41900	161900		9619.99	
6							
7	Inverse Matrix						
8	-1.4E-07	0.000019	-3.2E-05	6.1E-06			
9	-9.6E-05	0.000099	-3.5E-05	-2.1E-06			
10	0.000145	-0.00016	0.0001	-1.7E-05			
11	2.1E-08	-7.9E-06	4.9E-06	8.2E-06			
12							
13	Identity Matrix					Solution Matrix	
14	1	(0)	0	0		0.028618	
15	(0)	1	(0)	0		0.024705	
16	(0)	(0)	1	0		0.016878	
17	(0)	(0)	0	1		0.029799	
18							

equal number of rows and columns. The result of this operation is a second matrix that has the same dimensions as the first. For example, the inverse of the coefficient matrix appears in the range A8..D11.

- The Range ➤ Analyze ➤ Multiply Matrix operation is performed between two matrices and results in a third matrix. The number of columns in the first matrix must be the same as the number of rows in the second matrix. In this operation, 1-2-3 multiplies values in each row of the first matrix by the corresponding values in each column of the second matrix; the sums of these products become the elements of the third matrix. If the first matrix in the operation has $r1$ rows and $c1$ columns, and the second matrix has $r2$ rows and $c2$ columns, the resulting matrix will have $r1$ rows and $c2$ columns.

Identity Matrix By definition, the result of multiplying a matrix by its own inverse matrix is the *identity matrix*. As you can see in range A14..D17 of Figure 10.2, an identity matrix consists of values of 0 and 1, where the values of 1 are arranged in a diagonal from the upper-left to the lower-right corners of the matrix.

Due to the limits of precision in matrix operations, the values displayed as zero are actually very small positive or negative numbers. Notice that 1-2-3 encloses the small negative numbers in parentheses.

The identity matrix suggests an approach to solving the simultaneous equations. If the four equations can be rearranged so that one variable in each equation has a coefficient of 1 and the remaining variables have coefficients of 0, the resulting constants on the right sides of the equations are the solutions to the problem. Keep in mind that the identity matrix is the result of multiplying the coefficient matrix by its own inverse.

Solution matrix All this implies the basic rule that you use to solve simultaneous equations: the one-column *solution matrix* is found by multiplying the *inverse of the coefficient matrix* by the *constant matrix*, the column of values from the right sides of the original equations.

For example, consider the solution matrix displayed in range F14..F17 of Figure 10.2. This column of values is the result of using Range ➤ Analyze ➤ Multiply Matrix to multiply the inverse matrix in range A8..D11 by the constant matrix in F2..F5. Each element in the solution matrix is the value for one of the four *E*, *W*, *N*, or *S* variables.

Solving Simultaneous Equations

Returning now to the original curriculum expense worksheet, CURREXP.WK4 (see Figure 10.1), here are the steps for finding the correct percentage for each region:

1. Preselect the range of profit figures in B5..E8.

2. Choose Range ➤ Analyze ➤ Invert Matrix. In the resulting dialog box, the preselected range is displayed in the From text box.

3. In the To text box, enter a reference to cell A:B11. This is the upper-left corner of the range where 1-2-3 will generate the inverse matrix.

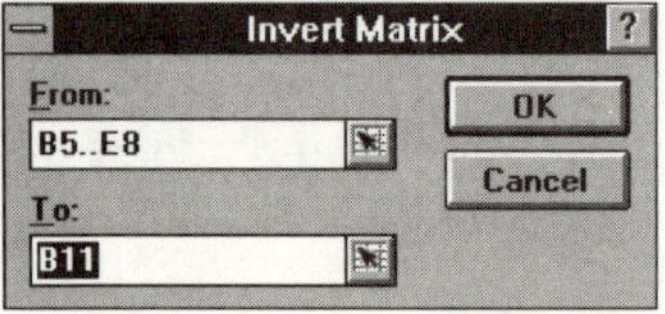

4. Click OK. The inverse matrix appears on the worksheet, as shown in Figure 10.3.

5. Preselect the inverse matrix, in range B11..E14.

6. Choose Range ➤ Analyze ➤ Multiply Matrix. In the resulting dialog box, the preselected range (of the inverse matrix) appears in

	A	B	C	D	E	F	G
1	Distributing the Cost of Curriculum Development						
2						Cost of	
3		Profits by Region				Curriculum	
4	Topic	Eastern	Western	Northern	Southern	Development	
5	Accountants	$111,200	$79,300	$59,500	$64,200	$8,058.76	
6	Doctors	$131,900	$116,900	$77,500	$96,700	$10,852.33	
7	Lawyers	$63,500	$81,500	$54,000	$88,400	$7,376.34	
8	Video Stores	$88,300	$63,200	$41,900	$161,900	$9,619.99	
9							
10							
11		-1.4E-07	0.000019	-3.2E-05	6.1E-06		
12		-9.6E-05	0.000099	-3.5E-05	-2.1E-06		
13		0.000145	-0.00016	0.0001	-1.7E-05		
14		2.1E-08	-7.9E-06	4.9E-06	8.2E-06		
15							
16	Region	% of Profit					
17	Eastern						
18	Western						
19	Northern						
20	Southern						

the First matrix text box. Enter the range of the constant matrix,
A:F5..A:F8, in the Second matrix text box. Then enter A:B17 in
the Output matrix text box. Click OK to complete the operation.

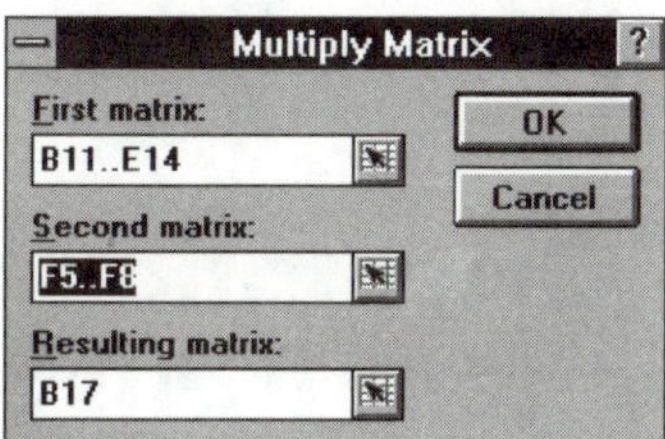

7. Preselect the range of the solution matrix, B17..B20, and click the
   Number Format SmartIcon on the Status bar. Select Percent
   from the list to format these figures as percentages. Your worksheet now appears as shown in Figure 10.4.

8. Click the SaveFile icon to save your work to disk.

In effect, you have now solved the four simultaneous equations. The values in range B17..B20 show the percentage to take from each region's
profits to cover the shared expense of curriculum development.

FIGURE 10.4

Producing the solution matrix

	A	B	C	D	E	F	G
1	Distributing the Cost of Curriculum Development						
2						Cost of	
3		Profits by Region				Curriculum	
4	Topic	Eastern	Western	Northern	Southern	Development	
5	Accountants	$111,200	$79,300	$59,500	$64,200	$8,058.76	
6	Doctors	$131,900	$116,900	$77,500	$96,700	$10,852.33	
7	Lawyers	$63,500	$81,500	$54,000	$88,400	$7,376.34	
8	Video Stores	$88,300	$63,200	$41,900	$161,900	$9,619.99	
9							
10							
11		-1.4E-07	0.000019	-3.2E-05	6.1E-06		
12		-9.6E-05	0.000099	-3.5E-05	-2.1E-06		
13		0.000145	-0.00016	0.0001	-1.7E-05		
14		2.1E-08	-7.9E-06	4.9E-06	8.2E-06		
15							
16	Region	% of Profit					
17	Eastern	2.86%					
18	Western	2.47%					
19	Northern	1.69%					
20	Southern	2.98%					

Now suppose that you would like to produce a table that shows the actual curriculum expense amount to be charged against the earnings for each conference topic in each region. For this table, you need to display the four percentages across a row, rather than down a column as they currently appear. Range ➤ Transpose is a convenient tool for accomplishing this task.

Changing the Orientation of a Table with Range ➤Transpose

Use Range ➤ Transpose to copy the row entries of a source range to the columns of a destination range, or, conversely, the column entries of a source to the rows of a destination. If the source range contains formulas, Transpose replaces those formulas with their current values in the destination range. (The original formulas in the source range are not affected.) The command also copies formats and display styles from the source to the destination range.

To produce the detailed table of curriculum expenses, you want to copy the percentages currently displayed in column range B17..B20 to row range B10..E10. (Note that these entries are simple values, not formulas.)

Because you have no further use for the inverse matrix in the curriculum expense worksheet, you'll begin this next exercise by deleting the matrix:

1. Preselect range B11..E14. Press the Del key on your keyboard to erase the entries in this entire range.

2. Preselect the range of labels in A5..A8 and click the CopyToClipboard icon. Then click cell A11 and click on the PasteFromClipboard icon to copy these labels to range A11..A14.

3. Preselect the range of percentages in B17..B20. Choose Range ➤ Transpose. The preselected range appears in the From text box. Enter A:B10 into the To text box and click OK to complete the operation.

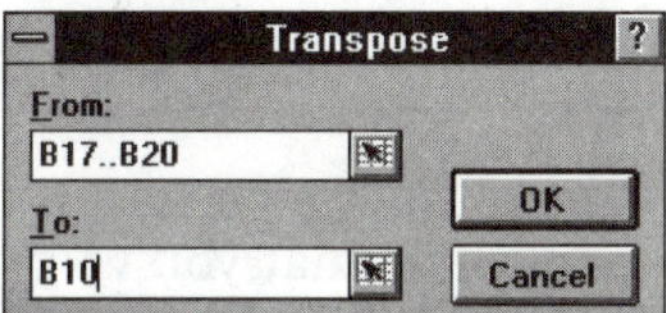

TIP   Another way to copy a range is to hold down the Ctrl key and drag it.

4. Enter the formula **+B5*B$10** into cell B11. Select B11..E14, first click the CopyDown icon, and then click on the CopyRight icon to copy the formula to the appropriate cells in columns B, C, D, and E.

5. Preselect range F11..B14. Click the Summation icon to enter @SUM formulas into column F; then click the Currency SmartIcon to apply this format to the entire range. Move the cell pointer to E1, out of the way of any data. Your worksheet now appears as shown in Figure 10.5.

6. Click the SaveFile icon to save your work to disk.

FIGURE 10.5

Producing the curriculum expense table

	A	B	C	D	E	F	G
1	Distributing the Cost of Curriculum Development						
2						Cost of	
3		Profits by Region				Curriculum	
4	Topic	Eastern	Western	Northern	Southern	Development	
5	Accountants	$111,200	$79,300	$59,500	$64,200	$8,058.76	
6	Doctors	$131,900	$116,900	$77,500	$96,700	$10,852.33	
7	Lawyers	$63,500	$81,500	$54,000	$88,400	$7,376.34	
8	Video Stores	$88,300	$63,200	$41,900	$161,900	$9,619.99	
9							
10		2.86%	2.47%	1.69%	2.98%		
11	Accountants	$3,182.33	$1,959.10	$1,004.22	$1,913.11	$8,058.76	
12	Doctors	$3,774.73	$2,888.00	$1,308.02	$2,881.58	$10,852.33	
13	Lawyers	$1,817.25	$2,013.45	$911.39	$2,634.25	$7,376.34	
14	Video Stores	$2,526.98	$1,561.35	$707.17	$4,824.49	$9,619.99	
15							
16	Region	% of Profit					
17	Eastern	2.86%					
18	Western	2.47%					
19	Northern	1.69%					
20	Southern	2.98%					

Notice that the expense totals that you've produced in range F11..F14 are the same as the original curriculum costs that you entered into F5..F8. These matching values confirm your solution for the simultaneous equations.

Now that you've created this worksheet, imagine that you want to send copies of it to each regional manager, highlighting the appropriate column of figures in each copy. One simple but effective way to draw attention to a particular range of data on a worksheet is to use Tools ➤ Draw.

Placing Graphic Shapes on a Worksheet

Use Tools ➤ Draw to insert a graph window in a worksheet file and draw an object or objects for subsequent display in a worksheet range. You can draw arrows, lines, circles, ellipses, polygons, squares, rectangles, text, and even freehand drawings.

In the following exercise you'll use Tools ➤ Draw to draw an ellipse around the curriculum expense figures for the Northern region:

1. Choose Tools ➤ Draw ➤ Ellipse.

2. Produce an approximation of the ellipse shown in Figure 10.6: move the mouse pointer to the upper-left corner of the middle column in the grid, and hold down the mouse button while you drag the mouse to the lower-left corner of the column. The ellipse appears as you draw it. Release the mouse button.

Drawing an ellipse around a range of worksheet cells. You can draw shapes on worksheets to call attention to figures.

	A	B	C	D	E	F	G	H
1	Distributing the Cost of Curriculum Development							
2						Cost of		
3		Profits by Region				Curriculum		
4	Topic	Eastern	Western	Northern	Southern	Development		
5	Accountants	$111,200	$79,300	$59,500	$64,200	$8,058.76		
6	Doctors	$131,900	$116,900	$77,500	$96,700	$10,852.33		
7	Lawyers	$63,500	$81,500	$54,000	$88,400	$7,376.34		
8	ideo Stores	$88,300	$63,200	$41,900	$161,900	$9,619.99		
9								
10		2.86%	2.47%	1.69%	2.98%			
11		$3,182.33	$1,959.10	$1,004.22	$1,913.11	$8,058.76		
12		$3,774.73	$2,888.00	$1,308.02	$2,881.58	$10,852.33		
13		$1,817.25	$2,013.45	$911.39	$2,634.25	$7,376.34		
14		$2,526.98	$1,561.35	$707.17	$4,824.49	$9,619.99		
15								
16	Region	% of Profits						
17	Eastern	2.86%						
18	Western	2.47%						
19	Northern	1.69%						
20	Southern	2.98%						
21								

3. Choose Style ➤ Lines and Color. Click the ↓ button to the right of Pattern and select the T pattern (in the upper-right corner), as shown in Figure 10.7. This assigns a Transparent background to the ellipse. Without it, the White background will cover up the figures on the worksheet.

4. Click the SaveFile icon to save your work to disk.

The worksheet now appears as shown in Figure 10.6. The ellipse circles the expense column for the Northern region. As you can see, this ellipse successfully highlights the target range of figures on your worksheet. If you want to include more objects, you can draw an arrow pointing to the column, and then add a unit of text to the worksheet.

Revising and deleting graphics To revise a graphic object produced by Tools ➤ Draw, simply click on any edge of the figure. In response, 1-2-3 redisplays the handles on the figure. To delete a graphic object from the worksheet, choose the figure and press the Del key.

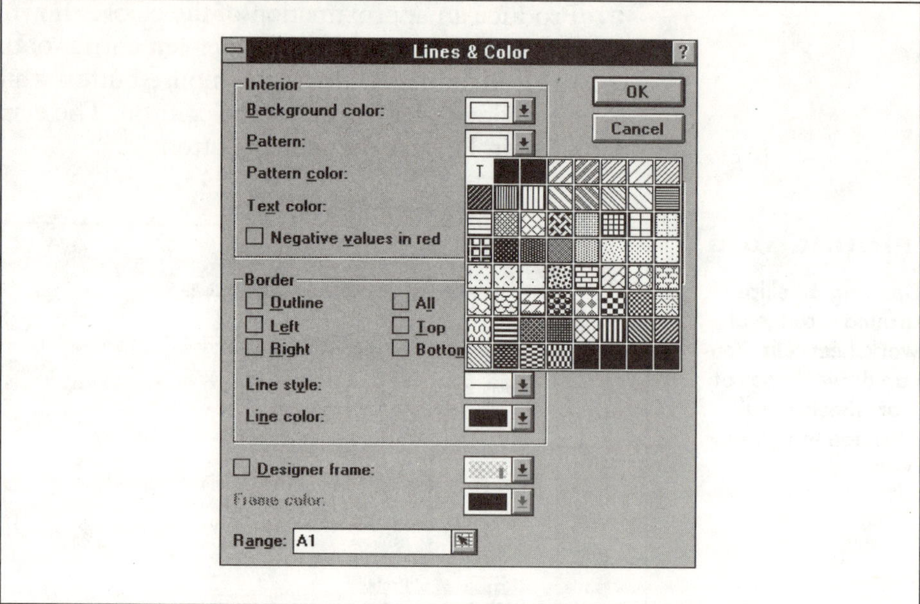

Parsing, or Transforming an Imported Text File into a Table

You can use the Range ➤ Parse command to *import* data into a 1-2-3 worksheet from a text file. A text file is made up of letters, digits, and printable symbols from the ASCII character code. Text files usually have a .TXT or .PRN file extension. The Range ➤ Parse command provides a simple way to transfer a text file of column-oriented information to a 1-2-3 worksheet.

The first step in the process is to select File ➤ Open. This command reads a text file from disk and copies it line by line into a worksheet. Each line of the text file is stored as a long label entry in a single cell of the worksheet.

Once the lines are in label-entry form, you can use the Range ➤ Parse command to separate the long labels into individual label and value entries.

Placing the Text File in the Worksheet

For the upcoming exercises:

1. Open the INSTRUCT.WK4 database that was developed earlier.

2. On sheet B, highlight A4..I20. Choose File ➤ Save As and save it as a text file.

To save the range only as a text file, follow these steps:

3. Use File ➤ Open to bring the INSTRUCT.WK4 worksheets back on-screen. Then click on the B tab to go to the B sheet.

4. Select the range of cells A4..I20.

5. Choose File ➤ Save As. The Save As dialog box appears, as in Figure 10.8. In the Save frame at the bottom of the dialog box, click on the Selected range only check box.

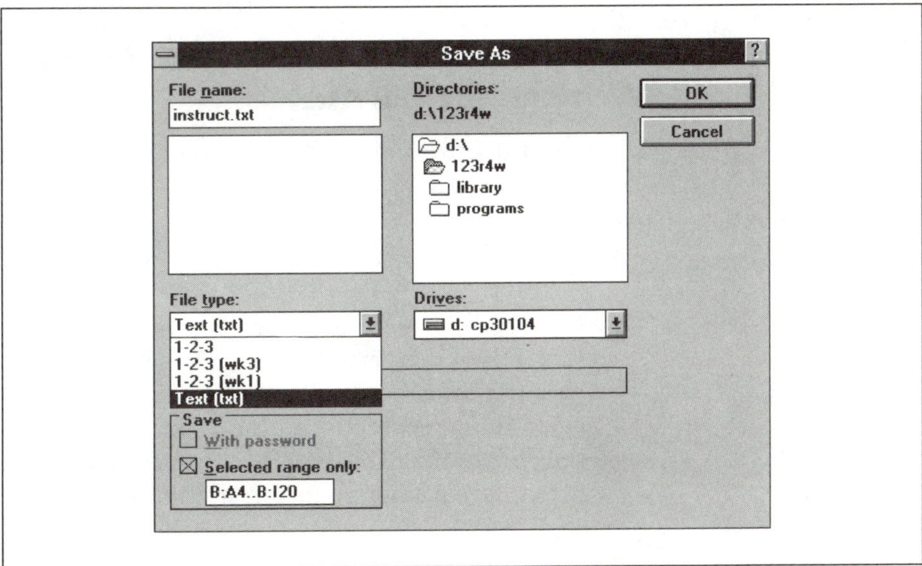

6. In File type box, select Text(txt) as the file type in which to save the ranges.

7. Click on the OK button or press ↵. To see the text file, you can open it with any word processing program.

Figure 10.9 shows the contents of the file. As you can see, the data values in each row are separated by spaces to align the columns. Keep in mind that this file was saved to disk in ASCII format, and the string and numeric fields alike are made up of sequences of ASCII characters.

FIGURE 10.9

The instructor database as a text file

```
S-149    Harris     P.   Dallas             S   Spreadsheet   $150    17    12-Feb-91
A-146    Daniels    A.   Atlanta            S   Accounting    $125    24    09-May-91
A-103    Perez      D.   Las Vegas          W   Accounting    $100     5    11-Jul-86
W-113    Porter     D.   Seattle            N   WP            $125    59    02-Aug-86
N-101    Schwartz   B.   Boston             E   Networks      $150   178    02-Mar-86
S-155    Roberts    P.   Chicago            N   Spreadsheet   $100    10    21-Aug-91
S-125    Ashford    W.   Washington, D.C.   E   Spreadsheet   $150   145    10-May-87
D-106    Weinberg   P.   Miami              S   Database       $75    59    18-Jan-86
W-119    Davis      G.   San Francisco      W   WP            $150   139    09-Jul-87
W-124    Meyer      J.   New York           E   WP            $150    85    05-May-87
W-145    Banks      S.   St. Louis          S   WP            $150    55    10-Jun-90
D-137    Sanchez    W.   Indianapolis       N   Database      $100    47    16-Apr-89
D-139    Porter     M.   Washington, D.C.   E   Database      $150    26    28-Mar-89
T-133    Ramirez    F.   Boston             E   Telecomm      $150    73    08-Feb-88
D-143    Cody       L.   Los Angeles        W   Database       $75    43    20-Jun-90
S-127    Gill       P.   Los Angeles        W   Spreadsheet   $100    25    22-Jun-87
T-128    Eng        R.   Albuquerque        S   Telecomm       $75    75    11-Oct-87
```

Converting the File to the 1-2-3 Worksheet Format

Here are the initial steps for converting a file like this one into the 1-2-3 worksheet format:

1. Use File ➤ New to open a new blank worksheet into which you can import the text file.

2. Choose File ➤ Open. Click on the ↓ button next to File type and select Text(txt,prn). Use the Drives and Directories boxes to navigate to the directory location of the existing text file. When you activate the correct directory, the name of the text file appears in the File name list box. (By default, this command looks for text files that have an extension name of .TXT or .PRN.)

3. When you find the target file name in the File _name list box, click on the name with the mouse. Click on the _Combine button instead of the OK button. The Combine Text File dialog box appears.

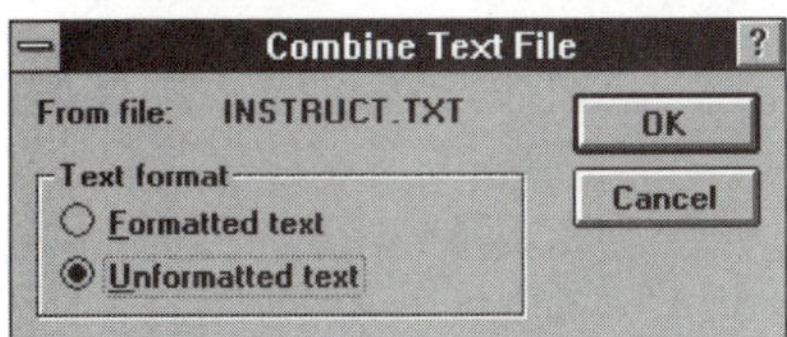

4. Select _Unformatted text and press ↵ or click on OK. In response, 1-2-3 enters the file into the current worksheet, starting from the location of the cell pointer. Each line of the text file becomes a long entry in a cell of the current column.

Parsing the Long Labels

For example, Figure 10.10 shows the instructor database imported from the text file in Figure 10.9. By looking in the contents box, you can see that the entire first line of the text file is stored in cell A1. The worksheet is of little use to you in this format. Your next step is to parse these long labels and make them individual data entries. The Range ➤ Parse accomplishes this step by developing a special _format line_ to represent the actual data structure of each data row.

Here are the steps for using the Parse command on the imported data shown in Figure 10.10:

1. Preselect the long data labels in column A, in range A1..A17.

2. Choose _Range ➤ _Parse. The Parse dialog box appears, as in Figure 10.11.

3. Click the _Create button to instruct 1-2-3 to develop a format line for the file. When you do so, the dialog box displays a format line, as in the figure. (Your screen will look different, as you selected multiple lines of data. Only one line is shown here for convenience.)

FIGURE 10.10

The instructor database imported from a text file

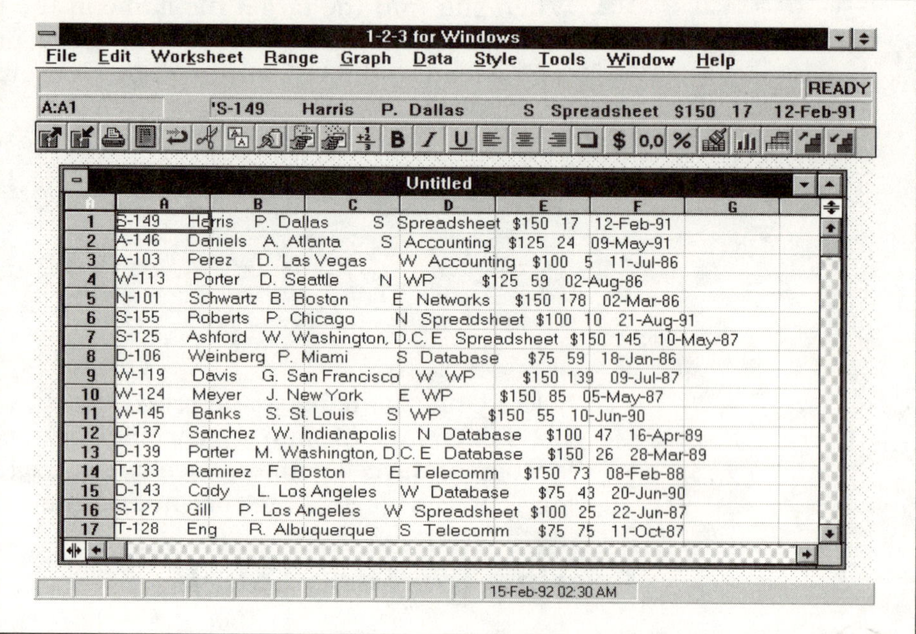

FIGURE 10.11

The Parse dialog box. Notice the format line for the imported file.

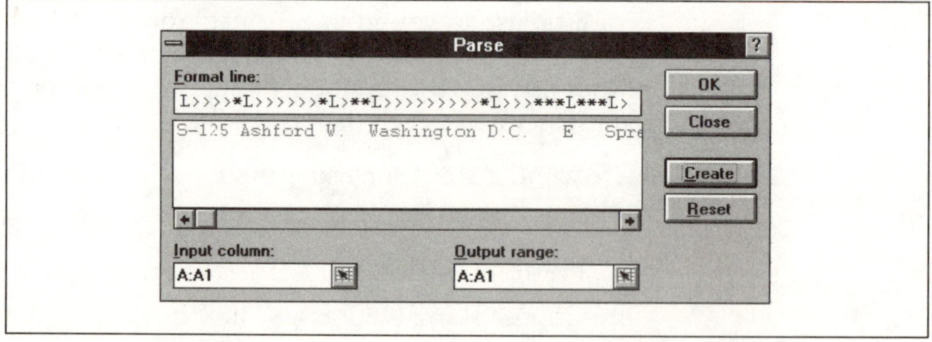

The format line The format line contains three types of characters: single letters (L, V, or D), right angle brackets (>), and asterisks (*):

L, D, T, *and* V	Represents the type of data in a given column, known as a *data block*. *L* stands for label, *V* for value, *D* for data, and *T* for time.
>	A sequence of right angle brackets represents the width of a data block.
*	A sequence of asterisks represents spaces between data blocks, or extra space for entries that extend beyond the data block width.

Beneath the format line, the dialog box displays a sample of the data as it will appear after parsing.

4. Use the scroll bar to scroll horizontally through the format line. As you can see, the letters *L*, *V*, and *D* represent data blocks containing labels, values, and dates, respectively. (In addition, 1-2-3 uses the letter *T* in a format line to represent time values.)

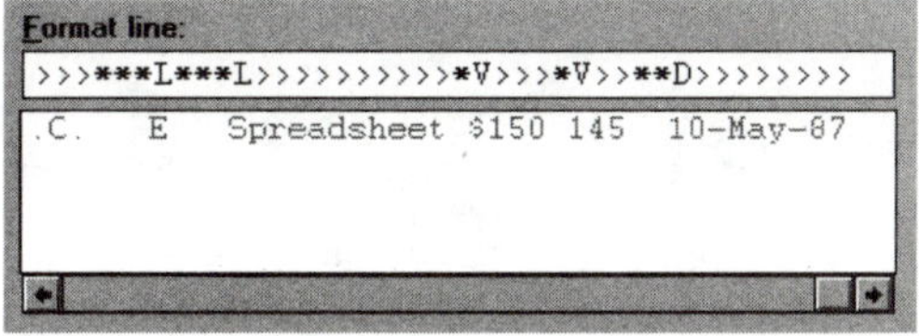

Editing the format line If the format line that 1-2-3 has developed does not meet your expectations for the parse, you can activate the line and edit it. For example, you can change the data type or increase the width of a data block. Moreover, you can use the letter *S* to tell 1-2-3 to ignore a data block.

5. When you are satisfied with the data structure represented in the format line, click the OK button to perform the parse.

Lotus enters the data blocks into individual columns of the worksheet. After you adjust column widths, the database looks like Figure 10.12. The first six columns have been entered as labels, and the final three as values. Notice that the date strings from the text file have been converted into date numbers. You can now format these numbers as dates.

NOTE

In the parsing process, 1-2-3 may generate an extra copy of a long label at the bottom of the database. To delete it, select the cell where this label is stored and press the Delete key.

Delimited and fixed field length files By the way, the Combine Text File dialog box offers two options, Formatted text and Unformatted text.

- <u>F</u>ormatted text reads in a *delimited text file* only. In a delimited text file, the data are broken into columns.

- <u>U</u>nformatted text reads in data from a *fixed field length file*. A fixed field length file is a text file in which all data values start at exactly the same column position.

FIGURE 10.12

The parsed database

	A	B	C	D	E	F	G	H	I
1	S-149	Harris	P.	Dallas	S	Spreadsheet	150	17	33281
2	A-146	Daniels	A.	Atlanta	S	Accounting	125	24	33367
3	A-103	Perez	D.	Las Vegas	W	Accounting	100	5	31604
4	W-113	Porter	D.	Seattle	N	WP	125	59	31626
5	N-101	Schwartz	B.	Boston	E	Networks	150	178	31473
6	S-155	Roberts	P.	Chicago	N	Spreadsheet	100	10	33471
7	S-125	Ashford	W.	Washington, D.C.	E	Spreadsheet	150	145	31907
8	D-106	Weinberg	P.	Miami	S	Database	75	59	31430
9	W-119	Davis	G.	San Francisco	W	WP	150	139	31967
10	W-124	Meyer	J.	New York	E	WP	150	85	31902
11	W-145	Banks	S.	St. Louis	S	WP	150	55	33034
12	D-137	Sanchez	W.	Indianapolis	N	Database	100	47	32614
13	D-139	Porter	M.	Washington, D.C.	E	Database	150	26	32595
14	T-133	Ramirez	F.	Boston	E	Telecomm	150	73	32181
15	D-143	Cody	L.	Los Angeles	W	Database	75	43	33044
16	S-127	Gill	P.	Los Angeles	W	Spreadsheet	100	25	31950
17	T-128	Eng	R.	Albuquerque	S	Telecomm	75	75	32061

Figure 10.13 shows the instructor database as a fixed field length file. Data files in this format are created from a variety of software environments. File ➤ Open ➤ Combine ➤ Formatted text reads a file into the current worksheet, and enters the data values into individual cells. You do not need to use Range ➤ Parse after using File ➤ Open ➤ Combine ➤ Formatted text.

FIGURE 10.13

The database as a
fixed field length file

```
"S-149","Harris","P.","Dallas","S","Spreadsheet",150,17,"12-Feb-91"
"A-146","Daniels","A.","Atlanta","S","Accounting",125,24,"09-May-91"
"A-103","Perez","D.","Las Vegas","W","Accounting",100,5,"11-Jul-86"
"W-113","Porter","D.","Seattle","N","WP",125,59,"02-Aug-86"
"N-101","Schwartz","B.","Boston","E","Networks",150,178,"02-Mar-86"
"S-155","Roberts","P.","Chicago","N","Spreadsheet",100,10,"21-Aug-91"
"S-125","Ashford","W.","Washington, D.C.","E","Spreadsheet",150,145,"10-May-87"
"D-106","Weinberg","P.","Miami","S","Database",75,59,"18-Jan-86"
"W-119","Davis","G.","San Francisco","W","WP",150,139,"09-Jul-87"
"W-124","Meyer","J.","New York","E","WP",150,85,"05-May-87"
"W-145","Banks","S.","St. Louis","S","WP",150,55,"10-Jun-90"
"D-137","Sanchez","W.","Indianapolis","N","Database",100,47,"16-Apr-89"
"D-139","Porter","M.","Washington, D.C.","E","Database",150,26,"28-Mar-89"
"T-133","Ramirez","F.","Boston","E","Telecomm",150,73,"08-Feb-88"
"D-143","Cody","L.","Los Angeles","W","Database",75,43,"20-Jun-90"
"S-127","Gill","P.","Los Angeles","W","Spreadsheet",100,25,"22-Jun-87"
"T-128","Eng","R.","Albuquerque","S","Telecomm",75,75,"11-Oct-87"
```

Performing Frequency Distribution Analysis

Use the Range ➤ Analyze ➤ Distribution command to do frequency distribution analysis. This command counts the number of worksheet entries that fall in specific numeric categories. To do a distribution analysis, you follow these general steps:

1. Begin by entering a progression of numbers, known as the *bin range*, in a worksheet column. These numbers express the numeric intervals into which you want to distribute the worksheet values.

2. Then you select the *values range*, or the range of worksheet values that will be the subject of the frequency distribution.

Given these two ranges, Range ➤ Analyze ➤ Distribution creates a new column of numbers representing the frequency count.

For example, Figure 10.14 shows a frequency distribution analysis on the instructor database. For the analysis, several fields in the database are temporarily hidden from view (using <u>S</u>tyle ➤ <u>H</u>ide), the Yrs field has been reformatted to display two places after the decimal point, and the instructor database appears in Worksheet A. As you'll recall, Yrs is a calculated field that shows the number of years each instructor has been working for Computing Conferences, Inc. The purpose of this analysis is to count the number of instructors whose length of employment falls in each of several categories appearing in bin range M7..M12:

- one year or less

- two years or less, but more than a year

- three years or less, but more than two years

- and so on

FIGURE 10.14

Performing a frequency distribution analysis

	A	B	C	J	L	M	N	O	P
1	Instructor Database								
2									
3	ID	Last	First	Yrs		Frequency Distribution:			
4	S-149	Harris	P.	0.97					
5	A-146	Daniels	A.	0.73		Years as	Number of		
6	A-103	Perez	D.	5.56		Instructor	Instructors		
7	W-113	Porter	D.	5.50		1	3		
8	N-101	Schwartz	B.	5.92		2	2		
9	S-155	Roberts	P.	0.45		3	2		
10	S-125	Ashford	W.	4.73		4	1		
11	D-106	Weinberg	P.	6.04		5	5		
12	W-119	Davis	G.	4.57		6	3		
13	W-124	Meyer	J.	4.75			1		
14	W-145	Banks	S.	1.64					
15	D-137	Sanchez	W.	2.79					
16	D-139	Porter	M.	2.85					
17	T-133	Ramirez	F.	3.98					
18	D-143	Cody	L.	1.62					
19	S-127	Gill	P.	4.61					
20	T-128	Eng	R.	4.31					

Once you have established the bin range, using the Range ➤ Analyze ➤ Distribution command is simple. Here are the steps to produce the frequency distribution shown in N7..N13:

1. Preselect the values range, in this case the data in the Yrs field, J4..J20.

2. Choose Range ➤ Analyze ➤ Distribution. The Distribution dialog box appears with the values range you preselected in the Range of values text box.

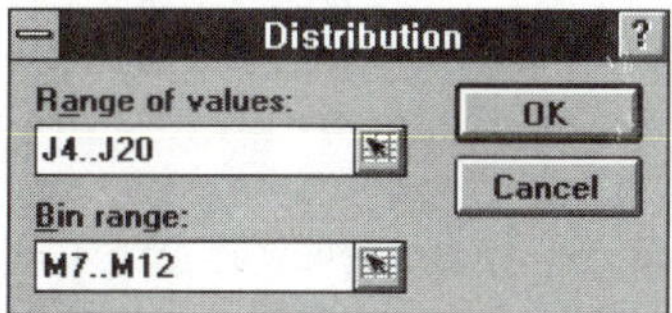

3. Enter the bin range as A:M7..A:M12 in the Bin range text box.

4. Click OK to complete the operation.

This command enters the frequency distribution into the column located immediately to the right of the bin range. In Figure 10.14, you can see that there are three instructors who have worked for one year or less, two instructors who have worked between one and two years, and so on. Notice that the frequency distribution range contains one more entry than the bin range. This final entry lists the number of value-range entries greater than the last entry in the bin range. In this example, one instructor has worked for more than six years.

Performing Regression Analysis

Regression analysis is an attempt to discover the strength of the mathematical correlation between two or more sets of data. For example, let's reopen the ADVER.WK4 file we created earlier. Column B of the worksheet in

Figure 10.15 shows the amount that Computing Conferences, Inc. spent on advertising for several computer-training conferences. Column C shows how many people attended those same conferences. The general question posed by this worksheet is clear: does attendance go up or down when the company spends more money on advertising? In other words, is there a correlation between advertising and attendance? In this regression analysis problem, attendance is the *dependent variable* because the goal of the analysis is to discover the extent to which attendance depends on advertising. Accordingly, advertising is called the *independent variable*.

You might recall working with this data in Chapter 6 when you studied XY graphs. Figure 6.24 displays an XY graph in which advertising dollars are plotted against attendance in an x-y coordinate system. This graph seems to show a relationship between the two data sets. In effect, an XY graph is a pictorial form of regression analysis. Suppose you were to draw a straight diagonal line somewhere through the middle of the plotted points in Figure 6.24. You might then formulate an approximate equation

FIGURE 10.15

Advertising and attendance data

	A	B	C
1	Computing Conferences, Inc.		
2	Attendance and Advertising		
3	*Computing for Video Stores*		
4			
5	Date	Advertising	Attendance
6	09-Jan-91	$5,000.00	154
7	21-Jan-91	$3,500.00	119
8	15-Feb-91	$6,000.00	174
9	07-Mar-91	$6,000.00	201
10	25-Mar-91	$3,500.00	136
11	03-Apr-91	$5,000.00	172
12	11-May-91	$3,500.00	112
13	28-May-91	$1,000.00	97
14	03-Jun-91	$1,000.00	86
15	29-Jun-91	$1,000.00	104
16	05-Sep-91	$7,500.00	235
17	11-Oct-91	$1,500.00	119
18	29-Oct-91	$2,500.00	137
19	05-Nov-91	$3,500.00	148

describing the relationship between advertising and attendance. The general equation for a straight line is

$$y = mx + b$$

where

- y is the dependent variable,

- x is the independent variable,

- m is the slope of the straight line that represents the relationship, and

- b is the y-intercept, or the value of y when x is zero.

To the extent that the equation you develop is a reliable description of the relationship between the two variables, you can use this equation to make predictions about the dependent variable.

Range ➤ Analyze ➤ Regression performs this same kind of analysis, but produces specific mathematical results rather than graphic approximations. Regression allows you to select a range containing one or more independent variables (known as the X-range) and one dependent variable (known as the Y-range). In addition, you specify an output range on your worksheet where the command can display the results of its analysis.

Filling in the Regression dialog box   Figure 10.16 shows the Regression dialog box. Here the X, Y, and Output ranges have been filled in with appropriate data for an analysis of the advertising and attendance worksheet.

TEXT/ CHECK BOX	ENTER
<u>X</u>range	The independent variables, in this case the range of advertising data in column B.
<u>Y</u>range	The dependent variables, in this case the range of attendance data in column C. Cell A:E5 is specified as the upper-left corner of the output range.

TEXT/ CHECK BOX	ENTER
Output range	Where you want to display the results of the analysis.
Y-intercept	A check in Compute or Set to zero:

- Compute calculates the actual y-intercept.

- Set to zero hypothesizes a value of zero for the yintercept.

For the advertising and attendance data, you want 1-2-3 to choose Compute and calculate the actual y-intercept; in theory, this value represents the expected attendance level when no money is spent on advertising.

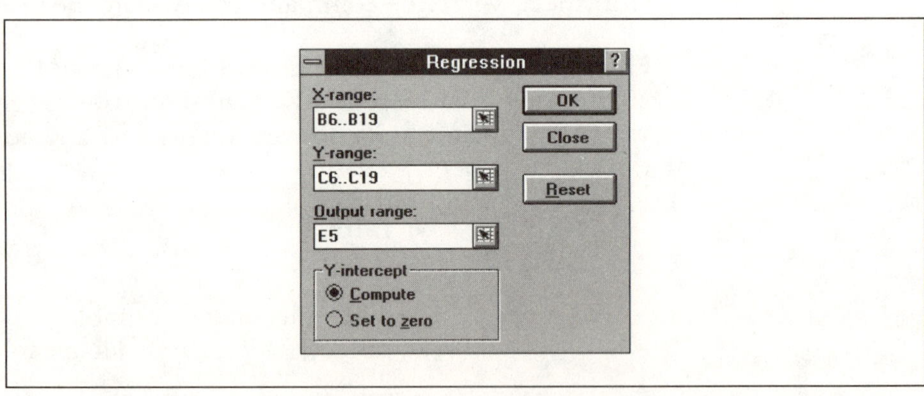

In Figure 10.17, you see the results of the regression analysis. At the top of the output table, the Constant value (displayed as 74.83875 in cell H6) is the y-intercept. Near the bottom of the table, the X Coefficient(s) value (displayed as 0.018738 in cell G12) is the slope of the line that theoretically

FIGURE 10.17

The output from a Regression analysis

	A	B	C	D	E	F	G	H	
1	Computing Conferences, Inc.								
2	Attendance and Advertising								
3	*Computing for Video Stores*								
4									
5	Date	Advertising	Attendance			Regression Output:			
6	09-Jan-91	$5,000.00	154		Constant			74.83875	
7	21-Jan-91	$3,500.00	119		Std Err of Y Est			15.7763	
8	15-Feb-91	$6,000.00	174		R Squared			0.869322	
9	07-Mar-91	$6,000.00	201		No. of Observations			14	
10	25-Mar-91	$3,500.00	136		Degrees of Freedom			12	
11	03-Apr-91	$5,000.00	172						
12	11-May-91	$3,500.00	112		X Coefficient(s)		0.018738		
13	28-May-91	$1,000.00	97		Std Err of Coef.		0.002097		
14	03-Jun-91	$1,000.00	86						
15	29-Jun-91	$1,000.00	104						
16	05-Sep-91	$7,500.00	235						
17	11-Oct-91	$1,500.00	119						
18	29-Oct-91	$2,500.00	137						
19	05-Nov-91	$3,500.00	148						
20									

describes the relationship between the two variables. Rounding these two values, you can formulate the equation for the line as:

$$y = 0.019x + 75$$

or as

$$\text{attendance} = 0.019 * \text{advertising} + 75$$

You can substitute actual advertising amounts into this equation to calculate the corresponding attendance projection. For example, according to this equation, attendance should be at a level of 75 people when no money is spent on advertising, or approximately 150 people when $4000 is spent.

Determining How Accurate the Analysis Is

Regression also displays output values that tell you how far you can rely on this regression analysis as a tool for predicting the behavior of the dependent variable:

- The R Squared value is a general measurement of the reliability of the analysis. For a strong correlation between the dependent and independent variables, the *R Squared* value is close to 1; for a weak correlation, the value is close to zero.

- The value labeled Std Err of Y Est (standard error of the *y* estimate) indicates the range of accuracy for calculated values of *y*. In Figure 10.17, the Std Err of Y Est value is approximately 16. This implies that any attendance value you calculate from the equation is accurate within a range of plus or minus 16.

- The value labeled Std Err of Coef. (standard error of the x coefficient) indicates the reliability of the slope calculation. The smaller this value is in relation to the X Coefficient(s), the better the reliability.

Exploring "What-If" Scenarios in a Worksheet

Table commands are a group of remarkably efficient tools for exploring multiple "what-if" scenarios in a worksheet. For example, consider the worksheet in Figure 10.18, which shows an abbreviated version of the conference worksheet you developed in Chapters 3 and 4. Most of the formulas on this worksheet depend directly or indirectly on the values entered for the attendance level and the per-person admission price. In Figure 10.18, these two key values appear in cells B4 and B5, respectively. By changing the values in one or both of these cells, you can explore how changing the attendance level and per-person admission price affects bottom-line profit (cell H19).

In some applications, you may want to build an entire table of what-if projections. For example, suppose you wanted to examine a table of profit calculations for a range of attendance and price levels in the conference worksheet. Such a table is shown in Figure 10.19. To create this table manually, you would have to enter many different values in cells B4 and B5 of the worksheet and copy each profit calculation that resulted from cell H19 to your table. Fortunately, this is exactly the kind of task that the What-if Table commands are designed to automate.

FIGURE 10.18

A shortened version of the conference worksheet

	A	B	C	D	E	F	G	H
1	Computing for Video Stores			Projected Revenues				
2	Place:	St. Louis			Attendance			$12,675.00
3	Date:	15-Oct-92			Video Sales		$35.00	$1,137.50
4	Attendance:	65			Total Revenues			$13,812.50
5	Price:	$195.00						
6					Projected Expenses -- Fixed			
7					Conference room			$1,500.00
8					Video production			$1,000.00
9					Promotion			$3,500.00
10					Travel			$800.00
11					Total Fixed Expenses			$6,800.00
12								
13					Projected Expenses -- Variable by Attendance			
14					Conference materials		$8.25	$536.25
15					Coffee and pastries		$3.25	$211.25
16					Box lunch		$4.75	$308.75
17					Total Variable Expenses			$1,056.25
18								
19					Projected Profit			$5,956.25
20								

FIGURE 10.19

A profit table, with varying price and attendance projections

	A	B	C	D	E
1	Profits		Price		
2			$145.00	$170.00	$195.00
3	Attendance	65	$2,706.25	$4,331.25	$5,956.25
4		75	$4,168.75	$6,043.75	$7,918.75
5		85	$5,631.25	$7,756.25	$9,881.25
6		95	$7,093.75	$9,468.75	$11,843.75
7		105	$8,556.25	$11,181.25	$13,806.25
8		115	$10,018.75	$12,893.75	$15,768.75
9		125	$11,481.25	$14,606.25	$17,731.25
10					

Choose Range ➤ Analyze ➤ What-if Table to see the options in the What-if Table dialog box. This dialog box is shown in Figure 10.20. Notice that the Number of variables pull-down box has three options: 1 (1-way), 2 (2-way), and 3 (3-way). The profit table in Figure 10.19 is an example of a two-way what-if table, which you'll learn to create shortly.

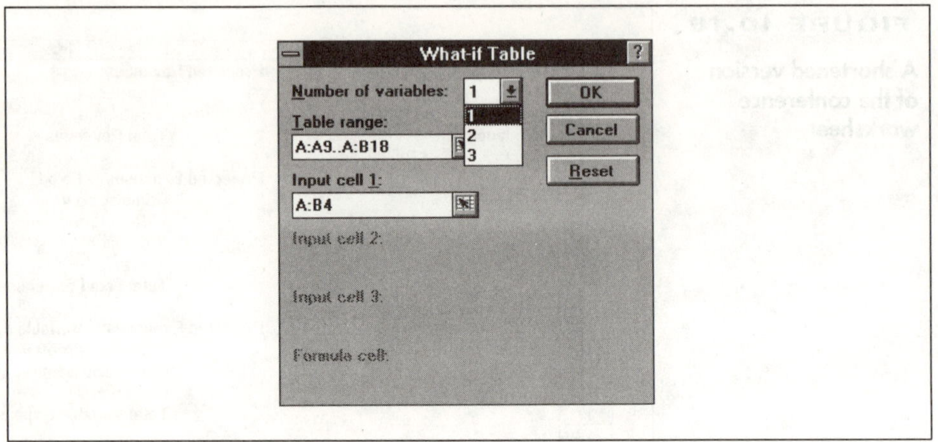

For the next few exercises in this chapter, you'll need your own copy of
the shortened conference worksheet. If you wish, you can create it by
reentering all the data and formulas in a new worksheet. Figure 10.21
shows the formulas you should enter into column H. Save this new file as
CONF2.WK4.

A	D	E	F	G	H	I
1	Projected Revenues:					
2		Attendance			+B4*B5	
3		Video Sales		$35.00	+G3*B4/2	
4		Total Revenues			@SUM(H2..H3)	
5						
6	Projected Expenses -- Fixed					
7		Conference room			1500	
8		Video production			1000	
9		Promotion			3500	
10		Travel			800	
11		Total Fixed Expenses			@SUM(H7..H10)	
12						
13	Projected Expenses -- Variable by Attendance					
14		Conference materials		$8.25	+$G14*$B$4	
15		Coffee and pastries		$3.25	+$G15*$B$4	
16		Box lunch		$4.75	+$G16*$B$4	
17		Total Variable Expenses			@SUM(H14..H16)	
18						
19	Projected Profit				+H4-(H11+H17)	

Combining Two Worksheet Files

To create your own copy of the shortened worksheet, you could also copy a range of data from the original CONF.WK4 file, and reformat and re-organize the worksheet to match the one in Figure 10.21. File ➤ Open ➤ Combine is a useful tool for performing this task. The command copies data to the current worksheet window from a worksheet file stored on disk, like so:

1. If necessary, choose File ➤ New to open a new blank worksheet.

2. Choose File ➤ Open. Use the Drives and Directories boxes to find the directory location of the CONF.WK4 file, and then select the file in the File name list box. Click on the Combine button. The Combine 1-2-3 File dialog box appears.

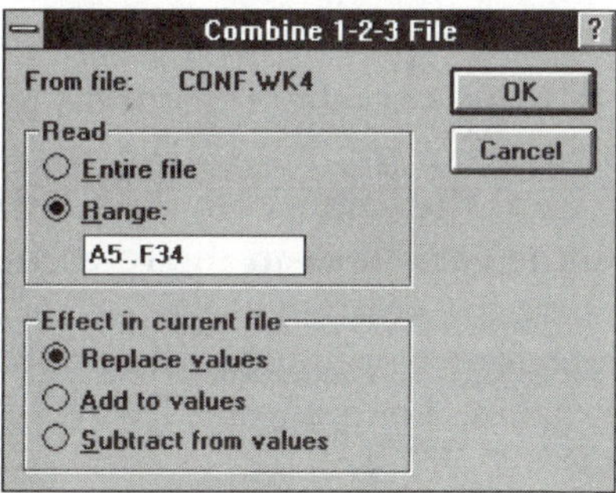

3. In the Read box, select the Range option, and enter **A5..F34** as the CONF.WK4 range from which to copy data. Click OK to complete the operation. In response, 1-2-3 copies the data from CONF.WK4 to your current worksheet.

4. Use Edit ➤ Delete to delete the final column of data and to delete extra blank rows from the worksheet.

5. Enter the label **Attendance:** in cell A4. Then move the ranges of data to their new positions on the worksheet, as shown in Figure 10.22. When you move the minimum attendance amount to its new position in cell B4, 1-2-3 will make the appropriate adjustments in all the worksheet's formulas. Confirm that these adjustments have been made correctly by entering a new attendance projection of **65** in cell B4.

FIGURE 10.22

Preparing for the
What-if Table 1-Way
command

	A	B	C	D	E	F	G	H
1	Computing for Video Stores			Projected Revenues				
2	Place:	St. Louis			Attendance			$12,675.00
3	Date:	15-Oct-92			Video Sales		$35.00	$1,137.50
4	Attendance:	65			**Total Revenues**			**$13,812.50**
5	Price:	$195.00						
6					Projected Expenses -- Fixed			
7					Conference room			$1,500.00
8	Attendance	Profit			Video production			$1,000.00
9		+H4-(H11+H17)			Promotion			$3,500.00
10	45				Travel			$800.00
11	55				**Total Fixed Expenses**			**$6,800.00**
12	65							
13	75				Projected Expenses -- Variable by Attendance			
14	85				Conference materials		$8.25	$536.25
15	95				Coffee and pastries		$3.25	$211.25
16	105				Box lunch		$4.75	$308.75
17	115				**Total Variable Expenses**			**$1,056.25**
18	125							
19					Projected Profit			$5,956.25
20								

Lotus recalculates the worksheet formulas that depend on this value, including the bottom-line profit. (In the end, the formulas in column H
should be essentially the same as those shown in Figure 10.21, although
you might see some variations in the reference formats.)

6. To complete your work, apply the appropriate formats and styles
   to the worksheet. Then choose File ➤ Save As and save the file on
   disk as CONF2.WK4.

Now you are ready to begin experimenting with the What-if Table
commands.

One-Way What-If Tables
for Experimenting with
One Variable

To create a one-way what-if table, you must be prepared to supply 1-2-3
with three kinds of information:

- A column of input values that 1-2-3 can insert one at a time into
  the worksheet calculations

- The input location where these values should be entered

- The formula that 1-2-3 should recalculate after each new input entry

For example, Figure 10.22 shows a range of attendance projections in A10..A18. The goal of the upcoming operation is to display the profit amount corresponding to each attendance value. To produce this information, 1-2-3 needs to insert each attendance figure into the input cell, B4, and then recalculate the formula that gives the profit. Accordingly, cell B9 contains a copy of the profit formula:

+H4–(H11+H17)

This formula represents the total revenues minus the sum of the fixed and variable expenses.

Entering the Input Values and Target Formula

You can use Range ➤ Analyze ➤ What-if Table successfully only after you enter the column of input values and the target formula. Here are the steps for producing the table:

1. Use Range ➤ Fill to enter integer values from **45** to **125** in increments of **10** into range A10..A18.

2. Enter the formula **+H4-(H11+H17)** into cell B9. Choose Style ➤ Number Format and select the Text format for this cell, so you can see the formula itself.

3. Enter the labels **Attendance** and **Profit** into cells A8 and B8, respectively. Right-justify the label in B8, and apply the bold style to cells A8, B8, and B9. Preselect the range B10..B18 and format these cells as Currency.

4. Preselect range A9..B18 and choose Range ➤ Analyze ➤ What-if Table.

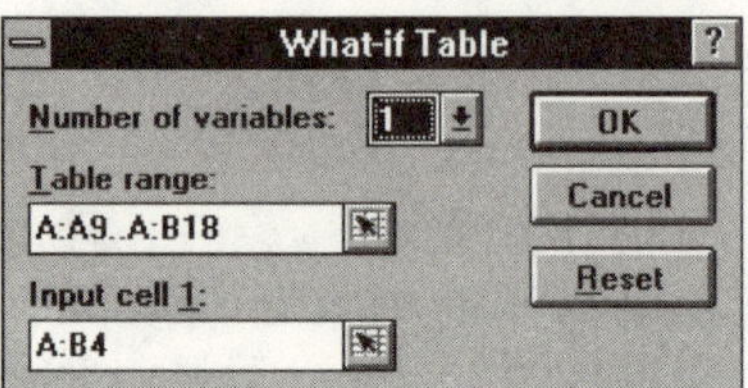

5. In the <u>N</u>umber of variables pull-down box of the What-if Table dialog box, choose 1. Enter a reference to cell **B4** in the Input cell <u>1</u> text box. Click OK to confirm.

6. Back on the worksheet, move the cell pointer to A7, out of the way of the what-if table.

7. Choose <u>F</u>ile ➤ Save <u>A</u>s and save this worksheet as TABLES.WK4. (The original file, named CONF2.WK4, remains unchanged on-disk for upcoming exercises.)

Lotus fills in the what-if table with a range of profit calculations in B10..B18, as you can see in Figure 10.23. Each of these figures represents the value that would appear in cell H19 of the worksheet if you were to enter the corresponding attendance value into cell B4. The What-if Table command has generated the entire column of figures in a single operation.

	A	B	C	D	E	F	G	H
1	Computing for Video Stores			Projected Revenues				
2	Place:	St. Louis			Attendance			$12,675.00
3	Date:	15-Oct-92			Video Sales		$35.00	$1,137.50
4	Attendance:	65			Total Revenues			$13,812.50
5	Price:	$195.00						
6					Projected Expenses -- Fixed			
7					Conference room			$1,500.00
8	Attendance	Profit			Video production			$1,000.00
9		+H4-(H11+H17)			Promotion			$3,500.00
10	45	$2,031.25			Travel			$800.00
11	55	$3,993.75			Total Fixed Expenses			$6,800.00
12	65	$5,956.25						
13	75	$7,918.75			Projected Expenses -- Variable by Attendance			
14	85	$9,881.25			Conference materials		$8.25	$536.25
15	95	$11,843.75			Coffee and pastries		$3.25	$211.25
16	105	$13,806.25			Box lunch		$4.75	$308.75
17	115	$15,768.75			Total Variable Expenses			$1,056.25
18	125	$17,731.25						
19					Projected Profit			$5,956.25
20								

Creating What-If Tables for More than One Formula

This command also allows you to create what-if tables for more than one formula at a time. For example, suppose you wanted to add a column to show the variable expenses corresponding to each projected attendance level. As shown in Figure 10.24, you would take the following steps:

1. Enter the formula **@SUM(H14..H16)** in cell C9.

2. Preselect range A9..C18.

3. Choose Range ➤ Analyze ➤ What-if Table again.

4. Specify B4 as the input cell and click OK.

The formatted results of this second formula appear in the range C10..C18.

A	A	B	C	
1	Computing for Video Stores			Proje
2	Place:	St. Louis		
3	Date:	15-Oct-92		
4	Attendance:	65		
5	Price:	$195.00		
6				Proje
7				
8	Attendance	Profit	Var. Exp.	
9		+H4-(H11+H17)	@SUM(H14..H16)	
10	45	$2,031.25	$731.25	
11	55	$3,993.75	$893.75	
12	65	$5,956.25	$1,056.25	
13	75	$7,918.75	$1,218.75	Proje
14	85	$9,881.25	$1,381.25	
15	95	$11,843.75	$1,543.75	
16	105	$13,806.25	$1,706.25	
17	115	$15,768.75	$1,868.75	
18	125	$17,731.25	$2,031.25	

Recalculating a What-If Table

The entries that 1-2-3 places in the what-if table are values, not formulas. They are therefore not subject to automatic recalculation when you make changes on the worksheet. However, 1-2-3 gives you a convenient way to repeat the last What-if Table command: simply press the F8 function key. For example, suppose you make some changes in the column of input values in A10..A18. After you revise the entries in this range, you can press F8 to produce a new version of the what-if table.

Try this exercise with the F8 key:

1. Use Range ➤ Fill to enter a new range of attendance projections into A10..A18. Enter values from **60** to **220** in increments of **20**.

2. Press the F8 function key. The new what-if table appears as shown in Figure 10.25.

A	A	B	C	
1	Computing for Video Stores			Proje
2	Place:	St. Louis		
3	Date:	15-Oct-92		
4	Attendance:	65		
5	Price:	$195.00		
6				Proje
7				
8	Attendance	Profit	Var. Exp.	
9		+H4-(H11+H17)	@SUM(H14..H16)	
10	60	$4,975.00	$975.00	
11	80	$8,900.00	$1,300.00	
12	100	$12,825.00	$1,625.00	
13	120	$16,750.00	$1,950.00	Proje
14	140	$20,675.00	$2,275.00	
15	160	$24,600.00	$2,600.00	
16	180	$28,525.00	$2,925.00	
17	200	$32,450.00	$3,250.00	
18	220	$36,375.00	$3,575.00	

Disabling F8 You can disable the F8 function key by choosing Range ➤ Analyze ➤ What-if Table ➤ Reset. Use this command to clear the What-if Table dialog box when you have produced the final version of the what-if table.

Two- and Three-Way Tables for Experimenting with More than One Variable

You can also produce what-if tables that calculate formulas in response to changes in two or three input cells. The 2Way and 3Way options in the What-if Table command are the tools you use for these tasks.

To prepare a two-way table, begin by entering a column of values for the first input cell, and a row of values for the second input cell. For example, suppose you want to generate a profit table for a range of attendance projections and a range of prices. To do so, you enter the attendance values down a column, just as you did for the one-way table. Then you enter the range of prices across a row at the top of the table range. In the upper-left corner cell of the table range, you enter the formula that 1-2-3 will use for calculating the what-if table.

In the following exercise, you'll generate a two-way what-if table in worksheet B of TABLES.WK4:

1. Choose <u>E</u>dit ➤ <u>I</u>nsert and select the <u>S</u>heet option. Click OK to add worksheet B to TABLES.WK4.

2. In cell B:B2, enter the formula **+A:H4-(A:H11+A:H17)**. Choose <u>S</u>tyle ➤ <u>N</u>umber Format, select the Text option, and click OK to display the formula itself in the cell. Apply the bold style to the cell, and widen column B so that the entire formula can fit in the column.

3. Enter **Prices** as an aligned-right label in B:C1. Then enter **Attendance** in cell B:A3. Apply the bold style to both labels.

4. Use Range ➤ Fill to enter a column of attendance projections into range B:B3..B:B12. Enter values from **45** to **135** in increments of **10**.

5. Use Data Fill again to enter a row of prices in the range B:C2..B:G2. Enter values from **145** to **245** in increments of **25**. Preselect range B:C2..B:G12 and select the Currency format for this range.

6. Preselect range B:B2..B:G12. Choose <u>R</u>ange ➤ <u>A</u>nalyze ➤ What-if Table. The What-if Table dialog box appears.

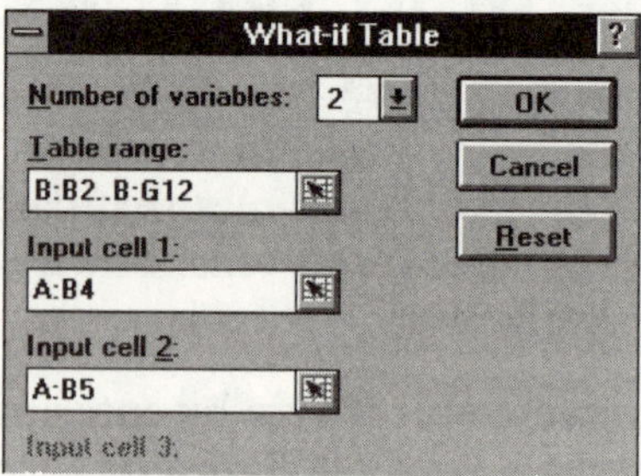

7. Choose 2 in the <u>N</u>umber of variables text box. The preselected range appears in the <u>T</u>able range text box. Enter **A:B4** as the reference for Input cell <u>1</u>, and **A:B5** as the reference for Input cell <u>2</u>. Click OK to confirm.

Figure 10.26 shows the resulting two-way what-if table. As you can see, 1-2-3 has calculated fifty different what-if scenarios in the conference

B	A	B	C	D	E	F	G
1			Prices				
2		+A:H4-(A:H11+A:H17)	$145.00	$170.00	$195.00	$220.00	$245.00
3	Attendance	45	($218.75)	$906.25	$2,031.25	$3,156.25	$4,281.25
4		55	$1,243.75	$2,618.75	$3,993.75	$5,368.75	$6,743.75
5		65	$2,706.25	$4,331.25	$5,956.25	$7,581.25	$9,206.25
6		75	$4,168.75	$6,043.75	$7,918.75	$9,793.75	$11,668.75
7		85	$5,631.25	$7,756.25	$9,881.25	$12,006.25	$14,131.25
8		95	$7,093.75	$9,468.75	$11,843.75	$14,218.75	$16,593.75
9		105	$8,556.25	$11,181.25	$13,806.25	$16,431.25	$19,056.25
10		115	$10,018.75	$12,893.75	$15,768.75	$18,643.75	$21,518.75
11		125	$11,481.25	$14,606.25	$17,731.25	$20,856.25	$23,981.25
12		135	$12,943.75	$16,318.75	$19,693.75	$23,068.75	$26,443.75
13							

worksheet. The profit figures resulting from these scenarios are displayed in range B:C3..B:G12.

Three-Way What-If Tables

A three-way what-if table is organized over a three-dimensional work-sheet range. Each worksheet in the range contains a column of entries for the first input cell and a row of entries for the second input cell, just like a two-way table. But instead of entering a formula in the upper-left corner of the table, you enter a value for the third input cell. Each worksheet in the three-dimensional range displays a different value in this cell. Rather than in the table range itself, you then specify the formula for the what-if table in the What-if Table dialog box.

For example, worksheets C, D, and E in Figure 10.27 have been prepared for a three-way what-if table. The purpose of this example is to generate profit scenarios by varying the values in three input cells:

- the attendance estimate (A:B4)

- the per-person admission price (A:B5)

- the cost of renting a conference room (A:H7)

Worksheet E

E	A	B	C	D	E	F	G	H
1		Room:						
2		$2,500.00	$145.00	$170.00	$195.00	$220.00	$245.00	
3	Attendance	65						
4		85						
5		105						
6		125						

Worksheet D

D	A	B	C	D	E	F	G	H
1		Room:						
2		$2,000.00	$145.00	$170.00	$195.00	$220.00	$245.00	
3	Attendance	65						
4		85						
5		105						
6		125						

Worksheet C

C	A	B	C	D	E	F	G	H
1		Room:						
2		$1,500.00	$145.00	$170.00	$195.00	$220.00	$245.00	
3	Attendance	65						
4		85						
5		105						
6		125						
7		145						

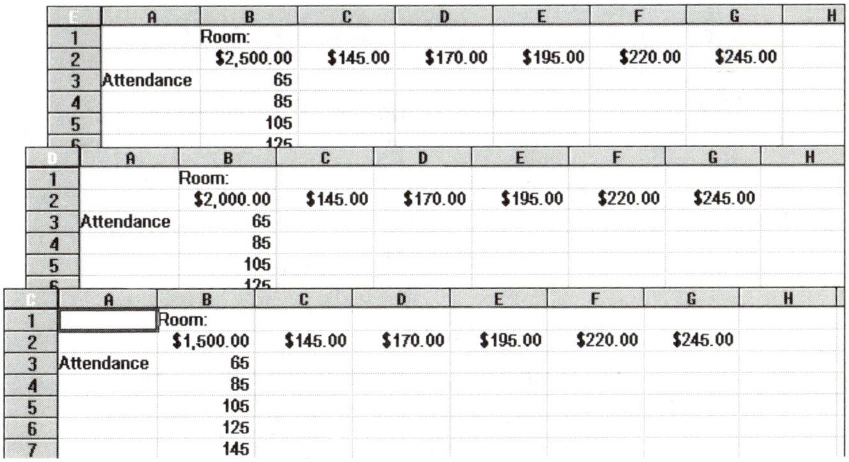

Range B3..B7 in each of the three worksheets displays the same column of attendance projections, and range C2..G2 displays the same row of conference prices. But cell B2 in each worksheet contains a different dollar amount for the conference room rental.

Here are the steps for creating this three-way what-if table in your own copy of the TABLES.WK4 worksheet:

1. With the cell pointer in worksheet B, choose Edit ➤ Insert and select the Sheet option. Enter **3** in the Quantity box and click OK.

2. Enter the labels and values into worksheet C, and format them as they appear in Figure 10.27. Then use the CopyToClipboard and PasteFromClipboard icons to copy the contents of worksheet C to worksheets D and E.

3. Enter a new value of **$2,000.00** in cell D:B2 and a new value of **$2,500.00** in cell E:B2.

4. Preselect the three-dimensional range C:B2..E:G7. To do so:

   a Select the two-dimensional range C:B2..C:G7 on worksheet C.

   b Hold down the Shift key and click on the folder tab for sheet E.

   c Click the PerspectiveView icon to view worksheets C, D, and E together in a single window. The selection looks like Figure 10.28.

5. Choose Range ➤ Analyze ➤ What-if Table. The What-if Table dialog box appears. It is shown in Figure 10.29.

6. Set Number of variables to **3**. The preselected three-dimensional range appears in the Table range text box.

7. Enter **A:H19** in the Formula cell text box. This is a reference to the profit formula in worksheet A.

8. Enter **A:B4** in the Input cell 1 box, **A:B5** in the Input cell 2 box, and **A:H7** in the Input cell 3 box. These are references to the attendance projection, the per-person admission price, and the conference room cost, respectively. When you finish all these entries, the Whatif Table 3-Way dialog box should look like the one in Figure 10.29. Click OK to confirm the entries in the dialog box.

FIGURE 10.28

Preselecting the three-dimensional range

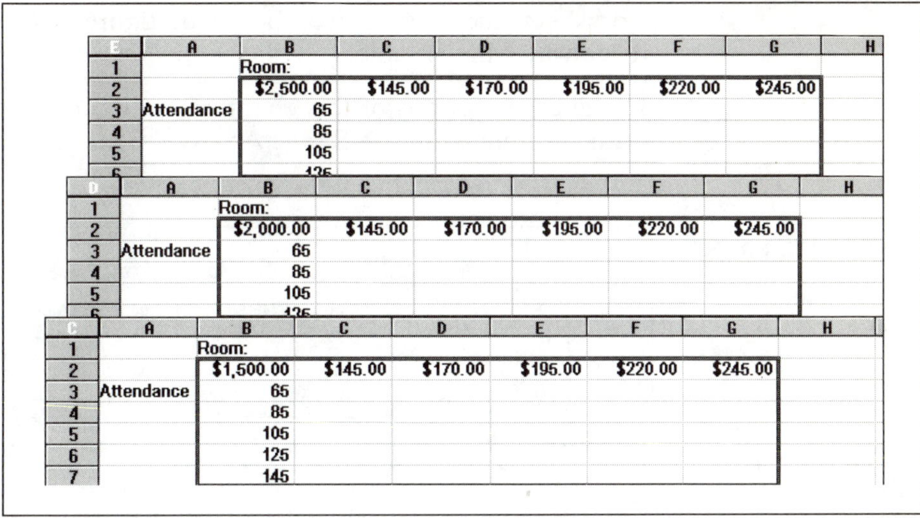

FIGURE 10.29

The What-if Table dialog box set for a three-way operation

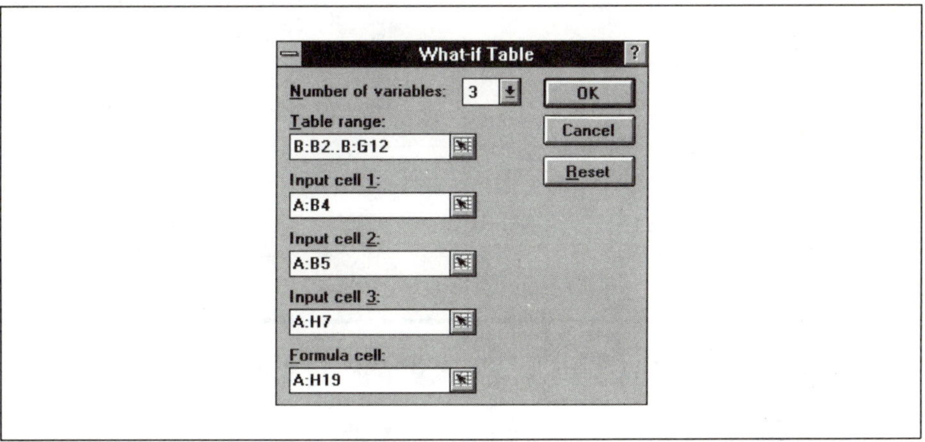

9. Back in the worksheet, preselect the three-dimensional range C:C3..E:G7 and click the Currency icon. Then press the Home key to position the cell pointer at C:A1.

10. Click the SaveFile icon to update the TABLES.WK4 file on disk.

Figure 10.30 shows the three-way what-if table that 1-2-3 creates. In this example, 1-2-3 has calculated 75 different scenarios for the conference worksheet and has copied the profit figure from each scenario to the three-way what-if table.

In the final sections of this chapter, you'll look at examples of two powerful commands in the Range Analyze menu: Backsolver and Solver.

FIGURE 10.30

A three-way what-if table

Sheet E:

	A	B	C	D	E	F	G	H
1		Room:						
2		$2,500.00	$145.00	$170.00	$195.00	$220.00	$245.00	
3	Attendance	65	$1,706.25	$3,331.25	$4,956.25	$6,581.25	$8,206.25	
4		85	$4,631.25	$6,756.25	$8,881.25	$11,006.25	$13,131.25	
5		105	$7,556.25	$10,181.25	$12,806.25	$15,431.25	$18,056.25	
6		125	$10,481.25	$13,606.25	$16,731.25	$19,856.25	$22,981.25	

Sheet D:

	A	B	C	D	E	F	G	H
1		Room:						
2		$2,000.00	$145.00	$170.00	$195.00	$220.00	$245.00	
3	Attendance	65	$2,206.25	$3,831.25	$5,456.25	$7,081.25	$8,706.25	
4		85	$5,131.25	$7,256.25	$9,381.25	$11,506.25	$13,631.25	
5		105	$8,056.25	$10,681.25	$13,306.25	$15,931.25	$18,556.25	
6		125	$10,981.25	$14,106.25	$17,231.25	$20,356.25	$23,481.25	

Sheet C:

	A	B	C	D	E	F	G	H
1		Room:						
2		$1,500.00	$145.00	$170.00	$195.00	$220.00	$245.00	
3	Attendance	65	$2,706.25	$4,331.25	$5,956.25	$7,581.25	$9,206.25	
4		85	$5,631.25	$7,756.25	$9,881.25	$12,006.25	$14,131.25	
5		105	$8,556.25	$11,181.25	$13,806.25	$16,431.25	$19,056.25	
6		125	$11,481.25	$14,606.25	$17,731.25	$20,856.25	$23,981.25	
7		145	$14,406.25	$18,031.25	$21,656.25	$25,281.25	$28,906.25	

Planning How to Meet Goals with the Backsolver Command

The Backsolver is a simple but valuable tool to use when you want to work backward through a worksheet scenario. When you have determined a bottom-line figure as your projection or goal, and you want to discover the input value necessary to achieve this goal, use the Backsolver command. For example, suppose you want to find the attendance level necessary to yield a total profit of $10,000 on the CONF2.WK4 worksheet. One way to find the correct attendance value would be to experiment with new entries in cell B4 until you find the value that gives a profit of $10,000. But this trial-and-error approach would be time-consuming, and the 1-2-3 Backsolver performs this task for you much more efficiently.

To use this command successfully, you supply three items of information:

- A worksheet cell with the target formula for the Backsolver operation

- The projected value that you want this formula to yield

- The cell with the input value that 1-2-3 will adjust in order to achieve the specified result from the target formula

In the following exercise, you'll experiment with the Backsolver on the CONF2.WK4 worksheet:

1. Close the TABLES.WK4 worksheet, and reopen the CONF2.WK4 worksheet from disk.

2. Choose <u>R</u>ange ➤ <u>A</u>nalyze ➤ <u>B</u>acksolver. The Backsolver dialog box appears.

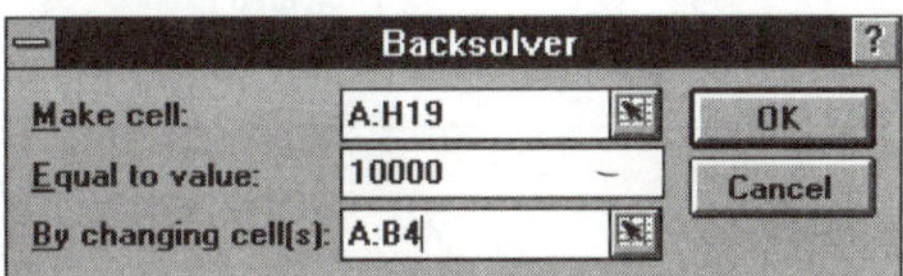

3. In the <u>M</u>ake cell text box, enter a reference to **A:H19**, the cell that contains the profit formula.

4. Enter **10000** in the <u>E</u>qual to value text box. This is the value that you want the profit formula to yield.

5. Enter a reference to cell **A:B4** in the <u>B</u>y changing cell text box. This cell contains the current attendance projection and is the cell that you want 1-2-3 to adjust in order to achieve the desired profit projection.

6. Click OK to perform the Backsolver operation.

7. Back on the worksheet, select cell B4, click the NumberFormat button in the status bar, and select Comma to display the contents of the cell as an integer if this is not already its format.

When you complete this operation, the worksheet looks like Figure 10.31. As you can see, an attendance level of about 86 people is necessary to achieve a profit of $10,000.

	A	B	C	D	E	F	G	H
1	Computing for Video Stores			Projected Revenues:				
2	Place:	St. Louis			Attendance			$16,692.99
3	Date:	15-Oct-92			Video Sales		$35.00	$1,498.09
4	Attendance:	86			Total Revenues			$18,191.08
5	Price:	$195.00						
6					Projected Expenses -- Fixed			
7					Conference room			$1,500.00
8					Video production			$1,000.00
9					Promotion			$3,500.00
10					Travel			$800.00
11					Total Fixed Expenses			$6,800.00
12								
13					Projected Expenses -- Variable by Attendance			
14					Conference materials		$8.25	$706.24
15					Coffee and pastries		$3.25	$278.22
16					Box lunch		$4.75	$406.62
17					Total Variable Expenses			$1,391.08
18								
19					Projected Profit			$10,000.00
20								

Producing Sophisticated Worksheet Scenarios with the Solver

The Solver command is designed to calculate meaningful variations in a worksheet in response to specific patterns that you formulate. This command is most often used on worksheets that contain interrelated formulas of some complexity. To set up a successful problem for the solver, you identify the following elements in your worksheet:

- *Adjustable cells.* Cells containing numeric values that you want the Solver to modify.

- *Constraint cells.* A range of cells containing logical formulas. You write these formulas to impose limits on the changes that the Solver can make in the adjustable values.

- *The optimal cell.* Optionally, a formula for which you want to find the optimum result within the constraints defined on your worksheet.

For example, consider Figure 10.32, a worksheet from one of the regional offices of Computing Conferences, Inc. To conduct its computer-training conferences, this office employs full-time instructors along with other instructors who work for the company on a short-term contractual basis. This worksheet analyzes the costs related to these two groups of workers. The goal of applying the Solver to this worksheet is to determine the most cost-effective mix of employee instructors and contract instructors.

FIGURE 10.32

Analyzing the mix of instructors

	A	B	C	D	E	F	G
1	Best Mix of Employee and Contract Instructors						
2					Per person	Total	
3	Employee Instructors			Salaries	$32,500.00	$130,000.00	
4		4		Benefits	$9,750.00	$39,000.00	
5				Support	$5,500.00	$22,000.00	
6							
7		Total annual hours of instruction:			2,496		
8		Annual teaching hours per employee:			360		
9		Hours remaining:			1,056		
10							
11	Contract Instructors			Hourly expense	$132.50	$139,920.00	
12		6		Support	$1,000.00	$6,000.00	
13				Supervision	$2,750.00	$16,500.00	
14							
15				Total Instructor Expense		$353,420.00	
16							
17	Constraints						
18		A minimum of 2 employees			1		
19		A maximum of 6 employees			1		
20		A total of 10 instructors			1		

At the present time, the regional office employ four full-time instructors and six contract instructors. Here is how the information about these two groups is organized in the worksheet:

CELLS	CONTENT
A2..F5	The costs related to the four full-time employees. Their individual salaries, benefits, and support costs appear in E3..E5. The totals for the four employees are calculated in F3..F5. Cell B4 displays the current number of employee instructors, 4.
B7..E9	Information about the number of hours of instruction. The total number of instruction hours planned for a given year is in E7. The number of hours assigned per year to each individual employee is in E8. A calculation of the number of remaining hours that must be assigned to contract instructors is in E9.
A11..F13	Information about the contract instructors. Cell B12 shows the current number of contract instructors, 6. The average hourly rate paid to these instructors appears in cell E11. The corresponding total cost of this hourly instruction for the year is in F11. Rows 12 and 13 show the support and supervision costs related to these contract instructors.
Row 15	The total costs for both groups of instructors is calculated in cell F15.

CELLS	CONTENT
A17..E20	The constraints that will apply to the Solver's calculations on this worksheet. There should be a minimum of two employee instructors, and a maximum of six. The combined number of employee and contract instructors is fixed at ten. The logical formulas expressing these constraints are in the range E18..E20; as you can see, all three formulas yield values of true for the current data.

Figure 10.33 displays the formulas that calculate the data and the constraints on this worksheet. In range F3..F5, the total employee expenses are calculated by multiplying individual expenses by the number of employees. Cell E9 computes the number of instruction hours assigned to contract instructors—the difference between the total annual hours and the total hours taught by employees. The range F11..F13 calculates the expenses related to contract instructors, and the @SUM function in cell F15 finds the total costs for all instructors. Finally, the constraint formulas appear in E18..E20.

Formulas behind the instructor-mix worksheet. Compare this worksheet to the one in Figure 10.32.

	A	B	C	D	E	F	G
1	Best Mix of Employee and Contract Instructors						
2					Per person	Total	
3	Employee Instructors			Salaries	$32,500.00	+$B$4*E3	
4		4		Benefits	$9,750.00	+$B$4*E4	
5				Support	$5,500.00	+$B$4*E5	
6							
7		Total annual hours of instruction:			2,496		
8		Annual teaching hours per employee:			360		
9		Hours remaining:			+E7-B4*E8		
10							
11	Contract Instructors			Hourly expense	$132.50	+E9*E11	
12		6		Support	$1,000.00	+$B$12*E12	
13				Supervision	$2,750.00	+$B$12*E13	
14							
15				Total Instructor Expense		@SUM(F3..F13)	
16							
17	Constraints						
18		A minimum of 2 employees			+B4>=2		
19		A maximum of 6 employees			+B4<=6		
20		A total of 10 instructors			+B4+B12=10		

Solver Definition dialog box When you choose Range ➤ Analyze ➤ Solver, a dialog box titled Solver Definition appears on the screen.

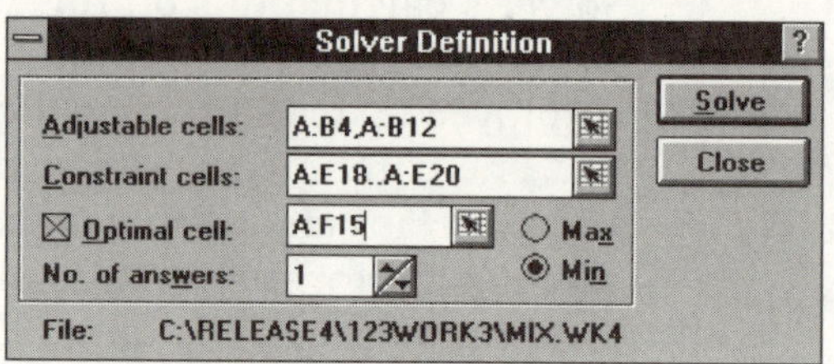

In this dialog box, you identify the worksheet locations of the adjustable values, the constraints, and the optimal formula in your Solver problem. For example, the correct references and ranges for the instructor-mix worksheet would be entered in the Solver Definition box like so:

Adjustable cells	B4, B12: the number of employee instructors and the number of contract instructors, respectively
Constraint cells	E18..E20: the constraint formulas
Optimal cell	F15: the location of the formula that calculates the total cost of instructors

The Solver can find the minimum or maximum value for the optimal formula. In this example, the option button labeled Min has been selected, because the goal of this analysis is to find the instructor mix that results in the least cost.

Once you have defined a problem by making the appropriate entries in the Solver Definition dialog box, you are ready to begin the analysis. To do so, click the Solve button in the Solver Definition dialog box.

Solver Progress box Depending on the number of adjustable cells and the complexity of the formulas on your worksheet, the Solver can take some time to complete its task. Accordingly, a box titled Solver Progress appears on the screen to keep you informed while the Solver completes the various steps of this procedure. First, this box displays the label "Analyzing problem…." Later, you see labels such as "Searching for answer #1."

The Solver Answer box When the analysis is finished, some important changes occur on the screen. The Solver actually makes changes in the worksheet locations that you designated as the adjustable cells. For example, the Solver has entered a new value of 6 in cell B4 as the optimal number of employee instructors, and a new value of 4 in cell B12 as the optimal number of contract instructors. The total expense associated with this optimal instructor mix is $346,020, as shown in cell F15. Moreover, a new dialog box named Solver Answer takes the place of the Solver Progress box.

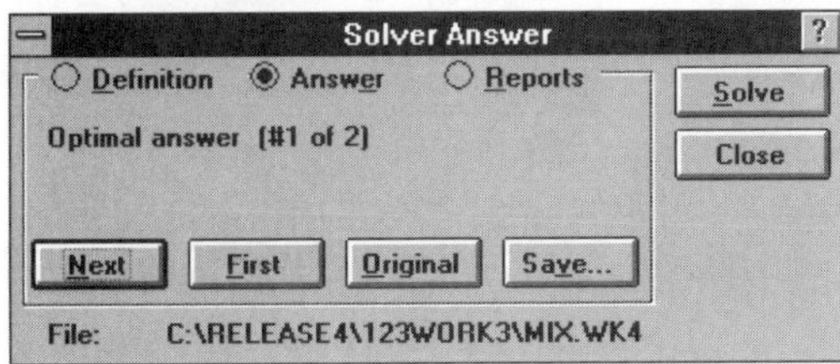

The Solver Answer dialog box contains an assortment of command buttons you can use to examine the results of the analysis. Click on the following buttons to obtain these different kinds of analyses:

BUTTON	USE
Next	Shows you the next-best answer the solver has found for your problem.
First	Takes you go back to the optimal answer.
Original	Displays the data values as they were displayed before the Solver analysis.

BUTTON	USE
<u>D</u>efinition	Returns you to the Solver Definition box.
<u>R</u>eports	Brings up the Solver Report dialog box. This dialog box offers a number of special-purpose reports from the analysis. The Solver generates each report individually; you request a report by selecting a report type from the dialog box and clicking OK. The reports are displayed in specially created worksheet files if you click on the <u>T</u>able button, or in dialog boxes on-screen if you select the <u>C</u>ell option.

<u>C</u>lose	Ends the Solver operation.

Summary

The Range ➤ Analyze menu offers a variety of commands and groups of commands for performing advanced mathematical calculations in organized worksheets. The Invert Matrix and Multiply Matrix commands are for solving simultaneous equations, represented as matrix tables in a worksheet. The Distribution command counts the worksheet entries that fit in numerical categories in a bin range. The Regression command analyzes the correlation between a dependent variable and one or more independent variables. The What-if Table commands produce one-, two-, and three-dimensional what-if tables representing multiple worksheet scenarios. The Parse command is essential for translating a column-oriented text file into the 1-2-3 worksheet format.

The Backsolver command finds the input value that produces a specified bottom-line result from a formula on your worksheet. Finally, in complex systems of worksheet formulas, the Solver facility can find data solutions that fit in specifically formulated constraints.

CHAPTER 11

Links between Files

**To create a link between the current worksheet
and a second worksheet,** 550

enter a formula with a file reference to the second worksheet.
The complete notation for a file reference contains the drive
name, directory path, file name, and extension of the second
worksheet, all enclosed in pairs of angle brackets (<< >>).
The file reference is followed by an ordinary range reference,
in the form <<*file*>>*range*. The purpose of the link is to copy
data from the second worksheet to the current worksheet, and
to update the current worksheet whenever the data changes
on the second worksheet.

**To use the Range Names list box to create
a reference to an open file,** 551

begin the formula entry with an appropriate operator, then
press the F3 function key to view the Range Names list box.
Double-click the name of a selected file reference to view the
range names defined in the file. Select the name that you want
to include in the reference. In response, 1-2-3 enters a complete file reference and range name into the formula.

**To update a destination file if the linked source
file is not currently open,** 557

open the destination file from disk, and choose Edit ➤ Links
➤ Update All.

**To create a worksheet that displays the sum
of data contained in other worksheets,**   559

choose File ➤ Open. In the File names list box, select one of
the worksheets from which you want to read data and click on
the Combine button. Select the Range option in the Read
frame, and enter the worksheet range from which you want to
read the data. In the Action box, choose the Add to values option and click OK. Repeat these steps for each file that you
want to add to the current worksheet. This command does not
establish links.

**To create a DDE link in which a 1-2-3 worksheet
is the source (or server) file,**   562

select a range of data in the worksheet and click the CopyTo-
Clipboard icon. Then move to the second application and select the location where you want to transfer the data. In the
second application, choose Edit ➤ Paste Link.

**To view the characteristics of a DDE link in which
a 1-2-3 worksheet is the client,**   567

choose Edit ➤ Links and select the name of the link you want
to view. The characteristics of the link are displayed in the Format information boxes.

MPORTANT categories of business data are often organized in different files on disk. Consider the following examples of how data is stored in a typical business:

- Accounting figures and calculations for a given year can be stored in twelve monthly worksheet files.

- Business information for a particular company might initially be collected in several regional files.

- Financial worksheets can appear in separate files for revenues, expenses, depreciations, deductions, and so on.

- Inventory data might be separated into files for product categories or inventory locations.

You can open several worksheet files at once in 1-2-3, so you could view the worksheet files listed above on the screen at once. Furthermore, 1-2-3 has a very important feature for integrating and coordinating the parts of a multifile application. You can establish *links* between worksheets. Once a link is in place, you can exchange information automatically between corresponding worksheet files.

How 1-2-3 Links Worksheets

Worksheet links are made by way of special formulas that include *file references* and range references. When 1-2-3 encounters such a formula, it transfers data to the current worksheet from the worksheet named in the file reference. The worksheet that contains the special linking formula is

called the *destination file*, and the worksheet named in the file reference—
the worksheet from which the data comes—is the called the *source file*.

Creating master worksheets In an application with many different
files, you can use links to create a *master worksheet* that consolidates the
information stored in several files. For example, the following are master
worksheets that present an overview of data stored in many different files:

- A year-end file with totals from twelve monthly files

- A corporate file with data from all regions

- A profit worksheet that calculates the bottom-line profit from data
  stored in various financial files

- A master inventory worksheet that consolidates information about
  several categories of products

To develop worksheets like these, you write formulas to link each source file
with a destination worksheet. Once a link is established, changes to data
stored in a source file are made automatically to the destination file. The
new data is transferred automatically to the cell in the destination file that
contains the link formula. In this chapter, you'll learn to write formulas to
integrate different parts of a multifile worksheet application.

1-2-3 and DDE The *dynamic data exchange* (DDE) feature in Windows
works exactly the same way. With programs that support DDE, you can
establish DDE links between documents in different Windows applications. A DDE link sends data from a source file to a destination file. Its
purpose is to update the destination file whenever a change is made to
the source file. Lotus 1-2-3 for Windows supports DDE in two directions: A 1-2-3 worksheet can be the source file or the destination file in
the link between two applications. Dynamic data exchange is discussed
in the second half of this chapter.

Preparing for the Exercises in this Chapter

For the exercises in this chapter, you'll work with files generated in the
four regions where Computing Conferences, Inc. operates. In this example, the central office has asked each regional manager to prepare a

monthly business summary worksheet. As you can see in Figure 11.1, each regional worksheet presents five items of information about regional business activity for the month of February, 1993.

FIGURE 11.1

Monthly business summaries from the four regions

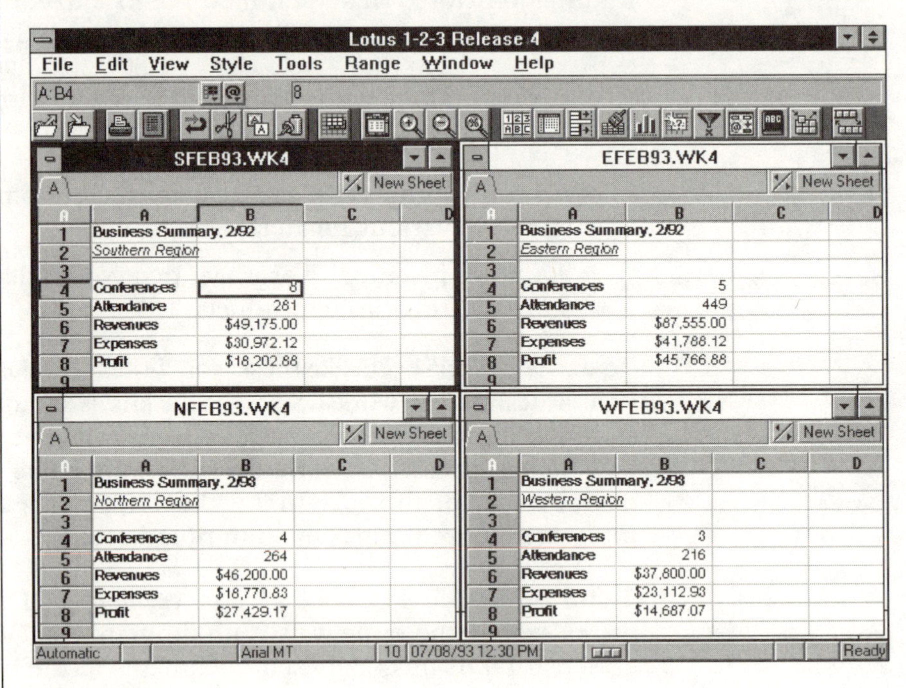

DATA CATEGORY	RECORDS
Conferences	The number of computer-training conferences conducted in the region
Attendance	The total number of people who attended the conferences
Revenues	The dollar revenues from the conferences
Expenses	The total expenses associated with conducting the conferences

DATA CATEGORY	**RECORDS**
Profit	The total profit for the month

The sample files in Figure 11.1 have been sized and positioned so you can see all four of them at once. To prepare for your work in this chapter, begin by creating copies of each file on your own computer. Here is an outline of the steps to follow:

1. If necessary, select File ➤ New to open a new worksheet window.

2. Enter the appropriate labels in column A of the new worksheet, and apply boldface, italic, and underlining styles as shown in Figure 11.1.

3. Preselect range A4..A8 and choose Range ➤ Name. Click Use Labels to assign these five labels as range names to the adjacent cells in column B.

4. Enter the first four numeric data items in column B:

   - the number of conferences
   - the attendance
   - the revenue amount
   - the expenses

5. Enter the formula **+REVENUES-EXPENSES** in cell B8. This calculates the region's total profit for the month.

6. Apply the currency format to range B6..B8. Increase the widths of columns A and B so that the labels and values in range A4..B8 can be viewed within their respective cells.

7. Choose File ➤ Save As and save the file under its appropriate name: NFEB93.WK4, SFEB93.WK4, WFEB93.WK4, and EFEB93.WK4 for the Northern, Southern, Western, and Eastern regions, respectively.

8. Resize and reposition each worksheet window so that you can view all four files at once. Use Window ➤ Tile.

Your screen should look like Figure 11.1. With the sample files displayed on-screen, you are ready to begin experimenting with 1-2-3 worksheet links.

Creating Links between Worksheets

To create links between worksheets, your first step is to enter the file and range references in the destination worksheet. This part of the chapter shows you how to do that, how to build a master worksheet, and how to update the destination worksheet when changes are made to source worksheets.

Entering the File and Range References

A reference to a cell or range on another worksheet consists of two parts: a file reference and a range reference. If the source file is currently open, all you have to do to make the file reference is enclose the name of the file in two pairs of angle brackets, like so:

```
<<file>>
```

The range appears immediately after the file reference:

```
<<file>>range
```

For example, the following formula copies the entry from cell A:A1 in an open file named SUMMARY:

```
+<<SUMMARY>>A:A1
```

When you enter this formula in a cell in the current worksheet, the contents of cell A1 in the SUMMARY worksheet appear in the destination cell.

Referencing an unsaved worksheet   In the special case of an unsaved worksheet named Untitled, the file reference is written by entering two pairs of angle brackets with no name between them. For example, here is a reference to cell A1 in the Untitled worksheet:

```
+<<>>A:A1
```

Unlike earlier versions of 1-2-3, you do not have to specify a range when referencing a single cell. For example, you can simple write +<<>>A:A1 to reference cell A:A1 in an Untitled worksheet, not +<<>>A:A1..A:A1.

Referencing an unopened worksheet If the source worksheet from which you want to get data is saved on disk but not currently open, include a complete path name and file name, including the extension, in the reference. For example, the following formula copies an entry from cell A1 of SUMMARY.WK4, a file stored in the \1-2-3R4W directory on drive D:

<<D:\1-2-3R4W\SUMMARY.WK4>>A:A1 is what follows

    +<<D:\1-2-3R4W\SUMMARY.WK4>>A:A1

Pointing to References with the Mouse and Keyboard

To enter a reference to an unopened file, you must type the reference directly from the keyboard. But if the source file is open, you can use mouse or keyboard pointing techniques to create the reference.

With the mouse The mouse pointing technique is the simplest. Once you have arranged your worksheets so that the source and destination files are both in view,

1. Select a cell on the destination worksheet.

2. Begin your formula with an operator (a plus sign, for example).

3. Click the mouse on the target location of the source worksheet. Lotus immediately provides a complete file reference and range reference.

4. Press ↵ to enter this reference in the current cell in the destination worksheet.

With the keyboard The keyboard pointing technique is more detailed:

1. Enter an operator such as a plus sign to begin the formula.

2. Press Ctrl-End to toggle 1-2-3 into Point mode. The word *Point* appears in the far right panel of the status bar.

Step 2 is unnecessary if the current destination file contains only one worksheet. However, if you are working with a multiple worksheet file, you must be in Point mode to point to another file.

3. Press Ctrl-PgUp to move the cell pointer to the next open file, or Ctrl-PgDn to point to the previous open file.

4. When the cell pointer is in the source file, use the arrow keys to point to the correct location in the file.

5. Continue writing your formula by entering another operator, such as a plus sign, or press ↵ to complete the formula entry.

Referencing a Named Range

If the target cell has been given a range name in the source file, you can use the F3 key to select a range name while you are building a formula. Pressing F3 is probably the simplest way to establish a link between two open files. After you press F3, you just choose a name from the Range Names list. For the regional summary files you created for this chapter, you defined range names. You can press F3 to build formulas, and that is what you will do in the upcoming exercise.

Building an Integrated Master Worksheet

Your goal in this exercise is to create a new summary worksheet with numeric totals from the four regional files. Here are the steps:

1. Preselect range A1..A8 in any one of the four files, and then click the CopyToClipboard icon.

2. Click the Minimize button on each worksheet in turn to reduce the files to icon size in the 1-2-3 window.

3. Choose File ➤ New to create a new worksheet file.

4. With the cell pointer at A:A1, click the PasteFromClipboard icon to paste the labels into column A of the new worksheet.

5. Enter the new label **Totals for Four Regions** in cell A2.

6. Resize the new worksheet to approximately the same dimensions as the other four worksheets, and reposition the worksheet near the center of the screen. Increase the widths of columns A and B.

7. Choose File ➤ Save As, and save the file to disk as TOTFEB93.WK4.

8. Select cell B4.

9. Type **+**, and press F3 to view the Range Names list. The list contains file references to the other four open worksheet files.

10. In the list box, double-click the reference to <<EFEB93.WK4>>.

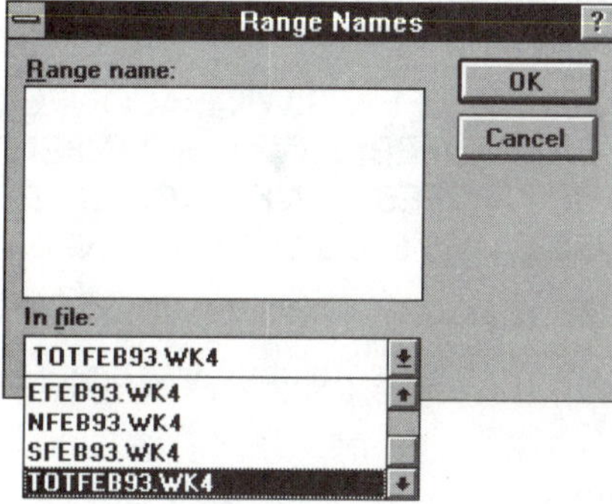

When you do so, the Range Names list box displays a list of the range names defined in this file.

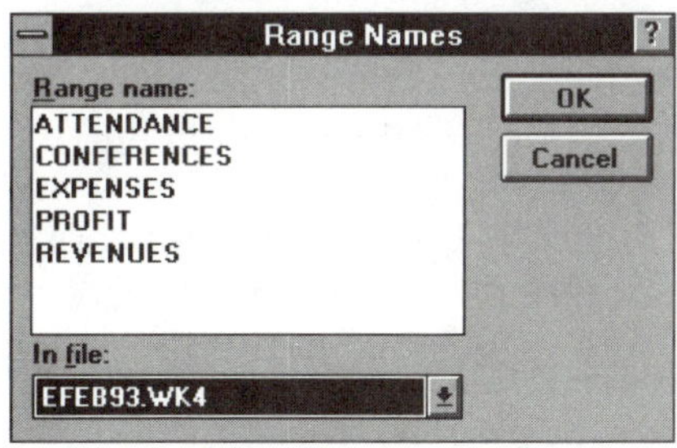

11. Select the range name CONFERENCES. A complete reference to the cell appears as follows:

+<<D:\1-2-3R4W\EFEB93.WK4>>CONFERENCES

To view the whole name, you can select the text box and press the → key repeatedly to scroll to the right. (In this example, the four files are saved in the \1-2-3R4W directory on drive D. The file references in your formula may be different, depending on the path location in which you have saved your files.)

12. Press ↵ to accept this as the first reference in your formula.

13. Repeat steps 10 and 11 three times, each time selecting a different file reference from the Range Names list box: first <<NFEB93.WK4>>, then <<SFEB93.WK4>>, and finally <<WFEB93.WK4>>.

When you are finished with these steps, the following formula appears in the contents box:

```
+<<D:\1-2-3R4W\EFEB93.WK4>>CONFERENCES+
<<D:\1-2-3R4W\NFEB93.WK4>>CONFERENCES+
<<D:\1-2-3R4W\SFEB93.WK4>>CONFERENCES+
<<D:\1-2-3R4W\WFEB93.WK4>>CONFERENCES
```

This formula finds the sum of the values stored in the cells named CONFERENCES in the four source worksheets.

TIP

You don't have to include the .WK4 file name extension in the << >> declaration. Leaving the file extension out makes it easier to read long formulas.

14. Press ↵ to complete the formula entry.

The TOTFEB93.WK4 worksheet appears as shown in Figure 11.2. As you can see, a total of 20 conferences were conducted in the four regions during the month of February, 1993.

15. Select B4..B8 and click the CopyDown SmartIcon.

Lotus copies the formula from cell B4, down to the cells in the range B5..B8. Because the original formula contains relative references to cells in the source worksheets, the references in the new copied formulas are automatically adjusted according to their positions in the column. For example, here

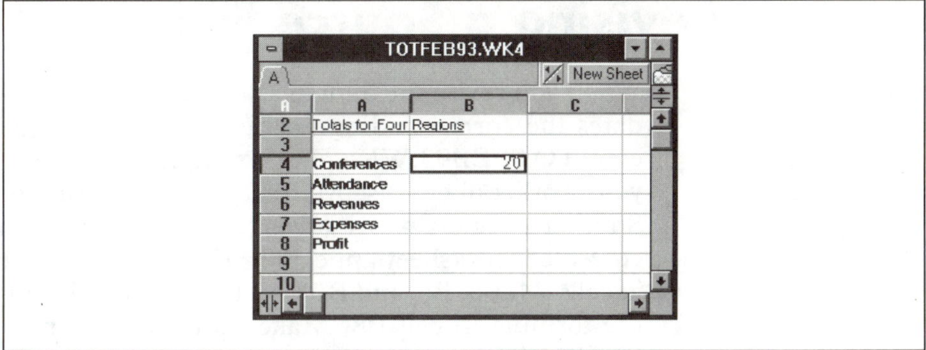

is the formula that 1-2-3 copies into cell B8 to calculate the total profit
from the four regional files:

```
+<<D:\1-2-3R4W\EFEB93.WK4>>PROFIT
+<<D:\1-2-3R4W\WFEB93.WK4>>PROFIT
+<<D:\1-2-3R4W\SFEB93.WK4>>PROFIT
+<<D:\1-2-3R4W\NFEB93.WK4>>PROFIT
```

16. Select cell B5 and give this cell the Comma number format. Then
preselect range B6..B8 and give these numbers the Currency format.

17. Click the SaveFile icon to save your work to disk.

When you complete these steps, the TOTFEB93.WK4 worksheet looks
like Figure 11.3. A quick look back at Figure 11.1 confirms that 1-2-3 has
successfully computed the data in the four source worksheets, including
the total number of conferences, total attendance, and the total revenues,
expenses, and profit.

A	A	B	C
1	Business Summary, 2/93		
2	Totals for Four Regions		
3			
4	Conferences	20	
5	Attendance	1,513	
6	Revenues	$302,955.00	
7	Expenses	$148,993.21	
8	Profit	$153,961.79	
9			
10			

Revising a Source File

When you revise the data in a source worksheet, 1-2-3 automatically updates the corresponding formulas in the destination worksheet, in this case TOTFEB93.WK4. For example, suppose you reach this point in your work, only to discover that one of the conferences conducted in the Southern region was inadvertently omitted from SFEB93.WK4. The corrected worksheet appears in Figure 11.4. As you can see, the entries in cells B4, B5, B6, and B7 have been changed, and 1-2-3 has recalculated the formula in cell B8. Make these changes now in your own copy of SFEB93.WK4:

1. Double-click the SFEB93.WK4 icon to view it again on-screen.

2. Make the four new entries in range B4..B7, as shown in Figure 11.4. Notice that the value in B8 is recalculated.

3. Click the SaveFile icon to save the new version of the file to disk.

4. Click the Minimize button on the SFEB93.WK4 window to reduce the file once again to icon size.

FIGURE 11.4

When you revise a source worksheet, the destination worksheet will be updated automatically.

A	A	B	C
1	Business Summary, 2/92		
2	Southern Region		
3			
4	Conferences	4	
5	Attendance	281	
6	Revenues	$49,175.00	
7	Expenses	$30,972.12	
8	Profit	$18,202.88	
9			

Now look at what has happened to TOTFEB93.WK4, shown in Figure 11.5. All the values in range B4..B8 have been revised to take account of changes to the source file. This demonstrates the advantage of linked worksheets: the destination file is updated when you revise the data in one or more source files.

To prepare for the next exercise, save the current version of TOTFEB93.WK4 and close the file. Also close all the source files except the worksheet for the Northern region, NFEB93.WK4.

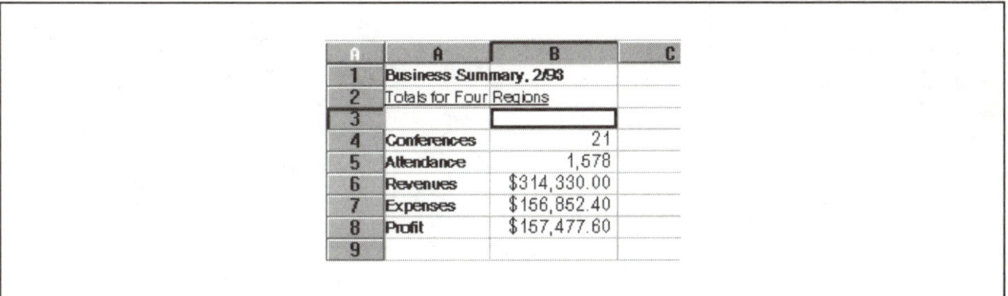

A	A	B	C
1	Business Summary, 2/93		
2	Totals for Four Regions		
3			
4	Conferences	21	
5	Attendance	1,578	
6	Revenues	$314,330.00	
7	Expenses	$156,852.40	
8	Profit	$157,477.60	
9			

Making Source File Revisions Appear on the Destination File

Sometimes you will make revisions to a source worksheet while the linked destination worksheet is not open. Likewise, you will sometimes open a destination worksheet without first opening the source worksheets. In either case, the links are still in place and the destination worksheet will be updated, but not automatically. To make sure that the destination file accurately reflects the data in the source files, you use the Edit ➤ Links command.

In the following exercise, you'll make a single revision to NFEB93.WK4, and then you'll close the file. Upon reopening TOTFEB93.WK4, you'll experiment with commands in the Links dialog box.

1. Double-click the icon representing NFEB93.WK4 to view the open worksheet file.

2. Enter the new value **56200** in cell B6. The entry is displayed in the currency format, as $56,200.00. In addition, 1-2-3 recalculates the profit formula in cell B8. The new version of the worksheet appears in Figure 11.6.

3. Click the SaveFile icon to update this file to disk, and then close the file.

4. Open TOTFEB93.WK4 from disk. Notice that the file is unchanged and exactly as it was in Figure 11.5. The worksheet has not yet accounted for the latest changes you made in NFEB93.WK4.

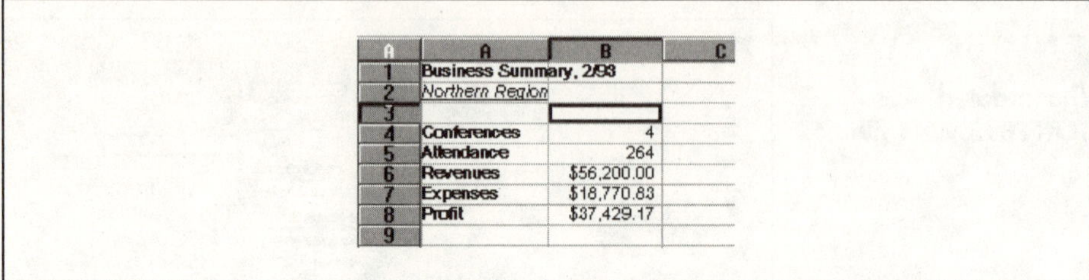

5. Choose Edit ➤ Links. The Links dialog box appears, as in Figure 11.7.

6. Change Link Type to File Links and choose Update All.

Lotus rereads the source files on disk and makes the revisions necessary in the current destination file. The TOTFEB93.WK4 file now appears as in Figure 11.8.

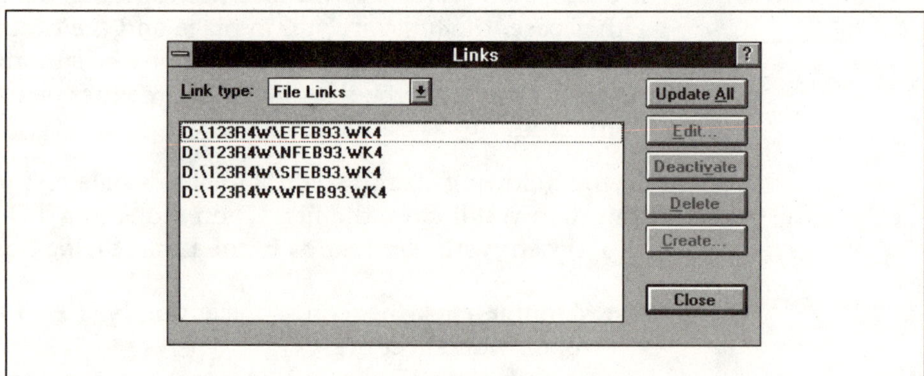

7. Move the cell pointer to C1, and then click the SaveFile icon to save the new version of this file to disk.

Now you have seen what you can do by creating links between sources files and a master destination file. TOTFEB93.WK4 integrates data from the four regional source files and can be updated whenever the data in one of the source files changes. Another way to create a totals worksheet that is similar *in appearance* is to use the File ➤ Open ➤ Combine command.

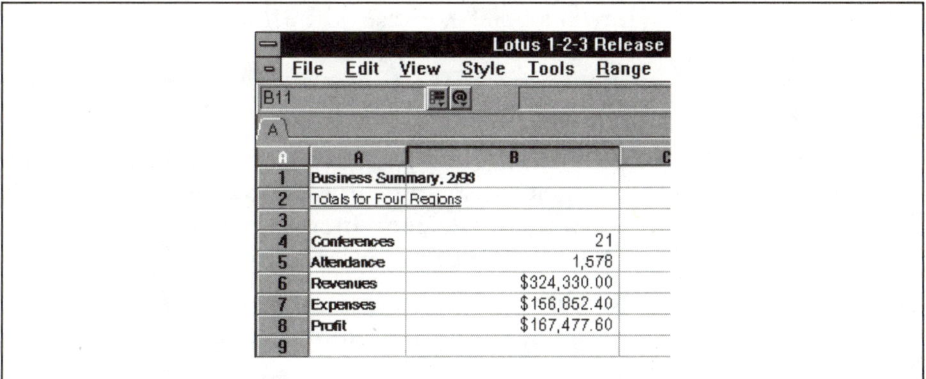

Adding Data from Different Worksheets without Using Links

The File ➤ Open ➤ Combine command reads data from a worksheet file on disk and incorporates the data in the current worksheet. Instead of creating a link between the current file and the file on disk, this command merely transfers data and enters it on the current worksheet. You used File ➤ Open ➤ Combine in Chapter 10 when you copied part of the CONF.WK4 worksheet to a new file.

Combine can also *add* data to values in specific cells of the current worksheet. Adding data this way requires careful planning to make sure the data values from disk are added in the right places. But the Combine option is useful when you want to create a totals worksheet without establishing links between source and destination worksheets.

NOTE

The Combine command does not link files. Changes made to one file that has been combined with another are not updated to the new, combined file.

Here is a brief exercise with this command:

1. On the TOTFEB93.WK4 file, preselect range A1..A8, and click the CopyToClipboard icon. Then close TOTFEB93.WK4.

2. With the cell pointer located in A1 of the Untitled worksheet, click the PasteFromClipboard icon to copy the labels to column A of the worksheet. Increase the widths of columns A and B. Then move the cell pointer to B4.

3. Choose File ➤ Open. Using the Drives, Directories, and File name boxes, find and select the file EFEB93.WK4.

4. Click on the Combine button. The Combine 1-2-3 dialog box appears, as in Figure 11.9.

5. Click the Replace values button in the dialog box.

6. Click the Range button in the Read frame and enter the range **B4..B8** in the Range text box. The dialog box now appears as shown in Figure 11.9. Click OK to complete the first Combine From operation.

7. Repeat steps 3 through 6 for the remaining three source files, NFEB93.WK4, SFEB93.WK4, and WFEB93.WK4. But this time choose Add to values rather than Replace values. Each operation adds the data from one of these files to the current worksheet.

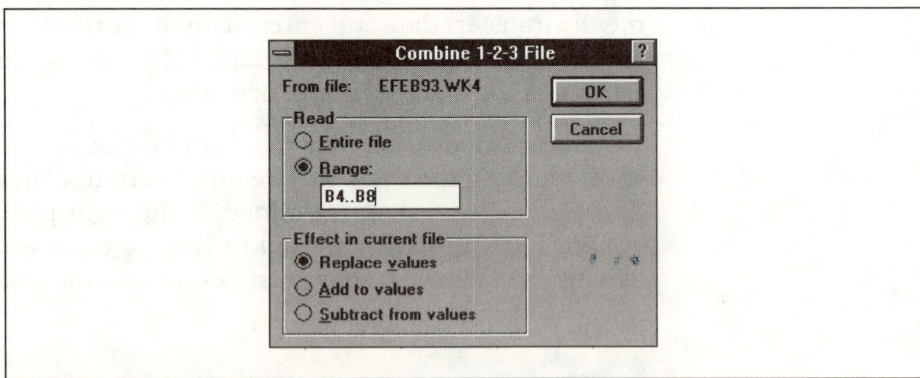

When you are finished, the data in the worksheet is the same as the data in Figure 11.8. However, the difference between this worksheet and TOTFEB93.WK4 is essential: the original worksheet contains formulas that link it to the source worksheets, but this new worksheet contains only data, with no formulas and no links.

Close this worksheet without saving it.

Creating Links between Documents in Different Applications

In the Windows environment, it is easy to *copy* data values from 1-2-3 worksheets to documents in other applications. The Clipboard is the key to this procedure:

1. Select a range of data in a 1-2-3 worksheet.

2. Choose Edit ➤ Copy to copy the data to the Clipboard.

3. Activate the other Windows application, and move in that application to the place where you want to copy the data.

4. Choose Edit ➤ Paste to insert the data from the Clipboard in the second application.

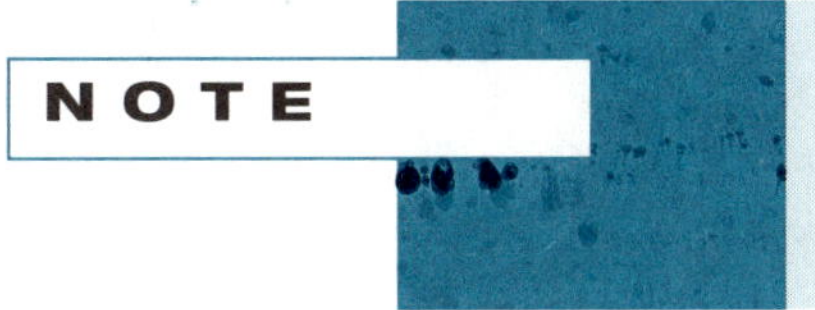

NOTE

The Paste command simply makes a copy of the data itself in the new location. It does not create a link of any kind.

A more powerful command, available in 1-2-3 and in many other Windows applications, is Paste Link. This command uses the dynamic data exchange (DDE) facility to establish a link between the two documents, one created in one application and the other created in another.

The server and the client In a DDE link, the source document is known as the *server* and the destination document is known as the *client*.

- The server document is located in the application where you choose Edit ➤ Copy.

- The client document is located in the new application where you choose Edit ➤ Paste Link to insert the copy and create the link.

While a DDE link is active in *automatic update* mode, data changes that are made to the server document are automatically sent to the client document.

Linking Data from 1-2-3 with another Application

Figure 11.10 shows the 1-2-3 application alongside Microsoft Word for Windows, a popular Windows word-processing program. The two application

FIGURE 11.10

Working with two applications in Windows

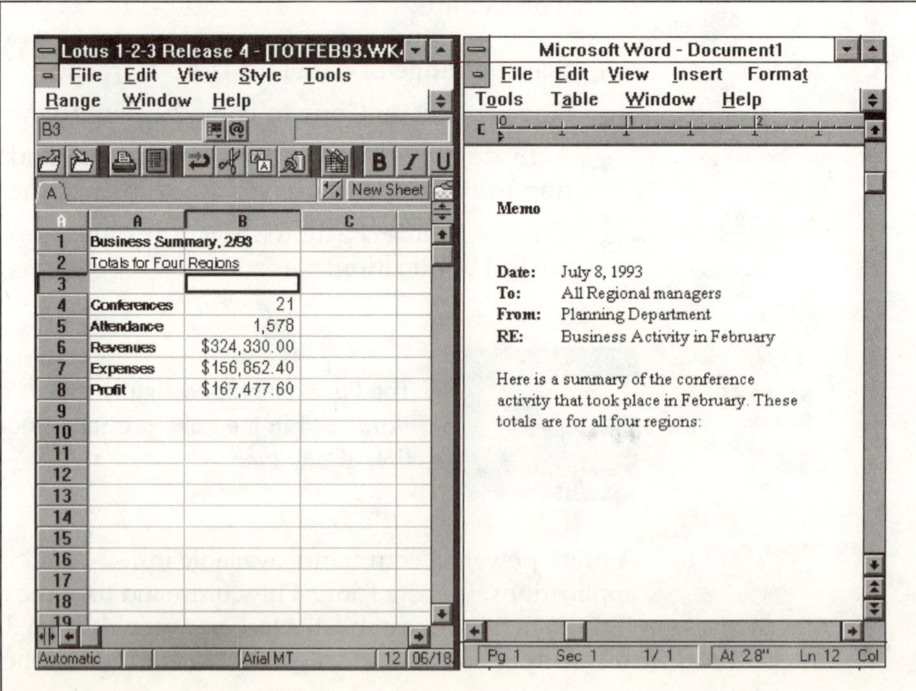

windows have been resized so that each occupies about half the screen. In the 1-2-3 window, you can see the TOTFEB93.WK4 worksheet. In the Word document window, you see the beginning of a memo to the regional managers of Computing Conferences, Inc.

Imagine that you are writing this memo and you have reached the point where you want to insert the data from the TOTFEB93.WK4 worksheet in the word-processed document. Because you anticipate changes in the worksheet data, you want to establish a DDE link between the worksheet and the document. Here are the steps to take:

1. Activate the worksheet window and preselect range A4..B8.

2. From the 1-2-3 main menu, choose <u>E</u>dit ➤ <u>C</u>opy, or simply click the CopyToClipboard icon.

3. Activate the Word document window and move the cursor to the end of the memo text.

4. From the Word main menu, choose <u>E</u>dit ➤ Paste <u>S</u>pecial. Word for Windows brings up the Paste Special dialog box.

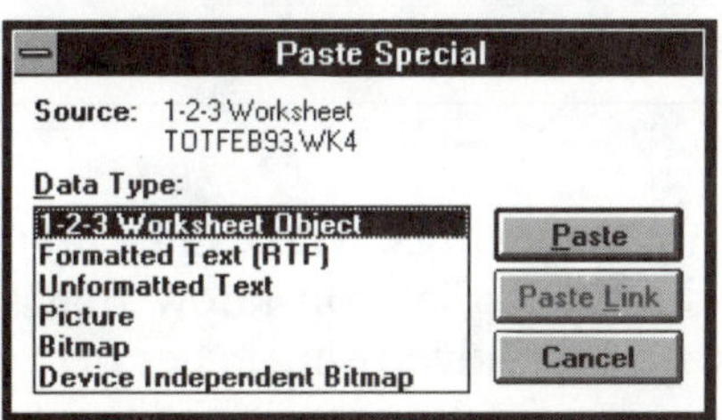

5. Change the entry in the <u>D</u>ata Type list box to 1-2-3 Worksheet Object.

6. Click on the Paste <u>L</u>ink button, rather than the <u>P</u>aste button, so that the link will be established in automatic update mode.

The data from the 1-2-3 worksheet appears as a table at the bottom of the Word document. (You can use the Table ➤ Column Width command in Word for Windows to change the column width and display the table more evenly.)

7. Reactivate the 1-2-3 window. At this point, the Windows desktop looks like Figure 11.11.

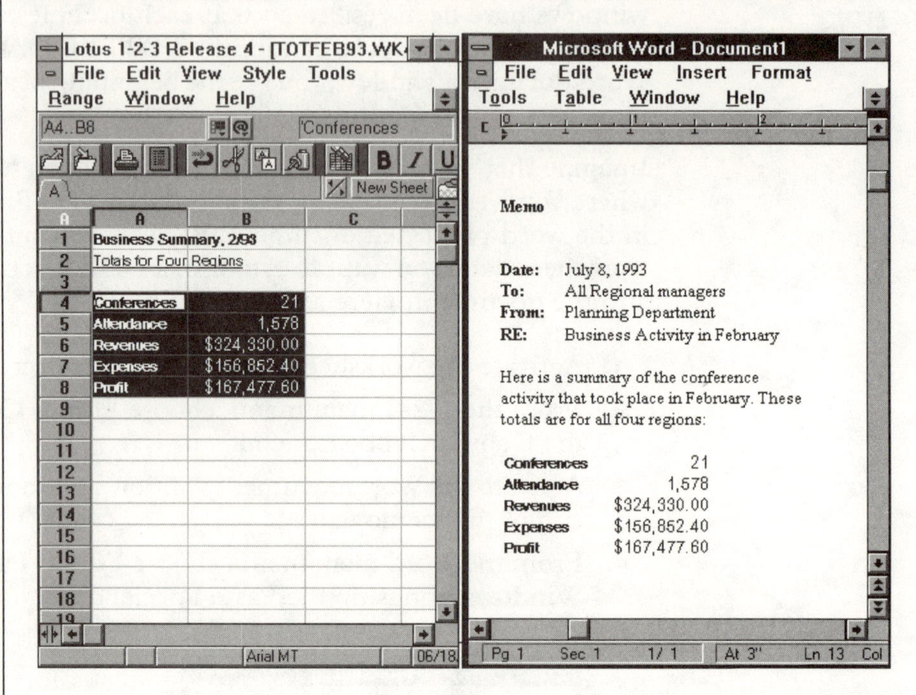

Suddenly your phone rings. Mary Garcia, the manager of the Western region, is on the line to let you know that she inadvertently omitted a $7000 expense item for advertising in her February worksheet. No problem, you tell her, you can fix the error right away.

8. Open the WFEB93.WK4 worksheet in the 1-2-3 window and select cell B7. As Figure 11.12 shows, the expense amount in the cell is $65,321.33.

9. Enter the revised figure into the cell, **$72,321.33**.

Several changes take place on the screen almost at once. First, a new profit figure is calculated in cell B8 of WFEB93.WK4. Then the new expense and profit figures are passed to the TOTFEB93.WK4 worksheet, which is linked to WFEB93.WK4 through formulas. Finally, the newly revised data is automatically sent to the memo document in Word, thanks to the DDE link between the document and the TOTFEB93.WK4 worksheet. The Windows desktop now appears as shown in Figure 11.13.

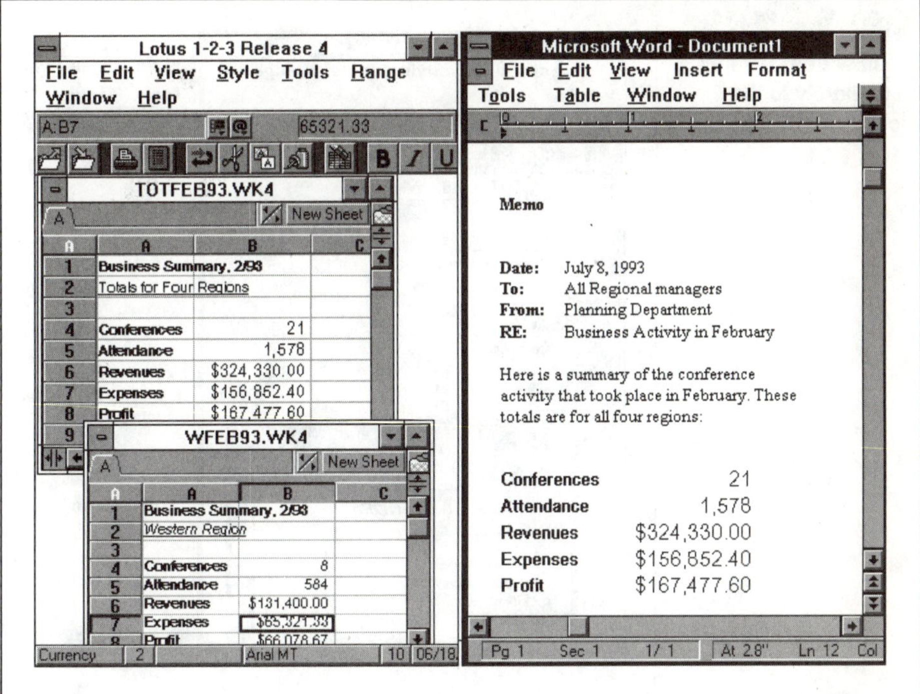

10. Save the revised worksheets in the 1-2-3 window. Then save and
print the memo document in the Word window.

WARNING

A DDE link is saved to disk with a document, but
the link is active only when both the source and
destination documents are open in the Windows
desktop.

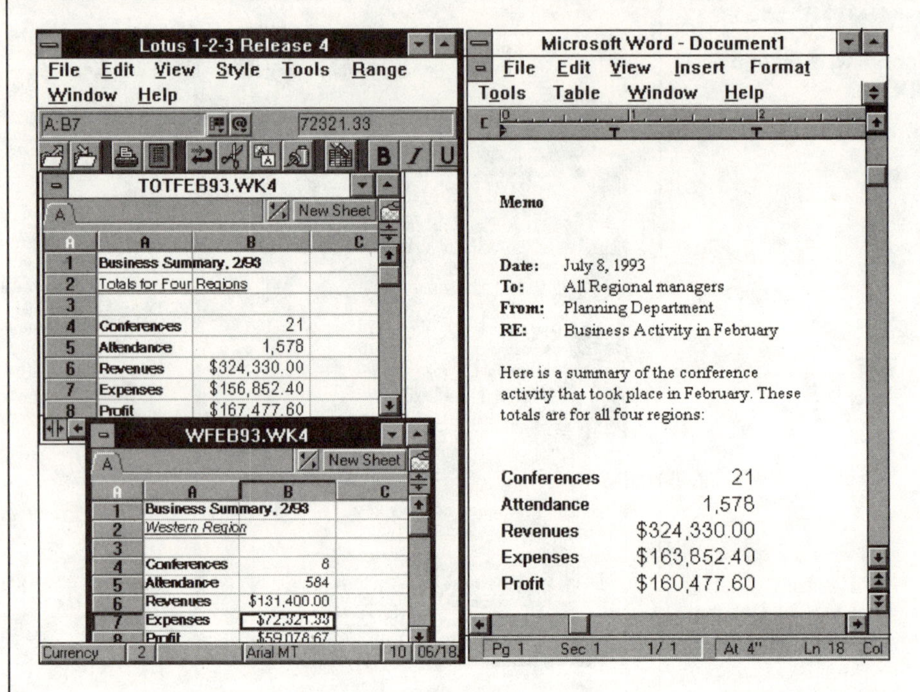

Linking Data from another Application with 1-2-3

In the previous example, the 1-2-3 worksheet was the source of the data in the DDE link. However, a 1-2-3 worksheet can also act as the client, or the destination, in the link. In other words, you can send and link data in another Windows application to a 1-2-3 worksheet. The steps for establishing the link are essentially the same, but reversed:

1. In the other application, select the data that you want to transfer to the 1-2-3 worksheet, and then choose Edit ➤ Copy to copy the data to the Clipboard.

2. Activate 1-2-3, and open the worksheet that is to be the client in the link.

3. Preselect the entire worksheet range to which you want to copy the data.

4. Choose Edit ➤ Links. The Links dialog box appears, as in Figure 11.14.

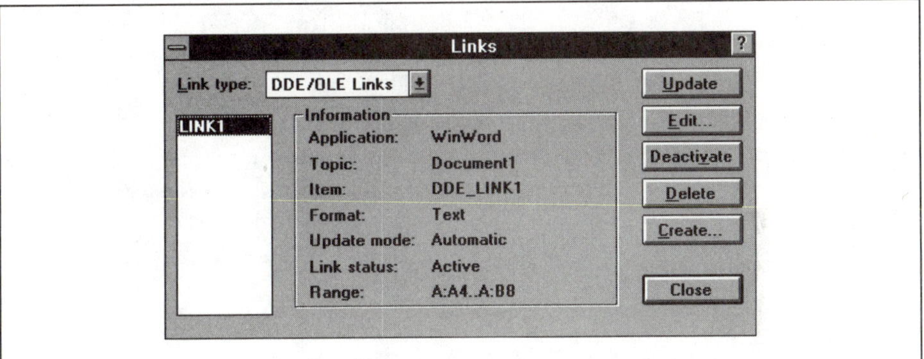

FIGURE 11.14

The Links dialog box for creating links with 1-2-3 as the client

5. Leave the Link Type set to DDE/OLE Links, and click on the Create button.

6. In the Create Link dialog box, the source application and the item you are linking are already selected, so just click on OK to accept the new link and return to the Links dialog box.

7. In the Links dialog box, click on OK to close the dialog and execute the link.

As a result of these steps, the data is copied from the source document, and a link is established in which the 1-2-3 worksheet is the client.

Modifying and Updating a Link

When 1-2-3 is the client, you can use Edit ➤ Links to create, modify, and update the link. For example, Figure 11.15 shows the Edit Link dialog box. that appears when you select Edit➤ Link ➤ Edit.It shows a description of an active link between a Microsoft Word document and the current 1-2-3 worksheet. The selected link has a default name of LINK1. In the Information

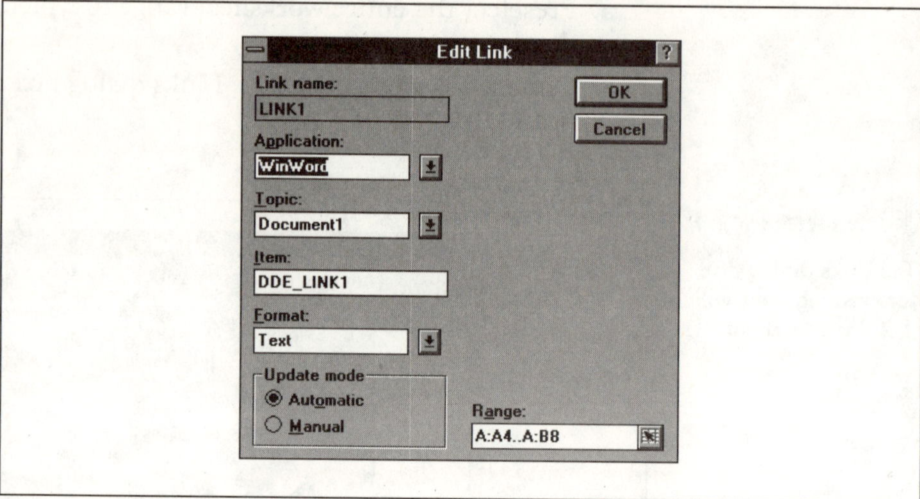

frame, information boxes describe the characteristics of the link. As you can see, the server in a DDE link is described by three elements:

SCROLL BOX	INFORMATION
Application	The name of the Windows program that is supplying the data.
Topic	The name of the document or worksheet that is the source of the data.
Item	The exact location of the target data in the source document or worksheet.

You can use the command buttons on the right side of the Links dialog box (see Figure 11.14) to perform actions related to this link or to modify the characteristics of the link.

BUTTON	USE
Update	Updates the link.
Edit	Brings up the Edit link dialog box for changing the attributes of a link.

BUTTON	USE
Deactivate	Switches the link into an inactive mode while retaining the link definition.
Delete	Removes the link between the two Windows documents and deletes the link definition altogether.
Create	Creates a link.

Switching to Manual Updates for Linked Documents

The Update button in the Links dialog box forces an update on a DDE link that is in *manual update* mode. You might sometimes prefer to work in this mode if you need to make many changes in the source document before updating the destination worksheet in 1-2-3. To switch a link to the manual update mode, follow these steps:

1. Choose Edit ➤ Links. In the Links dialog box (see Figure 11.14), select the name of the link that you want to change.

2. Click the Edit button. The Edit Links dialog box appears on the screen.

The Edit Link dialog box　This dialog box contains text boxes and option buttons representing the link characteristics that you can modify.

3. Click the Manual button in the Update mode frame. Click OK in the Edit Link dialog box.

4. Click Cancel to close the Edit Link dialog box.

Now the destination worksheet is no longer updated automatically in response to changes to the source document.

You don't have to select a target link to perform an update. Just click on the All Update button.

5. To force an update of the destination worksheet, choose Edit ➤ Links, select the name of the target link, and click the Update button. Click Close to close the dialog box.

Summary

The purpose of establishing a link between two files is to exchange data between the files and to ensure that the destination file is updated when a change is made to the source file.

A link between two worksheets is expressed as a formula that includes both a file reference and a range reference. The worksheet containing the formula is the destination file, and the worksheet named in the file reference is the source file. If the source and destination worksheets are both open, 1-2-3 automatically updates the destination file to account for changes in the source file. However, if you open the destination file when the source file is closed, you must choose Edit ➤ Links ➤ Update All to update the destination file.

Thanks to the Windows feature known as dynamic data exchange (DDE), you can also establish links between documents that are created in different Windows applications. To create such a link, choose Edit ➤ Copy to copy data from the source document to the Clipboard. Then move to the destination document and choose Edit ➤ Paste Link from the main menu of the second application. For example, you can use DDE to create a link between a source worksheet and a destination document in a word-processing program. While the link is active, the word-processed document is updated whenever you make changes in the worksheet data. When a 1-2-3 worksheet is the destination file in a DDE link, you use Edit ➤ Links to view or modify the characteristics of the link.

12

Macro

Programming

To view a help topic for any macro command,   **576**

type an open brace ({) into a worksheet cell and press F3. In the Macro Keywords dialog box, select a keyword in the list box and then press F1; the Macro Help window appears. Click on Search and enter any command name to view the corresponding help topic.

To create a custom menu for use in a macro performance,   **577**

enter a menu definition in a range of columns in the macro worksheet. Each column in the range describes one of the commands in your custom menu. Within a column, the first cell gives the command name, the second cell provides a description of the command, and subsequent cells contain the macro instructions that 1-2-3 will perform if the user selects this command from your menu. In the main part of the macro, use a {MenuCall} or {MenuBranch} command to display the custom menu on the screen. The menu appears in a custom dialog box.

To determine the correct format for a reference argument in a macro command,   **581**

keep in mind the rules that 1-2-3 follows for evaluating references in macros: by default, references that represent subroutines or branches of control are assumed to be located within the macro worksheet itself. All other references are assumed to be located within the worksheet that is current at the time of the macro run. To override these rules, you must include a file reference along with a cell or range reference as the argument in a macro command.

To create a conditional branch in a macro,   585

> use an {If} instruction to express the condition of the branch. The {If} command takes a single argument, a logical expression. Immediately following the {If} instruction, in the same cell of the macro worksheet, write a {Branch} command that identifies the destination of the branch. {Branch} takes a single argument, a reference to the macro location that receives control of the program if the branch is performed.

To locate a logical error in a macro,   588

> choose Tools ➤ Macro ➤ Single Step or Trace. Then run the macro and examine the contents of the Trace window as you move step by step through the program performance.

To write a macro that creates a text file,   599

> use the {Open} command to create the file on disk. This command takes two arguments, a string representing the file name, followed by a code letter indicating the file operation: R for read, W for write, M for modify, or A for append. Once the file is open, use a sequence of {Writeln} commands to write lines of text to the file. Each {Writeln} takes a single string argument. Finally, use the {Close} command to complete the write operations and to close the file. {Close} takes no arguments.

A programming language is a collection of tools designed to help you plan and perform tasks on your computer. Accordingly, a program is a sequence of steps, expressed in the commands and keywords of a particular language.

Macro programming is a broad and detailed subject. In fact, you'll find entire books devoted to techniques for writing macros. This chapter is a short follow-up to Chapter 9's introduction to macros and the basic concepts of macro programming. In the course of this chapter, you'll learn the most commonly used macro commands. You'll also work with two complete examples of macro programs:

- A schedule macro, which creates worksheets for keeping track of business appointments. You'll see three versions of this programming exercise, each illustrating different macro commands.

- A mailing list macro, which reads an address database and creates a text file of address labels from the database. This particular example is designed to work with the instructor database from Computing Conferences, Inc., but you can easily revise the program to create labels from the databases you use.

These examples illustrate general categories of programming tasks: data operations, input and output, decisions, loops, subroutine calls, and branches of control.

Introducing the 1-2-3 Macro Language

As you write a program, regardless of the language, you typically focus on these essential activities:

- Performing operations on specific types of data values, including numbers, strings, and logical values.

- Reading input from a variety of sources, and writing output to a variety of destinations. For example, an *interactive program* reads the user's input from the keyboard and displays output on the screen. Disk files can be both the source of input and the destination of output.

- Making decisions based on expressed conditions. A decision results in a choice between different options for the program's next action.

- Repeating the performance of a command or group of commands a specified number of times. Statements or commands that control repetition in a program are known as *loops*.

- Calling subroutines, or otherwise modifying the sequential line-by-line flow of control in a program. A subroutine performs a particular task and then returns control of the program to the location of the original call. In contrast, a *branch* command simply sends control of the program to a new location, with no expectation of a return.

The 1-2-3 macro language includes commands for performing these basic programming activities for use in worksheets, charts, and databases. The macro language also has a variety of important tools for utilizing 1-2-3 and Windows features, such as the Clipboard, external database connections, DDE, and window characteristics.

Macro commands   The macro language includes more than three hundred different commands, each represented by a unique keyword. As you learned in Chapter 9, macro commands appear within braces ({}), like so:

{Get Label}

Most macro commands require specific arguments, which may include numeric values, strings, logical expressions, or range references. Each argument is separated from the next by a semicolon (or by a separator character you select with Tools ➤ User Setup ➤ International).

For example, in Chapter 9 you worked with an input command named {Get-Label}. This command displays an input prompt in a custom text-input dialog box, and waits for the user to enter a string from the keyboard. When the user completes the string and presses ↵ (or clicks on OK), the {Get-Label} command copies the input to a specific cell location as a label entry.

Getting help with macro commands You can view an index of all the macro commands and a help topic describing any individual command. Follow these steps:

1. Type an opening brace character, {, into a worksheet cell.

2. While the Edit line is still active, press F3 to open the Macro Keywords dialog box.

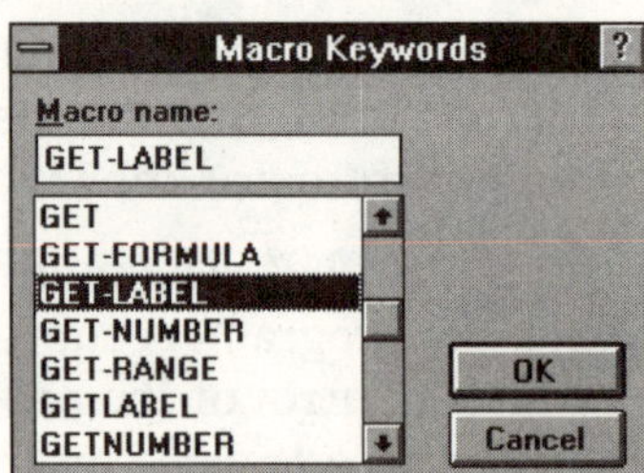

3. Click on a macro command in the list box below the Name text box and press F1.

The Help window displays complete information about the command, including the action it performs and the arguments it requires. For example, Figure 12.1 shows the Help window for the {GetLabel} command.

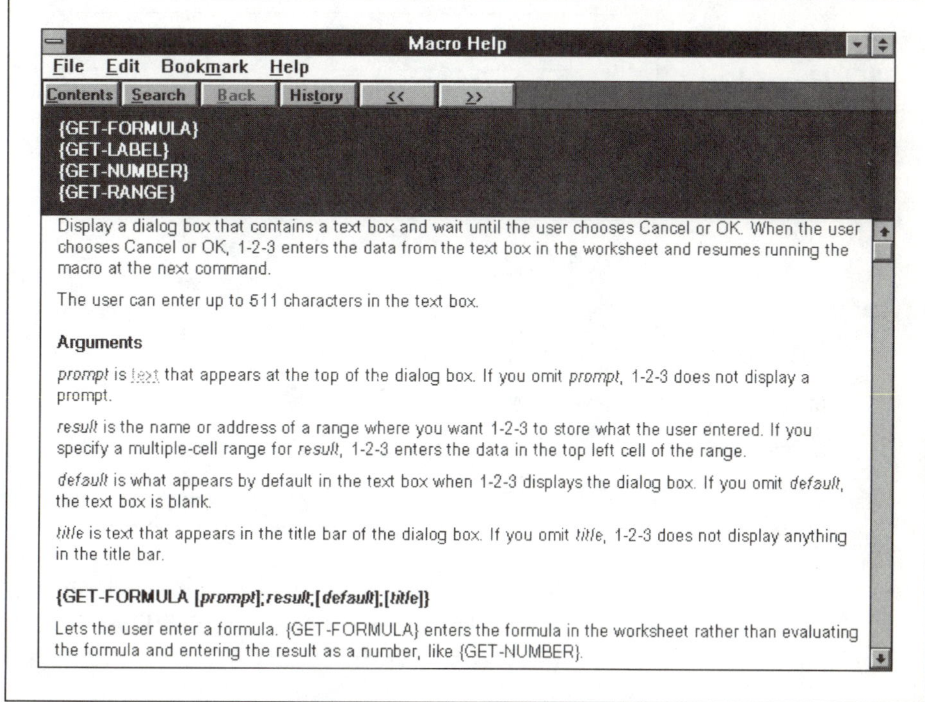

Writing Programs that Interact with the User

The schedule macro you'll build in this chapter creates worksheets in which you can record daily business activities. For example, the schedule worksheet in Figure 12.2 displays half-hour time slots from 6:00 AM to 6:00 PM. To create it, the program begins by choosing File ➤ New to open a new blank worksheet, and then proceeds to elicit your instructions for the format and contents of the worksheet. Specifically, the program lets you create a schedule worksheet for today, tomorrow, or the next day.

A schedule worksheet with half-hour time slots

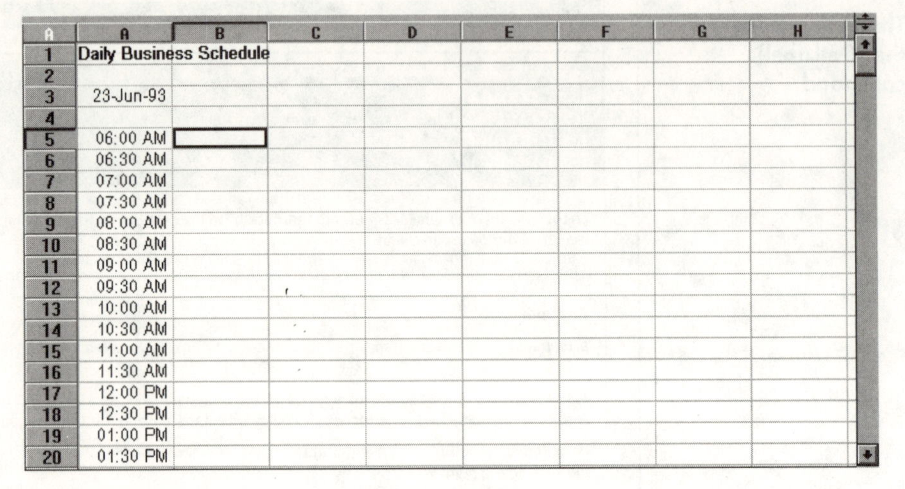

To elicit your instructions, the program displays an on-screen menu for choosing the day you want to schedule. The menu appears inside a custom dialog box, as shown in Figure 12.3. To make a selection in the menu, you can:

- Double-click on your choice

- Press ↑ or ↓ to highlight the option of your choice, and then press ↵

- Press 1, 2, or 3 to choose one of the options in the date menu

The date selection custom dialog box from the first version of the schedule macro

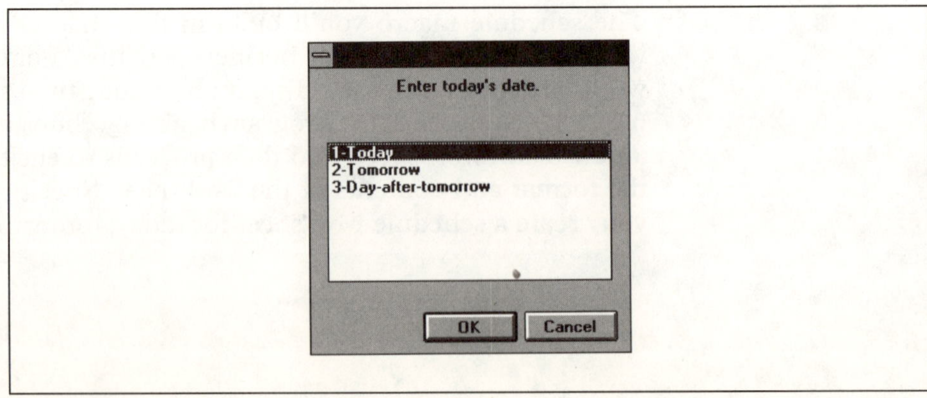

After you've created a schedule worksheet, the program moves the cell pointer to the first time slot, 6:00 AM. Then the program run is complete, and you can begin entering your appointments and activities on the worksheet.

The schedule macro itself appears in columns A through G of a worksheet that is stored on disk as S1.WK4. The main part of the worksheet, in columns A, B, and C, is shown in Figure 12.4. As you can see, the first cell in the macro, at B2, is named \S. You therefore begin a run of the program by pressing Ctrl-S.

	A	B	C
1		Schedule Macro	
2	\S	{File-New}Daily Business Schedule~{Style-Font-Attributes Bold;"On"}	Enter the title in bold.
3		{Down 2}{MenuCall DateMenu}{Style-Number-Format "DD-MMM-YY"}	Get the user's date choice.
4		{Down 2}{Anchor}{Down 48}~{Style-Number-Format "HH:MM AM/PM"}	Format the range.
5		{Fill ;"6:00";30;"18:00";"Minute"}	Fill with time values.
6		{Right}{Quit}	Select the first cell.
7			
8			
9			

How the Macro Program Works

This main part of the program consists of five lines of macro instructions. Here is a general description of what these lines do:

CELL LOCATION	WHAT THE PROGRAM DOES
B2	Chooses File ➤ New to create the worksheet, enters the title "Daily Business Schedule" into cell A1, chooses Style ➤ Font & Attributes, and selects the Bold option to display this title in boldface type.

CELL LOCATION	WHAT THE PROGRAM DOES
B3	Uses a macro command named {MenuCall} to display the date menu on-screen. The date you select is copied to the schedule worksheet. The program then chooses Range ➤ Number Format to apply an appropriate date format to the entry.
B4	Preselects the worksheet range in which the time entries will be displayed, and chooses Style ➤ Number Format to apply a time format to the entire range.
B5	The {Fill} instruction chooses Range ➤ Fill. (This command fills a selected range on the current worksheet with a sequence of values.) To specify the contents of this sequence, the macro must enter values for the Start, Step, and Stop text boxes in the Fill dialog box. Accordingly, the program enters 6:00 AM as the Start value and 6:00 PM as the Stop value. The program's entry for the Step text box is set to 30 minutes.
B6	Positions the cell pointer in column B, just to the right of the first time entry. The {Quit} command ends the macro.

The menu definition   To display a menu in a custom input dialog box, a macro must include a specially organized menu definition. A menu definition is a range of columns in which you describe the commands in a custom menu. In the S1.WK4 worksheet, such a definition appears in columns E through G, as shown in Figure 12.5. The definition for the date menu is in E2..G4. The {MenuCall} command in the main part of the program transfers control to this menu definition.

A	D	E	F	G
1	DateMenu	1-Today	2-Tomorrow	3-Day-after-tomorrow
2		Enter today's date.	Enter tomorrow's date.	Two days from today.
3		{Cell-Enter "@TODAY"}	{Cell-Enter "@TODAY+1"}	{Cell-Enter "@TODAY+2"}
4		{Return}	{Return}	{Return}
5				
6				
7				

Before you examine the precise structure of a menu definition, take the time to produce your own copy of the schedule macro.

1. Open a new blank worksheet for the macro, and carefully enter the range names, macro instructions, and comments into columns A through G of the worksheet, as shown in Figures 12.4 and 12.5.

Once you have finished typing the contents of the macro, here are the steps for completing your work:

2. Choose Range ➤ Name to assign the labels displayed in cell A2 to the adjacent cell in columns B. Then use the command again to assign the labels in D1 to the adjacent cell in column E.

3. Save the worksheet in the root directory of drive C as C:\S1.WK4.

When you finish your work, try running the macro a few times. Depending on your selections in the date menu, the macro produces a worksheet similar to the one in Figure 12.2.

Giving the User Menu Options to Select with {MenuCall}

As this program illustrates, a custom menu is a clear and efficient way to elicit instructions from the user during a macro run. The {MenuCall} command displays a menu on-screen and waits for the user to choose a menu option. The command takes one argument, a reference to the location of the menu definition:

{MenuCall *reference*}

The *reference* argument can identify the entire range of the menu definition, or simply the upper-left corner cell of the range. For example, the {MenuCall} command in the schedule macro can contain a reference to the named cell located at the beginning of the date menu definition:

    {MenuCall DateMenu}

A menu definition is a range of columns in which you describe the commands in a custom menu. Each column in the range is devoted to one command in the menu, and provides three kinds of information for the command:

- The first cell in the column gives the command name as it is to appear in the custom dialog box.

- The second cell in the column provides the command's description, which appears at the top of the custom dialog box when the command is highlighted. (See Figure 12.3 for an example of a command description.)

- Subsequent cells down the column provide the macro instructions that 1-2-3 performs if the user chooses this command.

For example, here is the complete definition for the first command in the date menu:

1-Today

Enter today's date

{Cell-Enter "@TODAY"}

{Return}

- The first cell contains the command's name as it appears in the menu: **1-Today.** (Here, the boldface display improves the clarity of the menu definition inside the macro worksheet itself; commands are not displayed in boldface inside the custom dialog box.)

- The second cell is the description of the command.

The two remaining cells are the macro instructions for this command:

- The first instruction enters the date number for today's date into the current cell.

- The second instruction, {Return}, returns control to the main part of the macro.

Using Subroutines

In effect, the {MenuCall} command treats each column in the menu definition as a subroutine. When the user chooses a command in the menu, {MenuCall} performs the instructions in the corresponding column of the menu definition. At the end of the subroutine, control of the program returns to the instruction located immediately after the original {MenuCall} command. The optional {Return} command at the end of each subroutine represents this return of control.

N O T E

The macro language also has a {MenuBranch} command that displays a menu on-screen. This command branches to the instructions for a selected command, but does not automatically return control to the main part of the macro.

A menu that you define in a macro can contain up to eight commands. In other words, 1-2-3 recognizes as many as eight columns of individual command definitions in the range. In the schedule macro, the date menu has three commands, defined in columns E, F, and G.

Take a brief look at the second and third columns in the date menu definition. The macro instruction corresponding to 2-Tomorrow is

    {Cell-Enter "@TODAY+1"}

located in cell F3, and the instruction for 3-Day-after-tomorrow is

    {Cell-Enter "@TODAY+2"}

located in cell G3. In other words, these two commands enter the date numbers for tomorrow's date and the next day's date, respectively.

In summary, each subroutine in the date menu definition enters a date in cell A3 of the schedule worksheet. When control of the program subsequently returns to the main part of the macro, the instruction {Style …} (in cell B3 of the macro worksheet) formats this entry as a date.

Entering a Specific Label or Value with {Cell-Enter}

The {Cell-Enter} command simply enters a label or a value into a specific cell:

{Cell-Enter *entry;reference*}

The label or value to be entered into the cell is identified by the first argument, *entry*, and the destination cell is optionally identified by the second argument, *reference*. For example, the following {Cell-Enter} command enters the date number for today's date in a cell named DATEENTRY:

{Cell-Enter @TODAY,DATEENTRY}

By default, {CellEnter} enters a value into the worksheet file that is current at the time the macro is running. However, this creates an interesting problem for the schedule macro, because the macro worksheet is *not* the current worksheet during a run of the program. The solution to this problem is to choose a correct format for the reference argument in the {Cell-Enter} command.

How 1-2-3 Evaluates References

In general, 1-2-3 follows two rules for evaluating references that appear as arguments in macro commands:

- In commands that send control of the program to a new location in the macro sheet—in other words, subroutine calls and branches of control—Lotus 1-2-3 evaluates range arguments as references to the macro worksheet itself.

- In all other macro commands, 1-2-3 evaluates range arguments as references to the worksheet that is current at the time the macro is running.

For example, the instruction {MenuCall DateMenu} expects to find a cell named DATEMENU on the macro worksheet itself, but the instruction {CellEnter @TODAY} makes an entry in the cell on the worksheet that is current at the time the macro is running.

Overriding Reference Defaults

To override these default rules for references in macro commands, you must supply a file reference as part of the cell address or range argument. Here is how you write the {Cell-Enter} command to enter a value or label in a cell location that is not in the current worksheet:

{Cell-Enter entry;<<*file*>>*reference*}

W A R N I N G

Because of the distinct rules for evaluating references in macro commands, reference arguments are a common source of errors in programs. If 1-2-3 interrupts a macro and displays an "Invalid range" error message, check to see if a reference argument in the current instruction needs a file reference.

Working with Decisions and Branches of Control

The second version of the schedule macro is similar to the first. But the second version of the macro employs a new technique for entering the range of time values into the schedule worksheet. Specifically, this version illustrates the use of a macro command named {If} to evaluate whether you want a time schedule in 60-, 30-, or 15-minute increments. Once you have indicated your preference, the program creates the appropriate time table.

Making a Program Decision with {If}

The {If} command expresses a decision in a macro, deciding whether to execute the macro commands on the same line (or cell). You can use this command to make a decision as to which time table to create in a macro. In some programming contexts, {If} may be the only appropriate tool for making particular kinds of decisions.

The main part of the new program appears in Figure 12.6, and the menu definitions are shown in Figure 12.7. To create this macro, you can start with your copy of the first version, S1.WK4, saving it as S2.WK4.

FIGURE 12.6

The second version of the schedule macro

A	A	B	C	D
1		Schedule Macro		
2	\S	{File-New}Daily Business Schedule~{Style-Font-Attributes Bold;"On"}	Enter the title in bold.	
3		{MenuCall TimeMenu}	Get the time choice.	
4		{Down 2}{MenuCall DateMenu}{Style-Number-Format "DD-MMM-YY"}	Get the user's date choice.	
5		{Down 2}{Anchor}{Down 48}~{Style-Number-Format "HH:MM AM/PM"}	Format the range.	
6		{If <<C:S2.WK4>>INCR="60"}{Fill ;"6:00";60;"18:00";"Minute"}	Fill with the 60 Minute values.	
7		{If <<C:S2.WK4>>INCR="30"}{Fill ;"6:00";30;"18:00";"Minute"}	Fill with the 30 Minute values.	
8		{If <<C:S2.WK4>>INCR="15"}{Fill ;"6:00";15;"18:00";"Minute"}	Fill with the 15 Minute values.	
9		{Right}{Quit}	Select the first time cell.	T
10				
11	INCR	60	The increment amount.	
12				

FIGURE 12.7

The three columns of menu definitions in S2.WK4

A	D	E	F	G
1	DateMenu	1-Today	2-Tomorrow	3-Day-after-tomorrow
2		Enter today's date.	Enter tomorrow's date.	Two days from today.
3		{Cell-Enter "@TODAY"}	{Cell-Enter "@TODAY+1"}	{Cell-Enter "@TODAY+2"}
4		{Return}	{Return}	{Return}
5				
6				
7				
8				
9	TimeMenu	Sixty-Minutes	Thirty-Minutes	Fifteen-Minutes
10		One-hour entries	Half-hour entries	Quarter-hour entries
11		{Let <<C:S2.WK4>>INCR;"60"}	{Let <<C:S2.WK4>>INCR;"30"}	{Let <<C:S2.WK4>>INCR;"15"}
12		{Return}	{Return}	{Return}
13				
14				

Here are the steps for making the appropriate revisions:

1. Enter new labels, instructions, and comments, as shown in Figure 12.6. Use <u>R</u>ange ➤ <u>N</u>ame to assign the labels in column A as the range names for the adjacent cells in column B. Adjust the widths of columns A, B, and C appropriately.

2. Enter the new subroutine for the TimeMenu option in the range D9..G12, as shown in Figure 12.7. Adjust the width of the columns accordingly.

3. Choose <u>F</u>ile ➤ <u>P</u>rotect, choose a password, and select the <u>S</u>eal file option. An *X* appears in the check box. Click OK.

4. Select cell B11 and choose <u>S</u>tyle ➤ <u>P</u>rotection and check the <u>K</u>eep data unprotected … option. Cell B11 is changed whenever you run the macro because it is the cell that the increment value is stored in.

5. Choose <u>F</u>ile ➤ <u>S</u>ave and save the new version of the macro as S2.WK4.

Now try running the macro two or three times. Now the program follows your instructions to produce a range of time entries in column A of the current schedule worksheet. But now the entries are produced by a {If} condition controlling 1-2-3's Range ➤ Fill command.

{If} command arguments   The {If} command takes a single argument, a logical expression that results in a value of true or false. This expression represents a decision that the macro makes during a performance. In the same cell as the {If} command, you always include a second macro command:

   {If *condition*}*command*

The result of {If} is as follows:

- If the *condition* is evaluated as true, 1-2-3 performs the *command* located in the same cell as the {If} instruction.

- If the *condition* is false, 1-2-3 skips the *command*, and instead continues to the next cell in the column of macro instructions.

Cell B6 in S2.WK4 contains a first example of an {If} instruction:

   {If <<C:S2.WK4>>INCR="60"}{Fill;"6:00";60;"18:00";"MINUTE"}

This command examines the current contents of the INCR cell in the macro worksheet. For the line to evaluate to true, the time increment must be equal to 60. Accordingly, if the expression

<<C:\S2.WK4>>Incr=60

is true, the subsequent {Fill} command will assign a new set of values to the currently selected range. However, if the entry in Incr is not equal to 60, the macro moves to the next command down the macro column.

{Branch} and {If}   Often the command located after {If} is a {Branch} command. {Branch} sends control of the program to a new location in the current macro. This instruction takes a single reference argument:

{Branch *reference*}

As usual, the *reference* argument can appear as a cell address or a range name. As long as the reference identifies a cell location in the current macro sheet, you do not need to include a file reference.

Debugging a Macro

The logical structure in a sequence of {If} and {Branch} statements presents many opportunities for error. Problems can result from a mistaken data entry, a faulty calculation, an incorrectly expressed condition, a misnamed cell, or any number of other common errors. In some cases, an error may actually cause an interruption in your program. Sometimes Lotus will stop the macro at a particular instruction and display an error message that identifies the problem. At other times, however, a macro completes its performance from beginning to end without interruption, but fails to produce the results you wanted. When this happens, you may need to examine the macro's actions step by step during a performance in order to identify the instruction that is causing the trouble.

To help you in this effort, 1-2-3 has two special menu commands named Tools ➤ Macro ➤ Single Step and Trace. These two commands represent features that you can turn on or off in advance of a given macro run. Both commands are off by default. In most debugging procedures, you use these two commands together. Figure 12.8 shows the Trace window when it is activated.

FIGURE 12.8

The Macro Trace window as it first appears on the screen

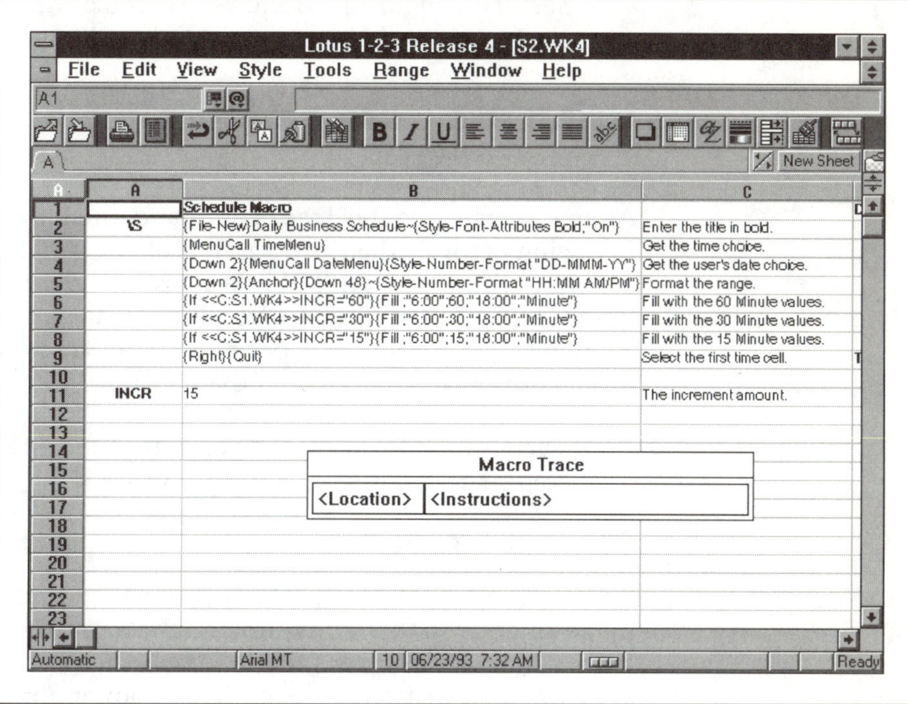

When you activate either Single Step or Trace, 1-2-3 modifies the action of the subsequent macro performance:

- If the Single Step command is active, 1-2-3 performs a macro in steps consisting of one instruction at a time. To proceed from one instruction to the next during the macro run, press any key on the keyboard.

N O T E   You can toggle in and out of the Single step mode by pressing Alt-F2 on the keyboard.

- If the Trace command is active, 1-2-3 displays a special Trace window on-screen. This window displays the cell location and the contents of each macro instruction that 1-2-3 is about to perform. Figure 12.8 shows the Trace window as it first appears on the screen, before you have started a macro's performance.

Using the Trace and Single Step Commands

As an exercise with the Trace command, imagine that you have made the following error in the third version of the schedule macro: rather than assigning the name S2.WK4 to represent the worksheet that INCR is found in, you have inadvertently left all macro instructions set to S1.WK4. If you want to experiment with Trace, you can actually create this error now in your copy of the program.

- Turn off the Protect mode and use Find & Replace to make all references to S2.WK4 read as S1.WK4.

When you next run the macro, 1-2-3 gives an error message.

As you think about this problem, your first guess may be that you have made an error in the {If} command that controls the looping. But a close look at this instruction fails to reveal the problem: the {If} condition appears to be written correctly. This is an opportunity to take advantage of the Trace command. Here is how to proceed:

1. Choose Tools ➤ Macro ➤ Trace.
2. Choose Single Step and place a check mark next to each menu command.
3. Press Ctrl-S to run the schedule macro again.
4. Press the spacebar (or any other key) repeatedly to step through the initial instructions of the program. Select options from both of the program's menus when they appear on-screen.
5. Pause when the Trace window first displays the instructions from cell B6, as shown in Figure 12.9. This is where you initially guessed the error was taking place.
6. Press the spacebar several more times.

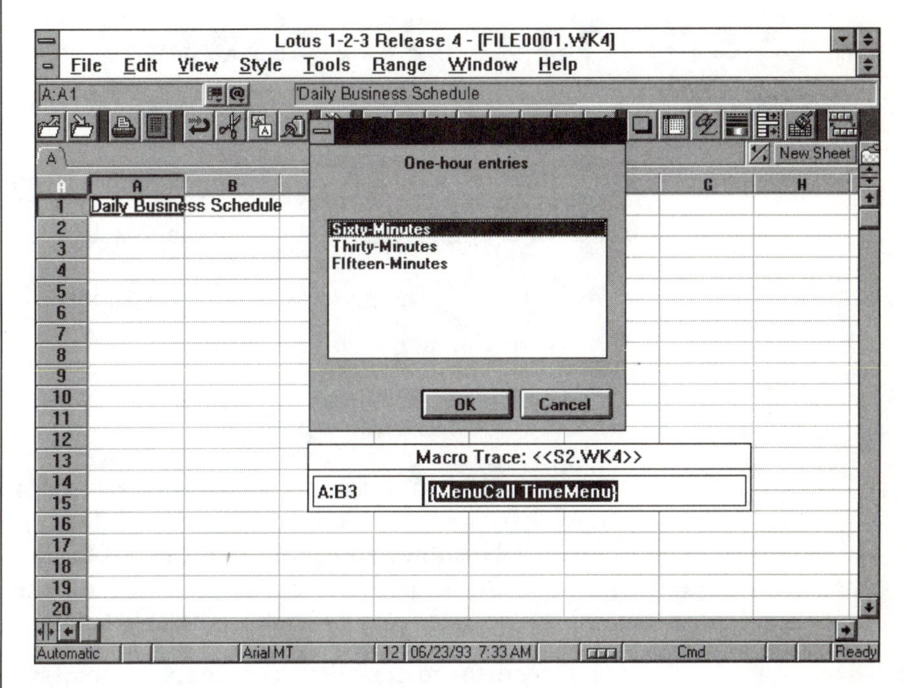

When the error occurs, an error message dialog box appears, telling you what the text of the macro is, the file it is called from, and the cell that the macro line is located in. When you change the reference to S1.WK4 back to S2.WK4 and rerun the macro, you will see that it goes smoothly past that point.

7. Choose Tools ➤ Macro ➤ Trace and Single Step, removing the check marks next to each.

8. Press Ctrl-S to try running the program again.

This time, the program runs as expected without the debugging help of Trace and Single Step. As you can see, the Trace and Single Step commands are simple features, but they can prove very helpful for finding a logical error in a macro.

To prepare for the next program, close the S2.WK4 worksheet and any schedule worksheets that you have created with the program.

Creating a Database Macro

There are many useful ways to apply macro programming to a 1-2-3 database. For example, you might write macros for the following purposes:

- To simplify the process of entering records into a database

- To automate queries on the database

- To produce special reports or lists from a database in formats that cannot otherwise be produced from 1-2-3

In the final programming exercise of this chapter, you'll work with a macro that creates a file of mailing labels from the instructor database. Figure 12.10 shows an example of this program's output. The program writes this list to disk as a text file, which can be used in your word-processing program to print gummed mailing labels.

You'll create the mailing list macro in the same worksheet file as the database itself. In the completed project, the database file contains five worksheets, A through E, with the following contents:

WORKSHEET	CONTENTS
A	The office database
B	The instructor database
C	A criteria range that tells 1-2-3 which instructors to pull out of the instructor database, as shown in Figure 12.11.
D	The output range, with fields for each instructor's first and last name, office address, city, state, and zip code, as shown in Figure 12.12.

```
W. Ashford
Computing Conferences, Inc.
222 Allen Street
New York, NY 10103


S. Banks
Computing Conferences, Inc.
11 Maple Street
Dallas, TX 75210


L. Cody
Computing Conferences, Inc.
432 Market Avenue
Los Angeles, CA 90028


A. Daniels
Computing Conferences, Inc.
11 Maple Street
Dallas, TX 75210


G. Davis
Computing Conferences, Inc.
432 Market Avenue
Los Angeles, CA 90028


R. Eng
Computing Conferences, Inc.
11 Maple Street
Dallas, TX 75210


P. Gill
Computing Conferences, Inc.
432 Market Avenue
Los Angeles, CA 90028


P. Harris
Computing Conferences, Inc.
11 Maple Street
Dallas, TX 75210


J. Meyer
Computing Conferences, Inc.
222 Allen Street
New York, NY 10103
```

WORKSHEET	CONTENTS
E	The mailing list macro, shown in Figure 12.13.

FIGURE 12.11

Preparing the instructor database for the mailing list macro

C	A	B	C	D	E	F	G	H	I	J
1	Criteria Range									
2										
3	Instructdb.Region									
4	+INSTRUCTDB.REGION=OFFICEDB.REGION									
5										

B	A	B	C	D	E	F	G	H	I	J
1				Instructor Database						
2										
3	ID	Last	First	City	Region	Specialty	Rate	Hrs	Contract	Yrs
4	S-125	Ashford	W.	Washington, D.C.	E	Spreadsheet	$150	145	10-May-87	4.7 A
5	W-145	Banks	S.	St. Louis	S	WP	$150	55	10-Jun-90	1.6 A
6	D-143	Cody	L.	Los Angeles	W	Database	$75	43	20-Jun-90	1.6 B

A	A	B	C	D	E	F	G	H
1	Regional Offices							
2								
3	Region	Address	City	State	Zip	Phone		Manager
4	E	222 Allen Street	New York	NY	10103	(212) 555-4678		Campbell, R.
5	N	Mills Tower, Suite 992	Chicago	IL	60605	(312) 555-8803		Logan, C.
6	S	11 Maple Street	Dallas	TX	75210	(214) 555-6754		Harvey, J.
7	W	432 Market Avenue	Los Angeles	CA	90028	(213) 555-9974		Garcia, M.

FIGURE 12.12

An output range containing instructors' names and office addresses

D	A	B	C	D	E	F
1	Output Range					
2						
3	Instructdb.First	Instructdb.Last	Officedb.Address	Officedb.City	Officedb.State	Officedb.Zip
4	W.	Ashford	222 Allen Street	New York	NY	10103
5	S.	Banks	11 Maple Street	Dallas	TX	75210
6	L.	Cody	432 Market Avenue	Los Angeles	CA	90028
7	A.	Daniels	11 Maple Street	Dallas	TX	75210
8	G.	Davis	432 Market Avenue	Los Angeles	CA	90028
9	R.	Eng	11 Maple Street	Dallas	TX	75210
10	P.	Gill	432 Market Avenue	Los Angeles	CA	90028
11	P.	Harris	11 Maple Street	Dallas	TX	75210
12	J.	Meyer	222 Allen Street	New York	NY	10103
13	D.	Perez	432 Market Avenue	Los Angeles	CA	90028
14	D.	Porter	Mills Tower, Suite 992	Chicago	IL	60605
15	M.	Porter	222 Allen Street	New York	NY	10103
16	F.	Ramirez	222 Allen Street	New York	NY	10103
17	P.	Roberts	Mills Tower, Suite 992	Chicago	IL	60605
18	W.	Sanchez	Mills Tower, Suite 992	Chicago	IL	60605
19	B.	Schwartz	222 Allen Street	New York	NY	10103
20	P.	Weinberg	11 Maple Street	Dallas	TX	75210

	A	B	C
1		Mailing List Macro	
2	\M	{Goto}Output1~{Down}	Goto output range.
3		{Open "C:\MAILLIST.TXT",W}	Open a new text file.
4	Loop	{Contents First,@CELLPOINTER("coord")}{Right}	Copy the first initial.
5		{Contents Last,@CELLPOINTER("coord")}{Right}	Copy the last name.
6		{Contents Address,@CELLPOINTER("coord")}{Right}	Copy the address.
7		{Contents City,@CELLPOINTER("coord")}{Right}	Copy the city.
8		{Contents State,@CELLPOINTER("coord")}{Right}	Copy the state.
9		{Contents Zip,@CELLPOINTER("coord")}{Left 5}{Down}	Copy the zip code.
10		{Writeln @TRIM(First)&" "&Last}	Write full name to file.
11		{Writeln "Computing Conferences, Inc."}	Write company name to file.
12		{Writeln Address}	Write address to file.
13		{Writeln @TRIM(City)&", "&@TRIM(State)&" "&@TRIM(Zip)}	Write city and state to file.
14		{Writeln ""}	Write blank line to file.
15		{Writeln ""}	Write blank line to file.
16		{If @CELLPOINTER("type")<>"b"}{Branch Loop}	Test for end of database.
17		{Close}	Close the text file.
18		{Quit}	End of program.
19			
20			

Building the Database Macro

Here are the instructions for preparing the database and creating this new macro:

1. Open your copy of the original INSTRUCT.WK4 file from disk. If necessary, choose Style ➤ Hide ➤ Show to unhide worksheet D.

2. Use Edit ➤ Delete ➤ Sheet to delete all the worksheets located after D. Then use Edit ➤ Insert ➤ Sheet to insert a new blank worksheet E.

3. Go to worksheet C. Clear the contents of row 4.

4. Go to worksheet D. Clear the current contents of the sheet.

The six new field names you see in row 3, as shown in Figure 12.12, will be entered automatically when the database is first queried and then joined.

5. Preselect range D:A3..D:F3. Choose Range ➤ Name and enter **OUTPUT1** as the name for this range. (Again, this is a new definition for an existing range name.) Click OK to confirm.

6. Choose <u>T</u>ools ➤ Data<u>b</u>ase ➤ <u>N</u>ew Query. Enter **INSTRUCTDB** in the Select <u>d</u>atabase table to query range text box and **OUT-PUT1** in the Select location for new <u>q</u>uery table range text box.

7. Click on the Choose <u>F</u>ields button, click on the Cl<u>e</u>ar All button, and then click on the <u>A</u>dd button.

8. In the Add Field dialog box, select First and click on OK to return to the Set Criteria dialog box, and then repeat this for the field named Last. Click on OK to close the dialog box and execute the query operation.

The instructors' names appear in the output range of worksheet D.

9. While the output query range is selected, choose <u>Q</u>uery ➤ <u>S</u>ort. Click in the <u>S</u>ort by list box and select Last, and then click on the Add <u>K</u>ey button. Click in the <u>S</u>ort by list box again and select First, click on the Add <u>K</u>ey button one more time and then click OK to complete the sort.

10. Choose <u>Q</u>uery ➤ <u>J</u>oin. Enter **OFFICEDB** in the <u>W</u>ith database Table text box and **Region** in the Join database Table and With database Table field list boxes. Click OK.

11. In the Choose Fields dialog box, in turn <u>C</u>lear the Last, Of-ficedb.Region, Phone, and Manager entries. Click on Address in the list box, click on the <u>A</u>dd button, select Last in the Choose Fields dialog box, and click on OK to close the box (this changes the order of the fields that are combined). Then click on OK twice to close the dialog box and execute the Join operation.

The Instructors address appears in the output range of worksheet D.

12. Choose <u>R</u>ange ➤ <u>N</u>ame, enter **Last** in the <u>N</u>ame text box. In the <u>R</u>ange text box enter **D:A4..D:A20**, and then click on the <u>A</u>dd button.

13. Enter the names and respective ranges for each of the columns of data in the output table as **First**, **Address**, **City**, **State**, and **Zip**, clicking on the <u>A</u>dd button for each and finally closing the dialog box by clicking on OK.

14. In column D of the macro worksheet, enter the following six labels:

CELL	ENTRY
E:D1	First
E:D2	Last
E:D3	Address
E:D4	City
E:D5	State
E:D6	Zip

15. Preselect range E:D1..E:D6 and click the Bold and AlignRight icons. Then use <u>R</u>ange ➤ <u>N</u>ame to assign these six labels as range names to the adjacent cells in column E.

Figure 12.14 shows what this range will look like after a run of the macro. As you can see, the macro uses this range to make a temporary copy of each record it reads from the output range of the database.

E	D	E	F
1	First	P.	
2	Last	Weinberg	
3	Address	11 Maple Street	
4	City	Dallas	
5	State	TX	
6	Zip	75210	
7			

16. Choose <u>F</u>ile ➤ Save <u>A</u>s to save the instructor database and the mailing list macro together under the name INSTMAIL.WK4.

Running the Database Macro

Now you are ready to run the macro:

- Press Ctrl-M to begin.

The macro begins by opening a new text file named MAILLIST.TXT in the root directory of drive C. Next, the macro moves record by record through the output range in worksheet D, copying the fields in each record to a temporary storage place in range E:D1..E:D6. After reading each record, the program reorganizes the fields in the format of a mailing label, and writes lines of text to the MAILLIST.TXT file. When all the addresses have been written, the program closes the file and the performance is complete.

To view the program's output:

1. Minimize the 1-2-3 window and start up the Windows accessory application Notepad.
2. In Notepad, choose File ➤ Open.
3. Select the MAILLIST.TXT file from the root directory of drive C.

When the Notepad opens the file, you'll see the list of mailing labels shown back in Figure 12.10. If you wish, you can print this list by choosing File ➤ Print.

4. Return to 1-2-3 now, and look again at the macro instructions in worksheet E.

{Contents} The program illustrates several new macro commands. For one, the {Contents} command copies data from one cell to another in a worksheet. This command takes two references as its arguments:

    {Contents *reference1;reference2*}

The command copies the contents of *reference2* to *reference1*. For example, here is how the mailing list program copies the first name field of each record to the cell named FIRST in worksheet E:

    {Contents First,@CELLPOINTER("coord")}

Notice that the mailing list program does not need to use file references in the {Contents} commands, because the macro is stored in the same file as the database.

Using Text File Commands in a Macro

The {Open}, {Writeln}, and {Close} commands are responsible for creating the text file on disk.

{Open} The {Open} command takes two arguments: a string representing the file name, and a single letter code representing the operation for which the file will be opened:

    {Open *file;code*}

The code argument can be R, W, M, or A, for reading, writing, modifying, or appending data. In the mailing list program, the MAILLIST.TXT file is opened for writing:

    {Open "C:\MAILLIST.TXT",W}

{Writeln} Once a file is open in this mode, the {Writeln} command sends a line of text to the open file. This command takes a single argument, a string or string expression:

    {Writeln *string*}

The mailing list program provides string arguments in a variety of formats for the {Writeln} command. For example, the argument in the program's first {Writeln} command is a concatenation of three strings, and includes a call to the @TRIM function to eliminate spaces from the end of the first string:

    {Writeln @TRIM(First)&" "&Last}

{Close} After the last line of text is written to the file, a {Close} command is necessary to complete the write operation and to close the file. This command takes no arguments.

Here is a summary of the instructions in the mailing list program:

CELL\RANGE	INSTRUCTION
E:B2	The macro selects the output range in worksheet D, and moves the cell pointer to the beginning of the first record in the range.
E:B3	The {Open} command creates the file MAILLIST.TXT on disk. (If a previous version of the file already exists, it is deleted.)
E:B4..E:B9	A sequence of {Contents} commands copies each field of the current record from the output range in worksheet D to the cells named FIRST, LAST, ADDRESS, CITY, STATE, and ZIP in worksheet E. At the end of this sequence, the cell pointer is positioned at the beginning of the next record in the output range.
E:B10..E:B15	A sequence of {Writeln} commands format the record as a mailing label, and write each line of the label to the open text file.
E:B16	An {If} instruction examines the contents of the current cell in the output range. If the cell is not empty, a {Branch} instruction sends control back up to the cell named LOOP, and the program once again begins reading a new record from the database. But if the cell is empty—that is, if the program has reached the end of the database—the {Branch} instruction is skipped.
E:B17	A {Close} instruction closes the text file.

CELL\RANGE	INSTRUCTION
E:B18	The {Quit} instruction represents the end of the program's performance.

This macro is easy to adapt for use in an address database for your own work. After each {Contents} command, the program uses {Right}, {Left}, and {Down} instructions to move the cell pointer to a new field or record in the output range. Then a subsequent {Contents} command uses the @CELLPOINTER function to identify the address of the current cell. To revise this program, you simply need to make sure that the movement of the cell pointer matches the structure of your own database. In addition, you may want to change the name of the output file in the {Open} command in cell E:B3. And, of course, you should revise the {Writeln} command in E:B11, which currently writes the name "Computing Conferences, Inc." as the second line of each mailing label.

Summary

The 1-2-3 macro language provides commands for major categories of programming activity. In this chapter, you've seen a selection of these macro commands:

Data operations The {Contents} command copies values from one cell to another.

Input and output In an interactive program, the {GetLabel} and {GetNumber} commands display input prompts in windows on the screen, and accept the user's input from the keyboard. In a data file program, the {Open}, {Writeln}, and {Close} commands together create a file on disk and write lines of text as output to the file.

Decisions The {If} statement makes a decision that results in a choice between alternative courses of action during the macro performance.

Loops The {For} command is the main tool for creating loops in a macro. But when the loop cannot be based on specific start, stop, and step values, you can instead use the {If} and {Branch} commands to form a loop.

Subroutines A subroutine call consists of a reference to the first cell in the subroutine, enclosed in braces. A {Branch} statement sends control of the program to a specified location without anticipating a return. Other commands that perform subroutines or branches include {For}, {MenuCall}, and {MenuBranch}.

This is just a small sampling of the many tools available in the 1-2-3 macro language. To explore the language further, study the wealth of information available on macro programming and on individual macro commands in the 1-2-3 Help window.

A

Installing Lotus 1-2-3 Release 4 for Windows

LOTUS 1-2-3 for Windows comes with an easy-to-use installation program named Install. It is stored on Disk 1 of the program disks that come with the 1-2-3 package. Run Install directly from Windows. While it is running, the program gives you complete instructions about the information you have to supply, and tells you when you need to swap disks. Install even has its own Help window that you can consult if you have questions during the installation procedure. When Install is finished, you will be ready to run 1-2-3.

Here are the steps for installing 1-2-3 on your computer:

1. If you are not in Windows, start it up now. Insert the Lotus 1-2-3 for Windows Install disk (Disk 1) into a floppy disk drive.

2. In the Windows Program Manager, pull down the File menu and choose the Run command. The Run dialog box appears on the screen.

3. In the Command Line text box, type **A:INSTALL** if you have inserted Disk 1 in drive A, or **B:INSTALL** if Disk 1 is in drive B.

4. Choose the OK button or press ↵.

At the outset, a message box informs you that Install is copying its own working files to your hard disk. A dialog box named Welcome to Install appears with the Lotus copyright notice.

5. After you have read the information in the box, choose the OK button to continue.

6. The Recording Name and Company Name box appears next on-screen. Enter your own name and a company name (if you are registering the program for a company) in the two text boxes provided. (After entering your name, press Tab to move to the Company Name text box, or just click anywhere in the Company

Name box with your mouse. Choose Help if you want more information.) The Install program uses these names to initialize and identify your copy of the 1-2-3 program.

7. When you have completed the two entries, choose OK to continue.

8. The subsequent dialog box asks you to confirm the two names you entered. Choose <u>Y</u>es if the entries are correct, or <u>N</u>o if you want to reenter them. When you choose <u>Y</u>es, a message tells you that Install is saving this information to disk.

Now the Install program's Main Menu is displayed. The menu box contains four icons, representing the four options of the menu.

9. Choose the first icon, labeled Install 1-2-3.

Choosing an Installation Procedure

A dialog box named Type of Installation appears, as shown in Figure A.1. The icons in this box represent three approaches to the installation process.

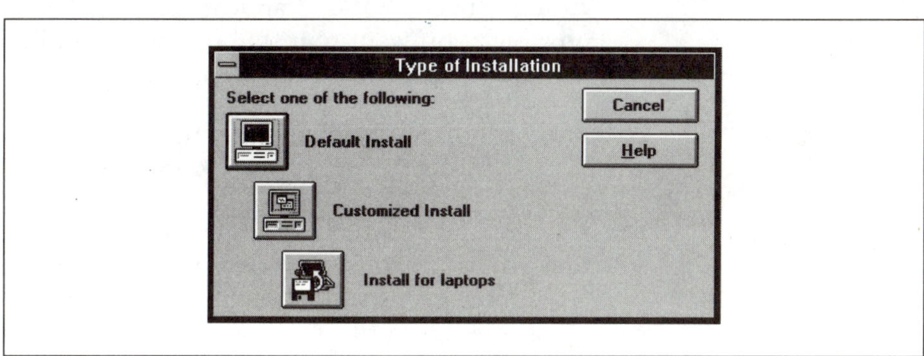

10. Choose the second icon, Customized Install.

The Customized Install dialog appears next, as shown in Figure A.2. In the Available drives and space box, the Install program shows the name of the drive that Windows is located in. By default, the Install program installs 1-2-3 to the same drive.

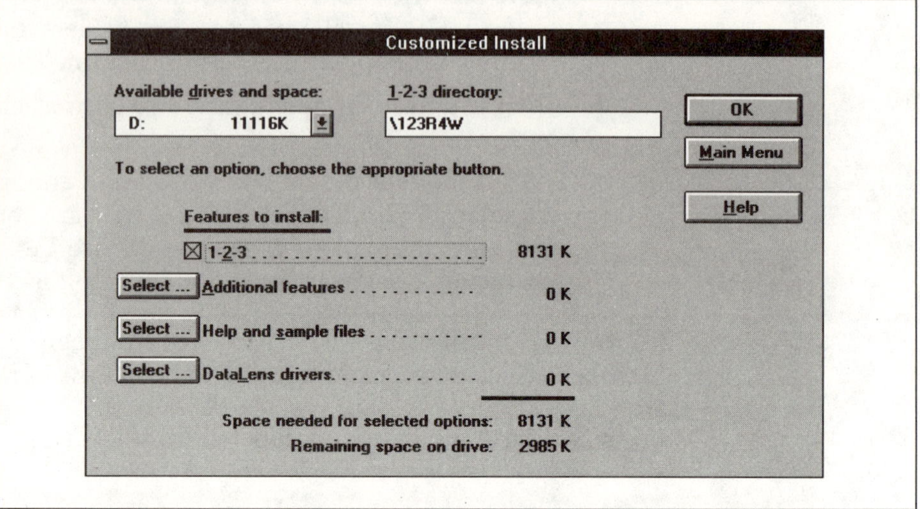

11. If you wish to save the program on a different drive, click the ↓ arrow next to this box. A dropdown list appears and shows you the hard drives available in your system. (Drives that do not have enough space for 1-2-3 appear in parentheses.) Choose the drive on which you want to install the program. For example, in Figure A.2, drive D has been selected.

The Program directory box shows the name of the default directory in which Install saves the program, \1-2-3R4W. Do not change this name.

12. Use the Customized Install dialog box to select the parts of 1-2-3 that you want to install. By default, the Installation includes the 1-2-3 program itself, a set of sample worksheets, and the DataLens Drivers.

TIP

Choose the Help command button if you want to know more about the various parts of the 1-2-3 package that you can install.

13. Choose OK to confirm your selections.

The Customized Install dialog box disappears and is replaced with a dialog box named Confirm Directory.

14. Choose the <u>Y</u>es button and the Install program creates the 123R4W directory on the drive that you have selected.

Next the Lotus Common Directory dialog appears. Here you can determine the directory where files used by all Lotus products are placed. In this dialog box, you can accept the default directory or select your own.

15. Either select your own directory or accept the default.

The 1-2-3 Application Icons dialog box appears next. This box displays the program icons that will appear inside the Lotus Applications group in the Windows Program Manager when you complete your installation.

16. Choose OK to accept these selections.

Next, the User Setup dialog box appears, as shown in Figure A.3. This box displays options that you can turn on or off for your installation.

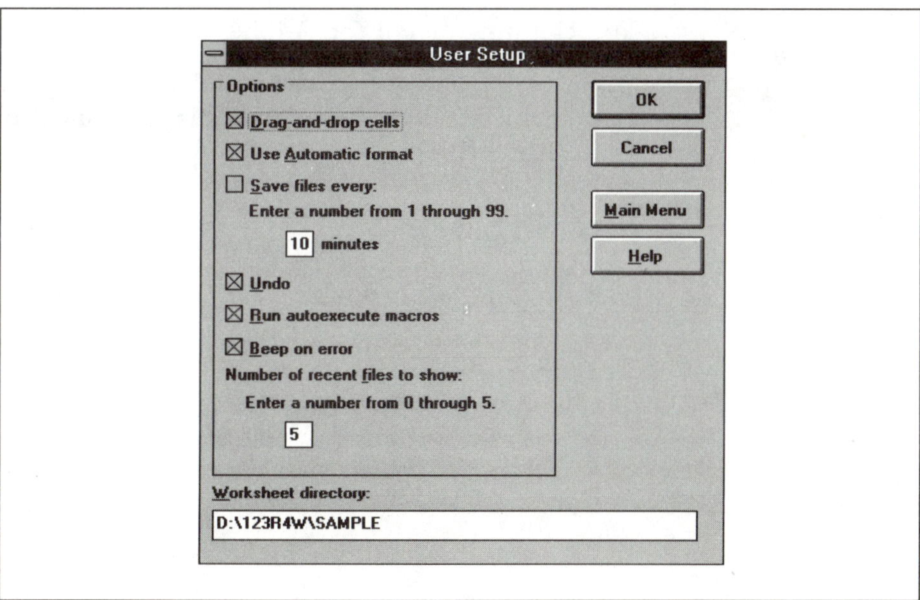

17. Choose any Setup options you want, and then choose OK.

Now the Install program begins copying the program files to your hard disk. This process takes several minutes. A dialog box named Transferring Files charts the progress of the installation. Whenever the Install program needs a new program disk, a message appears on the screen telling you which disk to insert in the floppy disk drive.

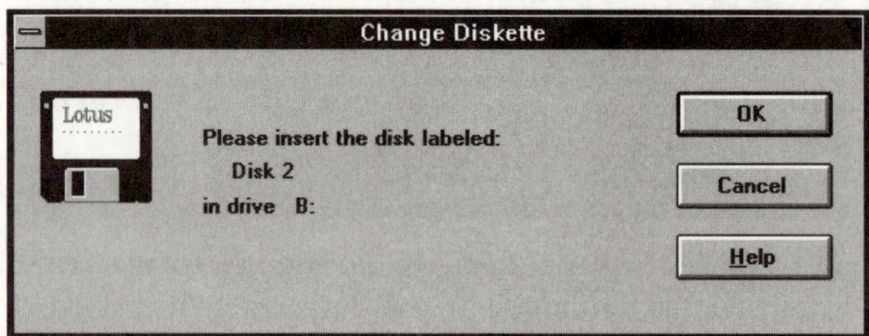

18. After you swap disks, choose the OK button to continue.

After the Install program transfers files from all the 1-2-3 program disks, the 1-2-3 installation is complete.

19. Read the Installation Finished box and then choose OK.

You can now install the Adobe Type Manager, which comes with the 1-2-3 package, if you want to.

Back in the Windows Program Manager, you will now find a group named Lotus Applications.

Starting 1-2-3

- To start 1-2-3, double-click the 1-2-3 for Windows icon.

Lotus 1-2-3
Release 4

Changing the Default Preferences Later

At any time while you are working in 1-2-3, you can change the default preferences you have selected during installation:

- Choose <u>T</u>ools ➤ <u>U</u>ser Setup to activate or disable the <u>U</u>ndo option or enter a new name for the default directory.

The User Setup dialog box is shown in Figure A.3.

APPENDIX

B

The @
Functions

THIS appendix describes all the 1-2-3 @ functions. Many functions listed here are explained in Chapter 5 as well in more detail.

@@(*reference*) returns the contents of the cell identified in *reference*. For example, if cell A1 contains the label entry E19, and the cell E19 contains the value entry 1-2-3, then **@@(A1)** returns the value 1-2-3.

@ABS(*value*) gives the absolute value of its numeric argument. For example, **@ABS(1-2-3)** and **@ABS(−1-2-3)** both return the value 1-2-3.

@ACCRUED(*settlement;issue;first-issue;coupon;[par]; [frequency];[b asis]*) returns the accrued interest for the values passed to the function. The first value passed is the *settlement* date-number. The second and third parameters are also date-numbers specifying the issue date and first interest payment date (in the future) of the note, respectively. The fourth value passed is the coupon rate. The three final parameters are optional. The first optional parameter is the security's *par* value, the second optional value is the number of payments per year, and the third is the means for calculating the number of days in a period.

@ACOS(*value*) returns the arccosine, or the angle in radians of a cosine argument. For example, **@ACOS(−1)** returns a value of π.

@ACOSH(*x*) returns a value, in radians, showing the arc hyperbolic cosine of the angle specified in the passed parameter.

@ACOT(*x*) returns a value, in radians, showing the arc cotangent of the angle specified in the passed parameter.

@ACOTH(*x*) returns a value, in radians, showing the arc hyperbolic cotangent of the angle specified in the passed parameter.

@ACSC(*x*) returns a value, in radians, showing the arc cosecant of the angle specified in the passed parameter.

@ACSCH(*x*) returns a value, in radians, showing the arc hyperbolic cosecant of the angle specified in the passed parameter.

@ASEC(*x*) returns a value, in radians, showing the arc secant of the angle specified in the passed parameter.

@ASECH(*x*) returns a value, in radians, showing the arc hyperbolic secant of the angle specified in the passed parameter.

@ASIN(*x*) returns the arcsine, or the angle in radians of a sine argument. For example, **@ASIN(1)** returns a value of $\pi/2$.

@ASINH(*x*) returns a value, in radians, showing the arc hyperbolic sine of the angle specified in the passed parameter.

@ATAN((*x*) returns the arctangent, or the angle in radians of a tangent argument. For example, the expression **@ATAN(1)★4** gives a value of π.

@ATANH(*x*) returns a value, in radians, showing the arc hyperbolic tangent of the angle specified in the passed parameter.

@ATAN2(*x;y*) returns the arctangent, or the angle in radians of a line in an (*x*,*y*) coordinate system. For example, **@ATAN2(1;1)** gives a value of $\pi/4$.

@AVEDEV(*list*) returns a value representing the average of the absolute deviation of the values in the list specified in the passed parameter.

@AVG(*list*) returns the average of the values in the list. The list argument can appear as any combination of values, addresses, ranges, or formulas.

@BESSELI(*x;n*) returns the modified Bessel function value of the integer specified in the first parameter raised to the order of the second value passed.

@BESSELJ(*x;n*) returns the Bessel function value of the integer specified in the first parameter raised to the order of the second value passed.

@BESSELK(*x;n*) returns the modified Bessel function value of the integer specified in the first parameter raised to the order of the second value passed.

@BESSELY(*x;n*) returns the Bessel, or Neumann, function value of the integer specified in the first parameter raised to the order of the second value passed.

@BETA(*z;w*) returns the beta value of the values z and w passed to the function.

@BETAI(*a*;*b*;*x*) returns the incomplete beta value of the values *z* and *w* passed to the function.

@BINOMIAL(*trials*;*successes*;*probability*;[*type*]) returns a value representing either the binomial probability mass function or the cumulative binomial distribution for the values passed in the function. The required parameters are the number of trials, the number of successes (in the trials), and the probability of success (0 or 1). Optionally, a fourth parameter specifying the value to be returned can be passed to the function.

@CELL(*info*;*reference*) supplies information about a cell at reference. The first argument, *info*, is a string that specifies the kind of information that **@CELL** will return. For example **@CELL("format",A1)** returns the current format of cell A1.

@CELLPOINTER(*info*) supplies information about the current location of the cell pointer. The argument is a string that specifies the kind of information the function will return. For example, **@CELLPOINTER("contents")** returns the contents of the current cell.

@CHAR(*integer*) returns a character from the LMBCS code. For example, **@CHAR(76)** returns "L".

@CHIDIST(*x*;*degrees-freedom*;[*type*]) returns the chi-square value for the two values passed. The two values represent the value to evaluate and the degrees of freedom used in determining the chi-square value. A third parameter, determining whether to return the chi-square value or a critical value that corresponds, is optional.

@CHITEST(*range1*;*range2*) returns the associated probability value for a chi-square test performed on the values in the two ranges specified in the first two parameters. The two ranges must be of the same size and must not contain any labels or blank cells, or a value of ERR will be returned.

@CHOOSE(*integer;list*) selects a value from a list or range of values. The first argument is a numeric offset, ranging from 0 to $n-1$, where n is the number of elements in the list. For example, **@CHOOSE(1;"one","two","three")** returns "two".

@CLEAN(*text*) returns a text string with nonprinting characters removed from the string specified in the single parameter.

@CODE(*string*) returns the LMBCS code for the first character in the string argument. For example **@CODE("L")** is 76.

@COLS(*range*) returns the number of columns in a *range*. For example, if the range name DB represents a database range, **@COLS(DB)** returns the number of fields in the database.

@COMBIN(*n;r*) returns the binomial coefficient for the two parameters specified.

@COORD(*worksheet;column;row;format*) supplies a cell reference. The arguments *worksheet*, *column*, and *row* are integers representing the elements of the reference. The format is an integer from 1 to 8 representing a reference format, where 1 is a completely absolute reference and 8 is a completely relative reference. For example, **@COORD(2,2,2,1)** gives the reference $B:$B$2.

@CORREL(*range1;range2*) returns a value equivalent to the correlation coefficient of the values in the two ranges specified in the two passed parameters.

@COS((*x*) gives the cosine of an angle, where the argument is expressed in radians. For example, **@COS(@PI)** is −1.

@COSH(*x*) returns a value showing the hyperbolic cosine of the angle specified in the passed parameter.

@COT(*x*) returns a value showing the cotangent of the angle specified in the passed parameter. The value passed is in radians.

@COTH(*x*) returns a value showing the hyperbolic cotangent of the angle specified in the passed parameter.

@COUNT(*list*) counts the number of cells that contain entries in a range or list of ranges.

@COV(*range1*;*range2*;[*type*]) will return the population or sample covariance for the values in the two ranges specified in the two required parameters. A third parameter specifying whether to return the population (the default) or sample covariance can be passed optionally.

@CRITBINOMIAL(*trials*;*probability*;*alpha*) returns the largest integer representing the cumulative binomial distribution that is less than the last parameter passed to the function. The first two parameters are the number of Bernoulli trials and the probability factor of success in a single trial. The third parameter is the criterion probability and is a value between 0 and 1.

@CSC(*x*) returns a value showing the cosecant of the angle specified in the passed parameter. The value passed is in radians.

@CSCH(*x*) returns a value showing the hyperbolic cotangent of the angle specified in the passed parameter.

@CTERM(*rate;futurevalue;presentvalue*) calculates the number of compounding periods required to reach a *futurevalue* amount, given a one-time investment of *presentvalue* and a fixed periodic interest rate.

@DATE(*year;month;day*) returns the date number corresponding to the date specified in its three integer arguments. For example, **@DATE(92,8,19)** returns 33835, the date number corresponding to 19-Aug-92.

@DATEDIF(*startdate;enddate;format*) returns the difference between the first date passed and the second date. The value returned can be days, months, or years, depending on the third parameter passed in **@DATEDIF**.

@DATEINFO(*date;attribute*) will return one of thirteen different pieces of information concerning the date number passed in **@DATEINFO**, according to the value (1–13) passed in the second parameter.

@DATEVALUE(*datestring*) returns the date number corresponding to a recognizable date string argument. For example **@DATEVALUE("19-Aug-92")** returns 33835.

@DAVG(*database;field;criteria*) calculates the average of selected values in a database range. The target database column is identified by *field*, which may appear as a field name in quotes, or a column offset number. The calculation includes all field entries in records that match the expressions in the criteria range.

@DAY(*datenumber*) returns an integer from 1 to 31, representing the day of the month of *datenumber*. For example, **@DAY(33835)** returns 19 from the date 19-Aug-92.

@DAYS(*startdate*;*enddate*;*[basis]*) will pass back the number of days between the first date specified and the second date. The value returned will vary according to the number (0–3) that is passed in the third parameter.

@DAYS360(*date1*;*date2*) returns the number of days between two dates, *date1* and *date2*. The subtraction is based on a 360-day year.

@DCOUNT(*database*;*field*;*criteria*) returns a count of selected values in a database range. The target database column is identified by *field*, which may appear as a field name in quotes, or a column offset number. The count includes all field entries in records that match the expressions in the criteria range.

@DB(*cost*;*salvage*;*life*;*period*) returns the depreciation value based upon the four values passed—*cost, salvage value, life,* and *period*.

@DDB(*cost*;*salvage*;*life*;*period*) calculates the double-declining-balance depreciation of an asset, given the original *cost,* the *salvage* value at the end of useful *life,* the *life* of the asset in years, and the target *period* for which the depreciation is to be calculated.

@DDELINK(*app*;*topic*;*item*;*[format]*;*[rows]*;*[cols]*;*[sheets]*) opens a dynamic data exchange (DDE) link with an open Windows application which will act as the server *app.* The parameter *app* is the application name, *topic* is the application file name, and *item* is the the item in the server application which you want to access. The first of the optional parameters, *format,* specifies the file format in the server application. The last three parameters, *rows, cols,* and *sheets,* specify how many rows, columns, and/or sheets to use in the destination worksheet.

@DECIMAL(*hexadecimal*) is used to determine the signed decimal value of the hexadecimal value passed to the function.

@DEGTORAD(*degrees*) converts the degrees value passed to the function into radians.

@DEVSQ(*list*) returns a sum value based on the values in the list specified in the passed parameter. The value is the sum of the squared deviation values for the list items.

@DGET(*database;field;criteria*) returns the field item from a single database record selected by the expressions in the criteria range. If two or more records match the criteria, **@DGET** returns an ERR value.

@DMAX(*database;field;criteria*) finds the largest value among selected entries in a database range. The target database column is identified by *field*, which may appear as a field name in quotes, or a column offset number. The largest value is selected from field entries in records that match the expressions in the criteria range.

@DMIN(*database;field;criteria*) finds the smallest value among selected entries in a database range. The target database column is identified by *field*, which may appear as a field name in quotes, or a column offset number. The smallest value is selected from field entries in records that match the expressions in the criteria range.

@DPURECOUNT(*input;field;criteria*) will return the number of cells in a database contain a value in the specified *field* (second parameter) which match the criteria specified in the third parameter.

@DQUERY(*"function"*;*arguments*) calls a function defined in an external database.

@DSTD(*database*;*field*;*criteria*) calculates the population standard deviation of selected values in a database range. The target database column is identified by *field*, which may appear as a field name in quotes or a column offset number. The calculation includes all field entries in records that match the expressions in the criteria range.

@DSTDS(*database*;*field*;*criteria*) calculates the sample standard deviation of selected values in a database range. The target database column is identified by *field*, which may appear as a field name in quotes or a column offset number. The calculation includes all field entries in records that match the expressions in the criteria range.

@DSUM(*database*;*field*;*criteria*) calculates the sum of selected values in a database range. The target database column is identified by *field*, which may appear as a field name in quotes or a column offset number. The sum includes all field entries in records that match the expressions in the criteria range.

@DVAR(*database*;*field*;*criteria*) calculates the population variance of selected values in a database range. The target database column is identified by *field*, which may appear as a field name in quotes or a column offset number. The calculation includes all field entries in records that match the expressions in the criteria range.

@DVARS(*database*;*field*;*criteria*) calculates the sample variance of selected values in a database range. The target database column is identified by *field*, which may appear as a field name in quotes or a column offset number. The calculation includes all field entries in records that match the expressions in the criteria range.

@D360(*date1;date2*) returns the number of days between two dates, *date1* and *date2*. The subtraction is based on a 360-day year.

@ERF(*lower;[upper]*) returns the error function value for the lower-bound value passed in the first parameter. An optional upper-bound value can be passed in the second parameter.

@ERFC(*x*) returns the complementary error function value for the value passed in the first parameter.

@ERFD(*x*) returns the derivative value of the error function for the value passed in the parameter.

@ERR returns the value ERR.

@EVEN(*x*) returns a value equivalent to the passed value rounded away from zero to the nearest even integer value.

@EXACT(*string1;string2*) returns a value of 1 (true) if *string1* is identical to *string2*, or a value of 0 (false) if the two strings are different.

@EXP(*x*) calculates e to the power of value. The natural constant e is given by **@EXP(1)** as 2.71828182845904524.

@EXP2(*x*) returns a value equivalent to the constant e (approximately 2.718282) raised to the value of the parameter passed in the function squared.

@FACT(*x*) returns the factorial value of the parameter passed to the function.

@FACTLN(*x*) returns the natural logarithm value of the factorial of the parameter passed to the function.

@FALSE returns the value 0, for false.

@FDIST(*x;degrees-freedom1;degrees-freedom2;[type]*) is used to determine the F-distribution value based on the numeric value specified in the first parameter, the degrees of freedom for the first sample in the second parameter, and the degrees of freedom in the second sample. Optionally, a fourth parameter can be specified controlling the value returned.

@FIND(*substring;string;pos*) searches for *substring*, starting from the offset position of *pos* inside *string*. If the search is successful, **@FIND** returns the offset location of the substring. For example, **@FIND("Co";"Computing Conferences";5)** returns a value of 10, the offset location of the second occurrence of "Co" in the string.

@FTEST(*range1;range2*) is used to determine the associated probability of a F-test performed on the two ranges of cells specified in the two passed parameters.

@FV(*payment;rate;term*) finds the future value of a series of equal periodic payment amounts over term periods at a fixed periodic interest rate.

@FVAL(*payment;rate;term;[type];[present value]*) returns the future value of an item based upon the present value (as specified in the optional fifth parameter). The required parameters are payments, interest, and term. Optionally, the type of payment (end or beginning of the period) can be specified in the fourth parameter.

@GAMMA(*x*) returns the gamma distribution value, accurate to six decimals, for the value passed in the parameter.

@GAMMAI(*x;n;complement*) returns the incomplete gamma value for the two values passed in the function.

@GAMMLN(*x*) returns the natural logarithm of the gamma value for the value passed in the single parameter specified in the function.

@GEOMEAN(*list*) returns a sum value of the geometric mean for the items in the list specified in the passed parameter.

@GRANDTOTAL(*list*) returns a value of the sum of the cells in the list specified in the passed parameter. The cells summed by **@GRANDTOTAL** are the cells containing the **@SUBTOTAL** function.

@HARMEAN(*list*) returns a value representing the harmonic mean of the items in the list specified in the passed parameter.

@HEX(*x*) is used to convert a signed numeric value to a hexa-decimal value.

@HLOOKUP(*value;table;row*) performs a lookup operation in a horizontally arranged lookup table. Specifically, the function finds the largest number in the top row of the table that is less than or equal to *value*, then looks down the corresponding col-umn to the cell located in *row*. **@HLOOKUP** returns the value in this target cell. (Alternatively, the function's first argument can appear as a string, in which case the first row of the lookup table contains labels.)

@HOUR(*timenumber*) returns an integer from 0 to 23, representing the hour of the decimal timenumber argument.

@IF(*expression*;*value1*;*value2*) returns *value1* if the logical expression is true, or *value2* if the expression is false. For example, **@IF(A1=0;"zero";"not zero")** returns zero if A1 contains a value of 0, or not zero if A1 contains a value other than 0.

@INDEX(*range*;*column*;*row*;*worksheet*) selects a label or a value from a worksheet table. The first argument, *range*, is the location of the table; and *column* and *row* are offset values identifying a cell location within the table. The optional *worksheet* argument refers to a table located on a different worksheet from the function itself.

@INFO(*info*) returns an item of information about the current 1-2-3 session. The *info* argument is a string that indicates the kind of information to be returned. For example, **@INFO("directory")** returns the current default directory path.

@INT(*value*) supplies the truncated integer portion of a numeric argument. For example, **@INT(@RAND*10)** gives random integers between 0 and 10.

@IPAYMT(*principal*;*interest*;*term*;*start-period*;[*end-period*];[*type*];[*future value*]) calculates the cumulative interest on a loan. The required parameters are the *principal*, *interest*, *term*, and *starting date*. You can optionally specify an ending date, type of payment (end or beginning of the period), and the future value of the principal.

@IRATE(*term*;*payment*;*present-value*;[*type*];[*future-value*];[*guess*]) returns a value equivalent to the periodic interest rate of an investment. The parameter specified in *term* is the

THE @ FUNCTIONS

number of compounding periods, *payment* is equivalent to the amount deposited, and *present-value* in the annuity of the investment. Optionally, the type of payment (end or beginning of the •period) can be specified in the fourth parameter. The optional parameter, *future-value*, specifies an amount which indicates a future value, but if not included, a value of zero is used. The *guess* parameter is what you "guess" the interest rate is.

@IRR(*guess*;*cashflows*) calculates the internal rate of return from a series of positive and negative cash flow amounts. The first argument is a reasonable guess for the internal rate of return, and the second is a reference to a worksheet range of positive and negative cash flow amounts.

@ISAAF(*name*) returns a value of 1 (true) if *name* is a defined add-in function currently in memory, or a value of 0 (false) if *name* is not defined.

@ISAPP(*name*) returns a value of 1 (true) if *name* is a defined add-in application, or a value of 0 (false) if *name* is not defined.

@ISERR(*reference*) returns a value of 1 (true) if the cell at reference contains the value ERR or a value of 0 (false) if it does not. (The function's argument can also appear as a value or expression.)

@ISFILE(*filename*) returns either a True or False value for the name of a file specified in the single value passed to the function. It determines whether the file already exists in the default directory or not.

@ISMACRO(*name*) returns either a True or False value for the name of an add-in macro specified in the single value passed to the function. It determines whether the add-in is a defined macro or not.

@ISNA(*reference*) returns a value of 1 (true) if the cell at *reference* contains the value NA or a value of 0 (false) if it does not. (The function's argument can also appear as a value or expression.)

@ISNUMBER(*reference*) returns a value of 1 (true) if the cell at *reference* contains a numeric value or is blank. If the cell contains a label entry, **@ISNUMBER** returns a value of 0 (false). (The argument of **@ISNUMBER** can also appear as a value, label, or formula.)

@ISRANGE(*reference*) returns a value of 1 (true) if *reference* is a valid range name or a correctly expressed reference.

@ISSTRING(*reference*) returns a value of 1 (true) if the cell at *reference* contains a label entry or a formula that produces a label. If the cell is blank or contains a number, **@ISSTRING** returns a value of 0 (false). (The argument of **@ISSTRING** can also appear as a value, label, or formula.)

@KURTOSIS(*range*;[*type*]) is used to determine the kurtosis of the values found in the range specified in the passed parameter.

@LARGE(*range*;*n*) returns the value that is the *n*th largest in the *range* specified in the first parameter. The value used to determine the *n*th is specified in the second parameter.

@LEFT(*string*;*n*) returns a substring consisting of the first *n* characters of string. For example, **@LEFT("Computing Conferences, Inc.";9)** returns the substring "Computing".

@LENGTH(*string*) returns the length, in characters, of its *string* argument. For example, **@LENGTH("Computing Conferences, Inc.")** returns 27.

@LN(*value*) supplies the natural logarithm of its argument, that is, the power of e that produces *value*.

@LOG(*value*) supplies the base-10 logarithm of its argument, that is, the power of 10 that produces *value*. For example, **@LOG(1000)** is 3.

@LOWER(*string*) returns a lowercase version of its string argument. For example, **@LOWER("Computing Conferences, Inc.")** returns "computing conferences, inc."

@MATCH(*cell;range;[type]*) returns the cell address of the first cell which matches the first parameter specified. The second parameter is a range to search. You can optionally specify the way that 1-2-3 evaluates the contents of each cell by passing a value or 0, 1, or 2 in the third parameter.

@MAX(*list*) returns the largest value in the *list*. The *list* argument can appear as any combination of values, addresses, ranges, or formulas.

@MEDIAN(*list*) returns a value representing the median value of the items in the list specified in the passed parameter.

@MID(*string;pos;n*) returns a substring consisting of *n* characters copied from *string*, starting at the position identified as *pos*. (The *pos* argument is the offset from the beginning of the *string*. The value of *pos* for the first character in the *string* is 0.) For example, **@POS("Computing Conferences, Inc.";10;11)** returns the substring "Conferences".

@MIN(*list*) returns the smallest value in the list. The *list* argument can appear as any combination of values, addresses, ranges, or formulas.

@MINUTE(*timenumber*) returns an integer from 0 to 59, representing the minutes in *timenumber*. The *timenumber* argument is a decimal time value. For example, **@MINUTE(0.1875)** returns 30, from the time 4:30 AM.

@MIRR(*range;finance-rate;reinvest-rate*) is the modified internal rate of return function returning the profits for the values specified. You specify a range containing the cash flow figures, the interest on the cash flow figures, and the interest on the reinvested funds.

@MOD(*numerator;denominator*) supplies the remainder from the division of two integers. For example, **@MOD(@TODAY;7)** gives a value from 0 to 6 representing the day of the week from Saturday to Friday.

@MONTH(*datenumber*) returns an integer from 1 to 12, representing the month of *datenumber*. For example, **@MONTH(33835)** returns a value of 8, identifying the month in the date 19-Aug-92.

@N(*reference*) returns a copy of the value in the first cell of the range identified by *reference*. If this cell does not contain a value, **@N** returns 0.

@NA returns the value NA (for "Not Available").

@NORMAL(*x;[mean];[std];[type]*) returns the normal distribution for the value passed in the single required parameter. The optional parameters are the mean of the distribution, the standard deviation of the distribution, and the type of calculation you want @NORMAL to perform.

@NOW supplies a combined date-and-time number representing the current date and time. For example, **@NOW** returns 33835.25 for the date 19-Aug-92 at 6:00 AM.

@NPER(*payments;interest;future-value;[type];[present-value]*) will tell you the number of periods required to reach a specified future value. The required parameters are *payments*, *interest*, and the *future value*. Optionally, you can specify the *type* of payments (end or beginning of the period) and the *present value*.

@NPV(*rate;cashflows*) finds the net present value of a series of future periodic cash flow amounts, positive or negative. The *rate* is the periodic rate of return. The *cashflows* argument is a range of cash flow amounts.

@ODD(*x*) returns a value equivalent to the passed value rounded away from zero to the nearest odd integer value.

@PAYMT(*principal;interest;term;[type];[future-value]*) will figure the amount of your payments. The required parameters of the function are the *principal*, *interest*, and *term*. You optionally specify the *type* of payments (end or beginning of the period) and the *future value* of the investment.

@PERCENTILE(*x*) returns the *n*th sample percentile in the range specified in the second parameter. The value of *n* is specified in the first parameter.

@PERMUT(*n;r*) returns a value representing the number of ordered sequences of the value passed in the second parameter that are found in the value specified in the first parameter.

@PI returns the value of π as 3.14159265358979324.

@PMT(*principal*;*interest*;*term*) calculates the periodic payment required to pay back a loan. The arguments are the original principal amount of the loan, the periodic rate, and the term of the loan. For a monthly payment result, the rate and term arguments must both be supplied as monthly amounts.

@PMTC(*principal*;*interest*;*term*) calculates the periodic payment required to pay back a loan based on Canadian mortgage conventions. The arguments are the original principal amount of the loan, the periodic rate, and the term of the loan. For a monthly payment result, the *rate* and *term* arguments must both be supplied as monthly amounts.

@POISSON(*x*;*mean*;[*cumulative*]) returns a Poisson distribution based on the parameters specified. The required parameters are the number of observed events and the expected number of events. Optionally, you can specify a value of 0 or 1 in a third parameter to indicate whether to return a value or values less than or equal to the first parameter or exactly the number of events in the first parameter.

@PPAYMT(*principal*;*interest*;*term*;*start-period*;[*end-period*];[*type*];[*future-value*]) returns the principal value of payments made on a loan. The required parameters of the function are the *principal*, *interest*, *term*, and *start date*. Optionally, you can specify the *ending date*, *type* of payments (end or beginning of the period), and the *future value* of the payments.

@PRANK(*x*;*range*;[*places*]) is used to determine the percentile of the value specified in the first parameter in the range of cells specified in the second parameter. The number of decimal places used in the returned value can be controlled by passing a value in the optional third parameter.

@PRICE(*settlement;maturity;coupon;yield;[redemption]; [frequency]; [basis]*) returns the price per $100 of value for investments which will pay a periodic interest. The first value passed is the settlement date-number. The second parameter is also a date-number specifying the maturity date (in the future) of the note. The third value passed is the coupon rate. The fourth value passed is the annual yield of the investment. The three final parameters are optional. The first optional parameter is the security's redemption value, the second optional value is the number of payments per year, and the third is the means for calculating the number of days in a period.

@PRODUCT(*list*) returns a value equal to all of the values in the specified argument multiplied against each other in sequence. The parameter passed can be a range or list of numeric values (each of the values in the list are separated from the following with a comma). For example, **@PRODUCT(1;2;4;8)** returns a value of 64.

@PROPER(*string*) returns a new string version in which the first letter of each word is capitalized. For example, **@PROPER ("computing conferences, inc.")** returns "Computing Conferences, Inc."

@PUREAVG(*list*) is used to find the average of the values in the *list* specified in the passed parameter, ignoring cells with no values.

@PURECOUNT(*list*) returns a value representing the number of cells in the list parameter that contain values, ignoring cells which do not contain values.

@PUREMAX(*list*) returns the contents of the cell which contains the largest numeric value from the list specified in the passed parameter, ignoring cells which do not contain values.

@PUREMIN(*list*) returns the contents of the cell which contains the smallest numeric value from the list specified in the passed parameter, ignoring cells which do not contain values.

@PURESTD(*list*) determines the population standard deviation for the values found in the list specified in the passed parameter, ignoring cells which do not contain values.

@PURESTDS(*list*) returns the sample standard deviation for the values found in the list specified in the passed parameter, ignoring cells which do not contain values.

@PUREVAR(*list*) determines the population variance for the values in the list specified in the passed parameter, ignoring cells which do not contain values.

@PUREVARS(*list*) returns a value equivalent to the sample variance for the values in the list specified in the passed parameter, ignoring cells which do not contain values.

@PV(*payment;rate;term*) finds the present value of a series of equal future cash flow amounts. The payment argument is the cash flow at the end of each period in *term*. The *rate* is the periodic rate of return.

@PVAL(*payments;interest;term;[type];[future-value]*) returns the present value of an investment. You must specify the *payments*, *interest*, and *term* of the investment. You can optionally specify the *type* of payments (end or beginning of the period) and the *future value* of the investment.

@QUOTIENT(*x;y*) returns an integer result of the first passed parameter divided by the second parameter.

@RADTODEG(*radians*) converts the *radians* value passed to the function into degrees.

@RAND returns a random decimal value between 0 and 1. Multiplying this function by a maximum value produces random numbers in a specified range. For example, **@INT(@RAND★100)** supplies random integers between 0 and 100.

@RANGENAME(*cell*) returns the name assigned to a range in which the cell pointer is currently located.

@RANK(*item;range;[order]*) returns a value equivalent to the relative size or position of the first parameter in the specified range. Specifying either 0 or 1 in the optional third parameter orders the position value in descending or ascending order, respectively.

@RATE(*futurevalue;presentvalue;term*) calculates the interest rate corresponding to a fixed future return of *futurevalue*, given an initial investment of *presentvalue* and a specified investment *term*.

@REFCONVERT(*reference*) is used to convert 1-2-3 column letters to numerical values or column numeric values to letters.

@REGRESSION(*X-range;Y-range;attribute;[compute]*) returns a statistical value for a linear regression based on the passed parameters. The three required parameters are an *X-range*, a *Y-range*, and an *attribute* value specifying an output value. Optionally, a value can be passed as a fourth parameter specifying the Y intercept.

@REPEAT(*string*;*n*) generates a string consisting of *n* copies of *string*. For example, **@REPEAT**("*^";5) produces the string *^*^*^*^*^.

@REPLACE(*string*;*pos*;*n*;*substring*) returns a copy of *string* in which the *n* characters starting from *pos* have been replaced by *substring*. For example, **@REPLACE**("Computing Instructors, Inc.";10;11;"Conferences") returns the string "Computing Conferences, Inc."

@RIGHT(*string*;*n*) returns a substring consisting of the last *n* characters of *string*. For example, **@RIGHT**("Computing Conferences, Inc.";4) returns the substring "Inc."

@ROUND(*value*;*place*) returns a rounded value. The first argument is the value to be rounded, and the second argument is the decimal place at which rounding will occur. If *place* is positive, rounding occurs at the right side of the decimal point; if negative, rounding occurs at the left of the decimal. If *place* is zero, **@ROUND** returns the nearest integer.

@ROUNDDOWN(*x*;[*n*];[*direction*]) returns a value equivalent to the passed value rounded down to the nearest multiple value of 10. A third value of either 0 or 1 can optionally be specified, controlling whether the value is rounded up (0) when negative or down (1).

@ROUNDM(*x*;*multiple*;[*direction*]) returns a value equivalent to the first passed value rounded to the nearest value specified in the second parameter. A third value of either 0 or 1 can optionally be specified, controlling whether the value is rounded up (0) or down (1).

@ROUNDUP(*x*;[*n*];[*direction*]) returns a value equivalent to the passed value rounded up to the nearest multiple value of 10. A third value of either 0 or 1 can optionally be specified, controlling whether the value is rounded down (0) when negative or up (1).

@ROWS(*range*) returns the number of rows in the specified range. For example, if the range name DB represents a database range (not including the top row of field names), **@ROWS(DB)** returns the number of records in the database.

@S(*reference*) returns a copy of the label in the first cell of a range identified by *reference*. If this cell does not contain a label, **@S** returns an empty string.

@SCENARIOINFO(*option*;*name*;[*creator*]) returns text information regarding the scenario you specify in the second parameter passed to the function. The first parameter specified can be one of seven keywords, each of which will cause a different piece of information to be returned. You can optionally specify the name of the creator of the scenario in a third parameter.

@SCENARIOLAST([*filename*]) will return the name of the last scenario of the specified file to be displayed. The *filename* is passed as the sole parameter in the function.

@SEC(*x*) returns a value showing the secant of the angle specified in the passed parameter. The value passed is in radians.

@SECH(*x*) returns a value showing the hyperbolic secant of the angle specified in the passed parameter.

@SECOND(*timenumber*) returns an integer from 0 to 59, representing the seconds in *timenumber*. The *timenumber* argument is a decimal time value.

@SEMEAN(*list*) returns the standard error of the sample mean for the values in the *list* specified in the passed parameter.

@SERIESSUM(*x;n;m;coefficient*) returns a series of values equivalent to the power of the first value specified in the function. The second value passed is the initial power to raise the first value, while the third value is the numeric value to increment the second value on each subsequent pass. The fourth value passed is a range of coefficients that the function multiplies by each subsequent value of the first parameter.

@SHEETS(*range*) returns the number of worksheets in the specified range.

@SIGN(*x*) returns a value of 1, 0, or −1 if the passed value is a positive, zero, or negative value, respectively.

@SIN(*angle*) gives the sine of an angle, where the argument is expressed in radians. For example, **@SIN(@PI)** is 0.

@SINH(*angle*) returns a value showing the hyperbolic sine of the angle specified in the passed parameter.

@SKEWNESS(*range*;**[***type***]**) is used to determine the skewness of the values in the list specified in the passed parameter. An optional parameter specifying whether to return the population skewness (the default) or the sample skewness can be passed in the second parameter.

@SLN(*cost;salvage;life*) calculates the straight-line depreciation of an asset, given the original cost, the salvage value at the end of useful life, and the life of the asset in years.

@SMALL(*range;n*) returns the value that is the *n*th smallest in the range specified in the first parameter. The value used to determine the *n*th is specified in the second parameter.

@SOLVER(*info*) returns information about the current Solver operation. For example, **@SOLVER("done")** returns a value of 1 if the Solver has completed its solution, 2 if the Solver is in the process of completing the solution, or 3 if the Solver is active but not in the process of finding a solution.

@SQRT(*value*) gives the square root of value. For example, **@SQRT(81)** is 9.

@SQRTPI(*x*) returns the square root of the passed parameter times π.

@STD(*list*) returns the population standard deviation of the values in the list. The *list* argument can appear as any combination of values, addresses, ranges, or formulas. @STD is calculated as the square root of @VAR.

@STDS(*list*) returns the sample standard deviation of the values in the list. The *list* argument can appear as any combination of values, addresses, ranges, or formulas. **@STDS** is calculated as the square root of **@VARS**.

@STRING(*value;n*) produces a string from a numeric argument. The first argument, *value*, is the number to be converted to a string; and the second argument, *n*, is the number of decimal places that will appear in the result. For example, **@STRING (1-2-3.456;1)** produces the string "1-2-3.5" as its result.

@SUBTOTAL(*list*) returns the total of all of the numeric values in the list specified in the passed parameter.

@SUM(*list*) returns the sum of the values in the list. The list argument can appear as any combination of values, addresses, ranges, or formulas.

@SUMPRODUCT(*list*) returns the sum of the products of corresponding values in a list of ranges. For example, **@SUMPRODUCT(RANGE1,RANGE2)** multiplies each value in RANGE1 by the corresponding value in RANGE2, and returns the sum of the products.

@SUMSQ(*list*) returns the sum of the square of all values in the list specified in the passed parameter.

@SUMXMY2((*range1*;*range2*) returns a sum value. The sum value is of the square of the difference between corresponding cells in the two ranges specified in the parameter list. The values in cells in *range2* are subtracted from the value of the corresponding cells in *range1*.

@SYD(*cost*;*salvage*;*life*;*period*) calculates the sum-of-the-years'-digits depreciation of an asset, given the original cost, the salvage value at the end of useful life, the life of the asset in years, and the target period for which the depreciation is to be calculated.

@TAN(*angle*) gives the tangent of an angle, where the argument is expressed in radians. For example, **@TAN(@PI/4)** is 1.

@TANH(*x*) returns a value showing the hyperbolic tangent of the angle specified in the passed parameter.

@TDIST(*x*;*degrees-freedom*;[*type*];[*tails*]) returns the Student's T-distribution. The first parameter can be either a critical value representing the cumulative T-distribution random variable or a probability value, depending upon the value passed in the optional third parameter (critical value is the default if no third parameter is specified). The second value is the degrees of freedom used in the calculation. The two optional parameters are the type of calculation and the the test is a one-tail test (1) or a two-tail test (2).

@TERM(*payment*;*rate*;*futurevalue*) calculates the number of equal *payment* amounts required to reach a specified *futurevalue*, given a fixed periodic interest rate.

@TIME(*hour*;*minutes*;*seconds*) returns the decimal time value corresponding to the time specified in its three integer arguments. For example, **@TIME(4;30;0)** returns 0.1875, the decimal corresponding to 4:30 AM.

@TIMEVALUE(*timestring*) returns a decimal time value corresponding to a recognizable time string. For example, **@TIMEVALUE("4:30 AM")** returns 0.1875.

@TODAY supplies a date number representing the current date. For example, **@TODAY** returns 33835 for the date 19-Aug-92.

@TRIM(*string*) returns a copy of string without extraneous spaces. **@TRIM** removes all spaces from the beginning and end of the string, and multiple consecutive spaces from inside the string.

@TRUE returns a value of 1 for true.

@TRUNC(*x*;[*n*]) returns a value representing the first parameter value truncated according to the value passed in the second parameter. If the optional parameter is a positive value, the decimal portion of the value is truncated. A negative value causes the portion of the value to the left of the decimal to be truncated. A value of 0 passed in the optional parameter truncates the first parameter value to an integer, the default if not specified.

@TTEST(*range1*;*range2*;[*type*];[*tails*]) returns the probability resulting from a Student's T-test on the two ranges specified in the two passed parameters.

@UPPER(*string*) returns an uppercase version of its string argument. For example, **@UPPER("Computing Conferences, Inc.")** returns "COMPUTING CONFERENCES, INC."

@VALUE(*string*) produces a number from a string of digits. For example, **@VALUE("9876")** returns the number 9876.

@VAR(*list*) returns the population variance of the values in the list. The *list* argument can appear as any combination of values, addresses, ranges, or formulas.

@VARS(*list*) returns the sample variance of the values in the list. The list argument can appear as any combination of values, addresses, ranges, or formulas.

@VDB(*cost*;*salvage*;*life*;*start*;*end*;[*factor*];[*switch*]) calculates the variable-rate declining-balance depreciation of an asset, given the original *cost*, the *salvage* value at the end of useful *life*, the *life* of the asset in years, the *start* and *end* of the target period for which the depreciation is to be calculated, the optional accelerated depreciation *factor*, and a value of true or false for the optional *switch* argument. If *factor* is omitted, the default is 200 percent, the same as the double-declining-balance method. If *switch* is true (the default), the calculation changes to the straight-line method to maximize depreciation in the final years of useful life.

@VERSIONCURRENT(*range*) returns the version name of the range specified in the specified parameter. The version is created when using the Version Manager with a 1-2-3 worksheet.

@VERSIONDATA(*option*;*cell*;*version-range*;*name*;[*creator*]) returns the contents of a cell in a specified range. The required parameters for the function are an *option* (either formula or value), the *cell* address, the *version-range*, and the *name* of the scenario. You can optionally specify the name of the *creator* in a final parameter. The version is created when using the Version Manager with a 1-2-3 worksheet.

@VERSIONINFO(*option*;*version-range*;*name*;[*creator*]) returns text information regarding the version you specify in the third parameter passed to the function. The first parameter specified can be one of seven keywords, each of which will cause a different piece of information to be returned, while the second parameter is version range name. You can optionally specify the name of the creator of the scenario in a fourth parameter.

@VLOOKUP(*value*;*table*;*column*) performs a lookup operation in a vertically arranged lookup table. Specifically, the function finds the largest number in the first column of the table that is less than or equal to *value*, then looks across the corresponding row to the cell located in the next column. **@VLOOKUP** returns the value in this target cell. (Alternatively, the function's first argument can appear as a string, in which case the first column of the lookup table contains labels.)

@WEEKDAY(*date-number*) will tell you what the day of the week is for the date passed in the function. If the value returned is 0 (zero), the day of the week is Monday, Saturday is 5, and so on.

@WEIGHTAVG(*data-range*;*weight-range*;[*type*]) returns a weighted average value for the cells in the *data-range* specified in the first parameter for corresponding weights specified in the matching *weight-range*. If a value of zero is passed in the optional type parameter, the average is figured using the sum of the values in *weight-range* (the default method if not specified), otherwise, the number of values in *data-range* are used.

@WORKDAY(*start-date*;*days*;[*holidays-range*];[*weekends*]) will return the date-number in the future or past that represents the number of days (in the future or in the past) passed in the second parameter added (or subtracted for negative or past days) to the date specified in the first parameter. You can also specify a number of holiday days to be excluded from the calculation. The date returned takes into account the days reserved for weekends.

@XINDEX(*range*;*column-heading*;*row-heading*;[*worksheet-heading*]) returns the contents of the cell located at the address passed to the function. The required parameters are a range, the column, and the row addresses. A fourth parameter can optionally be specified for the name of the desired worksheet to check.

@YEAR(*date-number*) returns an integer representing the year of *date-number*. For example, **@YEAR(33835)** returns 92, the year in 19-Aug-92.

@YIELD(*settlement*;*maturity*;*coupon*;*price*;[*redemption*]; [*frequency*]; [*basis*]) returns the yield on interest-bearing securities for the values passed to the function. The first value passed is the settlement date-number. The second parameter is a also a date-number specifying the maturity date (in the future) of the note. The third value passed is the coupon rate. The three final parameters are optional. The first optional parameter is the security's redemption value, the second optional value is the number of payments per year, and the third is the means for calculating the number of days in a period.

@ZTEST(*range1*;*mean1*;*std1*;[*range2*];[*mean2*];[*std2*]) is used to determine a probability based on a Z-test on one or two populations. The required parameters are a mandatory range to test, the known population mean, and the known population standard deviation. Optionally, you can specify a second range or second set of data, a known population mean, and a standard deviation for that range.

New Features

and Tools

in Release 4

LOTUS Corporation, drawing on its extensive experience in the world of spreadsheets, has made several important innovations in its upgrade to 1-2-3 for Windows Release 4. Heeding the advice of users and taking into account the innovations made by other software developers, Lotus has made extensive changes and additions to the look and feel of the new release.

The on-screen appearance of 1-2-3 Release 4 has changed dramatically. New tools have been added to the program. In this appendix we will look at the "new" 1-2-3 Release 4 for Windows.

The New Desktop

Lotus 1-2-3 Release 4 closely adheres to the standard Windows interface in its menu structure and the way in which you resize and move windows. The commands on the menu bar are more in line with other Windows programs. More SmartIcons are available than were available in Release 1, and they can be displayed anywhere on the desktop. Another change in the desktop is the status bar, which has been moved to the bottom of the window. And editing has been made even easier—now you can edit the contents of the cell directly in the cell.

New Menu Features

In previous versions of 1-2-3, a menu system now known as the 1-2-3 Classic menu was the standard. In the Classic menu and the 1-2-3 for Windows original menu as well, the entire menu bar changed when you switched between charts (graphs), worksheets, and database operations.

When, for example, you click on the frame of a chart or query to change operations in Release 4, only the sixth menu option (ordinarily Range) changes. You will see the menu option switch from Range to Chart to Query to Transcript when you select, respectively, the worksheet itself, a Chart object, the frame of a Query, or open the Macro Transcript window.

If you want, you can still access the 1-2-3 Classic menu. Just press the slash key (/) on your keyboard. The Classic menu gives traditional Lotus 1-2-3 users easier access to the world of 1-2-3 for Windows.

SmartIcons

Predefined graphical buttons called SmartIcons are now an integral part of 1-2-3. The SmartIcons are *hooks*, or simply buttons, used to get fast access to commonly used commands and macros. The SmartIcons shipped with 1-2-3 Release 4 are divided into seven groups organized around the commands and operations they are associated with. Look at the front and back inside covers of this book to see lists of SmartIcons.

Using a paint program, such as Windows Paintbrush, or the Edit Icon dialog box (available from Tools ➤ SmartIcons), you can create or edit your own SmartIcons. You can attach your own macros to the SmartIcon you've designed and place it on any SmartIcon bar. You can even create your own special SmartIcon bar or set of icons.

In the SmartIcons dialog box, opened when you choose <u>T</u>ools ➤ <u>S</u>martIcons, you can specify where the icon bar is displayed. You can display the SmartIcons across the top of the worksheet window, across the bottom, down either the left or right side, or as a floating window (which, like any good Windows object, can be moved, sized, or even closed).

Controlling What You See on the Worksheets and Screen

From the View menu option, you can select Set View Preferences to customize the appearance of worksheets on-screen. For example, if you want to have access at all times to SmartIcons and the status bar at the top of the screen, leave their check boxes selected in the Set View Preferences dialog box. At the same time, if you don't want to see the edit line, uncheck the check box next to the edit line prompt.

Charts (graphs) and other graphical objects are now placed directly in worksheets. If you prefer not to see the charts, however, you can control whether they are always visible or not in the dialog box. Moreover, you can turn off the scroll bars and grid lines, and worksheet frame and worksheet tabs, from the Set View Preferences dialog box.

Editing Cells Directly

When you want to edit the contents of a cell, you simply press the F2 function key on your keyboard. This is not new to Release 4, but with Release 4 you can edit the data in the cell right inside the cell. The contents box on the edit line below the main menu is still there, so you can use your old standby method. But now, when you make a change in the contents box on the edit line, you will see the changes being made in the cell simultaneously. Or, you can edit directly in the cell.

New Release 4 Features

Release 4 has changed the way charts (graphs) are drawn, the way drawings themselves are made, and the way you write macros. The new release also offers many more functions.

Charts

With Release 4, Lotus has made the use of charts, or graphs as they used to be referred to, easier then ever. The charts are now placed directly in your worksheet, not in a separate sheet as was the case before. As was mentioned earlier in this appendix, the display of the charts and other graphical objects can be switched on and off in the Set View Preferences dialog box.

When you click on the Chart SmartIcon or choose Tools ➤ Chart, you are presented with a crosshair pointer. Point-and-drag (with the left mouse button) the crosshair to create the frame of the chart. When you release the mouse button, a chart frame appears with a default bar chart inside. Sample headings and legends are provided. Click on any of the elements with the right mouse button and a context-sensitive pull-down menu appears. From there you can customize the chart.

Once you choose a chart object, the Range menu option disappears from the menu bar and is replaced with an option named Chart. Moreover, a SmartIcon set for creating charts appears on the SmartIcon bar.

Drawing in Release 4

If you need to emphasize a cell in a worksheet or an element in a chart, you can draw an object to call attention to it. Choose Tools ➤ Draw and select the form that you wish to add to the sheet. The objects used in drawing, like the objects of a chart, can be customized further by opening the Lines and Color dialog box and picking a format that will add emphasis to your presentation.

Whether you want to add ellipses or circles, squared or oblong shapes, text or arrows, lines, polygons, freehand figures, or buttons, the Tools ➤ Draw command opens the way to graphical excellence.

Improved Macro Language

This latest Release of 1-2-3 has made writing macros for automating your work even easier. Lotus 1-2-3 Release 4 now includes more than 300 macro commands.

Most macros can be created as easily as having 1-2-3 watch as you do a standard routine. While you work, 1-2-3 can record your keystrokes as you go along, even when you go to the menu bar and choose menu options, select ranges, or format ranges in a standard style.

All you have to do is choose Tools ➤ Macro ➤ Record. Lotus 1-2-3 will record your steps until you choose Tools ➤ Macro ➤ Stop Recording. You can even edit the recorded macro sequence in the Transcript window before adding the macro to your worksheet.

Additional @Functions

Lotus has added about 140 new @Functions. Using these functions can make financial, statistical, database, DDE, or other processes as easy as selecting the data to analyze and stepping back from the keyboard.

Speed Features in Release 4

A really great feature of Release 4 is the context-sensitive menu system available when you are using a mouse. When you point at any object of the worksheet—be it a cell, range of cells, a chart or drawing object, a row or column header, or whatever—clicking on the right mouse button immediately opens a special pull-down menu loaded with commands that can be used with the cell or object under the mouse pointer.

For example, when you click a drawing object, the pull-down menu offers Edit options (Cut, Copy, Paste, Clear), a Style option (Lines & Color), and drawing options (Bring to Front, Send to Back, Flip Left-Right, Flip Top-Bottom, and Group). When you click on a range of cells, the pull-down menu shows a different set of menu options drawn from all of the menu bar option menus.

External Tools that Come with Release 4

Lotus has provided two translator programs, 1-2-3 Translate and 1-2-3 Macro Translator, so you can use worksheet files and macros created in earlier versions of 1-2-3. The translator programs also help you use data developed in other programs. When you install Release 4, you are given the opportunity to install external programs along with 1-2-3. If you decide to install these programs, the Windows icons are placed in the Lotus Applications window along with the 1-2-3 icon.

The Lotus Dialog Box Editor is also included in the Lotus Applications window. The Lotus Dialog Box Editor lets you create your own custom dialog boxes and other interactive tools for use in Windows.

1-2-3 Translate

Lotus 1-2-3 Release 4 can automatically open worksheets created in earlier versions of 1-2-3, as well Symphony, dBASE III, Excel. However, if you want to use a database from dBASE II or a worksheet created in Multiplan, VisiCalc (and compatible programs), SuperCalc, or Enable, you will need to translate the file first using 1-2-3 Translate.

In 1-2-3 Translate, you will be required to make choices from a series of dialog boxes. From these dialog boxes, you choose the program that the data file was created with, enter the path to the directory where the file(s) are located, and select from a list of available files that match the file type selected in the first dialog box.

When you select 1-2-3 Release 3 in the From list box of the first dialog box, you may notice that the programs available in the To list box change. Now those programs are available in the From box. By selecting 1-2-3 Release 3 and an appropriate program name in the To list box, you can convert worksheets saved in Release 4 as Release 3 files to a data file compatible with the selected To file.

The 1-2-3 Translate programs can also be run from DOS as stand-alone programs. Whether run from Windows or DOS, the translator converts the data and compatible @Functions to the appropriate type when converting to or from 1-2-3 for Windows.

1-2-3 Macro Translator

While the 1-2-3 Translate programs will convert the data and formulas of other worksheets to a format compatible with 1-2-3 Release 4 for Windows, macros created in earlier versions of 1-2-3 for Windows and the DOS environment must be converted using the 1-2-3 Macro Translator. All macro commands can be automatically translated to Release 4 commands, but in these cases the original command is left in the macro for *debugging* later.

When you double-click on the 1-2-3 Macro Translator icon in the Lotus Applications window, the 1-2-3 Release 4 Macro Translator dialog box is brought to the front of your desktop.

A list of files to convert is shown in the Files (WK3) list box. If you do not see the file that you want to convert, select a different drive in the Drives pull-down box and/or a different directory from the Source directories list box on the right side of the File(s) to translate frame. Then highlight the name of the worksheet in the Files list box.

If you want to save the file with the translated macros in a drive or directory other than the current one (as shown in the File(s) to translate frame), make the needed changes in the Directory for translated files frame by selecting from the Drives pull-down box and/or the Target directories list box. When you are satisfied with all of your choices, click on the Translate button to continue.

If you are translating a file and the Target directory is the same as the Source directory, you will see a Warning dialog box cautioning you that a backup file will be made and the original will be overwritten. If you select the default option of Yes, the backup will be made and the translation will proceed. When it has completed, a message to that effect appears on screen. When you acknowledge the message by clicking on the OK button, you are returned to the 1-2-3 Release 4 Macro Translator dialog box.

If you have indicated that the Target directory is different from the Source directory, you will see no further messages after clicking on Translate until the translation complete message is displayed. Click on OK to return to the first dialog box. To close the macro translator and return to the Windows desktop, click on the Exit button.

Lotus Dialog Box Editor

For those individuals who would prefer to make their own dialog boxes for personal use or as a part of their businesses, Lotus has included the Lotus Dialog Box Editor. With this graphics editor, you can create your own dialog boxes to obtain interactive responses from a user.

As you create your dialog boxes, you can use a multitude of graphical objects for responses. Graphical objects, such as radio buttons, list boxes, bitmap graphics, combo boxes, and many other objects, can be used for recording data entries or user responses.

INDEX

Note: Boldfaced page numbers indicate definitions of terms and principal discussions of topics. Italicized page numbers indicate illustrations.

Symbols

& (ampersands), 267
<< >> (angle brackets), 550
* (asterisks)
  on format lines, 509
  in formulas, 32–33, 258
  for number overflow, 184
  in queries, **410–411**, *411*
@ (at signs)
  @@ function, 612
  for functions, 274
  in headers and footers, 241
\ (backslashes)
  in headers and footers, 241
  for macro range names, 453–454, 462
  for repeating characters, **190–191**, *191*

^ (carets)
  for aligning labels, 187
  in formulas, 32, 259
  in headers and footers, 241
: (colons), 23
{} (curly braces), 456
" (double quotation marks)
  for aligning labels, 148, 187
  for macro range names, 454
  for strings, 267
... (ellipses), 70, *70*
= (equal signs)
  in logical formulas, 263
  in queries, 408
forward slashes (/)
  in formulas, 32, 258
  for 1-2-3 Classic window, 22
> (greater than signs)
  on format lines, 509
  in Help window, 108

F

G

H

V

V on format lines, 509
Value Conversion macro, **473–476**
@VALUE function, **322**, *323*, **324**, 641
Value indicator, 25, 93, 126
Value text box for queries, 403
values, 24. *See also* numbers
    with charts, **347**, *347*
    color for, 234
    deleting, **121–123**
    entering, **25**
    on format lines, 509
    in formulas, 32
    logical, 263–264
values ranges for frequency distributions, **511–513**
@VAR function, 276, 641
variable-rate declining-balance depreciation function, **280–283**, 641–642
variables
    in regression analyses, 514
    in simultaneous equations, 494
variance functions, 276, 424, 621, 633, 641
@VARS function, 276, 641
@VDB function, **280–283**, 641–642
@VERSIONCURRENT function, 642
@VERSIONDATA function, 642
@VERSIONINFO function, 642
vertical bars (|), 190
vertical scroll bars, 10, 196
vertical window splitter, 99–100
View menu, 67, 647–648
    for charts, 362
    for freezing titles, 191–193
    for grid lines, 194
    for multiple worksheets, 15
    for single worksheets, 18
    for splitting windows, 100
VisiCalc program, translating files from, 650
@VLOOKUP function, **328–329**, 642

W

@WEEKDAY function, 642
@WEIGHTAVG function, 643
Welcome to Install dialog box, 604
what-if changes and scenarios, **27**, 491, **518–522**
    charts for, 41, **350–351**
    editing for, **38–39**, *38*, **169–170**
    with one variable, **522–527**, *524–525*
    recalculating, **526–527**, *526*
    with three variables, **529–532**, *532*
    with two variables, **527–529**, *528*
What-if Table dialog box, 492, 519, *520*, *524*, 528, *528*, 530, *531*
width of columns, 174, **181–185**
wildcards in criteria, **410–411**, *411*
{Window} macro key name, 457
Window menu, 101–102, *101*
windows, 4–5, 8, *8*
    application. *See* application window
    Help, **107–109**, *109*
    1-2-3 Classic, **22–23**, *22*
    Transcript, 68, **469–472**
    worksheet. *See* worksheet windows
Windows menu, 67
With password file option, 144
.WK4 extension, 37, 141
Word for Windows, linking data from, **562–565**, *566*

YES, YOU *CAN* DO WINDOWS.

964 pp. ISBN:842-4.

Mastering *Windows 3.1* is the most comprehensive start-to-finish Windows tutorial available today. And this Special Edition includes a special section that includes tips, tricks, and troubleshooting advice that alone is worth the price of the book.

Plus full coverage of all of the basics of Windows. Find out how to set up your desktop for ease of use, manipulate multiple windows and applications and more. You'll also find out about supercharging your system, running both Windows and DOS applications on your Windows 3.1 system.

There is also extensive coverage of advanced techniques, including TrueType font management, Dynamic Data Exchange (DDE) and Object Linking and Embedding (OLE) and multimedia support.

SYBEX. Help Yourself.

2021 Challenger Drive
Alameda, CA 94501
1-800-227-2346

SYBEX

MAKE A GOOD COMPUTER EVEN BETTER.

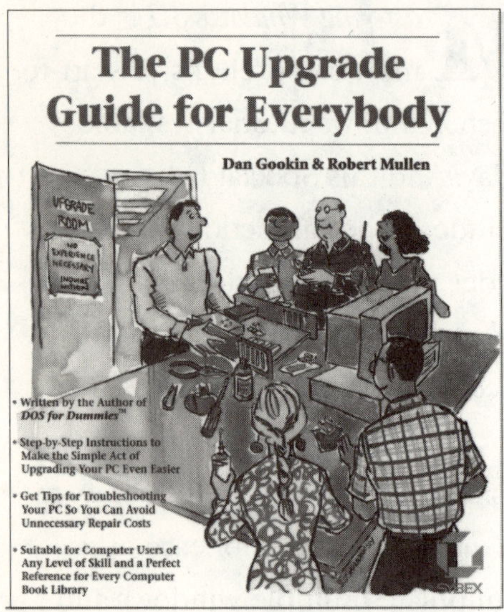

350pp. ISBN: 1301-X.

The *PC Upgrade Guide for Everybody* is the no-hassle, do-it-yourself PC upgrade guide for everyone. If you know the difference between a screwdriver and a pair of pliers, this book is for you.

Inside you'll find step-by-step instructions for installing hardware to make your computer even more fun and productive. Add memory chips, CD-ROM drives and more to your PC.

You'll also learn how to diagnose minor PC problems and decide whether to repair or replace faulty components —without schlepping your PC to the shop and paying big bucks.

SYBEX. Help Yourself.

2021 Challenger Drive
Alameda, CA 94501
1-800-227-2346

FREE BROCHURE!

Complete this form today, and we'll send you a full-color brochure of Sybex bestsellers.

Please supply the name of the Sybex book purchased.

____

How would you rate it?

_____ Excellent   _____ Very Good   _____ Average   _____ Poor

Why did you select this particular book?

_____ Recommended to me by a friend
_____ Recommended to me by store personnel
_____ Saw an advertisement in _______________________________
_____ Author's reputation
_____ Saw in Sybex catalog
_____ Required textbook
_____ Sybex reputation
_____ Read book review in _______________________________
_____ In-store display
_____ Other _______________________________

Where did you buy it?

_____ Bookstore
_____ Computer Store or Software Store
_____ Catalog (name: _______________________________)
_____ Direct from Sybex
_____ Other: _______________________________

Did you buy this book with your personal funds?

_____ Yes   _____ No

About how many computer books do you buy each year?

_____ 1-3   _____ 3-5   _____ 5-7   _____ 7-9   _____ 10+

About how many Sybex books do you own?

_____ 1-3   _____ 3-5   _____ 5-7   _____ 7-9   _____ 10+

Please indicate your level of experience with the software covered in this book:

_____ Beginner   _____ Intermediate   _____ Advanced

Which types of software packages do you use regularly?

_____ Accounting	_____ Databases	_____ Networks
_____ Amiga	_____ Desktop Publishing	_____ Operating Systems
_____ Apple/Mac	_____ File Utilities	_____ Spreadsheets
_____ CAD	_____ Money Management	_____ Word Processing
_____ Communications	_____ Languages	_____ Other _______________

(please specify)

Which of the following best describes your job title?

_____ Administrative/Secretarial   _____ President/CEO

_____ Director   _____ Manager/Supervisor

_____ Engineer/Technician   _____ Other _______________________
(please specify)

Comments on the weaknesses/strengths of this book: ______________________

____

____

____

____

Name ____

Street ____

City/State/Zip ____

Phone ____

PLEASE FOLD, SEAL, AND MAIL TO SYBEX

SYBEX, INC.
Department M
2021 CHALLENGER DR.
ALAMEDA, CALIFORNIA USA
94501

SYBEX

SEAL

1-2-3 SMARTICON SETS

Goodies SmartIcons

Icon	Name
	OpenFile
	SaveFile
	Print
	PrintPreview
	Undo
	CutToClipboard
	CopyToClipboard
	PasteToClipboard
	Versions&Scenarios
	Show/Hide
	ZoomIn
	ZoomOut
	ZoomDefault
	CompleteSequence
	SelectStyleTemplate
	SizeToWidest
	CopyStyleTo
	Chart
	Query
	Cross-Tabulate
	Audit
	SpellCheck
	CustomizeSmartIcons
	NextSet

Macro-Building SmartIcons

Icon	Name
	OpenFile
	SaveFile
	Print
	PrintPreview
	Undo
	CutToClipboard
	CopyToClipboard
	PasteToClipboard
	MacroRecordOn/Off
	SelectMacro
	Create/DeleteRangeName
	RunMacro
	TraceOn/Off
	StepOn/Off
	Show/HideTranscript
	DrawMacroButton
	InsertRange
	DeleteRange
	FindNextCellDown
	FindNextCellUp
	DialogBoxEditor
	MacroTranslator
	NextSet